THE GREAT WESTERN PICTURES II

by
James Robert Parish
and
Michael R. Pitts

The Scarecrow Press, Inc.
Metuchen, N.J., & London
1988

Library of Congress Cataloging-in-Publication Data

Parish, James Robert.
    Great western pictures II / by James Robert Parish
and Michael R. Pitts.
        p.   cm.
    ISBN 0-8108-2106-0
    1. Western films--History and criticism. I. Pitts,
Michael R. II. Title.
PN1995.9.W4P275   1988
791.43'09'093278--dc19   88-6528

ACKNOWLEDGMENTS

John Cocchi

Howard Davis

Dennis Deas

Steve Eberly

Film Favorites (Bob Smith,
    Charles Smith)

George Geltzer

Alex Gildzen

George A. Katchmer

Gary Kramer

The Library of Congress:

Motion Picture, Broadcasting
and Recorded Sound Division
(Katharine Loughney)

Doug McClelland

Alvin H. Marill

Jim Meyer

Peter Miglierini

Screen Facts Magazine (Alan G.
    Barbour)

T. Allan Taylor

Vincent Terrace

Dr. Raymond White

CONTENTS

INTRODUCTION

While the Western feature film appears to be almost dormant theatrically, the genre itself continues to be popular on television, video, and in revivals and so we continue our book series of updates of The Great ... Pictures series with this new volume on the Western. More than any of the other genres we have covered in this series, the Western provides a plethora of feature films, serials and telefeatures from which to choose and we have tried to include a wide variety of features from various aspects of the Western cinema. Like our other volumes, the word "Great" in the book's title does not necessarily refer to the individual films included, but the Western film genre as a whole.

Since THE GREAT TRAIN ROBBERY was filmed in 1903, and even before, the Western film has had a firm place in the heart of filmgoers and perhaps one of the reasons so few Westerns are produced today is that there is such a backlog of genre films to view that the Western, unlike most other types of cinema, has a more difficult time coming up with new kinds of plot twists to capture audience interest. Still the brief revival of the genre in the summer of 1985 with RUSTLERS' RHAPSODY, PALE RIDER, and SILVERADO proved there is still a theatrical audience for Westerns, and the fact that a large portion of the home video market is dominated by the defunct "B" Westerns demonstrates that the popularity of the genre will probably never fade.

The Great Western Pictures was published in 1976 and in that volume we examined many of the genre classics as well as other lesser efforts. In this follow-up book, we have included some of the Westerns produced since that date, but mainly have focused our discussion on a number of titles omitted from the initial volume because of space limitations and have added many other films which we feel will give a more rounded look at the Western film field. In doing so, we have covered such diverse areas as feature films, serials, and movies made for television, which are four reels or more in length.

When our initial volume was published it received uniformly good reviews and was well received by Western and general movie followers. Several reviewers, however, noted the lack of "B" Westerns in its pages and we have attempted to correct this by

devoting about one-half of the present volume to this popular art
form. Few books have looked seriously or in depth at the "B"
Western and we hope our examination of many of its titles will provide a better understanding of the reasons for the continuing
popularity of the low-budget series oater, which has not been in
production for more than three decades.

Like the other volumes in this series, this book looks at the
total spectrum of the Western film, covering titles which range
from classics to the bottom-of-the-barrel. Not only has the pro-
liferation of the home video field contributed to a wide viewing of
the low-budget Western but a number of television programs have
been produced in the past decade which have spotlighted this area.
One of the first of these was the syndicated "Roy Rogers Theatre"
in which Roy Rogers hosted a series of "B" Westerns. The PBS-TV
series, "Matinee at the Bijou," in its five-season run, featured
several "B" Westerns and serials, and that network has also been
responsible for the popular "Six-Gun Heroes" series hosted by Sunset Carson and now in its third season. Another network to produce
"B" Western TV programs is The Nashville Network, having turned
out "Tumbleweed Theatre," which has been greatly hurt by the use
of the inane Riders in the Sky as its hosts. The Nashville Network,
however, has compensated for this by producing the "Happy Trails"
series, starring Roy Rogers and Dale Evans, in which the two stars
present and discuss their feature films. This series is scheduled
to run for three seasons and encompass all of Roy Rogers' feature
films for Republic Pictures. Soon Gene Autry will be essaying the
same format on television. In addition, other television networks
like Christian Broadcasting Network (CBN) and the Satellite Program Network (SPN) have prominently featured low-budget
Westerns in their programming.

Thanks to videotape and the satellite networks, thousands of
Westerns, most of them low-budget, have been made available to
viewers in recent years and we have tried to include a representative number of them in this volume.

Finally, a word about a definition of the term "Western film."
Like most other types of movies, the Western has a broad founda-
tion, including not only sagebrush epics, but also northwoods and
south-of-the-border dramas as well as actioners with locales abroad
and Westerns produced and filmed on foreign soil. We have included
examples of all these types to give as rounded as possible a per-
spective of the Western motion picture art form. Also we have
taken the viewpoint that the Western refers to the boundary of the
American frontier; thus films like UNCONQUERED, dealing with the
French and Indian War, is included since the picture takes place in
territory which was then the Western boundary of the American
frontier.

Since we are both fans of the Western movie, this book has

provided us with a great deal of pleasure in its researching and writing and it has afforded us the opportunity to view and discuss several hundred Western movies. We hope this volume will give the viewer the same enjoyment and, as with our other volumes, we welcome additions, corrections, comments, etc. We hope that, a few years from now, we will be back with a third volume on Westerns. Until then, Happy Trails!

April, 1987

James Robert Parish
15101 Magnolia Boulevard #A-6
Sherman Oaks, CA 91403

Michael R. Pitts
512 North Street
Chesterfield, IN 46017

GREAT WESTERN PICTURES II

ABILENE TOWN (United Artists, 1946) 91 mins.

Producer, Jules Levey; associate producer, Herbert Biberman; director, Edwin L. Marin; based on the novel <u>Trail Town</u> by Ernest Haycox; screenplay, Harold Shumate; art director, Duncan Cramer; music director, Nat W. Finston; assistant director, Maurice Suess; songs, Fred Spielman and Kermett Goell; choreography, Sammy Lee; camera, Archie J. Stout; editors, Otho Lovering, Richard Heermance.

Randolph Scott (Dan Mitchell); Ann Dvorak (Rita); Edgar Buchanan (Bravo Trimide); Rhonda Fleming (Sherry Balder); Lloyd Bridges (Henry Dreiser); Helen Boice (Big Annie); Howard Freeman (Ed Balder); Richard Hale (Charlie Fair, the Saloon Keeper); Jack Lambert (Jeff Younger); Hank Patterson (Doug Neil); Dick Curtis (Ryker); Earl Schenck (Hazelhurst); Eddy Waller (Hannaberry).

Stoic Dan Mitchell (Randolph Scott), a one-time cattleman, is now the marshal of Abilene, Kansas, a wide open town at the end of a long cattle drive. Dan is at odds with local businessmen who want to maintain peace between the rowdy cowpunchers infesting the community and settlers who have migrated here for free government land. The marshal wants to help the settlers but gets little aid from county sheriff Bravo Trimide (Edgar Buchanan). Saloon keeper Charlie Fair (Richard Hale) is in league with Ryker (Dick Curtis), the leader of the trail herders, who vows revenge after the lawman beats him in a fight. When the cattlemen raid and burn settlers' homes, Dan learns that gunman Jeff Younger (Jack Lambert) led the forays and he sets out to corral him. Sherry (Rhonda Fleming), the pretty daughter of a local businessman (Howard Freeman), sells barbed wire to settler Henry Dreiser (Lloyd Bridges), and when Ryker and his men find their trail fenced off, they stampede their cattle and several people are killed. The cattlemen then arrive in town and cause havoc, but the settlers arrive in time to back Dan, who kills Ryker in a shootout. The vicinity is now safe for law-abiding citizens and Dan finds love with saloon singer Rita (Ann Dvorak).

ABILENE TOWN is a solid frontier saga, deftly outlining the struggle in the 1870s between wild and freedom-loving cattlemen and settlers who took advantage of free government land, thus fencing off the ranges. The film's structure owes much to its predecessor,

1

Jack Lambert and Randolph Scott in ABILENE TOWN (1946).

DODGE CITY (1938) (see B/V), which starred Errol Flynn, Olivia
de Havilland, and Ann Sheridan. As usual, taciturn Randolph Scott
makes a sturdy hero who here is given the opportunity for romance
with two contrasting types: comely, domestic-minded Rhonda
Fleming, and flashy saloon gal Ann Dvorak. It is Edgar Buchanan
who steals the show as the none too duty-prone county lawman who
prefers playing cards to enforcing the law. The film abounds in
good dialogue, such as Scott's evaluation of Dvorak's character:
"She tries too hard to be mean. Being mean comes natural." Or a
gambler's advice to Scott: "Why don't you let this town shoot it
out and die."

The picture's only drawback is too many extraneous saloon
numbers featuring ex-Warner Bros. star Ms. Dvorak.

ACES WILD see GHOST TOWN

AL JENNINGS OF OKLAHOMA (Columbia, 1951) C 77 mins.

Producer, Rudolph C. Flothow; director, Ray Nazarro; based
on the book by Al Jennings, Will Irwin; screenplay, George Bricker;

art director, Victor Greene; set decorator, Louis Diage; Technicolor
consultant, Francis Cugat; music director, Mischa Bakaleinikoff;
assistant director, Gilbert Kay; sound, Jack Goodrich; camera,
W. Howard Greene; editor, Richard Fantl.

Dan Duryea (Al Jennings); Gale Storm (Margo St. Claire);
Dick Foran (Frank Jennings); Gloria Henry (Alice Calhoun); Guinn
"Big Boy" Williams (Lon Tuttle); Raymond Greenleaf (Judge Jen-
nings); Stanley Andrews (Marshal Slattery); John Ridgely (Dan
Haines); James Millican (Ed Jennings); Harry Shannon (Fred
Salter); Helen Brown (Mrs. Salter); Robert Bice (Pete Kinkaid);
George J. Lewis (Sammy Page); Jimmie Dodd (Buck Botkin); Edwin
Parker (Doc Wrightmire); James Griffith (Slim Harris); William "Bill"
Phillips (Bill Mertz); John Dehner (Tom Marsden); Charles Meredith
(Judge Evans); William Norton Bailey (Robert Kyle); Louis Jean
Heydt (John Jennings); Harry Cording (Mike Bridges); Theresa
Harris (Terese).

Al Jennings lived for almost a century (1864-1962). He was
one of the last of the Western outlaws whose exploits were used by
O. Henry in several of his stories. A real-life outlaw, Jennings
(after release from prison in 1907 he became a lawyer) played himself as a real-life bandit in silent films and in the talkies undertook
several supporting roles. In SONG OF THE GRINGO (1936) (q.v.)
he portrayed a judge and star Tex Ritter later said it was Jennings
who taught him how to use a six-shooter properly. This screen
biopic of Jennings' early years is an overly romantic and basically
fictional rendering of his life of lawlessness but it was highlighted
by Dan Duryea's superb work in the title role, and Boxoffice
magazine termed the production "a fast-moving suspenseful story."

Brothers Al (Dan Duryea) and Frank Jennings (Dick Foran)
forsake their law practice in Kansas following a courtroom brawl
and head to the Oklahoma Territory to take up practice with
brothers Ed (James Millican) and John (Louis Jean Heydt). Once
there, Al tumbles for pretty New Orleans visitor Margo St. Claire
(Gale Storm), but Ed is shot by a corrupt politician (John Dehner)
and in trying to force a confession out of the killer, Al guns him
down. Al and Frank are then hunted by a posse and join forces
with outlaw gang leader Frank Slater (Herry Shannon), but Al
soon takes over the operation. When a reward is placed on the
brothers' heads, they move to New Orleans, which has no extradi-
tion laws. Al and Frank become cotton merchants and Al renews
his romance with Margo, who forgives him his past deeds. A railroad detective (John Ridgely) finds the brothers, so they decide
to return to Oklahoma for one more big heist and then go to
Mexico. After robbing a train they are captured and placed on
trial. They are defended by their judge father (Raymond Greenleaf), but a corrupt jury sentences Frank to five years in prison
and Al to life imprisonment. After enduring five years, Al is
pardoned by presidential order and returns to his Oklahoma law
practice.

Dan Duryea, Gale Storm and Dick Foran in AL JENNINGS OF OKLA-HOMA (1951).

ALBUQUERQUE (Paramount, 1948) C   89 mins.

Producers, William Pine, William Thomas, director, Ray En-right; based on the novel by Luke Short; screenplay, Gene Lewis, Clarence Upson Young; Cinecolor consultant, Gar K. Gilbert; art director, F. Paul Sylos; set decorators, Elias H. Reif, Vincent Taylor; assistant director, Howard Pine; makeup, Vern Murdock; music director, Darrell Calker; song, Calker; sound, Earl Sitar; camera, Fred Jackman, Jr.; editor, Howard Smith.

Randolph Scott (Cole Armin); Barbara Britton (Letty Tyler); George "Gabby" Hayes (Juke); Lon Chaney (Steve Murkil); Russell Hayden (Ted Wallace); Catherine Craig (Celia Wallace); George Cleveland (John Armin); Karolyn Grimes (Myrtle Walton); Bernard J. Nedell (Sheriff Linton); Russell Simpson (Huggins); Jody Gilbert (Pearl); Dan White (Jackson); Irving Bacon (Dave Walton); John Halloran (Matt Wayne); Walter Baldwin (Judge).

Former Texas Ranger Cole Armin (Randolph Scott) arrives in a small Lone Star State community in 1878 and finds that his cor-rupt uncle John Armin (George Cleveland) controls the area with the support of chief henchman and thug Steve Murkil (Lon Chaney). Opposed to his uncle's activities, Cole joins forces with Celia Wallace (Catherine Craig) and her brother Ted (Russell Hayden) in running

Catherine Craig and Randolph Scott in ALBUQUERQUE (1948).

their small transportation line, which is a rival to his uncle's freight business. To get Cole out of the way, the uncle imports siren Letty Tyler (Barbara Britton). When her ploys fail, he frames Cole for the robbery of a gold shipment from one of his stagecoaches, but this too fails and eventually Cole and the Craigs bring law and order to the town.

Although made economically by the Pine-Thomas unit at Paramount Pictures, this Cinecolor feature offers good production trappings and fine acting from its excellent cast. Still, Variety noted; "With all the basic ingredients to be exciting western filmfare, ALBUQUERQUE nevertheless misses." Probably the main reason the film failed to jell as solid entertainment is its too predictable narrative and leisurely direction, which diluted the excitement potential. Also the casting of George Cleveland as an arch-villain is amiss, as audiences liked the character actor for his typical lovable old man roles.

Despite being a pale Western, the movie caused some publicity when co-star Barbara Britton sued Paramount for $200,000 in damages because her name appeared in the film's credits and advertising in smaller letters than those for Randolph Scott. The suit was settled out of court, but as a result the studio cancelled the actress' term contract.

A.k.a.: SILVER CITY

ALIAS JOHN LAW (Supreme, 1935) 54 mins.

Producer, A. W. Hackel; director, Robert North Bradbury;

screenplay, Forbes Parkhill; camera, William Steiner.
Bob Steele (John Clark); Roberta Gale (Jean); Buck Connors
(Boots); Earl Dwire (The Kootney Kid); Bob McKenzie (Judge);
Steve Clark (Marshal John); Jack Rockwell (Marshal); and Roger
Williams, Jack Cowell, Horace Murphy.

The Kootney Kid (Earl Dwire), a notorious outlaw, finds a
letter addressed to John Clark (Bob Steele), telling him oil has been
discovered on the Lazy Dollar Ranch, which he has inherited, and
that the Western Oil Company wants to purchase the spread for
$75,000. The bad man poses as Clark to get the money. Mean-
while, John and his buddy Boots (Buck Connors) are trailed by a
marshal (Jack Rockwell) who thinks they are part of the Kid's
gang. In town, John meets his childhood sweetheart Joan (Roberta
Gale), who tells him about the oil discovery, and he goes to the
local courthouse to establish his claim to the property. There he
is detained but later escapes and goes in search of the marshal.
(He had saved the lawman's life earlier when one of the outlaws
tried to shoot him, and the marshal can prove John's identity.)
They find the lawman at a sheep camp but he is in serious condi-
tion. However, Boots, who is deaf and can read lips, uses a spy-
glass and sees the Kid and his gang nearby, splitting loot from a
robbery. John pursues the Kid and in a fight the outlaw falls to
his death from a hanging bridge. Returning to town, John establishes his identity and settles down with Joan.
Another in the long series (1324 to 1938) of features in which
compact Bob Steele starred for producer A. W. Hackel, ALIAS JOHN
LAW is packed with fine action and plot twists. Especially offbeat
is the story-line ploy of Boots relying on lip-reading to identify
the villain, and the finale fight between Steele and Dwire is well
executed.

ALONG THE GREAT DIVIDE (Warner Bros., 1951) 88 mins.

Producer, Anthony Veiller; director, Raoul Walsh; story,
Walter Doniger; screenplay, Doniger, Lewis Meltzer; music, David
Buttolph; art director, Edward Carrere; assistant director, Oren
Haglund; sound, Lewis Hewitt; camera, Sid Hickox; editor, Thomas
Reilly.
Kirk Douglas (U.S. Marshal Len Merrick); Virginia Mayo (Ana
Keith); John Agar (Billy Shear); Walter Brennan (Pop Keith); Ray
Teal (Lou Gray); Hugh Sanders (Frank Newcombe); Morris Ankrum
(Ed Roden); James Anderson (Dan Roden); Charles Meredith (The
Judge); Lane Chandler (Sheriff); Kenneth Macdonald (Crowley the
Rancher); Steve Clark (Witness); Carl Harbaugh (Jerome): Zon
Murray (Wilson the Witness); Sam Ash (Defense Counsel); Steve
Darrell (Prosecutor); Al Ferguson (Bailiff); Guy Wilkerson (Jury
Foreman).

U.S. Marshal Len Merrick (Kirk Douglas) is remorseful over

the death of his lawman father because he did not go with him on a dangerous mission which was the cause of the older man's death. Filled with guilt, he emphathizes with father figure/poor rancher Pop Keith (Walter Brennan), who is accused of cattle rustling and the murder of land baron Ed Roden's (Morris Ankrum) eldest son. Merrick must bring Keith in but prevents his lynching by Roden and his men, and with his two deputies, Billy Shear (John Agar) and Lou Gray (Ray Teal), heads into the desert to elude Roden and his men, accompanied by Pop's pretty daughter Ana (Virginia Mayo). Along the way Ana attempts to gain her father's release, even trying to romance Merrick, whom she dislikes. Roden and his men attack the party and deputy

Virginia Mayo and Kirk Douglas in ALONG THE GREAT DIVIDE (1951).

Shear is killed, but Merrick captures Roden's son Dan (James Anderson) and holds him hostage until they safely reach Santa Loma. There Pop Keith is tried and convicted for his alleged crimes, but Merrick proves it was Dan Roden who murdered his older brother because he was jealous of him. Pop is released and Merrick and Ana become romantically involved.

When ALONG THE GREAT DIVIDE was released, it failed to garner much critical praise. Variety termed it "Just fair entertainment," while the New York Times called it "...a strictly second-rate venture with all the seams and wheels showing." In retrospect, however, the movie holds up much better than its contemporary critics indicate. Well-paced by director Raoul Walsh, the movie keeps the viewer's attention with its interesting plot and characters, and it contains some rather sultry scenes between Kirk Douglas and Virginia Mayo in the desert, with the sexual content beautifully underplayed. The cast is quite good, although Kirk Douglas seemed ill at ease in his first time in the saddle.

AMBUSH TRAIL (Producers Releasing Corp., 1946) 60 mins.

Producer, Arthur Alexander; director, Harry Fraser; screenplay, Elmer Clifton; set decorator, Edward H. Reif; music director, Lee Zahler; sound, Glen Glenn; camera, Jack Greenhalgh; editor, Roy Livingston.

Bob Steele (Curley Thompson); Syd Saylor (Sam Hawkins); I. Stanford Jolley (Hatch Bolton); Lorraine Miller (Alice Rhodes);

Kermit Maynard, Charles King, Bob (John) Carson, Bob Steele, and Syd Saylor in AMBUSH TRAIL (1946).

Charles King (Al Craig); Bob "John" Carson (Ed Blane); Budd Buster (Jim Haley); Kermit Maynard (Walter Gordon); Frank Ellis (Frank Gwen); Edward Cassidy (Marshal Dawes).

Bob Steele had ridden the cinema trails for two decades when he came back to PRC in 1946 to star in his final quartet of "B" Westerns, before becoming a full-time character actor. (Steele had made a half-dozen "Billy the Kid" series actioners for the company in 1940-41 before joining Republic's "The Three Mesquiteers" and Monogram's "Trail Blazers" heroes). These final PRC Westerns, NAVAJO TRAIL, SIX-GUN MAN, AMBUSH TRAIL and THUNDER TOWN, cheaply produced, were lensed back-to-back by producer Arthur Alexander and director Harry Fraser, the latter writing most of the scripts. AMBUSH TRAIL, the third of the four releases, is typical of the series.

Power-mad land grabber Hatch Bolton (I. Stanford Jolley) schemes to take over the local range, aided by henchman Ed Blaine (Charles King) and his gang. Cattle rancher Curley Thompson (Bob Steele) is one of the men Holton tries to drive off, but Curley, along with his foreman Happy Hawkins (Syd Saylor) refuses to go and he comes to the aid of pretty Alice Rhodes (Lorraine Miller) and the other ranchers. Eventually Curley joins all the nearby ranchers into a fighting unit and they take on Holton and his gang and defeat them. Peace returns to the valley.

It is interesting to note that in these four PRC oaters, star Steele wore a thin mustache, something untypical of Western film heroes. At the time he was playing Canino in Raymond Chandler's

THE BIG SLEEP (1946) for Warner Bros. and since that assignment required a mustache, he refused to shave it off for these poverty row actioners.

ANOTHER MAN'S BOOTS see SQUARE DEAL SANDERSON

APACHE UPRISING (Paramount, 1966) C 90 mins.

Producer, A. C. Lyles; director, R. G. Springsteen; based on the novel Way Station by Harry Sanford; screenplay, Sanford, Max Lamb; music, Jimmie Haskell; assistant directors, Dale Coleman, Bob Templeton; camera, W. Wallace Kelley; editor, John Schreyer.

Rory Calhoun (Jim Walker); Corinne Calvet (Janice MacKenzie); John Russell (Vance Buckner); Lon Chaney (Charlie Russell); Gene Evans (Jess Cooney); Richard Arlen (Captain Gannon); Robert H. Harris (Hoyt Taylor); Arthur Hunnicutt (Bill Gibson); DeForest Kelley (Toby Jack Saunders); George Chandler (Jace Asher); Jean Parker (Mrs. Hawkes); Johnny Mack Brown (Sheriff Ben Hall); Donald Barry (Henry Belden); Abel Fernandez (Young Apache); Robert Carricart (Chico Lopewz); Paul Daniel (Old Antone).

With location shooting in Colorado's Vasquez Mountains, APACHE UPRISING is a tad more picturesque than most of the studio-bound entries producer A. C. Lyles churned out for Paramount in the mid- and late 1960s. Like the other series episodes, the movie is laced with veteran players, but its plot is overly complicated and director R. G. Springsteen fails to enliven the proceedings sufficiently to make it more than passable entertainment.

On his way to Lordsburg to pick up a mustang herd, Jim Walker (Rory Calhoun) is ambushed by warring Apaches but is saved by scout Bill Gibson (Arthur Hunnicutt). They find evidence of the marauding Apaches, but fail to convince the Army patrol they meet on the way to Apache Wells. In town, crook Vance Buckner (John Russell) plans to rob the stagecoach with the help of Jess Cooney (Gene Evans) and Toby Jack Saunders (De Forest Kelley). Jim and Bill ride the stage with driver Charles Russell (Lon Chaney) and at a way station Jim fights with Toby Jack over the latter's unflattering attentions to pretty passenger Janice MacKenzie (Corinne Calvert). Buckner arrives, however, and the outlaws take over the station. They intend to kill the passengers, but Jim convinces Buckner that an Indian (Paul Daniel) they have captured is actually an Apache chief and that his tribe will attack the station. Toby Jack murders Bill but is killed by the Apaches. Jim and Jancie escape, only to be captured by the tribe. They tell the Indians about their chief being held hostage, and the Indians agree to let them go, as well as Buckner and Jess. Jim trails the two outlaws and finds Jess murdered, but captures Buckner. The

DeForest Kelley, John Russell, Robert H. Harris, and Arthur
Hunnicutt in APACHE UPRISING (1966).

Apaches arrive and demand that Buckner be turned over to them,
but they allow Jim and Janice to go on to Lordsburg.
      The most diverting performances here are by Lon Chaney as
the happy-go-lucky stage driver and by rotund Johnny Mack
Brown as the town's lecherous lawman.

APACHE'S LAST BATTLE see OLD SHATTERHAND

THE APPLE DUMPLING GANG (Buena Vista, 1975) C 100 mins.

      Producer, Bill Anderson; director, Norman Tokar; based on
the book by Jack M. Buckham; screenplay, Don Tait; music, Buddy
Baker; art directors, John B. Mansbridge, Walter Tyler; assistant
director, Ronald R. Grow; sound, Herb Taylor, Frank Regula;
camera, Frank Phillips; editor, Ray deLeuw.
      Bill Bixby (Russell Donovan); Susan Clark (Magnolia Dusty
Clydesdale); Don Knotts (Theodore Ogilvie); Tim Conway (Amos);
David Wayne (Colonel T. R. Clydesdale); Slim Pickens (Frank
Stillwell); Harry Morgan (Homer McCoy); John McGiver (Leonard
Sharpe); Don Knight (John Wintle); Clay O'Brien (Bobby Bradley);
Brad Savage (Clovis Bradley); Stacy Manning (Celia Bradley).

      Following the death of their miner father, three orphans (Clay
O'Brien, Brad Savage, Stacy Manning) are left homeless and a pen-
niless gambler named Donovan (Bill Bixby) is convinced to take care
of them. To provide care, he talks frontier gal Magnolia (Susan
Clark) into a marriage of convenience. Meanwhile two bumbling

Tim Conway and Don Knotts in THE APPLE DUMPLING GANG (1975).

outlaws (Don Knotts, Tim Conway), who call themselves the Hash Knife Outfit, plan to fleece the gambler of a stake he has put together to build his dream gambling house in New Orleans. The children are supposed to go to San Francisco to live with relatives but Bixby does not have the money to take them there; it turns out, however, that the children have a valuable gold nugget taken from their late dad's mine. The Hash Knife boys learn about the gold and plot to heist it, but find themselves with rivals when outlaw Stillwell (Slim Pickens) arrives with his gang. Eventually the outlaws are defeated with the aid of the local lawman/justice of the peace/barber (Harry Morgan) and Donovan and Magnolia realize they are really in love and settle down to raise their three charges.

This "engaging gentle-humored comedy" (Variety) proved to be popular box-office fare and one of the Disney studio's more successful 1970s theatrical outings. With its amusing plot and harmless villains, THE APPLE DUMPLING GANG (the name derives from the youngsters' penchant for apple dumpling) was a winner with the family trade, grossing more than $16 million. As a result a sequel, THE APPLE DUMPLING GANG RIDES AGAIN, was issued in 1979. Here the three youngsters help the Hash Knife boys when they evoke the ire of a revengeful lawman (Kenneth Mars). The film was dull, although it grossed over $9 million. In 1982 the trio of siblings returned yet again in "Tales of the Apple Dumpling Gang," telecast January 16 on "Walt Disney's Wonderful World" television program on NBC-TV. Ed Begley, Jr., Arte Johnson, Keith Mitchell and Henry Jones headed the cast.

THE APPLE DUMPLING GANG RIDES AGAIN see THE APPLE DUMPLING GANG

ARIZONA see THE LAST ROUND-UP

ARIZONA BOUND see THE GUNMAN FROM BODIE

ARIZONA GUNFIGHTER (Republic, 1937) 56 mins.

Producer, A. W. Hackel; director, Sam Newfield; story, Harry F. Olmsted; screenplay, George H. Plympton; camera, Bob Kline; editor, S. Roy Luby.

Bob Steele (Colt Ferron); Jean Carmen (Beth Lorimer); Ted Adams (Wolf Whitson); Ernie Adams (Grizzly Barr); Lew Meehan (Snake Bralt); Steve Clark (Sheriff); John Merton (Farley); Karl Hackett (Durkin); A. C. Henderson (Governor Gray).

After the murder of his father over his Arizona ranch, young Colt Ferron (Bob Steele) confronts the two men (Karl Hackett, John Merton) he feels are responsible and shoots them, but he is himself

badly wounded. He is found by outlaw gang leader Wolf Witson
(Ted Adams), who helps him regain his health. Wolf wants to
settle down and breaks up his cattle rustling gang. But a member
of the bunch, Snake (Lew Meehan), wants them to continue and
take up bank robbing. Wolf deserts the gang and goes with Colt
and settles down at his ranch along with Witson's pretty daughter
Bess (Jean Carmen). Lawmen, however, arrest Wolf and Colt
thinks his absent associate has rejoined his gang until he finds out
that the man is in prison. When Snake kidnaps Bess, Colt convinces the governor to release Wolf and the two men rescue the girl
and bring about the gang's downfall.

Enhanced by a good plot and solid acting, ARIZONA GUN-
FIGHTER is one of Bob Steele's better starring vehicles and one of
the best of the 32 features he contracted for with producer A. W.
Hackel from 1934 to 1938. Director Sam Newfield, often deprecated
for his later Producer Releasing Corp. quickie oaters, here supplies strong direction, and the movie's acting is topnotch, especially
by star Bob Steele as the revengeful Colt, Ted Adams as the
reform-minded outlaw, and Lee Meehan as the dastardly villain.
Also spicing the proceedings is comely heroine Jean Carmen.

THE ARIZONA TERROR (Tiffany, 1931) 65 mins.

Producer, Phil Goldstone; director, Phil Rosen; screenplay,
John Francis [Jack] Natteford; art director, Ralph DeLacy; camera,
Arthur Reed; editor, Martin Cohn.

Ken Maynard (The Arizonan); Lina Basquette (Rancher's
Daughter); Hooper Atchley (Cole Porter); Michael Visaroff (Vasquez);
Nina Quartero (Lola); Charles King, Edmund Cobb, Tom London
(Henchmen); Fred Burns (Sheriff).

Following the 1930 termination of his Universal contract due to
the studio's belief that the program Western had no place in the
sound era, Ken Maynard signed with Tiffany Studios and made
eleven features there before trying a season with World-Wide and
then returning to Universal in 1933. THE ARIZONA TERROR is the
fourth of Ken's eleven Tiffany pictures and is a nicely done early
sound entry. It is actionful with nice locations and Michael Visaroff
is in especially good form as a good badman. In addition, the still
agile Maynard contributes a few of the stunts which had made him
so popular in the silent era.

Ken Maynard, a cowboy unjustly accused of a crime, is injured in an escape attempt and is taken in by a rancher and his
pretty daughter (Lina Basquette). While recuperating at their
ranch, he becomes aware of a plot by a crook (Hooper Atchley) to
take over the place. Aided by a kind-hearted bandit (Michael
Visaroff), he helps his benefactors. The villains are defeated.

AVENGING WATERS (Columbia, 1936) 57 mins.

Lina Basquette and Hooper Atchley in THE ARIZONA TERROR
(1931).

Producer, Larry Darmour; director, Spencer Gordon Bennet;
screenplay, Nate Gatzert; camera, James S. Brown, Jr.; editor,
Dwight Caldwell.
Ken Maynard (Ken Morley); Beth Marion (Mary Mortimer);
Ward Bond (Marv Slater); John Elliott (Charles Mortimer); Zella
Russell (Mrs. Eloise Smythe); Wally Wales (Slivers); Tom London
(Hoppy); Edward Hearn (Jim); Glenn Strange (Jake); Buffalo Bill,
Jr. (Ranch Hand); The Diamond K Ranch Boys (Entertainers); and
Edmund Cobb, Buck Moulton, Cactus Mack, Sterling Holloway, Jack
King, Buck Bucko, Bud McClure.

Crooked rancher Marv Slater (Ward Bond) seeks control of
the local water supply and is at odds with honest rancher Charles
Mortimer (John Elliott) and his pretty daughter (Beth Marion). A
cowboy (Ken Maynard), finding himself in the middle of the feud,
sides with Mortimer while romancing his daughter. Ken is captured
by Slater's gang and tied up in a remote cabin while the gang dyna-
mites a dam to flood the area. With the help of his horse Tarzan,
Maynard escapes in time to rescue the girl and bring the corrupt
Slater to justice.
AVENGING WATERS was the next-to-last "B" Western Ken
Maynard did for Columbia and he was quickly losing interest in his

screen career, opting to return to his first performing love, the circus. Overall, AVENGING WATERS is a decent entry, perked by Ward Bond's performance as the hateful and murderous Slater. The film, however, is lacking in the special effects department and the climactic flood is quite hokey, as is another scene ably described by Jon Tuska in Views & Reviews (Fall, 1969): "...Ken, supposedly being dragged to his death by a runaway horse, is saved by Tarzan coming up alongside and permitting him to catch hold of the stirrup and then gain the saddle. This was managed through rear view projection and, somehow, the attempt on Ken's part to grab hold of an obviously celluloid horse is hopelessly disappointing."

BAD COMPANY (Paramount, 1972) C 91 mins.

Producer, Stanley R. Jaffe; director, Robert Benton; screenplay, David Newman, Benton; music, Harvey Schmidt; production designer, Paul Sylbert; art director, Robert Gundlach; set decorator, Audrey Blasdel; assistant director, Howard Koch, Jr.; sound, Gene Cantamessa, Al Grimaglia; camera, Gordon Williams; editors, Ralph Rosenblum, Ron Kalish.

Jeff Bridges (Jake Rumsey); Barry Brown (Drew Dixon); Jim Davis (Marshal); David Huddleston (Big Joe); John Savage (Loney); Jerry Houser (Simms); Damon Cofer (Jim Bob Logan); Joshua Hill Lewis (Boog Bookin); Geoffrey Lewis, Raymond Guth, Ed Lauter, John Quade (Big Joe's Gang); Jean Allison, Ned Wertimer (Dixon's Parents); Charles Tyner (Farmer); Ted Gehring (Zeb); Claudia Bryar (Mrs. Clum); John Boyd (Prisoner); Monika Henreid (Min); Todd Martin (Sergeant).

During the Civil War, young Drew Dixon (Barry Brown) travels West to avoid fighting for the North, and once there teams with young con artist Jake Rumsey (Jeff Bridges). The duo becomes enmeshed in assorted adventures, including encountering an outlaw (David Huddleston) and his gang and a farmer (Charles Tyner) who prostitutes his young wife (Monika Henreid). With other youths, the two young men discover Western life is really rough and that death or the wrong side of the law seems a typical fate. Matters get worse when the Army hunts these "deserters" and the young men are stalked by a relentless lawman (Jim Davis).
Written by director Robert Benton and David Newman, who also scripted BONNIE AND CLYDE (1968), BAD COMPANY examines the harsh element of the "glamorous" West through the eyes of young drifters. The result "...is an excellent film which combines wry humor and gritty action with in-depth characterizations of two youths on the lam in the Civil War west" (Variety). Jeff Bridges and Barry Brown are fine as the raw-boned youths, although the film's best performances come from Jim Davis as the stern marshal and David Huddleston as the feisty gang leader.
Not everyone liked the picture, however, as can be seen from

Barry Brown, Jerry Houser, John Savage, Joshua Hill Lewis, and
Damon Coffer in BAD COMPANY (1972).

Deirdre Mack's comments in Films in Review (November, 1972):
"Bloody violence and an animal amorality mark this film, which never
makes up its mind whether it is a saga of adolescent boys or an expose showing the West was opened by the dregs of the U.S....
BAD COMPANY owes its failure to their [Benton, Newman] slack
screenplay." Phil Hardy in The Film Encyclopedia: The Western
(1983) observed, "Wildly overpraised for its realistic depiction of
life in the West, BAD COMPANY is, in fact, yet another grimly
ironic tale of the West. Unlike DIRTY LITTLE BILLY (1972) [see
B/V] or THE GREAT NORTHFIELD MINNESOTA RAID (1971) [see
B/V], films which complemented their unheroic views of the West
with muddy streets and the like, BAD COMPANY, with its blending
of the mythic and the comic, is full of quaint costumes and dusky,
dusty skies."

THE BAD MAN OF BRIMSTONE (Metro-Goldwyn-Mayer, 1938) 90
mins.

    Producer, Harry Rapf; director, J. Walter Ruben; story,
Ruben, Maurice Rapf; adaptors, Cyril Hume, Richard Maibaum;
camera, Clyde De Vinna; editor, Frank Sullivan.
    Wallace Beery (Trigger Bill); Virginia Bruce (Loretta Doug-
las); Dennis O'Keefe (Jeffrey Burton); Joseph Calleia (Ben); Lewis

Robert Barrat, Dennis O'Keefe, and Wallace Beery in THE BAD MAN
OF BRIMSTONE (1937).

Stone (Mr. Jackson Douglas); Guy Kibbee (Eight Ball Harrigan);
Bruce Cabot (Blackjack McCreedy); Cliff Edwards (Buzz McCreedy);
Guinn Williams (Vulch McCreedy); Arthur Hohl (Doc Laramie); Noah
Beery (Ambrose Crocker); John Qualen (Loco); Charley Grapewin
(Barney Lane); Robert Barrat (Hank Summers).

    Toward the twilight of his lengthy film career, popular
veteran star Wallace Beery turned more frequently to the Western
genre for his profitable screen vehicles, enjoying the good-bad man
characters he was so adept at portraying. Beery's boisterous,
quickly-produced films always received good production mountings
at Metro-Goldwyn-Mayer and his on-camera hamming made them enjoyable. Occasionally one of them developed into a really sturdy
production, such as THE BAD MAN OF BRIMSTONE. Variety rated
the film a "top-flight yarn" and added, "J. Walter Ruben's direction sets a heady pace and never lets up. He has inserted numerous suspenseful moments that are sure to go big."
    Wallace Beery capers as Trigger Bill, a notorious but good-
hearted bandit who commits a series of holdups with the aid of his
comrade, Ben (Joseph Calleia). Young boxer Jeffrey Burton (Dennis O'Keefe) arrives in Brimstone and begins romancing the
daughter (Virginia Bruce) of the local judge (Lewis Stone).

Trigger Bill, however, finds out young Jeff is his long, lost son and secretly supplies the money needed for the young man to become an attorney. Once Jeff receives his degree, he begins a law and order campaign which puts him at odds with Trigger Bill. When outlaws attempt to silence the lawyer, his dad comes to his rescue and brings peace to Brimstone.

Gruff-voiced Wallace Beery had made nearly two hundred films by the time he starred in THE BAD MAN OF BRIMSTONE, but he had lost none of his screen savvy and turned in an ingratiating performance, winning the audience's heart as the lovable bandit. In addition, the film launched the long and successful starring career of Dennis O'Keefe, who had been in Hollywood for several years as Bud Flanagan, bit player and script writer. The supporting cast, typical of M-G-M, is also substantial, especially Lewis Stone as the weak-willed judge and Bruce Cabot as the black-hearted villain.

THE BADGE OF MARSHAL BRENNAN (Allied Artists, 1957) 74 mins.

Producer, Albert C. Gannaway; associate producer, Thomas Hubbard; director, Gannaway; screenplay, Thomas G. Hubbard; music, Ramez Idriss; song, Hal Levy, Gannaway, and Idriss; assistant director, Lester Guthrie; camera, Charles Straumer; editor, Asa Clark.

Jim Davis (Jeff Harlan, the Stranger); Arleen Whelan (Murdock); Lee Van Cleef (Chad Doniphan); Louis Jean Heydt (Colonel Doniphan); Carl Smith (Sheriff); Marty Robbins (Felipe); Harry Lauter (Dr. Steve Hale); Douglas Fowley (Marshal Matt Brennan); Lawrence Dobkin (Chickamon); Rick Vallin (Deputy); Eddie Crandall (Pepe Joe); Darryl Buy (George); Edward Coleman (Governor).

Marshal Matt Brennan (Douglas Fowley) has been ambushed and left for dead. He is found by at-large fugitive Jeff Harlan (Jim Davis). Brennan dies and Harlan takes his identity and rides into a small town where the sheriff (Carl Smith) is caught between enforcing the law and taking orders from the local cattle baron, Colonel Doniphan (Louis Jean Heydt), and his trigger-happy son Chad (Lee Van Cleef). When the local veterinarian, Dr. Steve Hale (Harry Lauter), quarantines Doniphan's cattle, Harlan, now assumed to be Marshal Brennan, opposes the Colonel and is aided by the sheriff. Meanwhile Brennan is attracted to cafe owner Murdock (Arleen Whelan), who is also courted by Dr. Hale. Doniphan sends for a gunman (Lawrence Dobkin) to oppose Brennan, but in a shoot-out the gunman is killed, as is Chad, and the law prevails. By now Smith realizes Brennan is not who he says he is, but makes no effort to detain him when he leaves town, followed by Murdock.

In the mid and late 1950s, producer/director Albert C. Gannaway made a series of low-budget Westerns, most of them entertaining. THE BADGE OF MARSHAL BRENNAN, with its strong plot and topnotch cast is probably the best of the group. Jim Davis, giving

one of the best performances of his career, is especially effective
as the gunman-turned-lawman. Gannaway, who also produced
country music television programs, had a penchant for using country
music stars in his films and this one featured good work by Carl
Smith as the town marshal and Marty Robbins as Doniphan gang
member who reforms and is murdered as a result.

BADLANDS OF DAKOTA (Universal, 1941) 74 mins.

   Producer, George Waggner; director, Alfred E. Green; story,
Harold Shumate; screenplay, Gerald Geraghty; music, Hans J.
Salter; songs, Carson Robison, Shamus O'Connor, J. J. Stamford;
camera, Stanley Cortez; editor, Frank Gross.
   Robert Stack (Jim Holliday); Ann Rutherford (Anne Grayson);
Richard Dix (Wild Bill Hickok); Frances Farmer (Calamity Jane);
Broderick Crawford (Bob Holliday); Hugh Herbert (Rocky); Andy
Devine (Spearfish); Lon Chaney (Jack McCall); Fuzzy Knight
(Hurricane Harry); Addison Richards (General Custer); Bradley
Page (Chapman); Samuel S. Hinds (Uncle Wilbur); Dwight Latham,
Walter Carlson, Guy Bonham (The Jesters).

   In 1876 in Deadwood in the Dakotas at the time of a gold rush,
two brothers, Jim Holliday (Robert Stack) and Bob (Broderick
Crawford) love pretty Anne (Anne Rutherford). She marries Jim,
not knowing that Bob has been leading a gang which masquerades
as Indians to steal gold from local miners. Jim becomes the sheriff
but the Indians who have been blamed for the gold thefts go on the
warpath and attack the town. Wild Bill Hickok (Richard Dix) arrives and aids Jim in saving the settlement. Hickok remains and
romances frontier gal Calamity Jane (Frances Farmer) but Bob
hires gunman Jack McCall (Lon Chaney) to kill Hickok. Jim finally
realizes the truth about his brother and has a showdown with him.
In the gun battle it is Jane who shoots and kills Bob, bringing
peace to Deadwood.
   This conglomerate of Western action and pseudo-history holds
up well today, although contemporary critics were not thrilled by it.
The Baltimore Sun labeled it "Just a Western with a bigger budget
than usual, incongruously cast, and short on scenery." With its
slick Universal production-line look and a very able cast, plus
steady pacing from director Alfred E. Green, BADLANDS OF DAKO-
TA emerges as one of the better economy-line Westerns of the early
1940s. The movie is particularly strong in the acting department,
with especially memorable work by luminous Frances Farmer as the
boisterous, tough Calamity Jane; staunch Richard Dix as a flam-
boyant Wild Bill, and versatile Lon Chaney as the vicious killer.
Also noteworthy is Addison Richards' deftly underplayed appearance
as General Custer. The movie benefits from the unrestrained comedy
hijinks of Hugh Herbert, Andy Devine, and Fuzzy Knight, and more
particularly from several well-staged brawls.

BADMAN'S COUNTRY (Warner Bros., 1958) 85 mins.

Producer, Robert E. Kent; director, Fred F. Sears; screenplay, Orville H. Hampton; music, Irving Gertz; song, Robert E.
Kent; assistant director, Horace Hough; camera, Benjamin H. Kline;
editor, Grant Whytock.

George Montgomery (Pat Garrett); Neville Band (Butch Cassidy); Buster Crabbe (Wyatt Earp); Karin Booth (Lorna); Gregory
Walcott (Bat Masterson); Malcolm Atterbury (Buffalo Bill Cody);
Russell Johnson (The Sundance Kid); Richard Devon (Harvey Logan); Morris Ankrum (Mayor Coleman); Dan Riss (Marshal McAfee).

Pat Garrett (George Montgomery) leaves Lincoln County,
New Mexico for Abilene to marry Lorna (Karin Booth), planning to
ranch in California. Along the way an attempt is made on his life
by an outlaw friend of Billy the Kid, and in town the sheriff (Dan
Riss) tells him The Sundance Kid (Russell Johnson) has teamed
with Butch Cassidy (Neville Brand) and his Wild Bunch and they
intend to steal a half million dollars from the bank. Also in the
locale are Wyatt Earp (Buster Crabbe), Bat Masterson (Gregory
Walcott) and Buffalo Bill Cody (Malcolm Atterbury), and Garrett
enlists their expert aid in combatting the outlaws. Sundance and
his men try to kill Garrett but fail and in the climax the outlaws
are defeated. Garrett and Lorna are free to marry and move westward.

The best ingredient of BADMAN'S COUNTRY is its creative
use of historical figures (in a fictional plot) and the casting of
George Montgomery as Pat Garrett and Buster Crabbe as Wyatt
Earp. The two veteran Western stars breathe vitality into what
might otherwise have been a mundane actioner. Certainly Fred
Sears' direction is pedestrian and leading lady Karin Booth is
harshly photographed. The film does get off to a good start with
The Mellowmen singing the exciting title song over the opening
credits.

Neville Brand makes a particularly vicious Butch Cassidy in
BADMAN'S COUNTRY and it should be noted that two years before
he had portrayed the same character in THE THREE OUTLAWS.
That sadly arid Western had Cassidy and The Sundance Kid (Alan
Hale, Jr.) south of the border and trailed by a government agent
(Bruce Bennett).

THE BALLAD OF CABLE HOGUE (Warner Bros., 1970) C 121 mins.

Executive producer, Phil Feldman; producer/director, Sam
Peckinpah; screenplay, John Crawford, Edmund Penney; music,
Jerry Goldsmith; songs, Goldsmith and Richard Gillis; art director,
Leroy Coleman; set decorator, Jack Mills; assistant director, John
Gaudioso; sound, Don Rush; camera, Lucien Ballard; editors, Frank
Santillo, Lou Lombardo.

Jason Robards (Cable Hogue); Stella Stevens (Hildy); David

Warner (Joshua); Strother Martin (Bowen); Slim Pickens (Ben);
L. Q. Jones (Taggart); Peter Whitney (Cushing); R. G. Armstrong
(Quittner); Gene Evans (Clete); William Mims (Jensen); Kathleen
Freeman (Mrs. Jensen); Susan O'Connell (Claudia); Vaughn Taylor
(Powell); Max Evans (Webb); James Anderson (Preacher); Felix
Nelson (William).

Eccentric prospector Cable Hogue (Jason Robards) vows revenge on his evil partners, Bowen (Strother Martin) and Taggart
(L. Q. Jones), when the greedy duo leave him to die in the desert.
He finds a water hole near a stagecoach route and sets up a way
station, but shoots his first customer when he refuses to pay for
water. When lecherous revivalist Sloane (David Warner) arrives,
Cable leaves him to guard the site while he goes to town to file his
claim. When the stage line manager (R. G. Armstrong) refuses to
back him, he gets the needed funds from the local banker (Peter
Whitney). He also visits the town whore Hildy (Stella Stevens) but
fails to pay her. Soon Cable's business booms and when Hildy is
forced to leave town by its citizens, he gives her a home and they
fall in love. Eventually, though, she leaves him for a rich man and
Brown and Taggart arrive to take over Cable's operation. However,
he traps them in a snakepit and kills Taggart, but charitably lets
Bowen live. Cable is later killed in an automobile accident and the
locals eulogize him.
Made squarely tongue-in-cheek, THE BALLAD OF CABLE
HOGUE is a light-hearted Western from no-nonsense director Sam
Peckinpah, mainly known as a purveyor of screen violence. While
there is some rough action here, the movie relies more on character and motivation and the mystique of the vanishing romantic West.
The latter is particularly in evidence when the protagonist is run
down by a car, the auto symbolizing the advance of progress which
tames the raw West. An entertaining product, the movie is enhanced by Jason Robards' well modulated performance as the odd-
ball hero.

BANJO HACKETT: ROAMIN' FREE (Columbia Pictures/NBC-TV,
5/3/76) C 100 mins.

Producer, Bruce Lansbury; associate producer, Mel Swope;
director, Andrew V. McLaglen; teleplay, Ken Trevey; music, Morton
Stevens; art directors, Carl Brauner, Ross Bellah; costumes, Grady
Hunt; camera, Al Francis; editors, Dann Cahn, David Wages.
Don Meredith (Banjo Hackett); Ike Eisenmann (Jubal Winner);
Jennifer Warren (Mollie Brannen); Chuck Connors (Sam Ivory); Dan
O'Herlihy (Tip Conaker); Jeff Corey (Judge Janeway); Gloria
DeHaven (Lady Jane Gray); L. Q. Jones (Sheriff Tadlock); Jan
Murray (Jethro Swain); Anne Francis (Flora Dobbs); Slim Pickens
(Lijah Tuttle); David Young (Elmore Mintore); Richard Young (Luke
Mintore); Stan Haze (Blacksmith); John O'Leary (Mr. Creed); Jeff
Morris (Jack O'Spades); John Anderson (Moose Matlock); Kenneth

Jennifer Warren and Don Meredith in BANJO HACKETT (1976).

O'Brien (Wiley Pegram); Britt Leach (The Carpenter); Shirley
O'Hara (The Postmistress); Elizabeth Perry (Grace Nye); Doodles
Weaver (Old Turkey); Ben Bates, Walter Wyatt (Loggers); Albert
Able (Rudolph the Bettor); Faith Quabius (Ruttles); John McKee
(Official).

One-time Dallas Cowboys football quarterback turned sports-
caster/actor Don Meredith headlined this made-for-television movie
which also served as a pilot for a non-materializing series. Movies
on TV (1986) noted, "...Don's warmth helps in the early stages,
but the ex-athlete's lack of acting training shows before long." On
the other hand TV Movies (1985) opined, "Episodic film benefits
from Meredith's easygoing style, fine supporting cast."

In the 1880s, horse trader Banjo Hackett (Don Meredith)
takes his nine-year-old nephew Jubal Winner (Ike Eisenmann) out
of an orphanage and plans to give him a prize-winning Arabian
mare, but the horse is stolen by a bounty hunter (Chuck Connors)
and the duo set out to retrieve the animal. Along the way they experience many adventures before finally regaining the horse.

The outstanding aspect of this tepid telefeature is its sup-
porting cast: Chuck Connors, Dan O'Herlihy, Gloria De Haven,
Jeff Corey, Jan Murray, Anne Francis, L. Q. Jones, and Slim
Pickens--quite a grouping of veterans!

BAR 20 (United Artists, 1943) 54 mins.

Executive producer, Martin Starger; producer, Harry Sher-
man; associate producer, Lewis J. Rachmil; co-producer, William
Wittliff; director, Lesley Selander; based on characters created by
Clarence E. Mulford; screenplay, Morton Grant, Norman Houston,
Michael Wilson; assistant director, Glenn Cook; music director,
Irvin Talbot; art director, Ralph Berger; sound, Jack Noyes;
camera, Russell Harlan; editor, Carroll Lewis.

William Boyd (Hopalong Cassidy); Andy Clyde (California
Carlson); George Reeves (Lin Bradley); Dustine Farnum (Marie
Stevens); Victor Jory (Mark Jackson); Douglas Fowley (Slash);
Betty Blythe (Mrs. Stevens); Robert Mitchum (Richard Adams;
Francis McDonald (One Eye Quirt); Earle Hodgins (Tom); Topper
(The Horse).

The 44th entry in the long-running "Hopalong Cassidy"
series, BAR 20 boasts good direction from Lesley Selander and has
Robert Mitchum in one of his first sizable screen roles as the ranch
owner, while silent star Betty Blythe is featured as the heroine's
mother (Dustine Farnum is the real-life daughter of silent era leading man Dustin Farnum).

Hopalong Cassidy (William Boyd), California Carlson (Andy
Clyde) and Lin Bradley (George Reeves, later TV's Superman)
come across a stage holdup and try to help pretty Marie Stevens
(Dustine Farnum) and her mother (Betty Blythe), who have lost
their jewels. The chief suspects in the stickup are ranch owner

William Boyd, George Reeves, Andy Clyde, and Victor Jory in BAR 20 (1943).

Richard Adams (Robert Mitchum), Marie's fiancée, and Mark Jackson (Victor Jory), Richard's pal. Jackson is really the gang leader and he also wants Adams' ranch. Outlaw One Eye Quirt (Francis McDonald) is captured by the law but his own gang ambushes him. Before he dies he names Jackson as the culprit, but Adams refuses to believe him and he arrests Hoppy and his pals. Escaping, Hoppy poses as Quirt to trap Jackson. When the gang tries to kill him, Hoppy defeats them and captures their leader.

BAR 20 RIDES AGAIN (Paramount, 1936) 63 mins.

Producer, Harry Sherman; director, Howard Bretherton; based on the stories by Clarence E. Mulford; screenplay, Doris Schroeder, Gerald Geraghty; songs, Sam H. Stept and Dave Franklin; camera, Archie Stout.
William Boyd (Hopalong Cassidy); Jimmy Ellison (Johnny

Nelson); Jean Rouverol (Margaret Arnold); George "Gabby" Hayes (Windy Halliday); Frank McGlynn, Jr. (Red Connors); Harry Worth (Nevada); Howard Lang (Jim Arnold); Paul Fix (Gila); Ethel Wales (Clarissa Peters); J. P. McGowan (Buck Peters); Topper (The Horse).

    The third entry in the enduring "Hopalong Cassidy" series, BAR 20 RIDES AGAIN is a fast-paced, actionful drama highlighted by Harry Worth's strong performance as the Napoleon-imitating villain. The movie also introduces George "Gabby" Hayes in the role of Windy Halliday, the lovable old coot he would continue to play in sixteen more series episodes through THE FRONTIERSMAN (q.v.) in 1938. [Hayes played other characters in the first two series' films HOPA-LONG CASSIDY (1935) (see B/V) and THE EAGLE'S BROOD (1935), and in the fourth entry, CALL OF THE PRAIRIE (1936).]

    Hopalong Cassidy (William Boyd) is asked by pal Jim Arnold (Howard Lang), the owner of the SV Ranch, to halt a cattle-rustling gang run by the mysterious Nevada (Harry Worth). He also urges him to leave Johnny Nelson (James Ellison) at home so the lad will not pursue his romance with Jim's daughter Margaret (Jean Rouveral); the request makes Johnny angry. Hoppy takes Connors (Frank McGlynn, Jr.) with him to the SV Ranch, but finds Johnny already there. It develops that Johnny has a rival for Margaret's affection in local businessman George Purdue (Harry Worth), who is really the outlaw gang leader. Pretending to be a city slicker, and enlisting the aid of old prospector Windy Halliday (George "Gabby" Hayes), Hoppy finds the truth and locates the gang's hideout. Patching up his quarrel with Johnny, he ambushes the outlaws and in the skirmish Nevada is killed.

    Don Miller enthused in Hollywood Corral (1976), "BAR 20 RIDES AGAIN amply showed how good the Hoppys were capable of being, and as it evolved how good they were going to be. As before the main action was saved for the climax, but what a climax it was--a rousing pitched battle, preceded and introduced by a beautifully shot and cut montage, depicting the Bar 20 boys saddling and mounting, ready to ride to the rescue of Hopalong." It should be noted that Gluck's classical "Dance of the Furies" was used to heighten the excitement of the sequence.

BARBAROSA (Universal-Associated Film Distributors, 1982) C 90 mins.

    Producer, Paul N. Lazrus, III; co-producer, William D. Wittliff; director, Fred Schepisi; screenplay, Wittliff; art director, Michael Levesque; set decorator, Tok Roysden; music, Bruce Smeaton; assistant director, Tommy Thompson; camera, Ian Baker; editors, Don Zimmerman, David Ramirez.

    Willie Nelson (Barbarosa); Gary Busey (Karl); Gilbert Roland (Don Braulio); Isela Vega (Josephina); Danny De La Paz (Eduardo);

Gary Busey and Willie Nelson in BARBAROSA (1982).

Alma Martinez (Juanita); George Voskovec (Herman); Sharon Compton (Hilda); Howland Chamberlain (Emil).

Young farm youth Karl (Gary Busey) is on the run from vengeful relatives after he accidentally kills his brother-in-law. In the desert he is rescued by legendary bandit Barbarosa (Willie Nelson), who teaches him the art of survival and makes him his partner in his robbery sprees. Karl learns that the bandit is really married to Josephina (Isela Vega), the daughter of wealthy patron Don Braulio (Gilbert Roland) who has sworn to kill the outlaw because of the romance which produced a daughter (Alma Martinez). Although he seems to lead a charmed life, which includes clandestine visits to his wife, Barbarosa is eventually mortally wounded. To keep the man's legend alive, Karl, now a seasoned gunman, dresses like Barbarosa and raids Don Braulio's hacienda, leaving the peasants believing that their beloved bandit-hero is still functioning.

BARBAROSA is an excellent Western, one of the best yet to be offered in the 1980s. Unfortunately Universal Pictures did not know how to promote the feature and it languished theatrically, although it did find acceptance with audiences via television. The movie paints a harshly austere picture of the Old West, wrapped around the character of a Robin Hood-ish bandit. Ian Baker's cinematography of the parched desert environs is especially effective and adds authenticity to the film's theme of the murderous characters who encounter the movie's two protagonists.

Country music singer/songwriter Willie Nelson is outstanding in the title assignment, playing the character in a believable, easygoing manner and his work is matched by Gilbert Roland, giving his best screen performance in years, as the one-legged vengeful patron. Gary Busey, however, makes his character of the clumsy youth a bit too dense for the sudden change to manhood which takes place later in the proceedings.

THE BARON OF ARIZONA (Lippert, 1950) 96 mins.

Producer, Carl K. Rittleman; director/screenplay, Samuel Fuller; music, Paul Dunlap; assistant director, Frank Fox; makeup, Vernon Murdock; art director, Frank P. Sylos; set decorator, Ray Robinson; sound, Garry Harris; special effects, Don Steward; camera, James Wong Howe; editor, Arthur Hilton.

Vincent Price (James Addison Reavis); Ellen Drew (Sofia Peralta-Reavis); Beulah Bondi (Lona Morales); Vladimir Sokoloff (Pepito); Reed Hadley (Griff); Robert Barrat (Judge Adams); Robin Short (Lansing); Barbara Woodell (Carry Lansing); Tina Rome (Rita); Margia Dean (Marquesa); Edward Keane (Surveyor Miller); Gene Roth (Father Guardian); Karen Kester (Sofia as a Child); Joseph Green (Gunther); Fred Kohler, Jr. (Demming); Tristram Coffin (McCleary); Angelo Rosita (Angie); I. Stanford Jolley (Secretary of Interior); Terry Frost (Morelle); Zachary Yaconelli (Greco); Adolfo Ornelas (Martinez); Wheaton Chambers (Brother Gregory); Robert O'Neil (Brother Paul); Stephen Harrison (Surveyor's Assistant).

Advertisement for THE BARON OF ARIZONA (1950).

James Addison Reavis was an Arizona land office clerk in the 1870s who devised a scheme to claim a huge portion of the Arizona Territory by forging old Spanish land grant claims. So successful was his undertaking that the government offered him $25 million for his land claim before it was proven false. As a result he stood trial for his forgery and served time in prison. THE BARON OF ARIZONA is a substantial re-telling of this factual account, highlighted by Vincent Price's well-modulated performance as the crafty Reavis.

Land office clerk Reavis (Vincent Price) realizes he could own the entire Arizona territory by tampering with old Spanish land grants. He concocts an elaborate scheme to do so and this includes going to spain where he joins a monastery to forge documents located there. He dates his claim to 1850, says the Spanish government granted the Arizona Territory land to the Peralta family, and finds a poor child, Sofia (Karen Kester), who he insists is the real heir. He educates the girl, transforms her into an aristocrat and marries her when she becomes an adult (Ellen Drew). Then Reavis makes public his land title. The government sends a forgery expert (Reed Hadley) to fight Reavis' claim but a federal judge (Robert Barrat) holds a hearing and finds the government cannot disprove Reavis' contentions. Meanwhile panic spreads throughout the Territory as citizens fear they will lose their homes. Realizing he loves Sofia more than he wants Arizona or his title as Baron, Reavis confesses to his forgery but a mob almost hangs him. He is rescued and put on trial. He serves six years in prison. When he is released, Sofia is waiting for him.

Despite the use of stock footage and a narrative as grandiose as Reavis' scheme, THE BARON OF ARIZONA has a magnetic power that captures viewers' imagination.

BARQUERO (United Artists, 1970) C 108 mins.

Executive producer, Aubrey Schenck; director, Gordon Douglas; screenplay, George Schenck, William Marks; art director, Allen E. Smith; music, Dominic Frontière; assistant directors, Rusty Meek, Nat Holt, Jr.; special effects, Horace L. Hulburd, Allen Bastien; sound, Robert J. Miller, Bill Tremellen; camera, Gerald Finnerman, Dale Deverman; editor, Charles Nelson.

Lee Van Cleef (Travis); Warren Oates (Jake Remy); Forrest Tucker (Mountain Phil); Kerwin Mathews (Marquette); Mariette Hartley (Anna); Marie Gomez (Nola); Armando Silvestre (Sawyer); John Davis Chandler (Fair); Craig Littler (Pitney); Ed Bakey (Happy); Richard Lapp (Poe); Harry Lauter (Steele); Frank Babich (Roland); Armand Alzamora (Lopez); Terry Leonard (Hawk); Thad Williams (Gibson); Bennie Dobbins (Encow); Rita Conde (Layeta); Brad Weston (Driver).

With the arrival of the 1970s, movie audiences lost interest in the Western genre, although the cinema form would continue on for a few years before hitting a dry spell at decade's end. Sadly, BARQUERO never received the audience recognition it deserved, as it is a highly dramatic and entertaining oater which benefits from especially well modulated performances by Lee Van Cleef (as the hero for a change), Warren Oates as the villain, and Forrest Tucker as a mountain man who helps Van Cleef defeat the outlaw and his pals. Filmed in Colorado, the feature is a flavorful account deserving a revival.

After looting the town of Buckskin, Arizona, outlaw Jake Remy (Warren Oates) and his gang want to cross the Paria River into Mexico, and three gang members go to the little village of Lonely Dell to steal a ferry to take them across the river. They capture Travis (Lee Van Cleef), the boat owner, but he is rescued by Mountain Phil (Forrest Tucker); two of the outlaws are killed while the other one is captured. When Remy arrives, he finds all the citizens are being taken across the river by Travis but the boat owner refuses the outlaw's money to take him across. Remy captures Roland (Frank Babich), who returns from a hunting trip, and wants to exchange the hostage for the ferry passage. Travis refuses the offer even though Roland's wife offers to sleep with him. Travis and Mountain Phil swim the river, stampede the gan's horses and rescue Roland, and the latter's wife keeps her promise to Travis. To escape, Remy and his remaining men build a raft, but during the river crossing Travis arrives with his ferry boat filled with the town's citizens and they massacre the outlaws.

BATTLIN' BUCKAROO (Anchor Film, 1924) 5 reels

Director/screenplay, Alan J. Neitz; camera, Maurice Hughes.
Bill Patton (Jack Merrill); Peggy O'Day (Mary Stevens); Andrew Waldron (Judd Stevens); Lew Meehan (Buck Wheeler); Anthony Freadenthall (Tiny Summers); Fred Hank (Sheriff Brady).

One of the many silent film cowboy heroes whose careers were limited to the independent picture market was Bill Patton, who starred in a number of lower-budget Westerns for various production outfits. BATTLIN' BUCKAROO was done for Anchor and it is a low-grade but actionful entry sporting nice photography and attractive desert scenery. Star Bill Patton, however, was not much of a personality, being reminiscent of a silent Jimmy Wakely. When the sound era ushered in, Patton was reduced to supporting and bit parts, usually in the genre in which he had been a minor star.

Nestor Jack Merrill (Bill Patton) loves Mary Stevens (Peggy O'Day), the daughter of rancher Judd Stevens (Andrew Waldron). Stevens is being cheated by his crooked foreman Buck Wheeler (Lew Meehan), who puts the blame on Jack, saying he is involved with outlaws. To prove his innocence, Jack obtains the evidence to arrest Wheeler and his gang. It develops that Jack is a secret agent on the trail of the crooks. After bringing the gang to justice, Jack and Mary wed.

BELLE STARR (Twentieth Century-Fox, 1941) C 87 mins.

Associate producer, Kenneth Macgowan; director, Irving Cummings; story, Niven Busch, Cameron Rogers; screenplay, Lamar Trotti; Technicolor consultant, Natalie Kalmus; art directors, Richard Day, Nathan Juran; music, Alfred Newman; camera, Ernest Palmer, Ray Rennahan; editors, Robert Simpson.

Randolph Scott (Sam Starr); Gene Tierney (Belle Starr); Dana Andrews (Major Thomas Crail); John Shepperd [Shepperd Strudwick] (Ed Shirley); Elizabeth Patterson (Sarah); Chill Wills (Blue Duck); Louise Beavers (Mammy Lou); Olin Howland (Jasper Tench); Paul Burns (Sergeant); Joseph Sawyer (John Cole); Joseph Downing (Jim Cole); Howard Hickman (Colonel Thornton); Charles Trowbridge (Colonel Bright); James Flavin (Sergeant); Charles Middleton (Carpetbagger); Stymie Beard (Young Jake); Mae Marsh (Preacher's Wife); Kermit Maynard (Union Officer); Franklyn Farnum (Barfly); Cecil Weston (Mother).

BELLE STARR (Hanna-Barbera/CBS-TV, 4/20/80) C 100 mins.

Executive producers, Barry Krost, Joseph Barbera; producer, Doug Chapin; director, John A. Alonzo; teleplay, James Lee Barrett; art director, Robert Kinoshita; music, Dana Kaproff; camera, Alonzo; editor, David Garfield.

Elizabeth Montgomery (Belle Starr); Cliff Potts (Cole Younger); Michael Cavanaugh (Jesse James); Fred Ward (Ned Christie); Jesse Vint (Bob Dalton); Alan Vint (Grat Dalton); Gary Combs (Frank James); Geoffrey Lewis (Reverend Weeks); Sandy McPeak (Pratt); David Knell (Ed Reed); Geno Silva (Blue Duck); Michelle Stacy (Pearl Younger); Peter Hobbs (Jenkins); Morgan Paull (Latham); Sarah Cunningham (Mrs. Chandler); Stony Bower (Summerville); Burt Edwards (Bank Manager); James Burke (Fuller); Dee Cooper (Morris); Gilbert Combs (Baggage Clerk); Kate Williams (Woman); John Edwards (Stockyard Clerk).

Belle Starr (real name: Myra Belle Shirley, 1848-1889), one of the legends of the Old West, dipped into cattle rustling and was the girl friend of Cole Younger. Hardly an attractive female, Belle Starr has been glamorized on screen and has shown up in a number of features, ranging from COURTMARTIAL (1928) with Betty Compson to Pamela Reed playing the character in THE LONG RIDERS (q.v.) in 1981. In addition, Ruth Roman had the title role in BELLE STARR'S DAUGHTER (1948), with Isabel Jewell as Belle, a role she had done convincingly two years earlier in BADMAN'S TERRITORY. Both biopics of Belle Starr had her portrayed by beautiful actresses and neither was a true or satisfying account of the famed bandit's career.

The well-mounted 1941 Twentieth Century-Fox release presented Gene Tierney in the title assignment and her Belle was pictured as a Southern aristocrat who meets Rebel guerrilla leader Sam

John Shepperd [Shepperd Strudwick], Dana Andrews and Gene Tierney in BELLE STARR (1941).

Starr (Randolph Scott) at the end of the Civil War. The two fall in love and marry and continue their fight against Yankee injustice although the war has finished. They lead their gang in righting wrongs caused by the carpetbagging government but are hunted by an Army major (Dana Andrews). Finally Belle and Sam realize the Confederate cause in a lost one, but thanks to their activities the country is better off because of a better government policy for the defeated South.

Forty years later Elizabeth Montgomery (who had portrayed another famous female outlaw, Etta Place, in the 1974 telefilm MRS. SUNDANCE--see B/V) played the title role in the telefeature BELLE STARR, which took a more feminist view of the lady bandit's career. Here Belle is married with two children, but she is more attracted to the lawless life and ends up riding with the James and Dalton brothers gangs and falling in love with Cole Younger (Cliff Potts). While more sexually liberated than in the 1941 version, Belle Starr was no more accurately portrayed by the writers of this thin historical Western.

BELLS OF ROSARITA (Republic, 1945) 68 mins.

Executive producer, Armand Schaefer; associate producer,

Adele Mara, Dale Evans, George "Gabby" Hayes, and Roy Rogers in
BELLS OF ROSARITA (1945).

Eddy White; director, Frank McDonald; screenplay, Jack Townley;
music director, Morton Scott; music, Joseph Dubin; choreography,
Larry Ceballos; assistant director, John Grubbs; art director,
Hilyard Brown; set decorator, Earl B. Wooden; sound, Fred Stahl;
camera, Ernest Miller; editor, Arthur Roberts.

Roy Rogers (Himself); George "Gabby" Hayes (Gabby Whit-
taker); Dale Evans (Sue Farnum); Trigger (The Horse); Adele Mara
(Patty Phillips); Grant Withers (William Ripley); Janet Martin
(Rosarita); Addison Richards (Slim Phillips); Roy Barcroft (Max-
well); Earle Hodgins (Carnival Pitchman); Robert Mitchell Boys Choir
(Themselves); Bob Nolan and the Sons of the Pioneers (Themselves);
Wild Bill Elliott, Allan Lane, Donald "Red" Barry, Robert Livingston,
Sunset Carson, (Guest Stars); and Kenne Duncan, Rex Lease,
Earle Hodgins, Bob Wilke, Ted Adams, Wally West, Poodles Hanne-
ford, Helen Talbot, Charles Sullivan, Hank Bell, Forbes Murray,
Eddie Kane, Tom London, Marin Sais, Rosemond James, Marian
Kerrigan, Sam Ash, Craig Lawrence, Barbara Elliott, Mary McCarty,
Tom Plank, George Barton.

Crook Bill Ripley (Grant Withers) is after the ranch and circus
of pretty Sue Farnum (Dale Evans), whose late father was once his
partner. Ripley claims he is still owed money Sue's father borrowed
from him. In reality the money was repaid but Sue doesn't have the

receipt to verify the transaction. Meanwhile, Gabby Whittaker (George "Gabby" Hayes), an old friend of her father's, comes to help her and rival circus owner Slim Phillips (Addison Richards) suggests he and Sue merge their operations into one circus. Sue and Gabby meet film star Roy Rogers (himself), who is making a new movie in the area, and Ripley wants to sell him Sue's ranch. To stop Phillips from culminating his deal with Sue, which will save her ranch, Ripley has Slim kidnapped and Roy stays on to find out why the man was abducted. In order to get money to save her holdings, Roy suggests Sue put on a big benefit show and he persuades several Republic Western stars, Don "Red" Barry, Bill Elliott, Sunset Carson, Allan Lane, and Bob Livingston, to make guest appearances at the shindig. With the aid of Gabby, Roy finds the hideout where Phillips is being held and they rescue him. However, during the show, Ripley's henchman Maxwell (Roy Barcroft) blows up the bank's safe in order to get the receipts, and Roy and the other stars chase the gang and bring in Ripley and his henchmen.

Made on a larger than usual scale, this offbeat and illogical Roy Rogers series Western was packed with music and action. The songs were provided by Roy and Bob Nolan and the Sons of the Pioneers, plus the Robert Mitchell Boys Choir. The circus sequences also added zest to the proceedings, as did the appearance of the five Republic series Western stars (a plot ploy later used again in Monte Hale's OUT CALIFORNIA WAY, 1946 and Roy Rogers' TRAIL OF ROBIN HOOD, 1950, q.v.). The climax, with each of the stars (riding their famous mounts) corraling and defeating one of the bad guys, is well staged and exciting.

BETWEEN FIGHTING MEN (World-Wide, 1932) 59 mins.

Director, Forrest Sheldon; screenplay, Betty Burbridge, Sheldon; settings, Ralph DeLacy; camera; Ted McCord; editor, Dave Berg.

Ken Maynard (Ken); James Bradbury, Jr. (Wally); Ruth Hall (Judy); Wallace MacDonald (Butch Martin); Albert J. Smith (Thompson); Tarzan (The Horse); and John Pratt, Jack Perrin, Charles King, Walter Law, Edmund Cobb, Jack Kirk, Bud McClure, Roy Bucko, Jack Ward, Slim Whittaker, Robert Hortman.

Ken (Ken Maynard) and Wally (James Bradbury, Jr.) have been raised as brothers, although Ken was adopted by rancher Thompson (Albert J. Smith) when he was a boy. When sheepherders grab government land the cattlemen use for open range, a range war seems imminent. Ken and Wally try to prevent it. Meanwhile they both fall in love with Judy (Ruth Hall), the daughter of a sheepman murdered by Butch Martin (Wallace Macdonald), who was working for Thompson. Feeling remorse, Thompson takes Judy into his home, but when she finds out Martin was working for him, she leaves. Ken tries to convince her he hired

Martin but she doesn't believe him. Wally feels Ken is trying to steal Judy away from him and Martin gets him drunk and the two decide to route the sheepherders after Wally wings Ken in a saloon shootout. Ken follows with the sheriff and a posse. During a fight Wally is shot and Butch escapes, but Ken follows and captures him. Wally survives the shooting and Ken and Judy fall in love.

Sandwiched between his best work at Universal, Ken Maynard made features for Tiffany and World-Wide in the early 1930s. While these outings lacked the production values of his Universal features, they were solid programmers which kept him one of the most popular genre stars of the early 1930s. BETWEEN FIGHTING MEN is a good example of these films, with a literate script making for very pleasant viewing. Unlike most of Maynard's features, this one had surprisingly little action but it made good use of comedy. One particularly amusing sequence has Wally buying Judy a dress for the dance and Ken substituting a package containing a pair of long johns!

BETWEEN MEN (Supreme, 1933) 60 mins.

Producer, A. W. Hackel; director/screenplay, Robert North Bradbury; adaptor, Charles Francis Royal; assistant director, Barry Knight; camera, Bert Longnecker; editor, S. Roy Luby.
Johnny Mack Brown (Johnny Wellington); Beth Marion (Gale Winters); William Farnum (Wellington Rand); Earl Dwire (Trent); Lloyd Ingraham (Sir George Thorn); Frank Ball (Gentry Winters); Milburn Morante (Pete); Sherry Tamey (Trent's Pal).

Virginia blacksmith John Wellington (William Farnum) flees to the West, mistakingly thinking he is responsible for the death of his young son. Actually the boy was only hurt and was adopted by wealthy farmer Sir George Thorn (Lloyd Ingraham) who, two decades later, sends the now grown Johnny Wellington (Johnny Mack Brown) west to locate his granddaughter Gale (Beth Marion). She is the child of the daughter he disowned for marrying rancher Gentry Winters (Frank Ball). Gentry wants ranch hand Trent (Earl Dwire) to leave his pretty daughter alone, the man being employed by rancher Wellington Rand, the new identity of John Wellington. To get even, Trent and cohort (Sherry Tamey) rustle Winters' cattle and kidnap Gale. In the chase Winters is killed, but Johnny and prospector pal Pete (Milburn Morante) rescue the girl. Rand plans to get Trent for Winters' killing and hires Johnny to help him, but he doesn't like the young man's attentions to Gale. After a shootout with Trent's gang, Rand finds Johnny with the girl in a remote cabin and, thinking he has seduced her, Rand fights Johnny but during the fracas he sees a birthmark on the young man and realizes Johnny is his son. When Trent's gang surrounds the cabin, Rand wears Johnny's hat and goes out to meet them. He is shot, thus saving his son and the girl. In a shootout Johnny kills Trent and comes to the belated realization that Rand is his father. Gale goes back to Virginia with Johnny.

One of Johnny Mack Brown's first series Westerns, BETWEEN MEN is a stout production with a complicated plot, but it has the saving grace of a strong performance by William Farnum as Wellington Rand. Although much older than Johnny Mack Brown, the silent film star more than held his own with the younger man in their well-choreographed fight sequence. The movie has a few austere moments, including the shooting of the young boy at the beginning and a later trek as Johnny, Gale, and Rand are hunted in the desert by the murderous outlaws.

BEYOND THE LAST FRONTIER see RIDERS OF OLD SANTA FE

BIG BOY RIDES AGAIN (Beacon/First Division, 1935) 60 mins.

Producers, Max Alexander, Arthur Alexander; director, Al Herman; screenplay, William L. Nolte.
Guinn "Big Boy" Williams (Tom Duncan); Lafe McKee (Smiley Duncan); Bud Osborne (Windy); William Gould (Harding); Frank Ellis (Gunner); and Connie Bergen, Vic Potel, Charles K. French, Augie Gomez.

During the silent years of the 1920s, Guinn "Big Boy" Williams headlined a series of gallopers for various economy independent operations, but in the sound era he became a beloved character actor. In the mid-1930s, however, he top-lined a half-dozen Westerns for Beacon and the films were quite good considering their budget limitations. After viewing them one is saddened that Williams did not have more of a cowboy star career in talkies. The Hollywood Reporter noted of this production, "Here is a fast moving western, packing plenty of thrill action with the added punch of a mystery angle. The picture is well cast and directed...."
Cowboy Tom Duncan (Guinn "Big Boy" Williams) is called home by his rancher father (Lafe McKee), who has treasure buried on his spread and is attempting to prevent outlaws from locating it. Once home, Tom learns his dad has been murdered by the gang. The outlaws kidnap him, but he is rescued by his horse. At first he feels that a rival rancher (Charles K. French) is to blame for the troubles but he changes his mind after meeting the man's lovely daughter (Connie Bergen). His later kidnapper (Victor Potel) is actually the man who murdered his father and he brings the bad man and his gang to justice, finds love with Connie, and keeps the treasure.

BIG JAKE (National General, 1971) C 109 mins.

Producer, Michael Wayne; director, George Sherman; story/ screenplay, Harry Julian Fink, R. M. Fink; art director, Carl Anderson; set decorator, Raymond Moyer; music, Elmer Bernstein;

John Wayne and Maureen O'Hara in BIG JAKE (1971).

assistant director, Newton Arnold; special effects, Howard Jensen; sound, John Ferguson; camera, William Clothier; editor, Harry Gerstad.

John Wayne (Jacob McCandles); Richard Boone (John Fain); Maureen O'Hara (Martha McCandles); Patrick Wayne (James McCandles); Chris Mitchum (Michael McCandles); Bobby Vinton (Jeff McCandles); Bruce Cabot (Sam Sharpnose); Glenn Corbett (O'Brien); Harry Carey, Jr. (Pop Dawson); John Doucette (Buck Dugan); Jim Davis (Head of Lynching Party); John Agar (Bert Ryan); Gregg Palmer (John Goodfellow); Robert Warner (Will Fain); Jim Burke (Trooper); Dean Smith (Kid Duffy); John Ethan Wayne (Jake McCandles); Virginia Capers (Delilah); William Walker (Moses Brown); Jerry Gatlin (Stubby); Tom Hennesy (Saloon Brawler); Don Epperson (Saloon Bully); Everett Creach (Walt Devries).

Outlaw John Fain (Richard Boone) and his gang ride onto the ranch of Martha McCandles (Maureen O'Hara), kill several people, kidnap grandson Little Jack (John Ethan Wayne), and leave a ransom note demanding $1,000,000. While the Texas Rangers are called into the case, the woman sends for her estranged husband, land baron Jacob McCandles (John Wayne), to carry out the ransom delivery. Enlisting the aid of his sons James (Patrick Wayne), Michael (Christopher Mitchum) and Jeff (Bobby Vinton) and old Indian scout friend Sam Sharpnose (Bruce Cabot), McCandles sets out to rescue his grandson. Using the ransom as a ruse, Big Jake meets with Fain and while the Texas Rangers bungle the rescue, McCandles and his cohorts engage the outlaws in a shootout, the Indian dying in the fracas. The rescue attempt is executed successfully and Fain and his gang are exterminated.

Grossing a healthy $7,500,000 at the box office, BIG JAKE (originally called THE MILLION DOLLAR KIDNAPPING) is a big brawling John Wayne Western which is easy to view although very uncerebral. The film's chief appeal is its veteran star, the plot fashioned around the tried-and-true character of the tough, smart, just and larger-than-life role which John Wayne exemplified on the screen. The film moves well under George Sherman's steady direction and its Durango, Mexico locales are highlighted by William Clothier's magnificent cinematography. The screen reunion of Wayne and Maureen O'Hara (who appears only in the film's early scenes) is welcome and the supporting cast is sterling, especially Bruce Cabot as the wise old Indian tracker. With all its entertainment value, the movie's commercial success belongs entirely to its star, as Ellen Eyles noted in John Wayne and the Movies (1976), "It's Big Jake, alias John Wayne, who carries off the film, like the ransom chest, on his broad shoulders. Without him, it would have been in a minor bracket."

BILLY JACK (Warner Bros., 1972) C 115 mins.

Producer, Mary Rose Solti; director, T. C. Frank; screenplay,

Tom Laughlin and Delores Taylor in BILLY JACK (1972).

Frank, Terean Christin; music, Mendell Lowe; assistant directors, Mike Dmytryk, Joseph E. Rickards; camera, Fred Koenekamp, John Stephens; editors, Larry Heath, Marion Rothman.
    Tom Laughlin (Billy Jack); Delores Taylor (Jean Roberts); Clark Howat (Sheriff Cole); Bert Freed (Posner); Julie Webb (Barbara); Ken Tobey (Deputy); Victor Izay (Doctor); Debbie Schock (Kit); Stan Rice (Martin); Teresa Kelly (Carol); Katy Moffatt (Maria); Susan Foster (Cindy); Paul Bruce (Councilman); Lynn Baker (Sarah); Susan Sosa (Sunshine); David Roya (Bernard); Gwen Smith (Angela); John McClure (Dinosaur).

    The husband and wife team of Tom Laughlin and Delores Taylor made a quartet of feature films centered around the character of half-breed Indian and martial arts expert Billy Jack, played in all four films by Laughlin. The initial feature was a modern-day melodrama called BORN LOSERS, issued by American-International in 1967 and featuring Jane Russell. Next came BILLY JACK; it was originally issued by Warner Bros., but after failing to click, the movie was taken over by the Laughlins who redistributed it with great success (grossing $32.5 million). Somehow the unsubtle film hit a chord with the alienated war-weary younger generation which overlooked its strung-out plot, downright low-grade production values, and listless acting by leads Laughlin and Taylor. Only Kenneth Tobey as the villainous lawman contributes a credible performance.

BILLY JACK's anemic storyline tells of the half-breed Billy Jack (Tom Laughlin) returning to the West after being in Vietnam and trying to find peace. He becomes the champion of wild mustang herds hunted by dog meat manufacturers. He meets a young runaway (Julie Webb) and takes her to a school run by a liberal minded teacher (Delores Taylor) but runs into trouble with local ruffians incited by the town's racist sheriff (Kenneth Tobey). Eventually they overcome the local injustice, although the film ends with a shootout at the reservation school.

The financial success of BILLY JACK spawned two sequels: THE TRIAL OF BILLY JACK (1974) and BILLY JACK GOES TO WASHINGTON (1977). THE TRIAL OF BILLY JACK is a direct sequel to its predecessor and has Billy Jack (Tom Laughlin) getting out of prison for a murder he committed in the previous feature and heading to the hills where he was raised. There an old Indian (Gus Greymountain) teaches him to find the "inner peace of the third level," where he has a brief encounter with Jesus Christ. Returning to reality, Billy Jack then continues his crusade against the establishment. Running 170 minutes (it was cut to 144 minutes for TV showings), the film was labeled "one of the longest, slowest, most pretentious and self-congratulatory ego trips ever put on film" by Charles Champlin in the Los Angeles Times. The film grossed $7 million at the box-office.

While Warner Bros. released THE TRIAL OF BILLY JACK, the fourth and apparently final Billy Jack feature, BILLY JACK GOES TO WASHINGTON was released by Taylor-Laughlin in 1977 and bombed at the box office. Running 155 minutes, this laborious outing was a loose remake of the classic MR. SMITH GOES TO WASHINGTON (1939) and had Billy Jack fighting self-interest groups and corruption in the U.S. Senate. Needless to say, it had nothing to do with the Western genre despite the fact that it followed in the earlier "B" Western motifs of Roy Rogers' UNDER WESTERN STARS (1938) and Gene Autry's ROVIN' TUMBLEWEEDS (1939) (qq.v.).

In the midst of all these "Billy Jack" activities Tom Laughlin also made THE MASTER GUNFIGHTER (1975), a remake of the Japanese feature GOYOKIN (1966). Here he was a pacifist gunman (!) out to even the score with his father-in-law (Richard Angarda). The film's inanity is best exemplified by the fact that the direction is credited to Tom Laughlin's son Frank, then nine years old.

BILLY JACK GOES TO WASHINGTON see BILLY JACK

BILLY THE KID IN SANTA FE (Producers Releasing Corp., 1941) 66 mins.

Al St. John, Rex Lease, John Elliott, Bob Steele, and Hal Price in
BILLY THE KID IN SANTA FE (1941).

Producer, Sigmund Neufeld; director, Sherman Scott [Sam
Newfield]; screenplay, Joseph O'Donnell; art director, Melville De-
Lay; music, Johnny Lange, Lew Porter; camera, Jack Greenhalgh;
editor, Holbrook N. Todd.

Bob Steele (Billy the Kid); Al "Fuzzy" St. John (Fuzzy Q.
Jones); Rex Lease (Jeff); Marin Sais (Pat Walker); Dennis Moore
(Silent Don Vincent); Dave O'Brien (Texas Joe Vincent); Charles
King (Steve Barton); Karl Hackett (Davis); Steve Clark (Allen);
Hal Price (Sheriff); Frank Ellis (Hank Baxter); Kenne Duncan
(Scotty); Curley Dresden, Tex Palmer (Outlaws).

In 1940, the newly formed Producers Releasing Corporation
(PRC) signed Western film veterans Tim McCoy and Bob Steele to
star in individual series for the studio, McCoy doing seven features
for the 1940-41 season, while Bob Steele top-lined a half-dozen
features about a whitewashed Billy the Kid. BILLY THE KID IN
SANTA FE was the last of the group and it was typical--obviously
quickly made, speedy in action, seedy in appearance, and
benefitting from Steele's fine work in the lead, the comedy hi-jinks
of sidekick Al St. John, and a supporting cast choked full of genre
veterans. Following this July release, Steele departed PRC (he
would return for four more starring pictures in 1946, including
AMBUSH TRAIL, q.v.) to become part of Republic's "The Three
Mesquiteers" group. Buster Crabbe took over as Billy the Kid in
PRC's next entry, BILLY THE KID WANTED (1941). He would

continue the screen character for several more outings before the title character's name was altered to Billy Carson to appease parental protests about youngsters seeing an outlaw/killer as a film hero.

Billy the Kid (Bob Steele) is framed on a murder charge by crooks Baxter (Frank Ellis) and Texas Joe Vincent (Dave O'Brien). The corrupt local sheriff (Hal Price) plans to let Billy go and then shoot him, but the Kid's pals, Fuzzy (Al St. John) and Jeff (Rex Lease), break him out of jail. When Baxter double-crosses Vincent and kills him, Vincent's brother, reformed gunslinger Silent Don Vincent (Dennis Moore) vows revenge and sets out to murder each of the posse members responsible for his brother's death. Billy, however, gets the blame, although he has been hiding out at the ranch of Pat Walker (Marin Sais). Billy then has to find Texas Don but the latter does not want to have a showdown with Billy, an old friend, and lets the Kid capture him. The law, however, clears both Billy and Texas Don, since all the men he killed were wanted outlaws. Billy and his pals ride off in search of new adventures.

BILLY THE KID RETURNS see YOUNG BILL HICKOK

BLAZING ARROWS see FIGHTING CARAVANS

BLUE CANADIAN ROCKIES (Columbia, 1952) C 58 mins.

Producer, Armand Schaefer; director, George Archainbaud; screenplay, Gerald Geraghty; music, Paul Mehty; music conductor, Mischa Bakaleinikoff; camera, William Bradford; editor, James Sweeney.

Gene Autry (Himself); Pat Buttram (Rawhide); Gail Davis (Sandy Higbee); Carolina Cotton (Herself); The Cass County Boys (Themselves); Ross Ford (Tod Markley); Tom London (Pop Phillips); Mauritz Hugo (Mitchell); Don Beddoe (Cyrus Higbee); Gene Roth (Swede); John Merton (Frenchie); David Garcia (Indian Boy); Bob Woodward (Sergeant Midler); Billy Wilkerson (Dusty); Jody Gilbert (Guest).

Gene Autry was coming to the end of his cowboy star screen tenure when BLUE CANADIAN ROCKIES was issued late in 1952. It was his last feature with Pat Buttram, as Smiley Burnette would return as his sidekick for his remaining half-dozen big screen releases in 1953. Shot in attractive sepiatone in the beautiful redwood country of Northern California, the film is visually appealing and its storyline moves quickly in its under one-hour running time. In addition to the title song, Autry performs "Anytime" and Smiley Burnette's classic "Mama Don't Allow No Music," while the Cass County Boys and Carolina Cotton are featured in additional numbers.

Rancher Cyrus Higbee (Don Beddoe) dispatches his foreman Gene Autry (Himself) and bumbling Rawhide (Pat Buttram) to Canada

THE TALL TIMBER COUNTRY ECHOES THE FURY OF ALL-OUT AUTRY ACTION!

GENE AUTRY and CHAMPION

"BLUE CANADIAN ROCKIES"

GAIL DAVIS · CAROLINA COTTON
CASS COUNTY BOYS

A COLUMBIA PICTURE

to stop his headstrong daughter Sandy (Gail Davis) from marrying fortune hunter Tod Markley (Ross Ford). At Sandy's dude ranch lodge, Gene is hired to sing with the Cass County Boys (themselves), while Rawhide is taken on by caretaker Pop Phillips (Tom London), Higbee's one-time partner, as a wrangler. Gene finds out lumberman Mitchell (Mauritz Hugo) is unhappy because Sandy will not let him cut timber on Higbee lands and Gene and Rawhide have a run-in with two lumbermen, Swede (Gene Roth) and Frenchie (John Merton). Later, horses are stolen from the ranch, Markley, jealous of Gene, is knocked out, and Pop accuses him of being the rustler. While he is rounding up the horses, someone tries to shoot Gene; Markley is found with a gun, but denies firing the shot. Gene has the Mounties check the serial number on the weapon and, later, Mountie Sergeant Midler (Bob Woodward) is found murdered at the lodge. Markley confronts Mitchell at the lumber camp, since the gun was registered in his name, and a fight ensues. Gene saves Tod. Mitchell arms his men and attacks the lodge but Gene gets the draw on the lumbermen and stops the fight. He and Rawhide go after Pop Phillips who is behind all the trouble and who committed the murder. In a shootout, Pop is killed. Gene and Rawhide return home.

BOOT HILL BANDITS (Monogram, 1942) 58 mins.

Producer, George W. Weekes; associate producer, Anna Bell Ward; director, S. Roy Luby; screenplay, Arthur Durlam; music director, Frank Sanucci; camera, Robert Cline; editor, Roy Claire.

Ray "Crash" Corrigan (Crash); John King (Dusty); Max Terhune (Alibi); Jean Brooks (May Meadows); John Merton (Brand Bolton); Glenn Strange (Maverick); I. Stanford Jolley (The Mesquite Kid); Steve Clark (Sheriff); George Chesebro (Stover); Dick Cramer (Hawkins); Budd Buster (Mayor); Milt Moranti (Cameron); Jimmie Aubrey (The Drunk); Charles King (Outlaw); Elmer (The Dummy); and Carl Mathews, Tex Palmer, Merrill McCormack.

Series films have their ups and downs and "The Range Busters" grouping was no exception. One of its weaker links was BOOT HILL BANDITS, which was saddled with an uneven and hard to follow script and lackluster plot developments. Even the movie's three stars seem disinterested in the proceedings and the movie only perks up when Glenn Strange appears all too briefly as a madman prospector who double-crosses his crooked boss Harry Woods. One unbelievable sequence has Alibi (Max Terhune) captured by the bad guys and escaping by tricking his drunken guard (George Chesebro) into firing all the bullets from his six-shooter. Another script oddity has leading lady Jean Brooks' character called the "Songbird of the West" although she scarcely warbles at all.

The Range Busters (Ray "Crash" Corrigan, John King, Max Terhune) arrive in Sundance where the populace has been terrorized by a gang grasping for Wells Fargo gold shipments. The Mesquite

Kid (I. Stanford Jolley) challenges Crash (Corrigan) to a shootout and is killed, while the three lawmen aid the local sheriff (Steve Clark) in ferreting out the mysterious figure behind the murderous gang. They also become involved with a pretty saloon singer (Jean Brooks) who wants the gang brought to justice. The trio unmask the man behind the lawlessness, but not until he has been double-crossed by one of his underlings.

BOOTS OF DESTINY (Grand National, 1937)   59 mins.

Producer, M. H. Hoffman; director, Arthur Rosson; story, E. Morton Hough; screenplay, Rosson; camera, Tom Galligan; editor, Dan Milner.
Ken Maynard (Ken Crawford); Claudia Dell (Alice Wilson); Vince Barnett (Acey Deucy); Ed Cassidy (Harmon); Martin Caralga (Jose); George Morrell (Pedro); Tarzan (The Horse); Wally West (Stunts for Ken Maynard).

One of two productions Ken Maynard made for Grand National for producer M. K. Hoffman (he would do two more for Max and Arthur Alexander for that same studio), BOOTS OF DESTINY is an interesting minor league oater which uses a plot similar to the earlier Guinn "Big Boy" Williams' vehicle, LUCKY BOOTS (1935) (q.v.). Although an actionful picture, BOOTS OF DESTINY featured little action play from its star since Ken Maynard had broken his ankle in his first outing for Hoffman, TRAILIN' TROUBLE (1937), and was mostly doubled herein by actor/stuntman Wally West. This movie, budgeted at $30,000+, grossed more than twice that amount and is one of the star's better later starring solo vehicles.
Cowboys Ken Crawford (Ken Maynard) and Acey Deucy (Vince Barnett) ride onto a rustling-plagued ranch spread owned by Alice Wilson (Claudia Dell), who is working with her foreman Harmon (Ed Cassidy) to stop the lawlessness. Ken captures one of the rustlers but her foreman convinces Alice that Ken is the real rustler and he goes to jail. It turns out Harmon is the head of the gang and wants the ranch because it contains buried treasure. The gang raids the ranch and finds the booty, but Ken escapes from jail and rounds up the outlaws, recovering the famed Vasquez treasure for his attractive boss.

BORDER BADMEN (Producers Releasing Corp., 1945) 58 mins.

Producer, Sigmund Neufield; director, Sam Newfield; screenplay, George Milton; music director, Frank Sanucci; assistant director, William O'Connor; sound, Lyle Wiley; camera, Jack Greenhalgh; editor, Holbrook N. Todd.
Buster Crabbe (Billy Carson); Al "Fuzzy" St. John (Fuzzy Q. Jones); Lorraine Miller (Helen); Charles King (Merritt); Ralph Bennett (Deputy Spencer); Archie Hall (Gillan); Budd Buster (Evans);

Marilyn Gladstone (Roxie); Marin Sais (Mrs. Bentley); and Bud Osborne, Bob Kortman.

Between 1941 and 1946 Buster Crabbe and Al St. John starred in 42 low-budget PRC Westerns, with Crabbe's hero character undergoing a name change from Billy the Kid to Billy Carson. BORDER BADMEN is a representative series entry with its tawdry appearance countered by fast action and Al St. John's delightful pratfalls. Fuzzy Q. Jones (Al St. John) is the apparent heir to the Stockton estate and with his pal Billy Carson (Buster Crabbe) rides into Silver Creek where he is arrested for the murder of the man guarding the tollgate into town. Merritt (Charles King), the leader of a gang of crooks, who wants the estate for himself, lets Billy and Fuzzy go and on the road they meet Helen Stockton (Lorraine Miller), the actual heir to the estate. The trio is captured by Merritt's gang while the crook sets up Roxy (Marilyn Gladstone) as the "real" heir. Helen helps Billy and Fuzzy escape and with the aid of several of Helen's relatives, they rescue her from Merritt and round up the crooks. Helen earns the title to the estate while Fuzzy ends up with one dollar.

BORDER FEUD (Producers Releasing Corp., 1947) 55 mins.

Producer, Jerry Thomas; director, Ray Taylor; screenplay, Joe O'Donnell, Patricia Harper; camera, Milford Anderson; editor, Joe Gluck.
Lash LaRue (The Cheyenne Kid); Al "Fuzzy" St. John (Sheriff Fuzzy Q. Jones); Bob Duncan (Barton); Brad Slavin (Jim Condon); Kenneth Farrell (Bob Hart); Gloria Marlen (Carol Condon); Casey MacGregory (Jed Young); Ian Keith (Doc Peters); Mikel Conrad (Elmore); Ed Cassidy (Sheriff Steele).

BORDER FEUD is Lash LaRue's second starring picture for PRC, following his successful introduction as a headliner in LAW OF THE LASH (q.v.). The film contains plentiful action and moves quickly, despite an overuse of long shots of shooting, riding, and gun battles. Sidekick Al St. John repeats the comedy hill climbing gambit he first introduced in RIDERS OF DESTINY (1933) (see B/V).
In Red Gulch, Sheriff Fuzzy Q. Jones (Al St. John) is at odds with an outlaw known as The Tiger and two feuding families. Lawman Cheyenne Kid (Lash LaRue) comes to help him and masquerades as The Tiger to get the goods on the outlaw gang behind neighborhood trouble. He proves the resident doctor (Ian Keith) is the culprit.

BORDER GUNS see also BORDER MENACE

BORDER GUNS see also GHOST CITY

BORDER MENACE (Awyon, 1935) 55 mins.

Producer, Robert L. Horner; director, Jack Nelson; screenplay, Horner; camera, Frank Bender; editor, James Aubrey.
Bill Cody (Bill "The Shadow" Williams); Miriam Rice (Helen); George Chesebro (Chuck Adams); Jimmie Aubrey (Sheriff); Ben Corbett (Dragon); Frank Clark (Harris); Jim Donnelly (Milette).

"B" Western buffs consider BORDER MENACE the worst genre film ever made, which makes this production worth analyzing. Incompetently produced, poorly acted (!) and leadenly dull, BORDER MENACE is rank from start to finish, with no redeeming comedy relief. Slapped together perfunctorily, it remains a high-water mark of inept storytelling.
Secret Service agent Bill "The Shadow" Williams (Bill Cody) is investigating sabotage activities against a rancher (Jim Donnelly) and his pretty daughter Helen (Miriam Rice), whose range lands contain rich oil deposits. Williams determines that Chuck Adams (George Chesebro) and his gang are causing the trouble and that they are in the pay of dishonest banker Harris (Frank Clark). In a showdown with Adams, Williams defeats him, arrests Harris, and wins Helen's devotion.
Star Bill Cody appears disinterested, leading lady Miriam Rice lacks histrionic ability, and an older cast member appears three sheets to the wind in his big scene. One sequence has Cody combatting the bad guys and getting his black outfit torn. The torn shirt then appears, disappears, and reappears throughout the rest of the feature. The less said about Jimmie Aubrey's comedy the better; ditto for Ben Corbett as convict Dragon.
Actually BORDER MENACE is one of a trio of pictures Bill Cody did for Awyon, the others being BORDER GUNS and WESTERN RACKETEERS, all issued about the same time in the mid-1930s. All are bad, but at least BORDER GUNS has a likable if hammy performance by Franklyn Farnum in a good/bad guy role.

BORDER MENACE see also GHOST CITY

THE BORDER PATROL (Pathé, 1928) 4,598'

Producer, Charles R. Rogers; director, James P. Hogan; screenplay, Finis Fox; camera, Sol Polito; editor, Harry Marker.
Harry Carey (Bill Storm); Kathleen Collins (Beverly Dix); Phillips Smalley (Conway Dix); Richard Tucker (Earl Hanway); James Neill (Lefty Waterman); James Marcus (Captain Bonham).

United States border patrolman Bill Storm (Harry Carey) falls in love with heiress Beverly Dix (Kathleen Collins), who is unknowingly involved with crooks, one of whom is her father (Phillips Smalley). Bill tracks the gang to their hideout but the arrival of the girl causes his capture; however, she helps him to escape. As a result the gang takes Beverly along in their getaway and Bill gives chase. To stop the crooks, Bill boards a train which crashes with the gang's auto; the girl is unhurt and the crooks are captured. It develops that Beverly's father is a border patrol member working incognito to trap the gang.

Harry Carey was one of the screen's first Western stars, his genre career predating that of William S. Hart. During the 1920s he made a highly successful batch of oaters and this Pathé release is a pleasant example with lots of comedy, although not of the slap-stick variety. A modern-day Western with much footage shot in El Paso, Texas, BORDER PATROL spotlighted good cinematography and a well engineered finale chase sequence.

BORDER TREASURE (RKO, 1950) 60 mins.

Producer, Herbert Schlom; director, George Archainbaud; screenplay, Norman Houston; music, Paul Sawtell; music director, C. Bakaleinikoff; assistant director, John Pommer; art directors, Darrill Silvera, Harley Miller; makeup, Mel Burns, Gene Hibbs; sound, John Cass, Clem Portman; camera, J. Roy Hunt; editor, Desmond Marquette.

Tim Holt (Ed Porter); Jane Nigh (Stella); John Doucette (Bat); House Peters, Jr. (Rod); Inez Cooper (Anita Castro); Julian Rivero (Felipe); Ken MacDonald (Sheriff); Vince Barnett (Pokey); Robert Peyton (Del); David Leonard (Padre); Tom Monroe (Dimmick); Richard Martin (Chito Rafferty).

Cowboys Ed Porter (Tim Holt) and his pal Chito Rafferty (Richard Martin) help Anita Castro (Inez Cooper) transport valuables to aid the victims of a Mexican earthquake. An outlaw gang led by Bat (John Doucette) attacks the young woman's party as they leave her Arizona ranch and Chito is held hostage by the gang. Ed comes to his aid and later, in Los Alamos, Chito identi-fies Bat and he is jailed. Gang member Rod (House Peters, Jr.) then takes over the outlaw band and decides to leave Bat behind bars. With the aid of saloon singer Stella (Jane Nigh), they cap-ture the valuables. Anita accuses Ed and Chito of being part of the holdup. To clear up matters, Ed has Bat released so he will lead them to the stolen merchandise. At the outlaws' hideout, Bat has a showdown with Rod, and Ed, Chito and the law round up the gang and recover the treasure.

BORDER TREASURE is another solid actioner from the RKO-Tim Holt series. The film benefits from several first rate per-formances, especially Jane Nigh as the conniving Stella and John Doucette and House Peters, Jr. as the villains. The movie contains many brutal sequences, including the knock-down, drag-out saloon brawl between Tim Holt and John Doucette and the moment where the evil Bat captures Anita's employee Felipe (Julian Rivero) and mercilessly beats him with a whip.

BORDERLAND see IN OLD MEXICO

BORN TO BATTLE (Pathé, 1927) 4,875'

Director, Alvin J. Neitz; story/screenplay, L. V. Jefferson;
camera, Harold Wenstrom, David Smith.
   Bill Cody (Billy Cowan); Sheldon Lewis (Hank Tollivar); Barbara Luddy (Barbara Barstow); Nora Cecil (Ma Cowan); Olin Francis (Zack Barstow).

   Bill Cody is one of those "B" Western stars who headlined
actioners in both the silent and sound eras, but he is mostly known
for his talkies today and there he appears to be a weak hero,
physically not up to the rigors of the job. Although he starred in
Western series until 1936, his sound films aren't overly good and,
in fact, he appeared in what is considered the worst "B" Western
of all time, BORDER MENACE (1935), q.v. In silent films, however,
Cody was a fine hero whose movies interpolated comedy into the action format with pleasing results. BORN TO BATTLE is one of his
Pathé offerings, which ran from 1924 to 1927, after which he worked
at Universal. In this Pathé release, the star accomplishes much of
his own stunt work and uses a bullwhip, predating Lash LaRue's
on-screen gimmick by nearly two decades.
   Half-crazed Ma Cowan (Nora Cecil) wants revenge for the
death of her husband Jud, who she believes was killed by the Barstow family. To complicate matters, her son Billy (Bill Cody) is
romancing pretty Barbara Barstow (Barbara Luddy). Billy's uncle,
Hank Tollivar (Sheldon Lewis), wants a feud between the two
families so he can obtain both their ranches. He was the one who
killed Jud, with Zack Barstow (Olin Francis) as a witness. Tollivar
then murders Zack and Billy is blamed, but he escapes with the
help of his three brothers and returns to corner his uncle and his
gang. Tollivar escapes and Billy trails him to the Barstow ranch,
where the bad man has cornered Barbara. Billy stops him but his
mother kills the senior Barstow and Billy tells her the truth, ending
the feud.

THE BOSS COWBOY (Superior, 1934) 51 mins.

   Producer/director, Victor Adamson [Denver Dixon]; screen-
play, B. Burbodge [Betty Burbridge]; art director, Jack Cook;
camera, Byron Baker; editor, Francis Borroughs.
   Buddy Roosevelt (Dick Taylor); Frances Morris (Mary Ross);
Sam Pierce (Tom Ross); George Chesebro (Jack Kearns); Fay
McKenzie (Sally Nolan); Lafe McKee (Nolan); William McCormick
(Slim); Bud Osborne (Sheriff); Clyde McClary, Allen Holbrook
(Ranch Hands); Eva McKenzie (Ranch Woman).

   Buddy Roosevelt (real name: Kent Sanderson) rode the celluloid range in the mid-to-late 1920s for producer Lester F. Scott, Jr., who also headlined Wally Wales and Buffalo Bill, Jr. A big, handsome, rugged star, Roosevelt proved popular with the juvenile audiences of the silent era and he made the transition to sound easily, headlining a series for the low-grade Big Four outfit. Roosevelt's starring career, however, came to a close in 1934 when he made a quartet of bad oaters for producer/director Victor Adamson. THE BOSS COWBOY (the other three were: CIRCLE CANYON, LIGHTNING RANGE, and RANGE RIDERS) was a slow moving, tacky production rambling along with poorly staged fight and chase sequences and many unintentionally funny moments. Roosevelt did his best in a film where the camera was planted firmly in front of the actors as they read their lines; the script acceptable, but director Adamson was unable to bring it to life. Only Byron Baker's desert cinematography is a plus factor.

Pretty Sally Nolan (Fay McKenzie) returns home to the Flying N ranch after a five-year absence and she is met by her dad (Lafe McKee) and his foreman Dick Taylor (Buddy Roosevelt). Also at the station is Mary Ross (Frances Morris), who has come to see her brother Tom (Sam Pierce), whose foreman Jack Kearns (George Chesebro) is suspected by Nolan and Taylor of rustling. Later Ross sees a man he believes to be a rustler and takes aim at him, but it is Kearns who kills the man and makes Ross think he did the deed--the man turns out to be one of Nolan's cowpunchers. Meanwhile Kearns lusts for Mary; she is liked by Dick, who in turn attracts Sally. Dick finds a poster of a man wanted for murder and, realizing it is Kearns, alerts the local sheriff (Bud Osborne). When Kearns attempts to rob the Nolan ranch, Dick stops him, and after a lengthy cliff-side brawl, forces a confession from him. Love comes to Dick and Mary, and to Tom and Sally.

BOSS OF BOOMTOWN (Universal, 1944) 58 mins.

Associate producer, Oliver Drake; director, Ray Taylor; screenplay, William Lively; art directors, John B. Goodman, Abraham Grossman; songs, Johnny Marvin; camera, William Sickner; editor, Ted Kent.

Rod Cameron (Steve); Tom Tyler (Jim); Fuzzy Knight (Chatter); Vivian Austin (Dale Starr); Ray Whitley (Clark); Jack Ingram (Ridgeway); Robert Barron (Brett); Marie Austin (Minerva); Max Wagner (Dunne); Sam Flint (Cornwall); Dick Alexander (Yuma); The Bar-Six Cowboys (Themselves).

In the mid-1940s Universal tapped big Rod Cameron as its new Western star and the studio initiated his series with BOSS OF BOOMTOWN, teaming him with established genre headliner Tom Tyler and the studio's perennial sidekick, Fuzzy Knight, along with musical interludes by Ray Whitley and his Bar-Six Cowboys. This fast moving actioner spawned more starrers for Cameron, but he was destined for better things and after only a handful of "B" oaters, he was elevated to starring in big-budget productions.

Civil War cavalry sergeants Steve (Rod Cameron) and Jim (Tom Tyler) are friendly enemies who get into trouble with the Army just one day before their enlistments are up. Steve talks Jim into reenlisting but doesn't do so himself so he can aid Treasury man Cornwall (Sam Flint), who masquerades as an assayer, in investigating the gang behind a stagecoach mine payroll robbery. To prove he is an outlaw, Steve holds up another stage, gets in good with the gang, and finds it is run by mine owner Norton Brett (Robert Barron), aided by Ridgeway (Jack Ingram), who controls a gambling house recently inherited by pretty Dale Starr (Vivian Austin). Jim, Steve and Steve's pal Chatter (Fuzzy Knight) try to infiltrate the gang but the bandits double-cross them by drygulching Cornwall, and an Army sergeant (Max Wagner) arrests Jim and Chatter and takes them to the Army prison. Meanwhile the outlaws plan to heist an Army pay wagon, so Jim and Chatter break jail, with Steve and the sergeant on their trail, and the four team to save the payroll and arrest Brett and Ridgeway.

It should be noted that this film nicely interpolated action and music, the latter represented with a trio of tunes composed by veteran crooner Johnny Marvin, plus the perennial favorite "The Cowboy's Lament."

THE BOUNTY KILLER (Embassy, 1965) C 93 mins.

Executive producer, Pat B. Rooney; producer, Alex Gordon; director, Spencer Gordon Bennet; screenplay, R. Alexander, Leo Gordon; music, Ronald Stein; sound, Harry Lindgren; camera, Frederick E. West; editor, Ronald Sinclair.

Dan Duryea (Willie Duggan); Rod Cameron (Johnny Liam); Audrey Dalton (Carole); Richard Arlen (Ridgeway); Buster Crabbe (Mike Clayman); Fuzzy Knight (Luther); Johnny Mack Brown (Sheriff Green); Peter Duryea (Youth); Bob Steele (Red); Eddie Quillan (Pianist); Norman Wilis (Hank Willis); Edmond Cobb (Townsman); Duane Ament (Ben Liam); Grady Sutton (Minister); Emory Parnell (Sam); Daniel J. White (Marshall Davis); I. Stanford Jolley (Sheriff Jones); John Reach (Jeb); Red Morgan (Seddon); Dolores Domasin (Waitress); Dudley Ross (Indian); Ronn Delanor (Joe); Tom Kennedy (Waiter); G. M. "Bronco Billy" Anderson (Old Man).

In 1965 filmmaker Alex Gordon produced THE BOUNTY KILLER and REQUIEM FOR A GUNFIGHTER (q.v.) back-to-back at Paramount Pictures, the features being issued by Embassy Pictures. While both films were scant in production values, they were a treasure trove for genre followers, populated by a raft of veteran players, most associated with the Western in the bygone days of celluloid glory. Both features were directed by Western and serial veteran Spencer Gordon Bennet, who imbued them with good action and pacing.

THE BOUNTY KILLER tells of Willie Duggan (Dan Duryea), a mild-mannered Easterner who comes West and is beaten for talking

Fuzzy Knight, Buster Crabbe, and Dan Duryea in THE BOUNTY KILLER (1965).

with dance hall girl Carole (Audrey Dalton). Gunman Johnny Liam (Rod Cameron), however, comes to his rescue and Willie then gets a job delivering the miners' payroll for a transport operation. When Willie and his pal Luther (Fuzzy Knight) are attacked by robbers, Willie kills one of them and gets a reward, and he and Luther become bounty hunters. The duo capture murderous outlaw Mike Clayman (Buster Crabbe), but his gang kills Luther and wounds Willie, who is found by Carole's father (Richard Arlen), with the girl nursing him back to health. Although he loves Carole, Willie vows to revenge Luther's murder and continue his life as a bounty hunter. He kills Clayman but in the process accidentally murders an innocent man and himself becomes hunted. Willie finally decides to marry Carole but is gunned down by a younger bounty killer (Peter Duryea).

Of all the veteran performers in THE BOUNTY KILLER, Buster Crabbe is the most impressive in his performance as the cold-blooded killer Mike Clayman.

BRAND OF THE OUTLAWS (Supreme/William Steiner, 1936) 60 mins.

Producer, A. W. Hackel; director, Robert North Bradbury; screenplay, Forbes Parkhill; assistant director, Edwin Tyler; sound, Clifford Ruberg; camera, Bert Longenecker; editor, Don Milner.

Bob Steele (Gary Gray); Margaret Marquis (Verna Matlock); Jack Rockwell (Ben Holt); Charles King (Rufe Matlock); Virginia True Boardman (Mrs. Matlock); Edward Cassidy (Sheriff); Frank Ball (Doctor); and Bud Osborne, Bob Kortman.

When a lawman (Ed Cassidy) is shot by rustlers, young Gary Gray (Bob Steele) aids him and is hired by the gang, who he doesn't know are outlaws, to help brand cattle. When deputies led by Holt (Jack Rockwell) raid the camp, Bob is captured and Holt brands his chest. When the sheriff finds out he fires Holt, who is really the rustler chief. To gain revenge, Gary trails one of the gang, Rufe (Charles King), to his ranch and beats him in a fight, retrieving his horse and gun. Holt murders Rufe, blames Gary and at the same time romantically pursues Rufe's stepdaughter Verna (Margaret Morris), who rejects him. Gary escapes form mail and holds up the stage to save its money since Holt has been hired as the guard and plans to rob it himself. Gary returns the money to the express office and tells the sheriff the truth about Holt. In the finale, Holt and his gang are corraled, with Holt being killed. Gary and Verna fall in love.

Bob Steele's father, Robert North Bradbury, directed and wrote this actioner, as he did for many of his son's features, and overall it is a good release with lots of activity to please the star's followers. In 1937, Steele's features for producer A. W. Hackel would be issued by Republic and took on a slicker, more production-line quality lacking in his earlier outings.

BREED OF THE BORDER (Monogram, 1933) 60 mins.

Producer, Trem Carr; director, Robert North Bradbury; screenplay, Harry O. Jones.

Bob Steele (Speed Brent); Marion Byron (Joan Stafford); John Elliott (Judge Stafford); Ernie Adams (Joe Shaw); George "Gabby" Hayes (Chuck Wiggins); Fred Cavens (Fencer); and Henry Roquemore, Wilfred Lucas, Robert Cord, Perry Murdock.

Bob Steele's 1930s Westerns included many diverse plot machinations, probably more than those starring most cowboy heroes of the period. BREED OF THE BORDER is no exception: here the hero is a cowboy race car driver who is also an expert fencer. Otherwise the movie is average, with a hazy plot but plenty of action, especially in the climactic car race with a fast speed vehicle replacing the horse. Such ploys are not odd for Steele's films, as an earlier entry in his Monogram series for producer Trem Carr, HIDDEN VALLEY (1932), even includes the Goodyear blimp!

On the run from the law, escaped convict Joe Shaw (Ernie Adams) meets race car driver Speed Brent (Bob Steele), who takes

Bob Steele and Ernie Adams in BREED OF THE BORDER (1933).

him across the Mexican border. There Shaw takes revenge on Judge Stafford (John Elliott), the man who sent him to prison, by almost killing him. Shaw steals $50,000 worth of government bonds which the judge had purchased with the proceeds from the sale of his cattle. Joan Stafford (Marion Byron), the judge's niece, is an undercover government Secret Service agent working as a singer in a border night spot and she asks Speed and his pal Chuck Wiggins (George "Gabby" Hayes) to help recover the bonds. As a result, Speed and Chuck agree to lead a cattle drive across the border for Shaw, but when Shaw learns the truth he tries to escape. Speed chases him in his auto and Shaw is killed when his car goes off a cliff.

This film includes a well-mounted fencing sequence between Bob Steele and Fred Cavens, the latter one of Hollywood's best noted swordsmen.

BREED OF THE WEST (Big Four Film Corp., 1930) 60 mins.

Director, Alvin J. Neitz [Alan James]; story, Neitz, Henry Taylor; screenplay, Neitz; sound, Homer Ellmaker; camera, William Nobles; editor, Ethel Davey.

Wally Wales (Wally Weldon); Virginia Brown Faire (Betty Sterner); Buzz Barton (Jim Sterner); Robert Walker (Longrope

Wheeler); Lafe McKee (Mr. Sterner); Bobby Dunn (Shorty); Edwin [Edmund] Cobb (Sam Hardy); George Gerwin (Cook); Hank Bell (Sheriff Cole); and Art Mix, Frank Ellis, Slim Andrews.

Floyd Alderson Taliaferro came to films in the pre-World War I days and kicked around Hollywood for a decade before finding tenuous stardom in poverty row Westerns for producer Lester F. Scott's Action Pictures. It was Scott who changed his player's name to Wally Wales (a combination of Wally Reid and the Prince of Wales), and the handsome, lanky actor proved to be a fine addition to Tinsel Town's cowboy heroes, as evidenced by such starrers as GALLOPING ON (1925), (q.v.). Like many of his comrades, Wales found it rough going when talkies came in, but his voice was strong and he eventually landed a starring series at Big Four, a low-budget organization, and then supported other genre stars, although he did star in eight of the "Bud 'n' Ben" featurettes for Imperial in 1934 using the name Walt Williams. After appearing as Wally Wales in THE WAY OF THE WEST (Superior, 1935) the actor changed his screen name to Hal Taliaferro in 1936 and thereafter became a topnotch character actor, often appearing as a villain in Republic oaters before retiring from the screen in the early 1950s. He died in 1980 at the age of 85.

BREED OF THE WEST is one of Wally Wales' series for producer John R. Freuler's Big Four and it is poorly made, with more focus on romance than action. Wally Wales plays a ranch hand in love with his boss's (Lafe McKee) pretty daughter (Virginia Brown Faire) and at odds with the corrupt foreman (Robert Walker) who plans to rob the old man. Also involved is a young boy (Buzz Barton), actually the ranch owner's long-lost son.

BRET MAVERICK (Warner Bros. TV/NBC-TV, 12/1/81) C 100 mins.

Executive producer, Meta Rosenberg; supervising producer, Gordon Dawson; producers, Jeffrey Fischer, Charles Floyd Johnson; associate producer, Mark Horowitz; director, Stuart Margolin; teleplay, Gordon Dawson; costumes, Lee Dawson; makeup, Charles Roberson; art director, Scott Rittenour; music, J. A. C. Redford; theme song, Ed and Patsy Bruce, Glenn Ray; camera, Andrew Jackson; editors, George Rohrs, Diane Adler.

James Garner (Bret Maverick); Darleen Carr (Mary Lou Springer); Ed Bruce (Tom Guthrie); Ramon Bieri (Mr. Crow); John Shearin (Sheriff Mitchell Dows); Richard Hamilton (Cy Whitaker); Janis Paige (Mandy Packer); John McLiam (Doc Holliday); Stuart Margolin (Philo Sandine); Billy Kerr (Blue-Eyed Kid); Jack Garner (Jack); Louis DelGado (Shifty); Ed Bakey (Lyman Nickerson); Bill Cross (Dembro); Chuck Mitchell (Joe Dakota); Dwayne R. Campbell (Lucas); Ivan J. Rado (Wolfgang Miter); David H. Banks (Delta Fox); Tommy Bush (Deputy Sturgess); Norman Merrill, Jr. (Teller); Ruth Estler (Townswoman); Al Berry (Townsman); Kirl Cameron, Max Martin (Boys); Richard Moll (Sloate).

James Garner solidified his popularity as an actor in the role of Bret Maverick, which he played from 1957 to 1960 on the ABC-TV series "Maverick." Jack Kelly co-starred as his brother Bart and after Garner walked out of the series in 1960, Roger Moore was added as Cousin Beau Maverick; in 1961 Robert Colbert appeared briefly as a third Maverick brother, Brent, before Jack Kelly was left to go it alone until the series faded in 1962. In 1978 Garner and Kelly reappeared as the Maverick brothers in the ABC-TV tele-feature THE NEW MAVERICK, starring Charles Frank as still another brother, Ben. The telefilm spawned a series with Frank called "Young Maverick" the next year for a brief run. In 1981, James Garner had the title assignment in another telefeature, BRET MAVERICK, also a short-running series.

BRET MAVERICK opens with aging gambler Brett (James Garner) riding into the small Arizona town of Sweetwater and meeting Doc Holliday (John McLiam), who wants to win one last big game and give up gambling. Brett wins $100,000 and the local madam's (Janis Paige) saloon and decides to stay in Sweetwater. A young woman (Darleen Carr) who runs the local newspaper keeps after Maverick for a story and troubles begin for him when another gambler (Bill McKinney) steals his money from the local bank. With a fake Indian guide (Stuart Margolin) Bret sets out in search of the thief and is joined by the local sheriff (Ed Bruce) and the news gal. They retrieve the loot and the lawman joins Bret in running the Red Ox Saloon.

When the "Bret Maverick" series began on NBC-TV in 1982 Ed Bruce co-starred with James Garner. Bruce also co-wrote the show's title song and recorded it for MCA Records.

BRIGHAM YOUNG--FRONTIERSMAN (Twentieth Century-Fox, 1940) 112 mins.

Producer, Darryl F. Zanuck; associate producer, Kenneth Macgowan; director, Henry Hathaway; based on the book Children of God by Vardis Fisher; story, Louis Bromfield; screenplay, Lamar Trotti; music, Alfred Newman; song, Sam Coslow; art directors, William Darling, Maurice Ransford; special effects, Fred Sersen; camera, Arthur Miller; editor, Robert Bischoff.

Tyrone Power (Jonathan Kent); Linda Darnell (Zina Webb); Dean Jagger (Brigham Young); Brian Donlevy (Angus Duncan); Jane Darwell (Eliza Kent); John Carradine (Porter Rockwell); Mary Astor (Mary Ann Young); Vincent Price (Joseph Smith); Jean Rogers (Clara Young); Ann Todd (Mary Kent); Willard Robertson (Herbert Kimball); Moroni Olsen (Doc Richards); Marc Lawrence (Prosecutor); Stanley Andrews (Hyrum Smith); Frank Thomas (Hubert Crum); Fuzzy Knight (Pete); Dickie Jones (Henry Kent); Selmer Jackson (Caleb Kent); Frederick Burton (Mr. Webb); Russell Simpson (Major); Arthur Aylesworth (Jim Bridger); Chief Big Tree (Big Elk); Davidson Clark (Johnson); Claire Du Brey (Emma Smith); Tully Marshall (Judge); Dick Rich (Mob Leader); Ralph Dunn (Jury

Foreman); Edwin Maxwell (Leader); Edmund MacDonald (Elder);
George Melford (John Taylor); Charles Halton (Prosecutor); Lee
Shumway (Mobster); Frank LaRuse (Sheriff); Imboden Parrish (Man).

Producer Darryl F. Zanuck made this well-mounted feature on
an expensive (by 1940s standards) $2,500,000 budget and it remained
his favorite production. Based on Vardis Fisher's 1939 book Children
of God, the film eliminated the book's anti-Mormon stance and told a
straightforward history of the trek of the people of the Church of
Jesus Christ of the Latter-Day Saints to find a home in the West.
Lavishly constructed and finely acted, BRIGHAM YOUNG--FRONTIERS-
MAN is one of the best historical Western dramas produced by Hollywood and is sadly underrated, even today. It should be noted that
Twentieth Century-Fox appeared to have little faith in the film's
main theme: the word "Frontiersman" was added to the title and,
to further insure its box-office success, Tyrone Power and Linda
Darnell were given top star billing in roles little more than incidental
to the film's plot.

The narrative begins in Nauvoo, Illinois in 1839 where the
Mormons, led by founder Joseph Smith (Vincent Price), are about to
be obliterated by a mob of citizens because of the sect's practice of
polygamy. In the ensuing fight many Mormons are killed, including
the parents of young Zena (Linda Darnell), who loses her faith as
a result of the incident. Mormon Angus Duncan (Brian Donlevy) is
at odds with Smith because Duncan wants to remain in Illinois to
promote his own business interests, but Smith refuses to let him
compromise the faith. Smith, however, is arrested and put on trial.
His defense, led by Brigham Young (Dean Jagger), fails and he is
sentenced to die. Smith and his brother Hyrum (Stanley Andrews)
are lynched by a mob and the Mormons clandestinely escape under
cover of night over a frozen river and go West with Brigham Young
as their leader. Duncan, finding out that the locals plan to take
his property and kill him, also flees and joins the group, although
he continues to oppose Young. The people become disenchanted
with Young as he and scout Port Rockwell (John Carradine) lead
them across the plains. They are stopped by Indians but are per-
mitted to pass through by the chief (Chief Big Tree), and they
finally settle at the Great Salt Lake in Utah and plant crops. The
group nearly starves and at harvest time a plague of locusts
descends on their crops, but sea gulls arrive from the lake and eat
the insects. The Mormons are saved and become firmly rooted in
Utah.

Dean Jagger has the finest role of his career in the character
of Brigham Young and he dominates the film with his superb interpretation. Star Tyrone Power has only a passing assignment as a
young Mormon who takes in the homeless Zena, the roles adding the
only romantic interest in this historical drama of the frontier. The
movie was one of the less commercially popular of the historical
series produced by Darryl F. Zanuck; it was released the same year
as the studio's contemporary offering, THE GRAPES OF WRATH,
which did much better at the box office. In 1949 the National Society

of Social Studies re-edited the film into a 30-minute short subject
on religious tolerance, retitled it DRIVEN WESTWARD, and had it
shown in public schools. There is even a nine-minute short subject
entitled PRAIRIE SCHOONER derived from this feature.

One of the most dramatic and best presented sequences in
BRIGHAM YOUNG--FRONTIERSMAN is the climactic scene in which
the Mormons fight the hordes of locusts and are saved by the sea
gulls. This segment, lifted bodily, was color tinted and in the
1977 independent feature BRIGHAM, which starred Maurice Grand-
maison in the title role and featured Charles Moll as Joseph Smith.
New footage was added for a 1978 reissue of the film, but it had
few showings outside Utah.

BRONCO BILLY (Warner Bros., 1980) C 119 mins.

Executive producer, Robert Daley; producers, Dennis Hackin,
Neal Doborfsky; associate producer, Fritz Manes; director, Clint
Eastwood; screenplay, Dennis Hackin; art director, Gene Lourie;
set decorator, Ernie Bishop; costumes, Glenn Wright; assistant
director, Tom Joyner; music, Snuff Garrett; sound, Bert Hallberg;
special effects, Jeff Jarvis; camera, David Worth; editors, Ferris
Webster, Joel Cox.

Clint Eastwood (Bronco Billy); Sondra Locke (Antoinette
Lily); Geoffrey Lewis (John Arlington); Scatman Crothers (Doc
Lynch); Bill McKinney (Lefty LeBow); Sam Bottoms (Leonard
James); Dan Vadis (Chief Big Eagle); Sierra Pecheur (Lorraine
Running Water); Walter Barnes (Sheriff Dix); Woodrow Parfrey (Dr.
Canterbury); Beverlee McKinsey (Irene Lily); Douglas McGrath
(Lieutenant Wiecker); Hank Worden (Station Mechanic); William
Prince (Edgar Lipton); Pam Abbas (Mother Superior); Edye Byrde
(Maid Eloise); Douglas Copsey, Roger Dale Simmons (Reporters at
Bank); John Wesley Elliott, Jr. (Sanatorium Attendant); Chuck
Hicks, Bobby Hoy (Cowboys at Bar); Jefferson Jewell (Boy at
Bank); Dawneen Lee (Bank Teller); Lloyd Nelson (Sanatorium
Policeman); Don Mummert (Chauffeur); Tessa Richarde (Mitzi Fritz);
Tanya Russell (Doris Duke); Valerie Shanks (Sister Maria); Sharon
Sherlock (License Clerk); James Simmerhan (Bank Manager); Jenny
Sternling (Reporter at Sanatorium); Chuck Waters, Jerry Wills
(Bank Robbers).

Having long ago given up his job as a shoe salesman in New
Jersey, Bronco Billy (Clint Eastwood) ekes out a living as the
leader of a tattered Wild West show which appears in small towns
and fairs, often putting on charity performances for orphanages.
With sharp-shooter Billy is one-armed Lefty (Bill McKinney); ring-
master Doc (Scatman Crothers), draft-dodger roper Leonard (Sam
Bottoms), and Indian snake dancer Chief Big Eagle (Dan Vadis)
and his wife (Sierra Pecheur). Thrust upon this motley crew is
bitchy heiress Antoinette Lily (Sondra Locke), who has been thrown
out and disinherited by her husband (Geoffrey Lewis). Having

CLINT EASTWOOD

The most outrageous of 'em all.

BRONCO BILLY

CLINT EASTWOOD IS "BRONCO BILLY" STARRING SONDRA LOCKE
PRODUCED BY DENNIS HACKIN AND NEAL DOBROFSKY
EXECUTIVE PRODUCER ROBERT DALEY · ASSOCIATE PRODUCER FRITZ MANES
WRITTEN BY DENNIS HACKIN · DIRECTED BY CLINT EASTWOOD

PANAVISION® MUSIC SUPERVISED BY SNUFF GARRETT AND CONDUCTED BY STEVE DORFF
COLOR BY DELUXE® DISTRIBUTED BY WARNER BROS. A WARNER COMMUNICATIONS COMPANY

AVAILABLE ON ELEKTRA RECORDS AND TAPES. ©1980 WARNER BROS
ALL RIGHTS RESERVED

PG PARENTAL GUIDANCE SUGGESTED
SOME MATERIAL MAY NOT BE SUITABLE FOR CHILDREN

nowhere to go, the young woman reluctantly joins the show as an assistant to Billy's gun and knife act and falls in love with him. After many misadventures in trying to save the Wild West show, the group continues on its merry way.

While technically not a Western, BRONCO BILLY retains the feel of the genre and here director/star Clint Eastwood tries to show the larger-than-life hero figure in the guise of a man who means well but is almost always wrong. The romanticism of the Western hero, combined with the movie's interesting and eccentric, characters, makes the film "sophisticated enough and common enough to appeal to a broad audience" (Variety). While a third-rater, Eastwood's Bronco Billy is an honest man who attempts to do good (he gives youngsters a Saturday lecture on the evils of truancy), but if he accomplishes anything it is usually in spite of himself, not because of his efforts. One of the film's best segments occurs when Billy, needing money to keep the show going, attempts to rob a train, only to find himself and his horse easily outraced by a speeding freight train.

The special joy of BRONCO BILLY is its loving look at how heroes used to be.

BUCHANAN RIDES ALONE (Columbia, 1958) C 89 mins.

Producer, Harry Joe Brown; associate producer, Randolph Scott; director, Budd Boetticher; based on the novel, The Name's Buchanan; screenplay, Charles Lang; assistant director, Jerrold Bernstein; camera, Lucien Ballard; editor, Al Clark.

Randolph Scott (Buchanan); Craig Stevens (Abe Carbo); Barry Kelley (Lew Agry); Tol Avery (Simon Agry); Peter Whitney (Amos Agry); Manuel Rojas (Juan); L. Q. Jones (Pecos Hill); Robert Anderson (Waldo Peek); Joe De Santis (Esteban Gomez); Willam Leslie (Roy Agry); Jennifer Holden (K. T.); Nacho Galindo (Nacho); Roy Jensen (Jamp); Don C. Harvey (Lafe).

Riding into Agrytown, cowboy Buchanan (Randolph Scott), who has made a bankroll for himself in Mexico, aids Juan (Manuel Rojas), a poor Mexican who has killed the town bully in self-defense after the man assaulted his wife. For helping Juan, Buchanan is thrown in jail and the townfolk threaten to lynch both men. Buchanan comes to realize the town is controlled by the ruthless Agry family, led by Simon Agry (Tol Avery), aided by his loyal associate Abe Carbo (Craig Stevens). When he learns the members of the leading family are at odds over stolen money and their desire to control the area, Buchanan plays them off against each other, and after Juan is brutally murdered he acquires the money the boss man wants and holds them off. Eventually the Agrys are wiped out and Buchanan leaves the morally destitute community in the hands of Carbo.

In 1951 Randolph Scott formed a film company with producer Harry Joe Brown and in the next nine years they produced ten

Standing: Andy Devine, Kay Linaker, Phil Harris; seated: Lillian Cornell, Virginia Dale, Ellen Drew, Jack Benny in BUCK BENNY RIDES AGAIN (1940).

quality features; BUCHANAN RIDES ALONE was the penultimate entry. Without unnecessary romantic interest and lacking much action, the feature relies on character interplay to shoulder its theme, and it does so in a most satisfying manner. In addition to star Randolph Scott's stoical handling of the title role, the movie is highlighted by Lucien Ballard's superb color photography and a fine supporting cast, with Barry Kelly, Tol Avery, and brutish Peter Whitney effective as the sinister Agry brothers and L. Q. Jones very credible as their hired killer.

BUCK BENNY RIDES AGAIN (Paramount, 1940) 82 mins.

Producer/director, Mark Sandrich; story, Arthur Stringer; screenplay, William Morrow, Edmund Beloin; adaptor, Zion Myers; assistant director, Holly Morse; second unit director, Ben Holmes; choreography, LeRoy Prinz; songs, Frank Loesser and Jimmy McHugh; camera, Charles Lang; editor, LeRoy Stone.

Jack Benny (Himself); Ellen Drew (Joan Cameron); Eddie Anderson (Rochester); Andy Devine (Andy); Phil Harris, Dennis Day, Virginia Dale (Themselves); Lillian Cornell (Peggy); Theresa

Harris (Josephine); Kay Linaker (Brenda Tracy); Ward Bond, Morris Ankrum (Outlaws); Charles Lane (Charlie Graham); James Burke (Taxi Driver); Merriel Abbott Dancers (Themselves); Fred Allen (Offscreen Voice).

One of the running gags on Jack Benny's popular radio program was his pretending to be a Western hero, with series regular Andy Devine using the famous catch-phrase, "Hi ya, Buck." This motif was used to fashion the spritely comedy BUCK BENNY RIDES AGAIN, which made use of the radio star's cast of troupers and resulted in his most satisfying celluloid outing. Relying on radio techniques rather than established film story-line development, the feature was a series of comedy skits "all dovetailed together to provide some rousing fun and entertainment" (Variety). Benny fans were especially amused to see not only Benny's cast of regulars, but also some of the props used for comedy on the radio show, including his ancient Maxwell auto and Carmichael the polar bear.

During the summer recess from his enormously popular radio program, Jack Benny (himself) is turned down romantically by pretty singer Joan Cameron (Ellen Drew) and he accepts his bandleader Phil Harris's (himself) invitation to visit his Nevada ranch. Series regulars Andy Devine and Dennis Day (themselves) are also at the ranch, and Joan and her partners (Virginia Dale, Lillian Cornell) are singing at a nearby resort. Jack proves to be a greenhorn on the range and is not helped much in his endeavors by valet Rochester (Eddie Anderson). To impress Joan, Jack gets several ranch hands to intentionally lose a set-up brawl with him, but she sees through the facade. By accident Jack and Rochester get involved with two outlaws (Ward Bond, Morris Ankrum). Through a ruse Jack captures them with the aid of Carmichael the polar bear, and wins Joan.

A very funny film, BUCK BENNY RIDES AGAIN uses the caustic comments of Benny's radio rival, Fred Allen, on the soundtrack, thus setting up their screen pairing in Paramount's LOVE THY NEIGHBOR the next year. At Benny's insistence, BUCK BENNY RIDES AGAIN opened in Harlem. At the premiere Bill "Bojangles" Robinson introduced the film, declaring that Jack Benny was truly color blind because he gave Eddie Anderson better comedy lines than he gave himself in this feature.

BUFFALO BILL AND THE INDIANS, OR SITTING BULL'S HISTORY LESSON (United Artists, 1976) C 123 mins.

Presenter, Dino De Laurentiis; executive producer, David Susskind; producer/director, Robert Altman; based on the play Indians by Arthur Kopit; screenplay, Alan Rudolph, Altman; production designer, Tony Masters; art director, Jack Maxsted; assistant director, Tommy Thompson; music, Richard Baskin; sound, Richard Portman, Jim Webb, Chris McLaughlin; camera, Paul Lohmann; editors, Peter Appleton, Dennis Hill.

Geraldine Chaplin and Paul Newman in BUFFALO BILL AND THE
INDIANS, OR SITTING BULL'S HISTORY LESSON (1976).

Paul Newman (Buffalo Bill Cody); Joel Grey (Producer Sals-
bury); Kevin McCarthy (Publicist); Harvey Keitel (Nephew); Allan
Nicholls (Journalist); Geraldine Chaplin (Annie Oakley); John Con-
sidine (Frank Butler); Frank Kaquitts (Sitting Bull); Will Sampson
(William Halsey); Burt Lancaster (Ned Buntline); Robert Doqui
(Wrangler); Mike Kaplan (Treasurer); Bert Remsen (Bartender);
Denver Pyle (Indian Agent); Bonnie Leaders, Noelle Rogers,
Evelyn Lear (Singers); Pat McCormick (U.S. President); Shelley
Duvall (President's Wife).

In the mid-1880s, Buffalo Bill Cody (Paul Newman) packages
his Wild West Show throughout the East and Midwest and is the
toast of the country. He is already a legend in his time, and
writer Ned Buntline (Burt Lancaster) takes credit for creating this
popular image. Working with Bill in the show are his producer/
director (Joel Grey), publicist (Kevin McCarthy), his secretary and
nephew (Harvey Keitel), and a writer (Allan Nichols). The star
attraction of the show is Annie Oakley (Geraldine Chaplin), who
uses her husband/manager Frank Butler (John Considine) as a target. Chief Sitting Bull (Frank Kaquitts) joins the show with his
interpreter Halsey (Will Sampson), but when President Grover
Cleveland (Pat McCormick) comes to see the show he refuses to
talk with the Indians, who want to air their grievances to him.
After Sitting Bull dies, Buffalo Bill has bad dreams about which of

the two is the strongest and he comes up with a finale for the show
in which he defeats Halsey in a staged fight.

With its catch lines, such as "If God Wanted the Injuns to
Have This Land He Wouldn't Have Put Us Whites Here to Take It
Away From Them," this Robert Altman film attempts to be a Bicen-
tennial presentation, debunking the heroic figure of Buffalo Bill
Cody. Based on the Broadway play, it was filmed on the Stoney
Indian Reserve in Alberta, Canada. The movie portrays the
legendary frontiersman and showman as a drunken, lecherous bigot
who was also a phony. Paul Newman relished the role and threw
himself into a broad parody of Cody. The general public, however,
stayed away from this sorry comedy/drama in droves and its overall
effect was to punch more holes in Altman's reputation as a film
craftsman rather than in the larger-than-life legend of Buffalo Bill.

CAHILL see CAHILL, UNITED STATES MARSHAL

CAHILL, UNITED STATES MARSHAL (Warner Bros., 1973) C 103
mins.

Producer, Michael Wayne; director, Andrew V. McLaglen;
story, Barney Slater; screenplay, Harry Julian Fink, Rita M. Fink;
music, Elmer Bernstein; production designer, Walter Simonds; assistant director, Fred R. Simpson; camera, Joseph Biroc; editor,
Robert L. Simpson.

John Wayne (J. D. Cahill); Gary Grimes (Danny Cahill);
George Kennedy (Fraser); Neville Brand (Lightfoot); Clay O'Brien
(Billy Joe Cahill); Marie Windsor (Mrs. Green); Morgan Paull
(Struther); Dan Vadis (Brownie); Royal Dano (MacDonald); Scott
Walker (Ben Tildy); Denver Pyle (Denver); Jackie Coogan (Charlie
Smith); Rayford Barnes (Pee Wee Simser); Dan Kemp (Joe Meehan);
Harry Carey, Jr. (Hank); Walter Barnes (Sheriff Grady); Paul Fix
(Old Man); Pepper Martin (Hard Case); Vance Davis (Black Man);
Ken Wolger (Boy); Hank Worden (Undertaker); James Nusser (Doc-
tor); Murray MacLeod (Deputy Gordine); Hunter von Leer (Deputy
Jim Kane).

CAHILL, UNITED STATES MARSHAL is probably the least
satisfying of John Wayne's 1970s feature films and in many respects
one of his weakest Westerns. The movie attempts to reflect a contemporary theme, the alienation of youth due to parental neglect,
in the Western motif; the result is what Kevin Thomas of the Los
Angeles Times judged a combination of "toughness and sentimental
hokey." While the star has another of his stalwart on-camera roles
as the duty-bound lawman who neglects his family in deference to
his job, the film is plagued with a weak script which cannot be
salvaged by Wayne and his topnotch supporting cast. Despite
grossing a respectable $4,000,000+ at the box office it is a standard
Western at best. Thereafter the Duke left the genre for two tough

John Wayne and Gary Grimes in CAHILL, UNITED STATES MARSHAL
(1973).

crime melodramas, McQ (1974) and BRANNIGAN (1975), before his
final return to the Western mode for ROOSTER COGBURN (1975,
see B/V) and the classic finale of his career, THE SHOOTIST
(q.v.) in 1976.

    Lawman J. D. Cahill (John Wayne), trailing a gang of rob-
bers, corners them at night and brings them in with the loot they
have stolen. On the way home another outlaw (Chuck Roberson)
and his men attempt to steal the money, but Cahill calls their bluff
and returns safely to town. At home, he learns that bandit gang
leader Abe Fraser (George Kennedy) and his men have pulled a
bank robbery and that Cahill's two sons, Danny (Gary Grimes)
and Billy Joe (Clay O'Brien), are accomplices. With his Indian pal
Lightfoot (Neville Brand), Cahill sets out to catch Fraser and bring
his sons home. In the showdown, Cahill is injured, but his sons
come to his defense and get Fraser and the gang and also save
those outlaws falsely accused of crimes committed by the gang.

    Issued in Great Britain as CAHILL, the movie (produced as
WEDNESDAY MORNING) presents Wayne's character as a poor parent
whose sons are not innately bad, but have been forced to go along
with the outlaw gang.

CALAMITY JANE (CBS-TV, 3/6/84) C 100 mins.

Executive producer, Bernie Sofronski; producers, Herbert Hirschman, Jane Alexander; director, James Goldstone; teleplay, Suzanne Clauser; music, Fred Karlin; production designer, Albert Heschong; camera, Terry K. Meade; editor, Edward A. Biery.

Jane Alexander (Calamity Jane); Frederic Forrest (Wild Bill Hickok); Ken Kercheval (Buffalo Bill Cody); Walter Olkerwicz (Will Lull); Talia Balsam (Jean); Walter Scott (Charlie Burke); David Hemmings (Captain James O'Neill); Isabell Monk (Nell); Jack Murdock (Reverend Warren); Larry Cedar (Reverend Sipes); Doug Toby (Jackie); Laurie O'Brien (Mamie); Sara Abeles (Jean at age 7); Gillian Eaton (Mrs. O'Neill); Don Herpner (Barker); Jessica Nelson (Patty); Henry M. Kenrick (Station Boss); Gloria Henry, Mavis Neal Palmer (Ladies); Theresa DePaolo (Young Woman).

The story of Western legend Martha Jane Canary (1852-1903), known as "Calamity Jane," has been told on screen many times. This well produced telefeature attempts to set the story straight but does little more than muddy the waters surrounding the legend of the fast-riding, hard-drinking heroine who romanced Wild Bill Hickok and rode the western trails with her male counterparts. "She Rode Hard, She Drank Hard, She Loved Hard!" sang the blurbs for this CBS-TV movie. By now truth and fiction had blended to such a degree that the real substance of Calamity Jane will probably never be presented objectively.

Calamity Jane (Jane Alexander) falls in love and marries Wild Bill Hickok (Frederic Forrest) but he leaves her to join Buffalo Bill Cody's (Ken Kercheval) Wild West Show, not knowing that Jane is pregnant. She has the baby, gives it up to an Army captain (David Hemmings) and his wife, and continues her life. Bitter over losing her lover and giving up her baby, Jane leads a wild life, drinking, smoking, gambling, and stage driving. She marries a cowboy (Walter Scott) and eventually finds her grown daughter (Talia Balsam), although she never reveals that she is the girl's mother.

Suzanne Clauser adapted her novel about Calamity Jane, which in turn was based on Jane's letters to her daughter, for this telefilm, and star Jane Alexander served as co-producer. Variety judged the resulting feature an "uneven telefilm" while Judith Crist wrote in TV Guide, "With style and a very good cast, this CALAMITY JANE ranks as probably the first feminist Western--with something, however, for everyone."

CALAMITY JANE AND SAM BASS (Universal, 1949) C 85 mins.

Producer, Leonard Goldstein; associate producer, Aaron Rosenberg; director/story, George Sherman; screenplay, Maurice Geraghty, Melvin Levy; assistant director, John Sherwood; Technicolor consultants, Natalie Kalmus, Monroe Burbank; art directors, Bernard Herzbrun, Richard Riedel; set decorators, Russell A. Gausman, Al Fields; music director/orchestrator, Milton Schwarzwald; makeup,

Howard Duff and Yvonne De Carlo in CALAMITY JANE AND SAM
BASS (1949).

Bud Westmore, John Holden; costumes, Yvonne Wood; sound, Leslie
I. Carey, Glenn Anderson; camera, Irving Glassberg; editor,
Edward Curtiss.

 Yvonne De Carlo (Calamity Jane); Howard Duff (Sam Bass);
Dorothy Hart (Katherine Egan); Willard Parker (Sheriff Will Egan);
Norman Lloyd (Jim Murphy); Lloyd Bridges (Joel Collins); Marc
Lawrence (Dean); Houseley Stevenson (Dakota); Milburn Stone (Abe
Jones); Clifton Young (Link); John Rodney (Morgan); Roy Roberts
(Marshal Peak); Ann Doran (Mrs. Egan); Charles Cane (J. Wells);
Walter Baldwin (Doc Purdy); Paul Maxey (Underwood); George
Carleton (Mr. Sherman); Harry Harvey (Station Agent); Jack Ingram
(Mayes); Francis McDonald (Starter); Douglas Walton (Bookmaker);
Nedrick Young (Parsons); Russ Conway (Baggage Man); Jimmy
Ames (Blacksmith); Ezelle Pou1e (Woman Customer); Anthony Backus,
Pierce Lyden (Deputies); I. Stanford Jolley (Wilson); Stanley Bly-
stone (Cowboy); Roy Butler, Frank McCarroll, Charles Sullivan, Bob
Perry, James Linn, Bill Sundholm (Bits).

 Sam Bass (1851-78) and Calamity Jane Canary (1852-1903) are
legends of the Old West whose adventures have been recounted many
times on screen, usually resulting in more action than truth. One of

the better renderings of their frontier-days saga is CALAMITY
JANE AND SAM BASS, which although historically unreliable, does
provide good entertainment in appealing Technicolor under George
Sherman's stern helming, with likable performances from Yvonne De
Carlo and Howard Duff. In fact it is Yvonne De Carlo who makes
the film work with her larger-than-life portrayal of the hell-raising
but affection-craving cowgirl. She is far more alluring in the part
than Jean Arthur in THE PLAINSMAN (1936) (see B/V), Doris Day
in CALAMITY JANE (1953) or Jane Alexander in the telefilm CALAM-
ITY JANE (1953) or Jane Alexander in the telefilm CALAMITY JANE
(1984), q.v.

Easygoing cowboy Sam Bass (Howard Duff) arrives in a new
locale and becomes involved with the beautiful and sexy wild west
gal, Calamity Jane (Yvonne De Carlo). Jane tumbles for Bass but
he is more interested in racing his horse, as well as romancing the
respectable sister (Dorothy Hart) of the local sheriff (Willard
Parker). Bass enters his horse in a local race and it wins.
Crooked ranchers, upset at losing money in the race, have the
horse killed. Seeking revenge, Bass becomes an outlaw and gets
even with the ranchers, but the sheriff rides on his trail and the
lawman's sister rejects Bass; in turn, he finally realizes he loves
Calamity. It is too late, however, since the law catches up with
him and he is gunned down with Calamity at his side when he dies.

The death scene finale in CALAMITY JANE AND SAM BASS is
particularly effective and the movie is one of the few, despite its
historical faults, to portray Sam Bass accurately as something other
than a cold-hearted gunman.

CALL OF THE DESERT (Syndicate Pictures, 1930) 53 mins.

Director, J. P. McGowan; screenplay, Sally Winters; camera,
Hap Depew.

Tom Tyler (Rex Carson); Sheila LeGay (Jean Walker); Bud
Osborne (Todd Walker); Cliff Lyons (Nate Thomas); and Bobby
Dunn.

Tom Tyler (real name: Vincent Markowski) had a long screen
career as a cowboy star, lasting from 1926 to 1943, before turning
to character roles for another decade. A champion weight lifter,
he was a tall, athletic sagebrush hero whose assignments rarely
rose above the small studios and independent outfits which produced
cheap Westerns. From 1926 to 1929 he starred in oaters for Films
Booking Office (FBO) and from there he went to Syndicate Pictures and stayed until 1932 (the studio became Monogram Pictures
in 1931). CALL OF THE DESERT was Tyler's final silent film
(which was issued also in a sound-effects version with no dialogue).
A fairly entertaining and fast moving offering, the movie has an engrossing opening sequence of snow in the desert.

Rex Carson (Tom Tyler) and Todd Walker (Bud Osborne) head
into the desert searching for a mine claim left to Rex by his late

father. Todd steals the claim and injured Rex is taken to a ranch where he becomes enamored of pretty Jean Walker (Sheila LeGay), who is loved by foreman Nate Thomas (Cliff Lyons). Rex discovers that Todd is the girl's uncle, and Todd tells her that Rex is a crook and says the young man must prove his rightful mine claim. Jean, however, learns the truth and gets the local law on Rex's side when the young man defeats both Nate and Todd who are partners in the scheme. Rex wins Jean's love.

CALL OF THE PRAIRIE see BAR 20 RIDES AGAIN

THE CANYON OF MISSING MEN (Syndicate Pictures, 1930) 4,742'

Director, J. P. McGowan; screenplay, George H. Williams; camera, Hap Depew.
Tom Tyler (Dave Brandon); Sheila LeGay (Inez Sepulveda); Tom Forman (Juan Sepulveda); Bud Osborne (Slug Slagel); Cliff Lyons (Brill Lonergan); Bobby Dunn (Gimpy Lamb); Arden Ellis (Peg Slagel).

The penultimate of eight silent movies Tom Tyler churned out for Syndicate Pictures, CANYON OF MISSING MEN is only a fair outing, with mostly outdoor shots and too familiar scenery. The title refers to the outlaws' hideout in the film. Following CALL OF THE DESERT (q.v.), Tyler would do three talkies for Syndicate, then stay with the studio when it became Monogram Pictures.
Dave Brandon (Tom Tyler) is a member of an outlaw gang and is attracted by pretty Inez (Sheila LeGay), the daughter of ranch owner Juan (Tom Forman). When his cohorts plan to kidnap the girl and hold her for ransom, Dave stops them at first, but eventually they carry out their scheme and hold the girl prisoner. Having been arrested as part of the gang, Dave escapes in order to help Inez but finds out her father has also been captured and that the gang intends to blow up the entrance to the canyon where they are held hostage. Dave stops them and the sheriff rounds up the fleeing gang members, with Dave rescuing Inez and her father. Dave is then placed in Inez' custody.

THE CARAVAN TRAIL see LAW OF THE LASH

CARSON CITY KID (Republic, 1940) 56 mins.

Associate producer/director/story, Joseph Kane; screenplay, Robert Yost, Gerry Geraghty; songs, Peter Tinturin; camera, William Nobles; editor, Helen Turner.
Roy Rogers (Carson City Kid); George "Gabby" Hayes (Gabby Whittaker); Bob Steele (Lee Jessup); Noah Beery, Jr. (Warren);

Pauline Moore (Joby Gilby); Francis MacDonald (Laramie); Hal Talia-ferro (Harmon); Arthur Loft (Kirke); George Rosener (Tucker); Chester Gan (Wong); Trigger (The Horse); and Hank Bell, Ted Mapes, Jack Ingram, Jack Kirk, Jack Rockwell, Tom Smith, Art Dillard, Hal Price, Yakima Canutt, Kit Guard, Curley Dresden, Oscar Gahan, Chick Hannon, Al Taylor.

Following his sensational portrayal of the evil Curley in John Steinbeck's OF MICE AND MEN (1939), veteran sagebrush hero Bob Steele made a brief change to the wrong side of the law when he played villain Lee Jessup in this Roy Rogers' film. With near "A" production values, a fast moving script and fine direction by Joseph Kane, the movie was one of the best of the early Roy Rogers entries. The film is especially effective because of its cast, with Rogers on target in the title role, George "Gabby" Hayes providing comedy re-lief as the local lawman on the Kid's trail, Noah Beery, Jr. as a young miner swindled by Jessup, and pretty Pauline Moore as the saloon singer lusted after by the villain. It is Bob Steele, though, who dominates this motion picture in his special billed role as the wicked saloon owner.

In 1849 in Sonora, gambling house proprietor Lee Jessup (Bob Steele) controls the territory and is romancing his pretty singer Joby Gilby (Pauline Moore). His activities are opposed by the no-torious Carson City Kid (Roy Rogers) and his partner Laramie (Francis McDonald). When the two aid a young miner, Arizona (Noah Beery, Jr.), Laramie tries to rob the young man; the Kid stops him but in their escape, Laramie is captured by Jessup's gang. The local sheriff, Gabby Whittaker (George "Gabby" Hayes) jumps on the Kid's trail but the latter takes his horse and heads into town where he takes a job as a bouncer in Jessup's saloon and begins courting Joby. The Kid believes that Jessup is responsible for the death of his younger brother. Arizona comes to town and Jessup promptly gets him into a crooked poker game and fleeces him of his gold. The young man pretends to be the Kid, robs Jessup's safe and is arrested. At his trial in Jessup's saloon, the Kid appears and in a shootout kills Jessup. The Kid and Joby are free to wed.

CATTLE ANNIE AND LITTLE BRITCHES (Universal, 1981) C 97 mins.

Executive producers, John Daly, Derek X. Dawson; producer, Rupert Hitzig, Alan King; associate producer, David Korda; direc-tor, Lamont Johnson; based on the novel by Robert Ward; screen-play, David Eyre, Ward; music, Sanh Berti, Tom Slocum; production designer, Stan Jolley; set decorator, Dick Purdy; costume designer, Rita Riggs; assistant director, David Anderson; sound, Manuel Topete; camera, Larry Pizer; supervising editor, Robbe Roberts; editor, William Haugse.

Burt Lancaster (Bill Doolin); John Savage (Bittercreek New-comb); Rod Steiger (Tilghman); Diane Lane (Jenny); Amanda

Amanda Plummer, John Savage, and Diane Lane in CATTLE ANNIE AND LITTLE BRITCHES (1981).

Plummer (Annie); Scott Glenn (Bill Dalton); Redmond Gleeson (Red Buck); William Russ (Little Dick Raidler); Ken Call (George Weightman); Buck Taylor (Dynamite Dick); John Quade (Morgan); Perry Lang (Elrod); Steven Ford (Deputy Marshal); Mike Moroff (Deputy); John Hock (Bank Teller).

Small town teenage girls Jenny (Diane Lane) and Annie (Amanda Plummer) have overly romantic notions about riding with an outlaw gang. When the Doolin-Dalton gang, led by aging Bill Doolin (Burt Lancaster), bursts into town and pulls a stick-up, the girls follow them. Annie becomes the lover of gang member Bittercreek Newcomb (John Savage), while Jenny finds a father figure in Doolin. The gang, trailed by Lawman Tilghman (Rod Steiger), continues its bank robbing activities, but eventually breaks up, and Jenny sadly gives up her life with Doolin.

Filmed in 1979, CATTLE ANNIE AND LITTLE BRITCHES is a fanciful oater which Variety claimed "...will just give the public one more reason not to go to Westerns." Taken as just light entertainment, however, the feature is more than passable, especially for Amanda Plummer's work as the strong-willed Annie and Diane Lane's underplayed starry-eyed Jenny. Burt Lancaster is ingratiating as the likable bank robber Bill Doolin, although his characterization has little to do with the reality of the actual outlaw, and Rod Steiger is less hammy than usual as the non-stoppable lawman.

The film's most disappointing feature is the lack of interrelationship between the two young women and the outlaw band, except for the generally acceptable interplay between Lancaster's and Lane's characters. The finished product lacks the dash or production values associated with big-screen features of the period, although some of the Durango, Mexico locales are attractive.

CAVALRY (Republic, 1936) 63 mins.

Producer, A. W. Hackel; director/story, Robert North Bradbury; screenplay, George S. Plympton; camera, Bert Longenecker; editor, Roy Claire.

Bob Steele (Ted Thorne); Frances Grant (Betty Lee Harvey); Karl Hackett (Rance); William Welch (General John Harvey); Earl Ross (Colonel Lafe Harvey); Hal Price (Horace Leeds); Ed Cassidy (Bart Haines); Budd Buster (Jake the Wagon Boss); William Desmond (Major); Perry Murdock (Gang Member); Sam McDaniel (Mose); Etta McDaniel (Mammy); Hal Taliaferro (Conspirator); and Earl Dwire, Horace B. Carpenter.

At the end of the Civil War, guerrillas led by Rance (Karl Hackett) burn the plantation home of Betty Lee Harvey (Frances Grant); whose general father is thought dead, and Uncle Lafe (Earl Ross). Following the raid, the two leave their ex-slaves behind and join a wagon train moving West. Meanwhile Union soldier Ted Thorne (Bob Steele) returns General Harvey (William Welch) to his home and then goes to Washington, where the president orders him to head West and put down a conspiracy to start a new nation on the West Coast. Rance and his men are now working for Leeds (Hal Price), the leader of the conspiracy, and they attempt to steal an ammunition wagon on the train joined by Betty Lee and Uncle Lafe. Rance enlists the aid of the local Indians but Thorne has gotten on the gang's trail and convinces the local cavalry major (William Desmond) to send the Indians food. After a showdown with Thorne, Leeds decides the locals will not support his conspiracy and he and his men plot to wipe out the settlers and destroy the incoming telegraph lines. They lure the cavalry to the telegraph camp and plan to use the Indians for their scheme, but the Indians refuse to help Leeds and the crooks escape to the cabin home of Betty Lee and Uncle Lafe, where the cavalry captures them. Thorne has sent for General Harvey, who arrives for a reunion with his daughter and brother, and Betty Lee and Ted plan to wed.

CAVALRY is one of the strongest in the 32-picture series Bob Steele made for producer A. W. Hackel. It is an actionful entry with an intriguing plot and a series of fine performances, ranging from stalwart hero Steele to windbag villain Hal Price. The movie also contains a corker of a fight between Bob Steele and Karl Hackett, one obviously accomplished without doubles.

Charles Bronson in CHATO'S LAND (1972)

CHALLENGE OF THE FRONTIER see THE MAN OF THE FOREST (1933)

CHATO'S LAND (Universal, 1972) C 100 mins.

Producer/director, Michael Winner; screenplay, Gerald Wilson; art director, Manolo Manpaso; music, Jerry Fielding; assistant directors, Peter Price, Tony Tarruella; sound, Chris Kent; camera, Robert Paynter; editor, Freddie Wilson.
Charles Bronson (Pardon Chato); Jack Palance (Quincey Whitmore); Richard Basehart (Nye Buell); James Whitmore (Joshua Everette); Simon Oakland (Jubal Hooker); Ralph Waite (Elisa Hooker); Richard Jordan (Earl Hooker); Victor French (Martin Hall); William Watson (Harvey Lansing); Roddy McMillan (Gavin Malechie); Paul Young (Brady Logan); Lee Petterson (George Dunn); Rudy Ugland (Will Coop); Raul Castro (Mexican Scout); Sonia Rangan (Chato's Woman); Clive Endersby (Jacob Meade); Rebecca Wilson (Edna Malechie); Verna Harvey (Shelby Hooker); Sally Adez (Moira Logan).

Half-breed Apache Pardon Chato (Charles Bronson) rides into a small New Mexico town and is goaded into a fight which results in the death of the local lawman. The citizens form a posse led by Joshua Everette (James Whitmore) and ride out to Chato's desert home, rape and stake out his woman (Sonia Rangan) and burn his house. When his friend (Raul Castro) aids the woman, the posse burns him alive. Chato vows revenge on the posse members and as they chase him into the desert, the Apache uses the land he knows so well as his weapon, setting the posse members against each other as he kills them one by one. Finally Hooker (Simon Oakland) challenges the authority of Everette and kills him, and Hooker in turn is murdered by other posse members. Chato, however, continues to pick off the men until only one is left, and he runs deeper into the desert to die.

The basic theme of the hunted becoming the hunter has been utilized in films many times, particularly in THE LOST PATROL (1934), which RKO remade in 1939 as a Western called BAD LANDS (see B/V), and the theme would be used again in another Charles Bronson thriller, the gangster melodrama MR. MAJESTYK (1974), as well as in the star's DEATH HUNT (1981), q.v. CHATO'S LAND is notable for the first screen teaming of leading man Bronson and director Michael Winner; the two made many subsequent motion pictures together, including the DEATH WISH trilogy. The picture is also notable in that star Bronson speaks only fifteen lines of dialogue: two in English and thirteen in Apache. Populated with a fine supporting cast and well-paced with pleasing Spanish-lensed desert locales, CHATO'S LAND is a well modulated cat and mice thriller spiced with violence.

Films and Filming noted, "The screenplay is truthful, the direction understanding and the performances are unnerving." Variety opined, "Michael Winner takes a hard look at the early American West and comes up with a violence-drenched meller ... the film carries certain suspense, drive and grim realism, but lacks story development that would have made this a real winner."

CHEYENNE TAKES OVER see THE FIGHTING VIGILANTES

CHIP OF THE FLYING U see KING OF THE RODEO

CIRCLE CANYON see THE BOSS COWBOY

THE CISCO KID RETURNS see THE GAY AMIGO

CLANCY OF THE MOUNTED (Universal, 1934) twelve chapters

Producer, Henry MacRae; director, Ray Taylor; suggested by the poem by Robert W. Service; screenplay, Ella O'Neill, Basil Dickey, Harry Hoyt.
Tom Tyler (Sergeant Tom Clancy); Jacqueline Wells [Julie Bishop] (Ann Louise); Earl McCarthy (Steve Clancy); William

Desmond (Dave :Moran); Rosalie Roy (Maureen Clanch); W. L. Thomas ("Black" MacDougal); Leon Duval (Pierre LaRue); Francis Ford (Inspector Cabot); Tom London (Constable MacGregor); Edmund Cobb (Constable McIntosh); and Monte Montague, Frank Lackteen, Steve Clemente, Al Ferguson, William Thorne.

Chapters: 1) Toll of the Rapids; 2) Brother Against Brother; 3) Ambuscade; 4) The Storm; 5) A Desperate Chance; 6) The Wolf's Fangs; 7) The Night Attack; 8) Crashing Timber; 9) Fingerprints; 10) The Breed Strikes; 11) The Crimson Jacket; 12) Journey's End.

CLANCY OF THE MOUNTED was cowboy star Tom Tyler's final Western serial following his previous experiences in PHANTOM OF THE WEST (1930) and BATTLING WITH BUFFALO BILL (1931). He was also featured in a few other cliffhangers, and in the twilight days of his screen stardom he returned to the genre to play the title role superhero in THE ADVENTURES OF CAPTAIN MARVEL (1941) and THE PHANTOM (1943). CLANCY OF THE MOUNTED is an enjoyable, if somewhat old-fashioned, serial with a steady pace. The year before this serial was made Tom Tyler also played a Mountie in Monogram's HONOR OF THE MOUNTED.

Mountie Tom Clancy (Tom Tyler) is assigned to bring in his brother Steve (Earl McCarthy), accused of the murder of a miner. The deed was actually committed by Pierre LaRue (Leon Duval) and Black MacDougal (W. L. Thomas), who want the murdered man's goldmine. In tracking down Steve, Tom meets pretty Ann Louise (Jacqueline Wells), the murdered man's daughter, who now owns the mine. When LaRue and MacDougal attempt to eliminate her, Clancy realizes they are the culprits and brings them to justice, proving his brother's innocence.

Like most serials, this twelve-chapter entry has all kinds of momentary perils for the hero, including a blinding snowstorm, rampaging Indians, wild wolves, and dangerous river rapids.

CLEARING THE RANGE (Allied/Hollywood Pictures, 1931) 64 mins.

Producer, M. H. Hoffman, Jr.; director, Otto Brower; story, Jack Cunningham; dialogue, John Natteford; camera, Ernest Miller; editor, Mildred Johnson.

Hoot Gibson (Curt Fremont); Sally Eilers (Mary Lou Moran); Hooper Atchley (Lafe Kildare); Robert Homans (Dad Moran); Edward Peil (George "Slim" Allen); George Mendoza (Juan; Eva Grippon (Senora); and Edward Hearn, Maston Williams, Jack Byron.

When Universal terminated Hoot Gibson's contract in 1930 due to lack of interest in "B" Westerns, the star signed with independent producer M. H. Hoffman, Jr. and CLEARING THE RANGE was his first feature issued by Allied. Co-starring was his then-wife Sally Eilers, who had co-starred with him the year before in Universal's TRIGGER TRICKS. Here Sally Eilers has little to do as the heroine but her star was on the ascent while her husband's screen career was rapidly declining. Sadly this motion picture set the pace for Hoot's slow moving Allied series although it does contain fine photography by Ernest Miller and some well-delineated fight sequences.

Cowboy Curt Fremont (Hoot Gibson) tries to figure out who murdered his brother. The culprit is crooked banker Lafe Kildare (Hooper Atchley), and to gain sufficient evidence against him, Curt pretends to be a pacifist and refuses to fight. He also takes on the guise of the bandit El Capitan and gains access to Kildare's ledgers, proving he is a thief and the murderer.

COLORADO SERENADE (Producers Releasing Corp., 1946) C 68 mins.

Producer/director, Robert Emmett Tansey; screenplay, Frances Kavanaugh; songs, Eddie Dean, H. L. Canova, Sam Armstrong, Carle Hoefle; Cinecolor supervisor, Arthur Phelps; art director, Edward C. Jewell; assistant director, Harold Knox; sound, John Carter; camera, Robert Shackelford; editor, Hugh Winn.

Eddie Dean (Eddie); David Sharpe (Nevada); Roscoe Ates (Soapy Jones); Mary Kenyon (Sherry); Forrest Taylor (Judge Hilton); Dennis Moore (Duke Dillon); Abigail Adams (Lola); Warner Richmond (Dad Dillon); Lee Bennett (Mr. Trimble); Robert McKenzie (Colonel Blake); Bob Duncan (Ringo); Charles King (Deputy); and Bud Osborne.

Lawman Eddie Dean (himself) and his stuttering buddy Soapy Jones (Roscoe Ates) are working with Judge Hilton (Forrest Taylor) to rid Red Rock of outlaws who are stealing gold bars, melting them down, and then selling them as gold ore. The judge is also searching for his son, who many years before was kidnapped by outlaw Dillon (Warner Richmond) because the judge had sentenced the latter to jail. It develops the judge's son is really Duke Dillon (Dennis Moore), the owner of the local saloon and the leader of the outlaws along with Dillon, who he is convinced is his father. Arriving in the area is gunslinger Nevada (David Sharpe), who has a run-in with Eddie before going to work for Dillon. When he is told to kill the judge, he confides to Eddie that he is really working for the judge, but one of the gang (Bob Duncan) finds out and tells Duke, who plans to murder Nevada. When Eddie and Nevada find proof of the gang's activities at an abandoned mine, they are attacked by the outlaws but escape. In the finale, Dillon shoots his son and is in turn shot by Eddie.

The third Cinecolor film Eddie Dean made for PRC, COLORADO SERENADE could have used a faster-paced story-line and more tunes. The well-lensed movie is highlighted by actor/stuntman David Sharpe as Nevada, Dennis Moore as Duke and Warner Richmond as Dillon, plus a memorably-staged fight sequence between Eddie Dean and David Sharpe early on in the motion picture.

COLORADO SUNDOWN (Republic, 1952) 67 mins.

Associate producer, Edward J. White; director, William Whitney; story, Eric Taylor; screenplay, Taylor, William Lively; music, R. Dale Butts; camera, John Macburnie; editor, Tony Martinelli.

Rex Allen (Rex Allen); Koko (The Horse); Mary Ellen Kay (Jackie Reynolds); Slim Pickens (Slim); June Vincent (Carrie Hurley); Fred Graham (Dan Hurley); John Daheim (Dusty Hurley); Louise Beavers (Mattie); Chester Clute (Lawyer Davis); Clarence Straight (Postman); Republic Rhythm Riders (Themselves).

It has been claimed that the "B" Western for theatrical release was already in dire straits in the early 1950s before it was completely engulfed by television. This is not totally true, however, since a few really good films came out of the genre at the time, and one of the best, in that or any era, was COLORADO SUNDOWN, a Rex Allen starrer benefitting from a strong cast, excellent production values (despite stock footage), a budget in excess of $100,000, and stout direction from action ace William Witney. The film's main asset, however, is the acting of June Vincent in the villainous role of murderess Carrie Hurley. Slim Pickens, taking over for Buddy Ebsen, provides ample comedy relief.

Texas Ranger Rex Allen (himself) accompanies his pal Slim (Slim Pickens) to Colorado where the latter is an heir to a large ranch spread containing valuable timber. Also on hand is another heir, Jacqueline Reynolds (Mary Ellen Kay), and her servant Mattie (Louise Beavers). They are met by Carrie Hurley (June Vincent) and her brother Dan (Fred Graham), two other heirs who own a losing timber mill. Th two have been told by Forest Ranger Stocker (Russ Conway) that a bark beatle plague will close their operation. To keep him quiet, Carrie poisons him. When the will is read, each of the heirs gets one-third of the ranch, so the greedy Hurleys bring in their exconvict brother Dusty (John Daheim) who masquerades as Stocker and quarantines the area's timber with a bogus bark beatle claim. When Mattie sees Dusty steal a letter belonging to Rex, he shoots her, but Rex follows him to the Hurley mill where Carrie has given her brother poison tea. During a fight between the two men, Dusty dies and Carrie accuses Rex of murder and shoots him; but Rex is saved by Slim's arrival. In the finale fight with Rex, Dan drowns and Carrie is apprehended and must stand trial for homicide.

COMIN' AT YA (Filmways, 1981) C 91 mins.

Executive producers, Gene Quintano, Bruce Talbot; producer, Tony Anthony; co-producer, Stan Torchia; director, Ferdinando Baldi; story, Tony Petitto; screenplay, Lloyd Battista, Wolf Lowenthal, Quintano; music, Carlo Savina; art director/ costumes, Luciano Spadoni; special effects, Fred Unger; camera, Fernando Arirbus; editor, Franco Fraticelli.

Victoria Abril and Gene Quintano in COMIN' AT YA! (1981).

Tony Anthony (H. H. Hart); Gene Quintano (Pike); Victoria Abril (Abilene); Ricardo Palacios (Polk); Gordon Lewis (Old Man).

This spaghetti Western was the first 3-D feature to be released to theatres in some two decades, and the result was a surprising box-office success in America, resulting in a plethora of such 3-D cinema outings. The film itself, however, is disappointing and its 3-D Opti-max III proved to be visually irritating. The movie is also plagued with a violence-filled but dull plot-line and its gimmicky 3-D effects soon become tiring. Produced by star Tony Anthony, who had pre-viously been successful in the U.S. with his Italian oaters A STRANGER IN TOWN (1968) and THE STRANGER RETURNS (1968), the movie features such audience-involving activities as a villain thrown "right into" the theatre (thus the movie's title) and bats harassing a group of women.

The feature's very slim story has bad man Pike (Gene Quintano; the film's co-scripter) and his gang kidnap Abilene (Victoria Abril), the fiancée of Hart (Tony Anthony). The gang makes a practice of kidnapping women and then raping and torturing them, but even-tually Hart stops their activities and rescues his lady love.

CORNERED (Columbia, 1932) 58 mins.

Director, B. Reeves Eason; story, William Colt MacDonald; screenplay, Ruth Todd; camera, John Stimar; editor, Otto Meyer.

Tim McCoy (Tim Laramie); Raymond Hatton (Deputy Sheriff Jackson); Noah Beery (Red Slavens); Shirley Grey (Jane Herrick); Niles Welch (Rudi); Claire McDowell (Aunt); Walter Long (Slade); Wheeler Oakman (Deputy Red); Robert Kortman (Pete Fleming, the Foreman); Walter Brennan (Bailiff); Edmund Cobb, Tom London (Ranch Hands); and Artie Ortego, Jim Corey, Edward Peil, Ray Jones, Jack Evans, Blackie Whiteford.

Ranch foreman Rudi (Niles Welch) saves sheriff Tim Laramie (Tim McCoy) from an ambush. Both men like Jane Herrick (Shirley Grey) and when her rancher father is killed, Rudi is blamed and found guilty of the crime. Believing he will be lynched, Rudi escapes from jail and Tim resigns as sheriff and rides into the town where Rudi works for outlaw Red Slavens (Noah Beery), who once had trouble with the murdered man. Tim forces crooked deputy Jackson (Raymond Hatton), who is in cahoots with Slavens, to go against his cohort and Tim leads the cattlemen against Slavens' gang. Tim kills Red, who had murdered Herrick, and thus clears Rudi, who weds Jane.

CORNERED is a sturdy example of Tim McCoy's Columbia Pictures' series, executed on a moderate budget. Boasting the attractive heroine Shirley Grey and impressive trial and courtroom sequences, CORNERED is an illustration of just how good the "B" Western of the 1930s could be, when given proper care. The movie's bittersweet ending is also against the grain for "B" oaters of the period. Finally, Noah Beery is outstanding as the madman villain, Red Slavens, who insists there are only two things worth living for: 1) to kill or be killed, and 2) to get revenge.

COVERED WAGON TRAILS (Monogram, 1940) 52 mins.

Producer, Harry S. Webb; director, Raymond K. Johnson; screenplay, Tom Gibson; song, Johnny Lange and Lew Porter; camera, Edward Kull; editor, Robert Golden.

Jack Randall (Jack); Sally Cairns (Carol); David Sharpe (Ed Cameron); Lafe McKee (John Bradford); Budd Buster (Manny); Glenn Strange (Fletcher); and Kenne Duncan, Hank Bell, Frank Ellis, George Chesebro, Carl Mathews, Edward Hearn, Art Mix, Jack Montgomery, Frank McCarroll.

Jack Randall was the brother of Robert Livingston and starred in a low-budget "B" Western series for Monogram Pictures between 1937 and 1940, starting out as a singing cowboy and then as an action star, sans songs, for his total of twenty-two starrers. Randall was a fine actor and a likable cowboy hero. His movies proved popular and no doubt he would have continued as a sagebrush star

had he not interrupted his career for World War II military service.
In 1945 he returned to films for a bad guy role in the Universal
cliffhanger, THE ROYAL MOUNTED RIDES AGAIN, but died of a
heart attack (at the age of 39) while filming on location. COVERED
WAGON TRAILS came at the tail end of Randall's Monogram entries
and, like most of his final vehicles there, it was hampered by poor
production values.

The Cattlemen's Association does not want settlers in the
Prairieville area, and it hires outlaw Fletcher (Glenn Strange) and
his gang to keep them out. When the wagon train's horses are
poisoned, its leader (Lafe McKee) sends young Ed (David Sharpe)
into town to buy more mounts from the latter's brother Jack (Jack
Randall). Ed, however, is killed by Fletcher, who tells Jack that
Ed has absconded to Mexico with the money for the horses' purchase.
Jack and his pal Manny (Budd Buster), however, find the horses
Fletcher's gang has stolen and take them to the wagon strain. The
gang members escape, capture Jack and take him to Fletcher, who
he now realizes is the murderer of his brother. In a fight, Jack
holds off the gnag and Manny arrives with a posse to capture the
outlaws. Jack tells the local cattlemen the settlers will not hurt
their trade.

THE COWBOY AND THE SENORITA (Republic, 1944) 77 mins.

Producer, Armand Schaefer; associate producer, Harry Grey;
director, Joseph Kane; story, Bradford Ropes; screenplay, Gordon
Kahn; songs: Ned Washington and Phil Ohman, Consuelo Velasquez,
Bob Nolan, Tim Spencer; choreography, Larry Ceballos; music,
Walter Scharf; assistant director, Art Siteman; art director, Fred A.
Ritter; set decorator, Charles Thompson; sound, Vic Appel; camera,
Reggie Lanning; editor, Tony Martinelli.

Roy Rogers (Roy); Mary Lee (Chip Williams); Dale Evans
(Isobel Martinez); John Hubbard (Craig Allen); Guinn "Big Boy"
Williams (Teddy Bear); Fuzzy Knight (Fuzzy); Dorothy Christy
(Lulubelle); Lucien Littlefield (Judge Loomis); Hal Taliaferro (Fergu-
son); Jack Kirk (Sheriff); Cappell and Patricia, Jane Beebe and Ben
Rochelie, Tito and Corinne Valdez (Specialty Dancers); Bob Nolan
and the Sons of the Pioneers (Themselves), Trigger (The Horse);
and Rex Lease, Lynton Brent, Julian Rivero, Bob Wilke, Wally
West.

While looking for a job, cowboy Roy Rogers (himself) and his
pal Teddy Bear (Guinn "Big Boy" Williams) are accused of kidnapping
Chip Williams (Mary Lee), a young girl who has run away from home
in search of her late father's buried treasure. Escaping, Roy and
Teddy Bear find the girl. She vindicates them and they maneuver
a job on the ranch she owns with her relative, Isobel (Dale Evans).
The ranch houses a mine which gambling house proprietor Allen
(John Hubbard) wants for its high grade gold ore. Roy, Teddy
Bear, and The Sons of the Pioneers (themselves) find the hidden

gold and get it to the courthouse before Allen can complete buying the property, thus saving the ranch for Chip and Isobel.

THE COWBOY AND THE SENORITA was the first of a string of twenty features which Roy Rogers and Dale Evans made together. Formerly a big band vocalist, Dale Evans was actually the second female lead in this outing but she was soon Roy's co-star and after they were married in real life she became known in the film industry as "The Queen of the West." This production moves along fairly well, with amusing work by Guinn "Big Boy" Williams as Rogers' comedy sidekick. The film, however, was badly hampered by mediocre songs (e.g., "Enchilada Man," "What'll I Use Money For?") and production numbers and a vapid musical finale.

COWBOY CANTEEN (Columbia, 1944) 72 mins.

Producer, Jack Fier; director, Lew Landers; screenplay, Paul Gangelin, Felix Adler; art director, Lionel Banks; assistant director, Ray Nazarro; songs: Irving Bibo and Al Piantadosi, Sidney Arodia and Hoagy Carmichael, Walter G. Samuels and Saul Chaplin, Fred Rose, Jimmy Wakely; sound, James Thompson; camera, George Meehan; editor, Aaron Stell.

Charles Starrett (Steve Bradley); Jane Frazee (Connie Gray); Vera Vague [Barbara Jo Allen] (Vera); Tex Ritter (Tex Coulter); Guinn "Big Boy" Williams (Spud Marrigan); Dub Taylor (Cannonball); Emmett Lynn (Hank); Edythe Elliott (Mrs. Bradley); The Mills Brothers, Jimmy Wakely and His Saddle Pals; Buck, Chickie and Buck; Roy Acuff and His Smoky Mountain Boys and Girls, The Tailor Maids and Billy Hughes (Themselves); and Jeff Donnell, Dick Curtis.

Ranch owner Steve Bradley (Charles Starrett) is about to enter the Army for World War II service. To keep his ranch operating in his absence, he hires several hands without knowing who they are. The new workers turn out to be women, led by pretty Connie Gray (Jane Frazee). Steve is upset by the situation but is soon in the Army with his friend Spud Marrigan (Guinn "Big Boy" Williams). The two soldiers return home when Connie maneuvers the Army into assigning Steve and Spud to help her set up a canteen for local servicemen. It develops the girls working the ranch are members of an out-of-work vaudeville troupe and they convert the ranch's barn into a canteen and put on a big show.

Western fans, no doubt, found COWBOY CANTEEN a bit of a disappointment; it was basically a series of musical interludes sewn into a thin cowboy plot-line. Star Charles Starrett has little to do in the affair, but the movie is packed with genre names like Tex Ritter, Guinn "Big Boy" Williams, Dub Taylor, Max Terhune (and his dummy act), Jimmy Wakely and His Saddle Pals, and leading lady Jane Frazee, plus a variety of well known performers like Roy Acuff and His Smoky Mountain Boys, The Mills Brothers (in satin dungarees!), The Tailor Maids, and Chickie and Buck, plus the comedy antics of Vera Vague.

Don Miller in Hollywood Corral (1976) observed, "The melange blended together rather pleasantly, and its unpretentiousness made it as entertaining in its own way as some of the elephantine star-studded barges currently produced by every major studio. It wasn't much different from the average Starrett Western, except fifteen minutes extra length at 72 minutes and more expensive-looking sets that weren't about to collapse. But it was sold to exhibitors apart from the regular series."

CRASHING THRU see WYOMING ROUNDUP

THE CRIMSON TRAIL (Universal, 1935) 58 mins.

Producer, Irving Starr; director, Al Raboch; story, Wilton West; adaptor, Jack Natteford; camera, John Hickson.
Buck Jones (Billy Carter); Polly Ann Young (Kitty Bellaire); Carl Stockdale (Jim Bellaire); Charles K. French (Frank Carter); Ward Bond (Luke Long); John Bleiffer (Loco); Silver (The Horse); and Bob Kortman, Bud Osborne, Charles Brinley, Hank Pott, George Sowards, Paul Fix, Robert Walker.

Two rival rancher families, the Carters and the Bellaires, are at odds over cattle thefts and range land and Billy Carter (Buck Jones) returns home to find his father (Charles K. French) accused of killing his rival. Billy ends up falling in love with Bellaire's attractive daughter Kitty (Polly Ann Young). Billy feels that a lunatic, Loco (John Bleiffer), may be behind the rustling and murder, but he pinpoints Luke Long (Ward Bond) as the culprit. Long kidnaps Kitty and Buck tries to rescue her. Loco finds out where the girl is hidden and Long shoots him, but when the bad man and Billy are fighting, it is the dying Loco who kills Long, and the two families end their feud.
Buck Jones produced this effort in his Universal series and the results are good. As Phil Hardy determined in The Film Encyclopedia: The Western (1983): "Bleiffer, as the aptly named Loco, cackling and chuckling ... is the undisputed star of this extraordinary series Western. The plot is rudimentary but the staccato action scenes, like a midnight raid on a ranch, and Bleiffer's over-the-top vision of menace, are very powerful."

CUSTER'S LAST STAND (Stage & Screen, 1936) fifteen chapters

Producer, George M. Merrick; supervisor, Louis Weiss; director, Elmer Clifton; screenplay, George Arthur Durlan, Eddy Graneman, Robert Lively; assistant director, Adrian Weiss; music director, Hal Chasnoff; sound, T. Triplett; camera, Bert Longenecker; editor, Holbrook N. Todd, George M. Merrick.
Rex Lease (Kit Cardigan); William Farnum (Fitzpatrick); Reed

Howes (Tom "Keen" Blade); Jack Mulhall (Lieutenant Cook); Frank
McGlynn, Jr. (General Custer); Josef Swickard (Major Trent);
Creighton Hale (Hank); Lona Andre (Belle Meade); Nancy Caswell
(Barbara Trent); Dorothy Gulliver (Red Fawn); Ruth Mix (Mrs.
Elizabeth Custer); Helen Gibson (Calamity Jane); Chief Thunder-
cloud (Young Wolf); Bobby Nelson (Bobby); Marty Joyce (Buzz);
William Desmond (Wagon Boss); George Chesebro (Lieutenant
Roberts); Milburn Morante (Buckshkin); George Morrell (Sergeant
Flannigan); Howling Wolf (Sitting Bull); Robert Walker (Pete);
Walter James (Judge Hooker); Mabel Strickland (Mabel); Ted Adams
(Barney/Buffalo Bill); Carl Mathews (Curley/True Eagle; Allen
Greer (Wild Bill Hickok); Budd Buster (Major Ware); Barney Furey
(Sergeant Peters); James Sheridan (Jim); Chick Davis (Rain-in-the-
Face); Ken Cooper (Spike); Chief Big Tree (Medicine Man); Iron
Eyes Cody (Brown Fox); Ed Withrow (Blue Cow); Patter Poe (Crow
Scout); High Eagle (Crazy Horse); Cactus Mack (Lieutenant Weir);
Carter Wayne (Striker Martin).

Chapters: 1) Peril of the Plains: 2) Thundering Hoofs; 3)
Fires of Vengeance; 4) The Ghost Dancers; 5) Trapped; 6) Human
Wolves; 7) Demons of Disaster; 8) White Treachery; 9) Circle of
Death; 10) Flaming Arrow; 11) Warpath; 12) Firing Squad; 13) Red
Panthers; 14) Custer's Last Ride; 15) The Last Stand.

A scout for General Custer (Frank McGlynn, Jr.), Kit Cardigan (Rex Lease), tries to aid settlers attacked by Indians led by
Young Wolf (Chief Thundercloud), who is supported by renegade
Tom Blade (Reed Howes). The Indians have lost a sacred medicine
arrow which tells the location of a cave full of gold, and Blade assists them in its recovery. The arrow has been found by settlers
Major Trent (Josef Swickard) and his daughter Barbara (Nancy Caswell), but they do not know its importance. Custer and Cardigan
help the settlers who are being attacked by the Indians and create
a temporary peace. Nevertheless, Custer and his men are later
surrounded by the redskins and massacred at the Little Big Horn.
Following the defeat, Cardigan returns to kill Blade and brings
about a truce.

Made as the first Stage & Screen cliffhanger, CUSTER'S LAST
STAND is a ponderous entry filled with stock footage and is of
interest only because of its large veteran cast. (George Chesebro
is most impressive as a dishonest soldier who has a change of
heart.) The restaging of the Little Big Horn battle (stretched
between chapters fourteen and fifteen) is fairly well accomplished,
but overall the serial is disappointing.

In his series, "The Independent Sound Serial" in Film Fan
Monthly (February, 1968), James Stringham wrote, "The serial was
really a large-scale effort for an independent of the period. It
featured some unusually elaborate sets, particularly one of Fort
Henry, which were generously filled with players. Indian camps
and wagon trains were also used effectively for the picture's bigger
action scenes. The cast was outstanding, and the serial drew en-
thusiastic reviews on its first three chapters. Unfortunately, there

were another twelve chapters to go. The film quickly slowed after the fourth episode, and even the chapter climaxes became dull and often repetitious."

A 65-minute feature version of the serial was also issued and while such fare are usually speedy outings, this one moved at a snail's pace.

DALLAS (Warner Bros., 1950) C 94 mins.

Producer, Anthony Veiller; director, Stuart Heisler; screenplay, John Twist; music, Max Steiner; orchestrator, Murray Cutter; second unit director, B. Reeves Eason; Technicolor consultant, Mitchell Kovalaski; art director, Douglas Bacon; set decorator, George James Hopkins; costumes, Marjorie Best; assistant director, Chuck Hansen; sound, Oliver S. Garretson; camera, Ernest Haller, editor, Clarence Kolster.

Gary Cooper (Blade "Reb" Hollister); Ruth Roman (Tonia Robles); Steve Cochran (Bryant Marlow); Raymond Massey (Will Marlow); Barbara Payton (Flo); Leif Erickson (Martin Weatherby); Antonio Moreno (Felipe Robles); Jerome Cowan (Matt Coulter); Reed Hadley (Wild Bill Hickok); Gil Donaldson (Luis); Zon Murray (Cullen Marlow); Will Wright (Judge Harper); Monte Blue (The Sheriff); Byron Keith (Jason Trask); Jose Dominguez (Carlos); Steve Dunhill (Dink); Charles Watts (Bill Walter); Gene Evans (Drunk); Jay "Slim" Talbot (Stage Drive); Billie Bird (School Teacher); Frank Kreig (Politician); Tom Fadden (Mountaineer); Hal K. Dawson (Drummer); Buddy Roosevelt (Northerner); Alex Montoya (Vaquero); Dolores Corvall (Mexican Servant); Fred Graham (Lou); Charles Horvath, Wenn Wright, Carl Andre (Cowpunchers); Ann Lawrence (Mrs. Walters); O. Z. Whitehead (Settler); Mike Donovan (Citizen); Glenn Thompson (Guard); Dewey Robinson, Buddy Shaw (Prisoners); Fred Kelsey (Carter).

Three vicious brothers plunder a man's plantation and murder his family, and former Confederate officer Blade Hollister (Gary Cooper) vows revenge for his losses. He plans to trap the murderers and he is helped by the new local lawman Martin Weatherby (Leif Erickson): the two men exchange identities. At the rancho of wealthy Felipe Robles (Antonio Moreno), the lawman reveals the plans to the owner's pretty daughter Tonia (Ruth Roman), with whom he is in love. In town, Hollister kills the youngest of the outlaw brothers but is injured in the shootout and goes to the Robles hacienda to recover. There he and Tonia fall in love. He then trails the second brother, Bryant Marlow (Steve Cochran), and eliminates him. The third brother, Will Marlow (Raymond Massey), brings a renegade gang to the rancho and captures the Robles family. Hollister arrives in time to kill Will in a shootout.

Although finely photographed by Ernest Haller, and with a rousing score by Max Steiner and capable direction by Stuart Heisler, DALLAS is not a strong Cary Cooper vehicle. The chief flaw is that the star is too tame in the lead; perhaps his age was a factor or he was playing the assignment more for pathos than for action. In any event, Cooper was overshadowed by the on-camera villainy of Raymond Massey and Steve Cochran, just as sweet leading lady Ruth Roman was less entrancing to viewers than beautiful Barbara Payton as the saloon gal Flo.

The New York Times weighed, "Except for a few clever gimmicks that are dropped here and there, this is one of those two-gunman horse operas that comes right down from William S. Hart." In The Films of Gary Cooper (1972) Homer Dickens dubbed the movie "...an undistinguished western melodrama."

DARING DANGER (Columbia, 1932) 58 mins.

Director, D. Ross Lederman; screenplay, William Colt MacDonald, Michael Trevalyan; assistant director, Wilbur McGaugh; sound, Glen Rominger; camera, Benjamin Kline; editor, Otto Meyer.

Tim McCoy (Tim Madigan); Alberta Vaughn (Jerri Norris); Wallace MacDonald (Jughandle); Robert Ellis (Hugo Dusang); Richard Alexander (Bull Bagley); Vernon Dent (Pee Wee); Murdick MacQuarrie (Norris); Edward J. LeSaint (Boss); Edmund Cobb (Dusang's Brother); Art Mix (Gang Member); Max Davidson (Toby).

Bitter enemies Tim Madigan (Tim McCoy) and Bull Bagley (Richard Alexander) engage in a fist fight which culminates in a shootout, but before the gun battle, Bull removes the bullets from Tim's guns and shoots him, leaving him for dead. Tim, however, is only injured and after regaining his health, sets out to find Bull. The latter is working for the corrupt Dusang brothers (Robert Ellis, Edmund Cobb) who are after a rancher's (Murdock MacQuarrie) spread. Tim comes to the aid of the rancher and his pretty daughter (Alberta Vaughn), with whom he falls in love. He enlists the aid of the local bartender, Pee Wee (Vernon Dent), in helping him fight Bull and the Dusangs. Bull later murders Pee Wee, but Tim avenges the crime by killing Bull and bringing his crooked bosses to justice.

DARING DANGER is a pedestrian effort among Tim McCoy's generally good Western outings for Columbia. It is a picture best remembered for its parts, rather than as a whole. Among the more memorable scenes are the opening battle between Tim McCoy and villain Richard Alexander, the latter's murder of bartender Vernon Dent, McCoy's bringing provisions to the near-starving rancher and his daughter, and the humorous sequence where McCoy and Dent vocalize "I'll See My Susie Tonight," one of the few occasions the star sang in motion pictures. One surprising segment comes near the film's end when McCoy and Robert Ellis have a showdown in the latter's ranch house. It must have been extremely cold the day the scene was shot, because the breaths of both actors are clearly visible as they deliver their lines. Also of interest is the fact that usual series villain (and sometimes scripter) Wallace MacDonald,

later a Columbia Pictures producer, is cast as a drunk who is
really a Cattlemen's Association agent.

DAWN ON THE GREAT DIVIDE (Monogram, 1942) 63 mins.

Producer, Scott R. Dunlap; director, Howard Bretherton;
suggested by the story "Wheels of Fate" by James Oliver Curwood;
screenplay, Jess Bowers [Adele Buffington]; camera, Harry Newman;
editor, Carl Pierson.
Buck Jones (Buck Roberts); Rex Bell (Jack Carson); Ray-
mond Hatton (Sandy Hopkins); Mona Barrie (Sadie Rand); Robert
Lowery (Terry); Christine MacIntyre (Mary); Harry Woods (Jim
Corkle); Betty Blythe (Elmira Corkle); Robert Frazer (Judge
Corkle); Tristram Coffin (Rand); Jan Wiley (Martha); Dennis Moore
(Tony Corkie); Roy Barcroft (Loder); Silver (The Horse); and
Steve Clark, Reed Howes, Bod Osborne, I. Stanford Jolley, Artie
Ortego, George Morrell, Miburn Morante, Ray Jones.

Buck Jones died November 30, 1942 after suffering fatal burns
in Boston's Coconut Grove nightclub fire. The cowboy star had
escaped from the blaze, but returned to save others and lost his
life in the process, thus dying in the heroic manner he had portrayed so often on camera. Slightly more than two weeks after his
death, Monogram Pictures issued the star's final picture, DAWN ON
THE GREAT DIVIDE, a "B Plus" Western which proved to be a
fitting finale to a long and distinguished screen career. In the
production, Buck Jones portrayed Buck Roberts and Raymond Hatton was Sandy Hopkins, parts they had played in their Monogram
"Rough Riders" series. Co-star Tim McCoy, however, had left that
series to return to the Armed Forces for war duty and was replaced
by one-time genre star Rex Bell.
Buck Roberts (Buck Jones) leads a wagon train to Oregon,
the train filled with railroad supplies and carrying new settlers.
Buck is aided by pals Sandy Hopkins (Raymond Hatton) and Jack
Carson (Rex Bell). The train is attacked by Indians and makes its
way to a gambling town where Sadie Rand (Mona Barrie), the
operator of the local saloon, becomes enamored of Buck. He also
must contend with a romance between wagon passengers Terry
(Robert Lowery) and Mary (Christine McIntyre). Buck discovers
that the marauders attacking the train are not Indians but white
men dressed as such, and their leader is local businessman Jim
Corkle (Harry Woods). Buck and his pals defeat the attackers and
successfully complete their wagon train journey.
Variety termed DAWN ON THE GREAT DIVIDE one of Buck
Jones' "best films" and added "it's an all-around good job." Running
(at 70 minutes) longer than the average "B" Western and chock full
of fine players, the movie is both exciting and entertaining. It
could well have been the vanguard of a whole new Buck Jones series.

DAYS OF JESSE JAMES (Republic, 1939) 63 mins.

Producer/director, Joseph Kane; story, Jack Natteford; screenplay, Earle Snell; music director, Cy Feuer; songs, Peter Tinturin; camera, Reggie Lanning.

Roy Rogers (Roy); George "Gabby" Hayes (Gabby Whittaker); Donald Barry (Jesse James); Pauline Moore (Mary); Harry Woods (Captain Worthington); Arthur Loft (Sam Wyatt); Wade Boteler (Dr. Samuels); Ethel Wales (Mrs. Samuels); Scotty Beckett (Buster Samuels); Michael Worth (Frank Janes); Glenn Strange (Cole Younger); Olin Howland (Under-Sheriff); Monte Blue (Fields); Jack Rockwell (McDaniels); Fred Burns (Sheriff); Trigger (The Horse); and Bud Osborne, Jack Ingram, Carl Sepulveda, Forrest Dilon, Hansel Warner, Lynton Brent, Pasqual Perry, Eddie Acuff.

Railroad detective Roy Rogers (himself) is out to capture Jesse James (Donald Barry) and his gang. He runs afoul of an opportunistic sheriff (Harry Woods) and a crooked banker (Arthur Loft) who steals Gabby Whittaker's (George "Gabby" Hayes) money and then robs his own bank and blames Jesse. Roy sees through the ruse and enlists the aid of the famous outlaw in bringing the culprits to justice.

One of several pseudo-historical films Roy Rogers made early in his Republic series career, DAYS OF JESSE JAMES is excellent entertainment. Star Roy Rogers, however, takes a cinematic back seat to Donald Barry's performance as Jesse James. The same year Barry made a vivid impression as the doomed young outlaw in "The Mesquiteers" series outing, WYOMING OUTLAW (see B/V), and in 1940 he was launched into genre stardom with the serial THE AD-VENTURES OF RED RYDER (see B/V) before starring in his own Republic series. It should be noted that Roy Rogers played the famed outlaw in JESSE JAMES AT BAY (1941), while in DAYS OF JESSE JAMES, Glenn Strange contributes a fine characterization of another noted outlaw, Cole Younger. Songs in DAYS OF JESSE JAMES include "I'm the Son of a Cowboy," "Echo Mountain," and "Saddle Your Dreams."

THE DEAD DON'T DREAM see HOPPY'S HOLIDAY

DEATH HUNT (Twentieth Century-Fox, 1981) C 96 mins.

Executive producers, Albert S. Ruddy, Raymond Chow; producer, Murray Shostak; associate producer, Robert Baylis; director, Peter Hunt; screenplay, Michael Grais, Mark Victor; production designer, Ted Haworth; assistant director, Frank Ernst; costumes, Olga Dimitrov; music, Jerrold Immel; sound, Richard Lightstone; camera, James Devis; editors, Allan Jacobs, John F. Burnett.

Charles Bronson (Johnson); Lee Marvin (Sergeant Edgar Millen); Andrew Stevens (Alvin); Carl Weathers (Sundog); Ed

Charles Bronson and Ed Lauter (on ground) in DEATH HUNT (1981).

Lauter (Hazel); Scott Hylands (Pilot); Angie Dickinson (Vanessa);
Henry Beckman (Luce); William Sanderson (Ned Warren); Jon Cedar
(Hawkins); James O'Connell (Hurley); Len Lesser (Lewis); Dick
Davalos (Beeler); Maury Chaykin (Clarence); August Schellenberg
(Deak).

Based on an actual event, DEATH HUNT recounts how the
Canadian Mounties tracked trapper Albert Johnson, wanted for murder, into the Canadian wilds in 1931, using traditional methods as
well as initiating airplanes for the first time in a manhunt. The resulting motion picture is beautifully picturesque but largely unim-
pressive in its rendering of an exciting actual event. The film also
includes an unbelievable sequence in which Johnson survives the
dynamiting of his cabin. DEATH HUNT repeats the theme of man
using nature as his ally, the premise of two earlier Charles Bronson
vehicles, CHATO'S LAND (1972) (q.v.) and MR. MAJESTYK (1974).
Arriving at a remote frontier Canadian outpost, trapper Albert Johnson (Charles Bronson) witnesses a vicious dog fight and
thwarts it, saving the losing animal. The dog's owner, sadistic
Hazel (Ed Lauter), accuses him of stealing it and presses charges
against Johnson. Meanwhile men surround Johnson's cabin and in
the ensuing fight, one of them is killed. Mountie Sergeant Edgar
Millen (Lee Marvin) deserts the comforts of his whiskey and his mistress (Angie Dickinson) to chase Johnson through the Canadian
frontier along with rookie officer Adams (Andrew Stevens), veteran

Mountie Sundog (Carl Weathers) and Hazel and his men. The group, however, soon realizes Johnson is as much the hunter as the hunted as he begins eliminating Hazel's crew. The Mounties have a falling out with Hazel, who Millen learns is behind all the trouble. The chase by now has become a media event and an airplane is used to track Johnson. At the finale, Johnson escapes. Millen claims that a dead trapper, who has been murdering his cohorts, is actually the wanted man.

The Albert Johnson story was also picturized in 1972 as THE MAD TRAPPER, filmed in Canada by veteran director Tay Garnett. In 1976 Pacific International released the feature as CHALLENGE TO BE FREE and the raw-boned production starring Mike Mazurki in the title role was a big box-office winner, showing a far greater profit than the tepid returns for DEATH HUNT.

DEATH VALLEY see RIDERS OF DEATH VALLEY

THE DEERSLAYER (Republic, 1943) C 67 mins.

Producers, P. S. Harrison, E. B. Derr; director, Lew Landers; based on the novel by James Fenimore Cooper; screenplay, Harrison, Derr; adaptor, John W. Krafft; assistant director, Eddie Stein; camera, Arthur Martinelli; editor, George McGuire.

Bruce Kellogg (Deerslayer); Jean Parker (Judith Hutter); Larry Parks (Jingo-Good); Warren Ashe (Harry March); Wanda McKay (Hetty Hutter); Yvonne De Carlo (Wah-Tah); Addison Richards (Mr. Hutter); Johnny Michaels (Bobby Hunter); Phil Van Zandt (Briarthorn); Trevor Bardette (Chief Rivenoak); Robert Warwick (Chief Uncas); Many Treaties (Chief Brave Eagles).

THE DEERSLAYER (Twentieth Century-Fox, 1957) C 76 mins.

Producer/director, Kurt Neumann; based on the novel by James Fenimore Cooper; screenplay, Carroll Young, Neumann; music, Paul Sawtell, Bert Shefter; camera, Karl Struss; editor, Jodie Copelan.

Lex Barker (The Deerslayer); Rita Moreno (Hetty Hutter); Forrest Tucker (Harry Marsh); Cathy O'Donnell (Judith Hutter); Jay C. Flippen (Old Tom Hutter); Carlos Rivas (Chingachgook); John Halloran (Old Warrior); Joseph Vitale (Huron Chief); Rocky Shahan, Phil Schumacher, George Robotham, Carol Henry (Stunts).

THE DEERSLAYER (Schick Sunn Classics/NBC-TV, 12/18/78) C 78 mins.

Executive producers, Charles E. Sellier, Jr., James L. Conway; producer, Bill Conford; director, Dick Friedenberg; based on the novel by James Fenimore Cooper; teleplay, S. S. Schweitzer; music, Andrew Belling, Bob Summers; art director, Scott Lindquist;

Lex Barker and Rita Moreno in THE DEERSLAYER (1957).

camera, Paul Hipp; editor, Carl Kress.

Steve Forrest (Hawkeye); Ned Romero (Chingachgook); John Anderson (Hutter); Victor Mohica (Rivenoak); Joan Prather (Judith Hutter); Charles Dierkop (Hurry Harry March); Brian Davies (Lieutenant Plowden); Ted Hamilton (Sieur de Beaujour); Madeline Stowe (Hetty Hutter); Ruben Moreno (Tamenund); Betty Ann Carr (Wa-Wa-Ta); and Alma Bettran, Rosa Maria Hudson, Andrew William Lewis, Stephen Craig Taylor.

James Fenimore Cooper's classic 1841 novel The Deerslayer was first filmed as the serial LEATHERSTOCKING (1924), and in the sound era it was done as a feature film in 1943 and 1957, and as a television movie in 1978; none of the productions is worthy of the material.

Producers E. B. Derr and P. S. Harrison (publisher of Harrison's Reports) made THE DEERSLAYER in 1943 under the lax direction of Lew Landers. Republic took over its distribution and regretted the decision, as the low-budget entry received a critical lambasting. Don Miller noted in B Movies (1973), "...the action was crammed full of such unintended howlers as a band of horsemen riding point blank past an Indian ambush without receiving a scratch; a brave lying prone on a rock somehow managing to receive a wound in a part of his body completely obliterated from view; notable and frequent flaws in acting, dialogue, logic and exposition...." The movie's only redeeming features are good locations (Lake Arrowhead) handsomely filmed in color by Arthur Martinelli, and an early screen appearance by exotic Yvonne De Carlo.

The limp adaptation has hero Natty Bumppo, called the Deerslayer (Bruce Kellogg), aiding a pretty settler (Jean Parker) and her companions who are caught in the midst of an Indian war when an Indian princess (Yvonne De Carlo), promised to a young brave (Larry Parks), is kidnapped by a Huron tribe rival (Philip Van Zandt), who also burns the tribe's village. The Deerslayer then fights with his Indian brothers in defeating the Hurons and rescuing the Indian maiden.

The 1957 version is far better (by degree) than the 1943 entry, also enjoying striking cinematography, this time by Karl Struss. Here The Deerslayer (Lex Barker) and his Indian blood brother (Carlos Rivas) come to the aid of a frontier trapper (Jay C. Flippen) who lives with his daughters (Cathy O'Donnell, Rita Moreno) in a raft house in the midst of a river. It turns out the trapper is an Indian hater who for years has been taking Huron scalps, and the tribe wants revenge. One of the girls (Moreno) is actually a Huron adopted as a baby by the trapper and she returns to her people after her adopted father is killed in the attack.

THE DEERSLAYER was also translated into a TV movie in 1978 by Schick Sunn Classics as a sequel to their previous year's venture, LAST OF THE MOHICANS (q.v.). Here Hawkeye (Steve Forrest) and his blood brother Chingachgook (Ned Romero) aid an Indian chief (Victor Mohica) whose daughter has been kidnapped by a rival tribe. The mundane production was stretched another twenty-six minutes when the film was released for TV syndication.

DESERT GUNS see TRAIL'S END

THE DESERT RIDER (Sunset Productions, 1923) 4,700'

Director, Robert North Bradbury; screenplay, Frank Howard Clark; assistant director, Jack Pierce; camera, Bert Longenecker.
Jack Hoxie (Jack Sutherland); Frank Rice (Toby Jones); Evelyn Helson (Carolyn Grey); Claude Peyton (Rufe Kinkaid); Tom Lingham (Dan Baird); Walter Wilkinson (Mickey).

Jack Hoxie first came to films in the 1910s, billed as Hart Hoxie. In the early 1920s he starred in a series for Sunset Productions and from there went to Universal where he became one of the studio's most popular cowboy stars. As the silent era ended, Jack Hoxie retired, but he returned to films for a half dozen talkies in 1933 for Majestic before resuming his circus headlining career. Most critics are unkind to Hoxie, labeling him a cumbersome and oafish performer, but the likable actor obviously struck a positive chord in the hearts of youngsters in the silent era because he still has followers who delight in his films.

THE DESERT RIDER is one of the Sunset features which helped to solidify Jack Hoxie's screen status. Nevertheless, when the film was released in Great Britain in 1925 a trade paper reviewer complained it was "just another Western, with incidents that have been seen a hundred times before, made heavier by the cumbrous figure of the star and a general lack of inspiration."

Ranch owner Jack Sutherland (Jack Hoxie) finds Dan Baird (Tom Lingham) dying in the desert and learns the man has been shot and robbed of his gold claim map. He takes the man's motherless son (Walter Wilkinson) and plans to work the mine for the boy's benefit. Jack also rescues a young woman, Carolyn Grey (Evelyn Nelson), and tells her of his plans. Later he finds she has gone and that some of the gold is missing. He locates her with Rufe Kinkaid (Claude Peyton) and disarms the man. Carolyn informs Jack she has come from Kentucky to get revenge on Rufe and that he is Baird's murderer. Jack captures Baird, and he and Carolyn fall in love.

THE DEVIL HORSE see THE STRAWBERRY ROAN (1933)

DIAMOND CARLISLE see IN OLD SACRAMENTO

THE DISCIPLE (Kay-Bee-Triangle, 1915) 5 reels

Producer/director, Thomas H. Ince; screenplay, Barrett McCormack, Ince.

William S. Hart ("Shootin' Iron Parson" Jim Houston); Dorothy Dalton (Mary Houston); Thelma Salter (Alice Houston); Robert McKim (Doc Hardy); Charles K. French (Birdshot Bivens); Jean Hersholt (Man in Crowd).

Unlike the product of most silent screen Western stars, many of William S. Hart's movies are still extant. While Hart's movies are over-dramatic and overly heavy in morality, they mirror the Old West as it really was pictorially, with none of the frills and fancy trimmings or slick production values which developed in the 1920s and created a fantasy West that never existed. The frontier in Hart's movies did exist and his surviving films are a fine pictorial recreation of that rawboned time. THE DISCIPLE was directed by William S. Hart in the summer of 1915 under the supervision of Thomas H. Ince at a cost of slightly over $8,000.

"Shootin' Iron Parson" Jim Houston (William S. Hart) arrives in Barren Gulch with his pretty wife (Dorothy Dalton) and their little girl Alice (Thelma Salter). The town is controlled by gambler Doc Hardy (Robert McKim), who is turning the inhabitants against

the newcomer, and he starts romancing Mary and seduces her. As
Jim converts the town's heathens to religion, he learns that Mary
has run off with the gambler and he denounces God. When little
Alice becomes ill, however, Jim regains his faith and prays that his
wife will return. In a storm she comes to their house and Hardy
doctors the child, although Jim plans to kill him. Asked to choose
between the two men, Mary points to her child who is recovering
and Jim allows Hardy to go unharmed. He and Mary reconcile.

    The New York Dramatic Mirror judged the film "...a strong,
stirring exposition of primitive human emotions.... The picture is
replete with dramatic situations ... admirably handled by William S.
Hart and Dorothy Dalton...."

DOC (United Artists, 1971) C 95 mins.

    Producer/director, Frank Perry; screenplay, Pete Hamill; mu-
sic, Jimmy Webb; production designer, Gene Callahan; set decorator,
Manolo Mampaso; assistant director, Tony Tarruella; sound, Derek
Ball, Richard Vorisek; camera, Gerald Hirschfield; editor, Alan Heim.
    Stacy Keach (Doc Holliday); Faye Dunaway (Kate Elder); Har-
ris Yulin (Wyatt Earp); Mike Witney (Ike Clanton); Denver John
Collins (The Kid); Dan Greenburg (Editor).

    Producer/director Frank Perry attempted to recreate the events
leading up to and including the famous gun battle of the O.K. Corral
involving Wyatt Earp, Doc Holliday and the Clanton clan, and in
doing so tried to debunk the heroism of the lawmen and exonerate
the doings of the Clantons. The resulting psychological Western
was "all done at a leisurely pace, with dark photography and gritty
script" (F. Maurice Speed, Film Review 1972-73, 1972). While Perry's
jaundiced approach to history may not have appealed to purists, his
biggest error was in the staging of the famous shootout. Surprisingly the representation here is no more accurate than those that pre-
ceded it, thus negating any historical importance this feature sought.
    Self-centered Wyatt Earp (Harris Yulin) is the law in the wide
open town of Tombstone and intends to use the post to elevate his
position in life. He is allied with consumptive dentist Doc Holliday
(Stacy Keach), who falls in love with prostitute Kate Elder (Faye
Dunaway) who wants to settle down and raise a family. Opposing
Earp's less-than-good intentions is Ike Clanton (Mike Witney) and
his family, and Earp does all he can to get them out of his path.
Eventually Wyatt and Doc team to take on the Clantons at the O.K.
Corral and the latter are exterminated, but Doc finally realizes that
Kate's less-than-kind assessment of Wyatt is correct and he dis-
associates himself form the lawman.
    DOC has little to recommend it. It is not an appealing Western,
either visually or in its protagonists. The heroes are shown to be
worse than the villains and, while Stacy Keach and Faye Dunaway
are fair as Doc and Kate, Harris Yulin gives a vague performance
as the introspective and hard-as-nails Wyatt Earp. While Variety

was correct in assessing the film as "too intellectual for action fans," the trade paper should have added it was also boring!

DON AMIGO see THE GAY AMIGO

DON'T FENCE ME IN (Republic, 1945) 71 mins.

Supervising producer, Armand I. Schaefer; associate producer, Donald H. Brown; director, John English; screenplay, Darrell McGowan, Stuart E. McGowan; music director, Morton Scott; orchestrator, Dale Butts; choreography, Larry Ceballos; songs; Cole Porter, Milton Shore and Zeke Manners; Jack School and M. K. Jerome; Billy Hill, Larry Markes, Dick Charles, Eddie Delange, Freddie Slack, F. Victor, R. Herman, Bob Nolan; art director, Hilyard Brown; set decorators, John McCarthy, Jr., Marie Arthur; sound, Ed Borschell; camera, William Bradford; editor, Charles Craft.

Roy Roger (Roy Rogers); George "Gabby" Hayes (Gabby Whittaker); Dale Evans (Toni Ames); Robert Livingston (Jack Chandler); Moroni Olsen (Henry Bennett); Marc Lawrence (Cliff Anson); Lucille Gleason (Mrs. Prentiss); Andrew Tombes (Cartwright) Paul Harvey (The Governor); Tom London (The Sheriff); Douglas Fowley (Gordon); Stephen Barclay (Tracy); Edgar Dearing (Chief of Police); Bob Nolan and the Sons of Pioneers (Themselves); Trigger (The Horse); and Helen Talbot.

Cole Porter wrote the song "Don't Fence Me In" for Warner Bros.' patriotic all-star musical HOLLYWOOD CANTEEN (1944); in that feature it was performed by Roy Rogers, and Kate Smith thereafter had a best selling record with it on Columbia Records. The song was such a success that Republic Pictures used it as the title for one of Roy Rogers' series Westerns, issued the next year. The production proved to be a nice mixture of light drama interpolated with seven songs, including the title tune, "The Last Roundup," "Along the Navajo Trail," and "Tumbling Tumbleweeds," Bob Nolan's perennial classic which he and The Sons of the Pioneers had also sung in HOLLYWOOD CANTEEN.

Newspaper reporter Toni Ames (Dale Evans) is sent by her editor to the small Western town of Twin Wells to get a story about legendary outlaw Wildcat Kelly, who is buried on the outskirts of the community. At the R-Bar-R Dude Ranch, she meets old-timer Gabby Whittaker (George "Gabby" Hayes), who claims to have been Kelly's best pal, and ranch employees Roy Rogers (himself) and The Sons of the Pioneers (themselves). By accident, Toni finds out that Gabby is Wildcat Kelly. When her story breaks it interests the state's governor (Paul Harvey), since the state must now reopen the Kelly case. Crook Henry Bennett (Moroni Olsen) is also concerned because he committed a murder which he had blamed on the "dead" outlaw. Bennett sends henchman Cliff Anson (Marc Lawrence) to get rid of Gabby, but he only wounds him. Later Roy and The Sons of the Pioneers get a club booking and Gabby makes an appearance, with the sheriff clearing him of any wrongdoing. Roy and his pals corral Bennett's gang while Gabby personally captures the bad man. Roy and Toni realize they are in love.

George "Gabby" Hayes dominates this Roy Rogers vehicle which gives the star little to do other than sing several tunes and carry on a feud with reporter Dale Evans over her revealing the true Wildcat Kelly story.

DRAW (Astral/Bryna/HBO Premiere Films, 7/15/84) C 98 mins.

Executive producers, Harold Greenberg, Stuart B. Rekant; producer, Ronald M. Cohen; director, Steven Hilliard Stern; teleplay, Stanley Mann; production designer, Bill Brodie; music, Ken Wannberg; camera, Laszlo George; editor Ron Wisman.

Kirk Douglas (Handsome Harry H. Holland); James Coburn (Sam Starret); Alexandra Bastedo (Bess); Graham Jarvis (Wally Blodgett); Derek McGrath (Reggie Bell); Jason Michas (Moses); Len Birman (Ephraim); Maurice Brand (Mr. Gibson); Graham McPherson (Eugene Lippert); Vladimir Valenta (Mordecai Hurwitz); Linda Sorenson (Teresa); Gerard Parkes (Judge Nat Fawcett); Richard Donat (Sheriff Harmon); Frank Adamson (Bartender); Stuart Gillard (Dr. West); Miles Vasey (Charlie Tucker); James DeFelice (Bank Manager); James Forsythe (Bank Teller); Sherill De Marco (Sadie); Larry Musser (Townsman); Bonard Bain, Will Rowe, Brian Fustukian, Frank C. Turner (Poker Players); Brian George, Victor Bain (Banditos); Joan Hurley, Alan Stebbings, Vincent Gale (Acting Troupe); Steve Atkinson (Carpenter; Bob Supiene (Jose); Charlie Turner (Smith); Tom Dasko (Reggie's Tough); Miguel Neri, Bombo Ochica, Broderick Olson (Mariachi Players).

Kirk Douglas attempted to revive the small screen Western via this Home Box Office (HBO) Premiere Film first seen on pay cable television. But outside of the congenial ambiance created by the teaming of Douglas and James Coburn, the telefeature proved too predictable and tame. The film also borrowed bits and pieces from other genre efforts, making it seem "...like nothing so much as a ragbag of echoes" (Monthly Film Bulletin). Variety found the feature "Entirely predictable and without much suspense," but conceded, "It's a light entertainment, and both Douglas and Coburn give the audience their money's worth."

Aging gunman Handsome Harry Holland (Kirk Douglas) participates in a poker game in Bell City and ends up trying to collect an I.O.U. from the banker's son (Derek McGrath). The ensuing fracas concludes with the sheriff being killed. Injured in the shootout, Harry takes refuge in the local hotel and is ministered to by pretty Bess (Alexandra Bastedo), the ingenue with a touring acting company; he pretends that he is holding her hostage. The town's leading citizens demand Holland's arrest, but the deputy sheriff (Graham Jarvis) declines a showdown with Holland and instead sobers up once famous lawman Sam Starrett (James Coburn), who talks Harry into giving himself up instead of running away to Mexico with Bess, with whom he has fallen in love. The plan goes awry, however, when hanging Judge Nat Fawcett (Gerard Parkes) arrives with a score to settle with Harry. The gunslinger and the ex-marshal agree to a showdown and Sam shoots Harry. Sam then assists Bess in taking Harry's body to the desert for burial, but along the way Harry "revives" and the trio head south of the border.

DRIFTIN' RIVER (Producers Releasing Corp., 1946) 59 mins.

Producer, Robert Emmett Tansey; associate producer, Jerry Thomas; director, Tansey; screenplay, Frances Kavanaugh; songs: Johnny Bond and Eddie Dean; Lew Porter and Tansey; music arranger, Walter Greene; music director, Karl Hajos; assistant director, William L. Notle; art director, Edward C. Jewell; set decorator, Vin Taylor; sound, Buddy Myers; camera, Marcel Lipicard; editor, Hugh Winn.

Eddie Dean (Eddie); Roscoe Ates (Soapy); Shirley Patterson (J. C. Morgan); Lee Bennett (Tucson Browne); George Fawcett (Tennessee); Dennis Moore (Marino); Forrest Taylor (Mayor); Bob Callahan (Kensington); Lottie Harrison (Senora); Don Murphy (Captain Rogers); Lee Roberts (Trigger); Wiley Grant (Sam); Marion Carney (Mitzi); J. O. Smith, A. L. Smith, Edward F. Wallace (The Sunshine Boys); Flash (The Horse).

Eddie Dean had appeared in supporting roles in Westerns since the late 1930s, while carving out a successful career for himself as a singer, songwriter, recording artist, and radio performer. In the mid-1940s he finally landed lead roles in the "B" oaters HARMONY TRAIL (Meridian Pictures, 1944) and WILDFIRE (Screen Guild, 1945) before becoming the star of his own PRC series, which ran for nineteen entries from 1945 to 1948. In 1946 and 1947 he was voted one of the top ten money-making Western film stars by the Motion Picture Herald. While Eddie Dean's acting was sometimes deprecated and his starring vehicles were only average sagebrush tales at best, he was probably the finest singer ever to appear in Western motion pictures.

In DRIFTIN' RIVER, horse trader Eddie (Eddie Dean), along with his pal Soapy (Roscoe Ates), aids a beautiful young woman (Shirley Patterson) whose horse herd is being rustled by outlaws trying to halt the advance of the railroad. Eddie and Soap join the gang and expose the murderers who massacred an Army platoon carrying money to buy the young woman's herd.

DRIFTIN' RIVER was Eddie Dean's fourth PRC starring vehicle, and the first not in Cinecolor. Basically a slow drama, it greatly benefitted from appealing leading lady Shirley Patterson and two very fine songs: the title tune composed by Lew Porter and the film's producer/director, Robert Emmett Tansey; and "Way Back in Oklahoma," written by Eddie Dean and Johnny Bond.

DRIVEN WESTWARD see BRIGHAM YOUNG--FRONTIERSMAN

DRUM TAPS see TEX RIDES WITH THE BOY SCOUTS

THE DUDE BANDIT (Allied, 1933) 65 mins.

Producer, M. H. Hoffman, Jr.; director, George Melford; screenplay, Jack Natteford; assistant director, L. E. Tope; art director, Gene Hornbostel; camera, Harry Neumann, Tom Galligan; editor, Mildred Johnston.
Hoot Gibson (Ace Cooper/Tex); Gloria Shea (Betty Mason); Hooper Atchley (Burton); Skeeter Bill Robbins (Skeeter); Neal Hart (Jack); Lafe McKee (Brown); Gordon DeMain (Mason); Fred Burns (Sheriff); Art Mix (Art); and Fred Gilman, George Morrell, Merrill McCormack.

Using the name of Tex, Ace Cooper (Hoot Gibson) comes to investigate the death of Dad Mason (Gordon DeMain), who had money to pay off his debt to crook Burton (Hooper Atchley). Tex becomes "The Dude Bandit" and stops Burton from killing Betty Mason's (Gloria Shea) foreman, Skeeter (Skeeter Bill Robbins). Later when Betty and her neighbor, Brown (Lafe McKee), attempt to get their cattle away from Burton, Tex defeats the bad man and proves the latter was Mason's killer.
THE DUDE BANDIT was another in Hoot Gibson's Allied series for producer M. H. Hoffman, Jr. and like most entries in the group, it had low-grade production values and its plot rambled. As in the earlier SPIRIT OF THE WEST (q.v.), Hoot Gibson again masquerades as a none-too-bright character, and a further viewer annoyance is the presence of Skeeter Bill Robbins as Hoot's sidekick. Robbins was not long on talent and his underplayed type of humor was too much like that of Gibson's for the duo to complement each other.
One-time Western hero Neal Hart had one of his larger talking roles here as the villain's sidekick, while another former sagebrush star, Art Mix [George Kesterson], popped up in a bit part.

A DUEL A RIO BRAVO see GUNMEN OF THE RIO GRANDE

THE EAGLE see THE VIGILANTES ARE COMING

THE EAGLE'S BROOD see BAR 20 RIDES AGAIN

EL PASO KID (Republic, 1946) 54 mins.

Associate producer, Bennett Cohen; director, Thomas Carr; screenplay, Norman Sheldon; music director, Raoul Kraushaar; camera, Edgar Lyons; editor, William P. Thompson.

Sunset Carson (Sunset); Marie Harmon (Sally Stone); Hank Patterson (Jeff Winters); Edmund Cobb (Sheriff Frank Stone); Robert Filmer (Gil Santos); Wheaton Chambers (Dr. Hamlin); Zon Murray (Moyer); Tex Terry (Kramer); Charles Sullivan (Lowery); and Edward Cassidy, Bob Wilke, John Carpenter, Post Park.

In Laramie City, the citizens demand law and order, but are plagued by an outlaw gang who kill a townsman. Due to the murder, gang members Sunset Carson (himself) and Jeff Winters (Hank Patterson) desert the gang, and when the outlaws then hold up a stagecoach, the duo thwarts the robbery and Sunset is made the sheriff's (Edmund Cobb) deputy. Sunset and Jeff stop another attempted stage robbery but plan to double-cross the townspeople and steal a gold shipment. But the outlaws beat them to it and rob the express office, taking Sunset prisoner. He is shot while escaping and left for dead. But he is only wounded and returns to town, where he leads a posse to the gang's hideout. Sunset is pardoned by the governor and wins the hand of the sheriff's pretty daughter Sally (Marie Harmon).

EL PASO KID was the third from the last film in Sunset Carson's Republic series. Despite his screen exposure to date, he was still a mediocre actor at best, although he excelled as a rider and fighter and the movie is highlighted by a solid climactic fight. Otherwise the feature is a minor actioner and it demonstrated that Sunset Carson's star was definitely on the decline.

EL PASO STAMPEDE (Republic, 1953) 53 mins.

Producer, Rudy Ralston; director, Harry Keller; screenplay, Arthur Orloff; music, Stanley Wilson; camera, John MacBurnie; editor, Tony Martinelli.

Allan "Rocky" Lane (Himself); Black Jack (The Horse); Eddy Waller (Nugget Clark); Phyllis Coates (Alice Clark); Stephen Chase (Dr. Mason Ramsey); Roy Barcroft (Floyd Garnett); Edward Clark (Josh Bailey); Tom Monroe (Marty); Stanley Andrews (Marshal Banning); William Tannen (Joe); John Hamilton (Rancher).

After spending years in films doing everything from bits to leads to starring in serials, Allan Lane earned his own Western series at Republic Pictures in 1944. Two years later he replaced William Elliott in that studio's "Red Ryder" segments and did seven outings before returning to his own group of films in 1947, now billed as Allan "Rocky" Lane. For the next six seasons he did thirty-eight series Westerns, most of them above average. In 1953, the last year of his series, he was voted one of the top five

money-making Western film stars by the <u>Motion Picture Herald</u>. EL
PASO STAMPEDE was Allen Lane's final starring Western and it is
not one of the best of the series, although good enough for a fairly
high-level send off. Its plot-line is average and it contains lots of
stock footage, plus the re-use of the old ploy of having cattle
hidden in a valley behind a waterfall. To be noted is that although
he does not otherwise appear, a photograph of Grant Withers is
used to portray unseen rustler Jose Delgado.

At the time of the Spanish-American War, rustler Floyd Garnett
(Roy Barcroft) and his men hijack cattle herds intended for the Army. Special agent Allan "Rocky" Lane (himself) investigates and,
with the aid of pretty Alice Clark (Phyllis Coates) and sidekick
Nugget (Eddy Waller), learns that the local dentist (Stephen Chase)
is the brains of the operation. He rounds up the gang.

END OF THE TRAIL (Columbia, 1932) 59 mins.

Director, D. Ross Lederman; story/screenplay, Stuart Anthony;
camera, Benjamin Kline; editor, Otto Meyer.
Tim McCoy (Captain Tim Travers); Luanna Walters (Luanna);
Wheeler Oakman (Major Jenkins); Wade Boteler (Sergeant O'Brien);
Lafe McKee (Colonel Burke); Wally Albright (Timmy Travers); Chief
White Eagle (Indian Chief).

END OF THE TRAIL (Columbia, 1936) 70 mins.

Director, Erle C. Kenton; based on the story "Outlaws of
Palouse" by Zane Grey; screenplay, Harold Shumate; music director,
Morris Stoloff; camera, John Stumar; editor, Al Clark.
Jack Holt (Dale Brittenham); Louise Henry (Belle Pearson);
Guinn "Big Boy" Williams (Bob Hildreth); Douglass Dumbrille (Bill
Mason); George McKay (Ben Parker); Gene Morgan (Cheyenne);
John McGuire (Larry Pearson); Edward J. LeSaint (Jim Watrous);
Frank Shannon (Sheriff Anderson); Erle Keaton (Theodore Roose-
velt); and Hank Bell, Art Mix, Blackie Whiteford, Blackjack Ward,
Edgar Dearing.

It is ironic that two of the finest "B" Westerns of the 1930s
were unassuming productions made on a modest budget by cost-
conscious Columbia Pictures. The two films are not related: the
1932 entry is a Tim McCoy series vehicle, while the 1936 release
brought Jack Holt back to Columbia Pictures after an absence from
that studio for a season.

The Tim McCoy film is the star's definitive sound movie and
his personal statement on the plight of the American Indian. Filmed
in Lander, Wyoming and using local Indians in the production, the
movie is a compassionate study of how the Indians were being
treated by the whites. Among the highlights are the scenes where
star Tim McCoy uses sign language in his talks with the Indian

chiefs. McCoy had grown up in the West, knew the customs of the Indian nations and had worked as an Indian agent, which first brought him to Hollywood as an advisor on THE COVERED WAGON (see B/V) in 1921. In Views and Reviews (Volume 2, Issue 3, 1970), Jon Tuska called the film McCoy's "masterpiece of the talking picture era," and added, "It is scripted, acted, directed and photographed with such intensity of feeling, with such passion and dedication, that it stands out among not only McCoy's Westerns of the "Thirties, but among any Western Columbia was ever to make."

Tim McCoy stars as Captain Tim Travers, an Army scout assigned to a Montana fort to protect local prospectors following a gold strike on Indian lands. When Indians attack a wagon train, only Tim and fellow officer Jenkins (Wheeler Oakman) survive, and the latter, who has secretly been supplying guns to the Indians, tries to place the blame for the massacre on Tim. His commanding officer (Lafe McKee) doesn't want to believe the charges, but Jenkins plants false evidence which results in Tim's courtmartial. He leaves the service and takes his small son (Wally Albright) with him. When the boy is killed in a fracas with Jenkins and his men, Tim goes to live with the Arapahoes. There he falls in love with Luanna (Luana Walters), an Indian girl. Due to their treatment by the whites, the Indians want to declare war, but Tim tries to tell the chiefs that warfare against the whites is useless and that they will be slaughtered. Tim is captured by the soldiers and the Indians plan to attack the fort. In the ensuing fight, Jenkins is wounded and when dying, confesses to his crimes. Tim stops the attack but is shot. He recovers and becomes the local Indian agent.

Originally the character of Tim Travers dies at the film's finale, adding to the poignancy of the melodrama. However, Columbia Pictures feared fans would reject a film in which the hero dies, so they lensed a happy ending which in actuality doesn't harm the motion picture's overall effectiveness.

The 1936 Jack Holt END OF THE TRAIL is based on Zane Grey's story "Outlaws of Palouse," although it was reworked to the point where it was basically a remake of Casey Robinson's THE LAST PARADE (1930), set in a different time frame. In The Fabulous Holts (1976) Buck Rainey states, "The film was Jack's [Holt] last great solo western, a well-scripted, well-acted motion picture achieving high production values and tugging relentlessly at the heart strings of the viewer." Jean Arthur was set originally for the feminine lead, but was replaced by Louise Henry when Arthur was cast in another bigger-budgeted film.

Two young men grow up together and fight in the Spanish-American war. One (Jack Holt) loses an eye while saving his buddy's (Guinn "Big Boy" Williams) life. After the war they return to Texas and both of them fall in love with the same girl (Louise Henry). One of them (Holt) becomes a cattle rustler because his devil-may-care reputation prevents him from getting other work, while the other (Williams) becomes the sheriff who overlooks his friend's outlaw ways. The outlaw is idolized by the girl's younger brother (George McKay) and to ensure that he will go straight, the three move to California. But there the outlaw's enemy (Douglass Dumbrille) kills the boy and the outlaw vows revenge. He kills the culprit, but his sheriff friend is now forced to hunt him down and bring him to trial. At the finale, the outlaw is hanged.

ENEMY OF THE LAW (Producers Releasing Corp., 1945) 59 mins.

Producer, Arthur Alexander; director/screenplay, Harry Fraser; music director, Zee Zahler; camera, Jack Greenhalgh; editor, Holbrook M. Todd.
Tex Ritter (Tex Haines); Dave O'Brien (Dave Wyatt); Guy Wilkerson (Panhandle Perkins); Kay Hughes (Ruby Martin); Charles King (Charlie); Jack Ingram (Steve Martin); Frank Ellis (Red); Kermit Maynard (Mike); Henry Hall (Sheriff); and Karl Hackett, Edward Cassidy, Ben Corbett.

When James (Jim) Newill left PRC's "The Texas Rangers" series, the company signed Tex Ritter, who had just completed a tenure at Universal, to co-star with Dave O'Brien and Guy Wilkerson in the outings. Eight films were made for the 1944-45 season and in later years Tex Ritter expressed regret at having made these pictures. ENEMY OF THE LAW was the first of the eight films and a typical entry, with cheap production values and a meandering plot. On the plus side, it allowed Tex Ritter to perform "Teach Me to Forget" and "You Will Have To Pay."
Lawyer Tex Haines (Tex Ritter) and rangers Dave Wyatt (Dave O'Brien) and Panhandle Perkins (Guy Wilkerson) are tracking an outlaw gang who years before robbed a safe and hid the loot. Panhandle masquerades as a safecracker and gets in good with robber Charlie (Charles King), who is about to be double-crossed by another gang member, Steve Martin (Jack Ingram). Thanks to information obtained from Charlie, the trio recover the stolen money.

EXCEPT FOR ME & THEE see THE FRIENDLY PERSUASION (1975)

FALSE COLORS (United Artists, 1943) 64 mins.

Executive producer, Harry Sherman; producer, Lewis Rachmil; director, George Archainbaud; screenplay, Bennett Cohen; assistant director, Glenn Cook; art director, Ralph Berger; set decorator, Emile Kuri; sound, Jack Noyes; camera, Russell Harlan; editor, Fred Berger.
William Boyd (Hopalong Cassidy); Andy Clyde (California

Carlson); Jimmy Rogers (Himself); Tom Seidel (Bud Lawton/Kit
Mayer); Claudia Drake (Faith); Douglass Dumbrille (Mark Foster);
Robert Mitchum (Rip Austin); Glenn Strange (Sonora); Pierce
Lyden (Lefty); Roy Barcroft (Sheriff Clem Martin); Sam Flint
(Judge Stevens); Earle Hodgins (Lawyer Jay Griffen); Elmer
Jerome (Jed Stevens); Tom London (Townsman); Dan White (Bar
Spectator); George Morrell (Denton the Townsman); Topper (The
Horse); and Ray Jones, Bob Burns, Tom Smith.

While driving their cattle through the badlands, the Bar 20
wranglers are attacked by bushwackers. When one of the cowboys,
Bud (Tom Seidel), inherits his father's large ranch, he asks
Hopalong Cassidy (William Boyd) to help him set the place right.
Bud Lawton, however, is murdered by the bushwhackers and Hoppy
agrees to look after his sister (Claudia Drake) and the ranch.
Crooked banker Mark Foster (Douglass Dumbrille) is behind the
bushwackers and he hires a lookalike for Bud, Kit Mayer (Tom
Seidel), to impersonate the dead man in order to fool the girl and
take control of the property and its water rights. To get Hoppy
out of the way, Foster has him arrested on a bogus charge, but
Hopalong escapes, gets the goods on the banker and exposes the
imposter.
        Coming toward the end of the Harry Sherman-produced entries
in his long running "Hopalong Cassidy" series, FALSE COLORS is a
solid programmer with a good story, excellent photography, and
fine acting from its impressive cast. (Look for Robert Mitchum,
again portraying a bad guy.) The only weak link is Jimmy Rogers'
(Will's son) performance as Hoppy's sidekick Jimmy, this being his
first appearance in the role that would carry on for the final half-
dozen series segments. When Boyd revived the series in 1946
Rogers was replaced in the triad grouping by Rand Brooks, in a
recreation of the Lucky Jenkins character.

FANCY PANTS see RUGGLES OF RED GAP

THE FAR FRONTIER (Republic, 1949) C 67 mins.

        Associate producer, Edward J. White; director, William Whit-
ney; screenplay, Sloan Nibley; music, Dale Butts; music director,
Harry Scharf; songs, Jack Elliott; assistant director, Jack Lacey;
art director, Frank Hotaling; set decorators, John McCarthy, Jr.,
James Redd; Trucolor consultant, Sam Cohen; makeup, Steve
Drum; special effects, Roland Skeet; sound, Earl Crain, Sr.;
camera, Jack Martal; editor, Tony Martinelli.
        Roy Rogers (Himself); Gail Davis (Susan Hathaway); Andy
Devine (Judge Cookie Bullfincher); Francis Ford (Alf Sharper);
Roy Barcroft (Bart Carroll); Clayton Moore (Tom Sharper); Robert
Strange (Willis Newcomb); Holly Bane (Rocco); Lane Bradford
(Willie "Butch" Newcomb); John Bagni (Rollins); Clarence Straight

(Defendant); Edmund Cobb (Sheriff); Foy Willing and The Riders of the Purple Sage (Themselves); Trigger (The Horse); and Tom London.

A gang of smugglers, led by Willie "Butch" Newcomb (Lane Bradford) and Bart Carroll (Roy Barcroft), make a living by transporting deported gangsters back into the United States from Mexico, often leaving them to die once they have been paid for their services. Newcomb wants to buy out Alf Sharper (Francis Ford) and when his operation is uncovered by Alf's Border Patrolman son Tom (Clayton Moore), the young man is badly beaten, loses his memory, and the gang pins a murder on him. Cowboy Roy Rogers (Himself) and his pal Judge Cookie Bullfincher (Andy Devine) believe in Tom's innocence and eventually find out about Newcomb and his gang and thwart the villains.

THE FAR FRONTIER is a sharp, clever actioner which William Witney directed in a smooth, speedy fashion. Sloan Nibley's plot is particularly strong and villains Lane Bradford and Roy Barcroft dominate the proceedings. The supporting cast offers fine performances from Clayton Moore (in his pre-Lone Ranger days) as the wronged border patrolman and veteran Francis Ford as his loyal father. The movie is also more brutal than the average "B" Western of the time, especially in the early sequence where gangsters are being smuggled across the border in water barrels, and after an argument with Newcomb, the deported public enemies are left to suffocate after being dumped out of the truck carrying them. Later in the film, henchman Bart meets a similar fate when the barrels roll off a speeding truck and kill him.

FAST ON THE DRAW (Lippert, 1950) 57 mins.

Producer, Ron Ormond; director, Thomas Carr; screenplay, Ormond, Maurice Tombragel; camera, Ernest Miller; editor, Hugh Winn.

Jimmy Ellison (Shamrock); Russell Hayden (Lucky); Raymond Hatton (Colonel); Fuzzy Knight (Deacon/The Cat); Betty [Julia/Julie] Adams (Ann); Tom Tyler (Bandit Leader); George Lewis (Pedro); John Cason (Tex); Stanley Price (Carter); and Jimmy Van Horn, Bud Hooker, Ray Jones, I. Stanford Jolley.

FAST ON THE DRAW was the last of a half-dozen oaters starring one-time "Hopalong Cassidy" series regulars James Ellison and Russell Hayden. Produced by Ron Osmond and issued by Lippert, these thin proceedings were all directed by Thomas Carr in a four-week period using identical casts. None of the features was particularly satisfying, but FAST ON THE DRAW is one of the worst. Its only saving grace is having usual genre sidekick Fuzzy Knight as the movie's villain, a murderer called The Cat.

Years before, his lawman father and mother were bushwhacked by outlaws. Now Shamrock (James Ellison) is on the trail of the

Tom Tyler, Russell Hayden, I. Stanford Jolley, and John Cason in
FAST ON THE DRAW (1950).

killers, although he is afraid of guns and cannot bring himself to
fire upon anyone. With the aid of pal Lucky (Russell Hayden) and
a pretty girl (Betty [Julia/Julie] Adams) and two locals (Raymond
Hatton, Fuzzy Knight), he tries to locate the killer, whose gang he
has traced to the vicinity. Eventually he learns to use a gun adept-
ly and unmasks the gang leader--known as The Cat--who turns out
to be one of the men assisting him.

THE FIDDLIN' BUCKAROO see THE STRAWBERRY ROAN (1933)

$50,000 REWARD (Davis Distributing, 1924) 4,950'

Supervisor/director, Clifford S. Elfelt; screenplay, Frank
Howard Clark; camera, Bert Longenecker.
Ken Maynard (Tex Sherwood); Tarzan (The Horse); Esther
Ralston (Carolyn Jordan); Bert Lindley (Anthony Jordan); Edward
Peil (Buck Schofield); Lillian Leighton (Mrs. Miller); Charles New-
ton (Pa Miller); Frank Whitson (Asa Holman).

Tex Sherwood (Ken Maynard), a cowboy from Texas, comes to
Montana to register a title claim to land he has inherited. Two

crooked bankers (Edward Peil, Frank Whitson) want to land themselves because it is to be used for a reclamation and dam project. The crooks send their henchman to scare off Tex, but he foils them and meets Carolyn Jordan (Esther Ralston), who is taking her injured father's (Bert Lindley) place as construction supervisor. Tex records his claim, exposes the bankers as crooks, and earns $50,000 for the property. Ken and Carolyn then move to Texas.

$50,000 REWARD was Ken Maynard's first starring feature and the initial entry in a half-dozen features he made for Davis Distribution Division, which released its product through the state's rights Vital Exchanges. Fast paced and well done for a low-budget feature, this movie was a good start for Maynard's screen career, which would encompass more than 80 starring Westerns in the next two decades. Esther Ralston, also at the start of her film career, added her special brand of feminine allure as the more ambitious than usual leading lady.

FIGHTING CARAVANS (Paramount, 1931) 91 mins.

Directors, Otto Brower, David Burton; based on the novel by Zane Grey; adaptors, E. E. Paramore, Jr., Keene Thompson, Agnes Leahy; art director, Robert Odell; sound, Earle S. Hayman; camera, Lee Garmes; editor, William Shea.

Gary Cooper (Clint Belmet); Lily Damita (Felice); Ernest Torrance (Bill Jackson); Fred Kohler (Lee Murdock); Tully Marshall (Jim Bridger); Eugene Pallette (Seth); Roy Stewart (Couch); May Boley (Jane); James Farley (Amos); James Marcos (The Blacksmith); Eve Southern (Faith); Donald Mackenzie (Gus); Syd Saylor (Charlie); E. Alyn Warren (Barlow); Frank Campeau (Jeff Moffitt); Charles Winninger (Marshal); Frank Hagney (The Renegade); Jane Darwell (Pioneer Woman); Irving Bacon (Barfly); Harry Semels (Brawler); Iron Eyes Cody (Indian after Firewater); Merrill McCormick (Townsman); Tiny Sandford (Man at Wagon Train); Chief Big Tree (Indian in Opening Scene).

Zane Grey's well publicized novel Fighting Caravans (1929) was first brought to the screen in 1931 by Paramount as a big-budget production starring Gary Cooper, following his recent genre successes in THE VIRGINIAN (1929 - see B/V), THE TEXAN (q.v.) and THE SPOILERS (1930 - see B/V). Here Gary Cooper is cast as trail guide Clint Belmet, who leads a wagon train West with the help of pals Bill Jackson (Ernest Torrance) and Jim Bridger (Tully Marshall). On the train is headstrong French girl Felice (Lily Damita), with whom Clint falls in love. Trapper Lee Murdock (Fred Kohler) is afraid settlers will destroy his fur trace and he incites the Indians to attack the train, but they are defeated and Murdock is killed. The wagon train reaches its final destination. This film appears on TV as BLAZING ARROWS.

Three years after the release of FIGHTING CARAVANS, the film was remade by Paramount as WAGON WHEELS. This "B"

Gary Cooper and Lily Damita in FIGHTING CARAVANS (1931).

rendition interpolated a great deal of action footage from the original.
The plot-line is fairly identical, with scout Clint (Randolph Scott)
and cohorts Jim (Raymond Hatton) and Bill (Olin Howlin), leading a
wagon train to Oregon and fighting half-breed Murdock (Monte
Blue) and his warring Indian allies who attack the train but are
defeated. The romantic interest is supplied by Gail Patrick as attractive widow Nancy Wellington, who has a small son (Bill Lee).
For comedy relief, scout Jim is romanced by a man-hungry caravan
passenger (Jan Duggan).
    In keeping with the increasing usage of music in "B" Westerns,
several songs were used in the film, which featured Earl Conert and
the Singing Guardsmen. Stars Randolph Scott, Gail Patrick, Billy
Lee, Olin Howlin, and Raymond Hatton also sing the film's title tune,
while Jan Dugan does a comedy rendition of "Under the Daisies."

THE FIGHTING COWBOY (Superior Pictures, 1933) 58 mins.

    Producer, Victor Adamson; director, Denver Dixon [Adamson];
story/screenplay, L. V. Jefferson; sound, Herb Ficke; technical
director, Bart Carre; camera, Bydron Baker.
    Buffalo Bill, Jr. [Jay Wilsey] (Bill Carson); Genee Boutell

(Elizabeth Ryno); Allen Holbrook (Duke Neill); William Ryno (Cash Horton, the Miner); Marin Sais (Mary); Tom Palky (Buge); Bart Carre (Pete); Betty Butler (Saloon Girl); and Jack Evans, Boris Bullock, Hen Broeker, Hamilton Steele, Clyde McClary, Ernest Scott, Bud Baxter, Jack Bronston.

Cowpoke Bill Carson (Buffalo Bill, Jr.) discovers tungsten in an old gold chain, but town bully Duke Neill (Allen Holbrook) wants to steal it and has his pal Pete (Bart Carre) try to kill Bill by putting him on the wrong trail. The mine owner's (William Ryno) daughter Elizabeth (Genee Boutell) finds Bill dying of thirst in the desert and takes him to her dad's mine, where he tells them about the ore. Duke then plans to blow up the mine, but his scheme is foiled when Bill takes after the gang. Bill clears Elizabeth's dad of a phony murder charge, clearing the path for him and Elizabeth to fall in love.

One of a quartet of bottom-of-the-barrel sagebrushers Buffalo Bill, Jr. (real name: Jay Wilsey) made for poverty row producer/director/actor Victor Adamson, THE FIGHTING COWBOY is a sad state of affairs. Its only redeeming qualities are Byrdon Baker's cinematography and the shapely heroine.

Australian Victor Adamson began making independent Westerns in 1918 and continued in films until 1970, when he did a supporting role in his son's, Al Adamson, violent oater, FIVE BLOODY GRAVES (q.v.). Using a variety of names (e.g., Denver Dixon, Art Mix, Al Mix, Art James), he turned out scores of features and short subjects with no intrinsic and little entertainment value. Seen today, however, these efforts are amusing in their naive way. They also have some odd plot happenings, as in THE FIGHTING COWBOY, which contains the brutal scene of Buffalo Bill, Jr.'s shooting his horse when they become lost in the desert, or the sequence where the villain puts out his cigarette ash in a can of juice which a small child is drinking.

THE FIGHTING DEPUTY (Spectrum, 1937) 60 mins.

Producer, Jed Buell; associate producer, George H. Callaghan; director, Sam Newfield; story, Bennett Cohen; screenplay, William Lively; music supervisor, Abe Meyer; songs, June Hersey and Don Swander; camera, Robert Cline; editor, William Ness.

Fred Scott (Tom Bentley); Phoebe Logan (Alice Denton); Al St. John (Fuzzy); Marjorie Beebe (Peaches); Charles King (Scar Adams); Frank LaRue (Sheriff Bentley); Lafe McKee (Denton); Sherry Tansey, Chick Hannon (Henchmen); White King (The Horse); and Eddie Holden, Jack C. Smith.

A cowboy (Fred Scott) is in love with a rancher's daughter (Phoebe Logan), but she becomes upset when he tells her he is taking over as acting sheriff from his dad (Frank LaRue), who has been injured in gunplay with the vicious outlaw Scar Adams (Charles

King). The cowboy is unaware that Scar is the girl's black-sheep brother, and the girl refuses to marry him if he carries out his mission, after he trails the badman to her father's ranch. The cowboy agrees and he and the girl are wed. However, when Scar murders his sheriff father, the cowboy vows revenge and chases Scar into the mountains. Scar's rancher dad (Lafe McKee) dispatches his son. The cowboy and the girl settle down to a life of happiness while the cowpoke's buddy (Al St. John) finds his intended bride (Marjorie Beebe) has run away.

A fairly engaging entry in Fred Scott's minimal-budget series for producer Jed Buell and issued by Spectrum. THE FIGHTING DEPUTY benefits from the pleasant screen personality of robust crooner Fred Scott in tandem with the comedy highjinks of Al St. John. Although the movie's trio of songs, "A Hideaway in Happy Valley," "Yellow Moon" and "The Old Home Ranch," are minor, Scott delivers them in good form. Charles King provides one of his customary performances as the grimy and dastardly Scar Adams, whose totally immoral character is the highlight herein.

THE FIGHTING KENTUCKIAN (Republic, 1949) 100 mins.

Producer, John Wayne; director/screenplay, George Waggner; assistant director, Lee Lukather; music, George Antheil; costumes, Adele Palmer; art director, James Sullivan; set decorators, John McCarthy, Jr., George Milo; makeup, Bob Mark, Webb Overlander, Don Cash, Cecil Holland; special effects, Howard and Theodore Lydecker; sound, Dick Tyler, Howard Wilson; camera, Lee Garmes; editor, Richard L. Van Enger.

John Wayne (John Breen); Vera Ralston (Fleurette DeMarchand); Philip Dorn (Colonel Georges Geraud); Oliver Hardy (Willie Paine); Marie Windsor (Ann Logan); John Howard (Blake Randolph); Hugo Haas (General Paul DeMarchand); Grant Withers (George Hayden); Odette Myrtil (Madame DeMarchand); Paul Fix (Beau Merritt); Mae Marsh (Sister Hattie); Jack Pennick (Captain Dan Carroll); Mickey Simpson (Jacques); Fred Graham (Carter Ward); Mabelle Koenig (Marie); Shy Waggner, Crystal White (Friends).

In 1819 in the territory of Alabama, Kentucky rifleman John Breen (John Wayne) meets and romances Fleurette Marchand (Vera Ralston), the daughter of a French general (Hugo Haas) who has settled in the area with the officers and families of Frenchmen exiled from their homeland after Napoleon's defeat. Breen's sidekick, Willie Paine (Oliver Hardy), wants him to travel on, but John resigns his post to join society and court Fleurette. But he learns her family has promised her to Blake Randolph (John Howard), a rich man who has financed the settlers' stay in America. Breen finds that Randolph is in cahoots with George Hayden (Grant Withers), the leader of the rivermen, in cheating the settlers out of the lands granted to them by Congress. Breen exposes the plans and a battle results between the rivermen and the settlers, with

Odette Myrtil, John Wayne, and Vera Ralston in THE FIGHTING KENTUCKIAN (1949).

Hayden killing Randolph when he plans to halt the battle. Breen then chases and kills Hayden, with the Second Kentucky Riflemen arriving in time to defeat the rivermen. Breen and Fleurette are free to marry as they leave for his new military assignment.

John Wayne produced this well-financed frontier piece, with George Waggner directing from his own script. Overall, the film is one of John Wayne's lesser screen efforts and the New York Times correctly observed, "...if it is history, it is obscure and unconvincing." Wayne is properly stalwart in the title assignment and plays the part with a wry sense of humor. Oliver Hardy (sans Stan Laurel) provides many amusing moments as Breen's bumbling but well meaning sidekick, and the supporting cast is fine, although Vera Ralston is barely adequate in the feminine lead. The picture's best segment occurs rightly at the finale with the well-staged and actionful battle scenes backed by musical variations of "La Marseillaise."

THE FIGHTING SHERIFF (Columbia, 1931) 67 mins.

Producer, Sol Lesser; director, Louis King; story/screenplay,

Anthony Stuart; camera, Ted Tetzlaff.

    Buck Jones (Bob Terry); Loretta Sayers (Mary Cameron); Robert Ellis (Flash Holloway); Paul Fix (Jack Cameron), Silver (The Horse); Nena Quartero (Tiana); and Harlan Knight, Lillian Worth, Clarence Muse, Lilliane Leighton, Tom Bay.

    Following a hold-up, Red River lawman Bob Terry (Buck Jones) mortally wounds one of the robbers, Jack Cameron (Paul Fix), who asks him not to tell his sister Mary (Loretta Sayers) about his lawless activities. When Cameron dies in the sheriff's office, saloon proprietor Flash Holloway (Robert Ellis) is also there, and when Mary arrives to find her brother, he saves her from trouble at his saloon, the Hell's Delight Cafe. Meanwhile, the sheriff romances Mary. Soon Bob Terry discovers that the real culprit behind the outlaw gang is Flash, but he is blackmailed by Flash, who threatens to reveal to Mary who killed her brother. Still later the sheriff corrals Holloway and his gang, and with the evidence at hand, Mary realizes she loves Bob.

    THE FIGHTING SHERIFF was Buck Jones' eighth talking film and the final one in his first year at Columbia. This initial series for Harry Cohn's studio established Jones as the most popular genre star of the new talking era, and THE FIGHTING SHERIFF, with its solid script and plenty of action, provides ample reason for his popularity. In The Saga of Buck Jones (1975), Buck Rainey stated the movie was an "...honest-to-goodness, whirlwind western full of highway robberies, daredevil fights, and a grand exhibition of wild west riding."

THE FIGHTING TROOPER see NORTHERN FRONTIER

THE FIGHTING VIGILANTES (Eagle Lion, 1947) 61 mins.

    Producer, Jerry Thomas; director, Ray Taylor; screenplay, Robert B. Churchill; music, Walter Greene; music director, Dick Carruth; assistant director, Ira Webb; art director, Jack Mills; music, Walter Greene; makeup, George Bruce; sound, Glen Glenn; camera, Ernest Miller; editor, Hugh Winn.

    "Lash" LaRue (Marshal Cheyenne Davis); Al "Fuzzy" St. John (Marshal Fuzzy Q. Jones); Jennifer Holt (Abby Jackson); George Chesebro (Price Taylor); Lee Morgan (Sheriff); Marshall Reed (Check); Carl Matthews (Shanks); Russell Arms (Trippler); Steve Clark (Frank Jackson); John Elliot (Old Man); Felice Richmond (Old Woman).

    Marshals Cheyenne Davis (Lash LaRue) and Fuzzy Q. Jones (Al St. John) come to a town plagued by bandits, with businessman Price Taylor (George Chesebro) being robbed of his shipments. Frank Jackson (Steve Clark), another businessman, is arrested and later shot by a crooked lawman. In order to help Jackson's

daughter Abby (Jennifer Holt) prove her father's innocence,
Cheyenne and Fuzzy pose as vigilantes to solve the crimes. They
learn that Jackson had once opposed Taylor and had originally
started the local vigilantes. The two marshals then round up the
corrupt Taylor and his gang.

Mostly dull going except for an exciting climax, THE FIGHTING
vigilantes was Lash LaRue's seventh starring vehicle for Producers
Releasing Corp. It was followed by CHEYENNE TAKES OVER (1947),
after which the film company dissolved. LaRue and Al St. John
then contracted with producer Ron Ormond, who released his films
through Screen Guild.

UN FIUME DI DOLLARI see THE HILLS RUN RED

FIVE BLOODY GRAVES (Independent-International, 1969) C 88 mins.

Producer, Al Adamson; associate producer, John Cardos,
Robert Dix; director, Adamson; story/screenplay, Dix; sound, Robert
Dietz; camera, William Zsigmond; editors, William Faris, Peter Perry.

Robert Dix (Ben Thompson); Scott Brady (Jim Wade); Jim Davis
(Clay Bates); John Carradine (Boone Hawkins); Paula Raymond (Kan-
sas Kelly); John Cardos (Joe Lightfoot/Satago); Tara Ashton (Althea
Richards); Kent Osborne (Dave Miller); Vicki Volante (Nora Miller);
Denver Dixon (Rawhide); Ray Young (Horace Wiggins); Julie Ed-
wards (Lavina Wade); Fred Meyers (Driver); Maria Poloi (Little
Fawn); Gene Raymond (The Voice of Death).

Gunslinger Ben Thompson (Robert Dix), forever haunted by
the Voice of Death (Gene Raymond), badly abuses a prostitute and
then heads to the desert, where he rescues a woman (Vicki Volante)
from the sadistic half-breed Satago (John Cardos) and his band.
Later, the woman's husband (Kent Osborne) makes him leave and
the couple are butchered by the renegades. Satago then captures
a pretty Indian maiden (Maria Polo) and leaves her to die in the
desert. She is found by gun runner Clay Bates (Jim Davis), who
is in cahoots with Satago, and his moronic partner Horace (Ray
Young). Bates rapes and kills the bound girl. A covered wagon
driven by Rawhide (Denver Dixon) breaks down in the desert,
leaving its passengers stranded. They include lustful preacher
Hawkins (John Carradine), madam Kansas Kelly (Paula Raymond),
gambler Jim Wade (Scott Brady), and two prostitutes (Tara Ashton,
Julie Edwards). Eventually everyone except Ben Thompson and
Satago dies, and those two have a fight to the finish, with Thompson
emerging the winner. He is left to drift with the Voice of Death.

Billed as "The most sadistic and sensual slaughter the West
ever witnessed!" this economy production promised "Woman Scalped
Alive," "Men Fiendishly Tortured" and "Passionate Playgirls." While
this Independent-international release attempted to pander to
viewers' lowest demands, it was only successful in wasting a good

Scott Brady, John Cardos, and Robert Dix in FIVE BLOODY
GRAVES (1969).

cast. The film did boast attractive cinematography by William Zsigmond, with location shooting at Utah's Capitol Reef, and some of
the action sequences staged by one-time cowboy star John Carpenter are exciting. Also to be noted is that producer/director Al
Adamson's father, Victor Adamson (billed here as Denver Dixon),
has a featured role as Rawhide, the wagonmaster.
    TV title: GUN RIDERS

5 CARD STUD (Paramount, 1968) C 103 mins.

    Producer, Hal B. Wallis; associate producer, Paul Nathan;
director, Henry Hathaway; based on the novel Glory Gulch by Ray
Gaulden; screenplay, Marguerite Roberts; production designer,
Walter Tyler; set decorator, Ray Moyer; assistant director, Fred
Gammon; costumes, Leah Rhodes; music, Maurice Jarre; song, Jarre
and Ned Washington; W. H. Doane and F. C. Van Alstyne; makeup,
Adelbert Acevedo; sound, Harold Lewis; camera, Daniel L. Fapp;
editor, Warren Low.
    Dean Martin (Van Morgan); Robert Mitchum (Reverend
Jonathan Rudd); Inger Stevens (Lily Langford); Roddy McDowall
(Nick Evers); Katherine Justice (Nora Evers); John Anderson
(Marshal Dana); Ruth Springford (Mama Malone); Yaphet Kotto
(Little George); Denver Pyle (Sig Evers); Bill Fletcher (Joe Hurley);
Whit Bissell (Dr. Cooper); Ted De Corsia (Eldon Bates); Don Collier

Dean Martin and Robert Mitchum in 5 CARD STUD (1968).

(Rowan); Roy Jenson (Mace Jones); Boyd "Red" Morgan (Fred Carson); George Rowbothan (Stoney); Jerry Gatlin (Stranger); Charles B. Hayward (O'Hara); Louise Lorimer (Mrs. Wells); Hope Summers (Woman Customer).

In the small town of Rincon, Colorado, in 1880, a stranger is hung for cheating in a card game. One of the game players, Van Morgan (Dean Martin), tries to prevent the lynching but when he fails, goes to Denver. Meanwhile, a gold rush hits the community and with it comes self-proclaimed minister Jonathan Rudd (Robert Mitchum), who is actually the brother of the murdered man, seeking revenge on those who lynched his kin. When Van learns that two of the players in that fateful poker game have been murdered, he returns to Rincon and is told by bartender Little George (Yaphet Kotto) that his life is in danger. While trying to find the killer, Van romances madam Lily (Inger Stevens) and pretty local Nora Evers (Katherine Justice). Then two more participants in the game are killed. One of the surviving gamblers, Nick Evers (Roddy McDowall), Nora's brother, has told Rudd who the other players were, although it was he who instigated the hanging. Nick advises Rudd to kill Little George, which he does, but the bogus preacher discovers that it was Nick who was really the cause of the hanging, and shots him. During the final shootout with Van, Rud is killed.

Van once again goes to Denver.

Filmed on location in Durango, Mexico, 5 CARD STUD had the potent box-office combination of Dean Martin and Robert Mitchum to carry its lacklustre murder mystery plot set in the Old West. (The film grossed $4,250,000 in domestic rentals.) Mitchum is stoically impressive as the fake minister, a role not unlike his classic portrayal of the murderous clergyman in NIGHT OF THE HUNTER (1955 - see B/V). This Western suffers from its uneasy blend of low-key comedy and melodramatics, and is further hampered by too many lackadaisical performances.

FLAME OF SACRAMENTO see IN OLD SACRAMENTO

FRIENDLY PERSUASION (Allied Artists, 1956) C 137 mins.

Producer, William Wyler; associate producer, Robert Wyler; director, William Wyler; based on the novel by Jessamyn West; uncredited screenplay, William Wyler, West, Robert Wyler, Harry Kleiner; music, Dimitri Tiomkin; songs, Tiomkin and Paul Francis Webster; art director, Edward S. Haworth; set decorator, Joe Kish; costumes, Dorothy Jeakins; makeup, Emile La Vigne; assistant director Austin Jewell; technical adviser, Miss West; special effects, August Lohman; camera, Ellsworth Fredericks; editors, Robert Swink, Edward Biery, Jr., Robert Belcher.

Gary Cooper (Jess Birdwell); Dorothy McGuire (Eliza Birdwell); Marjorie Main (Widow Hudspeth); Anthony Perkins (Josh Birdwell); Richard Eyer (Little Jess); Robert Middleton (Sam Jordan); Phyllis Love (Mattie Birdwell); Mark Richman (Gard Jordan); Walter Catlett (Professor Quigley); Richard Hale (Purdy); Joel Fluellen (Enoch); Theodore Newton (Army Major); John Smith (Caleb); Mary Carr (Quaker Woman); Edna Skinner, Marjorie Durant, Frances Farwell (Widow Hudspeth's Daughters); Russell Simpson, Charles Halton, Everett Glass (Elders); Samantha (The Goose); Richard Garland (Bushwhacker); James Dobson (Rebel Soldier); John Compton (Rebel Lieutenant); James Seay (Rebel Captain); Diane Jergens (Elizabeth the Young Girl); Ralph Sanford (Business Man); Jean Inness (Mrs. Purdy); Nelson Leigh (Minister); Helen Kleeb (Old Lady); William Schallert (Young Husband); John Craven (Leader); Frank Jenks (Shell Game Man); Frank Hagney (Lemonade Vendor); Jack McClure (Soldier); Charles Courtney (Reb Courrier); Tom Irish (Young Rebel); Mary Jackson (Country Woman).

FRIENDLY PERSUASION (International Television Productions/Allied Artists, ABC-TV, 5/18/75) C 100 mins.

Executive producers, Emanuel L. Wolf, Herbert B. Leonard; producer/director, Joseph Sargent; based on the novels Friendly Persuasion and Except for Me and Thee by Jessamyn West; teleplay, William Wood; art director, James H. Spencer; music, John Cacavas;

theme song, Dimitri Tiomkin; camera, Mario Tosi; editors, Edward J. Forsyth, George Jay Nicholson.

Richard Kiley (Jess Birdwell); Shirley Knight (Eliza Birdwell); Clifton James (Sam Jordan); Michael O'Keefe (Josh); Kevin O'Keefe (Labe); Tracie Savage (Mattie); Sparky Marcus (Little Jess); Paul Benjamin (Swan Stebeney); Erik Holland (Enoch); Maria Grimm (Lily Truscott); Bob Minor (Burk).

A.k.a.: EXCEPT FOR ME & THEE

The threat of war comes to a small Southern Indiana community in 1862 and at a Quaker First Day Meeting, a Union officer asks for volunteers to fight the Confederacy. Young Quaker Josh Birdwell (Anthony Perkins), who does not believe in fighting, begins to doubt his own courage and convictions, but finds little support from his parents, Jess (Gary Cooper) and Eliza (Dorothy McGuire), who are faithful Quakers and do not believe in violence. When it is rumored that Morgan's Raiders are coming to the area, Josh joins the Home Guard in order to defend the locale, doing so against his mother's urging, although Jesse has come to realize that a person must follow his own convictions. In the skirmish, Josh is wounded and when he does not return home, his father goes to find him. In his search, he stumbles across his dying friend Sam Jordan

Gary Cooper and Richard Garland in FRIENDLY PERSUASION (1956).

(Robert Middleton). Enraged, Jess goes after the bushwackers who murdered his friend, but when he corners the man he cannot bring himself to kill him and lets him go. He then takes his wounded son home, with the youth realizing that he does have courage despite his dislike for violence.

Taken from Jessamyn West's 1945 novel and adapted by Michael Wilson (whose name was deleted from the final release credits due to his alleged Communist involvements), the William Wyler-directed epic is a delightful look at Quaker life in the Hoosier state in the Civil War era. Made with top production values and brimming over with uniformly fine performances, THE FRIENDLY PERSUASION was a big box-office success and one of Allied Artists most profitable productions. (The film grossed $5,050,000 in domestic release.) Filled with good humor and contrasting pathos, the movie deftly depicted the state of courage and its offshoots on the ever-expanding frontier, seen from the vantage point of non-violent Quakers caught in the grasp of war and its brutality.

In many respects this film was to be Gary Cooper's last substantial feature. While THE FRIENDLY PERSUASION deals with a serious subject it was lightened by several semi-comic episodes, the most pleasing of which centers around the visit of Jess Birdwell and his eligible son Josh to the farmhome of the earthy Widow Hudspeth (Marjorie Main) and her man-hungry unwed daughters.

The New York Times observed of this highly-praised production that it was "...a film of much sweetness, wisdom, warmth and real people, topped by a spurt of stirring drama and suspense..."

In 1975 International Television Productions and Allied Artists remade THE FRIENDLY PERSUASION as a television movie. Here William P. Wood's script combined the novel with another Jessamyn West book, Except for Me and Thee (1969), in a tale about an Indiana Quaker family which risks itself to help two runaway slaves. Richard Kiley was Jess Birdwell, Shirley Knight was his wife Eliza, and Michael O'Keefe was son Josh. While nowhere as good as the 1956 feature, the telefilm was more than adequate by small screen standards. For syndicated TV showing, the remake was retitled EXCEPT FOR ME AND THEE.

FROM NOON TILL THREE (United Artists, 1976) C 96 mins.

Producers, Mike J. Frankovich; director, Frank D. Gilroy; based on the novel by Gilroy; screenplay, Gilroy; production designer, Robert Clatworthy; art director, Dick Lawrence; set decorator, George Robert Nelson; Assistant director, Russ Saunders; music, Elmer Bernstein; song, Bernstein and Alan and Marilyn Bergman; sound, Arthur Piantadosi, Richard Tyler, Les Fresholtz, Al Overton; camera, Lucien Ballard; editor, Maury Winetrobe.

Charles Bronson (Graham Dorsey); Jill Ireland (Amanda Starbuck); Douglas V. Fowley (Buck Bowers); Stan Haze (Ape); Damon Douglas (Boy); Hector Morales (Mexican); Bert Williams

Charles Bronson in FROM NOON TILL THREE (1976).

(Sheriff); William Lanteau (Reverend Cabot); Betty Cole, Davis Roberts (Amanda's Servants); Fred Franklyn (Postmaster); Sonny Jones (Dr. Finger); Hoke Howell (Deke); Howard Brunner (Foster); Donald "Red" Barry (Outlaw Leader); Elmer Bernstein, Alan Bergman (Songwriters).

One of the most underrated Westerns of the 1970s, FROM NOON TILL THREE is a delightful send-up of the romantic period pieces of yore in its tale of a third-rate bandit who becomes a legend thanks to a book which details a three-hour love affair. Charles Bronson deftly handles the role of the amorous outlaw, and his real-life wife Jill Ireland--who usually arouses the ire of film critics--is delightful as the repressed widow who briefly becomes romantically alive. While lacking the action of a usual Charles Bronson opus, FROM NOON TILL THREE is a fragile but entirely satisfying Western comedy which deserved a better fate than it received (the public avoided the film, despite rather pleasant reaction from critics).

Outlaw Buck Bowers (Douglas Fowley) and his gang (Stan Haze, Damon Douglas, Hector Morales), including Graham Dorsey (Charles Bronson), ride into a seemingly deserted town and rob the bank, only to be massacred by the law. The situation turns out to be a nightmare, dreamed by Dorsey. However, on the way to the real stick-up, Dorsey's horse is lost and he takes sanctuary at the ranch of beautiful widow Amanda Starbuck (Jill Ireland). At first the two are distrustful, but they soon fall passionately in love and have a three-hour affair. When word arrives that the bank robbery has been foiled and that the gang will be hung, Amanda urges Graham to aid his comrades. Along the trail he meets a dentist (Sonny Jones), who is later mistaken for him since they have exchanged clothes. When the doctor is killed and everyone thinks Graham has died, Amanda agrees to let a writer (Howard Brunner) tell the story in a book, and it becomes a nationwide bestseller, making a hero of Dorsey. Having been jailed on a minor charge for a year, Graham now returns to Amanda. Rather than see his legend destroyed, she kills herself. No one will believe Dorsey concerning his identity until he is placed in an insane asylum where the other inmates accept him.

FRONTIER PONY EXPRESS (Republic, 1939) 58 mins.

Associate producer/director, Joseph Kane; screenplay, Norman Hall; music director, Cy Feuer; song, Walter G. Samuels; camera, William Nobles; editor, Gene Milford.

Roy Rogers (Himself); Mary Hart [Lynne Roberts] (Ann Langhorne); Raymond Hatton (Horseshoe); Edward Keane (Senator Lassiter); Noble Johnson (Cantrell); Monte Blue (Cherokee); Donald Dillaway (Brett Langhorne); William Royale (Garrett); Ethel Wales (Mrs. Murphy); Trigger (The Horse); and George Letz [Montgomery], Charles King, Bud Osborne, Fred Burns, Jack Kirk, Bob McKenzie, Ernie Adams, Hank Bell, Jack O'Shea.

In 1861 Missouri, Confederates plan to use the Pony Express to gain control of California for the South by issuing fake orders to Union soldiers. Corrupt Confederate Senator Lassiter (Edward Keane) pretends to be a Southern agent, but he really intends to set up his own Republic in California and he uses a Rebel spy, Brett Langhorne (Donald Dillaway), as his pawn. Pony Express rider Roy Rogers (Himself) rescues pretty Ann Langhorne (Mary Hart) from a runaway stagecoach and finds out she is Brett's sister. When his gang holds up the pony express payroll stage, Lassiter sets a benefit ball for the drivers and Ann agrees to work at the event. That night Roy, carrying secret papers, is attacked by the gang, but he defeats them. He believes Ann, who knew about his mission, is a Rebel spy, and she is arrested. When Lassiter schemes to rob a gold shipment, Brett finally sees through him and tries to stop him, but the Senator shoots the young man. Before he dies, Brett tells Ann the truth and asks her to persuade Roy to stop Lassiter. Roy takes the gold shipment to its destination and brings in Lassiter and his gang.

One of Roy Rogers' early starring features, FRONTIER PONY EXPRESS is an engaging film which moves quickly from start to finish in its 58-minute running time. Not only was Roy Rogers quickly establishing himself as a likable and popular sagebrush hero, but he also handled the unobtrusive musical interludes with finesse, this outing including a new tune, "Rusty Spurs," and an old faithful, "My Old Kentucky Home."

FRONTIER SCOUT <u>see</u> THE LONE RIDER IN TEXAS JUSTICE

THE FRONTIERSMAN (Paramount, 1938) 71 mins.

Producer, Harry Sherman; director, Lesley Selander; based on characters created by Clarence E. Mulford; screenplay, Norman Houston; additional dialogue, Harrison Jacobs; camera, Russell Harlan.

William Boyd (Hopalong Cassidy); George "Gabby" Hayes (Windy Halliday); Russell Hayden (Lucky Jordan); Evelyn Venable (June Lake); William Duncan (Buck Peters); Clara Kimball Young (Amanda Peters); Charles "Tony" Hughes (Judson Thorpe); Dickie Jones (Artie); Roy Barcroft (Sutton); Emily Fitzroy (Miss Snook); John Beach (Quirt); St. Brendan Boys Choir (School Kids); Topper (The Horse); and George Morrell, Jim Corey.

Too long and meandering, this unusual entry in the "Hopalong Cassidy" series plays much better on television, where it has been edited to 54 minutes, eliminating some of the footage devoted to the heroine schoolmarm and her boys' choir students. Containing beautiful scenery and a rousing music score, the movie features a slight romance between Hoppy and the leading lady (Evelyn Venable) and also presents silent film stars William Duncan (a semi-regular in

the early series entries as Bar 20 owner Buck Peters) and Clara
Kimball Young, the latter in a smallish role as Buck Peters' sister.
Bar 20 cattle are being rustled by crook Thorpe's (Tony
Hughes) gang and taken across the Mexican border. Thorpe falls
in love with pretty, dedicated school teacher June Lake (Evelyn
Venable), who is also liked by Hopalong Cassidy (William Boyd), the
Bar 20 foreman, and his pal Lucky Jenkins (Russell Hayden).
While a school function is taking place, Thorpe plans to have Sutton
(Roy Barcroft) rustle more Bar 20 cattle and then he plans to marry
the girl and leave the territory. When Sutton finds out that Thorpe
intends to break their rustling arrangement, he is shot by Thorpe,
who escapes, with Hoppy on his trail. The gang tries to rustle the
cattle, but the Bar 20 boys stop them. Hoppy captures Thorpe.
With the St. Brendans Boys' Choir playing the schoolchildren,
the inevitable choral serenading is worked into the scenario.

FUGITIVE VALLEY (Monogram, 1941) 60 mins.

Producer, George Weekes; director, S. Roy Luby; story,
Oliver Drake; screenplay, John Vlahos, Robert Finkle; music,
Frank Sanucci; camera, Robert Cline; editor, Roy Claire.
Ray "Crash" Corrigan (Crash); John King (Dusty); Max
Terhune (Alibi); Julie Duncan (Ann); Glenn Strange (Gray);
Robert Kortman (Red Langdon); Ed Brady (Doctor); Tom London
(Warren); Reed Howes (Brandon); Carl Mathews (Slick); Edward
Peil, Sr. (Jailer); Doye O'Dell (Jim); Elmer (The Dummy); and
Frank McCarroll.

Crash (Ray "Crash" Corrigan) is arrested in Texas and put
in jail, but his pal Dusty (John King) breaks him out along with
outlaw Red Langdon (Robert Kortman) and the trio head to Fugitive
Valley to join a gang led by the mysterious "Whip". They join the
gang's head man, Gray (Glenn Strange), in robbing a stagecoach
whose passengers include magician Hammino the Great, who is really
Alibi (Max Terhune), the third member of the Range Busters trio.
Together with Crash and Dusty, Alibi heads to the gang's hideout
to entertain the outlaws and there the former two fall for pretty
Ann (Julie Duncan), the doctor's assistant, who wants revenge
against Brandon (Reed Howes) for stealing her father's range land.
The Range Busters use pigeons to pass information on the gang on
to the law, but Gray gets suspicious and sets up a fake robbery.
During his magic act Alibi gets the drop on the bad guys and
Crash and Dusty head off the posse from an ambush. By the
finale, Brandon is arrested as being the brains behind the operation
and the Whip is unmasked as Ann, who is also a Pinkerton agent.
The seventh of two dozen "Range Busters" features for
Monogram, FUGITIVE VALLEY is one of the stronger efforts in the
series, highlighted by the delightful Max Terhune with his magic
act and repartee with dummy Elmer. There is a well-staged fight
between Ray Corrigan and Glenn Strange and the feature uses music

to good advantage, with series regular John "Dusty" King singing a few songs, as does noted country-western singer Doye O'Dell, who appears as one of the Whip's henchmen.

GALLOPING ON (Artclass Pictures, 1925) 50 mins.

Producers, Lester F. Scott; director, Richard Thorpe; screenplay, Frank L. Ingraham, Betty Burbridge; camera, Ray Reis.
Wally Wales (Wally Moore); Jessie Cruzon (Helen Jenkins); Louise Lester (Mrs. Moore); Charles Whitaker (Jack Bowers); Richard Belfield (Banker Brown); Gretchen Waterman (The Child); Art Phillips (Storekeeper); Lawrence Undergood (Sheriff Jenkins).

In the mid-1920s, Wally Wales starred in a series of cheap poverty row Westerns for producer Lester F. Scott's Action Pictures. Having been active in Hollywood for more than a decade, Wales proved to be a stalwart genre hero who manipulated his screen assignments with good grace and was especially adept in the action department. Wales continued on in films with the coming of sound, but was reduced to starring in the lowest grade actioners before changing his name to Hal Taliaferro and becoming a topnotch character actor, often appearing as a villain in the genre he once headlined.
GALLOPING ON is a fine example of Wally Wales' silent films and within the bounds of its limited production values, it is a good "B" entry.
Wally Moore (Wally Wales), returning home from five years in prison for a crime he did not commit, finds that his mother (Louise Lester) has lost their ranch and that the crooks who framed him have also stolen their cattle. The outlaws are controlled by corrupt banker Brown (Richard Belfield); his henchman, Jack Bowers (Charles "Slim" Whitaker), is stopped by Wally when he annoys pretty Helen Jenkins (Jessie Cruzon). As a result, Wally is returned to jail but the girl helps him to escape and he gains evidence that it was Bowers who committed the crime for which Wally was imprisoned. The gang robs the bank, but Wally captures them and establishes his innocence.

GANGSTER'S DEN (Producers Releasing Corp., 1945) 55 mins.

Producer, Sigmund Neufeld; director, Sam Newfield; screenplay, George Plympton; assistant director, Jack Vance; sound, Charles Atthouse; camera, Jack Greenhalgh; editor, Holbrook N. Todd.
Buster Crabbe (Billy Carson); Al "Fuzzy" St. John (Fuzzy Q. Jones); Sydney Logan (Ruth Lane); Charles King (Butch); Emmett Lynn (Webb); Kermit Maynard (Curt); Edward Cassidy (Sheriff); George Chesebro (Dent); I. Stanford Jolley (Horace Black); Karl Hackett (Taylor); Michael Owen (Jimmy Lane); Bob Casson (Burke);

Ed Cassidy, George Chesebro, and Buster Crabbe in GANGSTER'S DEN (1945).

Wally West (Deputy); Steve Clark (Bartender); Herman Hack (Mine Guard); Frank McCarroll (Gambler); Horace Carpenter (Barfly); Art Mix (Customer).

Billy Carson (Buster Crabbe) and pal Fuzzy Q. Jones (Al St. John) arrive in a small Western town where Fuzzy invests money in a saloon which turns out to be the headquarters of outlaws led by a crook (I. Stanford Jolley) who is out to take over the territory, including the ranch of a young woman (Sydney Logan). The duo eventually stop the crook's nefarious activities.

Another in the more than two-score PRC series Westerns co-starring Buster Crabbe and Al "Fuzzy" St. John, GANGSTER'S DEN is one of the better series efforts, although the gangsters herein are run-of-the-mill badmen and not members of a gang with machine guns and pin-stripe suits. Actually the movie relies a great deal on comedy, and in addition to Al St. John's usual pratfalls and mugging, the film showcases villain Charles King in a comedy role for a change of pace, and the actor proves just how deft he was at provoking laughter. In one scene, Charlie appears as a lovable drunk who stumbles into Fuzzy's saloon and Fuzzy tells him he is "big and ugly enough" to be his bodyguard. "I was a pretty baby," Charlie replies. Asked if he wants the bodyguard job, King inquires what it pays. "All your drinks and grub. Do you want the job?" asks Fuzzy. "Forget the grub and I do," Charlie announces.

GAUCHO SERENADE (Republic, 1940) 66 mins.

Associate producer, William Berke; director, Frank McDonald; screenplay, Betty Burbridge, Bradford Ropes; songs: Connie Lee, Gene Autry, John Marvin, John Redmond, James Cavanaugh, Nat Simon, Mack Davis, Dick Sanford, Sammy Mysels, Smiley Burnette; camera, Reggie Lanning; editor, Tony Martinelli.

Gene Autry (Gene); Smiley Burnette (Frog Milhouse); June Storey (Joyce); Duncan Renaldo (Gaucho); Mary Lee (Patsy); Clifford Severn, Jr. (Ronnie Willoughby); Lester Matthews (Alfred Willoughby); Smith Ballew (Buck Benson); Joseph Crehan (Martin); William Ruhl (Carter); Wade Boteler (Rancher); Ted Adams (Jenkins); Wendell Niles, The Velascos, Jose Eslava's Orchestra (Themselves); Champion (The Horse); and Fred Burns, Julian Rivero, George Lloyd, Edward Cassidy, Joe Dominguez, Olaf Hytten, Fred "Snowflakes" Toones, Gene Morgan, Jack Kirk, Harry Strang, Hank Worden, Kernan Cripps, Jim Corey, Tom London, Walter Miller.

Britisher ranch owner Alfred Willoughby (Lester Matthews) is sent to prison on a bogus charge by dishonest meat packers, and his young son Ronnie (Cliff Severn, Jr.) returns from London, believing that San Quentin, where his father is imprisoned, is the name of the family ranch. Ranch foreman Gene Autry (himself) and Frog Milhouse (Smiley Burnette) escort the boy home and, along the way, assist two runaway young women, Joyce (June Storey) and Patsy (Mary Lee). Back at the ranch, Ronnie becomes accustomed to the outdoor life. Meanwhile Gene attempts to clear his father, while romancing Joyce who is also attracted to a ranch hand (Smith Ballew). After the crooks try to kidnap the boy, Gene gets the goods on them and, using a locomotive, brings the bad guys to justice, frees Willoughby, and wins Joyce as the rival suitor goes to Hollywood to become a cowboy star.

Reissued as KEEP ROLLIN', GAUCHO SERENADE is one of the blandest of Gene Autry vehicles, filled with endless talk and too many songs. "This picture falls below the high Autry level, lacking in action and, additionally, being off in story values," noted Film Daily. Variety's reviewer recorded that in the 66-minute feature, the first horse was not mounted until the 44th minute, the first fist fight not begun until the 50th minute, and there was no gunfire until the 56th minute.

THE GAY AMIGO (United Artists, 1949) 62 mins.

Producer, Philip N. Krasne; associate producer, Duncan Renaldo; director, Wallace Fox; based on characters created by

O. Henry; screenplay, Doris Schroeder; art director, Frank Dexter; set decorator, Vin Taylor; assistant directors, Bud Messinger, Larry Chapman; makeup, Ted Larsen; music, Albert Glasser; sound, Ferrold Redd; camera, Ernest Miller; editor, Martin Cohn.

Duncan Renaldo (Cisco Kid); Leo Carrillo (Pancho); Armida (Rosita); Joe Sawyer (Sergeant McNulty); Walter Baldwin (Stoneham); Fred Kohler, Jr. (Brack); Kenneth MacDonald (Captain Lewis); George Denormand (Corporal); Clayton Moore (Lieutenant); Fred Crane (Duke); Helen Servis (Old Maid); Beverly Jons (Girl); Bud Osborne (Driver); Sam Flint (Paulsen).

Duncan Renaldo first portrayed O. Henry's famous Robin Hood of the Old West, the Cisco Kid,* in three 1945 features (THE CISCO KID RETURNS, IN OLD NEW MEXICO, SOUTH OF THE RIO GRANDE) with Martin Garralaga as his sidekick Pancho. For the next two years Gilbert Roland essayed the role in a half-dozen well-received programmers, but Renaldo returned to the part late in 1948 in THE VALIANT HOMBRE. He made five more "Cisco Kid" features (including the never-released DON AMIGO, 1949) before he and sidekick Leo Carrillo transferred their Cisco and Pancho roles to TV in 1951 and for the next five years appeared in more than 150 half-hour color episodes of "The Cisco Kid." These segments have proven to be among the most enduring, and endearing, of all Western television programs.

The Cisco Kid (Duncan Renaldo) and his sidekick Pancho (Leo Carrillo) find themselves blamed for a series of hold-ups and being hounded by U.S. Cavalry Sergeant McNulty (Joseph Sawyer). Cisco finds out that McNulty is in love with pretty señorita Rosita (Armida) and uses his charms to get information from the girl about the activities of his nemesis. Cisco and Pancho also stage a series of bogus hold-ups to smoke out the real culprits, who turn out to be a newspaper owner, Stoneham (Walter Baldwin), and blacksmith Brack (Fred Kohler, Jr.), who lead a gang disguised as Mexicans. Finally, after Cisco talks the greedy Stoneham and Brack into joining him on a robbery, he is able to bring in the crooks, proving to McNulty that he and Pancho are innocent.

THE GAY AMIGO is a swift-paced, light-hearted entertainment, depending far more on comedy and action than on violence in unfolding its narrative. Joseph Sawyer is particularly effective as the love-struck but dogged Cavalry sergeant.

GENERAL CUSTER AT LITTLE BIG HORN see WITH CUSTER AT THE LITTLE BIG HORN

DER GENERAL DAS GOLD see KAISER VON KALIFORNIEN

---

*Previous Hollywood on-screen Cisco Kids were Vester Pegg, Warner Baxter, and Cesar Romero.

THE GHOST CITY (Monogram, 1932) 60 mins.

Producer, Trem Carr; director/story, Harry Fraser; screenplay, Wellyn Totman; production manager; Paul Malvern; settings, E. R. Hickson; sound, Balsley and Phillips; camera, Archie Stout; editor, J. Logan Pearson.

Bill Cody (Bill Temple); Andy Shuford (Andy Blane); Helen Foster (Laura); Walter Miller (Blanc); Kate Campbell (Ruby Blane); Charles King (Buck); Walter Shumway, Jack Carlyle (Henchmen); Hank Bell (Blacksmith Joe Meeker); and Thomas Curran, Al Taylor.

Bill Cody prospered as a cowboy star in the silent era and had little difficulty adapting to talkies. But by the time of the sound era his star had descended and the best he could do was an anemic series for Monogram in 1931-32, followed by another weak grouping for Spectrum in the mid-1930s, along with a trio of the worst Westerns ever made: BORDER GUNS, BORDER MENACE, WESTERN RACKETEERS--these last three all for producer Robert Horner.

GHOST CITY is one of Bill Cody's better sound ventures. In his eight Monogram features he was co-starred with child actor Andy Shuford and the grouping was often tagged the "Bill and Andy" series. The movie contains quite a bit of action and a fairly suspenseful plot, although its finale is poorly staged and its title promises a mystery element which is not sufficiently developed. Film Daily commented, "This one was built for the thrill fans, and they piled plenty of gunplay and fights into the action which, keeps moving all the way."

Lawman Bill Temple (Bill Cody) comes to Boom Town to end the reign of terror of outlaw Blane (Walter Miller) and his gang, and plans to publish the truth about them in the town's newspaper. When his youngster pal Andy Blane (Andy Shuford) is injured by the gang, Bill straps on his guns to get even. He also has a score to settle with Blane for stealing the gold claim of his girl's (Helen Foster) father. He and Blane and the latter's henchman (Charles King) meet in a showdown, with Bill emerging the winner.

To be noted is that Andy Shuford does a good tap dance number in a saloon sequence.

GHOST TOWN (Commodore, 1936) 56 mins.

Producer, William Berke; director, Harry Fraser; screenplay, Monroe Talbot; assistant director, William Nolte; camera, Robert Cline; editor, Arthur Brooks.

Harry Carey (Cheyenne Harry); Ruth Findlay (Jane); Jane Novak (Rose); David Sharpe (Bud Ellis); Lee Shumway (Ed Morrell); Edward Cassidy (Sheriff); Roger Williams (Ed Gannon); Phil Dunham (Abe Rankin); Earl Dwire (Dan McCall); Chuck Morrison (Blackie Hawkes); Sonny (The Horse).

Arriving in deserted Ghost Town, Cheyenne Harry (Harry Carey) sees miner Dan McCall (Earl Dwire) being ambushed by crooks Blackie Hawes (Chuck Morrison, Ed Morrell (Lee Shumway) and Gannon (Roger Williams), who are after the money the old man obtained in a bank loan to work a new gold strike he discovered. Harry recovers the money before the trio can get it and the crooks leave the old man for dead, although he is only injured. Harry takes the man to safety but in town is arrested as a highwayman and jailed on suspicion of murdering McCall, since he still has the money in his possession. By a trick, Harry is released by the sheriff's daughter Jane (Ruth Findlay) and enlists the support of deputy Bud Ellis (David Sharpe) in aiding McCall. The two trail the crooks to the mine and after they enter a shaft, Harry follows them at one end while Bud and McCall are at the other. When the three see McCall they think it is his ghost. They run into Harry and overwhelm him, but he hits a plunger connected to dynamite and the ensuing explosion shuts off one end of the tunnel. The crooks, trapped, are arrested by the sheriff (Ed Cassidy) and his posse.

GHOST TOWN was one of six features Harry Carey made for producer William Berke in the mid-1930s; in all of them he played the character of Cheyenne Harry and rode Sonny the Marvel Horse. Also each movie was a continuation of the last. For example, at the end of ACES WILD (1936), Harry announces he is heading to a place called Ghost Town, thus leading into his adventures in this entry. While rather short on action, these Carey films for Commodore were well written and produced, considering their budget limitations. Naturally, their main asset was Harry Carey who, already in his mid-50s and having experienced a quarter of a century of genre stardom, was well experienced in shouldering this type of sagebrush adventure.

GIANT (Warner Bros., 1956) C 198 mins.

Producers, George Stevens, Henry Ginsberg; director, Stevens; based on the novel by Edna Ferber; screenplay, Fred Guiol, Ivan Moffat; music/music director, Dmitri Tiomkin; songs, Paul Francis Webster and Tiomkin; costumes, Marjorie Best, Moss Mabry; assistant director, Joe Rickards; camera, William C. Mellor; editors, William Hornbeck, Fred Bohanan, Phil Anderson.

Elizabeth Taylor (Leslie Benedict); Rock Hudson (Bick Benedict); James Dean (Jeff Rink); Mercedes McCambridge (Luz Benedict); Chill Wills (Uncle Bawley); Jane Withers (Vashti Snythe); Robert Nichols (Pinky Snythe); Dennis Hopper (Jordan Benedict, III); Elsa Cardenas (Juana); Fran Bennett (Judy Benedict); Carroll Baker (Luz Benedict, II); Earl Holliman (Bob Dace); Paul Fix (Dr. Horace Lynnton); Judith Evelyn (Mrs. Horace Lynnton); Carolyn Craig (Lacey Lynnton); Rodney Taylor (Sir David Karfrey); Alexander Scourby (Old Polo); Sal Mineo (Angel Oregon, II); Monte Hale (Bale Clinch); Mary Ann Edwards (Adarene Clinch);

Elizabeth Taylor and Rock Hudson in GIANT (1956).

Napoleon Whiting (Swazey); Charles Watts (Whiteside); Maurice Jara
(Dr. Guerra); Victor Millan (Angel Obregon, I); Pilar Del Redy
(Mrs. Obregon); Feliope Turich (Gomez); Sheb Wooley (Gabe Tar-
get); Francisco Villalobos (Mexican Priest); Ray Whitley (Watts);
Tina Menard (Lupe); Aha Maria Majalca (Petra); Mickey Simpson
(Sarge); Guy Teague (Harper); Natividad Vacio (Eusubio); Max
Terhune (Dr. Walker); Ray Bennett (Dr. Borneholm); Barbara
Barrie (Mary Lou Decker); George Dunne (Vern Decker); Slim Tal-
bot (Clay Hodgins); Tex Driscoll (Clay Hodgins, Sr.); Juney Ellis
(Essie Lou Hodgins); Charles Meredith (Minister); Noreen Nash
(Lona Lane); Rush Williams (Waiter); Bill Hale (Bartender); Tom
Monroe, Mark Hamilton (Guards); John Wiley (Assistant Manager);
Ina Poindexter (Young Woman); Carl Moore (Toastmaster); Ella
Ethridge (General's Wife); Paul Kruger (General); Eddie Baker
(Governor); Ethel Greenwood (Governor's Wife); Fernando Alvarado,
Tony Morella (Busboys); Julian Rivero (Old Man); Maxine Gates
(Mrs. Sarge); Richard and David Bishop (Jordan as an Infant);
Steven Kay (Jordan at Age Four); Mary Ann and Georgann Cashen
(Judy as an Infant); Christine Werner (Luz as an Infant); Judy
and Jill Lentz (Luz at Age Two); John Garcia (Angel as an Infant);
David Jiminez (Angel at Age Five); Colleen and Marlene Crane (Judy
II as an Infant); Wanda Lee Thompson (Judy II at Age Two); Per-
fideo Aguilar and Margaret Trujillo (Jordy IV as an Infant); Ramon
Ramirez (Jordy IV at Age Two).

In the 1920s, wealthy Texas rancher Jordan "Bick" Benedict,
II (Rock Hudson) visits Maryland to purchase thoroughbred horses
and there falls in love with Leslie Clinch (Elizabeth Taylor). He

marries the willful girl and brings her back to his huge Texas
spread, Reata, which he has inherited from his late father and which
is run by his spinster sister Luz (Mercedes McCambridge), who
takes an instant dislike to her new sister-in-law. Finally the two
women come to terms and Leslie is made welcome by a friendly neighbor (Jane Withers) and an old farmer (Chill Wills) who advises her
on how best to get along in her new environment. Leslie takes an
avid interest in her husband's business affairs as well as in politics
and the welfare of the poor Mexicans who exist on the ranch. When
Luz dies, Leslie takes over the day-to-day running of the ranch and
she and Bick raise a family. Bick, however, becomes jealous of her
motherly attentions to neurotic oil prospector Jett Rink (James Dean),
who falls in love with her. As the years pass and the Benedict
children grow up, one son (Dennis Hopper) decides to desert the
ranch for a career as a doctor and marries a Mexican girl (Elsa Cardenas), while Jett, who has become a rich oil man, marries daughter
Luz (Carroll Baker) as a substitute for Leslie. As he grows old,
Bick finally realizes that it will be up to one of his grandchildren
to carry on the family tradition of Reata.

Running in excess of three hours, GIANT proved to be a huge
box-office winner, grossing in excess of $14,000,000 and solidifying
the stardom of Rock Hudson, Elizabeth Taylor and James Dean, who
died in a car crash not long after the film's completion. This modern
day Western "...emerges on screen as a long, sprawling and tremendously vivid and engrossing movie that spouts a tawdry tragedy.
The picture flows fascinatingly..." (New York Times). The picture's
success, however, is due mainly to director George Stevens. As
Philip T. Hartung wrote in The Commonweal, "But in spite of the
good acting throughout GIANT, it is really producer-director
Stevens' picture. His is the triumph in correlating all the departments in this enormous film and capturing this portrait of time and
place."

GLI UOMINI DAL PASSO PESANTE see THE TRAMPLERS

GOIN' SOUTH (Paramount, 1978) C 101 mins.

Producers, Harry Gittes, Harold Schneider; director, Jack
Nicholson; screenplay, John Herman Shaner, Al Ramus, Charles
Shyer, Alan Mandel; assistant director, Michael Daves; production
designer, Toby Carr Rafelson; costumes, William Ware Theiss;
music, Van Dyke Parks, Perry Botkin, Jr.; sound, Arthur
Rochester; camera, Nestor Almendros; editors, Richard Chew, John
Fitzgerald Beck.
Jack Nicholson (Henry Moon); Mary Steenburgen (Julia Tate);
Christopher Lloyd (Towfield); John Belushi (Hector); Veronica Cart-
wright (Hermine); Richard Bradford (Sheriff Kyle); Jeff Morris (Big
Abe); Danny DeVito (Hog) Tracy Walter (Coogan); Gerald H. Rey-
nolds (Polty); Luana Anders (Mrs. Anderson); George W. Smith

Jack Nicholson in GOIN' SOUTH (1978).

(Anderson); Lucy Lee Flippin (Mrs. Haber); Ed Bagley, Jr.
(Haber); Maureen Byrnes (Mrs. Warren); B. J. Merholz (Warren);
Britt Leach (Parson Weems); Georgia Schmidt (Florence).

Jack Nicholson directed and played the lead role in this tired
Western semi-comedy and neither chore is performed with much
finesse. GOIN' SOUTH, while it contains a few amusing moments,
is simply not a very likable feature film. It is far too long at over
100 minutes, and except for leading lady Mary Steenburgen, its
characters have very little audience appeal. As a result, the production grossed slightly less than $5,000,000 at a time when infla-
tion was running wild at the box office.
Low-life, dirty outlaw Henry Moon (Jack Nicholson) is chased
across the U.S./Mexican border, captured by a posse, and returned
to town for hanging. At the last minute, Henry discovers a local
ordinance which will save him, if an eligible lady will marry him.
Finally pretty but prim rancher Julia Tate (Mary Steenburgen)
agrees to wed the outlaw and plans to use him to get gold out of
her mine before it is taken over by the railroad. About all she
gains from the deal, however, is to be raped on her wedding night,
as Moon proves to be utterly shiftless. Finally, his old gang and
ex-lover Hermine (Veronica Cartwright) arrive on the scene, planning
to use Moon in their latest scheme. But he turns on them and wins

circumspect Julia's affections.

Outside of appealing performances by Mary Steenburgen and Veronica Cartwright, along with well-etched cameos by such fine character players as Luana Anders and Lucy Lee Flippen, GOIN' SOUTH has little to recommend it. Jack Nicholson mugs broadly but does little else in the lead, and John Belushi is totally wasted in a background role as one of the gang members. Not serious, and certainly not very funny to most viewers, GOIN' SOUTH is one of the most mixed-up and least satisfying Westerns to emerge from the 1970s.

GOLD (Majestic, 1932) 48 mins.

Director, Otto Brower; story, Jack Natteford; screenplay, Scott Darling; sound, Carl Crain; camera, Art Reed, Charles Marshall; editor, S. Roy Luby.

Jack Hoxie (Jack); Alice Day (Marian); Hooper Atchley (Peter Kramer); Tom London (Sheriff); Robert Kortman (Outlaw); Lafe McKee (Jeff); Dynamite (The Horse); and Jack Byron, J. C. Clifford.

Jack Hoxie was one of the more popular screen cowboys in the 1920s but he retired from films with the coming of the sound era. Financial troubles forced him to make a half-dozen "B" Westerns for Majestic in 1932. These features were well executed and their budgets were more on a par with those of the major studios than with the poverty-row oaters of the day. Hoxie was an engaging screen personality, but not an overly good actor and he seemed a bit ill at ease in these outings. His best work was done in the silent years. Nevertheless, Hoxie has been treated unjustly by some film historians and a viewing of these last talkies reveal him to be a pleasant player who had a deservedly large following.

Cowboy Jack (Jack Hoxie) shares a gold claim with a man who is murdered by the vicious Peter Kramer (Hooper Atchley) and his gang. The dead man's daughter, Marian (Alice Day), however, blames Jack for the murder and the cowboy must prove his innocence. He captures Kramer, dresses him in the clothes of another miner whose claim he has bought, and the gang mistakenly murders its leader. Jack is exonerated and he and Marian pursue their courtship.

The highlight of this production is its austere finale, with villain Hooper Atchley tied to a wagon, garbed like his intended victim, and being gunned down by his own men.

GOLD RAIDERS see THE OUTLAW IS COMING

THE GOLDEN STALLION (Republic, 1949) C 67 mins.

Associate producer, Edward J. White; director, William Witney,

Jack Hoxie, Alice Day, and Lafe McKee in GOLD (1932).

screenplay, Sloan Nibley; music, Nathan Scott; orchestrator, Stanley
Wilson; songs: Sid Robin, Foy Willing, Nathan Gluck, Anne Paren-
tean, Eddie Cherkose, Sol Meyer, Jule Styne; assistant director.
Jack Lacey; makeup, Bob Mark, Steve Drumm; art director, Frank
Hotaling; set decorators, John McCarthy, Jr., James Redd; special
effects, Howard and Theodore Lydecker; camera, Jack Marta; editor,
Tony Martinelli.
    Roy Rogers (Himself); Dale Evans (Stormy Billings); Estelita
Rodriguez (Pepita Valdez); Pat Brady (Sparrow Biffle); Douglas
Evans (Jeff Middleton); Frank Fenton (Sheriff); Greg McClure (Ben);
Dale Van Sickel (Ed Hart); Clarence Straight (Spud); Jack Sparks
(Guard); Chester Conklin (Old Man); Riders of the Purple Sage
(Themselves); Trigger (The Horse); and Dale Van Sickel.

    Diamond smugglers led by hotel owner Jeff Middleton (Douglas
Evans) use a herd of wild horses to carry gems across the Mexican
border. They run afoul of horse trainer Roy Rogers (Himself),
who leases a ranch from Dale Evans (Herself) and Estelita Rodriguez
(Herself) to train horses from the herd. After a fight, Roy defeats
Ned Hart (Guy McClure), Middleton's henchman, and Trigger brings
in the mare leader of the horses. That night Hart tries to steal the
mare; she kills him and Roy is blamed for the crime. He is convicted and sent to prison. Middleton, who pretends to be Dale's

friend, buys Trigger in an auction and trains him to lead the horse herd, but Trigger escapes with a mare who has his colt and then dies. Three years pass, the colt is grown, and the smuggling racket continues. Roy returns to Oro to await parole but breaks jail and Middleton aids the posse in trying to capture him. It turns out to be a trick set up by Roy and the lawman to intercept the smuggling ring and bring Middleton to justice. Finally Roy and Trigger are reunited.

Highlighted by solid direction by William Witney, a literate script by Sloan Nibley, and Jack Marta's sharp color cinematography, THE GOLDEN STALLION should have been a better picture than it is. However, it is hampered by the obvious use of backdrops and especially by the lowjinks "comedy" antics of Pat Brady and his jeep Nellybelle. Spotlighting the beautiful horse Trigger and assorted equestrian tricks, as was done to better advantage in the earlier MY PAL TRIGGER (1946), the movie, too long at 67 minutes, is on the dull side. It plays better when cut to the standard TV running time of 54 minutes.

GRAND CANYON TRAIL (Republic, 1948) C 67 mins.

Associate producer, Edward J. White; director, William Witney; screenplay, Gerald Geraghty; music, Nathan Scott; music director, Morton Scott; songs, Jack Elliott, Foy Willing; art director, Frank Hotaling; set decorators, John McCarthy, Jr., James Redd; assistant director, Jack Lacey; sound, T. A. Cameron; special effects, Howard and Theodore Lydecker; camera, Reggie Lanning; editor, Tony Martinelli.

Roy Rogers (Himself); Jane Frazee (Carol Martin); Andy Devine (Cookie Bullfincher); Robert Livingston (Bill Regan); Roy Barcroft (Dave Williams); Charles Coleman (J. Malcolm Vanderpool; Emmett Lynn (Ed Carruthers); Ken Terrell (Mike Delsing); James Finlayson (Sheriff); Tommy Coats (Bannister); Foy Williams and the Riders of the Purple Sage (Themselves); Trigger (The Horse); and Zon Murray.

Crook Bill Regan (Robert Livingston) and his henchman Dave Williams (Roy Barcroft) are trying to find the location of a rich vein of silver which has been discovered by old-timer Ed Carruthers (Emmett Lynn). The duo capture the old man, try to force him to talk, and keep him prisoner in a ghost town. The owner of the town, Carol Martin (Jane Frazee), arrives on the scene after being rescued from a runaway stagecoach by cowboy Roy Rogers (Himself). When the old man's disappearance is discovered, Roy and the local sheriff, Cookie Bullfincher (Andy Devine), attempt to locate him and eventually find out what Regan is up to. But when Ed is found murdered, it is Roy who is blamed and arrested. He escapes to prove his innocence and when a lawman (Jimmy Finlayson) is brought in to arrest him, they accidentally stumble across the old man's mine. Regan's guilt is soon proved.

With its satisfying blend of action, comedy and suspense, GRAND CANYON TRAIL stands out as one of Roy Rogers' better starring vehicles, enhanced by William Witney's rapidly paced direction and the good interplay between hero Rogers, sidekick Andy Devine and pretty heroine Jane Frazee. Unlike some of Roy Rogers' mid-1940s films, which subjugated action for heavy-handed production numbers, this outing places action and drama first. It nicely interpolates a few songs by the star and by Foy Willing and the Riders of the Purple Sage, the latter a replacement for the Sons of the Pioneers.

THE GREAT ADVENTURES OF WILD BILL HICKOK (Columbia, 1938) fifteen chapters

Producer, Jack Fier; associate producer, Harry Webb; directors, Mack V. Wright, Sam Nelson; story, John Peere Miles; screenplay, George Rosener, Charles Arthur Powell, George Arthur Durlam, Dallas Fitzgerald, Tom Gibson; music, Abe Meyer; camera, George Meehan, Ben Kline; editor, Richard Fantl.

Gordon Elliott (U.S. Marshal Wild Bill Hickok); Monte Blue (Cameron); Carole Wayne (Ruth Cameron); Frankie Darro (Jerry); Dickie Jones (Bud); Sammy McKim (Boots); Kermit Maynard (Kit Lawson); Roscoe Ates (Snake Eyes); Monty Collins (Danny); Reed Hadley (Blakely); Chief Thunder Cloud (Gray Eagle); Ray Mala (Little Elk); Walter Wills (Bruce); J. P. McGowan (Scudder); Eddie Waller (Stone); George Chesebro (Metaxa); Alan Bridge (Blackie); and Slim Whitaker, Walter Miller, Lee Phelps, Robert Fiske, Earle Hodgins, Earl Dwire, Ed Brady, Ray Jones, Edmund Cobb, Art Mix, Hal Taliaferro, Blackie Whiteford.

Chapters: 1) The Law of the Gun; 2) Stampede; 3) Blazing Terror; 4) Mystery Canyon; 5) Flaming Brands; 6) The Apache Killer; 7) Prowling Wolves; 8) The Pit; 9) Ambush; 10) Savage Vengeance; 11) Burning Waters; 12) Desperation; 13) Phantom Bullets; 14) The Lure; 15) Trail's End.

Columbia Pictures' fourth chapterplay, THE GREAT ADVENTURES OF WILD BILL HICKOK, launched the starring career of Gordon Elliott, later to become better known as Bill Elliott, Wild Bill Elliott, William Elliott, and again Bill Elliott. Having been in films since the silent days, Elliott had been playing bits in big features and villains in "B" affairs, but he came into his own in the role of Wild Bill Hickok and developed into one of the screen's most popular and dependable cowboy stars. While this serial was flawed in its production, it moved at a good clip and Elliott was outstanding in the lead, ably supported by villainous Monte Blue and one-time genre star Kermit Maynard as an army scout.

In Abilene, U.S. Marshal Wild Bill Hickok (Gordon Elliott) is attempting to stop an outlaw gang called the Phantom Raiders which rustles cattle herds driven along the Chisholm Trail from Texas. Needing help, Hickok organizes area youngsters into a band called

the Flaming Arrows. Also assisting him is army scout Kit Lawson
(Kermit Maynard), who saves a wagon train attacked by the Raiders.
Hickok and Lawson then team with the Flaming ARrows to trap the
renegade gang. With the aid of an army detachment the Phantom
Raiders are captured, allowing the cattle herds to enter Abilene.

THE GREY FOX (UA Classics, 1982) C 90 mins.

Producer, Peter O'Brian; director, Phillip Boros; screenplay,
John Hunter; music, Michael Baker; camera, Frank Tidy; editor,
Ray Hall.

Richard Farnsworth (Bill Miner); Jackie Burroughs (Kate
Flynn); Wayne Robson (Shorty) Ken Pogue (Jack); David Petersen
(Louis).

William Miner was a stagecoach robber who was dubbed "The
Gentleman Bandit" and whom the Pinkerton Detective Agency credits
with originating the term "Hands Up." After serving 33 years in
San Quentin, Miner was released from prison but was soon back at
his old calling, this time robbing trains. He was again captured and
sent to prison but escaped, never to be heard from again. The last
years of Miner's escapades were chronicled by one-time documentary
director Phillip Boros, in his commercial film debut. Overall this
$3,000,000 production is quite impressive, probably the best Western
of the 1980s.

At San Quentin, Bill Miner (Richard Farnsworth) is released
from prison, having spent over three decades there for his stagecoach robberies. He finds the world much modernized. His former
occupation no longer exists because the stage lines have been replaced by trains. He goes to Washington State to live with his
younger sister but cannot cope with the life of an oyster picker and
after viewing the film THE GREAT TRAIN ROBBERY, decides to
return to the bandit life. After his initial robbery attempt is foiled,
he steals a horse, escapes into British Columbia and, teaming with
the none-too-bright drifter Shorty (Wayne Robson), pulls off a
successful robbery. Using the name George Edwards, Miner goes
with Shorty to a small town where a former inmate acquaintance,
Jack (Ken Pogue), owns various properties. Jack puts the two men
to work in his mine and gives them the cover of being mining en-
gineers. There Miner becomes a respectable citizen and falls in love
with spunky photographer Kate Flynn (Jackie Burroughs). With a
Pinkerton agent on his trail, Miner again teams with Shorty and consumptive Louis (David Peterson) to accomplish another train robbery.
It nets them only $17, and in attempting to escape the trio is cap-
tured by the Mounties. Miner is sentenced to 25 years in prison,
but later escapes and is never found. Kate moves to Chicago and is
later seen in the company of a man resembling Miner as she tours
Europe.

Told in a series of well-staged vignettes surrounding the

character of Bill Miner and his robbery activities, THE GREY FOX is an appealing feature. "It is the kind of nice, small family audience film without glittering stars or obviously commercial concessions that needs careful handling," decided <u>Variety</u>. Unfortunately the film did not receive the proper exposure.

Richard Farnsworth, a one-time stuntman turned actor, who was nominated as best supporting actor for another Western, COMES A HORSEMAN (1978), is the main catalyst holding the film together. His likable, easy-going performance as the Robin Hood-ish Miner contrasts sharply to the violence caused by the character's deeds. He is shown as a decent, kind man whose amoral activities are aimed at capitalistic targets such as the railroads and the banks.

GRIZZLY AND THE TREASURE (Gold Key/James T. Flocker Enterprises, 1975) C 98 mins.

Producer/director, James T. Flocker; screenplay, no credit; music, William Loose; animal sequences director, Monty Cox; camera, David E. Jackson.
Scott Beach (Narrator); Andrew Gordon (Kidd); Robert Sheble (Ezra); Susan Backlinie (Eve); and Terry Bough, Mark Ostrander.

In the 1890s, Ezra (Robert Sheble), a prospector, takes his pretty wife Eve (Susan Backlinie) and their ten-year old son Kidd (Andrew Gordon) into the wilds of Alaska in search of gold. In the remote Klondike, Ezra, with the aid of a nugget-hunting raccoon, makes a big find and begins mining his claim while his wife and son try to adapt to their new environment, the boy finding a pal in a young bear. Winter sets in and the family is soon stranded as blizzard after blizzard pelts the area. Ultimately, Ezra is injured, their food supply runs low, and it is up to the boy to trek to the nearest settlement for help. While he is gone, his mother is forced to shoot their old pack horse for food. On his journey, the boy loses his way in a storm and nearly dies before being rescued by the son of an Indian trapper. When the boy is well enough, he leads a rescue party to the cabin and saves his folks. His mother buries the gold they mined, because it has brought them only bad luck.
One of a number of wholesome travelogue-type adventures set in the north country, GRIZZLY AND THE TREASURE is minimal cinema, in terms of plot and production, but its location shooting and fine photography by David E. Jackson make it a visual delight. The scene with the mother and her son bathing in the river with their pet bear is a good example, as is the entire panorama shooting of the beautiful Alaskan terrain.

GUN GRIT (Atlantic, 1936) 53 mins.

Director, Lester Williams [William Berke]; screenplay, Allen

Hall, Gordon Phillips; music, Lee Zahler; camera, Robert Cline; editor, Arthur Brooks.

Jack Perrin (Bob Blake); Ethel Beck (Jean); David Sharpe (Dave); Starlight (The Horse); Braveheart (The Dog); Roger Williams (Mack); Ralph Peters (Dopey); Frank Hagney (Henry Hess); Jimmy Aubrey (Murphy); Edward Cassidy (Tim Hess); Phil Dunham (Looey); Oscar Gahan (Don); Earl Dwire (Joe Hess); Horace Murphy (Sully); Baby Lester William Berke (Bobby Hews); Budd Buster (Henchman).

For seventeen years during the 1920s and 1930s, Jack Perrin starred in "B" Westerns, easily making the transition to sound pictures but never becoming a top-echelon genre star. During the Thirties he even used other screen names, such as Richard Terry and Jack Gable, and took small parts in other stars' vehicles. He proved to be an enduring player who worked for a variety of companies such as Universal, Big Four, Reliable, Syndicate and Astor, for which he made the "Bud 'n Ben" shorts before coming to the end of the trail as a star in a series for Atlantic for producer William Berke. Appearing with Perrin in this final batch was his beautiful horse Starlight, who had been with him since the silent days.

GUN GRIT is a fairly typical starring vehicle for Jack Perrin, emphasizing his handsome features and daring heroics. Really as much a gangster film as a Western, this low-cost feature, with lots of obvious Hollywood locales, told of big city racketeers heading West to sell "protection" to cattlemen, and FBI agent Bob Blake (Jack Perrin) being assigned to stop the racket.

GUN PLAY see LUCKY BOOTS

GUN RIDERS see FIVE BLOODY GRAVES

GUN SMOKE (Paramount, 1931) 56 mins.

Director, Edward Slomans; story/screenplay, Grover Jones, William Slavens McNutt; camera, A. J. Stout.

Richard Arlen (Brad Farley); Mary Brian (Sue Vancey); William Boyd (Kedge Darvas); Eugene Pallette (Stub Waltack); Charles Winninger (Tack Gillup); Louise Fazenda (Hampsey Dell); Brooks Benedict (Spot Skee); William Arnold (Mugs Maransa); J. Carroll Naish (Mink Gordon); Stanley Mack (Jassy Quinn); Guy Oliver (Pusey Meed); William V. Mong (Strike Jackson); James Durkin (J. K. Horton); Anne Shirley (Horton's Daughter); Willie Fong (Chinese Cook); and Jack Richmond.

Big city gangsters led by Kedge Darvas (William Boyd) feel the heat from the law and transfer to a small Idaho town where the

locals mistake them for big-time investors and make them welcome.
The machine-gun-laden hoodlums attempt to take over the town
through sheer force, but are opposed by local Brad Farley (Richard
Arlen), who helps his fellow citizens to defeat the gangsters, showing
Westerners superior to the minions of the lawless.

    The chief interest of this 56-minute feature is that it combines
the then popular genres of the Western and ganster films, albeit
none too homogeneously. Violent for its time, the movie is surprisingly slow despite its compact unfolding which gives little opportunity for character delineation, such as the romance between
Richard Arlen and Mary Brian. Underplayed comedy by Eugene
Pallette, Louise Fazenda, and Charles Winninger provides some zest,
as does the focal finale fight sequence between Arlen and Boyd (the
latter would become a Western stalwart in his enduring "Hopalong
Cassidy" series).

THE GUNFIGHTER (Triangle, 1916) five reels

    Producer, Thomas H. Ince; director, William S. Hart; screen-
play, Monte J. Katterjohn; art director, Robert Brunton; camera,
Joseph August.
    William S. Hart (Cliff "The Killer" Hudspeth); Margery Wilson
(Norma Wright); Roy Laidlaw (El Salvador); Joseph J. Dowling (Ace
High Larkins); Milton Ross (Cactus Fuller); George Stone (Jimmy
Wright); J. P. Lockney (Colonel Ellis Lawton).

    By the time THE GUNFIGHTER was released early in 1917,
William S. Hart had made nearly three dozen Westerns for Thomas
H. Ince since 1914 and had solidified his position as the screen's
premiere cowboy. Hart's films were gritty and realistic, presenting
a pictorial look at the Old West as the star remembered it in its
twilight days. THE GUNFIGHTER presented Hart in a part he obviously relished, and played many times--that of the outlaw re-
deemed by the good side of his nature, usually with the aid of a
fine woman. In this regard, Louis Reeves Harrison wrote in the
Moving Picture World, "He [Hart] has played it so often that one
might get the impression that he would not be effective in any other
part, whereas he could really be more impressive in a purely human
characterization, that of a man with complex impulses and qualities,
rather than the purely heroic, long since shelved by dramatists and
novelists as lacking verisimilitude...."
    In the gold rush community of Desert pass, outlaw gang
leaders Cliff "The Killer" Hudspeth (William S. Hart) and El Salvador (Roy Laidlaw) fight for domination. The latter's henchman
Cactus (Milton Ross) carries out a successful hold-up and brags how
he will defeat Hudspeth. But Cliff arrives as the Golden Fleece
saloon and in a later shoot-out in the streets, Cactus is murdered.
As he is leaving town, Cliff is denounced as a cold-blooded
murderer by pretty milliner Norma Wright (Margery Wilson). In
anger the gang leader abducts her and takes her to his mountain

William S. Hart and Margery Wilson in THE GUNFIGHTER (1916).

retreat, where he gets drunk. The woman's words and purity, plus the effect of the drink, make Hudspeth sorry for his past deeds. The young woman persuades him to promise he will not again kill. Not long afterwards Cliff is pardoned and is assigned to bring in El Salvador, who then burns Desert Pass and kidnaps Norma. Cliff follows El Salvador to the mountains and rescues the heroine, but is mortally wounded while killing his opponent.

THE GUNMAN (Monogram, 1952) 52 mins.

Producer, Vincent M. Fennelly; director, Lewis Collins; screenplay, Fred Myton; assistant director, Melville Shyer; dialogue director, Stanley Price; sound, Frank Webster; camera, Ernest Miller; editor, Sam Fields.

Whip Wilson (U.S. Marshal Whip Wilson); Fuzzy Knight (Blinkey); Rand Brooks (Jud); Terry Frost (Duke Kirby); I. Stanford Jolley (Dan Forrester); Phyllis Coates (Anita Forrester); Lane Bradford (Gatlin); Gregg Barton (Longley); Russ Whiteman (Sheriff); Richard Avonde (Blake); and Robert Bray.

U.S. Marshals Whip Wilson (Himself) and Jud (Rand Brooks) are called in by the citizens of the New Mexico territory town of Eagle Pass to stop the lawlessness caused by an outlaw gang. The leaders of the local citizens and ranchers wanting law and order are newspaper editor Dan Forrester (I. Stanford Jolley) and his daughter Anita (Phyllis Coates). Their drunken printer Blinkey (Fuzzy Knight) innocently gives information about the coming of the lawmen to three outlaws (Lane Bradford, Gregg Barton, Richard Avonde). They attempt to ambush Whip and Jud, but fail. Once in town, the two lawmen realize that supposedly upright citizen Duke Kirby (Terry Frost) is behind the gang, since he is wanted for murder in Texas. In a shoot-out with Whip, Kirby is killed and the lawmen break up the gang, leaving the members with the local sheriff (Russ Whiteman) to stand trial.

An average entry in Monogram's Whip Wilson series, THE GUN-MAN (originally entitled TEXAS MARSHAL) came near the end of the 22 films Whip Wilson made for Monogram between 1949 and 1952. A handsome cowboy with a good singing voice and fairly adept with a bullwhip, Wilson did not catch on as a Western star. Apparently Monogram did not think him strong enough to carry films alone and he had various sidekicks over his three seasons, including Andy Clyde, Jim Bannon, Tommy Farrell, Lee Roberts, and Fuzzy Knight.

THE GUNMAN FROM BODIE (Monogram, 1941) 62 mins.

Producer, Scott R. Dunlap; director, Spencer G. Bennet; screenplay, Jess Bowers [Adele Buffington]; music, Edward J. Kay; assistant director, Chris Benton; technical director, Vin Taylor; camera, Harry Newmann; editor, Carl L. Pierson.

Buck Jones (Buck Roberts/Bob "Bodie" Bronson); Tim McCoy (Tim McCall); Raymond Hatton (Rusty); Christine McIntyre (Alice Borden); Dave O'Brien (Joe Martin); Robert Frazer (Wyatt); Charles King (Steve); John Merton (Bill Cook); Silver (The Horse); and Jerry Sheldon, Jack King, Earl Douglas, Warren Jackson, Billy Carro, Frederick Gee.

THE GUNMAN FROM BODIE was the second of eight films in Monogram's "The Rough Riders" series which teamed genre favorites Buck Jones and Tim McCoy with Raymond Hatton as a trio of hard-riding law enforcers of the Old West. Made on a week's schedule with budgets around $60,000+, the films were economical but full of action. This release is the best-written of the series and one of the most atmospheric. (Because it was shot in tandem with ARIZONA BOUND, 1941, the first of the series, there is much overlapping of costumes and scenery.) This movie also boasts superior supporting cast performances, including Dave O'Brien singing the song "Little Tenderfoot."

In a house during a thunderstorm, lawman Buck Roberts (Buck Jones) stumbles across a murdered family and a surviving baby. He learns that rustlers in the valley have been killing homesteaders. To prove that crook Wyatt (Robert Frazer) is behind the lawlessness, he masquerades as gunman Bodie Bronson. Meanwhile, U.S. Marshal Tim McCall (Tim McCoy) arrives to investigate the situation, as does their cohort Rusty (Raymond Hatton), who goes to work for attractive ranch owner Alice Borden (Christine MacIntyre), who is in love with Joe (Dave O'Brien). Eventually Buck and Tim arrest Wyatt for his crimes.

GUNMEN OF THE RIO GRANDE (Allied Artists, 1965) C 86 mins.

Producer, Ike Zingarmann [Italo Zingarelli]; director, Tulio Demicheli; story, Chen Morrison; screenplay, Gene Luotto, Giovanni Simonell, Zingarelli, Natividad Zaro, Guy Lionel, Tulio Demicheli; art directors, Angelo de Amicio, Luis Arguello, A. Dea; music, Angelo Francesco Lavagnino; sound, Alessandro Sarandrea, Mario Amari; camera, Guglielmo Mancori, Mario Capriotti.

Guy Madison (Marshal Wyatt Earp/Laramie); Madeleine Lebeau (Jennie Lee); Gerard Tichy (Zack "The Snake" Williams); Fernando Sancho (Pancho Bogan); Carolyn Davys (Clementine Hewitt); Olivier Hussenot (Judge); Massimo Serato (Leo); and Benyt Deus, Dario Michaelis, E. Marn, H. Morrow, Xan Das Bolas, Alvaro de Luna, Juan Majan, Natividad Zaro.

Early in the spaghetti Western craze, U.S. star Guy Madison starred in the French-Italian-Spanish co-production, GUNMEN OF THE RIO GRANDE, as Marshal Wyatt Earp. Madison adds a great deal of zest to the proceedings and is well supported by genre favorite Fernando Sancho as a good-bad guy. The film has a fairly literate script, moves well, and benefits from well-staged

action sequences, including the segment where Earp uses a wagon full of gun powder to decimate the bandits who badly outnumber his own men.

Jennie Lee (Madeleine Lebeau) owns a mine in Mexico but is threatened with foreclosure by Zack "The Snake" Williams (Gerard Tichy), who is trying to gain control of all the local property. The young woman writes to Wyatt Earp and asks his help in stopping the bad man. Taking the name of Laramie, Earp heads south of the border to aid Jennie. Earp convinces her to stick it out and begins thwarting Williams' evil machinations. Williams hires bandit leader Pancho Bogan (Fernando Sancho) to eliminate Earp, but in a shoot-out most of his men are killed. In order to silence Pancho, who respects Earp more than he does his employer, Williams shoots the bandit in the back. Dying Pancho asks Earp to avenge his death and, in a climactic shoot-out, Earp kills Williams and restores peace.

Filmed in Spain, the motion picture received some U.S. release by Allied Artists. Abroad it had a variety of titles: in Spain it was called EL SHERIFF DEL O.K. CORRAL and JEANNIE LEE HAS UNA NUOVA PISTOLA; while in Italy it was titled SFIDA A RIO BRAVO [Duel at Rio Bravo]; and in France, A DUEL A RIO BRAVO.

GUNS AND GUITARS (Republic, 1937) 58 mins.

Producer, Nat Levine; supervisor, Robert Becke; director, Joseph Kane; story/screenplay, Dorrell and Stuart McGowan; camera, Ernest Miller.

Gene Autry (Gene); Dorothy Dix (Marjorie); Smiley Burnette (Frog Milhouse); Tom London (Conner); Charles King (Sam); Champion (The Horse); J. P. McGowan (Morgan); Earl Hodgins (Professor Parker); Frankie Marvin (Shorty); Eugene Jackson (Eightball); Jack Rockwell (Sheriff); Ken Cooper (Deputy); Tracy Lane, Wes Warner, Jim Corey, Frank Stravenger (Henchmen); Harrison Greene (Dr. Schaefer); Pascale Perry (Hall); Bob Burns (Jenkins); and Bob Burns, Jack Don, Tracy Layne, Frank Stravenger, Jack Kirk, Audry Davis, Al Taylor, George Morrell Sherry Tansey, Jack Evans, George Plues, Denver Dixon, Wes Warner, Jim Corey.

From 1937 to 1942, when he entered World War II service, Gene Autry was voted the number one Western star in the Motion Picture Herald poll of the Top Ten Money-Making Stars. One of the reasons he retained his popularity was that he appeared in solid features such as GUNS AND GUITARS, a film which mixed well the elements of music and action, resulting in topnotch entertainment. Released in 1936, when Autry was listed third in the Exhibitors' poll, GUNS AND GUITARS was one of the motion pictures which solidified the popularity of both Autry and the screen singing cowboy.

Released in the summer of 1936, this movie tells of a crooked cattleman (J. P. McGowan) who tries to have a ban lifted on the driving of herds between counties despite a cattle fever quarantine. Arriving on the scene is Professor Parker's (Earle Hodgins) medicine show with star singer Gene Autry (Himself). Gene, volunteering to stop the lawlessness caused by the cattleman and his gang, runs for sheriff, after proving he is innocent of killing the last office holder. He is elected and rounds up the bad guys.

GUNS AND GUITARS, Gene Autry's eighth starring feature, was directed by Joseph Kane, who helmed him in his first, TUMBLING TUMBLEWEEDS, the year before. It was produced by Nat Levine, the filmmaker who discovered Autry and gave him his first starring role in the Western/science fiction serial, THE PHANTOM EMPIRE (1934). The movie was scripted by the brother team of Dorrell and Stuart McGowan, the sons of veteran actor/director J. P. McGowan, who played the villain herein. In GUNS AND GUITARS, Gene sings, among other songs, "Ridin' All Day" and the title tune.

THE HALLELUJAH TRAIL (United Artists, 1965) C 167 mins.

Producer, John Sturges; associate producer, Robert E. Relyea; director, Sturges; based on the novel by Bill Gulick; screenplay, John Gay; assistant director, Jack N. Reddish; art director, Cary Odell; costumes, Edith Head; music, Elmer Bernstein; song, Bernstein and Ernie Sheldon; maps, DePatie-Feleng; sound, Robert Martin; special effects, A. Paul Pollard; camera, Robert Surtees; editor, Ferris Webster.

Burt Lancaster (Colonel Thadeus Gearhart); Lee Remick (Cora Templeton Massingale); Jim Hutton (Captain Paul Slater); Pamela Tiffin (Louise Gearhart); Donald Pleasence (Oracle Jones); Brian Keith (Frank Wallingham); Martin Landau (Chief Walks-Stooped-Over); John Anderson (Sergeant Buell); John Dehner (Narrator); Tom Stern (Kevin O'Flaherty); Robert J. Wilkie (Chief Five Barrels); Jerry Gatlin, Larry Duran (Brothers-in-Law); Jim Burk (Elks-Runner); Dub Taylor (Clayton Howell); John McKee (Rafe Pike); Helen Kleeb (Henrietta); Noam Pitlik (Interpreter); Carl Pitti (Phillips); Bill Williams (Brady); Marshall Reed (Carter); Caroll Adams (Simons); Ted Markland (Bandmaster).

Termed a "lusty, gusty western comedy with screwball situations" by Variety, which also (wrongly) predicted "hefty grosses foreseen," THE HALLELUJAH TRAIL turned out to be an enfeebled, limp attempt to lampoon the Western genre. Despite an interesting if slight premise and a superb supporting cast, plus steady direction by John Sturges and fine camera work by Robert Surtees, the movie turned out to be a box-office bust and this highly promoted Cinerama release was one of the most disappointing Westerns of the 1960s. The blame for its dramatic failure can be placed on its seemingly endless narrative (the movie's release times varied from 168 to 156 minutes) and Burt Lancaster's miscasting in the pivotal lead role. The tongue-in-cheek main part would have been much

Lee Remick in THE HALLELUJAH TRAIL (1965).

better suited to John Wayne, who could have handled this vital comedy assignment capably.

In the winter of 1867 the city of Denver is faced with a whiskey shortage and Oracle Jones (Donald Pleasence) schemes to bring in 40 wagons full of liquor before the city is snowed in for the season. The local newspaper editor (Whit Bissell), a non-drinker, writes to Cora Templeton Massingale (Lee Remick), the leader of the area's temperance league, about the shipment, and three Sioux Indian chiefs (Martin Landau, Robert J. Wilkie, Jim Burk) also get wind of the shipment being headed by distiller Frank Wallingham (Brian Keith). The cavalry forces Colonel Thadeus Gearhart (Burt Lancaster) to escort Cora and her temperance women workers, who intend to stop the shipment, while another cavalry company led by Captain Paul Slater (Jim Hutton) must protect the wagon train. The Indians decide to hijack the shipment and the Denver citizens, led by Clayton Howell (Dub Taylor), plan to escort it to safety. When Irish teamsters go on strike, the way is open for an Indian attack on the train, but a sandstorm prevents it and the Indians then kidnap the temperance women and demand the whiskey as ransom. An exchange is arranged but the wagon train runs into trouble, coming into territory where there is quicksand. Oracle uses underwear to mark the safe trail for the wagon train but the recently released women remove the markers and, when the train's horses stampede, dump barrels of champagne, and the corks pop, sounding like gunfire. The Indians surround the wagon train, the cavalry surround the Indians, and Wallingham drives the train into quicksand, with the wagons sinking. Gearhart and Cora, who have fallen in love, decide to marry, as do Slater and Louise (Pamela Tiffin), Gearhart's daughter and a temperance worker. As everyone heads home, Oracle and Wallingham remain, waiting for the whiskey to resurface.

HANDS ACROSS THE BORDER (Republic, 1943) 72 mins.

Associate producer, Harry Grey; director, Joseph Kane; screenplay, Bradford Ropes, J. Benton Cheney; music director, Walter Scharf; orchestrator, Marlin Skiles; choreography, Dave Gould; songs, Hoagy Carmichael, Ned Washington, Phil Ohman; art director, Fred Ritter; set decorator, Charles Thompson; assistant director, Art Siteman; sound, Earl Crain, Sr.; camera, Reggie Lanning; editor, Tony Martinelli.

Roy Rogers (Himself); Trigger (The Horse); Bob Nolan and the Sons of the Pioneers (Themselves); Ruth Terry (Kim Adams); Guinn "Big Boy" Williams (Teddy Bear); Onslow Stevens (Brock Danvers); Mary Treen (Sophie Lawrence); Joseph Crehan (Jeff Adams); Duncan Renaldo (Juan Moraiva); Frederick Burton (Colonel Ames); LeRoy Mason (Mac Morelay); Larry Steers (Colonel Carter); Julian Rivero (Señor Morales); Janet Martin (Rosita Morales); The Wiere Brothers (Themselves); and Roy Barcroft, Kenne Duncan, Jack Kirk, Jack O'Shea, Curley Dresden.

Crook Brock Danvers tries to deprive horse rancher Jeff Adams (Joseph Crehan) of a cavalry contract by hijacking his horses, but cowboy Roy Rogers (Himself) and his pal Teddy Bear (Guinn "Big Boy" Williams) arrive on the scene and, after several mishaps, go to work for Adams. Roy rides his horse Trigger in a race for the contract, wins it, and brings the corrupt Danvers to justice.

Although a fairly actionful Western, speedily directed by Joseph Kane, HANDS ACROSS THE BORDER was a sad portent of things to come in the Roy Rogers Republic series: the film's plot was subordinated to its songs (by Hoagy Carmichael et al.) and after all the skimply plotline threads are tied together, the film anti-climactically concludes with an elaborately staged production number. It is said that studio chieftain Herbert J. Yates saw "Oklahoma!" on the Broadway stage and was so impressed with the production that he ordered these musical trappings for Roy Rogers. For the next several years the popular star was saddled with more music than action, until director William Witney took over the series reins in 1946 and reversed the situation.

Fortunately HANDS ACROSS THE BORDER is a strong production and is able to keep both the action and musical numbers in proper proportion. In addition to star Roy Rogers and Bob Nolan and the Sons of the Pioneers, leading lady Ruth Terry sang "Girl with High Button Shoes" and some good comedy was supplied by the Wiere Brothers. Also Guinn "Big Boy" Williams was seen to advantage as Roy's sidekick Teddy Bear. It is too bad he did not remain with the Rogers' series.

THE HANGING TREE (Warner Bros., 1959) C 106 mins

Producers, Martin Jurow, Richard Shepherd; director, Delmer Daves; based on the novel by Dorothy M. Johnson; screenplay, Wendell Mayes, Halsted Welles; art director, Daniel B. Cathcart; set decorator, Frank Miller; makeup, Gordon Bau; music, Max Steiner; orchestrator, Murray Cutter; song, Mack David and Jerry Livingston; assistant director, Russell Llewellyn; costumes, Marjorie Best; Miss Schell's costumes, Orry-Kelly; camera, Ted McCord; editor, Owen Marks.
Gary Cooper (Doc Joseph Frail); Maria Schell (Elizabeth Mahler); Karl Malden (Frenchy Plante); Ben Piazza (Rune); George C. Scott (Dr. George Grubb); Karl Swenson (Tom Flaunce); Virginia Gregg (Edna Flaunce); John Dierkes (Society Red); King Donovan (Wonder); Slim Talbot (Stage Driver); Guy Wilkerson (Home Owner); Bud Osborne (Horseman); Annette Claudier (Dance Hall Girl); Clarence Straight (Dealer).

From the opening credits, with Marty Robbins singing the title tune (which was Oscar-nominated), until the well-staged hanging scene climax, THE HANGING TREE is a topnotch production dealing with the raw frontier and its inhabitants. In many ways it is a late 1950s counterpart to the stark reality of the West as portrayed in the silent days by William S. Hart. Filmed in Yakima, Washington, the movie has a wonderful pioneer flavor about it, enhanced by Ted McCord's spectacular color cinematography and Delmer Daves' steady, deliberate direction. Gary Cooper is especially effective as the doctor haunted by his past, and the movie's action sequences are well-executed and exciting. Overall THE HANGING TREE is one of the best Westerns of the 1950s and deserves more accord than it has received in recent years.
Frontier physician Doc Frail (Gary Cooper), who has known too much tragedy in his life, comes to the rawboned mining community of Skull Creek in Montana. There he saves young Rune (Ben Piazza) from a posse that plans to hang him and helps the young man regain his strength. He also treats pretty Elizabeth Mahler (Maria Schell), who has suffered shock and blindness as a result of exposure following a stagecoach robbery. After helping the young woman become healthy again, Doc grubstakes her and her partners, Frenchy Plante's (Karl Malden) and Rune's, gold claim. The trio strike it rich, but Frenchy tries to rape the girl and Doc

Gary Cooper and Ben Piazza in THE HANGING TREE (1959).

kills him. The bloodthirsty locals vow to hang him, but the young woman stops them by giving them her mine in return for the doc's life.

Taken from Dorothy M. Johnson's novelette of 1957, which had won the Western Writers of America's Spur Award, the movie was "one of 1959's 'sleepers'; no one expected it to be as good or as well played as it was" (Homer Dickens, The Films of Gary Cooper, 1971). To be noted is that future Academy Award winner George C. Scott made his film debut in this production.

HARMONY TRAIL see DRIFTIN' RIVER

HARRY TRACY--DESPERADO (IMC, 1982) C 100 mins.

Producer, Ronald I. Cohen; director, William A. Graham; screenplay, David Lee Henry; production designer, Karen Bromley; camera, Allen Daviau; editor, Ron Wisman.

Bruce Dern (Harry Tracy); Helen Shaver (Catherine Tuttle); Michael C. Gwynne (Dave Merrill); Gordon Lightfoot (Morrie Nathan).

Al Jennings and Harry Tracy were two of the Old West's last

legendary outlaws, but Al Jennings reformed and had a long career thereafter, a portion of which was fictionalized in AL JENNINGS OF OKLAHOMA (q.v.). Harry Tracy, however, met the fate of most outlaws and was hunted and killed by the law. HARRY TRACY-- DESPERADO retells the story of the outlaw and was lensed in British Columbia. Bruce Dern in the title role was not overly effective and the movie itself was not very satisfying. Variety reported, "Film is told in a succession of rather brief episodes and never works up much spirit or excitement. The dialog is flat, the establishment of moods is tepid."

Known to be a friend of the poor and gallant with women, Harry Tracy (Bruce Dern) becomes involved in a life of crime and for a time travels with a painter (Michael C. Gwynne), but Harry is forced to shoot him when the man tries to turn him over to the law. On the run, Tracy falls in love with the daughter (Helen Shaver) of a deceased judge, and she joins him for a time as he flees from state to state in the northwest, all the time being pursued by a lawman (Gordon Lightfoot--the Canadian singer making his film debut). Eventually a posse of over fifty men corners Tracy and he is killed in the ensuing fight.

The life of Harry Tracy (1870-1902) was first brought to the screen at the end of the silent era in TRACY THE OUTLAW (1928), and the story is basically the same except that at the finale Tracy (Jack Hoey) takes his own life with his last bullet rather than be captured by the law.

HAUNTED TRAILS (Monogram, 1949) 58 mins.

Supervisor producer, Eddie Davis; director, Lambert Hillyer; screenplay, Adele Buffington; music director, Edward J. Kay; camera, Harry Neumann; editor, James C. Fuller.

Whip Wilson (Whip); Andy Clyde (Trigger Winks); Reno Browne [Blair] (Marie Martel); Dennis Moore (Phil Rankin); I. Stanford Jolley (Joe Rankin); William Ruhl (Gorman); John Merton (Sheriff Charley Coons); Mary Gordon (Aunt Libby); Steve Clark (Foreman Lou); Myron Healey (Lasser); Milburn Morante (Cookie); Eddie Majors (Deputy Jed); Bud Osborne (Tom Craig); Bill Potter (Deputy); Carl Mathews (Red); Thornton Edwards (Blacksmith); Chuck Roberson (Ed); Carol Henry (Outlaw); Ben Corbett (Townsman).

Whip Wilson starred in 22 Monogram features between 1949 and 1952. He was a rather likable cowboy hero, who, like Lash LaRue, depended on a bullwhip as his primary weapon. He also sang in his first few entries, but later the singing interludes were dropped from the formula. HAUNTED TRAILS is one of the better series efforts, with a literate script by Adele Buffington and some fine character work by sidekick Andy Clyde, shown here in a reformer-type role, reminiscent of his work in the classic "Hopalong Cassidy" feature, THREE MEN FROM TEXAS (1940) (q.v.).

Dennis Moore and Whip Wilson in HAUNTED TRAILS (1949).

Outlaws murder Whip Wilson's (Himself) brother and he gets on their trail and finds out that brothers Phil (Dennis Moore) and Joe Rankin (I. Stanford Jolley) are after a ranch and are killing off all the hands so they can bring in a bogus heir, Wink (Andy Clyde). Wink, however, reforms after Whip does him a favor and he agrees to aid the rightful owner, Marie Martel (Reno Browne), in gaining the spread. The Rankins later capture the girl but Whip and Wink rescue her and Whip kills the three men responsible for his brother's death.

The plot for this "B" outing calls for star Whip Wilson to be much more vengeful than usual for the lead in this type of fare. When he kills the three men responsible for his brother's death, after each shooting he crosses the dead man's name off the wanted posters. Director Lambert Hillyer, whose career goes back to William S. Hart films from the silent days and on to some of Buck Jones' best early talkies, does a fine job helming this low-budget actioner, embuing it with sufficient interesting touches to make it well above average for a feature in this dying genre.

HAWMPS (Mulberry Square Productions, 1976) C 126 mins.

Executive producer, A. Z. Smith; producer, Joe Camp;

Jim Hampton in HAWMPS (1976).

co-producer, Ben Vaughn; director, Camp; story/screenplay,
William Bickley, Michael Warren; production designer, Harland
Wright; set decorator, Ned Parsons; assistant director, Terry
Donnelly; stunt coordinator, George Fisher; sound, Bruce Shearin;
camera, Don Reddy; editor, Leon Seith.

James Hampton (Lieutenant Howard Clemmons); Christopher
Connelly (Uriah Tibbs); Slim Pickens (Sergeant Naman Tucker);
Denver Pyle (Colonel Seymour Hawkins); Gene Conforti (Hi Jolly);
Mimi Maynard (Jennifer Hawkins); Jack Elam (Bad Jack Cutter);
Lee de Broux (Fitzgerald); Herb Vigran (Smitty); Jesse Davis
(Mariachi Singer); Frank Inn (Cook).

Following the amazing screen success of BENJI (1974), Mulberry Square Productions turned to an actual event for its next
family-oriented comedy, an 1850s cavalry experiment using camels
for transportation in the Southwest rather than horses. With a
likable cast of non-star names and a pleasant story-line, HAWMPS
resulted in a good fun film which was a little too long (it originally
ran 126 minutes and was later cut to 113 minutes). Also, the title
characters had none of the appeal of the little canine Benji, and the
next year the studio reverted to the successful dog formula in FOR

THE LOVE OF BENJI.

At a remote Southwest desert Army outpost Lieutenant Howard Clemmons (James Hampton) receives the bad news that his unit is to be deployed by the government in an experiment involving the use of camels instead of horses for desert transportation and travel. His cohort, Sergeant Uriah Tibbs (Christopher Connelly), tries to convince the men at the post that the experiment will go well. Also arriving on the scene is Arabian "camel doctor" Hi Jolly (Gene Conforti) who, with Clemmons' and Tibbs' aid, manages to outfit the Army's first camel corps. There are those at the fort who oppose the plan, including the abrasive Sergeant Naman Tucker (Slim Pickens) and the fort's commanding officer (Denver Pyle). The latter's daughter, Jennifer (Mimi Maynard), is in love with Clemmons and urges him to petition her father to allow the camels' stay at the fort. The final test for the camels comes when they are used to track down the evil outlaw Bad Jack Cutter (Jack Elam), who is so bad that even his fellow desperadoes have run him out of town. With Jack captured, the camels prove their worth and Clemmons and Jennifer plan to wed.

One of the nicer aspects of HAWMPS (the Texas drawl pronunciation of humps) is its on-location shooting in such diverse southwest locales as Old Tucson, Arizona's Texas Canyon (the one-time winter camping grounds for Geronimo), and the scenic Arizona desert sand dunes.

HEART OF ARIZONA (Paramount, 1938) 68 mins.

Producer, Harry Sherman; director, Lesley Selander; based on the story by Clarence E. Mulford; screenplay, Norman Houston; camera, Russell Harlan.

William Boyd (Hopalong Cassidy); George "Gabby" Hayes (Windy Halliday); Russell Hayden (Lucky Jenkins); John Elliott (Buck Peters); Billy King (Artie); Natalie Moorhead (Belle Starr); Dorothy Short (Jacqueline Starr); Stephen Alden Chase (Dan Ringo); John Beach (Sheriff Hawley); Lane Chandler (Trimmer Winkler); Leo MacMahon (Twister); Topper (The Horse); and Lee Phelps, Bob McKenzie.

Crooks are after Buck Peters' (John Elliott) prime breeding stock and steal them while Lucky Jenkins (Russell Hayden) takes an injured girl (Dorothy Short) back to her outlaw mother Belle Starr (Natalie Moorhead). Belle's foreman (Stephen Alden Chase), the culprit behind the rustling, tries to put the blame on Hopalong Cassidy (William Boyd), but Hoppy finds out the truth. After Belle's cattle are rustled, he is able to round up the gang with the help of the Bar 20 wranglers. In the shoot-out Belle is killed.

The fifteenth entry in the "Hopalong Cassidy" series, this outing boasted memorable location photography, lots of action, and a surprisingly sad finale.

HEART OF THE WEST (Paramount, 1937) 63 mins.

Producer, Harry Sherman; director, Howard Bretherton; based on the story by Clarence E. Mulford; adaptor, Doris Schroeder; song, Sam Coslow and Victor Young; camera, Archie Stout.

William Boyd (Hopalong Cassidy); Jimmy Ellison (Johnny Nelson); George "Gabby" Hayes (Windy Halliday); Lynn Gabriel (Sally Jordan); Sidney Blackmer (Big John Trumbull); Charles Martin (Jim Jordan); John Rutherford (Tom Paterson); Warner Richmond (Johnson); Walter Miller (Whitey); Ted Adams (Saxon); Fred Kohler (Bartom); Robert McKenzie (Tim Grady); Topper (The Horse); and John Elliott.

Hopalong Cassidy (William Boyd) and his pal Johnny Nelson (James Ellison) become involved with two landowners who are fighting over the same grazing territory. They join up with Jim Jordan (Charles Martin), his pretty daughter Sally (Lynn Gabriel), and their whip-carrying ranch foreman Windy Walliday (George "Gabby" Hayes) in opposing rival Big John Trumbull (Sidney Blackmer), who they discover is the head of a cattle rustling gang. In a showdown between the two factions, Trumbull is killed in a cattle stampede.

The sixth entry in the long-running "Hopalong Cassidy" series, HEART OF THE WEST is a bit on the slow side, even with its fairly compact running time of one hour, although it does pick up considerably at the climax. The film is highlighted by good cinematography (by Archie Stout) of pleasant scenery, and co-star James Ellison singing the title song over the credits.

HEAVEN'S GATE (United Artists, 1981) C 219 mins.

Executive producers, Denis O'Dell, Charles Okum; producer, Joann Carelli; director/screenplay, Michael Cimino; art director, Tambi Larsen; music, David Mansfield; costumes, Allen Highfill; choreography, Eleanor Fazan; assistant directors, Michael Grillo, Brian Cook; camera, Vilmos Zsigmond; editors, Tom Rolf, William Reynolds, Lisa Fruchtman, Gerald Greenberg.

Kris Kristofferson (Averill); Christopher Walken (Champion); John Hurt (Irvine); Sam Waterston (Canton); Brad Dourif (Mr. Eggleston); Isabelle Huppert (Ella); Joseph Cotten (The Reverend Doctor); Jeff Bridges (John H. Bridges); Roseanne Vela (Beautiful Girl); Ronnie Hawkins (Wolcott); Geoffrey Lewis (Trapper).

HEAVEN'S GATE has the dubious distinction of having lost more money than any other Western (and perhaps any other feature film)--some $35-$40,000,000. The brainchild of director/scripter Michael Cimino (who gained critical acclaim for his 1978 melodrama THE DEER HUNTER), the movie began filming in the spring of 1979 as THE JOHNSON COUNTY CATTLE WAR and finished principal photography a year later. The bulk of the footage was shot in

HEAVEN'S GATE (1981).

Montana and the Harvard prologue lensed at Oxford University, England. Originally running 225 minutes, the film was cut and re-cut before finally getting national release in the spring of 1981 with a print lasting about 150 minutes. Having taken a critical shellacking the previous November when previewed, the film proved a box-office dud, grossing only $1,500,000 in initial distribution. Since then the film has become a video cassette cult favorite; a lesson in what not to do when creating a Western picture.

Beyond the financial and critical hassling, one is hard pressed to discern how $40,000,000+ was spent, unless it remained on the cutting room floor. The film's plot is simplistic, although the movie is at its best in period detail and in its recreation of the raw frontier.

The narrative tells of a wealthy young man (Kris Kristofferson) who graduates from Harvard University and migrates West in the latter part of the 19th century. In Wyoming the settlers are being harassed by land barons and the railroad, who want them out of the way at any cost. The young man joins the fight on the side of the oppressed, becoming the marshal. As a result the whore (Isabelle Huppert) whom he loves but must share with a gunslinger (Christopher Walken) is brutally raped and murdered. A bloody showdown occurs between the two factions, although neither side is victorious.

Despite the simplistic plot, HEAVEN'S GATE never was able satisfactorily to unfold its story and it becomes engulfed in its own detail and its oblique moralizing. The film, however, does have its moments, and it is visually stunning thanks to Vilmos Zsigmond's superb cinematography. The opening scenes of Joseph Cotten's speech at Harvard are also memorable, as is the appealing performance of Isabelle Huppert as the young prostitute innocently caught between the two warring factions.

Writing in Time magazine, Richard Corliss complained that the final edited version of HEAVEN'S GATE was unsatisfactory: "The film's coda no longer baffles, it disappoints...." He adds that the film's original "brazen visual virtuosity ... can still be seen, in postcard glimpses ... but they are subordinated to a small story and to Cimino's notion of Hollywood Marxism: the poor are better than the rich because they are more photogenic." The Film Year Book 1981 (1982), edited by Al Clark, said, "Cimino's folly turned out to be neither the all-eclipsing masterwork he clearly intended nor the irredeemable turkey his critics dismissed ... it is a triumph of style over context: marvelous set pieces, millions of authentic looking extras and a real sense of small bloody struggles in a big country ... without at any stage making one interested in the people who participate in them." As Phil Hardy discerns in The Film Encyclopedia: The Western (1983), "Cimino's main failing is his inability to balance the epic and the personal.... Cimino's characters are never fully integrated into the epic design of his film, and the movie accordingly seems strangely cold because of it."

It should be noted, however, that HEAVEN'S GATE was lauded abroad, particularly in France, where Jean-Pierre Coursedon wrote in Cinema '81 magazine (January, 1981) that the motion picture was a masterpiece which had been cut up because it was too realistic about the West and the American dream. In 1982, France gave the 225-minute version of the film its only full-blown release.

The artistic, financial, and political contretemps enmeshing this film was the detailed subject of the controversial best-selling book Final Cut (1985) by Steven Bach.

HELL BENT FOR LEATHER (Universal, 1960) C 82 mins.

Producer, Gordon Kay; director, George Sherman; based on the novel by Ray Hogan; screenplay, Christopher Knopf; music, William Lava, Irving Gertz; camera, Clifford Stine; editor, Milton Carruth.

Audie Murphy (Clay); Felicia Farr (Janet); Stephen McNally (Deckett); Robert Middleton (Ambrose); Rad Fulton (Moon); Jan Merlin (Travers); Herbert Rudley (Perrick); Malcolm Atterbury (Gamble); Joseph Ruskin (Shad); Allan "Rocky" Lane (Kelsey); John Qualen (Old Ben); Eddie Little Sky (William); Steve Gravers (Grover); Beau Gentry (Stone); Bob Steele (Jared).

Taking its title from the lyrics in the title theme to the popular

Audie Murphy and Felicia Farr in HELL BENT FOR LEATHER (1960).

television Western series "Rawhide," this Audie Murphy vehicle, with its tarnished tale of an innocent man hunted for a murder he did not commit, has medium entertainment value. With an outstanding supporting cast and expertly helmed by genre veteran George Sherman, it proved to be "...a fair enough entry for its intended market though noticeably lacking in the sort of usual heroics that go to make an exciting Western" (Variety).

Travers (Jan Merlin) escapes after committing a murder and cowboy Clay (Audie Murphy) is blamed for the crime. Local lawman Deckett (Stephen McNally) knows the accused man is innocent but plans to bring him in and get credit for solving the crime. Clay, however, escapes and takes pretty Janet (Felicia Farr) with him as a hostage. During their flight from the lawman and his posse, she comes to believe in his innocence. It is also the young woman who pieces together the puzzle and discovers that Travers is the real murderer, allowing for Clay to be set free.

Veteran Western lovers will especially like HELL BENT FOR LEATHER because it is filled with long-time genre players, including two former "B" Western stars: Allan "Rocky" Lane and Bob Steele.

HELL-FIRE AUSTIN (Tiffany, 1932) 70 mins.

Producer, Phil Goldstone; director/story, Forrest Sheldon;

screenplay, Betty Burbridge; camera, Ted McCord, Joe Novak.

Key Maynard (Ken Austin); Ivy Merton (Judy Brooks); Nat Pendleton (Bouncer); Charles LeMayne (Edmunds); Tarzan (The Horse); and Allan Roscoe, Jack Perrin, William Robyns, Lafe McKee, Fargo Bussey, Bud McClure, Lew Meehan, Ben Corbett.

The eleventh and final entry in Ken Maynard's Tiffany series, HELL-FIRE AUSTIN is one of the star's best talkies. Not only does it feature an interesting plot-line, but it contains a great deal of action, the type which made Maynard one of the most popular cowboy movie stars of the late 1920s. Astride his beautiful horse Tarzan, Ken Maynard performs many of the daring stunts and complex riding sequences which endeared him to movie action lovers.

After World War I, soldier Ken Austin (Ken Maynard) and his pal Bouncer (Nat Pendleton) return home to Texas on a freight train. Instead of receiving a big welcome, the two ex-soldiers end up on the chain gang for ordering a big meal in a cafe and then not being able to pay for it. While incarcerated, Ken spots the beautiful horse Tarzan which is owned by pretty ranch owner Judy Brooks (Ivy Merton). She plans to enter the horse in a cross-country race and use the prize money to pay off her debts to rival rancher Edmunds (Charles LeMayne). Observing Ken's affinity for the horse, she has him paroled into her custody so he can ride Tarzan in the sweepstakes race. Edmunds, however, plans to grab the ranch, but during a raid Ken and Bouncer take the horse to safety. During the ride Ken is bushwhacked by the crook's men, but he still manages to win the race, saves Judy's ranch and earns her love.

THE HERO OF PINE RIDGE see YODELIN' KID OF PINE RIDGE

HEROES OF THE SADDLE see ROLL ON, TEXAS MOON

HEROES OF THE WEST (Universal, 1932) twelve chapters

Producer, Henry MacRae; director, Ray Taylor; story, from "The Tie That Binds" by Peter B. Kyne; adaptor, Ella O'Neill; continuity, George Plympton, Basil Dickey, Joe Roach.

Noah Beery, Jr. (Noah Blaine); Diane Duval (Ann Blaine); Onslow Stevens (Tom Crosby); William Desmond (John Blaine); Martha Mattex (Martha Blaine); Philo McCullough (Rance Judd); Harry Tenbrook (Butch Gole); Frank Lackteen (Buckskin Joe); Edmund Cobb (Bart Eaton); Jules Cowles (Missouri); Francis Ford (Captain Donovan); Thunderbird (The Horse); and Grace Cunard, Chief Thundercloud.

Chapters: 1) Blazing the Trail; 2) The Red Peril; 3) The Avalanche; 4) A Shot from the Dark; 5) The Hold-Up; 6) Captured by the Indians; 7) Flaming Arrows; 8) Frontier Justice; 9) The Iron

Master; 10) Thundering Death; 11) Thundering Hoofs; 12) End of the Trail.

Contractor John Blaine (William Desmond) is attempting to build a railroad across the West and is aided by his son Noah (Noah Beery, Jr.), daughter Ann (Diane Duval), and engineer Tom Crosby (Onslow Stevens). Crooks led by Rance Judd (Philo McCullough) try to sabotage his operation; they use people working in Blaine's camp to undermine the job, and also incite the Indians to attack the work crews. Young Noah and Crosby (who is romancing Ann) unite to defeat the crooks and Blaine is able to successfully complete the project.

Taken from the Peter B. Kyne story, "The Tie That Binds," the serial is a colorful entry, but lacks the Universal polish which highlights its remake WINNERS OF THE WEST (q.v.) eight years later. In fact, quite a bit of stock footage from this version reappears in the revamp version, including several well-staged Indian chase sequences. Ray Taylor directed this version and co-directed the 1940 edition with Ford Beebe.

HIDDEN VALLEY see BREED OF THE BORDER

THE HILLS RUN RED (United Artists, 1967) C 89 mins.

Producers, Emmano Donati, Luigi Carpentieri; director, Lee W. Beaver [Carlo Lizzano]; screenplay, Dean Craig; art director, Aurelo Crugnola; music, Leo Nichols [Ennio Morricone]; song, Nichols and Audrey Nohra; camera, Antonio Secchi; editor, Ornella Micheli.

Thomas Hunter (Jerry Brewster); Henry Silva (Mendez); Dan Duryea (Getz); Nando Gazzolo (Ken Seagall); Nicoletta Machiavelli (Mary Ann Seagall); Gianna Serra (Hattie); Loris Loddi (Tim); Geoffrey Copleston (Horner); Paolo Magalotti (Stayne); Tiberio Mitri (Federal Sergeant); Vittorio Bonos (Gambler); Mirko Valentin (Sancho); Guglielmo Spoletini (Pedro); Guido Celano (Burger); Mauro Mannatrizio (Mitch the Soldier); Gianluigi Crescenzi (Carson).

"They Meet and the Hills Run Red" is the tagline for this violent Italian Western which was lensed as UN FIUME DI DOLLARI [A River of Dollars] and issued in Europe in 1966. One of the better of its ilk, the film especially benefits from strong performances by its three stars: Thomas Hunter, Henry Silva, and Dan Duryea; the latter is especially impressive as the mysterious stranger helping the hero.

When the Civil War ends, Rebel soldiers Jerry Brewster (Thomas Hunter) and Ken Seagall (Nando Gazzolo) hold up an army payroll; Brewster leads troops away while Seagall escapes with the money. Brewster, however, is captured and is sent to prison for five years. When he is released, he finds that Seagall is now a wealthy but hated land baron who was responsible for the death of Brewster's wife and the abduction of his infant son. When Seagall learns of Brewster's release, he hires gunslinger Mendez (Henry Silva) to kill him. In the subsequent ambush a mysterious stranger named Getz (Dan Duryea) saves Brewster, yet makes it appear he was killed. Together Getz and Brewster plan Seagall's downfall. They learn that his men plan to raid a small town, so they organize the locals to defend it. During the fight which follows, Brewster is wounded but is saved and cared for by Mary Ann (Nicoletta Machiavelli), Seagall's daughter. Seagall, realizes that Brewster is still alive and in the showdown between the two, Getz aids Brewster and Seagall and Mendez are killed, as is the innocent Mary Ann. Brewster finds his son and Getz, who is really a government agent, makes him the town's sheriff.

HIRED GUN see WYOMING ROUNDUP

HIS BROTHER'S GHOST (Producers Releasing Corp., 1945) 54 mins.

Producer, Sigmund Neufeld; director, Sam Newfield; screen-play, George Plympton; assistant director, Harold E. Knox; sound, Arthur Smith; special effects, Ray Mercer; camera, Jack Greenhalgh; editor, Holbrook N. Todd.
Buster Crabbe (Billy Carson); Al "Fuzzy" St. John (Fuzzy Q. Jones/Andy Jones); Charles King (Thorne); Karl Hackett (Doc Parkard); Archie Hall (Deputy Sheriff Bentley); Roy Brent (Yaeger); Bud Osborne (Magill); John Cason (Jarrett); Frank McCarroll (Madison); George Morrell (Foster).

Outlaws are terrorizing the area around Andy Jones' (Al St. John) ranch and he calls in Billy Carson (Buster Crabbe) to help him. Billy is captured by the gang, but later escapes. The outlaws, however, go to Andy's ranch and shoot him. Badly injured, he sends for his brother Fuzzy (Al St. John), whom he asks to impersonate him. Andy dies but later two of the outlaws see Fuzzy and think he is Andy's ghost, but Thorne (Charles King), the gang chief, has them dig up Andy's remains to prove he is dead. Billy and Fuzzy then capture a gang member (John Cason), who confesses that Thorne and the doctor (Karl Hackett) who treated Andy are the gang leaders. When another outlaw member (Bud Osborne) and the doctor are captured, they implicate the town's deputy sheriff (Archie Hall) in the crimes. Billy and Fuzzy then set out to stop the gang from raiding area sharecroppers. In a showdown, the lawman is captured but Thorne shoots him. Billy chases the bad man who has taken Fuzzy hostage. Fuzzy escapes, and Billy finally corners Thorne. At the finale, Fuzzy ends up as the town's judge and sheriff and he sentences the lawbreakers to life in prison.
A compact effort in PRC's "Billy Carson" series with Buster

Crabbe and Al St. John, this fast-moving picture greatly benefits from St. John's work in dual roles; he is especially good in a dramatic part for a change. Good riding sequences also lift the film, which suffers from an insignificant outlaw gang and no real leading lady in the narrative. Also of interest is the darkly photographed scene in which the outlaws dig up Andy Jones' corpse, certainly a grisly, out-of-the-ordinary activity for a 1940s Western.

HIS FIGHTING BLOOD (Ambassador, 1935) 60 mins.

Producers, Maurice H. Conn, Sigmund Neufeld; director, John English; based on the story by James Oliver Curwood; screenplay, Joseph O'Donnell; camera, Jack Greenhalgh; editor, Richard G. Gray.

With: Kermit Maynard, Polly Ann Young, Ted Adams, Paul Fix, Joseph Girard, Ben Hendricks, Jr., Frank O'Connor, Charles King, Frank LaRue, Ed Cecil, Theodore Lorch, Jack Cheatham, Rocky (The Horse), Jack Kirk, Chuck Baldra, Glenn Strange (The Singing Constables).

The seventh of eighteen starring films Kermit Maynard made for producer Maurice H. Conn and issued by Ambassador Pictures, HIS FIGHTING BLOOD relies more on dramatics than action to fulfill its entertaining plot. Film Daily newspaper noted, "There is more drama and less fighting than in the regular Westerns, but there is enough action to keep things interesting throughout." Especially good was Paul Fix in another of his weasel-type roles.

Kermit Maynard longs to be a Mountie but loses his chance when his younger brother (Paul Fix) goes to the wrong side of the law and participates in a hold-up. Kermit takes the blame, thinking it will make his sibling see the right path, and goes to jail. The brother, however, puts together a gang and during a heist one of them is mortally wounded. Before he dies the man confesses to Kermit's innocence and he is released from prison. Now able to join the Mounties, Kermit ends up hunting his brother's gang. It appears that Paul has been killed, but he tries to murder Kermit in order to silence him, but finds he cannot do the deed. He is himself shot and he dies from the wounds, as Kermit forgives him.

In 1927 Kermit Maynard, the stuntman/brother of Ken Maynard, starred in a half-dozen gallopers for Rayart Pictures and was billed as Tex Maynard. In 1934 he began his Ambassador series of well-received movies, mostly with northwoods settings and allegedly based on James Oliver Curwood's works, that lasted until 1938. Thereafter Kermit did supporting parts in motion pictures. Although cheaply assembled, the Ambassador series overall is pleasant, displaying Kermit Maynard as an appealing performer.

HONOR OF THE WEST (Universal, 1939) 60 mins.

Producer, Trem Carr; associate producer, Paul Malvern;

director, George Waggner; screenplay, Joseph West; songs, Fleming
Allan; camera, Harry Neumann.

Bob Baker (Bob Barrett); Marjorie Bell (Diane); Carleton
Young (Russ); Jack Kirk (Heck Clayborn); Dick Dickenson (Luke
Grimes); Frank O'Connor (Butch); Reed Howes (Deputy Tom); Glenn
Strange (Bat Grimes); Forrest Taylor (Walker); and Murdock
McQuarrie.

Bob Baker was brought in by Universal Pictures in 1937 to
replace Buck Jones, who had left the studio after a contract dispute. A likable performer with a decent singing voice, Bob Baker
never fit into the groove as a Western star. To make matters more
disappointing, the series' associate producer, Paul Malvern, had
tried to hire a young singer/actor named Len Slye to replace Buck
Jones, but he was vetoed in favor of Baker. Baker lasted only
two seasons as a Universal star, but in 1938 Slye, redubbed Roy
Rogers, made his first starring picture for Republic and the rest
is history.

Lawman Bob Barrett (Bob Baker) is under pressure from
ranchers to get rid of a rustling operation which is secretly being
led by Heck Clayborn (Jack Kirk). When Bob's deputy (Reed
Howes) is murdered by gang member Luke Grimes (Dick Dickinson),
the man's brother Bat (Glenn Strange) vows revenge. Hoping to
thwart Bat's plans, Bob makes him his deputy, but at the ranch of
suspected gang leader Whitley (Carleton Young), Bat kills Luke.
Upset over the action, Bob resigns his job and Bat becomes the
marshal. When Whitley heads for the border, Bob follows him.
They are ambushed by the gang and, joined by Bat, they shoot it
out with the rustlers, killing Clayborn and disposing of the gang.

During the course of the action star Bob Baker is given
screen time to romance and warble frequently to comely Marjorie
Bell (who later becomes better known as Marge Champion).

HOODED HORSEMEN see MYSTERY OF THE HOODED HORSEMEN

HOPALONG CASSIDY RETURNS see MYSTERY OF THE HOODED
HORSEMEN

HOPPY'S HOLIDAY (United Artists, 1947) 70 mins.

Executive producer, William Boyd; producer, Lewis J. Rachmil;
director, George Archainbaud; based on characters created by
Clarence E. Mulford; story, Ellen Corby, Cecile Kramer; screenplay,
J. Benton Cheney, Bennet Cohen, Ande Lamb; assistant director,
George Tobin; art director, Harvey T. Gillett; set decorator,
George Mitchell; music, David Chudnow; sound, Frank Hansen;
camera, Mack Stengler; editor, Fred W. Berger.

William Boyd (Hopalong Cassidy); Andy Clyde (California

Carlson); Rand Brooks (Lucky Jenkins); Andrew Tombes (Mayor Patton); Leonard Penn (Danning); Jeff Corey (Jed); Mary Ware (Gloria); Donald Kirke (Sheriff); Hollis Bane (Ace); Gil Patrick (Jay); Frank Henry (Bart); Topper (The Horse).

Hopalong Cassidy (William Boyd), California Carlson (Andy Clyde) and Lucky Jenkins (Rand Brooks) arrive in Mesa City for a celebration. After a bank robbery, California accidentally is handed the stolen loot and is arrested for the crime. The real criminals, however, retrieve the money and Hoppy goes after them, capturing the culprits and proving California's innocence.

HOPPY'S HOLIDAY was the third entry in the "Hopalong Cassidy" series following its return to the screen in 1946 with distribution through United Artists. Star William Boyd now controlled the rights to the title character but this outing was not as strong as the two initial entries, THE DEVIL'S PLAYGROUND (1946) and FOOL'S GOLD (1947). HOPPY'S HOLIDAY does have a neat climax, with the outlaws using a horseless carriage for a getaway vehicle; naturally, the good guys on horseback prove superior to the new technology--all of which is a little morality lesson about the goodness of the Old West versus the modern age.

Nine more "Hopalong Cassidy" features followed, some with exotic titles like UNEXPECTED GUEST (1947), SINISTER JOURNEY (1948) and THE DEAD DON'T DREAM (1948), but most were tepid and lacking in solid production values. The series shut down in 1948 and Boyd transferred the films to television distribution where a new "Hopalong Cassidy" craze took place. Thereafter, the dozen United Artists features were cut to 26 minutes each and were used as segments of "Hopalong Cassidy" (NBC-TV, 1949-51). Some of the titles actually play better in the truncated version.

HOSTILE COUNTRY (Lippert, 1950) 59 mins.

Executive producer, Robert Lippert; producer, Ron Ormond; associate producer, Ira Webb; director, Thomas Carr; screenplay, Ormond, Maurice Tombrage; art director, Fred Preble; set decorator, Theodore Offenbecker; assistant director, F. O. Colings; music director, Walter Greene; sound, Glen Glenn, Harry Eckles; camera, Ernest Miller; editor, Hugh Winn.

Jimmy Ellison (Shamrock); Russell Hayden (Lucky); Raymond Hatton (Colonel); Fuzzy Knight (Deacon); Betty [Julia/Julie] Adams (Ann Greene); Tom Tyler (Tom); George J. Lewis (Knowlton); John Cason (Ed); Stanley Price (Sheriff); Stephen Carr (Curt); Dennis Moore (Pete); George Chesebro (Oliver); Bud Osborne (Agate); Jimmy Martin (Fred); J. Farrell MacDonald (Mr. Lane); I. Stanford Jolley (Bartender); Cliff Taylor (Taylor); and George Sowards, Judith Webster, Jimmy Van Horn.

"Hopalong Cassidy" alumnus James Ellison and Russell Hayden were teamed as the Irish cowboys by producer Thomas Carr for a

half-dozen "B" Westerns for Lippert release; the films were shot
back-to-back with almost identical casts, including leading lady Betty
Adams, later better known as Julia/Julie Adams. In the supporting
casts were one-time sidekicks Raymond Hatton and Fuzzy Knight and
former genre stars Tom Tyler, George J. Lewis and Dennis Moore,
along with perennial bad guys, John Cason, George Chesebro, Bud
Osborne, and I. Stanford Jolley.

HOSTILE COUNTRY (shown on TV as OUTLAW FURY) is a
typical entry in the group, with a mundane plot hampered by too
many drawn out sequences. The film, however, used minimal stock
footage and it contained intriguing camera work by Ernest Miller plus
a dandy villainous duo called the Brady boys, well etched by Tom
Tyler and John Cason.

Shamrock (James Ellison) and Lucky (Russell Hayden) arrive
in a remote territory where Shamrock is to take half-interest in his
stepfather's ranch. They find themselves involved in a range feud.
When he shoots a man in self defense, crooks lead Shamrock to believe that the dead man was his stepfather, though the latter is actually a prisoner of the gang who want to ranch and the man's
money. Shamrock and Lucky discover the truth, defeat the gang,
and then aid pretty Ann Greene (Betty Adams) in transporting her
horses to market to raise the money she needs to save her ranch.

HOT LEAD (RKO, 1951) 60 mins.

Producer, Herman Scholm, director, Stuart Gilmore; screenplay, William Lively; art directors, Albert S. D'Agostino, Feild Gray;
set decorators, Darrell Silvera, John Sturtevant; music, Paul Sawtell; music director, C. Bakaleinikoff; assistant director, Bert Spur-
lin; sound, John Cass, Clem Portman; camera, Nicholas Musuraca;
editor, Robert Golden.

Tim Holt (Tim); Joan Dixon (Gail Martin); Ross Elliott (Dave
Collins); John Dehner (Turk Thorne); Paul Marion (Dakota); Lee
MacGregor (Bob); Stanley Andrews (Warden); Paul E. Burns (Duke);
Kenneth MacDonald (Sheriff); Robert Wilke (Stoney Dawson);
Richard Martin (Chito Rafferty).

Like serials, the "B" Western was coming to the end of the
trail in the early 1950s and most of the studios which still hung on
to the genre greatly diluted their films' entertainment value by budget corner-cutting. RKO Radio did not do this with its Tim Holt
series and thus the long-running Holt features (1940-1952) were just
as good as the end of the series as at the beginning. A good
example of this is HOT LEAD, a well made effort which spotlighted
a particularly effective rail station shoot-out between the good guys
and an outlaw gang.

Cowboys Tim (Tim Holt) and Chito Rafferty (Richard Martin)
stop a gold shipment robbery at Trailhead's depot, but one of their
cohorts is killed in the melee by a gang led by Turk Thorne (John
Dehner). Thorne then figures another angle by arranging the

Richard Martin and Tim Holt in HOT LEAD (1951).

parole of Dave Collins (Ross Elliott), a telegrapher he plans to use to give him needed messages on valuable shipments. Once released, Dave refuses to work for Thorne, who then murders the depot's telegrapher (Paul E. Burns) and plants the blame on Dave. The latter, meanwhile, has fallen in love with pretty Gail Martin (Joan Dixon), the owner of the ranch where Tim and Chito work. When the outlaws capture Gail and Dave, Tim and Chito are able to rescue the girl but find out that Thorpe and his men have taken Dave with them on a train expedition. With the aid of the law, Tim and Chito defeat the gang in a final confrontation.

HUNT TO KILL <u>see</u> THE WHITE BUFFALO

THE HURRICANE EXPRESS <u>see</u> MYSTERY MOUNTAIN

IDAHO (Republic, 1943) 70 mins.

Associate producer, Joseph Kane; production supervisor, Harry Grey; director, Kane; screenplay, Roy Chanslor, Olive Cooper; music director, Morton Scott; songs: Tim Spencer, Jesse Stone, Roy

Rogers and Fred Rose, Bob Nolan; art director, Russell Kimball; set decorator, Charles Thompson; assistant director, Art Siteman; sound, Fred Stahl; camera, Reggie Lanning; editor, Arthur Roberts.

Roy Rogers (Himself); Smiley Burnette (Frog Milhouse); Bob Nolan and the Sons of the Pioneers (Themselves); Trigger (The Horse); Virginia Grey (Terry); Harry J. Shannon (Judge Grey); Ona Munson (Belle Bonner); Dick Purcell (Duke Springer); Onslow Stevens (Chief Hanger); Arthur Hohl (Spike Madagan); Hal Taliaferro (Bud); Robert Mitchell Boys Choir (Themselves); and Rex Lease, Tom London, Jack Ingram, James Bush.

When Gene Autry entered the military service during World War II, the action left Roy Rogers as Republic's number one Western star, soon to be dubbed "King of the Cowboys." As a result Rogers would become the top moneymaking Western star for the next decade. Beginning with IDAHO, Harry Grey took over as production supervisor for the Rogers' films, replacing Joseph Kane who remained as director. Grey had worked with Autry, as had Smiley Burnette, who temporarily replaced George "Gabby" Hayes as Roy's comedy sidekick. Also with this production, Roy began sporting flashy outfits which hardly benefitted a cowboy, but despite this his popularity continued to zoom. IDAHO, which was focused more on melodramatics and music rather than action, is a good film which helped to consolidate the star's screen popularity.

Judge Gray (Harry Shannon) is being blackmailed by two ex-convicts who know that he was once the famous outlaw, Tom Allison. Also involved is gambling house proprietress Belle (Ona Munson). When these three attempt to force the judge to help them rob a bank and he refuses, they pin a murder on him. When his true identity is revealed, he is arrested. The crooks then try to kill the judge, but state ranger Roy Rogers (Himself) rescues him. The outlaws then plot to stage a payroll robbery and blame the judge and Roy for it. Roy foils the plan and captures the crooks. Since the ranch kids helped in the capture, Roy gives them the reward which is used to save the judge's ranch.

IN OLD CHEYENNE (Republic, 1941) 56 mins.

Producer/director, Joseph Kane; story, John Krafft; screenplay, Olive Cooper; music director, Cy Feuer; song, Sol Meyer and Jule Styne; camera, William Nobles; editor, Charles Craft.

Roy Rogers (Steve Blane); George "Gabby" Hayes (Arapahoe Brown); Joan Woodbury (Dolores Casino); J. Farrell MacDonald (Tim Casey); Sally Payne (Squeak); George Rosener (Sam Drummond); William Haade (Davidge); Hal Taliaferro (Pete); Jack Kirk (Rufe); Bob Woodward, Jim Corey (Outlaws); George Lloyd (Smitty); Billy Benedict (Vendor); Jack O'Shea (Barfly); Edward Piel, Sr. (Conductor); Merill McCormick (Townsman); and Ted Mapes, Fred Burns, Ben Corbett, Nick Thompson.

New York Inquirer newspaper reporter Stephen Blane (Roy Rogers) is dispatched to Wyoming to get the scoop on a cattle war between cattlemen and outlaw Arapahoe Brown (George "Gabby" Hayes). Cattleman Sam Drummond (George Rosenor), who wants all the settlers out of the area, is really behind all the conflict, and Brown saves Blane from being hung after he is captured by Drummond's gang. Drummond's men try to kill newspaperman Tim Casey (J. Farrell MacDonald) and attack the settlers, but are stopped by Blane, Brown and other settlers.

An entertaining and actionful Western, this Roy Rogers series entry is a bit different from the later, more standardized productions starring the singing cowboy and his horse Trigger. Here Rogers does not use his own name. George "Gabby" Hayes does not portray the character of Gabby Whittaker, although William Haade is cast as a character called Gabby, and Spanish dancer Dolores Casino (Joan Woodbury) ends up being engaged to Rogers' reporter character (a switch from the usual Rogers finale). The movie, nevertheless, is typical in some ways: it has the Republic gloss and workmanlike production values and the fast and steady directorial hand of the much-underrated Joseph Kane.

IN OLD MEXICO (Paramount, 1938) 67 mins.

Producer, Harry Sherman; director, Edward D. Venturini; based on a story by Clarence E. Mulford; screenplay, Harrison Jacobs; camera, Russell Harlan; editor, Robert Warwick.

William Boyd (Hopalong Cassidy); George "Gabby" Hayes (Windy Halliday); Russell Hayden (Lucky Jenkins); Paul Sutton (The Fox); Betty Amann (Janet Leeds); Jane [Jan] Clayton (Anita Gonzales); Al Garcia (Don Carlos Gonzales); Glenn Strange (Burk); Trevor Bardette (Colonel Gonzales); Anna Demetrio (Elena); Tony Roux (Pancho); Topper (The Horse) and Fred Burns.

In Mexico, Hopalong Cassidy (William Boyd), Lucky Jenkins (Russell Hayden) and Windy Halliday (George "Gabby" Hayes) are visiting a rancho where they try to stop rustlers and locate the murderer of a young man. Hoppy suspects that a pretty houseguest (Betty Amann) is involved in the lawlessness and she turns out to be the sister of the bandit leader, The Fox (Paul Sutton). The latter's men corner Hoppy, Lucky and Anita (Jane Clayton), the daughter of the ranch owner, but wounded Windy gets word to the rancho and they are saved and the gang captured.

A leisurely outing in the "Hopalong Cassidy" series, this feature is slowly paced but contains nice location scenery. Don Miller noted in Hollywood Corral (1976), "IN OLD MEXICO was a semi-sequel to BORDERLAND (1937) and merited more than the usual amount of attention because it was not made like a Western at all, but rather resembled a suspense drama in construction and execution, with more than the obligatory number of interior sequences." Leading lady Jane Clayton, married to series co-star Russell Hayden

Russell Hayden and Jan Clayton in IN OLD MEXICO (1938).

at the time, later shortened her name to Jan Clayton before finding success on Broadway in CAROUSEL and later in television's "Lassie" series.

IN OLD NEW MEXICO <u>see</u> THE GAY AMIGO

IN OLD OKLAHOMA (Republic, 1943) 100 mins.

Associate producer, Robert North; director, Albert S. Rogell; based on the story "War of the Wildcats" by Thomas Hurtle; screenplay, Ethel Hill, Eleanore Griffin; song, Sol Meyer and Walter Scharf; art director, Russell Kimball; set decorator, Otto Siegel; assistant director, Phil Ford; special effects, Howard Lydecker, Jr.; sound, Richard Tyler; camera, Jack Marta; editor, Ernest Nims.

John Wayne (Dan Somers); Martha Scott (Catherine Allen); Albert Dekker (Jim "Hunk" Gardner); George "Gabby" Hayes (Desprit Dean); Marjorie Rambeau (Bessie Baxter); Dale Evans (Cuddles Walker); Grant Withers (Richardson); Sidney Blackmer (Teddy

Roosevelt); Paul Fix (The Cherokee Kid); Cecil Cunningham (Mrs.
Ames); Irving Bacon (Ben); Byron Foulger (Wilkins); Anne O'Neal
(Mrs. Peabody); Richard Graham (Walter); and Lane Chandler,
Robert Warwick, Harry Shannon, Arthur Loft, Stanley Andrews,
Harry Woods, Bud Geary, LeRoy Mason, Will Wright, Fred Graham,
Tom London, Edward Gargan, Kenne Duncan, Hooper Atchley, Em-
mett Vogan, Wade Crosby, George Chandler, Curley Dresden, Roy
Barcroft, Jack Kirk, Slim Whitaker, Dick Rich, Yakima Canutt,
Shirley Rickert, Oril Taller, Linda Scott, Juanita Colteaux, Jess
Cavan, Charles Agnew, Pat Hogan, Bonnie Jean Harley, Pearl Early,
Linda Brent, Rhonda Fleming.
      A.k.a. WAR OF THE WILDCATS

      In 1906 schoolteacher Cathy Allen (Martha Scott), forced to
leave her hometown after writing a racy novel, relocates to a small
Oklahoma oil community where she draws the attentions of cowboy
Dan Somers (John Wayne) and oilman Jim Gardner (Albert Dekker).
The two men become immediate rivals for her affection. Cathy lives
at the local hotel run by motherly Bessie Baxter (Marjorie Rambeau).
The corrupt Gardner attempts to lease oil rich Indian lands. Dan
advises the tribe against the transaction and the Indians ask him to
take control of their oil leases. The government approves the
agreement but specifies that Dan must deliver the oil in Tulsa by a
certain date. Gardner does everything in his power to stop him, including sabotage and attempting to turn Cathy against Dan. On the
deadline day, however, Dan and his men get the oil to Tulsa and he
and Cathy are reunited. Realizing he has lost both the oil lease
and Cathy, Gardner joins forces with Dan.
      Although not terrific in its plot, IN OLD OKLAHOMA--better
known under its reissue title of WAR OF THE WILDCATS--is
probably one of John Wayne's more memorable Republic features.
It is a big, handsome production which moves constantly from start
to finish, with exceedingly strong performances from John Wayne as
the hero, Albert Dekker as his nemesis and lovely Martha Scott as
the beautiful bone of contention. The supporting cast is also very
good, especially George "Gabby" Hayes and Marjorie Rambeau in
their earthy characterizations. Jack Marta's cinematography is another plus and the final scenes of Wayne's oilmen racing their cargo
to market, fighting Dekker's minions, and battling a raging brush
fire are especially exciting.

IN OLD SACRAMENTO (Republic, 1946) 89 mins.

      Associate producer/director, Joseph Kane; based on the story
"Diamond Carlisle" by Kane; screen story, Jerome Odlum; screenplay, Frances Hyland; music director, Morton Scott; music/orches-
trator, Dale Butts; choreography, Fanchon; songs: Andrew B.
Sterling and Charles B. Ward; Bruce Siever and Jean Lenoir; Fred
Gilbert; Charles Maxwell; Barney Fagin; Will Cobb and Gus Edwards;
art director, James Sullivan; set decorators, John McCarthy, Jr.,

Earl Wooden; assistant director, Rollie Archer; special effects,
Howard and Theodore Lydecker; camera, Jack Marta; editor, Fred
Allen.

William Elliott (Johnny Barrett); Constance Moore (Belle
Malone); Hank Daniels (Sam Chase); Ruth Donnelly (Zebby Booker);
Eugene Pallette (Jim Wales); Lionel Stander (Eddie Dodge); Jack
LaRue (Laramie); Grant Withers (Captain Marc Slayter); Bobby Blake
(Newsboy); Charles Judels (Marchetti); Paul Hurst (Stage Driver);
Victoria Horne (Ma Dodge); Dick Wessel (Oscar); and Hal Taliaferro,
Jack O'Shea, H. T. Tsiang, Marshall Reed, Wade Crosby, Eddy
Waller, William Haade, Boyd Irwin, Lucien Littlefield, Ethel Wales,
Elaine Lange, William B. Davidson, Ellen Corby, Fred Burns.

After toiling in "B" Westerns for Columbia and Republic for
eight years, Bill Elliott was elevated to "A" productions by Republic
in 1946, and in the next four years starred in ten high-budget
features, beginning with IN OLD SACRAMENTO. It is claimed that
Elliott was not particularly pleased with the movie since he felt it
would lose him his following among youngsters. At any rate, when
the Republic package ended in 1950, he went to Allied Artists for a
series of "B" Westerns, some of which are quite good. He closed
out his film career in the mid-1950s with a half-dozen detective
features for Allied Artists.

IN OLD SACRAMENTO stars Elliott (now billed as William Elliott) as gambler Johnny Barrett, who uses gaming as a cover for
his real enterprise, that of being the notorious road agent Spanish
Jack. In frontier Sacramento he falls in love with pretty saloon
chanteuse Belle Malone (Constance Moore), but she is also romanced
by young miner Sam Chase (Hank Daniels). Although he loves Belle,
Johnny realizes he cannot make her happy. He takes part in one
last robbery, but leads the sheriff and his posse to the scene and
is killed, leaving Belle and Sam to a life of contentment.

William Elliott proved to be a very strong lead in top-budget
films and IN OLD SACRAMENTO (reissued as FLAME OF SACRAMEN-
TO) he was also bolstered by a topnotch supporting cast, including
Ruth Donnelly, Eugene Pallette, Lionel Stander, Jack LaRue and
Grant Withers. No doubt, however, Elliott's fans (especially the
younger ones) were disappointed to see their hero killed off at the
finale.

This was the third screen retelling of Kane's story "Diamond
Carlisle." Previous versions were DIAMOND CARLISLE (1922) with
George Chesebro and THE CARSON CITY KID (1940) (q.v.) with
Roy Rogers.

IN OLD SANTA FE (Mascot, 1935) 64 mins.

Producer, Nat Levine; director, David Howard; story, Wallace
MacDonald, John Rathmell; adaptors, Culbert Clark, James Guren;
songs, M. M. Hathaway and Floyd Ray; Gene Autry and Smiley
Burnette; Bernie Grossman and J. Harold Lewis; camera, Ernie

Miller, William Nobles; editor, Thomas Scott.
    Ken Maynard (Himself); Evalyn Knapp (Lila Miller); H. B.
Warner (Mr. Miller); Kenneth Thomson (Chandler); Wheeler Oakman
(Tracy); George "Gabby" Hayes (Cactus); Gene Autry (Himself);
Tarzan (The Horse); Smiley Burnette, Frankie Marvin (Entertainers);
and Wheeler Oakman, George Chesebro, George Burton, Jack Rock-
well, Jim Corey, Jack Kirk, Edward Hearn, Frank Ellis, Horace B.
Carpenter.

    Cowboy Ken Maynard (Himself) and sidekick Cactus (George
"Gabby" Hayes) are nearly run down by pretty Lila Miller (Evalyn
Knapp) and her fast car, and they end up working at her father's
(H. B. Warner) dude ranch. Also staying at the vacation spot are
crooks Chandler (Kenneth Thomson) and Tracy (Wheeler Oakman),
who are planning to rob Miller of his gold during a stagecoach
heist. Meanwhile, Chandler is romancing Lila, who has also drawn
Ken's attentions. Ken learns of the gangster's activities and
thwarts their plans, but not before they get him falsely accused
of their crimes. Finally, Ken corrals the hoodlums who have also
been blackmailing Miller, a one-time cohort of the gangsters who
has gone straight, and Ken wins Lila's affections.
    IN OLD SANTA FE is an important Western in several
respects. It was the beginning of the singing cowboy features of
the 1930s in that it had a singing hero (star Ken Maynard, who
had been singing in his features since the advent of sound, was
dubbed herein by Bob Nolan of The Sons of the Pioneers fame) in
a modern setting of the West battling big city gangsters. It was a
plot motif which would soon dominate the genre and replace the
sagebrush yarns of earlier times. The feature also marks the apex
of Ken Maynard's screen popularity because, after making another
Mascot produciton--the serial MYSTERY MOUNTAIN, q.v.--he was
let go because of his temper and drinking problems, and his
popularity began a slow decline. Finally, this film marks the
screen debut of popular radio singer and recording artist Gene
Autry, seen here in two sequences entertaining at the dude ranch,
along with sidekicks Smiley Burnette and Frankie Marvin. After
a bit part in MYSTERY MOUNTAIN, Autry replaced Maynard as the
lead in the science fiction/Western/musical serial, THE PHANTOM
EMPIRE (1935), and changed the entire status of the "B" Western,
renewing its popularity and launching the singing cowboy craze.

THE INCREDIBLE ROCKY MOUNTAIN RACE (Schick Sunn Classic/
NBC-TV, 12/17/77) C 100 mins.

    Executive producer, Charles E. Sellier, Jr.; producer, Robert
Stambler; director, James L. Conway; teleplay, David O'Malley, Tom
Chapman; music, Bob Summers; art director, Charles Bennett;
camera, Henning Schellerup; editor, John F. Link, II.
    Christopher Connelly (Mark Twain); Forrest Tucker (Mike
Fink); Larry Storch (Eagle Feather); Jack Kruschen (Jim Bridger);

Mike Mazurki (Crazy Horse); Parley Bear (Farley Osmond); Whit Bissell (Simon Hollaway); Bill Zuckert (Mayor Calvin Mercer); Don Haggerty (Sheriff Benedict); Sam Edwards (Milford Petri); Sandy Gibbon (Virginia City Sheriff); William Kazele (Burton); John Hansen (Bill Cody); and Robert Easton, Greg Brickman, Thomas Chapman, Hugh Burritt, Prentiss Rowe, Warren Ewing, David O'Malley, Allen Wood, Michael Roud, Earl Smith, Dennis Williams.

The citizens of St. Joseph, Missouri, are in a quandary over what to do about feuding Mark Twain (Christopher Connelly) and his arch-rival Mike Fink (Forrest Tucker). Hoping to get the two out of town for good, they set up a cross-country race between them, the winner being the first one to make it to California after collecting an assortment of items (a payroll train's conductor's cap, the moccasins of an Indian chief, a Pony Express rider's saddlebag, etc.) along the way. The competition starts with Fink racing out of town in a stolen stagecoach, but not knowing that Twain is a passenger. Along the way Fink is aided by addled Indian Eagle Feather (Larry Storch).

While it has no historical importance, this telefeature from Sunn International is a fun frolic with a jovial plot and delightfully zany performances by Forrest Tucker and Larry Storch, one-time co-stars of the TV Western series, "F Troop." Besides Mark Twain, the vid-pic also involves such historical figures as Jim Bridger (Jack Kruschen) and Chief Crazy Horse (Mike Mazurki).

THE INDIAN FIGHTER (United Artists, 1955) C 80 mins.

Producer, William Schorr; associate producer, Samuel P. Norton; director, Andre de Toth; story, Ben Kadish; screenplay, Frank Davis, Ben Hecht; music, Franz Waxman; songs, Waxman and Irving Gordon; art director, Wiard Ihnen; assistant directors, Tom Connors, Jr., Jack Voglin; camera, Wilfrid M. Cline; editor, Richard Cahoon.
Kirk Douglas (Johnny Hawks); Elsa Martinelli (Onahti); Walter Abel (Captain Trask); Walter Matthau (Wes Todd); Diane Douglas (Susan Rogers); Eduard Franz (Red Cloud); Lon Chaney (Chivington); Alan Hale (Will Crabtree); Elisha Cook (Briggs); Michael Winkelman (Tommy Rogers); Harry Landers (Grey Wolf); William Phipps (Lieutenant Blake); Buzz Henry (Lieutenant Shaeffer)/ Ray Teal (Morgan); Frank Cady (Trader Joe); Hank Worden (Crazy Bear); Lane Chandler (Head Settler).

Kirk Douglas embarked on a career as a movie producer when his Bryna Productions made THE INDIAN FIGHTER In 1955. Douglas not only played the leading role, he also hired his former wife Diana Douglas to play one of his on-screen romances. The result was an entertaining feature which was colorful but "more derring-do than dramatic" (Variety). The New York Times judged that the film was "...a lively adventure, if not setting fresh standards for Westerns."

Kirk Douglas and Elsa Martinelli in THE INDIAN FIGHTER (1955).

In 1870 the Army hires frontier scout Johnny Hawks (Kirk Douglas) to guide a wagon train to Oregon. Along the way the train is detained by Sioux Indians who will no longer allow whites to cross their territory because gold-hungry settlers have tried to steal the tribe's hidden riches. Hawks, however, signs a treaty with the chief, Red Cloud (Eduard Franz), and falls in love with pretty Indian maiden Onahti (Elsa Martinelli). Two white renegades, Todd (Walter Matthau) and Chivington (Lon Chaney), kill a tribal member and trouble erupts, forcing Hawks to take measures to restore peace; he even engages in victorious hand-to-hand combat with the chief's brother, Grey Wolf (Harry Landers). In a showdown with the villains, Hawks kills Chivington and captures and turns Todd over to Red Cloud. The chief permits the train to continue its journey following Hawks' marriage to Onahti.

In addition to skilled performances form its cast, Wilfred M. Cline's color cinematography of the on-location Oregon settings was a big plus. Remembered by many viewers were Martinelli's "nude" bathing scenes.

IRON MOUNTAIN TRAIL (Republic, 1953) 53 mins.

Associate producer, Edward J. White; director, William Witney;

story, William Lively; screenplay, Gerald Geraghty; camera, Bud
Thackery; editor, Tony Martinelli.
    Rex Allen (Himself); Koko (The Horse); Slim Pickens (Himself);
Grant Withers (Roger McCall); Nan Leslie (Nancy Sawyer); Roy Bar-
croft (Nate Orrin); Forrest Taylor (Sam Sawyer); Alan Bridge
(Marshal); John Hamilton (Circuit Judge); George H. Lloyd (John
Brockway).

    Although he appeared near the end of the trail for the
theatrical "B" Western, Rex Allen quickly established himself as
one of the most popular stars in a diminishing field. In the years
1952-54 he was ranked number three in the Motion Picture Herald's
poll of top money-making Western stars. A pleasant on-screen
personality and singer, Allen later carved out a very successful
career for himself as a movie narrator (mainly for the Disney organization) and doing television commercials. IRON MOUNTAIN TRAIL is
a typical Rex Allen starrer, well-made and entertaining, but
plagued with too much stock footage in order to keep its budget
trim.
    Post Office Inspector Rex Allen (Himself) is assigned to learn
why mail is lost in clipper ship transportation and a race is planned
for the contract between a rival stage line and the clipper ship.
The ship-line owner Roger McCall (Grant Withers) tries to sabotage
the race. When his henchman (Roy Barcroft) kills one of the stage
line owners, the man's partner, Sawyer (Forrest Taylor), is arrested for the crime. McCall has a crooked judge (John Hamilton)
convict Sawyer and sentence him to die. The man's daughter, Nancy
(Nan Leslie), tries to convince Allen of her father's innocence.
Outlaws then destroy the stage line's road and Rex rides to San
Diego with the mail. He is ambushed, but with the aid of the stage
driver (Slim Pickens), captures McCall's henchman, who confesses
to the murder. Rex then rides back with the confession, saves
Sawyer and captures McCall, the swiftness of his ride establishing
the Pony Express.
    To be noted is that villainous henchman Roy Barcroft has a pet
monkey named Marie. Another animal in the film--Rex Allen's horse
Koko--was billed on screen as "The Wonder Horse of the Movies."

THE IRON RIDER (Goodwill, 1926) 60 mins.

    Producer, Yakima Canutt; director/screenplay, Jacques Jac-
card; camera, Harry McGuire; editor, Francis Mulligan.
    Yakima Canutt (Yak Halliday); Elsa Benham (Anita Nelson
Parsons); James Corey (Larbun); Lee Sepulveda (Morgan); Alfred
Hewston (Flash Clayton); Nelson McDowell (Dunk); Les Bates
(Sheriff); Boy (The Horse); Lad (The Dog).

    Academy Award winner Yakima Canutt was considered the
greatest stuntman in the history of motion pictures. He also has
many credible performances as a villain in "B" Westerns. During

the silent days, he was the star of oaters made by such poverty row outfits as Arrow, Bell, and Goodwill. Canutt was the chief asset of these below-average outings, especially with his knack for trick riding and stunt work, but he was also a fine actor and a handsome celluloid hero. His deep, rough-sounding voice, however, would type him as a bad guy during the sound era, and thus he turned more and more to stunting. THE IRON RIDER is a typical Yakima Canutt starrer from the silent days, a rough-hewn and overly dramatic entry ("Up your cur and get going," read one of its title cards) but Canutt is the whole show--and he makes it worth watching.

Gambler Tex Clayton (Alfred Houston) is also cowboy Yak Halliday's (Yakima Canutt) girl (Elsie Benham). Yak stops him but needs money to get married. He decides to gamble and is cheated and loses what money he has, plus his horse (Boy). When he finds out he was cheated, he takes back the animal, and a drunk (Nelson McDowell), run out of town by crooks, tells him there is a reward for the capture of the gang. Now Yak has a plan to earn money. He confronts the outlaws and in the shoot-out between Yak and the gang, only Knife Morgan (Lee Sepulveda) survives. Yak captures him, wins the reward money, and gets married.

THE IRON SHERIFF (United Artists, 1957) 73 mins.

Producer, Jerome C. Robinson; director, Sidney Salkow; screenplay Seeleg Lester; music/music director, Emil Newman; assistant director, Ralph E. Black; wardrobe, Einar Bourman; art director, William Ross; sound, James Thompson; camera, Kenneth Peach; editor, Grant Whytock.

Sterling Hayden (Sheriff Sam Galt); Constance Ford (Claire); John Dehner (Roger Pollock); Kent Taylor (Quincy); Darryl Hickman (Benjie Galt); Walter Sande (Ellison); Frank Ferguson (Holloway); King Donovan (Leveret the Telegrapher); Mort Mills (Sutherland); Peter Miller (Jackson); Kathy Nolan (Kathi); I. Stanford Jolley (Walden); Will Wright (Judge); Ray Walker (Bilson); Bob Williams (Tilyou).

"From His Leather-Tough Skin to His Cold-Steel Guts he was all cast iron ... and then he began to crack ... she could clear his name ... but only if she'd dirty her own!... A shot and deadly as the bullets that screamed from his gun!" So read the ad lines from THE IRON SHERIFF.

Benjie Galt (Darryl Hickman), the son of town marshal Galt (Sterling Hayden), is accused of murdering a way station attendant over a money shipment. Most of the townspeople feel the young man will be acquitted because he is the lawman's son. During the trial, Benjie is defended by lawyer Pollock (John Dehner) who maintains Benjie's innocence, while the prosecutor (Frank Ferguson) calls the sheriff to the stand and the lawman recounts how the dying man

AS
HOT
AND
DEADLY
AS
THE
BULLETS
THAT
SCREAMED
FROM
HIS
GUN!

THE IRON SHERIFF

STARRING
STERLING HAYDEN
CONSTANCE · JOHN · KENT
FORD · DEHNER · TAYLOR
DARRYL HICKMAN · WALTER SANDE · FRANK FERGUSON
KING DONOVAN · MORT MILLS · PETER MILLER
Written by   Directed by   Produced by
SEELEG LESTER · SIDNEY SALKOW · JEROME C. ROBINSON
A GRAND PRODUCTIONS, INC. Presentation
Released thru UNITED ARTISTS

Advertisement for THE IRON SHERIFF (1957).

named his son as the culprit. The lawman has further problems because the local newspaper editor (Kent Taylor) is after the lawman's
girlfriend (Constance Moore) and uses his newspaper to convict Benjie. Galt, however, investigates the killing further and learns that
telegrapher Leveret (King Donovan) was the only other person who
knew about the money shipment. He gets a confession out of Leveret,
thus freeing his son.

With the plot twist of a lawman giving evidence which will hang
his own son, THE IRON SHERIFF is a particularly strong "B" melodrama, with a good script and a fine cast. Relying far more on
dramatics than action, the film contains some excellent performances,
especially from Kent Taylor as the jealous newspaper publisher,
Walter Sande as another lawman, and King Donovan as the actual
murderer. Cinematographer Kenneth Peach does a capable job of
distracting the viewer from the fact that the film is a mainly studio-
bound production.

JENNIE LEE HAS UNA NUOVA PISTOLA see GUNMEN OF THE RIO GRANDE

JESSE JAMES (1928) see THUNDERING HOOFS

JESSE JAMES AT BAY see DAYS OF JESSE JAMES

JESSE JAMES AT BAY see YOUNG BILL HICKOK

JESSI'S GIRLS (Manson Distributing Corp., 1975) C 84 mins.

Producers, Michael F. Goldman, Al Adamson; director, Adamson; screenplay, Budd Donnelly; music, Don McGuinnis; assistant director, John D'Amato; special effects, Gregg Auer; camera, Gary Graver; editor, John Winfield.

Sondra Currie (Jessica Hartwell); Geoffrey Land (Sheriff Clay); Ben Frank (Frank Brock); Rod Cameron (Rufe); Regina Carroll (Claire); Jennifer Bishop (Rachel); Ellen Stern (Kana); Joe Cortese (Baldry); Jon Shank (Slime); Biff Yeager (Link); Gavin Murrell (Indian); Rigg Kennedy (Seth Hartwell); William Hammer (Shag); Hugh Warden (John); Joe Arrowsmith (Teller); John Durren (Moose).

In Arizona in 1879 newly married Seth Hartwell (Rigg Kennedy) and his bride Jessica (Sondra Currie) are ambushed by outlaw Frank Brock (Ben Frank) and his gang; Seth is murdered and Jessica brutally raped and left for dead. The young woman, however, survives and makes her way to the camp of an old prospector, Rufe (Rod Cameron), who takes care of her and teaches her to ride and shoot. Coming across a prison wagon, Jessica frees three female prisoners, Claire (Regina Carroll), Rachel (Jennifer Bishop), and Kana (Ellen Stern). The quartet head to the outlaw's camp for revenge. There three of the gang are killed, as is Rachel, while Claire sleeps with an Indian (Gavin Murrell) who was the gang's prisoner. Kana then kills the brave and fights with Claire. When Jessica breaks them up, she rides off to warn Brock, her former lover. Claire then leaves Jessica, who must face Brock alone, since he kills Kana. At the showdown, Claire returns with the local sheriff (Geoffrey Land) and the gang is totally destroyed, although Claire dies in the gun battle. The sheriff then turns on Jessica and tries to abscond with the gang's stolen loot, but Jessica gets the upper hand.

The film was released in Great Britain as WANTED WOMEN and the British Monthly Film Bulletin opined, "WANTED WOMEN is a shell of a movie--a formulary outline that follows, disconcertingly enough, in the hoofprints of HANNIE CAULDER, all the way from rape to revenge. Working on a threadbare shoestring, director Al Adamson reprises his credit footage of Jessie's [sic] galloping across the

plains more than once, and economises more blatantly with the offensive score, which fills nearly every minute of screen time and
quite literally makes the film a painful experience."

For the record, this otherwise shoddy production does contain
a fine Rod Cameron performance as the sage prospector.

THE JUDGMENT BOOK see TRAIL'S END

KAISER VON KALIFORNIEN (Tbis-Rota, 1936) 80 mins.

Producer/director, Luis Trenker; based on the play and opera
Der General Das Gold by Bruno Frank; screenplay, Trenker; music,
Giuseppe Recce; camera, Albert Benitz.

Luis Trenker (J. A. Sutter); Victoria von Ballasko (Anna);
Warner Konig (Rudolph); Karl Zwingmann (Emil); Elsie Autinger
(Mrs. Duebbelt); Melanie Mareschowsky (Amalie); Bernard Minetti
(The Stranger); Luis Gerold (Ermattinger); Paul Verhoewen (Billy);
Hans Zesch-Ballot (Gouvernor Alvaredo); Marcella Albani (His Wife);
Walther Franck (Castro); Reginald Pasch (Marshall); August Eich-
horn (Harper); Bertha Drews (Chansonette); Alex Golling (Kewen);
Heinrich Marlow (Thompson).

In 1936 Universal issued its costly box-office flop, SUTTER'S
GOLD (see B/V), starring Edward Arnold in the title role of John
Sutter. This lavish, but strung-out super production recounted how
Johann August Sutter, a Swiss immigrant, built an empire for himself
in California, only to have it stolen from him because gold was dis-
covered on his lands in 1848. Around the time Universal was making
this film, Adolf Hitler's Germany made its own version, produced by
Luis Trenker, who also portrayed John Sutter. (Ironically, when
Universal originally intended to have Russian director Sergei M.
Eisenstein direct this big-budget film, Luis Trenker was considered
for the title assignment.)

KAISER VON KALIFORNIEN relates the same story as the Universal feature, with Sutter (Luis Trenker) here identified as a German merchant, coming to California, setting up a colony and building
an empire through land grants, only to be cheated by huntry gold
seekers when the precious metal is found in a mill stream on his
property. Although he is legally in the right, the courts side with
the might of the claim jumpers and Sutter loses everything.

Based on Bruno Frnak's play and opera Der General Das Gold,
this West German production is photographically vivid with its on-
location footage shot in the California deserts. Variety, however,
said the German film "suffers by comparison" with the U.S. feature,
but added, "Production moves along with more alacrity and suspense
than usually uncovered in German cinemas. Gold rush sequences at-
tain a certain amount of force." This Nazi-era production predates
the popular West German Westerns of the 1960s--based on the works
of Karl May--which themselves gave impetus to the spaghetti Western
craze later in the decade.

KEEP ROLLIN' see GAUCHO SERENADE

KENNY ROGERS AS THE GAMBLER (Kragen & Co/CBS-TV, 4/8/80)
C 100 mins.

Executive producer, Ken Kragen; producer, Jim Byrnes; associate producer, John Marias; director, Dick Lowry; based on the
song by Don Schlitz; story, Cort Casady, Byrnes; teleplay, Byrnes;
music, Larry Cansler; art directors, Allen E. Smith, Richard Sawyer;
camera, Joseph Biroc; editor, Jerrold L. Ludwig.
Kenny Rogers (Brady Hawkes); Christine Belford (Eliza);
Bruce Boxleitner (Billy Montana); Harold Gould (Arthur Stobridge);
Clu Gulager (Rufe Bennett); Lance LeGault (Doc Palmer); Lee Pur-
cell (Jennie Reed); Ronnie Scribner (Jeremiah); Noble Willingham
(Conductor); Bruce Fischer (Tabor); Borah Silver (Botkin); Lew
Brown (Johnson); Lee Pual (George); Robert Lussier (Busienssman);
Edward Walsh (Charlie Rose); Marianne Gordon (Dallas); Dave Cass
(Winters); Cathy Worthington (Lilly); Jerry Wills (Rufe's Man); Neil
Summers (Polo); Charles Knapp (Shuster); Ed Bakey (Eli).

KENNY ROGERS AS THE GAMBLER--THE ADVENTURE CONTINUES
(Lion Share/CBS-TV, 11/28/83) C 200 mins.

Producers, Dick Lowry, Ken Kragen; supervising producer,
Neil T. Maffeo; director, Lowry; based on the song by Don Schlitz;
teleplay, Jim Byrnes; music, Larry Cansler; production designer,
Paul Peters; camera, James Pergola; editors, Bernard Balmuth,
Byron "Buzz" Brandt.
Kenny Rogers (Brady Hawkes); Bruce Boxleitner (Billy Mon-
tana); Linda Evans (Kate Muldoon); Johnny Crawford (Masket);
Charlie Fields (Jeremiah); David Hedison (Garson); Bob Hoy (Juno);
Brion James (Reece); Paul Koslo (Holt); Cameron Mitchell (Colonel
Greeley); Mitchell Ryan (Charlie McCourt); Gregory Sierra (Silvera);
Ken Swofford (Witchita Pike); Harold Gould (Stowbridge); Macon
McCalman (Rawlins Sheriff); Lee Paul (Pettibone); Roy Jenson
(Hatch); Gary Cox (Sergeant Norton); Ann Gillespie (Young Saloon
Girl); Marianne Gordon (Dallas); Bill Hart (Daniels); Kelly Junker-
mann (Young Gambler); Hank Kendrick (Colonel Collins); Joe Mas-
sengale (Grau); Cliff McLaughlin (Evans); Gene McLaughlin (Simms);
Patrick O'Brien (Jenkins); John Putch (Hanging Deputy); Lelan
Rogers (Swenson); Roy Rogers (Drunk); Monty Simons (Baggage
Guard); Earl Smith (Forbes); John Tatum (Horseman); Bob Terhune
(Thayer); Henry Wills (Rand); Bunky Young (Pioneer Woman);
Cathy Worthington (Lilly); Ron Colby (Haines Sheriff); Debbie At-
kinson (Girl on Street); Randy Patrick (Orville); Whitney Rydbeck
(Teller).

Kenny Rogers first came to prominence in the late 1960s and
early 1970s as a member of the popular singing group, The First
Edition. By the late 1970s he had gone solo and had a big success

in 1977 with the country song "Lucille." In 1979 he scored big with the semi-narrative song, "The Gambler," and its success prompted TV movie makers to star him in the telefilm KENNY ROGERS AS THE GAMBLER (1980). It was so successful that it briefly held the title of most-watched made-for-TV movie. Due to its rating success, the movie spawned a sequel three years later, KENNY ROGERS AS THE GAMBLER--THE ADVENTURE CONTINUES, which teamed Rogers with Linda Evans, who had impacted so positively as the mature beauty in the teleseries "Dynasty."

KENNY ROGERS AS THE GAMBLER featured the singing star as a gambling man who returns to the southwestern town where the woman (Christine Belford) he never married lives with their son. The gambler knows that his enemies are waiting there for him. He is aided by a younger gambler (Bruce Boxleitner) and eventually the two tame the town. Having little to do with the Grammy award-winning song, the telefilm had little substance.

KENNY ROGERS AS THE GAMBLER--THE ADVENTURE CON-TINUES was originally aired in two parts and emerged as a colorful, if overdrawn attempt to duplicate the rating formula of the original. Here the gambler's (Kenny Rogers) son is kidnapped by outlaws and Rogers teams with his fellow gamester (Bruce Boxleitner) and a gun-toting beauty (Linda Evans) to track down the gang and rescue the lad.

For his third TV Western, Kenny Rogers deserted the Old West for the modern one in WILD HORSES (1985), q.v. In early 1987, plans were announced for the singer to start in yet another follow-up to KENNY ROGERS AS THE GAMBLER.

THE KENTUCKIAN (United Artists, 1955) C 104 mins.

Producer, Harold Hecht; director, Burt Lancaster; based on the novel The Gabriel Horn by Felix Holt; screenplay, A. B. Guthrie, Jr.; music, Bernard Herrmann; songs, Irving Gordon; music director, Roy Webb; assistant director, Richard Mayberry; camera, Ernest Laszlo; editor, William B. Murphy.

Burt Lancaster (Big Eli); Dianne Foster (Hannah); Diana Lynn (Susie); John McIntire (Zack); Una Merkel (Sophie); Walter Matthau (Bodine); John Carradine (Fletcher); Donald MacDonald (Little Eli); John Litel (Babson); Rhys Williams (Constable); Edward Norris (Gambler); Lee Erickson (Luke); Clem Bevans (Pilot); Lisa Ferraday (Woman Gambler); Douglas Spencer, Paul Wexler (Fromes Brothers); Whip Wilson (Lancaster's Double).

Burt Lancaster helmed this production as well as starring in it, and the overall results were not commendable. While the film does recreate the feeling of the 1820s frontier, its story is not particularly interesting, nor are its main protagonists very intriguing. The film does have some interesting supporting character roles (e.g., John Carradine as a none-too-honest peddler and Una Merkel as a frontier woman), and it is at its best in depicting life on the frontier, but at its worst when trying to be more than just passing entertainment.

Widower Big Eli (Burt Lancaster) plans to migrate to Texas in the 1820s with his young son Little Eli (Donald MacDonald). Trekking through Kentucky, they meet Hannah (Dianne Foster), a servant girl, and Susie (Diana Lynn), a school teacher. Big Eli also finds that the area is threatened by bully Bodine (Walter Matthau) and he decides to fight the bad man. Eventually he and his son settle in the area and quit their roaming.

The New York Times commented that the film "...shifts gears repeatedly, first entangling Lancaster with civilization and a civilized girl, Diana Lynn, then jumps with joy, then bursts into violence, then broadens into near-burlesque) and continually back and forth. It's best when Lancaster is simply bucking and brawling athletically."

THE KID FROM KANSAS see ROAD AGENT

THE KID'S LAST RIDE (Monogram, 1941) 55 mins.

Producer, George W. Weeks; director, S. Roy Luby; screenplay, Earle Snell; songs, Harry Tobias, Jean George, Roy Ingraham; camera, Robert Cline; editor, Roy Claire.

Ray "Crash" Corrigan (Crash); John King (Dusty); Max Terhune (Alibi); Luana Walters (Sally Rall); Edwin Brian (Jimmy Rall); Al Bridge (Sally Rall); Edwin Brian (Jimmy Rall); Al Bridge (Harmon); Glenn Strange (Bart); Frank Ellis (Wash); John Elliott (Disher); George Havens (Johnny); Elmer (The Dummy); and Tex Palmer, Carl Matthews, George Morrell.

"They wouldn't be scared and they couldn't be chased ... and they'd rather fight than eat!" is how the ads ran for this "Range Busters" episode, the fifth segment in the Monogram series and the first of the group where the trio are law officers. The overall production is satisfactory, although the plot drags. Two songs, "Call of the Wild" and "It's All a Part of the Game," are well interpolated into the action.

As a cover-up, The Range Busters (Ray "Crash" Corrigan, John King, Max Terhune) are called into a town by crook Harmon (Al Bridge), who has control over Jimmy Rall (Edwin Brian), the brother of schoolmarm Sally Rall (Luana Walters). Jimmy owes Harmon gambling debts and the crook and his partner Bart (Glenn Strange) uses him to gain information about where local ranchers hide their money from cattle sales. Harmon and Bart were once outlaws and Jimmy's late judge father sentenced their partner to hang; for revenge Harmon wants the Rall ranch and he intends to see Jimmy at the end of a rope. When the gang commits its latest robbery attempt, the Range Busters stop them and Bart is killed and Jimmy injured. Sally tries to rescue Jimmy, who dresses like Crash, but he is ambushed and shot by the gang. Crash captures Harmon, while Dusty and Alibi round up the rest of the outlaws.

KILLER ON A HORSE see WELCOME TO HARD TIMES

KING OF THE RODEO (Universal, 1929) 5,509'

Producer, Hoot Gibson; director, Henry MacRae; story, Bertha M. Bower; continuity, George Morgan; titles, Bower, Harold Tarshis; art director, David S. Garber; camera, Harry Neumann; editor, Gilmore Walker.
Hoot Gibson (Chip, the Montana Kid); Kathryn Crawford (Dulcie Harlan); Slim Summerville (Slim); Charles K. French (Chip, Sr.); Monty Montague (Weasel); Joseph W. Girard (Harlan); Jack Knapp (Shorty); Harry Todd (J. G.); Bodil Rosing (Mother).

Chip (Hoot Gibson) finds that a rival rancher has been stealing from his father's (Charles K. French) horse herd, but his dad orders him back to college. When he refuses, he is told to "...pack your things and drift." Chip goes to Chicago and becomes a rodeo performer known as the Montana Kid. He falls in love with Dulcie Harlan (Kathryn Crawford), the daughter of the rodeo owner. Chip wins many events and becomes a top star, but dishonest rider Weasel (Monty Montague) robs the box office and even steals Chip's shirt. Mistaken for the thief, Chip chases the culprit and captures him, and wins Dulcie's love. He is reunited with his family.
KING OF THE RODEO is a semi-sequel to star Hoot Gibson's earlier CHIP OF THE FLYING U (1926) (see B/V), one of several screen version of Bertha M. Bower's standby story. Here Hoot's character is billed as the "new Chip of the Flying U," with Charles K. French portraying a much older Chip Bennett. Coming at the finale of the silent film era, KING OF THE RODEO is a lighthearted Hoot Gibson outing with lots of action and rodeo footage and the exciting climax of Gibson chasing the villain on a motorcycle.

KING OF THE SIERRAS (Grand National, 1938) 55 mins.

Producer, George A. Hirliman; director, Samuel Diege; story, Frank Gay; screenplay, Scott Darling; camera, Jack Greenhalgh, Jr., Tom Gailigan.
Hobart Bosworth (Uncle Hank); Harry Harvey, Jr. (Tom); Frank Campeau (Jim); Harry Harvey, Sr. (Pete); Sheik (Whitey the Horse); Jack Lindell (Trainer); Rex (El Diablo the Horse).

The term "horse opera" has always referred to Westerns, but KING OF THE SIERRAS is a horse opera in the real sense, because its protagonists are horses. The narrative is framed by Uncle Hank (Hobart Bosworth) telling young Tom (Harry Harvey, Jr.) in detail how a wild horse, El Diablo (Rex), protects his lady love from the advances of a rival steed, Whitey (Sheik).

This sewn-together outing interpolates older footage of the horse star Rex, whose movie career dates back to the silent days, into the newer footage with scenery-chewing veteran Hobart Bosworth and a small supporting cast. Variety noted the story "...allows for no women, no runaway stagecoaches, no hip-shooting gunmen," and concluded, "It's fable styled, good for youngsters...."

Rex, "The King of the Wild Horses," starred in over two dozen features during the silent days, mostly for producer Hal Raoch, who also headlined him in the Pathé serial THE DEVIL HORSE (1926). (Footage from this chapterplay would be used repeatedly for action shots in movies of the sound era.) The celebrity horse, however, was also quite active in the 1930s, especially in serials such as THE VANISHING LEGION (1931), THE LAW OF THE WILD (1934) and THE ADVENTURES OF REX AND RINTY (1935), all for Nat Levine's Mascot Pictures.

THE LARAMIE KID (Reliable, 1935) 57 mins.

Producer, Bernard B. Ray; associate producer/director, Harry S. Webb; story, C. C. Church; screenplay, Carl Krusada, Rose Gordon; assistant director, William Nolte; camera, J. Henry Kruse; editor, Fred Bain.

Tom Tyler (Tom Talbot); Alberta Vaughn (Peggy Bland); Al Ferguson (Jim Morley); Murdock McQuarrie (Dad Bland); George Chesebro (Ed Larkin); Snub Pollard (Shorty); Steve Clark (Sheriff); Artie Ortego, Budd Buster (Henchman); Nelson McDowell, James Aubrey (Convicts); Wally Wales (Guard).

Returning home after a year's absence, Tom Talbot (Tom Tyler) informs his girl Peggy Bland (Alberta Vaughn) that he does not have enough money to marry her. He is told that the local banker, Morley (Al Ferguson), intends to marry her and that he holds the mortgage on her father's (Murdock MacQuarrie) ranch. Tom is in town when outlaws rob the bank and he is mistaken for one of them. Morley is at the Bland ranch when the robbers ride by and when the law arrives, he points them in the wrong direction. Tom then turns himself in and gets the reward money for the payment of the Bland mortgage. In prison, he saves the life of Shorty (Snub Pollard), who turns out to be one of the gang and tells Tom that Morley staged the robbery to hide his own thefts of bank funds. During a prison break, Tom escapes and returns home, where Dad Bland shelters him from the law. Mary, meanwhile, finds the outlaws' hiding place, where gang member Larkin (George Chesebro) has been deserted by his cohorts because he is badly injured. Before he dies, he confesses the truth to her. Tom comes to her rescue and the sheriff (Steve Clark) and a posse capture the outlaws.

The cast is the best aspect of THE LARAMIE KID, one of

nineteen features cowboy star Tom Tyler made for distributor William Steiner between 1934 and 1936. Especially good are Al Ferguson as the treacherous banker, Murdock MacQuarrie as the heroine's father, and silent screen comedian Snub Pollard as the jailbird.

THE LAST BULLET see RUN OF THE ARROW

THE LAST DAYS OF FRANK AND JESSE JAMES (NBC-TV, 2/16/86) C 100 mins.

Executive producer, Joe Cates; producer, Phillip Cates; director, William A. Graham; teleplay, William Stratton; music, Paul Chihara; stunt coordinator, Mike Eledsoe; makeup, Norma Gerson; costume designer, Faye Sloan; production designer, David Gropman; set decorator, Leslie Morales; sound, Bill Daly; camera, Tony Imi; editor, Patrick McMahon.

Johnny Cash (Frank James); Kris Kristofferson (Jesse James); Ed Bruce (Major Edwards); Gail Youngs (Anna Young); David Allan Coe (Whiskeyhead Ryan); Andy Stahl (Dick Liddil); June Carter Cash (Mother James); Willie Nelson (General Jo Shelby); Marcia Cross (Sarah Hite); Darrell Wilks (Bob Ford); Margaret Gibson (Zee James); James Sinclair (Charlie Ford); Cherie Elledge Grapes (Martha Bolton); Peter Bradshaw (Wood Hite); Earl Pooderall (Squire Farnum); Jack Barlow (Uncle George Hite); Mac Bennett (Clarence Hite); John Brown (Gentleman); Dan Butler (New York Reporter); Glen Clark (Angry Man); David Cobb (Dr. Samuel); Bruce Darnaham (Sedalia Reporter); Ed Evans (Governor Tom Crittenden); Marshal Falwell (Jim Ward); Buck Ford (William Pinkerton); Donnie Fritts (Jury Foreman); Lecille Harris (Bartender); Mary Jane Harrill (Actress); Dan Hoffman (Conductor Westfall); John Jay Hecker, Jr. (John Phillip); Slick Lawson (Ed Kelly); William Newman (Sheriff Timberlake); John Jackson Routh (Jesse at Age 3); Jimmy Tittle (Jim McDaniels); Denis Tucker (Bud McDaniels); Charlie Williams (Judge).

The adventures of Jesse and Frank James have been recounted on film numerous times and yet another airing of the good and bad times of the famous outlaws seemed a bit superfluous. Overall, though, this TV film sustains interest. With the catchlines "The most wanted men in the West. By the law ... and by the ladies!" the production pegs its appeal to country music stars in the lead assignments. When the ratings were tallied, this telefilm took third place to a 1983 theatrical release, MR. MOM, and the premiere of a Robert Mitchum telefeature, THOMPSON'S LAST RUN.

The movie opens with the shooting of Jesse James (Kris Kristofferson) by psychopathic gang member Bob Ford (Darrel Wilks), and then jumps in flashback to 1877 when Jesse and Frank James (Johnny Cash) decide to retire and lead normal lives. Frank changes his name to Bob Woodson and becomes a farmer while Jesse,

still woman-hungry and greedy for money, calls himself John Davis
Howard and attempts domesticity. The two, however, cannot shake
the outlaw life and soon re-form their gang and continue their lawless activities until Jesse is killed, although loyalty by gang members saves Frank's hide.

Judith Crist in TV Guide labels the film "a rich and illuminating
story" and Daily Variety judged, "Vidpic clearly shows the two men
and their accomplices were not heroes, but their story remains a part
of Americana. As dramatic fodder, the two outlaws steal the show."
Kris Kristofferson is more than passable as Jesse while fellow country
music stars Willie Nelson, Ed Bruce, and David Allan Coe all contrib-
ute finely etched cameo appearances. The most embarrassing performances are turned in by stilted Johnny Cash and his wife, June
Carter Cash, who "portrays" the James boys' one-armed mother.

THE LAST BULLET see RUN OF THE ARROW

THE LAST HARD MEN (Twentieth Century-Fox, 1976) C 103 mins.

Executive producer, William Belasco; producers, Walter Seltzer,
Russell Thacher; director, Andrew V. McLaglen; based on the novel
Gun Down by Brian Garfield; screenplay, Guerdon Trueblood; music,
Jerry Goldsmith; art director, Edward Carfagno; set decorator, Bob
Signorelli; assistant director, Jack Roe; stunt coordinator, Joe
Canutt; sound, Don Bassman, William Teague; camera, Duke Callag-
han; editor, Fred Chulack.

Charlton Heston (Sam Burgade); James Coburn (Zach Provo);
Barbara Hershey (Susan Burgade); Jorge Rivero (Cesar Menendez);
Michael Parks (Sheriff Noel Nye); Larry Wilcox (Mike Shelby); Mor-
gan Paull (Portugee Shiraz); Thalmus Rasulala (George Weed); Bob
Donner (Lee Roy Tucker); John Quade (Will Gant); Christopher
Mitchum (Hal Brickman).

Years earlier, famous lawman Sam Burgade (Charlton Heston)
was the cause of outlaw Zach Provo's (James Coburn) wife's death
during a shoot-out. Vowing revenge, Provo escapes from prison
and forms a gang composed of Cesar Menendez (Jorge Rivero),
Mike Shelby (Larry Wilcox), Portugee Shiraz (Morgan Paull), George
Weed (Thalmus Rasulala), Lee Roy Tucker (Bob Donner), and Will
Gant (John Quade). To provoke the wrath of the now-retired
Burgade, Provo abducts and sexually misuses his daughter Susan
(Barbara Hershey). Young Sheriff Nye (Michael Parks), who re-
gards Burgade as a relic from the past, still enlists the man's help
and together they rescue Susan and bring in the outlaws.

Like THE SHOOTIST (q.v.) from the same year, THE LAST
HARD MEN examines the changing picture of the West, here contrasting old-time lawman Burgade and the newer-type lawman as
represented by Sheriff Nye in their combat with traditional outlaw
Provo and his gang of misfits. All of the characters depicted here

are tough and believable, especially Barbara Hershey as the atypical heroine, a self-reliant young woman who realizes her fate rests primarily in her own hands and that she cannot overly depend on rescue from her father or the law.

With well-defined characterizations, in-depth direction by Andrew V. McLaglen, and exciting stunt coordination by Joe Canutt, the film evolves as quite an entertaining enterprise. Like most Westerns (and other genre films) of the 1970s, the movie is quite violent. Variety defended this, stating, "Though the violence is disturbing, it is acceptable in context as a reflection of survival ethics among hard-boiled western characters, viewed with relative realism and lack of sentimentality."

LAST OF THE MOHICANS (Shick Sunn Classics/NBC-TV, 11/23/77)
    C 100 mins.

Executive producer, Charles E. Sellier, Jr.; producer, Robert Stambler; director, James L. Conway; based on the novel by James Fenimore Cooper; teleplay, Stephen Lord; music, Bob Summers; art director, Charles Bennett; camera, Henning Schellerup; editors, Jim Webb, Steve Michael.

Steve Forrest (Hawkeye); Ned Romero (Chingachgook); Andrew Prine (Major Heyward); Don Shanks (Uncas); Robert Tessier (Magua); Jane Actman (Alice Morgan); Michele Marsh (Cora Morgan); Robert Easton (David Gamut); Whit Bissell (General Webb); and Dehl Berti, John G. Bishop, Beverly Rowland, Coleman Lord.

Films made from James Fenimore Cooper's 1841 novel Last of the Mohicans were detailed in the Base Volume, but since then, a new version of the classic tale has appeared, released by Schick Sunn Classics as part of its "Classics Illustrated" teleseries. When shown on NBC-TV, the film ran 100 minutes, but it was trimmed by 10 minutes when syndicated.

Frontiersman Natty Bumpo, known as Hawkeye (Steve Forrest), teams with his Indian blood brothers Chingachgook (Ned Romero) and Uncas (Don Shanks) in helping a British officer (Andrew Prine) escort two comely young women (Jane Actman, Michele Marsh) through the wilderness to a frontier settlement. Along the way they are threatened by the evil Magua (Robert Tessier) and his Mohawk warriors, but eventually the group reaches its destination.

The reviews for this telefeature were mixed. Movies on TV (1986) questioned, "Do you need another inferior version of James Fenimore Cooper's classic frontier yarn about Hawkeye and his Indian friends?" while TV Movies (1986) thought it "Sturdy ... with [Steve] Forrest fine as the stalwart Hawkeye. Above average." The telefilm resulte din a sequel, THE DEERSLAYER, q.v., the next year. Again produced by Schick Sunn Classics in its "Classics Illustrated" series, the TV film re-teamed Steve Forrest and Ned Romero while James L. Conway, director of the initial film, was co-executive producer.

Steve Forrest and Don Shanks (right) in THE LAST OF THE MO-
HECANS (1977).

Jean Heather and Gene Autry in THE LAST ROUND-UP (1947).

THE LAST ROUND-UP (Columbia, 1947) 77 mins.

Producer, Armand Schaefer; director, John English; story, Jack Townley; screenplay, Townley, Earle Snell; music supervisor, Paul Mertz; songs: Johnny Burke and James Monaco; Allan Roberts and Doris Fisher; David Kapp; music director, Mischa Bakaleinikoff; assistant director, Earl Bellamy; art director, Harold MacArthur; set decorator, Frank Tuttle; sound, Hugh McDowell; camera, William Bradford, editor, Aaron Stell.

Gene Autry (Himself); Jean Heather (Carol); Ralph Morgan (Mason); Carol Thurston (Lydia Henry); Mark Daniels (Matt Mason); Bobby Blake (Mike); Russ Vincent (Jeff Henry); George "Shug" Fisher (Marvin); Trevor Bardette (Indian Chief); Lee Bennett (Goss); John Halloran (Taylor); Sandy Sanders (Jim); Roy Gordon (Smith); Silverheels Smith (Sam Luther); Frances Rey (Cora Luther); Bob Cason (Carter); The Texas Rangers (Themselves); Champion, Jr. (The Horse); and Dale Van Sickle, Billy Wilkinson, Ed Piel, Sr., George Carleton, Don Kay Reynolds, Nolan Leary, Ted Adams, Jack Baxley, Steve Clark, Chuck Hamilton, Bud Osborne, Frankie Marvin, Kernan Cripps, Jose Alvarado, J. W. Cody, Iron Eyes Cody, Blackie Whiteford, Robert Walker, Virginia Carroll, Arline Arhuletta, Louis Crosby, Brian O'Hara, Rodd Redwing, Alex Montaya.

Gene Autry returned from active duty in World War II and in 1946 made a quartet of Republic films before switching allegiance to Columbia Pictures, where his initial entry was THE LAST ROUND-UP. With its use of action footage from ARIZONA (1940), the movie was too long at 77 minutes and on the arid side, with the star very stiff, although the movie does include an amusing television sequence. The film relied more on drama than music--something not done by Autry in a long time--and genre followers consider it one of his better post-war vehicles.

Government agent Gene Autry (Himself) tries to relocate an Indian tribe so that an aqueduct can be built to irrigate their presently worthless lands and make them suitable for crops. Crooked land baron Mason (Ralph Morgan) tries to halt the project, which will interfere with his scheme to take over open range lands. He attempts to start an Indian uprising but is thwarted by Autry.

Some sources claim THE LAST ROUND-UP is Gene Autry's favorite of his 93 screen appearances.

LAW OF THE LASH (Produces Releasing Corp., 1947) 53 mins.

Producer, Jerry Thomas; director, Ray Taylor; screenplay, William L. Notte; assistant director, T. O. Collings; set decorator, Louis Diage; sound, Glen Glenn; camera, Robert Cline; editor, Norman A. Cerf, Hugh Winn.

Al "Lash" LaRue (The Cheyenne Kid); Al "Fuzzy" St. John (Fuzzy Q. Jones); Lee Roberts (Lefty); Mary Scott (Jane Hilton); Jack O'Shea (Decker); Charles King (Sheriff); Cirl Matthews

(Blackie); Matty Roubert (Pee Wee); John Elliott (Dad Hilton);
Charles Whittaker (Bart); Ted French (Smitty); Richard Cramer
(Bartender); Brad Slaven (Sam).

After a few small parts in films, Al LaRue caused a sensation
portraying the good/bad man character of the Cheyenne Kid in
PRC's SONG OF OLD WYOMING (1945), a Cinecolor opus starring
Eddie Dean. LaRue again supported Eddie Dean in THE CARAVAN
TRAIL and WILD WEST (both 1946) before PRC launched him in his
own movie series; he was billed first as Al "Lash" LaRue and then
simply as Lash LaRue. The new star (LAW OF THE LASH) was his
initial starring vehicle) quickly developed a loyal screen following
and after PRC's demise in 1947 he signed with producer Ron Ormond,
who issued his films first through Screen Guild and then Realart
before the series came to a halt in 1953. LaRue went into television
and then toured with various circuses before drifting in and out of
show business. In the mid-1980s, he made a dramatic comeback as
the star of low-budget science fiction thrillers.
     U.S. Marshal The Cheyenne Kid (Al "Lash" LaRue), along
with his cohort Fuzzy Q. Jones (Al St. John), arrives in Temekula,
where outlaws are running off citizens and taking over the small
town. Cheyenne and Fuzzy aid the locals in getting resettled and
go after the gang, led by crook decker (Jack O'Shea). The duo
brings the villains to justice and Cheyenne wins the love of a pretty
settler (Mary Scott).
     To be noted is that LAW OF THE LASH cast perennial Western
film bad man Charles King in a good guy role. The movie also
amply demonstrates star LaRue's agility with a bullwhip, which gave
him the nickname Lash. Finally, all of LaRue's starring roles were
with Al St. John, the famous silent movie comedian who had created
the screen role of Fuzzy Q. Jones in the late 1930s while working
with Fred Scott at Spectrum Pictures and had carried it over to
PRC where he costarred with such screen cowpokes as Bob Steele,
George Houston, and Buster Crabbe.

LAW OF THE NORTHWEST (Columbia, 1943) 57 mins.

     Producer, Jack Fier; director, William Berke; screenplay,
Luci Ward; art directors, Lionel Banks, Arthur Royce; set decorator,
James M. Crowe; assistant director, William O'Connor; sound, Charles
Althouse; camera, Benjamin Kline; editor, Jerome Thoms.
     Charles Starrett (Mountie Steve King); Shirley Patterson
(Michel Darcy); Arthur Hunnicutt (Arkansas); Stanley Brown (Neal
Clayton); Douglas Leavitt (George Bradley); Donald Curtis (Frank
Mason); Douglas Drake (Paul Darcy); Davison Clark (Tom Clayton);
Reginald Barlow (Jean Darcy).

     Mountie Steve King (Charles Starrett) and his pal Arkansas
(Arthur Hunnicutt) aid a contractor (Stanley Brown) in the north
woods who must complete a road so it can be used to transport

minerals and materials required for the war effort. His construction
efforts, however, are sabotaged by a dishonest contractor (Douglas
Leavitt) who wants to discredit his rival. The mounties put a stop
to the man's illegal activities and get the roadway completed on
schedule.

Another in the long-running Charles Starrett Columbia Pictures series, this one has the cowboy hero back in the saddle as
a Mountie, a part he played on and off in the first years of his
studio actioners. Deftly interpolating contemporary war effort needs
into its plot, the movie is highlighted by Benjamin Kline's attractive
outdoor cinematography. He would soon be promoted to be the
series director.

LAW OF THE PAMPAS see OUTLAWS OF THE DESERT

LAW OF THE WEST (Sono Art-World Wide, 1932) 55 mins.

Producer, Trem Carr; director/story/screenplay, Robert North
Bradbury; sound, John Stransky; camera, Archie Stout, Will Cline;
editor, Charles Hunt.

Bob Steele (Bob Carruthers); Nancy Drexel (Sally Tracy);
Ed Brady (Lee Morgan); Hank Bell (Dad Carruthers); Charles West
(Clem Tracy); Earl Dwire (Butch); Dick Dickinson (Buck); Rose
Plummer (Mrs. Carruthers); Frank Ellis (Deputy).

A young boy is kidnapped from his lawman father (Ed Brady)
by Clem Tracy, the head (Charles West) of an outlaw gang. Eighteen
years later the young man (Bob Steele) is a member of the gang and
Clem plans to use him for revenge by having the youth murder his
own father; the boy is led to believe that the outlaw is his dad.
The plot is foiled when the young man romances a pretty girl (Nancy
Drexel) and eventually wants to settle down and rid himself of a
life of crime. He also identifies his real father and saves him from
the outlaws.

Although this Bob Steele action entry is full of typical fights,
chases, and shootings, it contains quite a bit of melodrama and
emotional interplay not always associated with the "B" oater. Bob
Steele, an excellent performer, handles both aspects of this offering
in good form. The Film Daily trade paper approved: "Worthy
Western [which] gets over usual human interest punch along with
plenty action and fight stuff."

The movie was quite topical in its early scenes of the young
boy being abducted by outlaws, as the Lindburgh kidnapping case
was prominent at the time. The famous crime took place March 1,
1932 and by the end of the month this Trem Carr production was
playing in theatres.

LEATHERSTOCKING see THE DEERSLAYER

THE LEGACY OF THE INCAS see THE TREASURE OF SILVER LAKE

THE LEGEND OF THE LONE RANGER (Universal/Associated Film
Distribution, 1981) C 98 mins.

Executive producer, Martin Starger; producer, Walter Coblenz;
associate producer, Linda Francis; director, William A. Fraker;
based on stories and characters created by George W. Trendle, Fran
Striker; screenplay, Ivan Goff, Ben Roberts, Michael Kane, William
Roberts; adaptor, Jerry Berloshon; music, John Barry; production
designer, Albert Brenner; art director, David M. Haber; set
decorator, Phillip Abramson; costume designer, Noel Taylor, as-
sistant director, Charles Okun; sound, William Randall; camera,
Laszlo Kovacs; editor, Thomas Stanford.
Klinton Spilsbury (The Lone Ranger); Michael Horse (Tonto);
Christopher Lloyd (Cavendish); Matt Clark (Sheriff Wiatt); Juanin
Clay (Amy Striker); Jason Roberds (President Grant); John Bennett
Perry (Dan Reid); David Hayward (Collins); John Hart (Lucas
Striker); Richard Farnsworth (Wild Bill Hickok); Lincoln Tate
(General Custer); Ted Flicker (Buffalo Bill Cody); Marc Gilpin
(Young John Reid); Patrick Montoya (Young Tonto); James Keach
(Dubbed Voice of The Lone Ranger).

THE LEGEND OF THE LONE RANGER was doomed from the
start. Fans of the series became enraged in the late 1970s when
the Wrather Corporation, owner of the rights to the Fran Striker
character, went to court to force Clayton Moore, who played the
character on TV from 1949 to 1952 and 1954 to 1957, as well as in
two feature films (see B/V), to abandon the Lone Ranger trademark
mask in personal appearances. The corporation's "epic" film soon
went into production, but was plagued with all kinds of problems,
ranging from an ever-growing budget to the need for James Keach
to dub the hero's dialogue, to bad publicity surrounding the film's
star, Klinton Spilsbury. Added to this was the protest staged by
Clayton Moore's fans about his treatment by the Wrather Corporation, and the courts and the loyalists threatened boycotts of the
finished feature. When the Western was finally unveiled in 1981 it
was a financial bust, with the Wrather Corporation losing millions
(some say between 20 and 30 million dollars--making it the second
biggest loser of the decade behind HEAVEN'S GATE, q.v.), and
the film was quickly forgotten. In 1985 Clayton Moore and the
Wrather Corporation came to a settlement and the star resumed wearing the mask in personal appearances, never having lost the public's belief that he was and IS the only Lone Ranger.
The narrative opens with the retelling of the childhood of the
Lone Ranger and how he adopted the mask and teamed with Indian
sidekick Tonto (Michael Horse). The story shifts to how the two
saddle pals oppose a corrupt railroad baron (Christopher Lloyd) who
dreams of ruling Texas and has a mad plan to kidnap President Grant
(Jason Robards) while he is on a Mexican hunting trip with such

Klinton Spilsbury and Michael Horse in THE LEGEND OF THE LONE
RANGER (1981).

notables as Wild Bill Hickok, Buffalo Bill Cody, and General George
Armstrong Custer. The Lone Ranger and Tonto thwart the evil
machinations and save the President, as well as Texas.

THE LEGEND OF THE LONE RANGER is mired down by its
many deficiencies. Running just under 100 minutes, the feature
seems endless. So much footage was shot and reshot that the story
gets lost somewhere on the cutting room floor and the film crawls
along for fifty minutes before the Lone Ranger ever puts on his
mask, leaving the last half of the feature to relate its mundane adventure. While Laszlo Kovacs' cinematography is attractive, William
A. Fraker's (who contributed the near classic MONTE WALSH, q.v.,
a decade before) direction is almost non-existent. While some of the
stunt work and action sequences are quite satisfying, they have little
to do with the context of the feature and seemed spliced into the
story-line arbitrarily. The less said the better about Klinton Spilsbury's performance, which ranges from stalwart to camp to comic
without being successful at any of these ranges. One-time TV Lone
Ranger John Hart (he played the part on TV between 1954 and 1956)
has a small role in the proceedings, while Jason Robards attempts to
breathe life into the production with a hammy, overblown stab at
playing Grant.

Edward Arnold, Nelson Eddy, Charles Butterworth, and Virginia
Bruce in LET FREEDOM RING (1939).

LET FREEDOM RING (Metro-Goldwyn-Mayer, 1939) 85 mins.

Producer, Harry Rapf; director, Jack Conway; screenplay,
Ben Hecht; songs: Edward Heyman and Sigmund Romberg; Chet
Forrest, Bob Wright, and R. Drigo; Leon and Otis Rene; Foster
Carling and Phil Ohman; camera, Sidney Wagner; montage, John
Hoffman; editor, Frederick Y. Smith.
Nelson Eddy (Steve Logan); Virginia Bruce (Maggie Adams);
Victor McLaglen (Chris Mulligan); Lionel Barrymore (Thomas Logan);
Edward Arnold (Jim Knox); Guy Kibbee (David Bronson); Charles
Butterworth (The Mackerel); H. B. Warner (Rutledge); Raymond
Walburn (Underwood); Dick Rich (Bumper Jackson); Trevor Bar-
dette (Gagan); George F. Hayes (Pop Wilkie); Louis Jean Heydt
(Ned Wilkie); Sarah Padden (Ma Logan); Eddie Dunn (Curly); C. E.
Anderson (Sheriff Hicks).

In the late 1800s, crusading lawyer Steve Logan (Nelson Eddy)
returns home after graduating from Harvard University and finds

that local ranchers, including his crippled father (Lionel Barrymore), who leads them, are being forced to sell their lands to corrupt land baron Jim Knox (Edward Arnold). To infiltrate Knox's organization, Steve pretends to join forces with him. In doing so he alienates his dad, his friends, and his sweetheart (Virginia Bruce). He secretly starts a newspaper to discredit Knox and is aided by sly saloon pianist Mackerel (Charles Butterworth) and a dying gambler (H. B. Warner). Eventually Steve brings about Knox's downfall, but not before engaging in hand-to-hand combat with the latter's railroad gang boss Chris Mulligan (Victor McLaglen). With the menace under control, Steve is free to settle down with his lady love.

LET FREEDOM RING, filled with the usual Metro-Goldwyn-Mayer glossy production values, was Nelson Eddy's seventh starring vehicle and one of his most successful solo screen enterprises. The stalwart baritone appeared in several pioneer and Western features, such as NAUGHTY MARIETTA (1935)--which brought him to stardom as Jeanette Macdonald's singing partner--THE GIRL OF THE GOLDEN WEST (1938, see B/V), NEW MOON (1940), KNICKERBOCKER HOLI-DAY (1940), and NORTHWEST OUTPOST (1947, q.v.). In LET FREEDOM RING Eddy contributes one of his best screen characteri-zations and is also in top voice in a number of songs, including "Love's Serenade," "Dusty Road," "When Irish Eyes Are Smiling," and "America."

The feature was distributed at a time when patriotism was on the rise and greatly benefitted from public sentiment, although it was a topnotch, if top-heavy, production on its own. As Variety assessed, "LET FREEDOM RING is momentous. It's packed with b.o. [box-office] potentialities and audience appeal."

LIGHTNING RAIDERS (Producers Releasing Corp., 1945) 60 mins.

Producer, Sigmund Neufeld; director, Sam Newfield; screen-play, Elmer Clifton; camera, Jack Greenhalgh; editor, Holbrook N. Todd.

Buster Crabbe (Billy Carson); Al "Fuzzy" St. John (Fuzzy Q. Jones); Mady Laurence (Jane); Henry Hall (Wright); Steve Darrell (Hayden); I. Stanford Jolley (Kane); Karl Hackett (Murray); Roy Brent (Phillips); Marin Sais (Mrs. Murray); Al Ferguson (Lorrin).

Outlaws hold up a stagecoach and steal papers which make Fuzzy Q. Jones (Al St. John) a big land owner. Billy Carson (Buster Crabbe) arrives and he and Fuzzy recover the mail from the bandits and investigate the hold-up. The town's banker Hayden (Steve Darrell) leads the gang which steals mail in order to gain properties for the banker, who then forecloses on local ranchers. The crooks try to pin the robberies on Billy and Fuzzy but they turn the tables on the gang and capture them, proving Hayden's guilt by blowing up his office safe and exposing the evidence which sends the culprits to jail.

Coming toward the end of the lengthy PRC "Billy Carson"

series, LIGHTNING RAIDERS is a cheap but pleasing feature, high-lighted by an amusing scene of Fuzzy accidentally swallowing Mexican jumping beans. Marin Sais, once a genre leading lady, but now maturing, was now playing supporting parts like her Mrs. Murray role here.

LIGHTNING RANGE see THE BOSS COWBOY

LIGHTS OF OLD SANTA FE (Republic, 1944) 78 mins.

Associate producer, Harry Grey; director, Frank McDonald; screenplay, Gordon Kahn, Bob Williams; music, Morton Scott; choreography, Larry Ceballos; songs: Tim Spencer; Sunny Skylar and Gabriel Ruiz; Ken Carson; Jack Elliott; Bob Nolan; camera, Reggie Lanning; editor, Ralph Dixon.

Roy Rogers (Himself); George "Gabby" Hayes (Gabby Whit-taker); Dale Evans (Marjorie Brooks); Lloyd Corrigan (Marty Mal-zely); Richard Powers (Frank Madden); Claire Du Brey (Rosie McGerk); Arthur Loft (Bill Wetherbee); Roy Barcroft (Ken Fergu-son); Lucien Littlefield (The Judge); Sam Flint (The Sheriff); Bob Nolan and the Sons of the Pioneers (Themselves); Trigger (The Horse).

Gabby Whittaker and Marjorie Brooks (Dale Evans) run a failing rodeo; their rival Frank Madden (Richard Powers) has a successful one and wants to buy out Marjorie. Madden dislikes his musical acts--Roy Rogers and the Sons of the Pioneers (Themselves) --and fires them, whereupon Gabby gives them employment. On the eve of her marriage to Madden, Roy proves that Madden is trying to sabotage Marjorie's rodeo and Madden is arrested. Promoter Bill Wetherbee (Arthur Loft) buys out Madden and he and Marjorie com-bine their shows into a single successful rodeo.

LIGHTS OF OLD SANTA FE is only a fair film in the Roy Rogers' Republic canon, although it does possess a beautiful title song and a very fine performance by Richard Powers (himself a one-time genre star billed as Tom Keene) as the villainous Madden. Typical of this period of Roy Rogers' films, this production has no real dramatic climax, but rather a big rodeo/musical finale.

THE LONE RANGER see THE LEGEND OF THE LONE RANGER

THE LONE RIDER IN TEXAS JUSTICE (Producers Releasing Corp., 1942) 58 mins.

Producer, Sigmund Neufeld; director, Sam Newfield; screen-play, Steve Braxton [Sam Robins]; songs, Johnny Lange and Lew Porter; editor, Holbrook N. Todd.

George Houston (Tom Cameron); Al "Fuzzy" St. John (Fuzzy Q. Jones); Dennis Moore (Smokey); Wanda McKay (Kate Stewart); Claire Rochelle (Nora); Karl Hackett (Stewart); Curley Dresden, Steve Clark, Ray Davis (Ranchers); and Dirk Thane, Horace B. Carpenter, Frank Ellis, Merrill McCormack, Ray Jones.

Opera singer George Houston, who was Wild Bill Hickok in Grand National's FRONTIER SCOUT (1938), starred in eleven "Lone Rider" films for PRC. While these productions were hurt by the studio's makeshift production values, they were lifted by Houston's able acting and fine singing and by Al St. John's comedy antics in his continuing characterization of Fuzzy Q. Jones. THE LONE RIDER IN TEXAS JUSTICE is a good example of the series. It is fast-paced and exciting, despite a complicated plot. Wanda McKay makes a comely heroine and, in an ironic bit of casting, one-time genre leading lady Claire Rochelle is seen as the villain.
    The Lone Rider, Tom Cameron (George Houston), and his pal Fuzzy Q. Jones (Al St. John) try to buy Stewart's (Karl Hackett) ranch and learn that the man is being framed as a cattle rustler. They assist their sheriff friend Smokey (Dennis Moore) in the case and Tom is mistaken for the rustler. Later Tom and Fuzzy learn that Nora (Claire Rochelle) is the widow of the real rustler and that she is the gang leader, whose members pose as padres. Tom solves the caper, saving the Stewart ranch for daughter Kate (Wanda McKay) following her dad's murder.

LONE STAR (Metro-Goldwyn-Mayer, 1952) 94 mins.

Producer, Z. Wayne Griffin; director, Vincent Sherman; based on the story by Borden Chase; screen story, Howard Estabrook; screenplay, Chase; music, David Buttolph; art director, Cedric Gibbons, Hans Peters; camera, Harold Rosson; editor, Ferris Webster.
    Clark Gable (Devereaux Burke); Ava Gardner (Martha Ronda); Broderick Crawford (Thomas Craden); Lionel Barrymore (President Andrew Jackson); Beulah Bondi (Minniver Bryan); Ed Begley (Senator Anthony Demmett); William Farnum (Senator Tom Crockett); Lowell Gilmore (Captain Elliott); Moroni Olsen (Sam Houston); Russell Simpson (Senator Maynard Cole); William Conrad (Mizette); James Burke (Luther Kilgore); Ralph Reed (Bud Yoakum); Ric Roman (Curau); Victor Sutherland (President Anson Jones); Jonathan Cott (Ben McCulloch); Charles Cane (Mayhew); Nacho Galindo (Vincente); Trevor Bardette (Sid Yoakum); Harry Woods (Dellman); Dudley Sadler (Ashbel Smith); George Hamilton (Noah); Roy Gordon, Stanley Andrews, William E. Green (Men); Earle Hodgins (Windy Barton); Warren MacGregor (Rancher); Rex Lease, Davison Clark (Senators); Chief Yowlachie (Indian Chief); Emmett Lynn (Josh); Tony Roux (Chico).

In the years after the landmark GONE WITH THE WIND (1939),

Clark Gable, Ava Gardner, Broderick Crawford in LONE STAR
(1952).

megastar Clark Gable's screen career had its ups and downs, but
one of his better showcases came in the lusty and actionful LONE
STAR, a delightful pseudo-historical drama with Gable at his best
as a Texas freedom fighter combatting his rival, Broderick Crawford.
Unfortunately the screen teaming of Gable and Ava Gardner amounted
to little; the feminine star had only a minor role as window dressing
(but did have the opportunity to sing "Lovers Are Meant to Cry").
The film was filled with historical inaccuracies such as having Andrew
Jackson as president in 1845, when he left office in 1837. Made at
a time when Hollywood was combatting the "Red" purge, Borden
Chase's script is ultra-patriotic and high-falutin. Director Vincent
Sherman was not always able to rise above the lavish production
mountings and keep the story rolling at a heady pace.

President Andrew Jackson (Lionel Barrymore) assigns adventurer Devereaux Burke (Clark Gable) to go to Texas and convince
Sam Houston (Moroni Olsen) that the independent state should join
the U.S. When Indians attack Burke's party, he is joined in the
fight by Thomas Craden (Broderick Crawford), who opposes annexation because he secretly plots to become the dictator of Texas. The
Indians are staved off, but when Craden learns Burke's plan, he
sets a trap for him. Meanwhile Burke finds Houston making a treaty

with local Indians and tells him of his order from his old friend
Jackson. On his way to Austin, Burke is ambushed by Craden's
men, but escapes. In Austin, he meets lovely Martha Ronda (Ava
Gardner), the local newspaper editor, who has sided with Craden
because she thinks Houston opposes annexation. Burke and Craden
become rivals for the woman as well as for Texas, but when Craden's
true plans are learned, Martha turns against him and aids Burke in
defeating the would-be dictator.

Variety noted that LONE STAR has a "strong star-name trio
and a good action plot" while the New York Times offered, "The
picture moves consistently, under Vincent Sherman's direction. For
all the fanciful trimmings of Borden Chase's script, it packs punch,
color and tang.... Gable, with plenty of space to move around in,
was never Gabler."

LONE STAR PIONEERS (Columbia, 1939) 54 mins.

Producer, Larry Darmour; director, Joseph Levering; screenplay, Nate Gatzert; camera, James S. Brown, Jr.; editor, Dwight
Caldwell.

Bill Elliott (Pat Barrett); Dorothy Gulliver (Virginia); Charles
Whittaker (Buck); Charles King (Pete); Lee Shumway (Bill); Budd
Buster (Crittenden); Jack Ingram (Cole); Harry Harvey (Eph);
Buzz Barton (Chuck); Frank LaRue (Joe); and David Sharpe, Frank
Ellis, Budd Buster, Kit Guard, Merrill McCormack, Jack Rockwell,
Tex Palmer.

In Texas after the Civil War, guerrillas raid supply wagons
and federal marshal Pat Barrett (Bill Elliott) is sent to stop the
lawlessness. He masquerades as outlaw Bob Cantrell and joins the
gang who hold a rancher (Budd Buster), his daughter (Dorothy
Gulliver) and son (David Sharpe) prisoner on their homestead,
which the gang is using as its headquarters. When the gang attempts to rob a wagon train, the lawman and his pal Cole (Jack
Ingram) arrive with a posse and the outlaws are captured.

LONE STAR PIONEERS is an early series starring effort for
Bill Elliott and the Larry Darmour-produced oater is well made but
has a draggy plot. Elliott would go on to make much more actionful
films in this series, and later for Republic. An offbeat bit of casting is that of Jack Ingram. Usually a genre bad man, here he is
the hero's sidekick.

THE LONESOME TRAIL see OKLAHOMA CYCLONE

THE LONG RIDERS (United Artists, 1980) C 100 mins.

Executive producers, James Keach, Stacy Keach, producer,
Tim Zinnemann; director, Walter Hill; screenplay, Bill Bryden,

Steven Philip Smith, Stacy Keach, James Keach; music, Ry Cooder;
production designer, Jack T. Collis; art director, Peter Romero;
set decorator, Richard Goddard; costumes, Tom Bronson; assistant
director, Peter Gries; sound, James Webb, Chris McLaughlin;
camera, Ric Waite; editors, David Holden, Freeman Davies.

David Carradine (Cole Younger); Keith Carradine (Jim
Younger); Robert Carradine (Bob Younger); James Keach (Jesse
James); Stacy Keach (Frank James); Dennis Quaid (Ed Miller);
Randy Quaid (Clell Miller); Kevin Bropohy (John Younger); Harry
Carey, Jr. (George Arthur); Christopher Guest (Charlie Ford);
Nicholas Guest (Bob Ford); Shelby Leverington (Anne Ralston);
Felice Orlandi (Mr. Reddick); Pamela Reed (Belle Starr); James
Remar (Sam Starr); Fran Ryan (Mrs. Samuel); Savannah Smith
(Zee); Amy Stryker (Beth); James Whitmore, Jr. (Mr. Rixley);
John Bottoms (Mortician); West Buchanan (McCorkindale).

Yet another screen retelling of the sordid exploits of the
Younger-James gang is detailed in this visually gripping Western.
Director Walter Hill brought this property to the screen with great
care for period authenticity, although its historical merits are a
bit dubious. The focal interest and prime box-office gimmick is
the casting of acting brothers in the roles of real-life outlaw siblings. Also the film provides some viewer interest with the interplay between the various famous outlaws, the origins of their
criminal activities as a result of their Civil War experiences, their
relationships with assorted women, the actual planning and execution
of their heists, and finally, their nearly uncanny knack for eluding
the law.

The film opens long after the James and Younger brothers
have teamed to form their famous outlaw band, associated with the
Miller and Ford brothers. While the outlaws form an uneasy alliance
with Cole Younger (David Carradine) as their leader, it is Jesse
James (James Keach) who rises to prominence as the gang's notori-
ety--greatly propelled by the press--grows. The gang also has
good luck in fending off the law as they engage in a series of robberies. Finally they decide to rob the bank of the peaceful community of Northfield, Minnesota. But the locals are alerted to their
whereabouts and when the robbery takes place, the citizens turn on
them. Many of the gang are killed, but Jesse and Frank (Stacy
Keach) escape. Jesse is later gunned down by gang member turn-
coat Bob Ford (Nicholas Guest).

Variety reported, "Attempted by young hands, the pic is
striking in several ways ... but narrative is episodic in the extreme and disparate artistic qualities fail to completely jell into satisfactory whole." Phil Hardy in The Film Encyclopedia: The Western
(1983) observed, "...if the film's intentions are unclear and masked
in the complicated storyline of deceit and betrayal ... stylistically
the film is a triumph. Hill, for the first time directing a script not
written by himself, remoulds his material to produce an almost ab-
stract film, beautiful looking, but very thin."

LOST RANCH (Victory, 1939) 57 mins.

Producer/director, Sam Katzman; screenplay, Basil Dickey; camera, Bill Hyer; editor, Holbrook N. Todd.
Tom Tyler (Wade); Jeanne Martel (Rita Carroll); Marjorie Beebe (Minnie); Howard Bryant (Happy); Ted Lorch (Merkle); Slim Whittaker (Sheriff); Forrest Taylor (Garson); Lafe McKee (Carroll); Roger Williams (Terry).

Pretty Rita (Jeanne Martel) and her friend (Marjorie Beebe) come west to find Rita's missing father (Lafe McKee) and the secret he harbors. The women are attacked by outlaws but are saved by lawman Tom Wade (Tom Tyler). Later the outlaws knock out Tom and abduct Rita. Tom and his pal Happy (Howard Bryant) track the girl, who leaves a trail of beads as a clue. At the outlaw hide-out, her prison father tells her the gang are smugglers. To throw the law off the track, the gang leader, Garson (Forrest Taylor), lets Rita write a letter to her friend claiming she is all right. Rita, however, puts a code in the message and when Tom breaks the code, he follows Rita's trail and finds the hideout. She and her father are rescued, and Garson and his gang are captured.
LOST RANCH was one of eight films Tom Tyler did for low-budget producer Sam Katzman's Victory Pictures. In most of the group, he played Tom Wade, an agent for the Cattlemen's Protective Association. All of these efforts were shoddy--this one was even directed by Katzman, one of the few films actually helmed by the prolific penny-pinching filmmaker. The movie takes place mostly outdoors (which saved on building interior sets) and action is prevalent from start to finish. Here Tyler is more of an athlete than an actor, while his then-wife, Jeanne Martel, is quite comely as the heroine. This Victory series proved to be Tom Tyler's final solo Westerns. He would return often to the genre, but usually in supporting roles, although he did headline Republic's "The Three Mesquiteers" series from 1941 to 1943.

LUCKY BOOTS (Beacon/Equity, 1935) 59 mins.

Producer, Arthur Alexander; director, Al Herman; screenplay, William L. Nolte; camera, William Hagen; editor, Myron Marsh.
Guinn "Big Boy" Williams (Bill Williams); Marion Shilling (Meg Holt); Frank Yaconelli (Frank); Wally Wales (George Holt); Charles K. French (Old John Holt); Tom London (Meeker); Roger Williams (Cal); Gordon Griffith (Mark); Barney Beasley (Pete); Julian Rivero (Pedro); Si Jenks (Cowpoke); and Dick Botiller.

After a Mexican bandit is killed, his treasure is buried on a ranch and outlaw Meeker (Tom London) intends to locate it. Cow-pokes Bill Williams (Guinn "Big Boy" Williams) and Frank (Frank Yaconelli) ride into the area and Bill finds a pair of boots which he keeps, not knowing that they belong to a murdered land owner. The man's daughter Meg (Marion Shilling) and her brother George (Wally Wales) take over the ranch and Bill and Frank are hired as ranch hands. Meeker discovers that the key to the treasure is hidden in one of the boots and he attempts to steal them, but Bill finds the clue and digs up the treasure. Meeker and his gang chase Bill and Frank to the ranch house, where they are captured by the law. Bill and Meg pursue their courtship.

Originally called GUN PLAY, this poverty row oater was one of a brief series starring Guinn "Big Boy" Williams and released through Beacon. Considering its slight budget, the movie is a decent one, highlighted by a good story and a pleasing star. Usually a sidekick comedy relief during the sound era in "B" Westerns and a fine character player in "A" productions, Guinn "Big Boy" Williams starred in some three dozen silent sagebrush yarns for bottom-of-the-barrel outfits like DiLorenzo and Aywon.

MACHO CALLAHAN (Avco Embassy, 1970) C 99 mins.

Producers, Martin C. Schute, Bernard L. Kowalski; director, Kowalski; story, Richard Carr; screenplay, Clifford Newton Gould; music, Pat Williams; production designer, Ted Marshall; assistant directors, Jesus Marin, Manuel Munoz; sound, Jose Carles; camera, Gerald Fisher; editors, Frank Mazzola, Fabien Todjmann, Jerry Taylor.

David Janssen (Macho Callahan); Jean Seberg (Alexandra Mountford); Lee J. Cobb (Duffy); James Booth (Harry Wheeler); Pedro Armendariz, Jr. (Juan Fernandez); David Carradine (David Mountford); Richard Anderson (Senior Officer); Matt Clark (Jailer); Diane Ladd (Girl); Richard Evans (Mulvey); Bo Hopkins (Yancy); Robert Morgan (McIntyre).

Held as a prisoner by the Confederates during the Civil War, Macho Callahan (David Janssen) escapes form a prison camp by blowing up the gate. He is determined to eradicate Duffy (Lee J. Cobb), whom he holds responsible for his forced army enlistment and later imprisonment. In a small Texas town, Callahan fights with one-armed Confederate veteran David Mountford (David Carradine) and kills the man while the latter's wife Alexandra (Jean Seberg) watches helplessly. Alexandra offers $1,000 to anyone who will kill Callahan and she meets Duffy, who agrees to help, but Callahan kills him. Alexandra dogs Callahan's trail and hires gambler Harry Wheeler (James Booth) to do the job. Callahan escapes and later, when she corners him, she fails to kill him herself and he rapes her. The woman falls in love with him. Later Wheeler and his gang of bounty hunters overtake Callahan, and he and his friend Juan Fernandez (Pedro Armendariz, Jr.) are murdered, leaving Alexandra to grieve over her second lost love.

With location filming in Mexico, MACHO CALLAHAN is a picturesque and well-made Western which appears to be a Hollywood attempt to incorporate more violence than the then popular Spaghetti

David Janssen and Jean Seberg in MACHO CALLAHAN (1970).

Westerns imported from Europe. The film reeks with mayhem and, despite respectable performances by the leads, soon becomes tiresome in its repeated excursions into brutality, murder, and rape. The film also continued the jinx of American actress Jean Seberg, who failed to establish a foothold in her homeland despite critical success in European-made motion pictures. This was her second Western effort following her failure to create much of an impression in the big-budgeted musical, PAINT YOUR WAGON (see B/V) the year before.

MACKENNA'S GOLD (Columbia, 1969) C 128 mins.

Producers, Carl Foreman, Dmitri Tiomkin; director, J. Lee Thompson; based on the novel by Will Henry; screenplay, Foreman; second unit director, Tom Shaw; assistant director, David Salven; music, Quincy Jones; orchestrator, Leo Shuken, Jack Hayes; song, Jones and Freddie Douglass; production designer, Geoffrey Drake; art directors, Drake, Cary Odell; set decorator, Alfred E. Spencer; stunt co-ordinator, Buzz Henry; costumes, Norma Koch; sound, Derek Frye, William Randall, Jr.; special effects, Geoffrey Drake, Abacus Productions (John Mackey, Bob Cuff), Willis Cook, Larry Butler; camera, Joseph MacDonald; second unit camera, Harold

Wellman; additional camera, Mackey, Don Glouner, Farciot Edouart, Richard Moore; editor, Bill Lenny.

Gregory Peck (MacKenna); Omar Sharif (Colorado); Telly Savalas (Sergeant Tibbs); Camilla Sparv (Inga); Keenan Wynn (Sanchez); Julie Newmar (Hesh-Ke); Ted Cassidy (Hachita); Lee J. Cobb (The Editor); Raymond Massey (The Preacher); Burgess Meredith (The Storekeeper); Anthony Quayle (Older Englishman; Edward G. Robinson (Old Adams); Eduardo Ciannelli (Prairie Dog); Dick Peabody (Avila); Rudy Diaz (Besh); Robert Phillips (Monkey); Shelley Morrison (Pima Squaw); J. Robert Porter (Young Englishman); John Garfield, Jr. (Adams' Boy); Pepe Callahan (Laguna); Madeleine Taylor Holmes (Old Apache Woman); Duke Hobbie (Lieutenant); Victor Jory (Narrator).

Issued at the same time as John Wayn'e Oscar-winning TRUE GRIT (see B/V) and Sergio Leone's ONCE UPON A TIME IN THE WEST (see B/V), MacKENNA'S GOLD was lost in the shuffle between these big-budgeted productions. Despite its expensive mounting and star-studded cast, it was termed only a "standard western" (Variety) when released, and now has almost been forgotten. Nevertheless, the production is still worth viewing, mainly for Joseph MacDonald's cinematography in such diverse locales as Oregon, Utah and Arizona's Canyon de Chelly and Glen Canyon. To gain box-office impetus, the feature had scattered road show engagements in 70mm, but the gimmick failed to enlist viewer interest.

In 1874 Arizona sheriff MacKenna (Gregory Peck) learns the whereabouts of a canyon where Apache gold is hidden. Along the way he is ambushed by old Apache chief Prairie Dog (Eduardo Ciannelli) and is forced to shoot him. Before he dies the old man gives MacKenna a map of the canyon. MacKenna memorizes and burns the map, but is captured by outlaw Colorado (Omar Sharif) and his band, and they force him to take them to the canyon, threatening to murder their hostage, Inga (Camilla Sparv), the daughter of a local judge. Local citizens buoyed with gold fever join them and are pursued by Apaches. The Indians, in turn, are sought by the cavalry, who are also after Colorado and his men. Eventually all these factions have a showdown and only MacKenna, Colorado, Inga and two Apaches, Hesh-Ke (Julie Newmar) and Hachita (Ted Cassidy), survive. The band is also joined by Colonel Tibbs (Telly Savalas), who has slaughtered his own command in order to find the gold. Along the way the jealous Hesh-Ke is killed because of her desire for MacKenna, and Hachita murders Tibbs, but is himself shot by Colorado. The treasure is located and Colorado and MacKenna fight to the death, but the Apaches arrive and their stampeding horses start an avalanche which buries the canyon and its gold. His saddlebags filled with gold, MacKenna rides away with Inga on Tibbs' horse, but vows someday to kill Colorado.

A much simpler and tremendously more effective study of gold greed is Humphrey Bogart's THE TREASURE OF THE SIERRA MADRE (1948--See B/V).

Roy Rogers and Clay O'Brien in MACKINTOSH & T.J. (1975).

MACKINTOSH & T.J. (Penland, 1975) C 96 mins.

Producer, Tim Penland; director, Marvin J. Chomsky; screen-play, Paul Savage; music, Waylon Jennings; art director, Alan Smith; assistant director, Claude Binyon, Jr.; camera, Terry Mead; editor, Howard Smith.

Roy Rogers (Mackintosh); Clay O'Brien (T.J.); Billy Green Bush (Luke Jenkins); Andrew Robinson (Coley Phipps); Joan Hackett (Maggie Jenkins); James Hampton (Cotton); Dennis Fimple (Schuster); Luke Askew (Cal); and Larry Mahan, Walter Barnes, Edith Atwater, Ted Gehring, Jan Harrell, Dean Smith, Ron Hay, Guich Koock, Autry Ward, Steve Ward, Troy Ward.

"Roy Rogers Returns ... A Family Film About a Pair of Cow-boys on a Texas Ranch" read the catchlines for this independent picture which brought Roy Rogers back to the big screen after a long hiatus. Set in contemporary Texas, where the jeep had re-placed the cowboy's horse, the movie was highlighted by a fine per-formance by veteran Roy Rogers as a drifting, easy-going philo-sophical cowpoke and by background music by Waylon Jennings and Willie Nelson. "The movie falters, however, in its slow-paced script and uneven direction by Marvin J. Chomsky, focusing too much on homespun philosophy from Rogers, square dancing and other repe-titious aspects of ranch life, and not enough on the bronc-riding, coyote-hunting and brawling action sequences," judged Boxoffice trade magazine. Although the movie was given limited theatrical re-lease in the Midwest in the fall of 1975, it did not have its official debut until early in 1976 and then met with modest box-office returns. It was reissued theatrically in 1985, giving new audiences an opportunity to evaluate Roy Rogers' dignified comeback performance. To be noted is that Waylon Jennings performed the songs here, not singing cowboy Rogers.

Aging Bible-carrying cowboy Mackintosh (Roy Rogers) meets a fourteen-year old youth, T.J. (Clay O'Brien), who wants to see the Pacific Ocean, and the two find work on a ranch where Mackintosh's experience quickly gains him respect. There is underlying trouble on the spread, though, because one of the cowboys, Coley Phipps (Andrew Robinson), lusts after ranch owner Luke Jenkins' (Billy Green Bush) wife Maggie (Joan Hackett), and often watches her undress. When one of the drunken hands tells Jenkins his wife has been seeing Mackintosh, the two have a fight at a square dance. That night Jenkins catches Phipps watching his wife and in a fight the ranch owner is killed. The ranch hands blame Mackintosh for the murder, track him down and try to drown him, but T.J. comes to his rescue. When Phipps is found hanging from a windmill, the men realize their mistake. Mackintosh and T.J. plan to head West to the ocean.

THE MAD TRAPPER see DEATH HUNT

A MAN ALONE (Republic, 1955) C 95 mins.

Director, Ray Milland; story, Mort Briskin; screenplay, John Tucker Battle; music, Victor Young; camera, Lionel Lindon; editor, Richard I. Van Enger.

Ray Milland (West Steele); Mary Murphy (Nadine Corrigan); Ward Bond (Sheriff Gil Corrigan); Raymond Burr (Stanley); Arthur Space (Dr. Mason); Lee Van Cleef (Clantin); Alan Hale (Anderson); Douglas Spencer (Slocum); Thomas B. Henry (Maybanks); Grandon Rhodes (Luke Joyner); Martin Garralaga (Ortega); Kim Spalding (Sam Hall); Howard J. Negley (Wilson).

Academy Award-winning actor Ray Milland turned director for A MAN ALONE, in which he also played the title role. Unlike most thespians-turned-helmsmen, Milland proved to be a deft director and continued to direct items such as the suspense films, LISBON (1956) and THE SAFECRACKER (1957), a good science-fiction item, PANIC IN YEAR ZERO (1962), and the satisfying courtroom melodrama, HOSTILE WITNESS (1970). A MAN ALONE was his best directorial outing and he carved out a most satisfying feature film, one which relied more on the pictorial than dialogue. In fact, Milland does not speak for the first third of the film as he cements the movie's premise sans words. Don Miller wrote in Focus on Film (Autumn, 1972): "As director, Milland wisely resists any temptation to indulge in camera virtuosity but presents his story, which becomes quite intricate, in a straightforward manner."

Wes Steele's (Ray Milland) horse breaks its leg as he crosses

Ray Milland and Mary Murphy in A MAN ALONE (1955).

the desert. On foot, he finds a stagecoach whose passengers have been robbed and murdered. In town he seeks sanctuary in a house after realizing that he is being sought for the hold-up and killings. The house belongs to the town's lawman, Sheriff Gil Corrigan (Ward Bond), who has been quarantined with yellow fever. The sheriff is being nursed by his pretty daughter Nadine (Mary Murphy) and she and the fugitive fall in love. The girl wants to help him prove his innocence and the two find out that the sheriff is in cahoots with crooked banker Stanley (Raymond Burr), whose men carried out the robbery and murders. The lawman eventually has a change of heart and turns on Stanley. He and Steele bring down the banker and his cohorts.

In addition to Milland's direction and performance, A MAN ALONE is highlighted by Mary Murphy's fine work and by Lionel Lindon's outstanding TruColor cinematography.

A MAN CALLED HORSE (National General, 1970) C 115 mins.

Producer, Sandy Howard; director, Elliot Silverstein; story, Dorothy M. Johnson; screenplay, Jack DeWitt; music, Leonard Roseman, Lloyd One Star; production designer, Dennis Lynton Clark;

art director, Phil Barber; set decorator, Raul Serrano; assistant director, Terry Morse, Jr.; second unit director, Yakima Canutt; special effects, Frederico Fartan, Tim Smythe; sound, Rafael Esparza; camera, Robert Hauser; editor, Philip Anderson.

Richard Harris (John Morgan); Dame Judith Anderson (Buffalo Cow Head); Jean Gascon (Batise); Manu Tupou (Yellow Hand); Corinna Tsopei (Running Deer); Dub Taylor (Joe); William Jordan (Bent); James Gammon (Ed); Edward Little Sky (Black Eagle); Lina Marin (Thorn Rose); Tamara Garina (Elk Woman); Michael Baseleon (He-Wolf); Manuel Padilla (Leaping Buck); Iron Eyes Cody, Richard Fools Bull, Ben Eagleman (Medicine Men); Terry Leonard (Striking Bear).

A trilogy of feature films have been built around the exploits of aristocratic Englishman Lord John Morgan, played in all three features by Richard Harris, and his rejection of civilization for the life of an Indian warrior. The initial production, A MAN CALLED HORSE, grossed $6.5 million at the box office and inspired its two sequels.

A MAN CALLED HORSE opens with John Morgan (Richard Harris) on a hunting expedition in the Dakotas in the early 1800s and being captured by Sioux Indians. They murder his party but return him to their camp because he has blond hair. There Chief Yellow Hand (Manu Tupou) gives him to an old squaw, Buffalo Cow Head (Judith Anderson), as a slave. A fellow prisoner (Jean Gascon), a Frenchman, warns him not to try to escape, so Morgan decides to learn the language and customs of the tribe. During a fight with a Shoshone war party he kills two scouts of the rival tribe and is accepted as a brave man. Morgan falls in love with Yellow Hand's daughter, Running Deer (Corinna Tsopei), but before he can marry her, he has to endure the terrible torture of being hung by the skin of his chest for the masochistic Sun Vow initiation ceremony. After their marriage, Yellow Hand is killed by the Shoshones and Morgan murders the rival tribe's chief, but in the confrontation the pregnant Running Deer dies. Morgan then agrees to become Buffalo Cow Head's son and the tribe's new chief because of his bravery. When the old squaw dies, he returns to England.

In the 1976 sequel, THE RETURN OF A MAN CALLED HORSE, John Morgan (Richard Harris) finds himself restless with upper-crust life in England and returns to the tribe (now called the Yellow Hands) for a year, but finds they have disappeared. From trappers he learns that the tribe has been run off their land by rival Rickaree Indians in the pay of Zenas Morro (Geoffrey Lewis) and his trappers, who want the area for their fur trade. Morgan locates the tribe and chides them for not reclaiming their lands, but Elk Woman (Gale Sondergaard) says that only through pain and suffering can they defeat those who have taken their homes. Morgan undergoes again the agonizing torture of being hung in mid-air by his chest skin to prove to the tribe that they must fight for their land. When others fail to aid the Yellow Hands in their fight with the Rickarees, Morgan leads his blood brothers in defeating the rival Indians and then trains the

women of the tribe to fight. They attack and destroy the trappers'
headquarters and reclaim their lands. Morgan decides to spend the
rest of his life with the Yellow Hands.

The British Monthly Film Bulletin labeled this indulgent sequel
"pointless" and "self-indulgent," and further complained, "As a study
of authentic tribal behaviour among North American Indians, Irv
Kershner's film is even less convincing and more condescending than
its precursor, while John Morgan's motivation in going native seems
rooted not so much in a mystical empathy with the Yellow Hands as
in a profound boredom with fox-hunting. In any event, the film's
anthropological pretensions are at length abandoned in favour of a
more conventional scenario which owes most to THE MAGNIFICENT
SEVEN [see B/V] but never achieves the same style or effect...."

Although the box-office receipts of the second entry were far
less than from the first, in 1983 TRIUMPHS OF A MAN CALLED
HORSE appeared. But here star Richard Harris appears only briefly
as John Morgan, who is murdered by gold-seeking settlers. His half-
breed son Koda (Michael Beck) takes over as chief to preserve the
tribe's Black Hills home. Morgan's spirit, however, appears at times
to counsel his son in his quest. Although the movie recreates the
plight of the Indian against encroaching settlers and has excellent
cinematography, the film is certainly the weakest of the trilogy and
met with near indifference from moviegoers. Beyond the scenery,
the film's only other asset is Rita Coolidge singing the title song,
"He's Comin' Back."

MAN FROM MUSIC MOUNTAIN (Republic, 1938) 58 mins.

Associate producer, Charles E. Ford; director, Joseph Kane;
story, Bernard McConville; screenplay, Betty Burbridge, Luci Ward;
songs, Peter Tinturin, Jack Lawrence, Eddie Cherkose, Smiley Burnette, Gene Autry, Johnny Marvin, Fred Rose; camera, Jack Marta;
editor, Lester Orlebeck.

Gene Autry (Himself); Smiley Burnette (Frog Milhouse); Carol
Hughes (Helen); Sally Payne (Patsy); Ivan Miller (Scanlon); Edward
Cassidy (Brady); Lew Kelly (Bowdie Bill); Howard Chase (Abbott);
Albert Terry (Buddy); Frankie Marvin (Larry); Earl Dwire (Martin);
Lloyd Ingraham (Harmon); Lillian Drew (Mrs. Chris); Al Taylor
(Hank); Joe Yrigoyen (Pete); Polly Jenkins and Her Plowboys (Them-
selves); Champion (The Horse); and Gordon Hart, Rudy Sooter,
Harry Harvey, Meredith McCormack, Chris Allen.

MAN FROM MUSIC MOUNTAIN (Republic, 1943) 71 mins.

Associate producer, Harry Grey; director, Joseph Kane;
screenplay, Bradford Rope, J. Benton Chaney; songs, Tim Spencer,
Bob Nolan, Smiley Burnette; assistant director, Art Siteman; art
director, Russell Kimball; set decorator, Charles Thomas; sound,
Earl Crain, Sr.; music director, Morton Scott; camera, William

Bradford; editor, Russell Kimball.

Roy Rogers (Himself); Trigger (The Horse); Bob Nolan and the Sons of the Pioneers (Themselves); Ruth Terry (Laramie Winters); Paul Kelly (Victor Marsh); Ann Gillis (Penny Winters); George Cleveland (Sheriff Joe Darcey); Pat Brady (Pat); Renie Riano (Christina Kellog); Paul Harvey (Arthur Davis); Hank Bell (Dobe Joe); Jay Novello (Barker); Hal Taliaferro (Slade); and I. Stanford Jolley, Jack O'Shea, Tom Smith, Charles Morton.

MAN FROM MUSIC MOUNTAIN is one of two titles (the other is RED RIVER VALLEY) shared by Republic Pictures' two top cowboy stars, Gene Autry and Roy Rogers. Autry first used the title in 1938 when he headlined a musical Western with a plot-line centered around the effects of the Boulder Dam project. Variety weighed the film "just about the best to date" in the Autry series, and added, "It has everything that makes for real entertainment values. Its excellent story, diverging far from the beaten formula path, is as modern as tomorrow's newspaper, yet retains the vitality and atmosphere of the west, with intriguing musical numbers woven into it with a fine sense of proportion."

A gang of crooks try to take advantage of drought-plagued farmers by reviving a ghost town with the promise of stringing power lines to it from the recently completed Boulder Dam. The gullible farmers sell their properties, give the crooks their money and move to the new location, and almost lose out until cowboy Gene Autry (Himself) and his buddy Frog Milhouse (Smiley Burnette) aid the people in making the town a success. The duo also expose the crooks and bring them to justice.

The 1943 Roy Rogers vehicle, called TEXAS LEGIONNAIRES on television, is also a modern-day story. It tells of radio singer Roy Rogers (Himself) returning to his home town, only to have the celebration spoiled by a cattlemen-versus-sheepmen feud which is being fueled by rancher Victor Marsh (Paul Kelly), who wants to control the range. Roy suspects Marsh of causing the trouble and with the help of The Sons of the Pioneers (Themselves) he is able to get the needed evidence to round up the gang and end the long-time feud. This version proved to be actionful and entertaining and not overly plagued with poorly interpolated musical production numbers.

THE MAN FROM SNOWY RIVER (Hoyts Distribution, 1982) C 102 mins.

Executive producers, Michael Edgley, Simon Wincer; producer, Geoff Burrowes; director, George Miller; based on the poem by A. B. "Banjo" Paterson; screenplay, John Dixon, Fred Cullen; art director, Leslie Binns; music, Bruce Rowland; camera, Keith Wagstaff; editor, Adrian Carr.

Kirk Douglas (Harrison/Spur); Jack Thompson (Clancy); Tom Burlinson (Jim Craig); Sigrid Thornton (Jessica Harrison); Lorraine Bayly (Rosemary); Chris Haywood (Curly); Tony Bonner (Kane);

Sigrid Thornton and Tom Burlinson in THE MAN FROM SNOWY
RIVER (1982).

Gus Mercurlo (Frew); Terence Donovan (Henry Craig); A. B.
"Banjo" Paterson (David Bradshaw).

Although Kirk Douglas has dual roles in this Australian-lensed
Western, it is third-billed Tom Burlinson who is the star of this Out
Back oater in his characterization of a youth growing to manhood in
frontier Australia. A beautifully photographed (by Keith Wagstaff),
posh production based on the legendary Aussie poem by A. B.
"Banjo" Paterson, the movie proved to be a world-wide box-office
force and showed that the Western genre, left to die on the vine in
Hollywood, could still provide good, vibrant entertainment in the
1980s.

Shot in the Great Dividing Range in Victoria, the adventure
tells of Jim Craig (Tom Burlinson), a young man coming to the ranch
of wealthy Harrison (Kirk Douglas) and finding himself made the
protégé of expert horseman Clancy (Jack Thompson), who teaches
him the horse business. Jim also falls in love with Harrison's
freedom-loving daughter Jessica (Sigrid Thornton) but her father
disapproves of the relationship. In the Out Back, the young man
encounters Spur (Kirk Douglas), a one-legged prospector who is
really the brother of Harrison, and learns that the two men have a

bitter hatred for one another. Spur, however, aids Jim in his romance with Jessica, and she runs away with the young man, only to
be pursued by her dad and his men.

A "rattling good adventure story" (Variety), THE MAN FROM
SNOWY RIVER is a highly entertaining feature, both in plot and
production. Its scenery is a delight and the movie is quickly
paced and finely acted. The climax, involving a chase with more
than three dozen cowboys and nearly one hundred horses charging
over the beautiful Australian terrain, is one of the most exciting
sequences seen in a Western in many years.

MAN OF ACTION (Columbia, 1933) 57 mins.

Director, George Melford; story, William Colt MacDonald;
screenplay, Robert Quigley; music, Otto Meyer; camera, John W.
Boyle; editor, John Boyle.

Tim McCoy (Tim Barlowe); Caryl Lincoln (Irene Summers);
Julian Rivero (Don Miguel); Wheeler Oakman (Sheriff); Walter
Brennan (Sommers); Joseph Girard (Matt Caldwell); Stanley Bly-
stone (Masters); Ted Adams (Deputy); Lafe McKee (Matt Sherman).

A bandit robs a bank and is shot, but the stolen money is
not recovered. Ranger Tim Barlowe (Tim McCoy) and his pal Don
Miguel (Julian Rivero) come home and become involved in the mystery,
and the sheriff (Wheeler Oakman) is very antagonistic towards Tim.
Tim learns that Matt Caldwell (Joe Girard) hired a man to shoot bank
clerk Sommers (Walter Brennan) after having signed a large bank
note to get another man's (Stanley Blystone) ranch and the banker's
pretty daughter (Caryl Lincoln), and also because the banker had
evidence against Caldwell. Tim unravels the mystery and exposes
the rancher as the culprit.

With its murder mystery theme, MAN OF ACTION is one of Tim
McCoy's better Columbia series Westerns and in Views & Reviews
(Winter, 1971), Jon Tuska judged it "a superbly delightful film."
Played mostly on the light side by its fine cast, the movie is very
entertaining. The only drawback is the economical inclusion at the
finale of stock footage from other Tim McCoy features. Sidekick
Julian Rivero, who teamed nicely with McCoy, sings a few love songs
and Walter Brennan appears briefly as the murdered banker.

THE MAN OF THE FOREST (W. W. Hodkinson, 1921) 6,800'

Producer, Benjamin B. Hampton; based on the novel by Zane
Grey; screenplay, Howard Hickman, Richard Schayer, W. H. Clifford;
camera, Joseph A. Dubray.

Carl Gantvoort (Milt Dale); Claire Adams (Helen Raynor);
Robert McKim (Harvey Riggs); Jean Hersholt (Lem Beasley); Harry
Lorraine (Al Auchincloss); Eugenia Gilbert (Bessie Beasley); Frank
Hayes (Los Vegas); Charlotte Pierce (Bo Raynor); Charles B.

Murphy (Snake Anson); Frederick Starr (John Wilson); Tote DuCrow (Lone Wolf).

MAN OF THE FOREST (Paramount, 1926) 5,187'

Presenters, Adolph Zukor, Jesse L. Lasky; associate producer, B. P. Schulberg; director, John Waters; based on the novel by Zane Grey; screenplay, Fred Myton; adaptor, Max Marcin; camera, Edgar Schoenbaum.
Jack Holt (Milt Dale); Georgia Hale (Nancy Raynor); El Brendel (Horace Pipp); Warner Oland (Clint Beasley); Tom Kennedy (Sheriff); George Fawcett (Nancy's Uncle); Ivan Christie (Snake Anson); Bruce Gordon (Jim Wilson); Vester Pegg (Moses); Willard Cooley (Deputy Sheriff); Guy Oliver, Walter Ackerman (Deputies); Duke R. Lee (Martin Mulvery).

MAN OF THE FOREST (Paramount, 1933) 63 mins.

Director, Henry Hathaway; based on the novel by Zane Grey; adaptors, Jack Cunningham, Harold Shumate; art director, Earl Hedrick; camera, Ben Reynolds.
Randolph Scott (Brett Dale); Verna Hills (Alice Gaynor); Harry Carey (Jim Gaynor); Noah Beery (Clint Beasley); Barton MacLane (Mulvey); Buster Crabbe (Hegg); Guinn "Big Boy" Williams (Big Casino); Vince Barnett (Little Casino); Tom Kennedy (Sheriff); Blanche Friderici (Mrs. Forney); and Tempe Piggot, Frank McGlynn, Jr., Duke Lee, Lew Kelly, Merrill McCormack.

Zane Grey's 1920 novel The Man of the Forest has been picturized three times, the first time in 1921 by Zane Grey Pictures and issued by Hodkinson. This silent edition has a rancher (Harry Lorraine) send his two nieces, Helen (Claire Adams) and Bo (Charlotte Pierce), into the forest to hunt for stray cattle with the help of Milt Dale (Carl Gantvoort). Milt and Helen begin romancing, which upsets Harvey Riggs (Robert McKim), who has been sent to their ranch to get away from drink, but becomes involved with bootlegger Beasley (Jean Hersholt) who is plotting to gain control of the ranch spread. Beasley frames Milt on a forgery charge, kidnaps the two young women and tries to poison the rancher, but is shot by one of his cowboys. Milt rescues Helen and Bo and is cleared of charges. He and Helen continue their courtship.

Five years later Paramount remade MAN OF THE FOREST as a Jack Holt silent film. The revamped plot has woodsman Milt Dale (Jack Holt) learning that crook Beasley (Warner Oland) is planning to kidnap attractive Nancy Raynor (Georgia Hale), who is about to inherit her dying uncle's (George Fawcett) ranch. To prevent this, he takes the girl to his remote cabin, but she outmaneuvers him and has him arrested. After her uncle dies, Nancy is romanced by Beasley but she mistrusts him; he forces her to accompany him to his ranch. Dale escapes from jail and in a fight at Beasley's place, the latter is killed. Nancy realizes her love for Dale.

Rugged Jack Holt starred in several well-budgeted movies in the 1920s based on Zane Grey works and this is considered the best of the three movies adapted from The Man of the Forest. In fact, quite a bit of footage from this production was used in the 1933 remake and Tom Kennedy played the sheriff in both features.

In the 1933 version, highlighted by beautiful scenic locations and excellent cinematography, crook Beasley (Noah Beery) intends to steal the forest land of ex-convict Jim Gaynor (Harry Carey) and plots to kidnap his niece Alice (Verna Hillie) so that Jim cannot sign the land over to her. Gaynor's woodsman friend Brett Dale (Randolph Scott) learns of the scheme and, to save the girl, takes her to his cabin. Beasley, in the meantime, murders Jim Gaynor and Brett is convicted of the crime. The murdered man's ranch hands decide to break Brett out of jail. Beasley, meanwhile, makes advances to Alice, but her landlady (Blanche Frederici) stops him. Brett breaks jail and with two of the ranch workers (Guinn "Big Boy" Williams, Vince Barnett) saves the girl; they take refuge in a warehouse and have a shoot-out with Beasley's gang. Beasley later captures the girl, but Brett saves her again and the landlady, Beasley's ex-mistress, shoots the gang leader. Brett and Alice fall in love. Although the plot is very melodramatic (not surprising considering the origin), Henry Hathaway's direction and the performances lend it a winning sincerity. This production was revived by Favorite Films in the 1940s as CHALLENGE OF THE FRONTIER.

MAN OF THE WEST (United Artists, 1958) C 100 mins.

Producer, Walter M. Mirisch; director, Anthony Mann; based on the novel by Will C. Brown; screenplay, Reginald Rose; music, Leigh Harline; song, Bobby Troup; art director, Hillyard Brown; set decorator, Ed Boyle; assistant director, Richard Moder; costumes, Yvonne Wood; makeup, Emil La Vigne; sound, Jack Solomon; camera, Ernest Haller; editor, Richard Heermance.

Gary Cooper (Link Jones); Julie London (Billie Ellis); Lee J. Cobb (Dock Tobin); Arthur O'Connell (Sam Beasley); Jack Lord (Coaley); John Dehner (Claude); Royal Dano (Trout); Robert Wilke (Ponch); Jack Williams (Alcutt); Guy Wilkerson (Conductor); Chuck Roberson (Rifleman); Frank Ferguson (Marshal); Emory Parnell (Gribble); Tina Menard (Mexican Woman); Joe Dominguez (Mexican Man).

MAN OF THE WEST, the first of Gary Cooper's final quartet of Westerns, was definitely the weakest of the group, although one of the four involved only a cameo role in ALIAS JESSE JAMES (1959--see B/V). The violent movie's title tune was written by Bobby Troup and sung by his wife, Julie London, the movie's leading lady.

One-time outlaw Link Jones (Gary Cooper), now a respectable

rancher, is on an Arizona stagecoach and his mission is to hire a schoolmarm for his town. Also on board are dance hall songstress Billie Ellis (Julie London) and gambler Sam Beasley (Arthur O'Connell). The stage is held up by outlaws and Link realizes it is his old gang, now led by his sadistic uncle, Doc Tobin (Lee J. Cobb). To save his fellow passengers, Link pretends to rejoin the group. Doc tells him to go with the gang to the nearby town of Lasso to rob the bank. Link, however, hates his past and his former cohorts and kills one of them in a shoot-out. In a final showdown he is also forced to gun down Doc. Billie, who has fallen in love with Link, goes her own way, respecting him, while Link continues his search for a town teacher.

Very deliberately paced, with Gary Cooper too old for the lead role, the film made scant box-office impact. One of the movie's staunchest supporters is Phil Hardy in The Film Encyclopedia: The Western (1983), whose verdict was: "In contrast to the Westerns he [director Anthony Mann] made with James Stewart ... MAN OF THE WEST is a far more desperate film.... The result is Mann's most powerful film, a movie whose characters are stripped of all but their elemental natures."

THE MAN WHO LOVED CAT DANCING (Metro-Goldwyn-Mayer, 1973)
     C 114 mins.

Producers, Martin Poll, Eleanor Perry; director, Richard C. Sarafian; based on the novel by Marilyn Durham; screenplay, Perry; music, John Williams; art director, Edward C. Carfagno; set decorator, Ralph S. Hurst; assistant director, Les Sheldon; sound, Charles M. Wilborn, Harry W. Tetrick; camera, Harry Stradling, Jr.; editor, Tom Rolf.

Burt Reynolds (Jay Grobart); Sarah Miles (Catherine Crocker); Lee J. Cobb (Lapchance); Jack Warden (Dawes); George Hamilton (Crocker); Bo Hopkins (Billy); Robert Donner (Dub); Sandy Kevin (Ben); Larry Littlebird (Iron Knife); Nancy Malone (Sudie); Jay Silverheels (The Chief); Jay Vareta (Charlie); Sutero Garcia, Jr. (Grobart's Son).

Running away from an unhappy marriage, Catherine Crocker (Sarah Miles) is kidnapped by outlaw gang leader Jay Grobart (Burt Reynolds) and his cohorts, Dawes (Jack Warden) and Billy (Bo Hopkins), after the three men have robbed a train. For a time Jay, who killed the man who raped his Indian wife, must keep his two partners from raping the woman, but she soon falls in love with Jay and he returns her affections. The group, however, is being dogged by Wells Fargo operative/bounty hunter Lapchance (Lee J. Cobb), who is accompanied by the woman's husband (George Hamilton). In an argument Dawes badly beats Billy and he dies from internal bleeding. Jay is forced into a showdown with Dawes as he and Catherine are being chased by the Wells Fargo agent.

While the title of this film taken from Marilyn Durham's novel

(1972) refers to Grobart's dead Indian wife, the movie positions its
narrative from the point of view of the kidnapped woman, who
changes from an unhappy, repressed female into a woman of passion
when aroused by the outlaw. Beautifully lensed by Harry Stradling,
Jr., the movie is far more enjoyable for its scenic value than its
convoluted story-line, told in penny-dreadful fashion. Overall the
acting is above par, especially Jack Warden as the sadistic Dawes.
The box-office returns were as marginal as the film's entertainment
values, despite the publicity engendered by the real-life emotional
intrigue among some of the talent involved in this production.

THE MAN WHO SHOT LIBERTY VALANCE (Paramount, 1962) 123
mins.

    Producer, Willis Goldbeck; director, John Ford; based on a
short story by Dorothy M. Johnson; screenplay, James Warner Bellah,
Goldbeck; music, Cyril Mockridge; art directors, Hal Pereira, Eddie
Imazu; makeup, Wally Westmore; assistant director, Wingate Smith;
sound, Philip Mitchell; camera, William H. Clothier; editor, Otho
Lovering.
    John Wayne (Tom Doniphon); James Stewart (Senator Ranson
Stoddard); Vera Miles (Hallie Stoddard); Lee Marvin (Liberty
Valance); Edmond O'Brien (Dutton Beabody); Andy Devine (Link
Appleyard); Ken Murray (Dr. Willoughby); Jeanette Nolan (Nora);
John Qualen (Peter); Willis Bouchey (Jason Tully); Carleton Young
(Maxwell Scott); Woody Strode (Pompey); Denver Pyle (Amos Car-
ruthers); Strother Martin (Floyd); Lee Van Cleef (Reese); Robert
F. Simon (Handy Strong); O. Z. Whitehead (Ben Carruthers); Paul
Birch (Mayor Winder); Joseph Hoover (Hasbrouck); Leonard Baker
(Man); Larry Finley (Bar X Man); Daniel Borzage, Ralph Volkie
(Townsmen); Anna Lee (Mrs. Prescott); Charles Morton (Drummer);
Mike Edward Jauregui (Drummer); Byron "Slim" Hightower (Shotgun);
Jack Williams, Charles Hayward, Chuck Roberson, Mario Arteaga
(Henchmen); George "Shug" Fisher (Kaintuck); Ted Mapes (High-
pockets); Ronald "Jack" Pennick (Bartender); Bob Morgan (Rough-
rider); Earle Hodgins (Clute Dumfries); Monte Montana (Politician
on Horseback).

    It is not difficult to argue that THE MAN WHO SHOT LIBERTY
VALANCE was John Ford's last great Western [thereafter in the
genre he would only do one sequence in HOW THE WEST WAS WON
(1962--see B/V) and his finale cater, CHEYENNE AUTUMN (1964--
see B/V)]. THE MAN WHO SHOT LIBERTY VALANCE also ranks as
one of the great Westerns of the 1960s. According to Sight and
Sound, the elements of this feature "...all combine to make THE
MAN WHO SHOT LIBERTY VALANCE look like THE WESTERN."
    In the small town of Shinbone, Senator Ranse Stoddard (James
Stewart) arrives with wife Hallie (Vera Miles) to attend the funeral
of Tom Doniphon (John Wayne). With a little urging from the press
and Hallie's consent, the senator relates (in flashback) why Tom was

Edmond O'Brien, John Wayne, and James Stewart in THE MAN WHO
SHOT LIBERTY VALANCE (1962).

so important to each of them. Decades before, greenhorn Ranse arrives in Shinbone, only to be beaten and robbed by gunman Liberty
Valance (Lee Marvin) and he is taken care of by rancher Tom, with
whom Valance is afraid to fight. Valance is working for corrupt
ranchers who oppose statehood for the area, while Tom and most of
the locals want the law and order which will come with the status.
Tom takes Ranse to a nearby cafe where he is cared for by the
owner (John Qualen) and his wife (Jeannette Nolan), and there he
meets waitress Hallie, Tom's lady friend. Ranse then goes into
business as a lawyer at the office of the local newspaper editor (Edmond O'Brien) and they win sufficient delegates to attend the Territorial convention and fight for statehood. Valance comes to town
and brutally batters the newspaper editor. In anger Ranse takes up
a gun--which he does not know how to use--and goes to meet
Valance. Hallie, now in love with Ranse, begs Tom to intercede.
In the showdown Tom kills Valance, but it appears that Ranse did
the deed and he becomes a hero, which launches his political career.
When he learns that Hallie loves Ranse, Tom tells Ranse the truth
about the shooting but urges him to keep it a secret for Hallie's
sake and for his own career, which will aid the new state. When the
account is concluded, the newsman decides he will not use it because the legend, not the truth, is better copy.
     "When the legend becomes a fact, print the legend," is the

final line in THE MAN WHO SHOT LIBERTY VALANCE, and in many ways this sums up the picture's theme as well as many aspects of the film genre. The Western is most successful and appealing when it has a larger-than-life hero, an approach that has sustained its popularity for some seven decades. Only in the past few years, when this kind of image has faded from the genre, has the Western motion picture faded also. Certainly THE MAN WHO SHOT LIBERTY VALANCE is not lacking in heroism, or its antithesis, seen here in the character of murderous Liberty Valance, with Lee Marvin providing one of his staunchest characterizations as one of the rottenest villains ever created for a Western. Of course, John Wayne scores in the opposite vein as the hero who sacrifices his love and reputation to secure safety for his state and its people.

Phil Hardy wrote in The Film Encyclopedia: The Western (1983): "This is a key work. More than any other, this film, with its extended treatment of the garden/civilization versus the wilderness/nature theme that is so central to Ford, articulates its director's sombre gainsaying of what once he had so gaily celebrated.... The film's sombre dignity is made the more so by Ford's even-handed treatment of his leading characters ... as he watches both bend to the inevitability of historical process." In his study, John Ford (1968), Peter Bogdanovich judged the film Ford's "most important film of the sixties." In it "...he seems to be making his final statement on the western.... It is perhaps the most mournful, tragic film Ford has made."

MASON OF THE MOUNTED (Monogram, 1932) 59 mins.

Producer, Trem Carr; director/screenplay, Harry Fraser; production manager, Paul Malvern; camera, Archie Stout; editor, J. Logan Pearson.

Bill Cody (Bill Mason); Andy Shuford (Andy); Nancy Drexel (Marion Kirby); LeRoy Mason (Calhoun); Jack Carlyle (Luke Kirby); Earl Dwire (Dwire); James Marcus (Sheriff); Joe Dominguez (Riveras); and Gordon McGee, Captain Art Smith, Blackie Whiteford, Nelson McDowell, Dick Dickinson, Frank Hall Crane, Jack Long.

After a trapper is murdered and the gunman injures him, wounded Canadian Mountie Bill Mason (Bill Cody) crosses into the United States to find the killer. In horse-raising country, he meets young Andy (Andy Shuford), who has run away from home. He befriends the lad and learns that the area is plagued by a gang of horse thieves run by Calhoun (LeRoy Mason) and his cohort Riveras (Joe Dominguez). In town, Bill meets Andy's cousin Marion (Nancy Drexel) and her father Luke Kirby (Jack Carlyle), whose horse herd has been the outlaws' target. When one (Earl Dwire) of the gang members is captured, the locals encourage Bill to bring in the rest of the gang. He now suspects that Calhoun is the man he is after. When Calhoun and his men come to rescue their cohort, Bill and the vigilantes capture the gang, but Calhoun escapes. In a chase he is

knocked from his horse and overcome. Bill finds a watch chain in
his possession which belonged to the murdered trapper, proving that
Calhoun is the culprit. Bill returns to Canada with his prisoner
and Marion promises to wait for him.

During the 1931-32 season, Bill Cody co-starred with young
Andy Shuford in eight films for producer Trem Carr in the "Bill and
Andy" series. In quality, they range from poor (OKLAHOMA JIM,
q.v.) to fair, like this one and THE GHOST CITY (q.v.). With
production manager Paul Malvern's penchant for attractive locales,
the film is pleasant to see, especially during the early snowscape
footage, and Archie Stout's cinematography is always a major plus.
Nevertheless, the plot is only average and the movie is weakened by
poor editing and obtrusive stock footage.

THE MASTER GUNFIGHTER see BILLY JACK

MELODY OF THE PLAINS (Spectrum, 1937) 53 mins.

Producer, Jed Buell; associate producer, George H. Callaghan;
director, Sam Newfield; screenplay, Bennett Cohen; music supervisor, Abe Meyer; songs, Don Swander and June Hershey; camera,
Robert Kline; editors, Arthur Brooks, William Hess.

Fred Scott (Steve Connor); Al "Fuzzy" St. John (Fuzzy);
Louise Small (Molly Langley); Hal Price (Gorman); Lew Meehan
(Starr); Charles "Slim" Whitaker (Cass); Lafe McKee (Langley);
David Sharpe (Bud Langley); Bud Jamison (Cook); and Carl
Mathews, George Fisk, George Morrell.

When it comes to the cowboy crooners of the 1930s there is
little doubt that the best of them, strictly as a singer, was Fred
Scott. From 1936 to 1939 he headlined a dozen features for Spectrum, the final three being produced by comedy star Stan Laurel.
A thirteenth feature, RIDIN' THE TRAIL, was produced but did not
get released until 1940, when Arthur Ziehm issued it following the
demise of Spectrum. Although cheaply made, Scott's oaters were
pleasing to fans, and the star proved to be a rugged screen cowboy
with an exceptionally fine voice. Although he had been in motion
pictures since 1920, Fred Scott spent several years in the early
1930s with the San Francisco Opera.

MELODY OF THE PLAINS was the third release in Scott's
series and it has historical import for genre fans in that this was
the film in which famous silent film comedian Al St. John created his
beloved "Fuzzy" characterization, a role he was to perfect in the
1940s in his PRC outings with Bob Steele, George Houston, Buster
Crabbe, and Lash LaRue.

MELODY OF THE PLAINS opens with a cattle drive led by
rancher Steve Connor (Fred Scott) and his pals Fuzzy (Al St. John)
and Bud Langley (David Sharpe), the latter being involved with
outlaws Cass (Charles "Slim" Whitaker) and Starr (Lew Meehan).

When the outlaws attack the camp Bud has a change of heart and
fires a warning shot. Cass kills him, but in the fight Steve thinks
he fired the fatal shot. Steve gives up his herd and he and Fuzzy
drift into a small town where crooked realtor Gorman (Hal Price) is
trying to force rancher Langley (Lafe McKee) off his range. Steve
defeats Gorman in a fight and is hired by the old man and his
pretty daughter Molly (Louise Small). He discovers that they are
Bud's father and sister. Cass and Starr, who work for Gorman, go
to work for Langley so they can more easily rustle his cattle. Cass
tries to seduce Molly and when Steve stops him, Cass tells them
that Steve killed Bud. Langley orders Steve off his ranch, but
Steve figures out who really did the killing, forces a confession
from Starr, and stops Cass and Gorman from taking the ranch.
Steve and Molly become engaged.

MEN WITHOUT LAW (Columbia, 1930) 65 mins.

Producer, Harry Cohn; associate producer, Sol Lesser; director, Louis King; story, Lewis Seiler; screenplay, Dorothy Howell;
art directors, Edward Jewell, Edward Shulter; assistant director,
Mac V. Wright; sound, John Livadary, Ben Harper; camera, Ted
McCord; editor, Ray Snyder.

Buck Jones (Buck Healy); Tom Carr (Tom Healy); Harry
Woods (Murdock); Fred Burns (Sheriff Jim); Fred Kelsey (Deputy
Sheriff); Sid [Syd] Saylor (Hank); Carmelita Geraghty (Juanita Del
Rey); Lydia Knott (Mrs. Healy); Victor Sarno (Senor Del Rey);
Silver (The Horse); and Ben Corbett, Lafe McKee, Art Mix [George
Kesterson].

In 1930, Buck Jones returned to the screen for Sol Lesser's
Beverly Productions, which released its features through Columbia
Pictures. These early talkies are among the best "B" Westerns
made, and MEN WITHOUT LAW, a solid entry, is the third in the
series. It is a fine example of just how well the "B" oater could
adapt to the demands of the sound medium. The film's success is
also due to star Buck Jones, a fine actor and stalwart hero; one of
the top guns in the cowboy film genre for over two decades. Sporting a literate plot and solid acting, MEN WITHOUT LAW contains a
well-lighted climactic fight sequence, and also interpolated engaging
songs like "La Paloma" and "Bury Me Not on the Lone Prairie."

Returning home from World War I, Buck Healy (Buck Jones)
finds his younger brother Tom (Tom Carr) has been accused of
being involved in a bank robbery. On his way to see his mother
(Lydia Knott), Tom is captured by outlaw gang leader Murdock
(Harry Woods). Buck is arrested in Tom's place but later escapes
from jail. Buck too is caught by Murdock, who takes his papers
and heads for Mexico masquerading as Buck to get money from the
Del Rey family, whose son Buck befriended in France. Buck and
Tom make their getaway from the gang and Buck heads to Casa Del
Rey, but the family doubts his story. Later Buck proves his

identity to daughter Juanita (Carmelita Geraghty), but Murdock carries off the girl. Buck follows them and is cornered by Murdock's gang. Buck's horse Silver helps him to escape and he chases the gang to its hideout, defeating Murdock and helping the posse lasso the gang.

THE MISSOURI BREAKS (United Artists, 1976) C 126 mins.

Producers, Elliott Kastner, Robert M. Sherman; director, Arthur Penn; screenplay, Thomas McGuane; music, John Williams; production designer, Albert Brenner; art director, Stephen Berger; set decorator, Marvin March; assistant director, Malcolm Harding; second unit director, Michael Moore; sound, Richard Vorisek, Jack Solomon, Dennis Maitland; camera, Michael Butler; second unit camera, Rex Metz; editors, Jerry Greenberg, Stephen Rotter, Dede Allen.

Marlon Brando (Lee Clayton); Jack Nicholson (Tom Logan); Kathleen Lloyd (Jane Braxton); Randy Quaid (Little Tod); Frederick Forrest (Cary); Harry Dean Stanton (Calvin); John McLiam (David Braxton); John Ryan (Si); Sam Gilman (Hank); Steve Franken (Lonesome Kid); Richard Bradford (Pete Marker); James Greene (Hellsgate Rancher); Luana Anders (Rancher's Wife); Danny Goldman (Baggage Clerk); Hunter Von Leen (Sandy).

The screen teaming of Marlon Brando and Jack Nicholson was considered big news in the mid-1970s, especially in a film to be directed by Arthur Penn. The result, however, was a disappointing, over-long feature. The viewer is "...seriously drawn to it on its upfront elements, but leaves with a depressing sense of waste. Penn is doing his number, Brando his, Nicholson, his... Maybe the whole thing is just one big joke" (Variety).

Pompous land baron David Braxton (John McLiam) rules the range in Montana and his henchman Peter Marker (Richard Bradford) hangs Sandy (Hunter Von Leen), a young horse thief. To avenge the young man's death the leader of his gang of horse rustlers, Tom Logan (Jack Nicholson), buys a nearby ranch and with his gang--Little Tod (Randy Quaid) and Calvin (Harry Dean Stanton)-- begins rustling Braxton's horse herd. Logan meets Braxton's pretty and loner daughter Jane (Kathleen Lloyd), and they have an affair which grows stronger as he decides he prefers being a farmer to rustling. Braxton then hires iconoclastic gunman Lee Clayton (Marlon Brando) to eliminate Logan and he does wipe out Logan's gang. However, in a shoot-out, it is Clayton who is killed, and Braxton fails in his own attempt to shoot Logan.

Marsha McCreadie wrote in Films in Review (August-September 1976), "The photography is beautifully elegiac, picking up one of the movie's themes; the music jarringly absurdist, underscoring another. Everyone, including the viewer, is left slugging it out on his or her own. No wonder Brando runs wild, burlesquing his role(s) in a brilliant but out-of-kilter performance. Nicholson struggles heroically

Jack Nicholson and Marlon Brando in THE MISSOURI BREAKS (1976).

with what amounts to a non-part. THE MISSOURI BREAKS leaves us fascinated, but baffled."

MONTANA <u>see</u> SAN ANTONIO

MONTANA MOON (Metro-Goldwyn-Mayer, 1930) 90 mins.

Producer/director, Malcolm St. Clair; story/continuity, Sylvia Thalberg, Frank Butler; dialogue, Joe Farnham; art director, Cedric Gibbons; songs: Nacio Herb Brown and Arthur Freed; Herbert Stothart and Clifford Grey; gowns; Adrian; sound, Paul Neal, Douglas Shearer; camera, William Daniels; editors, Carl L. Pierson, Leslie F. Wilder.

Joan Crawford (Joan Prescott); John Mack Brown (Larry); Dorothy Sebastian (Elizabeth); Ricardo Cortez (Jeff); Benny Rubin ("The Doctor"); Cliff Edwards (Froggy); Karl Dane (Hank); Lloyd Ingraham (Mr. Prescott).

Statuesque Joan Crawford first appeared in Westerns opposite Tim McCoy in M-G-M's WINNERS OF THE WILDERNESS (1927--see B/V) and LAW OF THE RANGE (1928), and her first sound galloper was MONTANA MOON, which also was Johnny Mack Brown's first talkie Western. Joan Crawford would not return to the genre for nearly a quarter of a century until she starred in Republic's offbeat

222 / MONTE WALSH

but highly regarded JOHNNY GUITAR (1954). MONTANA MOON, with location filming in the San Jacinto mountains, is an acceptable mixture of the Western and operetta trimmings. Mordaunt Hall in the New York Times judged it "An interminable, amateurish talking picture with spasmodic snatches of melody...." Photoplay magazine, more in tune with the timbre of the proceedings, opined, "Joan Crawford, still untamed, on a ranch. And what a tango she does with Ricardo Cortez! Frolicsome." The film boasts a trio of pleasant Nacio Herb Brown and Arthur Freed tunes: "Sing a Song of Old Montana," "The Moon Is Low" and "Happy Cowboy."

The self-centered, spoiled daughter of rich rancher Prescott (Lloyd Ingraham), beautiful Joan Prescott (Joan Crawford), is bored with life and yearns only for a good time. She travels home to Montana from New York but at a stopover before reaching her father's ranch, leaves the train, planning to catch another back to the city. She wanders into the camp of handsome cowboy Larry (Johnny Mack Brown), who has come to Montana from Texas. Liking Larry, Joan forgets about her train trip; the two fall in love and decide to marry. Prescott is happy about the engagement as he feels the steady Larry will be good for his daughter. After the wedding, a big western-style party is given for the young couple and during the proceedings Joan does a torrid tango with gigolo Jeff (Ricardo Cortez). This throws Larry into a rage and he hits Jeff. In anger Joan leaves to go to New York, but Larry pursues her and in the guise of bandits he and his cowboys hold up the train. He takes Joan back to the ranch for a life of happiness together.

MONTE WALSH (National General, 1970) C 99 mins.

Producers, Hal Landers, Bobby Roberts; director, William A. Fraker; based on the novel by Jack Schaefer; screenplay, Lukas Heller, David Zelag Goodman; music, John Barry; song, Barry and Hal David; production designer, Al Brenner; set decorator, Phil Abramson; assistant director, Jack Roe; sound, Jerry Kosloff; camera, David M. Walsh; editor, Dick Brockway.

Lee Marvin (Monte Walsh); Jeanne Moreau (Martine Bernard); Jack Palance (Chet Rollins); Mitch Ryan (Shorty Austin); Jim Davis (Cal Brennan); John "Bear" Hudkins (Sonny Jacobs); Ray Guth (Sunfish Perkins); John McKee (Petey Williams); Michael Conrad (Dally Johnson); Tom Healon (Sugar Wyman); Ted Gehring (Hal Henderson); Bo Hopkins (Jumpin' Joe Joslin); Matt Clark (Rufus Brady); Billy Bush (Powder Kent); Allyn Ann McLerie (Mary Eagle); John McLiam (Fightin' Joe Hooker); Charles Tyner (Doctor); Guy Wickerson (Old Man); Roy Barcroft (Proprietor); Richard Farnsworth, Fred Waugh (Cowboys).

Cowboys Monte Walsh (Lee Marvin) and Chet Rollins (Jack Palance) ride into the town of Harmony and ranch manager Cal Brennan (Jim Davis) offers them a job. Later they meet old pal Shorty Austin (Mitchell Ryan) and the trio go into town, where

John "Bear" Hudkins and Lee Marvin in MONTE WALSH (1970).

Monte sees his mistress Martine Bernard (Jeanne Moreau) while Chet
romances widow Mary Eagle (Allyn Ann McLerie), who owns a hardware store.   When Shorty loses his ranch job he gets into a saloon
brawl and kills the local sheriff.   Chet settles down and marries the
widow.   Martine, meanwhile, has moved on to another town and
Monte follows her and asks her to marry him, but she refuses.
Getting drunk, Monte comes across a carnival horse and tries to
tame it, nearly tearing up the town of Charleyville in the attempt.
He is offered a job with the carnival but is too proud to take it,
and returning to Harmony he learns that Shorty has killed Chet
while robbing the hardware store.   Monte intends to bring in Shorty,
but he hears that Martine is very ill and goes to Charleyville where
he finds she has died and that Shorty is waiting there for him.   In
the shootout, Monte kills Shorty.

There is a memorable scene in MONTE WALSH where Chet Rollins advises the stubborn protagonist that the day of the cowboy has
ended and that he should settle down to a quiet life.   This is the
crux of the plot background of MONTE WALSH, which delves into
the drudgery of the lives of three range hands caught in the changing world of the late 1880s, with the coming of the modern age, a
depression in the cattle business, and the termination of westward
expansion.

Grossing only slightly more than $2,000,000 at the box office,
MONTE WALSH is an interesting study enhanced by fine characterizations and good pacing.   Unfortunately overlooked when it was
released, it is one of the better genre outings of the 1970s.

MOTHER LODE (Agamemnon Films, 1982) C 101 mins.

Executive producer, Peter Snell; producer, Fraser Clarke
Heston; associate producer, Les Kimber; director, Charlton Heston;
screenplay, Fraser Clarke Heston; production designer, Douglas
Higgins; art director, Michael Bottom, James H. Crow; second unit
director, Joe Canutt; music, Ken Wannberg; wardrobe, Maureen
Hiscox, Linda Langdon; makeup, Jamie Brown, Phyllis Newman;
camera, Richard Leiterman; editor, Eric Boyd Perkins.

Charlton Heston (Silas McGee/Ian McGee); Nick Mancuso (Jean
Dupre); Kim Basinger (Andrea Spalding); John Marley (Elijah);
Dale Wilson (Gerard Elliot); Ricky Zantolas (George Patterson);
Marie George (Elijah's Wife).

When his pal George Patterson (Ricky Zantolas) disappears in
the mountains of British Columbia while looking for gold, bush pilot
Jean Dupre (Nick Mancuso) goes in search of him accompanied by
the man's girl friend, Andrea Spalding (Kim Basinger).   In a
dilapidated plane, they crash-land on a lake in the vicinity where
George disappeared and meet Elijah (John Marley), a local inhabitant
who warns them to turn back.   They keep going on foot, however,
and find the mine of Silas McGee (Charlton Heston), who has been
mining the area for two decades.   He tells them there is no gold

there but that he is hunting for silver. Jean comes to disbelieve him and feels that Silas has done away with George, who may have found the mother lode. It turns out that Silas and his twin brother Ian (Charlton Heston) have been working the mine together. When Silas, who did murder George, tries to kill the couple, Ian is able to rescue Andrea and Jean escapes on his own and he kills Ian, who he believes is Silas. When Silas kidnaps the girl and takes her deep into the mine, Jean pursues him and when a flood is set off in the caverns, he uncovers the mother lode. Eventually he and Andrea escape and in the process Silas is killed. Jean and Andrea, now in love, return to civilization without the gold.

Charlton Heston, who directed this feature from his producer son's screenplay, is quite menacing as the murderous Silas and gives the motion picture its main interest. Not to be overlooked is Richard Leiterman's cinematography (especially the aerial shots, the mine sequences, and the views of the Cassiar Mountains in British Columbia) and second unit director Joe Canutt's well-executed action sequences.

THE MOUNTAIN MEN (Columbia, 1980) C 102 mins.

Presenter, Martin Ransohoff; executive producer, Richard R. St. Johns; producers, Martin Shafer, Andrew Scheinman; associate producer, Cathleen Summers; director, Richard Lang; screenplay, Fraser Clarke Heston; music, Michel Legrand; production designer, Bill Kenney; set decorator, Rick T. Gentz; second unit director, Joe Canutt; sound, Glenn Anderson, Les Fresholtz; camera, Michael Hugo; second unit camera, Herb Pearl; editor, Eve Ruggiero.

Charlton Heston (Bill Tyler); Brian Keith (Henry Frapp); Victoria Racimo (Running Moon); Stephen Macht (Heavy Eagle); John Glover (Nathan Wyeth); Seymour Cassel (La Bont); David Ackroyd (Medicine Wolf); Cal Bellini (Cross Otter); Bill Lucking (Jim Walker); Ken Ruta (Fontenelle); Victor Jory (Iron Belly).

Veteran frontiersman Bill Tyler (Charlton Heston), who has spent most of his life in the wilds, meets and takes up with a young Indian maiden, Running Moon (Victoria Racimo), who has fled from her husband, the sadistic Heavy Eagle (Stephen Macht). The Indian tries to regain the young woman and she and Tyler are forced to fight members of the tribe and to flee into the wilderness in attempt to escape. Along the way, they meet Tyler's old friend, fellow woodsman Henry Frapp (Brian Keith). He aids them, but is killed in a fight, although the young woman eventually wins her freedom.

While THE MOUNTAIN MEN is not an unlikable Western it is devoid of much character development or fluid script. The film's main thesis is that frontier life was raw and hard and to survive one had to be cunning and kill or be killed. As is to be expected, the movie is very violent and is filled with excessive profanity. Neither Charlton Heston nor Brian Keith appear overly comfortable in their roles, with Heston trying to make the best of the situation,

while Keith compensates in his usual way--hamming up his scenes.
While Victoria Racimo and Stephen Macht are acceptable in their
Indian roles, it is veteran Victor Jory's brief appearance as the
aged Iron Belly that elicits the film's most satisfying performance.
Variety complained about the abundant mayhem in this over-
long feature: "Screenplay by star's son Fraser Clarke Heston is
loaded with vulgarities that seem excessive for the genre, and scene
after scene dwells on bloody hand-to-hand battles between Indians
and the grizzled trappers played by Heston and sidekick Brian
Keith." Just as needless was the scene where Heavy Eagle sodomizes
Running Moon as punishment for one of her escape attempts.

MUSTANG COUNTRY (Universal, 1976) C 79 mins.

Producer/director/screenplay, John Champion; music, Lee
Holdridge; song, Holdridge and Joe Henry; set decorator, Peter
Young; assistant director, Frank Arrigo; sound, Rodney Haykin;
camera, J. Barry Herron; editor, Douglas Robertson.
Joel McCrea (Dan); Robert Fuller (Griff); Patrick Wayne (Tee
Jay); Nika Mina (Nika).

Filmed in Alberta, Canada, MUSTANG COUNTRY marked Joel
McCrea's return to the screen in his first major role since his acclaimed performance in RIDE THE HIGH COUNTRY (see B/V) in
1961. In the interim he did a cameo appearance in CRY BLOOD,
APACHE (1970) and narrated the Academy Award-winning documentary, THE GREAT AMERICAN COWBOY (1974). While Boxoffice
magazine claimed "...the outdoor adventure is strictly on a juvenile
level in dialog and action," the film sported nice scenery and a
strong performance by Joel McCrea, making it ideal family fare.
This has proven to be the star's last screen appearance to date.
Aging but still rugged rancher and ex-rodeo champion Dan
(Joel McCrea) hunts for the wild black stallion Shoshone along the
Montana-Canadian border in 1925. Two cowboys (Robert Fuller,
Patrick Wayne) rope the animal but lose him and eventually give up
the chase. The rancher manages to rope the horse but is dragged
into a river and is saved by his dog, Luke. He is also helped by
a young Indian boy (Nika Mina), an orphan who has run away from
school and who also wants to capture the horse so he can sell him
and give the money to his widowed grandmother. The rancher and
the boy set out corral the mustang by building a fence, but the
horse easily jumps over it. When a huge grizzly bear attacks them,
the two escape, but the rancher's loyal dog is killed. Later the
rancher's horse Rosey gets stuck in a mud-filled gully and the wild
mustang aids them in rescuing her. They go back to Dan's ranch
and find it has burned. There the rancher kills the grizzly in a
showdown and asks the boy to stay on with him.
One of the most enjoyable aspects of MUSTANG COUNTRY is
that the film contains nothing offensive to its audience. The movie
recounts the adventures in capturing a mustang and battling a

Joel McCrea and Nika Mina in MUSTANG COUNTRY (1976).

grizzly, but has no vile villains or obscene language or nudity or any other such activities that some filmmakers deemed "necessary" by the mid-1970s.

THE MYSTERIOUS DESPERADO (RKO, 1949) 60 mins.

Producer, Herman Schlom; director, Lesley Selander; screen-play, Norman Houston; music, Paul Sawtell; camera, Nicholas Musuraca; editor, Les Millbrook.

Tim Holt (Tim); Richard Martin (Chito); Edward Norris (Ramon); Movita Castaneda (Luisa); Robert Livingston (Jordan); Frank Wilcox (Stevens); William Tannen (Barton); Robert B. Williams (Whittaker); Kenneth MacDonald (Sheriff); Frank Lackteen (Pedro); Leander DeCordova (Padre).

From 1940 to 1952 Tim Holt starred in a series of well-done sagebrush yarns for RKO Radio, the movie benefitting from decent production values, usually interesting scripts, fine casts, and an appealing leading man who was capable of holding his own in classic

features like THE MAGNIFICENT AMBERSONS (1942) and THE
TREASURE OF SIERRA MADRE (1948--see B/V). Many feel that Tim
Holt's best films came toward the end of his career, in the late
1940s, and THE MYSTERIOUS DESPERADO certainly substantiates
this opinion. With its flavorful mystery element, engrossing plot-
line, and a fair amount of action, the movie is a good illustration of
the TIM HOLT series at its best.

Cowboy Tim (Tim Holt) helps his pal Chito (Richard Martin)
claim the rancho of his late uncle. Arriving in Santo Domingo, the
two are attacked by Jordan (Robert Livingston) and Barton (William
Tannen), whom they defeat in a saloon fight. That evening, they
obtain entry to the deserted hacienda and Chito is set upon by a
mysterious man who turns out to be his cousin Ramon (Edward Norris). They learn that Ramon's father, the owner of the estate, has
been murdered by a gang led by Stevens (Frank Knox), the public
administrator who had notified Chito of his inheritance. Ramon tells
them that he and his father disagreed over his intention to marry
pretty Luisa (Movita Casteneda). The sheriff (Kenneth MacDonald)
and Stevens arrive with a posse to arrest Ramon, claiming that he
killed his father. Ramon escapes, and Stevens then tells Chito he
has sole claim to the rancho. Later he has Jordan and Barton shoot
Chito, but Tim comes to his rescue. The sheriff captures Ramon at
the local mission, where he came to meet Luisa. Tim entraps
Stevens' henchmen but Jordan escapes. Tim stops the sheriff and
Stevens from hanging Ramon and takes them to the rancho where
Chito holds Barton prisoner; the latter confesses Stevens' crooked
activities. In a shoot-out, Stevens, Jordan, and the gang are captured, and Ramon and Luisa plan to wed.

MYSTERY MOUNTAIN see IN OLD SANTA FE

MYSTERY MOUNTAIN (Mascot, 1934) twelve chapters

Producer, Nat Levine; supervisor, Victor Zobel; directors,
Otto Brower, B. Reeves Eason; story, Sherman Lowe, Barney
Sarecky, Eason; screenplay, Bennett Cohen, Armand Schaefer; mu-
sic, Lee Zahler; sound, Terry Kellum; camera, Ernest Miller, William
Nobles; editors, Earl Turner, Walter Thompson.

Ken Maynard (Ken Williams); Verna Hillie (Jane Corwin); Ed-
ward Earle (Blayden); Edmund Cobb (The Rattler); Lynton Brent
(Matthews); Syd Saylor (Breezy); Carmencita Johnson (Little Jane);
Lafe McKee (Mr. Corwin); Al Bridge (Henderson); Edward Hearn
(Lake); Bob Kortman (Hank); Gene Autry (Cowboy); Tarzan (The
Horse); and Smiley Burnette, Wally Wales, Tom London, Philo
McCullough, George Chesebro, Steve Clark, Frank Ellis, James
Mason, Lew Meehan, Jack Rockwell, Art Mix, William Gould.

Chapters: 1) The Rattler; 2) The Man Nobody Knows); 3)
The Eye That Never Sleeps; 4) The Human Target; 5) Phantom Outlaws; 6) The Perfect Crime; 7) Tarzan the Cunning; 8) The Enemy's

Stronghold; 9) The Fatal Warning; 10) The Secret of the Mountain;
11) Behind the Mark; 12) The Judgment of Tarzan.

A masked fiend known only as The Rattler wants all the land
around Mystery Mountain. He kills anyone who gets in his way and
uses an outlaw gang, none of whom know his true identity, to carry
out his commands. The B & L Railroad begins constructing a tunnel
that will put the local Corwin Transportation Company out of
business and the owner (Lafe McKee) is murdered by The Rattler,
leaving pretty daughter Jane (Verna Hillie) to carry on the operation. Arriving on the scene is cowboy Ken Williams (Ken Maynard),
actually an undercover agent, aided by fellow operative Breezy (Syd
Saylor). The two assist Jane and get on the trail of The Rattler,
who changes his disguises via a series of rubber face masks he has
made of several local people, including Ken. Ken locates The
Rattler's headquarters deep in Mystery Mountain and in a showdown
destroys the lair and its advanced electrical equipment, escaping
just as the place explodes and buries The Rattler in its rubble.
    MYSTERY MOUNTAIN, a twelve-chapter serial, was the first
of many projects Ken Maynard was supposed to undertake for Nat
Levine's Mascot Pictures. However, his only other effort for the
studio was to be the feature IN OLD SANTA FE (1934) (q.v.) before
he quit the company after squabbling with Levine. Gene Autry, who
appeared in both of Maynard's Mascot's, was elevated to the star's
role in the third production, THE PHANTOM EMPIRE (1935).
MYSTERY MOUNTAIN was a big financial success, largely due to
Maynard's popularity. The serial cost about $80,000, with one-half
of that amount going to the star's salary, and it grossed more than
ten times its cost.
    Overall the movie is a rawboned affair, choppy in parts, but
full of action, with Ken Maynard continuing his larger-than-life
portrayal of a Western hero. The gimmicky device of the villain
employing intricate facial disguises was common to Mascot cliffhangers, as witnessed in such outings as THE HURRICANE EXPRESS
(1932).

MYSTERY OF THE HOODED HORSEMEN (Grand National, 1937)
    59 1/2 mins.

    Producer, Edward F. Finney; director, Ray Taylor; screen-
play, Edmund Kelso; music, Frank Sanucci; songs: Tex Ritter,
Fred Rose, Michael David, Sanucci; camera, Gus Peterson; editor,
Fred Bain.
    Tex Ritter (Tex Martin); Iris Meredith (Nancy); Horace
Murphy (Stubby); Charles King (Blackie); Earl Dwire (Sheriff);
Forrest Taylor (Norton); Joseph Girard (Dan Farley); Lafe McKee
(Tom Wilson); White Flash (The Horse); Ken Cards, Ray Whitley
and His Range Ramblers (Themselves); Jack Smith (Brown); Chick
Hannon (Pete); Hebe Snow [Hank Worden] (Deputy); Oscar Gahan
(Bartender).

The eighth film in Tex Ritter's starring series for Grand National, MYSTERY OF THE HOODED HORSEMEN is a flavorful mystery-cowboy picture which includes a snappy heroine (Iris Meredith), sterling camera work and memorable scenic locales, and only a small amount of stock footage. The film contains two of Tex Ritter's better known melodies: "Ride, Ride, Ride" and "Ridin' Old Paint." As Kate Cameron penned in the New York Daily News, "Tex's songs are given a good play in the picture and the cowboy puts them over effectively."

A group of masked riders kill Tom Wilson (Lafe McKee) for his mine and cowboys Tex Martin (Tex Ritter) and Stubby (Horace Murphy) help his daughter Nancy (Iris Meredith) learn why he was murdered. The sheriff (Earl Dwire), however, does not trust the do-gooders and Tex must infiltrate the gang. He is arrested, but Stubby breaks him out of jail. Tex then leads the vigilantes against the hooded horsemen and in their chase the vigilante leader (Forrest Taylor) is shot by the head (Joe Girard) of the outlaws. Tex and the law enforcers bring the gang to justice.

British release title: HOODED HORSEMEN.

MYSTERY RANCH (Reliable, 1934) 56 mins.

Producer, Bernard B. Ray; director, Ray Bernard [Ray]; story, J. K. Henry; screenplay, Rose Gordon, Carl Krusada; assistant director, B. Raymond; sound, J. S. Westmoreland; camera, J. Henry Kruse; editor, Fred Bain.

Tom Tyler (Tom Morris); Roberta Gale (Mary Henderson); Louise Cabo (Mrs. Henderson); Jack Gable [Jack Perrin] (George Andrews); Frank Hall Crane (Percy Jenkins); Charles King (Sam); Tom London (Blake); George Chesebro (Kern).

Tom Morris, who writes Western novels, receives a letter from ranch owner Mrs. Henderson (Louise Gabo) and her daughter Mary (Roberta Gale) informing him that his tales are far too tame. They invite him to their Mystery Ranch to witness the real West for himself. Tom travels there with his secretary Percy (Frank Hall Crane) and soon realizes that the women are toying with him, arranging a series of "happenings" including a lynching, a runaway horse, a fake feud, and a shoot-out. Tom, tongue-in-cheek, tells the women all of this is not enough action for him. Meanwhile gold thieves Blake (Tom London) and Kern (George Chesebro) arrive at the ranch and leave a bag which Tom and Percy discover contains gold bullion. As a lark, they plan to switch the gold for scrap metal and have Percy disguise himself as a hold-up man and kidnap Mary, with Tom riding to the rescue. Foreman Sam (Charles King) overhears the plot, switches the gold again and takes Mary himself, telling her it is all a gag to fool Tom. The law arrives looking for the two crooks and Tom leads them to the bogus gold. The sheriff arrests him, thinking he is a part of the gang. Tom escapes and comes to Mary's rescue, defeating Sam and returning the bullion.

One of nineteen starrers Tom Tyler made for producers Harry S. Webb and Bernard B. Ray, MYSTERY MOUNTAIN starts out in good form and for its first half pleasantly kids the Western film genre. With the introduction of crooks, though, the film's shoddy production values show through and the movie concludes as one of the less satisfying entries in the inexpensive series.

THE MYSTIC WARRIOR (Warner Bros. Television/ABC-TV, 5/20-21/84) C-250 mins.

Executive producers, David L. Wolper; Stan Margulies; producer, Paul Freeman; director, Richard T. Heffron; based on the novel Hanta Yo and other material by Ruth Beebe Hill; teleplay, Jeb Rosebrook; music, Gerald Fried; production designer, Mort Rabinowitz; camera, Stevan Larner; editors, Michael Eliot, Richard McCullough.
Robert Beltran (Ahbleza the Adult); Devon Ericson (Heyatawin); Rion Hunter (Tonweya); Victoria Racimo (Napewaste); Nick Ramos (Olepi); James Remar (Pesla); Ned Romero (Wisa); Ron Soble (Wanagi); Will Sampson (Wambli); Roger Campo (Young Pesla); Hortensia Colorado (Heyatawin's Mother); Brigitte Gault (Kipanna); Patty Kotero (Wicahpi); Ivan Naranjo (Ogle); Branscombe Richmond (Miyaca); Rita Rogers (Cankuna); Joanelle Nadine Romero (Zitkala); Geno Silva (Huste); Doug Toby (Young Ahbleza); David Yanez (Young Tonweya); George Aguilar (Kungi Yuha Leader); Henry K. Bal (Siyo Breed); Joshua Gallegos (Psa Leader); Darwin V. Mitchell (Sungmani); Tony Russel (Red Lake); Frank Sotonoma Salsedo (Sinte); Sonny Skyhawk (Heyatawin's Father).

"The saga of the first Americans. Fighting to survive in an undiscovered land. The legend of a leader whose vision built the future from the past," read the blurbs for this ABC-TV telefeature based on the book Hanta Yo (1979) by Ruth Beebe Hill and "other material." Set in the early 1800s, the telefilm relates the daily lives and tribal customs of the Mahto, a Great Plains tribe belonging to the family of the Oglala Dakota, or Sioux. the project had begun in 1979 but the work on which it was based drew the ire of Indian purists and historians and the producers became embroiled in a controversy which lasted for several years, with the production finally being completed in 1983.
The story centers around young Ahbleza (Doug Toby), the son of the Mahto chief Olepi (Nick Ramus), a youth who is courageous and an obvious future leader. When he grows to manhood Ahbleza (Robert Beltran) is chosen by the tribe's medicine man Wanagi (Ron Soble) to be his successor. He also falls in love and marries Heyatawin (Devon Ericson). Following the death of his father, Ahbleza becomes the tribe's chief and leads them in battle against their enemies. Eventually, however, the young chief realizes the need to unite the Plains tribes against the white man who has brought misery with guns and liquor. Personal tragedy also follows Ahbleza, who

eventually undergoes spiritual and physical renewal through personal torture, although he fails to save his tribe.

"The depiction of Indian life as more complex than usually portrayed was an interesting plus, but the tale of Ahbleza confronting his ultimate destiny was strangely devoid of dramatic intensity," wrote Variety. Judith Crist determined in TV Guide, "...eventually the mix of anthropology, mysticism and Western 'action' becomes tedious."

THE NAKED DAWN (Universal, 1955) C 82 mins.

Associate producer, James Q. Radford; director, Edgar G. Ulmer; screenplay, Nina and Herman Schneider; music/music conductor, Herschel Burke Gilbert; song, Gilbert and William Copeland; assistant director, Raoul Pagel; camera, Frederick Gately; editor, Dan Milner.

Arthur Kennedy (Santiago); Betta St. John (Maria); Eugene Iglesias (Manuel); Charlita (Tita); Roy Engel (Guntz).

In his book about George Sanders, A Dreadful Man (1979), actor/author Brian Aherne discussed working with director Edgar G. Ulmer on the feature THE CAVERN (1965), and correctly assessed Ulmer by saying he was "...a rather florid, temperamental character who had much experience and some talent but so far not much success." Over the years many highbrow critics, particularly the French, have lionized Ulmer's canon of films and one of the most praised of these is his 1955 Western, THE NAKED DAWN. This film possesses a poetic-like quality, but its thin story-line, lack of action, and only average emoting reduce it to being only of passing interest. While the feature does boast scenic Mexican locales well-filmed by Frederick Gately in Technicolor, Variety correctly assessed that the motion picture "...never rises above the dualer entertainment classification."

Outlaw Santiago (Arthur Kennedy) is on the run from the law and stops at the farm of poor Mexican Manuel (Eugene Iglesias) and his pretty wife Maria (Betta St. John). Santiago enlists the aid of the farmer in helping him retrieve the money he has hidden from the robbery of a freight train. Meanwhile Manuel develops a plan to kill the outlaw and keep the riches for himself, while Maria decides to run away with Santiago to escape poverty. None of the plans are realized, however, because lawman Guntz (Roy Engel) tracks Santiago to the farm and in a shoot-out both men die.

THE NAKED DAWN is pleasant on the eye, as is heroine Betta St. John, but it is a slow-moving drama with too much talk. The only diversion, except the final shoot-out, is a sequence in a cantina where the Mexican farmer and his wife celebrate their supposed new-found fortune and singer Charlita performs the song "Ali Hombre."

THE NAKED SPUR see THE OUTLAW JOSEY WALES

William S. Hart (left) in THE NARROW TRAIL (1918).

THE NARROW TRAIL (Paramount, 1918) five reels

     Producer, William S. Hart; director, Lambert Hillyer; screenplay, Hart; camera, Joseph August.
     William S. Hart (Ice Harding); Sylvia Bremer (Betty Werdin); Milton Ross ("Admiral" Bates); Robert Kortman ("Moose" Halloran); Fritz (The Horse).

     Outlaw Ice Harding (William S. Hart) and his gang capture a wild pinto and Ice tames the horse and names it King. The gang then holds up a stagecoach and the passengers include San Francisco gangster Bates (Milton Ross) and his niece Betty Werdin (Sylvia Bremer). Ice refuses to take the girl's jewelry and later meets her again in Saddle City, where he poses as a rich rancher. Bates intends to cheat Ice out of his money but the girl won't help and Bates returns to San Francisco. Later Ice goes there to find Betty, but thug Moose Halloran (Robert Kortman) spots him and he and his gang scheme to mug Ice on the waterfront; but in a saloon it is Ice who is victorious and there he also rescues Betty. Back in Saddle City, the two decide to go to the right side of the law and they plan a fresh life together, using $1,000 Ice wins in a horse race with King.
     THE NARROW TRAIL, the initial William S. Hart production for Artcraft, is one of the star's best known features because it has received wide distribution in recent years to the home market, via

both film and video cassette. The movie is tightly directed by Lambert Hillyer and contains outstanding cinematography by Joseph August, along with Hart's typical stern performance as the outlaw. At the time of its release, the New York <u>Dramatic Mirror</u> evaluated, "In THE NARROW TRAIL William S. Hart has a film offering of exceptional merit, if suspense and climax go to constitute merit. The story builds with quickening tempo to a crescendo finish which leaves one breathless, and through all the hurry and agitation of movement it unfolds a simple tale of the heart--or of two hearts, rather--which is profoundly moving and convincing." Nearly a half century later, George N. Fenin and William K. Everson wrote in <u>The Western</u> (1962): "It was not only one of Hart's best films, but also a sort of synthesis of all that he had expressed before: sentiment, reformation, action, a love for his horse. The climactic race contained some of the best riding shots of Hart ever taken...."

NEAR THE RAINBOW'S END <u>see</u> NEVADA BUCKAROO

'NEATH CANADIAN SKIES <u>see</u> TRAIL OF THE MOUNTIES

NED KELLY (United Artists, 1970) C 101 mins.

Producer, Neil Hartley; director, Tony Richardson; screenplay, Richardson, Ian Jones; production designer, Jocelyn Herbert; art director, Andrew Sanders; song, Shel Silverstein; assistant director, Andrew Grieve; camera, Gerry Fisher; editor, Charles Rees.
Mick Jagger (Ned Kelly); Clarissa Kaye (Mrs. Kelly); Mark McManus (Joe Byrne); Ken Goodlet (Superintendent Nicholson); Frank Thring (Judge Barry); Bruce Barry (George King); Tony Bazell (Mr. Scott); Allen Bickford (Dan Kelly); Robert Bruning (Sergeant Steele); Alexander Cann (McInnes); David Copping (Curnow); Diane Craig (Maggie Kelly); Gerry Duggan (Father O'Shea); Geoff Gilmour (Steve Hart); Anne Harvey (Mrs. Devine); Serge Lazareff (Wild Wright); Alexi Long (Grace Kelly); Susan Lloyd (Kate Kelly); Nigel Lowell (Captain Standish); Clifford Neate (Living); Jessica Noad (Mrs. Scott); Marilyn Sanderson (Fitzpatrick); Ken Shorter (Aaron Sherritt); Lindsay Smith (McIntyre); Peter Summer (Tom Lloyd); Doreen Warburton (Mrs. Jones); Janne Wesley (Caitlyn).

Ned Kelly, probably the nearest Australian counterpart to America's Jesse James, is a legendary figure from the frontier days Down Under. The Australian-made biopic of the notorious outlaw, directed and co-scripted by Tony Richardson, caused some stir at the time of its production because of the offbeat casting of Mick Jagger (of The Rolling Stones) in the title role. Although the resulting picture made little headway in the genre, or with the general public for that matter, NED KELLY is not an unsatisfying feature and is memorable for its gritty realism in capturing Australia's frontier times. Mick Jagger's interpretation of the morose Kelly is surprisingly good, and the movie's soundtrack--containing several Nashville-oriented tunes performed by country singer Waylon Jennings-- adds life to the proceedings.

Set in Australia in the middle of the last century, the story tells of teenager Ned Kelly (Mick Jagger) being sent to prison on trumped up charges because of his lowly station in life, his father having been deported there for stealing two hogs. After three years behind bars, young Kelly returns home to find his mother (Clarissa Kaye) engaged to American George King (Bruce Barry), a horse thief, and his two brothers in jail for stealing cattle. Ned wants to go legitimate and operate a sawmill, but British policeman Fitzpatrick (Martyn Sanderson) doctors a drink he is having in a bar and arrests him for drunkenness. After his new jail sentence, Kelly joins his brother Dan (Allen Bickford) and King in stealing horses. When Fitzpatrick and his men follow them, they ambush and kill the lawman. When he finds his pregnant mother has been accused of murder, Ned offers himself in her place, but the authorities refuse. Using self-made suits of armor, the gang eludes the law, but later they are trapped and killed in a saloon; all except Ned, who is captured and hanged.

THE NEVADA BUCKAROO (Tiffany, 1931) 59 mins.

Producer, Trem Carr; director, John P. McCarthy; screenplay, Wellyn Totman; editor, Len Wheeler.
Bob Steele (Buck); Dorothy Dix (Joan); George Hayes (Cherokee); Ed Brady (Slade); Glen Cavander (Hank); Billy Engle (Elmer); Artie Ortego (Alex); Merrill McCormick, Al Taylor (Bits).

Cowboy Buck (Bob Steele) and his pal (George Hayes) have been working on the wrong side of the law with two outlaws (Glen Cavander, Billy Engle) and they decide to go straight after Buck falls in love with a stage owner's (Ed Brady) pretty daughter (Dorothy Dix). The duo get jobs protecting the stage, but their two ex-pals rob it and then accuse Buck of being in on the heist. When the outlaws murder his pal, Buck agrees to help the law bring the men to justice. Once this is accomplished, he settles down with his lady love.
Bob Steele made his sound film debut in 1930 in NEAR THE RAINBOW'S END for Tiffany, and starred in seven more features for that studio. They varied in quality; some, like SUNRISE TRAIL (1931), are quite stilted, while others, such as this film and OKLAHOMA CYCLONE (q.v.), move well and are very entertaining. NEVADA BUCKAROO benefits greatly from Wellyn Totman's strong script and John PJ. McCarthy's speedy direction. Film Daily noted, "It works up to some very fast action and surprise stuff that will satisfy the thrill lovers."

NIGHT TIME IN NEVADA (Republic, 1948) C 66 mins.

Associate producer, Edward J. White; director, William Witney; screenplay, Sloan Nibley; music, Dale Butts; music director, Morton Scott; songs: Richard W. Pascoe, Will E. Dulmage, H. O'Reilly Clint, Tim Spencer, Edward Morrissey, Bob Nolan; assistant director, Jack Lacey; art director, Frank Hotaling; set decorators, John McCarthy, Jr., Charles Thompson; makeup, Bob Marks; sound, Herbert Norsch; special effects, Howard and Theodore Lydecker; camera, Jack Marta; editor, Tony Martinelli.

Roy Rogers (Himself); Adele Mara (Joan Andrews); Andy Devine (Cookie Bullfincher); Grant Withers (Ran Farrell); Marie Harmon (Toni Bordon); Joseph Crehan (Casey); George Carleton (Jason Howley); Holly Bane (Mort Oakley); Steve Darrell, Hank Patterson (Tramps); Jim Nolan (Jim Andrews); Bob Nolan and the Sons of the Pioneers (Themselves); Trigger (The Horse).

Sixteen years earlier, Ran Farrell (Grant Withers) murdered his partner over a mine claim, and now the dead man's daughter, Joan Andrews (Adele Mara), appears to claim her share of the mine's proceeds. Farrell then decides to steal Roy Rogers' (Himself) and the Sons of the Pioneers' (Themselves) cattle in order to pay off his debts, and he pretends to be Joan's father. Roy, however, suspects Farrell of the crimes and discovers the truth. When the bad man traps Roy on a train and tries to kill him, local lawman Cookie Bullfincher (Andy Devine) arrives with the Sons of the Pioneers and Farrell is killed in the fight.

Grant Withers' strong work as the villain dominates this exciting Roy Rogers' entry, which is well-helmed by William Witney. Other highlights of the picture are comely Adele Mara as the heroine and the picture's attractive Trucolor photography.

NOOSE FOR A GUNMAN (United Artists, 1960) 90 mins.

Producer, Robert E. Kent; director, Edward L. Cahn; story, Steve Fisher; screenplay, James B. Gordon; art director, Bill Glasgow; assistant director, Herbert S. Greene; sound, Ben Winkler; camera, Al Cline; editor, Grant Whytock.

Jim Davis (Case Britton); Lyn Thomas (Della Haines); Ted de Corsia (Cantrell); Walter Sande (Tom Evans); Barton MacLane (Carl Avery); Harry Carey, Jr. (Jim Ferguson); Lane Chandler (Ed Folsey); John Hart (Barker); Leo Gordon (Link Roy); Bill Tannen (Willetts); Bob Tetrick (Anders); William Remick (Man on Stage Coach); Kermit Maynard (Carter); William Challee (Gorse); Cecil Weston (Mrs. Franklyn).

Gunfighter Case Britton (Jim Davis) is forced to leave his small-town Western home after killing the two sons of land baron Tom Evans (Walter Sande) because they murdered his brother. He finds out that gang leader Cantrell (Ted de Corsia) is in league with

Bob Tetrick, William Challee, James Anderson, and Jim Davis in
NOOSE FOR A GUNMAN (1960).

Evans in planning to rob the town bank and he returns to stop the
plot, but meets opposition from the locals before he is proved correct
and aids them in bringing the culprits in.

Series Westerns had long been assimilated by the small screen,
while "A"-budget sagebrushers were mostly of the psychological
variety by the time this low-budget programmer was released. A
no-frills production with a stalwart hero, comely heroine and
dastardly but colorful villains, NOOSE FOR A GUNMAN harkened
back to the good old action days of the genre. Its somewhat tiresome story is compensated for by a good cast and sturdy direction.

Variety noted, "Audiences will be able to anticipate most of
the action, gestures and character decisions, but they will have a
rough time figuring out most of the motivations, if they bother to
be discriminating about it all."

NORTH OF THE BORDER see TRAIL OF THE MOUNTIES

NORTH TO ALASKA (Twentieth Century-Fox, 1960) C 122 mins.

Producer/director, Henry Hathaway; based on the play Birth-day Gift by Laszlo Foder; adapted from an idea by John Kafka; screenplay, John Lee Mahin, Martin Rackin, Claude Binyon; art directors, Duncan Cramer, Jack Martin Smith; set decorators, Walter M. Scott, Stuart A. Reiss; music, Lionel Newman; orchestrators, Urban Thielmann, Bernard Mayers; choreography, Josephine Earl; song, Russell Faith, Robert P. Marcucci and Peter DeAngelis; assistant director, Stanley Hough; makeup, Ben Nye; costumes, Bill Thomas; second unit director, Richard Talmadge; sound, Alfred Burzlin, Warren B. Delaplain; special camera effects, L. B. Abbott, Emil Kosa, Jr.; sound, Alfred Bruzlin, Warren B. Delaplain; camera, Leon Shamroy; editor, Dorothy Spencer.

John Wayne (Sam McCord); Stewart Granger (George Pratt); Ernie Kovacs (Frankie Canon); Fabian (Billy Pratt); Capucine (Michelle "Angel"); Mickey Shaughnessy (Boggs); Karl Swenson (Lars); Joe Sawyer (Commissioner); Lilyan Chauvin (Jenny); Kathleen Freeman (Lena); John Qualen, Fortune Gordien (Lumberjacks); Stanley Adams (Breezy); Stephen Courtlegh (Duggan); Douglas Dick (Lieutenant); Jerry O'Sullivan (Sergeant); Ollie O'Toole (Mack); Frank Faylen (Arnie); Fred Graham (Ole); Alan Carney (Bartender); Peter Bourne (Olaf); Hobo (Clancy the Dog); Kermit Maynard (Townsman); Esther Dale (Picknicker).

Prospector Sam McCord (John Wayne) and partner George Pratt (Stewart Granger) make a big gold strike in Alaska, and Sam uses the money to go to Seattle to get better machinery for their claim and to bring back George's fiancée Jenny (Lilyan Chauvin). On the boat Sam meets crook Frankie Canon (Ernie Kovacs), who tries to fleece him out of $500, and Sam throws him off the barge along with George's younger brother Billy (Fabian). Canon then befriends both Billy and George, who has remained behind to build a cabin for his bride, and sells George a bogus diamond ring for Jenny. In Seattle, Sam finds that Jenny is already married and in a saloon he meets Michelle (Capucine). He conceives the idea of bringing her back for George, but the girl thinks Sam wants her. When she learns the truth, Michelle throws away the money Sam has given her and in Nome she meets up with Canon, her former lover. He tries to persuade the girl to help him steal Sam and George's mine, but she refuses. Canon continues his plot, however, when he finds out that his drunken porter (Mickey Shaughnessy) once had a trapline across the McCord-Pratt gold claim. Later at the goldmine, Sam and George leave to aid a fellow prospector from claim jumpers and Billy makes advances to Michelle. Upon their return, George, who is upset, throws Michelle and Sam off the property, but later Michelle tells him the truth. He tries to patch up things between her and Sam, but his partner and Billy turn against them. Soldiers arrive to tell the two men that the mine has been impounded due to Canon's cross-filing on the area, and Sam is arrested when he tries to take his share of the mine. Fed up, Michelle plans to return to Seattle. When Sam discovers the truth behind the cross-filing, he and George and Billy take after the porter and Canon and defeat them in a street brawl. As the boat whistle announces Michelle's departure, Sam admits he loves her and the three men go to the boat, where she decides to remain with Sam.

"This is a bouncy, richly enjoyable comedy that set a pattern for most of Wayne's films since, showing him fully at ease with humorous material and marking the beginning of a much broader style to his playing," assessed Allen Eyles in John Wayne and the Movies (1976). Actually the movie was conceived as a straightforward adventure melodrama but its makers realized its lighthearted potential and switched it to a brawling comedy, with exceedingly good results. Despite its two hours-plus running time, the film never drags; it is lushly photographed, and very entertaining. John Wayne and Stewart Granger are nicely teamed as the two gold prospector partners, while Capucine is effective as the feisty heroine and the villainy of Ernie Kovacs and Mickey Shaughnessy is never threatening. The film grossed $5,000,000 in domestic box-office rentals.

NORTHERN FRONTIER (Ambassador, 1935) 56 mins.

Producer, Maurice Conn; director, Sam Newfield; suggested by the story "Four Minutes Late" by James Oliver Curwood; adaptor, Barry Barringer; camera, Edgar Lyons; editor, Jack English.

Kermit Maynard (Trooper MacKenzie); Eleanor Hunt (Beth Braden); Russell Hopton (Duke Milford); J. Farrell MacDonald (Inspector Stevens); LeRoy Mason (Bull Stone); Ben Hendricks, Jr. (Federal Agent Sam Keene); Gertrude Astor (Mae); Rocky (The Horse); Tyrone Power (Mountie); and Dick Curtis, Kernan Cripps, Jack Chisholm, Lloyd Ingraham, Lafe McKee, Artie Ortego, Walter Brennan.

NORTHERN FRONTIER was the second of eighteen feature films Kermit Maynard made for producer Maurice Conn's Ambassador Pictures between 1934 and 1938. The younger brother of Ken Maynard, Kermit had previously headlined a half-dozen silent oaters for Rayart in 1927, where he was billed as Tex Maynard. In his Ambassador series, Kermit was usually cast as a Mountie and most of the films were allegedly based on works by popular author James Oliver Curwood. THE FIGHTING TROOPER (1934) opened the series and NORTHERN FRONTIER followed and "was a definite improvement over the first" (Don Miller, Hollywood Corral, 1976).

Gangsters led by Duke Milford (Russell Hopton) have come north into Canada and the head of the Mounties, Inspector Stevens (J. Farrell MacDonald), assigns trooper MacKenzie (Kermit Maynard) to work with U.S. federal agent Keene (Ben Hendricks, Jr.) in rounding up the racketeers who are heading a counterfeiting operation. Working incognito, MacKenzie infiltrates the gang and also romances pretty Beth Braden (Eleanor Hunt). After getting the goods on the hoodlums, the mountie rounds up the gangsters.

Film buffs should be on the lookout for Tyrone Power, who

Nelson Eddy and Peter Gurs (trumpeter) in NORTHWEST OUTPOST
(1947).

appears briefly as a Mountie, while Walter Brennan also has a minor
role as a north country denizen.

NORTHWEST OUTPOST (Republic, 1947) C 91 mins.

Producer/director, Allan Dwan; story, Angela Stuart; adaptor,
Laird Doyle; music, Rudolf Friml; songs, Friml and Edward Hey-
man; music director, Robert Armbruster; camera, Reggie Lanning;
editor, Harry Keller.
Nelson Eddy (Captain James Laurence); Ilona Massey (Natalie
Alanova); Joseph Schildkraut (Count Igor Savin); Elsa Lanchester
(Princess Tanya); Hugo Haas (Prince Nickolai Balinin); Lenore Ul-
ric (Baroness Kruposny); Peter Whitney (Volkoff); Tamara Shayne
(Olga); Erno Verebes (Kyril); George Sorel (Baron Kruposny);
Rick Vallin (Dovkin); American GI Chorus (Convicts); Peter Gurs
(Trumpeter).

The year before Republic Pictures was financially overwhelmed
by Orson Welles' near-incomprehensible version of MACBETH (1948),
the studio almost suffered a similar monetary fate with its attempt to
revive the movie operetta with Rudolf Friml's original score for
NORTHWEST OUTPOST. A slow beginning nearly doomed the
feature, although its "Plot setting is fresh and novel enough to
offset the frequently stilted dialog and familiar situations" (Variety).

Nelson Eddy, in his final film appearance, does well and is particularly good in handling Friml's pretty melodies, but war-weary
audiences simply did not want sugary historical musicals. As Harry
Banta judged in his article on Nelson Eddy in Films in Review (February, 1974), "The background for the opening titles revealed a
nearly becalmed ship on the high seas, with male chorus singing a
dirge-like hymn a capella. The film never overcame this dreary beginning and the critics made fun of it."

    The film is set in 1830s California in territory claimed by Rus-
sia, and U.S. Army Cavalry Captain James Laurence (Nelson Eddy)
arrives in the area as the vanguard of a mission to take the territory for the United States. He finds the Russian fort stronghold
under the command of the dense Prince Nickolai Balinin (Hugo Haas)
and his dizzy wife Princess Tanya (Elsa Lanchester). The fort is
actually a prison camp for political outcasts, including Count Igor
Savin (Joseph Schildkraut), who has been thrown out of his native
land for treason. In order to save his co-conspirator, Savin had
forced the man's daughter Natalie (Ilona Massey) to marry him and
she has now come to the area to free her husband, although she
does not love him. Logan finds the Russians have developed a
lucrative fur and lumber trade, but are harassed by Indians. Meanwhile he meets and falls in love with Natalie. Through his own evil
machinations, Savin is killed, the Russians are overthrown, and
Laurence and Natalie plan a life together.

OKLAHOMA BLUES (Monogram, 1948) 56 mins.

    Producer, Louis Gray; director, Lambert Hillyer; screenplay,
Bennett Cohen; music director, Edward J. Kay; assistant director,
Eddie Davis; art director, Vin Taylor; sound, Earl Sitar; camera,
Harry Neumann; editors, Fred Maguire, John C. Fuller.

    Jimmy Wakely (Himself); Dub Taylor (Cannonball); Virginia
Belmont (Judy); George Lewis (Slip Drago); Zon Murray (Matt Drago);
I. Stanford Jolley (Beasley); Steve Clark (Sheriff Oldring); Frank
LaRue (Judge); Milburn Morante (Amos); Charles L. King, Jr.
[Charles King] (Gabe); J. C. Lytton (State Commissioner Walton);
Richard [Dick] Reinhardt (Joe); Arthur Smith (Pete); Don Weston
(Ray); and Bob Woodward.

    When outlaws Slip Drago (George Lewis) and Matt Drago (Zon
Murray) hold up the stage he is riding, State Commissioner Walton
(J. C. Lytton) has second thoughts about making Rainbow's End the
county seat. The local undertaker, Beasley (I. Stanford Jolley), is
behind all the lawlessness because he wants the county government
in nearby Yuba, since his holdings there will make him wealthy.
In Rainbow's End, local character Cannonball (Dub Taylor) tells of
a fictitious bandit called the Melody Kid and claims he is his pal
Jimmy Wakely (Himself). Pretty Judy (Virginia Belmont), owner of
the local cafe, refuses to serve Jimmy because she thinks he is the
Melody Kid, but later Jimmy stops Slip when he starts a fight in the

Jimmy Wakely, Dub Taylor, and Steve Clark in OKLAHOMA BLUES (1948).

establishment. As a result the local judge (Frank LaRue) makes Jimmy deputy marshal after the Dragos sideline the sheriff (Steve Clark). The Dragos, however, set Jimmy up on a false murder charge, but Cannonball aids in his escape from jail. Later, Jimmy is captured by the Drago gang. The sheriff and Cannonball lead a posse to the outlaws' headquarters and by a ruse Jimmy causes their capture. As a result, Rainbow's End becomes the county seat as Jimmy and Cannonball ride out of town.

OKLAHOMA BLUES came towards the end of the trail in Jimmy Wakely's Monogram series, which ran from 1944 to 1949. By this time, veteran Republic producer Louis Gray had taken over the series and the films now relied more on plot and action than music. This was a liability for the star, who was a superb singer but a mediocre actor at best. In previous films, Dennis Moore and John James had played strong second leads to Wakely, but none was present here.

OKLAHOMA CYCLONE (Tiffany, 1930) 66 mins.

Producer, Trem Carr; director/screenplay, John P. McCarthy;

adaptor, Ford Beebe; settings, R. R. Hickson; assistant director, Terry Murdock; camera, M. A. Anderson; editor, Fred Allen.

Bob Steele (Jim Smith/Oklahoma Cyclone); Nita Rey (Carmelita); Al St. John (Slim); Charles L. King (McKim); Hector Sarno (The Don); Slim Whittaker (Rawhide); Shorty Hendrix (Shorty); Emilio Fernandez (Panchez Gomez); and Hector Sarno, Fred Burns, Cliff Lyons, John Ince.

Cowboy Jim Smith (Bob Steele) arrives at the rancho of The Don (Hector Sarno) and corrupt foreman McKim (Charles King) hires him, thinking he is the notorious bandit, "The Oklahoma Cyclone." McKim, however, warns him to stay away from the Don's pretty daughter Carmelita (Nita Rey), whom McKim loves. Jim, nevertheless, serenades the girl with his songs and guitar, which makes the foreman jealous. McKim is really the leader of a local outlaw gang which includes ranch hand Slim (Al St. John). The latter befriends Jim since he dislikes McKim. Jim joins the gang and they rob a bank and head to a cantina south of the border where they hold a lawman (Fred Burns) prisoner. The man is Jim's father, but Jim pretends not to know his dad. McKim suspects a ruse and later catches Jim attempting to set his father free. In a fight between McKim and Jim in the cantina, the mortally-wounded Slim kills McKim as Carmelita arrives with a posse.

OKLAHOMA CYCLONE, Bob Steele's second talkie, holds up well today, being more actionful and speedy than most oaters from this period. For its limited budget, the movie is lushly made, especially with its hacienda sequences. Music plays a big part in the picture, with star Bob Steele playing the guitar and singing two tunes, "Song of the Range" and "Let Me Live Out on the Prairie," plus a bit of a then popular Tin Pan Alley song, "Roll, Roll, Rollin' Along." As a result, Bob Steele was one of the first singing Western stars, predating John Wayne's Lone Star-Monogram series by three years and Gene Autry by four years. In addition to these early Bob Steele Tiffany releases, music was used by Ken Maynard in his initial Universal films, and Charles Delaney sang in his 1930 Syndicate starrer, THE LONESOME TRAIL, issued at the same time as OKLAHOMA CYCLONE.

OKLAHOMA JIM (Monogram, 1931) 53 mins.

Producer, Trem Carr; director/story, Harry Fraser; screenplay, G. A. Durlam.

Bill Cody (Oklahoma Jim Kirby); Marion Burns (Betty Rankin); Andy Shuford (Jerry); William Desmond (Lacey); Franklyn Farnum (Army Captain); Earl Dwire (Sergeant); Iron Eyes Cody (War Eagle); and Gordon DeMain, J. W. Cody, Ann Ross, Art Ortego, White Eagle.

Bill Cody was one of those lower-rung Western film stars whose career lasted from the silents into the talkies, and from 1925 to 1936

he headlined some three dozen "B" oaters for a variety of studios.
Like many of his contemporaries: (e.g., Wally Wales, Yakima
Canutt), Cody made a better appearance in silent films than in
talkies, and in the sound era he worked mainly for low-grade outfits like Syndicate, Spectrum and Aywon, appearing for the latter
in junk entries like BORDER MENACE (1935) (q.v.).

OKLAHOMA JIM, one of Cody's first talkies, is one of his
better-budgeted starrers, but this Monogram production is slow
moving, poorly recorded, and contains too much stock footage. In
it, Bill Cody stars as gambler Oklahoma Jim, headquartered in a
saloon owned by crook Lacey (William Desmond). The latter seduces
a pretty Indian maiden and she commits suicide. He decides to
clear out, but is stopped when his late partner's niece, Betty Rankin (Marion Burns), arrives and attracts the attention of Oklahoma
Jim. Both Jim and Lacey are blamed for the death of the Indian
girl. At the Indian camp Lacey runs and is killed, leaving Jim to
a life of happiness with Betty.

OLD SHATTERHAND (Constantin, 1964) C 122 mins.

Producer, Artur Brauner; director, Hugo Fregonese; screenplay, Ladislas Fodor, Robert A. Stemmle; music, Riz Ortolani;
camera, Siegfried Hold; editor, Alfred Srp.

Lex Barker (Old Shatterhand); Pierre Brice (Winnetou);
Daliah Lavi (Paloma); Guy Madison (Bradley); Ralf Wolter (Sam Haw-
kens); Gustave Rojo (Bush); Rik Battaglia (Dixon); Kitti Mattern
(Rosemary); Alain Tissier (Tununga); Charles Fawcett (General
Taylor).

After General Taylor (Charles Fawcett) leaves for Washington,
outlaws and their Comanche Indian comrades pose as Apaches and
pillage small ranches in an effort to discredit the Apaches and steal
their pasture lands. Two witnesses to the attacks are escorted by
scout Old Shatterhand (Lex Barker) to a cavalry patrol led by Captain Bradley (Guy Madison). The patrol is later attacked, with two
Apaches killed in the fracas. Old Shatterhand feels there is
treachery involved and he goes to his blood brother, Apache chief
Winnetou (Pierre Brice), for guidance. When yet another person is
killed, Shatterhand suspects Bradley of being responsible for the
raids. Winnetou's son (Alain Tissier) is arrested on a murder
charge by Bradley and the Apaches attack the fort when they find
out that Old Shatterhand has also been detained. During the battle
the chief's son blows up the fort's ammunition supply, but is killed.
The battle ceases when General Taylor returns, arrests Bradley,
and finalizes a treaty between the Apaches and the government.

Also called APACHE'S LAST BATTLE, OLD SHATTERHAND was
the third 1960s West German film to be based on the public domain
characters created by Karl May. The 122-minute feature was made
on location in Yugoslavia and was filmed in 70 mm Super Panorama. It
was first issued in the U.S. in 1964 as OLD SHATTERHAND and was

Pierre Brice in OLD SHATTERHAND (1964).

reissued here in 1968 as the 98-minute SHATTERHAND. When it was first distributed, Variety noted, "...director Hugo Fregonese has given this the typical American action slant. The screenplay is the weakest thing about OLD SHATTERHAND."

Of all the Karl May-derived features this one had the most commercial appeal stateside, because not only did Lex Barker star in it, but the film also featured Guy Madison as well as the lovely international leading lady Daliah Lavi.

THE OLD TEXAS TRAIL <u>see</u> RIDERS OF OLD SANTA FE

OLD YELLER (Buena Vista, 1957) C 83 mins.

Producer, Walt Disney; director, Robert Stevenson; based on the novel by Fred Gipson; screenplay, Gipson, William Tunberg; music, Oliver Wallace; art director, Carroll Clark; second unit director, Yakima Canutt; camera, Charles P. Boyle; editor, Stanley Johnson.

Dorothy McGuire and Tommy Kirk in OLD YELLER (1957).

Dorothy McGuire (Kate Coates); Fess Parker (Jim Coates); Tommy Kirk (Travis Coates); Kevin Corcoran (Arliss Coates); Jeff York (Bud Searcy); Beverly Washburn (Lisabeth Searcy); Chuck Connors (Burn Sanderson).

In 1869 Texas, rancher Jim Coates (Fess Parker) leaves his family for three months to embark on a cattle drive. His wife Katie (Dorothy McGuire) and sons Travis (Tommy Kirk) and Arliss (Kevin Corcoran) must now run the spread. A stray dog comes to the ranch and Arliss adopts him; before long the animal proves to be a good watchdog and becomes the family pet. A cowboy (Chuck Connors) arrives to claim the dog as his, but he realizes how much the boys are attached to the animal and trades him for a horned toad. Later Travis takes the dog--now dubbed Old Yeller--on a wild pig hunt and the dog ends up fighting the razorbacks when Travis falls out of a tree trying to rope one of the porkers. Both Travis and the dog are badly hurt, but both mend. Travis is forced to kill the dog when it becomes evident that he has contracted rabies from the pigs. Neighbor Bud Searcy (Jeff York) has a female dog who has had pups by Old Yeller and his daughter Lisabeth (Beverly Washburn) offers Travis one of them, but he refuses the animal. When his father returns home he tells Travis that events in life, like Old Yeller's death, must be faced. The boy finally accepts the pup as his own.

"OLD YELLER is a lovely film, under the able guidance of Robert Stevenson, who treats his subject with dignity and understatement that brings out all the emotion inherent in the story. In less skilled hands the same material could have been cloying and phony; his film never sinks to that level" (Leonard Maltin, The Disney Films, 1973).

OLD YELLER is particularly effective in its recreation of family ranch life in the post-Civil War period in Texas and it includes interesting character performances, especially by Jeff York as the bombastic neighbor. Although a leisurely executed feature, the movie has well staged action scenes--the work of second unit director Yakima Canutt.

OLD YELLER grossed more than $8,000,000 at the box office and several years later resulted in a follow-up, OLD SAM (1963), which again casts Tommy Kirk and Kevin Corcoran as the Coates brothers. With neighbor Lisabeth (Marta Kristen) they are captured by Indians, and the boys' dog, Sam, and their uncle (Brian Keith) effect a rescue.

ONLY THE VALIANT (Warner Bros., 1951) 104 mins.

Producer, William Cagney; director, Gordon Douglas; based on the novel by Charles Marquis Warren; screenplay, Edmund H. North, Harry Brown; music, Franz Waxman; orchestrator, Leonard Krab; assistant director, William Kissell; art director, Wiard Inhen; set decorator, Armor E. Marlowe; costumes, Leah Rhodes; sound, Leslie

Now *WARNER BROS.* *present*

GREGORY PECK

...*as Captain Lance who gave Fort Invincible its name!*

The more desperate his fight on the desert's 'scorching sands, the more adored he was in her arms

ONLY THE VALIANT

ALSO STARRING
BARBARA PAYTON · WARD BOND **WITH** **GIG YOUNG · LON CHANEY**
SCREEN PLAY BY EDMUND H. NORTH AND HARRY BROWN **MUSIC BY FRANZ WAXMAN**
FROM THE NOVEL BY CHARLES MARQUIS WARREN
DIRECTED BY **DISTRIBUTED BY**
GORDON DOUGLAS · WILLIAM CAGNEY Prod. · WARNER BROS.

and ON THE WAY
"CAPTAIN HORATIO HORNBLOWER"
COLOR BY TECHNICOLOR

and!
"A STREETCAR NAMED DESIRE"

G. Hewitt; camera, Lionel Linden; editors, Walt Hannemann, Robert
S. Seiter.

Gregory Peck (Captain Richard Lance); Barbara Payton (Cathy
Eversham); Ward Bond (Corporal Timothy Gilchrist); Gig Young
(Lieutenant William Holloway); Lon Chaney (Trooper Kebussyan);
Neville Brand (Sergeant Ben Murdock); Jeff Corey (Joe Harmony);
Warner Anderson (Trooper Rutledge); Steve Brodie (Trooper Onstot);
Dan Riss (Lieutenant Jerry Winters); Terry Kilburn (Trooper Sax-
ton); Herbert Heyes (Colonel Drumm); Art Baker (Captain Jennings);
Hugh Sanders (Captain Eversham); Michael Ansara (Tucsos); Nana
Bryant (Mrs. Drumm).

Following a muted attempt to establish an acting career for
himself in the shadow of his famous brother James, William Cagney
turned to film production and one of his efforts was this early 1950s
psychological Western. It was an illustration of Freud out West.
The film is laced with fine performances and an underlying sexual
frustration played against the burning desert heat. It proved to be
more intelligent and cerebral than filmgoers were used to or wanted.

Assigned to go into the desert to thwart an Apache attack,
stern Captain Richard Lance (Gregory Peck) is leading a squad of
half a dozen men who hate his straight-laced ways as well as each
other. They are: Trooper Kebussyan (Lon Chaney), a murderous
Bedouin Arab; sadistic Sergeant Ben Murdock (Neville Brand);
Trooper Rutledge (Warner Anderson), who was thrown out of West
Point; trooper Onstot (Steve Brodie), who has attempted desertion;
drunkard Corporal Gilchrist (Ward Bond); and frightened recruit
Saxton (Terry Kilburn). Along the way the men pick up Indian attack survivor Cathy Eversham (Barbara Payton), whose blatant
charms set the men off against each other. Lance tries to save the
woman and his cohorts from themselves and the marauding redskins.

Perhaps the greatest weakness of ONLY THE VALIANT is its
too keen interest in the psychological interplay between the story's
diverse characters, a departure from the tried-and-true traditions
of the Western genre. If a bit more effort had been made to beef
up the action, the movie could have been more than a hazy adult
melodrama.

OREGON TRAIL (Universal/NBC-TV, 1/10/76) C 100 mins.

Producer, Michael Gleason; associate producer, Carl Vitale;
director, Boris Sagal; teleplay, Gleason; music, David Shire; art
director, Norman R. Newberry; camera, Jack Woolf; editors, Jamie
Caylor, Larry Strong.

Rod Taylor (Evan Thorpe); Blair Brown (Jessica Thorpe);
David Huddleston (Painted Face Kelly); Douglas V. Fowley (Eli
Thorpe); Andrew Stevens (Andrew Thorpe); Tony Becker (William
Thorpe); Gina Maria Smika (Rachel Thorpe); G. D. Spardlin (Thomas
Hern); Linda Purl (Deborah Randal); George Kermas (Trenchard);
Eddie Little Sky (Sioux Brave); Robert Karnes (Hatcher); Jerry

Rod Taylor and Blair Brown in THE OREGON TRAIL (1976).

Hardin (Macklin); Wilford Brimley (Ludlow); Hoke Howell (Vaughn); Walker Edmiston (George Cutter); John Wyler (Reverend Turner).

In the early 1840s farmer Evan Thorpe (Rod Taylor) leaves his midwest home and travels west with his wife Jessica (Blair Brown) and three children (Andrew Stevens, Tony Becker, Gina Maria Smika). The family joins a wagon train headed to Oregon and Evan is soon elected its wagon master. En route, the pioneers face an outbreak of plague, hostile environments, and attacking Indians. Evans, with the aid of old-timer Eli Thorpe (Douglas V. Fowley), does his best to keep the train together so they will reach their destination safely.

Rod Taylor is especially good as the wagon master in this made-for-TV feature and is complemented by Blair Brown as his understanding wife and Douglas V. Fowley as the crusty relative.

While THE OREGON TRAIL was aired at the start of 1976 it was some twenty months later at the beginning of the 1977-78 video season that the NBC-TV series, "The Oregon Trail," debuted. Rod Taylor repeated his role as Evan Thorpe as did Andrew Stevens, Tony Becker and Gina Maria Smika as his offspring. In the show, Thorpe was a widower attracted to pretty wagon train passenger Margaret Devlin (Darleen Carr). Also starring in the program was Charles Napier as wagon train scout Luther Sprague. The low-rated series was canceled before the year was out.

OREGON TRAIL SCOUTS (Republic, 1947) 58 mins.

Associate producer, Sidney Picker; director, R. G. Springsteen; based on the comic strip by Fred Harman; screenplay, Earle Snell; art director, Paul Youngblood; set decorator, John McCarthy, Jr.; assistant director, Joe Kramer; music director, Mort Glickman; sound, William E. Clark; camera, Alfred Keller; editor, Harold R. Minter.

Allan "Rocky" Lane (Red Ryder); Bobby Blake (Little Beaver); Martha Wentworth (The Duchess); Roy Barcroft (Bill Hunter); Emmett Lynn (Bear Trap); Edmund Cobb (Jack); Earle Hodgins (Judge); Edward Cassidy (Bliss); Frank Lackteen (Running Fox); Billy Cummings (Barking Squirrel); Jack Kirk (Stage Coach Driver); Blackjack (The Horse); and Jack O'Shea, Chief Yowlachie.

In 1946 Allan "Rocky" Lane took over the role of Red Ryder in SANTA FE UPRISING and made seven series entries before reverting back to a regular Western format in 1948. OREGON TRAIL SCOUTS brought into play the characters of The Duchess (Martha Wentworth), Ryder's aunt, and his Indian boy pal, Little Beaver (Bobby Blake). The film had plenty of action, despite its juvenile approach and inexpensive look.

A group of hoodlums led by Bill Hunter (Roy Barcroft) tries to steal trapping rights from local Indians by kidnapping young Indian boy Little Beaver (Bobby Blake) from the sideshow man (Emmett

Lynn) who years before had taken in the youth after the gang had stolen him from his Indian chief grandfather. Red Ryder (Allan "Rocky" Lane) also wants the trapping rights and comes to the aid of the Indians and helps them round up the gang and free Little Beaver.

OUT WEST WITH THE HARDYS (Metro-Goldwyn-Mayer, 1938) 84 mins.

Director, George B. Seltz; based on characters created by Aurania Rouverol; screenplay, Kay Van Riper, Agnes Christine Johnston, William Ludwig; camera, Lester White; editor, Ben Lewis.

Lewis Stone (Judge Hardy); Mickey Rooney (Andy Hardy); Cecilia Parker (Marian Hardy); Fay Holden (Mrs. Hardy); Ann Rutherford (Polly Benedict); Sara Haden (Aunt Milly); Don Castle (Dennis Hunt); Virginia Weidler ("Jake" Holt); Gordon Jones (Ray Holt); Ralph Morgan (Bill Northcote); Nana Bryant (Dora Northcote); Tom Neal (Aldrich Brown); Anthony Allan (Cliff Thomas).

Cecilia Parker, Mickey Rooney, Fay Holden, Lewis Stone, Virginia
Weidler, and Sara Haden in OUT WEST WITH THE HARDYS (1938).

The fifth in the long-running and exceedingly popular "Andy
Hardy" series, OUT WEST WITH THE HARDYS was the third entry
with the established repertory group of Lewis Stone as avuncular
Judge Hardy, Mickey Rooney as teenager Andy, Cecilia Parker as
older sister Marian, Fay Holden as homey Mrs. Hardy, Sara Haden
as helpful Aunt Milly, and Anne Rutherford as Andy's patient girl,
Polly Benedict. Switching the locale of the series from the mythical
small town of Carvel to a Western ranch added zest to the proceedings. the film's subplots--Andy's rivalry with young tomboy Jake
(Virginia Weidler) and Marian's romance with the girl's older foreman
brother (Gordon Jones)--bring a great deal of viewing pleasure.
"Picture is studded with entertaining factors throughout its unfolding.
Nicely paced and with smoothness in development, it has numerous
comedy moments in both situation and dialog, and provides opportunity for excellent performances by Mickey Rooney, Lewis Stone and
little Virginia Weidler" (Variety).
     The Hardy family receives an invitation to visit a Western
ranch as the Judge (Lewis Stone) comes to the aid of rancher friend
Bill Northcote (Ralph Morgan), whose spread is in danger of going
under as a result of the underhanded shenanigans of a neighbor involving water rights. At the ranch pretty sister Marian falls in love

with foreman Ray Holt (Gordon Jones) while the latter's little sister, tomboy "Jake" (Virginia Weidler), manages to outwit show-off Andy Hardy (Mickey Rooney) at every turn. Eventually the Judge uses the law to regain Northcote's water rights, Andy and Jake come to terms, and Marian realizes she does not really love Ray. The family happily returns to Carvel and normalcy.

THE OUTCAST (Republic, 1954) C 90 mins.

Associate producer, William J. O'Sullivan; director, William Witney; based on a story by Todhunter Ballard; screenplay, John K. Butler, Richard Wormser; music, R. Dale Butts; camera, Reggie Lanning; editor, Tony Martinelli.

John Derek (Jet Cosgrave); Joan Evans (Judy Polsen); Jim Davis (Major Cosgrave); Catherine McLeod (Alice Austin); Ben Cooper (The Kid); Taylor Holmes (Andrew Devlin); Nana Bryant (Mrs. Banner); Slim Pickens (Boone Polsen); James Millican (Cal Prince); Bob Steele (Dude Rankin); Nacho Galindo (Curly); Harry Carey, Jr. (Bert); Bill Walker (Sam Allen); Robert "Buzz" Henry (Zeke Polsen); Nicolas Coster (Asa Polsen).

Young Jet Cosgrave (John Derek) returns home to claim his late father's ranch, only to find that his crooked uncle, Major Cosgrove (Jim Davis), has taken possession of it, claiming that the old man's will left it to him. Jet is convinced the will is a forgery and tries to find the valid document. He is helped by pretty Judy Polsen (Joan Evans), who wants to marry him. Jet, however, is badly beaten by Major's hired gunmen, Cal Prince (James Millican) and Dude Rankin (Bob Steele), and is helped by Alice Austin (Catherine McLeod), his uncle's fiancée, who develops a yen for Jet. Finally Jet finds the real will and in a showdown eliminates his vicious uncle.

After making nearly forty feature "B" Westerns with Roy Rogers and Rex Allen at Republic, the dying studio assigned director William Witney to "A" productions and THE OUTCAST was the first of these, done in color. Francis M. Nevins, Jr., in his chapter on William Witney in Close Up: The Contract Director (1976), called the film "a superb Western," while Variety noted it "...has enough action footage to sustain general interest."

THE OUTCAST is a highly effective film with its basic good-versus-evil plot-line. The romantic angle receives a twist, with the hero having to decide between the young woman and the more experienced girl friend of his evil uncle. Jim Davis breathes the most life into this feature as the calculating, murderous uncle who will undertake anything to keep his property. His work is complemented by James Millican and Bob Steele as the tough hired gunmen.

OUTLAW FURY see HOSTILE COUNTRY

John Derek, Slim Pickens, and Robert "Buzz" Henry in THE OUTCAST (1954).

THE OUTLAW JOSEY WALES (Warner Bros., 1976) C 135 mins.

Producer, Robert Daley; director, Clint Eastwood; based on the novel Gone to Texas by Forrest Carter; screenplay, Phil Kaufman, Sonia Chernus; music, Jerry Fielding; production designer, Tambi Larsen; set decorator, Chuck Pierce; assistant director, Jim Fargo; stunt coordinator, Walter Scott; sound, Tex Rudloff, Bert Hallberg; camera, Bruce Surtees; editor, Ferris Webster.

Clint Eastwood (Josey Wales); Chief Dan George (Lone Watie); Sondra Locke (Laura Lee); Bill McKinney (Terrill); John Vernon (Fletcher); Paula Trueman (Grandma Sarah); Sam Bottoms (Jamie); Geraldine Keams (Little Moonlight); Woodrow Parfrey (Carpetbagger); Joyce Jameson (Rose); Sheb Wooley (Cobb); Royal Dano (Ten Spot); Matt Clarke (Kelly); John Verros (Chato); Will Sampson (Ten Bears); William O'Connell (Carstairs); John Quade (Comanchero Leader).

At the end of the Civil War, Union renegades raid the farm of Josey Wales (Clint Eastwood), which is located on the Missouri-Kansas border, killing his wife and young son and leaving him for dead. The farmer then sets out for revenge and goes to a Confederate fort where the commander (John Vernon) has been tricked into surrender by the Union leader (Bill McKinney) of the renegades, with most of the Rebel soldiers being shot. Wales again escapes and on the trail meets an elderly Indian chief (Chief Dan George) who has left the reservation. Together they go to Mexico, with the

Clint Eastwood in THE OUTLAW JOSEY WALES (1976).

Union men in pursuit. When marauders attack the wagon of a pretty settler (Sondra Locke) and try to rape her, Wales comes to her rescue and the young woman, her grandmother (Paula Trueman) and a Navajo girl (Geraldine Keams) join their party. They rebuild a run-down, abandoned ranch and the group settles in. When the Union leader finds them, he is killed in a shoot-out with Wales. The former Confederate fort commander, forced to ride with the renegades, tells Josey he will turn in a false report that Josey has been killed. Wales looks forward to a peaceful life tilling the earth.

THE OUTLAW JOSEY WALES marked Clint Eastwood's first Western in some time and it would be his last until PALE RIDER (q.v.) in 1985. He directed this long and austere tale of revenge and it is overall a satisfying piece of work. Especially memorable are the interchanges between Eastwood and philosophical Chief Dan George and the brutal sequence where the ruffians try to rape Locke. Some observers noted a strong resemblance between this film and the Anthony Mann-directed, James Stewart Western, THE NAKED SPUR (1952), which also had an eye-for-an-eye motif and extolled the nourishing, regenerative effect of the earth.

THE OUTLAW JOSEY WALES grossed $13,500,000 in domestic film rentals.

THE OUTLAW'S DAUGHTER (Twentieth Century-Fox, 1954) C 76
    mins.

    Producer/director, Wesley Barry; screenplay, Sam Roeca; music, Raoul Kraushaar; camera, Gordon Avil; editor, Ace Herman.
    Bill Williams (Jess); Jim Davis (Dan); Kelly Ryan (Kate);

Bill Williams, Kelly Ryan in OUTLAW'S DAUGHTER (1954).

Elisha Cook (Tulsa); George Cleveland (Lem); Guinn "Big Boy" Williams (Moose); Nelson Leigh (Dalton); Sara Hayden (Mrs. Merrill); George Barrows (Rock); Zon Murray (Duke the Bartender); Zabudea (Mexican Dancer); Dick Powers (Bank Manager); Regina Gleason (Eastern Girl); Sam Flint (Doctor); Eugene Anderson, Jr. (Rider); Paul Stader, Danny Fisher (Stunt Men).

Economically directed and produced by Wesley Barry (a former child actor), THE OUTLAW'S DAUGHTER "stands quite a few notches above average" (Variety) for a "B" Western programmer of the mid-1950s. Sam Roeca's script keeps the action pulsating, and the work of the three leads, Bill Williams, Jim Davis and Kelly Ryan (in the title assignment), is compelling and well supported by character actors Elisha Cook and Guinn "Big Boy" Williams.

Outlaw Jess (Bill Williams) murders famous highwaymen James Dalton and the latter's daughter (Kelly Ryan) moves to a new locale where she falls in love with the local lawman Dan (Jim Davis). The girl, Kate Dalton, later comes to believe that Dan killed her father. When Jess turns up, the sheriff tries to arrest him and the girl not only helps him escape, but departs with him. She joins his outlaw gang, but the men are hunted by Dan and his posse and after a shoot-out Jess is killed. Only Kate survives. She learns who really killed her father and, although Dan offers to set her free, she insists upon returning to town to stand trial for her crimes.

THE OUTLAWS IS COMING (Columbia, 1965) 89 mins.

Producer/director/story, Norman Maurer; screenplay, Elwood Ullman; art director, Robert Peterson; set decorator, James M. Crowe; music, Paul Dunlap; assistant director, Don Gold; makeup, Joe Dibella; special effects, Richard Albain; sound, James Z. Flaster, Win Hancock, William Bernds; camera, Irving Lippman; editor, Aaron Nibley.

Larry Fine, Moe Howard, Joe De Rita (The Three Stooges); Adam West (Kenneth Cabot); Nancy Kovack (Annie Oakley); Mort Mills (Trigger Mortis); Don Lamond (Rance Roden); Rex Holman (Sunstroke Kid) Emil Sitka (Mrs. Abernathy/Witch Doctor/Cavalry Colonel); Henry Gibson (Charlie Horse); Murray Alper (Chief Crazy Horse); Tiny Brauer (Bartender); Joe Bolton (Rob Dalton); Bill Camfield (Wyatt Earp); Hal Fryer (Johnny Ringo); Johnny Ginger (Billy the Kid); Wayne Mack (Jesse James); Ed T. McDonnell (Bat Masterson); Bruce Sedley (Cole Younger); Paul Shannon (Wild Bill Hickok); Sally Starr (Belle Starr); and Marilyn Fox, Sidney Marion, Audrey Betz, Jerry Allan, Lloyd King.

Following their resurgence in popularity after the release of their old two-reel comedies to television by Screen Gems, The Three Stooges returned to the big screen in a series of economy features. THE OUTLAWS IS COMING is the best of the lot. The film is a fast-paced comedy romp tailored to the Stooges' brand of ultra slapstick

Moe Howard, Joe De Rita, and Larry Fine in THE OUTLAWS IS
COMING.

comedy and, unlike some of their outings, it holds up very well.
Made as THE THREE STOOGES MEET THE GUNSLINGERS, the film
had the added box-office novelty of including TV children shows'
hosts from around the country in cameo appearances.

A Boston wildlife magazine publisher sends his editor (Adam
West), along with a trio of bungling pressmen (The Three Stooges),
West to stop the buffalo slaughter. Once there, the quartet has
run ins with several famous gunmen, including Billy the Kid (Johnny
Ginger), Johnny Ringo (Hal Fryar), and Cole Younger (Bruce
Sedley), and try to stop the outlaws' attempts to bring about an
Indian uprising. Eventually the men are saved by sharpshooter
Annie Oakley (Nancy Kovack), the gang leaders attempt to reform,
and the editor plans to marry Oakley.

Dubbed a "fast slapstick western, a natural for trio's particu-
lar market" by Variety, THE OUTLAWS IS COMING proved to be The
Three Stooges' final theatrical feature. (Their unfinished feature
KOOKS TOUR in 1970 was later edited for home film and tape

distribution.) The Stooges in their long career did many take-offs on the Western genre, including the feature ROCKIN' IN THE ROCKIES (1945) and GOLD RAIDERS (1951), along with such short subjects as: HORSE COLLARS (1935), WHOOPS I'M AN INDIAN (1936), GOOFS AND SADDLES (1937), YES, WE HAVE NO BONANZA (1939), ROCKIN' THROUGH THE ROCKIES (1940), CACTUS MAKES PERFECT (1942), PHONY EXPRESS (1943), OUT WEST (1947), PUNCHY COWPUNCHERS (1950), MERRY MAVERICKS (1951), and SHOT IN THE FRONTIER (1954).

OUTLAWS OF THE DESERT (Paramount, 1941) 66 mins.

Producer, Harry Sherman; director, Howard Bretherton; based on characters created by Clarence E. Mulford; screenplay, J. Benton Cheney, Bernard McConville; music director, Irvin Talbot; music, John Leipold; camera, Russell Harlan; editor, Carroll Lewis.
William Boyd (Hopalong Cassidy); Brad King (Johnny Nelson); Andy Clyde (California Carlson); Forrest Stanley (Charles Grant); Jean Phillips (Susan Grant); Nina Guilbert (Mrs. Jane Grant); Lulu Deste (Marie Karltza); Albert Morin (Nickie Karltza); George Woolsey (Major); George Lewis (Yussuf); Duncan Renaldo (Sheik Suleiman); Joan Del Val (Faran El Kaker); Mickey Elssa (Salim); Jamiel Hasson (Ali); Topper (The Horse).

Hopalong Cassidy (William Boyd), California Carlson (Andy Clyde) and Johnny Nelson (Brad King) travel from their Bar 20 ranch in the West to Arabia to aid in the purchase of horses for rancher Grant (Forrest Stanley), and become embroiled in desert warfare when Grant is kidnapped. With the aid of a friendly sheik (Duncan Renaldo), the trio set Grant free and end the fighting.
Although purists cringe, "B" Westerns have not always stayed put on the range. Not only have cowboys gone east to combat gangsters, and north into Canada and south of the border into Mexico; they have also traveled abroad occasionally. In 1939 the "Hopalong Cassidy" entry LAW OF THE PAMPAS took place in Argentina and this outing moved the saddle pals to North Africa, both preceding the Range Busters going to the Philippines in the topical TEXAS TO BATAAN (1942). Despite impressive desert photography and a fine performance by Duncan Renaldo as Sheik Suleiman (and the diverting presence of Luli Deste as his harem girl), OUTLAWS OF THE DESERT is a meandering feature. It is probably the reason the Bar 20 cowpokes stayed on home soil thereafter.

OVERLAND BOUND see RANCHERS AND RASCALS

OVERLAND MAIL (Universal, 1942) fifteen chapters

Producer, Henry MacRae; directors, Ford Beebe, John Rawlins;

story, Johnston McCulley; screenplay, Paul Huston; camera, William Sickner, George Robinson.

Lon Chaney (Jim Lane); Helen Parrish (Barbara Gilbert); Noah Beery, Jr. (Sierra Pete); Don Terry (Buckskin Billy Burke); Bob Baker (Young Bill Cody); Noah Beery (Frank Chadwick); Tom Chatterton (Tom Gilbert); Charles Stevens (Puma); Robert Barron (Charles Darson); Harry Cording (Sam Gregg); and Marguerite De La Motte, Ben Taggart, Jack Rockwell, Riley Hill, Carleton Young, Ethan Laidlaw, Jack Clifford, Chief Thundercloud, Chief Many Treaties.

Chapters: 1) A Race with Disaster; 2) Flaming Havoc! 3) The Menacing Herd; 4) The Bridge of Disaster; 5) Hurled to the Depths; 6) Death at the Stake; 7) The Path of Peril; 8) Imprisoned in Flames; 9) Hidden Danger; 10) Blazing Wagons; 11) The Trial of Terror; 12) In the Claws of the Cougar; 13) The Frenzied Mob; 14) The Toll of Treachery; 15) The Mail Goes Through.

Frontiersmen Jim Lane (Lon Chaney) and Sierra Pete (Noah Beery, Jr.) are assigned to investigate problems with mail delivery in the La Paz country, where the franchise belongs to Tom Gilbert's (Tom Chatterton) Overland Company. They learn that Indian renegades are attacking the lines, robbing and destroying stage-coaches and ambushing pony express riders. They come upon a hold-up and rescue Gilbert's daughter Barbara (Helen Parrish). They also run across their old friend Buckskin Billy Burke (Don Tery), who is working with two men (Robert Barron, Harry Cording) who are actually in the pay of businessman Frank Chadwick (Noah Berry); he is behind the lawlessness because he wants the franchise for himself. Billy joins Jim and Sierra in fighting the crime makers and they learn that Chadwick is responsible for all the area's troubles. In a showdown, Chadwick's gang is defeated and he is killed trying to escape. Jim becomes the operations manager for the stage line and plans to wed Barbara.

Following the success of THE WOLFMAN (1941), Lon Chaney became Universal Pictures' most popular screen star. The studio kept him active in a variety of roles, usually in horror films and Westerns, and here he headlined his seventh and final serial, his fourth for co-director Ford Beebe, who kept the cliffhanger's fifteen chapters galloping at a swift pace. Noah Beery (senior) contributed another of his rich, hammy characterizations as the arch-villain Chadwick, and the serial was further enhanced by star Chaney's ob-vious relish for his athletic hero role.

THE PAINTED TRAIL (Monogram, 1938) 50 mins.

Producer, Robert Emmett Tansey; director, Robert Hill; screen-play, Robert Emmett; assistant director, Eddie Saeta; sound, Glen Glenn; camera, Bert Longenecker.

Tom Keene (Tom); Eleanore Stewart (Alice); LeRoy Mason (Duke); Walter Long (Driscoll/Pecos Kid); Jimmy Eagles (Sammy);

Harry Cording, Lon Chaney, Jr. and Noah Beery, Sr. in OVERLAND MAIL (1942).

Forrest Taylor (Jackson); Harry Harvey (Reed); Ernie Adams (Nosey); Bud Osborne (Spud); Glenn Strange (Sheriff); Frank Campeau (Marshal); and Tom London, Bob Kortman, Dick Cramer.

After starring in a topnotch series for RKO between 1931 and 1933, Tom Keene returned to the Western fold in 1937 for four Monogram outings. Where Keene was once criticized for his florid acting at RKO he was now a much more subdued and believable hero, and it is too bad that the series did not endure longer. In 1941 he was back at the studio for another eight features but they lacked the production values of his earlier films there. Don Miller noted in Hollywood Corral (1976) that at a short fifty minutes this feature was "succinct and swift." He added, "The Robert Emmett [Tansey] script had a favorite gimmick of the author's, a climactic gun battle with the hero on one side of the border, the baddie (Walter Long) on the other. Hero plugs villain across the border-line. It was used several times, and always worked well."

Federal agent Tom (Tom Keene) is sent by a U.S. marshal (Frank Campeau) to Laredo near the Mexican border to bring to justice an outlaw gang involved in cattle rustling and smuggling. With fellow officers Reed (Harry Harvey) and Jackson (Forrest

Taylor) he takes on the guise of the notorious bad man, The Pecos
Kid, and joins the gang led by Driscoll (Walter Long), who is employed by the evil Duke (LeRoy Mason). In the meantime, Tom
meets his childhood sweetheart Alice (Eleanore Stewart) and swears
her to silence. Working with the gang, Tom is arrested by the
local sheriff (Glenn Strange), but the outlaws break him out of
jail. He goes to the Mexican police and makes arrangements for the
capture of the gang, but he is spotted by one of the outlaws and
is hunted by Driscoll, who is the real Pecos Kid. In a shoot-out
Driscoll is killed by Tom, who goes to the gang's hideout and arrests
them. Tom renews his romance with Alice.

PALE RIDER (Warner Bros., 1985) C 116 mins.

Executive producer, Fritz Manes; producer, Clint Eastwood;
associate producer, David Valdes; director, Eastwood; screenplay,
Michael Butler, Dennis Shryack; assistant directors, Valdes, L. Dean
Jones, Jr.; production designer, Edward Carfagno; set designer,
Bob Sessa; set decorator, Ernie Bishop; music, Lennie Nichaus;
makeup, Barbara Guedel; stunt co-ordinator, Wayne Van Horn;
sound, C. Darin Knight; camera, Bruce Surtees; editor, Joel Cox.
Clint Eastwood (Preacher); Michael Moriarty (Hull Barret);
Carrie Snodgrass (Sarah Wheeler); Christopher Penn (Josh LaHood);
Richard Dysart (Coy LaHood); Sydney Penny (Megan Wheeler);
Richard Kiel (Club); Doug McGrath (Spider Conway); John Russell
(Marshal Stockburn); Charles Hallahan (McGill); Marvin J. McIntyre
(Jagou); Fran Ryan (Ma Blankenship); Richard Hamilton (Jed
Blankenship); Graham Paul (Ev Gossage); Chuck LaFont (Eddie
Conway); Jeffrey Weissman (Teddy Conway); Allen Keller (Tyson);
Tom Oglesby (Elam); Herman Poppe (Ulrik Lindquist); Kathleen
Wygle (Bess Gossage); Terrence Evans (Jake Henderson); Jim Hitson
(Biggs); Loren Adkins (Bossy); Tom Friedkin (Miner Tom); S. A.
Griffin (Deputy Folke); Jack Radosta (Deputy Grissom); Robert
Winley (Deputy Kobold); Billy Drago (Deputy Mather); Jeffrey
Josephson (Deputy Sedge); John Dennis Johnston (Deputy Tucker);
Mike Adams, Clay Lilley, Gene Hartline, R. L. Tolbert, Cliff Happy,
Ross Loney, Larry Randles, Mike McGaughty, Gerry Gatlin (Horse-
men); Lloyd Nelson (Bank Teller); Jay K. Fishburn (Telegrapher);
George Orrison (Station master Whitey); Milton Murrill (Porter);
Mike Munsey (Dentist/Barber); Keith Dillin (Blacksmith); Wayne Van
Horn (Stage Driver); Fritz Manes, Glenn Wright (Stage Riders).

By the mid-1980s the Western appeared to be dead and buried,
at least in regard to U.S. theatrical features. Suddenly a trio of
big-budgeted oaters appeared: RUSTLERS RHAPSODY, SILVERADO
(qq.v.) and PALE RIDER. None proved to be a blockbuster or
critically satisfying. PALE RIDER was the most popular (grossing
over $40,000,000 in domestic rentals at the box office) due to the
star/director Clint Eastwood, who returned to the genre for the
first time in nearly a decade after having done THE OUTLAW JOSEY

WALES (q.v.) nine years before.

A rootless loner called Preacher (Clint Eastwood) arrives in a remote mining locale to find the local prospectors up against a ruthless hydraulic mining tycoon (Richard Dysart) and his corrupt son (Christopher Penn). Preacher boards with the earnest leader (Michael Moriarty) of the miners and soon finds that the man's fiancée (Carrie Snodgrass) and her teenage daughter (Sydney Penny) are in love with him, and the girl tries to seduce him. Preacher, however, is more intent in righting the area's wrongs and is soon up against the mining tycoon's hired gunman (John Russell), whom he defeats eventually in a gun battle. Preacher then rides away.

Very similar in plot to the classic SHANE (see B/V), the movie was shot in the Sun Valley Hills of Idaho and sports gorgeous photography by Bruce Surtees. As a Western, PALE RIDER is acceptable but nothing more, and star Eastwood appears to be reprising the mystical loners he did so well in his enduringly popular spaghetti Westerns for Sergio Leone in the 1960s. In the Los Angeles Times, Michael Wilmington termed the movie "a reflexive Western," and added, "It assumes the audience is somewhat familiar with the sources; Stevens, Ford, Hawks, Leone and even Kurosawa ... PALE RIDER's pleasures lie in its games with traditionalism, its ironic, playful attitude. Eastwood tries consciously for a poetry of action and images and, amazingly, he often succeeds."

PANAMINT'S BAD MAN see RAWHIDE

PARDNERS (Paramount, 1956) C 86 mins.

Producer, Paul Jones; director, Norman Taurog; based on a story by Mervin Fapp; screen story, Jerry Davis; screenplay, Sidney Sheldon; music, Frank De Vol; songs, Sammy Cahn and James Van Heusen; choreography, Nick Castle; assistant director, Michael D. Moore; costumes, Edith Head; camera, Daniel Fapp; editor, Archie Marshek.

Jerry Lewis (Wade Kingsley, Jr.); Dean Martin (Slim Mosely, Jr.); Lori Nelson (Carol Kingsley); Jackie Loughery (Dolly Riley); John Baragrey (Dan Hollis); Jeff Morrow (Rio); Agnes Moorehead (Mrs. Kingsley); Lon Chaney, Jr. (Whitey); Mickey Finn (Red); Douglas Spencer (Smith); Philip Tonge (Footman); Milton Frome (Hawkins); Richard Aherne (Chauffeur); Lee Van Cleef (Gus); Stuart Randall (Carol's Cowhand); Scott Douglass (Salvin); Jack Elam (Pete); Bob Steele (Shorty).

Dean Martin and Jerry Lewis' penultimate starring effort, PARDNERS, is a loose remake of 1936's RHYTHM ON THE RANGE (see B/V), starring Bing Crosby, Frances Farmer, Martha Raye, and Bob "Bazooka" Burns. Norman Taurog directed both pictures and the first one is decidedly the better, although critical reaction to the remake has been mixed. At the time of its release, the New

Dean Martin and Jerry Lewis in PARDNERS (1956).

York Times wrote of Martin and Lewis, "...they both seem pretty
tired in some contrived sound and fury meant to kid horse opera
cliches and succeeding fitfully." On the other hand, Leonard
Maltin wrote in Movie Comedy Teams (1970) that it "...turned out
to be one of the comedy duo's better endeavors, with some truly
funny scenes of the pardners Out West...."
    When lawmen Slim Mosely (Dean Martin) and Wade Kingsley
(Jerry Lewis) are shot down by bad men in the Old West, the
latter's wife (Agnes Moorhead) takes her infant son back East and
she becomes a wealthy businesswoman. Years later Mosley's son
(Dean Martin) comes East to get financial help from the woman and,
with her mama's boy Junior (Jerry Lewis) in tow, heads back to
Carsonville to avenge the deaths of their fathers. There the duo
find themselves up against bad men Dan Hollis (John Baragrey) and
Pete Rio (Jeff Morrow) and their henchmen Whitey (Lon Chaney)
and Shorty (Bob Steele). After several misadventures in the
Western town they eliminate the lawlessness and Slim finds love with
pretty Carol (Lori Nelson) while Junior ends up with Dolly (Jackie
Loughery).
    While Martin and Lewis may have been the headliners of this
tepid genre spoof shot in widescreen VistaVision, it is villains John
Baragrey, Jeff Morrow, Lon Chaney, and Bob Steele who provide
the major interest.

PARTNERS (RKO-Pathé, 1932) 58 mins.

Director, Fred Allen; story/screenplay, Donald W. Lee; assist-
ant director, Dave Lewis; music, Arthur Lange; sound, Richard
Tyler; camera, Harry Jackson; editor, Walter Thompson.
Tom Keene (Dick Barstow); Nancy Drexel (Jean Morgan); Otis
Harlan (Morgan); Victor Potel (Carry-All Roach); Bobby Nelson
(Bud); Lee Shumway (Chet Jarvis); Billy Franey (Deputy Len);
Carleton Young (Deputy); Ben Corbett (Rider); Flash (The Horse).

Horse raiser Dick Barstow (Tom Keene) rescues old man Roach
(Victor Potel) and his grandson (Bobby Nelson) from ruffians led by
Chet Jarvis (Lee Shumway). The old man loans Dick money for his
ranch and then is killed, and Dick is blamed for the shooting. He
escapes from the sheriff and his posse and finds out that Jarvis, who
is after pretty Jean Morgan (Nancy Drexel), who in turn likes Dick,
is the real killer. He comes to the auction of his horses and proves
Jarvis is the murderer. Dick then adopts the boy and plans to
marry Jean.
Around 1930, leading man George Duryea changed his screen
name to Tom Keene and headlined a series of well-executed Westerns
for RKO, of which PARTNERS is representative. Keene's RKO
series ended in 1933 and he deserted the genre for a time, but returned in the late 1930s and early 1940s for two Monogram programs
before switching his name to Richard Powers in the mid-1940s and
becoming a character actor. He reverted to the name Tom Keene in
a comeback attempt in the mid-1950s. He died in 1963.

PASSION (RKO, 1954) C 84 mins.

Producer, Benedict Borgeaus; director, Allan Dwan; story,
Joseph Leytes, Beatrice A. Dresher, Miguel Padilla; screenplay,
Leytes, Dresher, Howard Estabrook; art director, Van Nest Polglase;
set decorator, John Sturtevant; costumes, Gwen Wakeling; music,
Louis Forbes; camera, John Alton; editor, Carlos Lodato.
Cornel Wilde (Juan Obregon); Yvonne De Carlo (Rosa Melo/
Tonya Melo); Rodolfo Acosta (Salvador Sandro); Raymond Burr (Cap-
tain Rodriguez); Lon Chaney (Castro); John Qualen (Gaspar Melo);
Anthony Caruso (Sergeant Munoz); Frank De Kova (Martinez);
Peter Coe (Colfre); John Dierkes (Escobar); Richard Hale (Don
Domingo); Rozene Kemper (Senora Melo); Rosa Turich (Maracuita);
Stuart Whitman (Bernal Vaquaro); James Kirkwood (Don Rosendo);
Robert Warwick (Money Lender); Belle Mitchell (Senora Carrisa);
Alex Montoya (Manuel Felipe); Zon Murray (Barca).

In Spanish California, grasping land baron Captain Rodriguez
(Raymond Burr) uses henchman Castro (Lon Chaney) and his gang
to murder ranchers and take their lands. Vaquero Juan Obregon
(Cornel Wilde) rides to the hacienda of his father-in-law (John
Qualen) and finds that the ranch has been raided and that his wife
Rosa (Yvonne De Carlo) and their small daughter have been
murdered. The only survivor is his wife's twin sister, Tonya

Cornel Wilde and Yvonne De Carlo in PASSION (1954).

(Yvonne De Carlo), and she forms an uneasy alliance with Juan in seeking revenge. Eventually the couple track Rodriguez and Castro to the Nevada mountain range. Juan kills both men and he and Tonya return home for a life together.

Made on an $800,000 budget by veteran director Allan Dwan, with lensing at various Hollywood lots to take advantage of standing sets (the Spanish buildings were on the Warner Bros. lot), the movie was a naive, contrived and slow-paced melodrama saved by John Alton's color photography and a good cast. Striking Yvonne De Carlo was particularly effective in dual roles and Lon Chaney engaging as the sadistically evil henchman Castro. One particularly well-done scene was Tonya recognizing Castro's maniacal laughter and pinpointing him as the killer of her sister and niece. The film's highlight comes appropriately at the finale when Wilde tracks and kills Burr in the snowy Nevada highlands.

THE PHANTOM BULLET (Universal, 1926) 6,148'

Presenter, Carl Laemmle; director, Clifford S. Smith; based on the novel Click of the Triangle T by Oscar J. Friend; adaptor, Curtis Benton; camera, Harry Neumann.

Hoot Gibson (Tom "Click" Farlane); Eileen Percy (Jane Terrill); Allan Forrest (Don Barton); Pat Harmon (Bill Haynes); Nelson McDowell (Zack Peters); William H. Turner (Judge Terrill); John T. Prince (Tom Farlane, Sr.); Pee Wee Holmes (Short); Rosemary Cooper (Dolores).

During the 1920s, Hoot Gibson was second only to Tom Mix in cowboy film popularity and it is claimed that at his height in the mid- and late 1920s, Hooter earned some $14,500 weekly. In many respects Hoot Gibson was not a typical Western star of the time, as he rarely toted a gun, did not dress in fancy duds, and although his oaters were fast-paced they were also light-hearted and comical. THE PHANTOM BULLET is a good example of Hoot Gibson at his most popular, the movie being well photographed with good locations and the narrative bolstered by an exciting car chase and rescue sequence at its finale.

Cowboy Tom "Click" Farlane, who fancies himself a photographer, learns that his father has been killed mysteriously and he returns home to Texas. To track the murderer, he pretends to be none too bright. He meets Jane Terrill (Eileen Percy), who is also liked by ranch foreman Barton (Alan Forrest). When Click tries to take a picture of Jane and himself, he is almost killed by a phantom bullet and he thinks Bill Haynes (Pat Harmon) is the man he is after. When the photograph is developed, it shows Barton trying to kill Click. The foreman kidnaps Jane, and Click pursues them and saves her as Barton's auto tumbles over a cliff.

THE PHANTOM EMPIRE <u>see</u> IN OLD SANTA FE

THE PHANTOM RANCHER (Colony, 1940) 61 mins.

Producers, Max Alexander, Arthur Alexander; director, Harry Fraser; screenplay, Bill Lively; music, Lew Porter; camera, William Hyers; editor, Fred Bain.

Ken Maynard (Ken Mitchell); Dorothy Short (Ann); Harry Harvey (Gopher); Ted Adams (Collins); Dave O'Brien (Luke); Tom London (Parker); John Elliott (Markham); Reed Howes (Lon); Steve Clark (Burton); Karl Matthews (Hank); Sherry Tansey (Doc); Tarzan (The Horse); and Wally West, George Morrell, Herman Hack.

After the end of his Columbia Pictures' contract in 1936, cowboy hero Ken Maynard signed with producers Max and Arthur Alexander for four Westerns for Grand National release, and following the demise of that studio he and the two brother-producers did another four programmers for Colony. THE PHANTOM RANCHER was Maynard's penultimate solo starring vehicle, although in terms of its plot it was one of his most pedestrian films, salvaged by the star donning a mask and cape to become an avenger in the Old West. It resulted in an entertaining entry with the star still in agile hero, although by this time he was getting too heavy.

Cowboy Ken Mitchell (Ken Maynard) returns home to take over his late uncle's ranch and finds that the man was hated in the area for stampeding his cattle over farm land. He also learns that crook Collins (Ted Adams) intends, with the aid of his henchman (Dave O'Brien), to grab the ranch for himself. To save the spread and bring the villains to justice, Ken masquerades as a masked phantom and captures the outlaw gang.

THE PHANTOM RANGER (Monogram, 1938) 54 mins.

Producer, Maurice Conn; director, Sam Newfield; story, Stanley Roberts, Joseph O'Donnell; screenplay, O'Donnell; camera, Jack Greenhalgh; editor, Richard Wray.

Tim McCoy (Tim Hayes); Suzanne Kaaren (Joan Doyle); Karl Hackett (Sharpe); John St. Polis (Pat Doyle); John Merton (Bud); Harry Strang (Jeff); Charles King (Dan); Dick Cramer (Barton); Tom London (Reynolds); Jimmie Aubrey (Telegraph Operator); and John Merton, Dick Cramer, Herb Holcombe, Harry Strang, Wally West, Horace B. Carpenter, Sherry Tansey, George Morrell, Herman Hack.

Mining engineer Sharp (Karl Hackett) keeps engraver Pat Doyle (John St. Polis) a prisoner to make bogus money, and the Secret Service sends agent Tim Hayes (Tim McCoy) westward to track the gang which is swamping the country with its counterfeit currency. In Topec, Arizona, Doyle's daughter Joan (Suzanne Kaaren) pretends to be Spanish dancer Dolores Lopez in order to find her father, and Tim joins her in the quest by masquerading as a road agent to get in with the gang. G-men arrive on the scene and aid Tim in rounding up the gang, and Sharp is killed by falling off a cliff. Tim and Joan marry.

The last of four Westerns Tim McCoy made for Monogram, and budgeted at about $60,000, THE PHANTOM RANGER is a low-grade but pleasant modern-day Western which nicely incorporates the gangster film motif into its Western scenario. Although a straight dramatic film, THE PHANTOM RANGER ends on a light note, with the hero and heroine marrying and the groom paying the telegrapher (Jimmie Aubrey) to announce the event, unintentionally using a bogus bill.

PINTO RUSTLERS (Reliable, 1937) 60 mins.

Producer, Bernard B. Ray, associate producer, Harry S. Webb; director, Henri Samuels [Harry S. Webb]; screenplay, Robert Tansey; assistant director, R. G. Springsteen; sound, Johnnie Eilers; camera, William Hyer; editor, Fred Bain.

Tom Tyler (Tom Dawson); George Walsh (Nick); Al St. John (Mack); Catherine Cotter (Ann Walton); Earl Dwire (Bud Walton); William Gould (Inspector); George Chesebro (Spud); Roger Williams (Lugo); Bud Osborne (Buck); Murdock McQuarrie (Dad); Charles Whittaker (Sheriff); and Milburn Morante, Sherry Tansey.

From 1934 to 1936 veteran "B" Western star Tom Tyler headlined nineteen features for Reliable Pictures, a low-grade outfit controlled by producer Bernard B. Ray and director Harry S. Webb, who helmed this entry using the name Henri Samuels. Unlike most of the films in this group, PINTO RUSTLERS is a solid feature, actionful and well photographed by William Hyer. Unfortunately, the bulk of the series was hampered by "...jumbled storylines, aimless meandering about in quest of an excuse to start the action, and supporting performances of often amateur stature. Through it all Tyler's manly presence did much, if not enough, to overcome the pall. Even Tyler was victimized by sloppy staging of the action scenes" (Don Miller, Hollywood Corral, 1976).

Tom Dawson's (Tom Tyler) father is murdered by rustlers. Tom pretends to be an outlaw and joins the gang to gain needed evidence to catch the murderer, who turns out to be gang leader Nick (George Walsh).

THE PIONEER SCOUT (Paramount, 1928) 56 mins.

Directors, Lloyd Ingraham, Alfred L. Werker; screenplay, Frank M. Clifton; titles, Garrett Graham; camera, Mack Stengler; editor, Duncan Mansfield.

Fred Thomson (Fred); Nora Lane (Mary Baxter); William Courtwright (Old Bill); Tom Wilson (Handy Anderson).

"Thrill-Swept Romance of the Early West" is how Paramount

catchlined this popular Fred Thomson starrer which "strives for variety by having Thomson play a dual role" (Photoplay magazine). Sadley, the movie was to be the third from the last to star the popular sagebrush hero who died the year this feature was issued.

Scouts Fred (Fred Thomson) and Old Bill (William Courtright) arrive in Last Chance with news of an Indian uprising. The uprising is actually instigated by hook-handed Handy Anderson (Tom Wilson), whose gang masquerades as Indians and attacks wagon trains. Fred meets pretty settler Mary Baxter (Nora Lane) and her father and tells them to wait to join a larger train before going further westward. The next day Fred participates in a Fourth of July race and his wagon is nearly sabotaged by Anderson, but Fred's horse Silver King comes to his rescue. Fred beats Anderson in the race and gains a kiss from Mary, who has also caught the bad man's lustful eye. That night Anderson and his men capture Fred and then send a note to Mary's father telling him to start their wagon train westward. Silver King frees his master from the shack where he is held prisoner and Fred organizes a posse and goes after the caravan. They stop Anderson's gang from attacking the train and in a fight Fred defeats Anderson and saves Mary.

To be noted is the scene with a runaway wagon in which star Fred Thomson leaps from his horse to the axle of a wagon drawn by four horses going at full gallop.

THE PIONEER TRAIL (Columbia, 1938) 54 mins.

Producer, Larry Darmour; director, Joseph Levering; story/ screenplay, Nate Gatzert; camera, James H. Brown, Jr.

Jack Luden (Beezy); Joan Barclay (Alice); Slim Whittaker (Curley); Leon Beaumont (Joe); Hal Taliaferro (Smokey); Marin Sais (Belle); Eva McKenzie (Ma Allen); Hal Price (Baron Waite); Dick Boteler (Pedro); Tom London (Sam Hardin); Tuffy (The Dog); and Art Davis, Fred Burns, Bob McKenzie.

Having ridden the sagebrush trial in the silent days and in the early talkies, Jack Luden briefly returned to genre stardom at Columbia in the late 1930s, in a quartet of oaters as the studio was experimenting with various players in hopes of successfully replacing Tim McCoy. Luden, however, was a lackluster performer and he was usually upstaged in his brief series by a none-too-attractive mutt named Tuffy. PIONEER TRAIL, one of the better of the Luden outings, nicely interpolates high-budget action footage from another film and contains an amusing performance by Slim Whittaker as a dense gang leader who is ably abetted by Marin Sais as his sharp-tongued mistress.

Cattlemen pool their herds for a big drive to be led by Breezy (Jack Luden), the foreman for a rancher (Hal Price) and his lovely daughter (Joan Marclay). A loutish bandit, Curley (Slim Whitaker), and his partner (Hal Taliaferro), in cahoots with the former's cafe-owner girlfriend Belle (Marin Sais), plan to rustle the herd. The

Joan Barclay in THE PIONEER TRAIL (1938).

two crooks capture Breezy and try to bribe him into bringing the
cattle into their hands, but he refuses. He is kept prisoner in an
old bunkhouse, but is rescued by his dog Tuffy. Breezy returns
to the drive, makes sure his men are well armed, and when the raid
is made, he causes the cattle to stampede through the town, bringing
about the crooks' downfall.

PLAINSONG (Ed Stabile, 1982) C 76 mins.

    Producer, Tiare Stack; director, Ed Stabile; based on the
diary of Sara Charity Karker; screenplay, Stabile; music, Bill Peek,
Brian Eno, Meredith Monk; sound, Ed Novick; camera, Joe Ritter;
editor, Stabile.
    Jessica Nelson (Mary Jessop); Teresanne Joseph (Sara Charity
Karker); Lyn Traverse (Trish Howler); Steve Geiger (Tom Logan);
Sandon McCall (Frank Logan); Carl Kielblock (Harve Fletcher);
Michael Stabile (Ralph Karker); John Pasquale (Fred Payne); Lynn
Bettelli (Lucy Bennett).

    Like the historic THE GREAT TRAIN ROBBERY (1903), this
feature was filmed in the wilds of New Jersey (over a period of
several years), but it is a drab, forlorn affair which made little
impression when theatrically released. Based on the life of a pioneer
woman caught in the midst of range warfare in Kansas just after the
Civil War, the film chronicles the interwoven lives of three female
settlers. "The mix of ethnography and six guns is unsatisfying.
Events and characters appear unmotivated as a result of sketchy
characterization and [director] Ed Stabile constantly changes the
focus of his action, making the narrative difficult to follow"
(Variety).
    Young Sara Charity Karker (Teresanne Joseph) comes to Kan-
sas in 1866 with several other women, all of whom are married to
local men and have children. When a farmer is killed in a skirmish
with cattlemen, the other settlers unite to fight the invaders and a
full scale range war ensues. After several of the farmers are killed
by the cattle baron's hired gun, Sara goes to the law but it does
not protect her and she is murdered, as are several other townsfolk,
by the gunslinger.
    To complicate PLAINSONG's downbeat storyline, the movie is
told in flashback by a young boy who witnesses the murder of Sara
Karker. Thus the climax comes at the start of the production,
negating any excitement it might have built in telling its story.

POWDER RIVER RUSTLERS (Republic, 1950) 60 mins.

    Associate producer, Gordon Kay; director, Philip Ford;
screenplay, Richard Wormser; music, Stanley Wilson; camera, John
MacBurnie; editor, Robert M. Leeds.
    Allan "Rocky" Lane (Himself); Eddy Waller (Nugget Clark);

Gerry Ganzer (Louise Manning); Roy Barcroft (Bull Macons);
Francis McDonald ("Sears" Williams); Cliff Clark (Lucius Stratton);
Douglas Evans (Devereaux); Bruce Edwards (Bob Manning);
Clarence Straight (Telegraph Operator); Ted Jacques (Blacksmith);
Tom Monroe (Guard); Stanley Blystone (Rancher); Black Jack (The
Horse); and Eddie Parker, Herman Hack.

Government agent Allan "Rocky" Lane (Allan "Rocky" Lane)
is sent to investigate a scheme by a gang of crooks to bilk money
from local citizens to build a needed bridge. The scheme is actually
being masterminded by the town tailor (Francis McDonald), but
Rocky solves the caper with the aid of local prospector Nugget
(Eddy Waller).

Although it contains obvious stock shots, POWDER RIVER
RUSTLERS is one of the more actionful Allan "Rocky" Lane features.
Discussing the Lane entries in Hollywood Corral (1976), Don Miller
noted, "Perhaps the Lane that could be chosen as most representative of the bunch is POWDER RIVER RUSTLERS ... [Richard]
Wormser's script gives the illusion of movement even where none
exists, and Lane and Waller are in top form. The climactic struggle
between Lane and McDonald is unusually realistic, with McDonald
driving a pair of pinking shears into Lane's shoulder; it drew a
gasp from the audience."

PRAIRIE OUTLAWS see WILD WEST

PRAIRIE SCHOONER see BRIGHAM YOUNG--FRONTIERSMAN

THE PRESCOTT KID (Columbia, 1936) 55 mins.

Producer/director, David Selman; supervisor, D. Ross Lederman; story, Claude Rister; screenplay, Ford Beebe; camera, Benjamin Kline.

Tim McCoy (Tim Hamlin); Sheila Mannors (Delores Ortega);
Joseph Sauers [Sawyer] (Willoughby); Alden Chase (Walton);
Hooper Atchley (Banner); Albert J. Smith (Frazier); Harry Todd
(Dr. Haley); Walter Brennan (Stage Driver); Carlos De Valdez
(Ortega); Ernie Adams (Red Larson); Steve Clark (Crocker); and
Slim Whittaker, Charles King, Bud Osborne, Art Mix, Tom London,
Edmund Cobb, Lew Meehan, Jack Rockwell.

After he had completed his successful Western series at Columbia in 1933, that studio put Tim McCoy into eight action dramas,
leaving Buck Jones as the studio's sole big-name oater star. In
1934 Jones came back to Universal and, since McCoy's non-Westerns
had not been overly successful, he returned to the genre with THE
PRESCOTT KID, directed by David Selman and supervised by D.
Ross Lederman, who by then preferred to have his name associated

with bigger-budget productions. In Views and Reviews (Winter, 1971), Jon Tuska wrote of this feature, "Background music during chase and romantic sequences was used to very good effect, with special attention paid to lighting and close-ups. Consistent in plot, with logical development and fine camera work, PRESCOTT KID set a high standard for the series.... [The film] was one of the very first Westerns to ever use background music during chase sequences and, as such, pre-dating Harry Sherman's HOP-A-LONG CASSIDY [Paramount, 1935--see B/V], has some little historical importance beyond its entertainment value."

When cowboy Tim Hanlon (Tim McCoy) arrives in San Lorenzo, the locals think he is a lawman who has come to smoke out a nest of cattle thieves. Pretty Delores Ortega (Sheila Mannors) confides to Tim that her father is about to lose his ranch to saloon owner Bonner (Hooper Atchley), who really works for supposedly respectable businessman Ed Walton (Alden Chase). Tim learns the truth about the two men from captured outlaw Red Larson (Ernie Adams), but during the interrogation the latter is shot by an outsider. The crooks try to dispose of Tim as he gets evidence to bring them to justice. Real lawman Willoughby (Joseph Sawyer) arrives and in a showdown he and Tim defeat the two bad guys.

THE PURPLE HILLS (Twentieth Century-Fox, 1961) C 60 mins.

Producer/director, Maury Dexter; screenplay, Edith Cash Pearl, Russ Bender; music, Richard LaSalle; assistant director, Frank Parmenter; camera, Floyd Crosby; editor, Jodie Copelan. Gene Nelson (Sheppard); Kent Taylor (Barnes); Danny Zapien (Chito); Medford Salway (Young Brave); Russ Bender (Deputy); Joanna Barnes (Amy Carter); Jerry Summers (Martin); John Carr (Beaumont).

Filmed on location in Arizona's Apacheland and co-scripted by featured performer Russ Bender, this Maury Dexter-produced and -directed oater is a compact feature which proves that the "B" movie had not lost its ability to entertain with the coming of the 1960s. The film is enhanced by a professional cast, with Kent Taylor stealing the limelight as the money-hungry outlaw.

With the setting in 1870s Arizona, outlaw Beaumont (Jack Carr) is shot by cowpoke Gil Shepard (Gene Nelson), who comes to town to collect the reward on the dead man. There he finds that the outlaw's partner, Johnny Barnes (Kent Taylor), also wants the money. The deceased's teenage brother Martin (Jerry Summers), meanwhile, arrives with lovely guardian Amy Carter (Joanna Barnes), looking for revenge for his sibling's death. The sheriff (Russ Bender) decides to take all concerned to the outlaw's burial site, and along the way Amy falls in love with Gil. At the grave site they find that the Apaches, who thought Beaumont a kind of god, have taken the corpse. Barnes murders the sheriff but himself is mortally wounded when the Apaches attack the party. Before he

Kent Taylor, Joanna Barnes, and Gene Nelson in THE PURPLE
HILLS (1961).

dies Barnes holds off the Indians so that the others can escape,
and once they reach safety, Martin no longer craves revenge.
Gil realizes Amy is more important than money.

QUANTRILL'S RAIDERS (Allied Artists, 1958) C 65 mins.

Producer, Ben Schwalb; director, Edward Bernds; screenplay,
Polly James; music, Marlin Skiles; assistant director, Ralph Black;
wardrobe, Elmer Ellsworth; camera, William Whitley; editor, William
Austin.
Steve Cochran (Westcott); Diane Brewster (Sue); Leo Gordon
(Quantrill); Gale Robbins (Kate); Will Wright (Judge); Kim Charney
(Joel); Myron Healey (Jarrett); Robert Foulk (Hager); Glenn
Strange (Todd); Lane Chandler (Sheriff); Guy Prescott (Major);
Dan M. White (Fred).

During the Civil War the Confederacy wants to acquire the
ammunition stored at the Union arsenal in Lawrence, Kansas. A
Confederate major (Guy Prescott) sends officer Westcott (Steve
Cochran) to meet with guerrilla leader Quantrill (Leo Gordon) and
make arrangements for the raid. Westcott works undercover as a

horse trader for the army to set up the raid, but when he finds out
the ammunition has been moved he tries to thwart the raid. The
bloodthirsty Quantrill plans to carry it out in order to gain revenge
on those who harmed him in the past. He imprisons Westcott but the
latter escapes and alerts the people in Lawrence about the raid.
During the fight Quantrill is killed.

Historically QUANTRILL'S RAIDERS is inaccurate. The guerrilla leader was denounced by the South long before the Lawrence
raid and the Confederacy would not have enlisted his aid. Further,
the film shows just a few men in his band during the attack, when
in reality more than 400 Quantrill gang members plundered the small
community. Finally, Quantrill did not die in the raid but lived on
to carry out other such activities.

Outside its factual faults, the movie does provide good entertainment and Leo Gordon is particularly effective in the title role,
as is Steve Cochran as the spy. "A tight, showmanly piece of film-
making, QUANTRILL'S RAIDERS packs plenty of movement in its
comparatively short footage and is probably the best yet of films on
this guerrilla leader turned out in recent years" (Variety). While
we do not argue with the reviewer's opinion of the film's entertainment value, many feel the best version of the Quantrill story is
DARK COMMAND (1940) (see B/V).

RACHEL AND THE STRANGER (RKO, 1948) 92 mins.

Executive producer, Jack J. Gross; producer, Richard H.
Berger; director, Norman Foster; based on the novel Rachel by
Howard Fast; screenplay, Waldo Salt; art directors, Albert S.
D'Agostino, Jack Okey; set decorators, Darrell Silvera, John Sturte-
vant; music director, C. Bakaleinikoff; songs, Roy Webb and Salt;
assistant director, Harry Mancke; makeup, Gordon Bass; Miss
Young's costumes, Edith Head; sound, Earl Wolcott, Terry Kellum;
special effects, Russell A. Cully; camera, Maury Gertsman; editor,
Les Milbrook.

Loretta Young (Rachel); William Holden (Big Davey); Robert
Mitchum (Jim); Gary Gray (Davey); Tom Tully (Parson Jackson):
Sara Haden (Mrs. Jackson); Frank Ferguson (Mr. Green); Walter
Baldwin (Gallus); Regina Wallace (Mrs. Green); Frank Conlan
(Jebez).

In the early 1800s frontiersman Big Davey (William Holden)
finds it difficult to raise his small son (Gary Gray) following the
death of his beloved wife. For $22 he buys an indentured servant,
Rachel (Loretta Young), to be his new wife, but he informs her he
only wants her to help raise the boy and take care of his home.
Rachel moves into Davey's cabin and is welcomed to the area by the
local parson (Tom Tully) and his wife (Sara Haden), but her husband remains aloof. Romance does come into Rachel's life when she
meets Davey's friend Jim (Robert Mitchum), a vagabondish hunter
attracted to the ladies. He romances Rachel and in doing so, shows

William Holden and Loretta Young in RACHEL AND THE STRANGER (1948).

Davey just how important his new wife is to him. When Indians threaten the settlement, Davey and Jim lead the fight against them and are aided by Rachel. After the Indians have been thwarted, Jim continues to roam while Davey and Rachel settle down to a life of happiness together.

This "engaging and unpretentious show" (Time) is at its best in its recreation of the raw frontier and in the performances of the three leading players. Loretta Young is especially effective as the porcelain-looking bondswoman who proves to be tough, passionate and loyal. The supporting cast is quite effective and delightfully recreates the camaraderie of frontier pioneers.

Third-billed Robert Mitchum was getting much headline attention at the time of this film's release as a result of his being jailed on marijuana charges, and the publicity did not hurt this feature's box-office receipts. In addition, the film required Mitchum to be a guitar-strumming troubadour type in his romancing of Loretta Young and he sang several ditties in the feature. In fact, the film's title theme, "Rachel," and one of its songs, "O-He-O-Hi-O-Ho," were recorded by Mitchum for Decca Records.

RAIDERS OF SUNSET PASS see RIDERS OF OLD SANTA FE

RAINBOW'S END (First Division, 1935) 60 mins.

Director, Norman Spencer; screenplay, Rollo Lloyd; camera, Gilbert Warrenton; editor, Ralph Dietrich.
Hoot Gibson (Neil Gibson, Jr.); June Gale (Ann Ware); Oscar Apfel (Gibson, Sr.); Warner Richmond (Stark); Ada Ince (Owen Gibson); Charles Hill (Bert); Stanley Blystone (Dorgan); and John Elliott, Henry Rocquemore, Fred Gilman, Charles Hill.

A cowboy named Neil Gibson, Jr. (Hoot Gibson) wins a saddle in a rodeo but has trouble with his businessman father (Oscar Apfel), and after a barroom brawl he and his pal (Buddy Roosevelt) are put on a freight train. At a Western train station they meet the lady (June Gale) boss of a ranch on which his father holds the mortgage. The boys get jobs on the spread but crooked lawyer Stark (Warner Richmond) tries to get the businessman to foreclose on the ranch. The cowboy is made foreman and is told he must take all the cattle to market in order to save the place. After the herd is on its way, the lawyer's henchman steals the herd's sale money from the foreman's pal. Neil, Jr. proves Stark is a crook, saves the ranch, and plans to wed his pretty boss.

RAINBOW'S END and SUNSET RANGE (q.v.) were two above-average features Hoot Gibson made for First Division Pictures between his Allied oaters for M. H. Hoffman and his final solo starring series for Walter Futter's Diversion Pictures. A modern Western with plenty of comedy, RAINBOW'S END has a good story and entertains nicely. Although cheaply produced, its low budget does not show.

To be noted is that June Gale (of the singing Gale Sisters) was then Mrs. Hoot Gibson in real life.

RANCHERS AND RASCALS (William Steiner, 1925) 4,600'

Producer, William Steiner; director, Leo Maloney; screenplay, Ford Beebe.

Leo Maloney (Harvey Martin); Josephine Hull (Helen Williams); Evelyn Thatcher (Mrs. Williams); Barney Furey (Williams); Patricia Darling (Young Wife); Tom London (Simons); Bud Osborne (Yates); Whitehorse (Indian); Bullet (The Dog).

During the 1920s Leo Maloney starred in a series of popular two-reel Westerns for the independent market, also directing from scripts by Ford Beebe. In the mid-1920s the two began doing features for William Steiner and at the advent of the sound era, Maloney produced and directed (as well as co-starring in) the first independent Western of the sound era, OVERLAND BOUND (1929), proving that the genre could adapt to the new sound process. Maloney, however, died soon after the film was completed.

RANCHERS AND RASCALS, one of the features Maloney did for William Steiner, is typical of his oaters in that it interspersed action and comedy for a breezy effect. Rancher Harvey Martin (Leo Maloney) intends to wed pretty Helen Williams (Josephine Hill). The girl and her bad-tempered mother (Evelyn Thatcher) visit the Martin ranch to make wedding preparations. Two men (Tom London, Bud Osborne) who have a grudge against Martin encounter a young woman (Patricia Darling) and her child. The woman has run away from her husband and the two men make it appear that Martin is her lover. When he finds the runaway at his ranch, Martin conceals her and tries to keep his fiancée and her mother from finding her, but fails. Eventually the ruse is uncovered and Harvey and Helen are reunited.

The film was released in Great Britain in late 1926 as ROGUES OF THE WEST.

RANCHO DELUXE (United Artists, 1975) C 93 mins.

Producer, Elliott Kastner; director, Frank Perry; screenplay, Thomas McGuane; music, Jimmy Buffett; art director, Michael Haller; assistant director, Charles Okun; sound, Al Gramaglia, William J. Randall; camera, William A. Fraker; second unit camera, David L. Butler, Roger M. Montgomery; editor, Sid Katz.

Jeff Bridges (Jack McKee); Sam Waterston (Cecil Colson); Elizabeth Ashley (Cora Brown); Charlene Dallas (Laura Beige); Clifton James (John Brown); Slim Pickens (Henry Beige); Harry Dean Stanton (Curt); Richard Bright (Burt); Patti D'Arbanville (Betty Fargo); Maggie Wellman (Mary Fargo); Bert Conway (Wilbur Fargo); Richard McMurray, Danna Hansen (McKee's Parents); Doria Cooke (McKee's Ex-Wife); Patti Jerome (The Madam).

Following his divorce, Jack McKee (Jeff Bridges) leaves his well-to-do family life to become a vagabond and teams with equally alienated Indian Cecil Colson (Sam Waterson). The two survive by rustling pompous rancher John Brown's (Clifton James) cattle from his Montana ranch. Fed up with the thefts, Brown and his city-bred wife Cora (Elizabeth Ashley) retain the services of range detective Henry Beige (Slim Pickens), and he arrives at the ranch with his niece Laura (Charlene Dallas). The lawman, however, appears to be senile and the two rustlers enlist the aid of two ranch workers (Harry Dean Stanton, Richard Bright) in pulling off a big cattle-rustling operation. But Laura, who has been romancing one of the workers (Stanton), gets the information to her uncle and he rounds up the two thieves and they are sent to a state prison farm. It develops that Beige was only using his alleged senility to fool the rascals, and that Laura is not his niece but one of his operatives.

Variety called RANCHO DELUXE "an amiable, lightweight comedy ... [which] has a very good cast and an easy charm. But the humor is too throwaway when it isn't laid on with a trowel; the plotting is more of a series of sketches; and the end result is an uneven little film...." While the movie is generally pleasant, it is better for its parts than as a whole. Particularly memorable is Slim Pickens' performance as the supposedly doddering range detective, and almost as amusing is the scene where his "virginal niece" seduces the ranch hand.

Scripter Thomas McGuane used the basic story-line for this modern-day Western comedy again the next year for his straight period piece Western, THE MISSOURI BREAKS (q.v.), but of the two RANCHO DELUXE is more entertaining.

RANCHO NOTORIOUS (RKO, 1952) 89 mins.

Producer, Howard Welsch; director, Fritz Lang; based on the story by Sylvia Richards; screenplay Daniel Taradash; production designer, Wiard Ihnen; music, Emil Newman; songs, Ken Darby; assistant director, Emmett Emerson; production supervisor, Ben Hersh; camera, Hal Mohr; editor, Otto Ludwig.

Marlene Dietrich (Altar Keane); Arthur Kennedy (Vern Haskell); Mel Ferrer (Frenchy Fairmont); Lloyd Gough (Kinch); Gloria Henry (Beth); William Frawley (Baldy Gunder); Lisa Ferraday (Maxine); John Raven (Chuck-A-Luck Dealer); Jack Elam (Gary); George Reeves (Wilson); Frank Ferguson (Preacher); Francis McDonald (Harbin); Dan Seymour (Comanche Paul); John Kellogg (Factor); Rodric Redwing (Rio); Stuart Randall (Starr); Roger Anderson (Red); Charles Gonzales (Hevia); Felipe Turich (Sanchez); Jose Dominguez (Gonzales); I. Stanford Jolley (Deputy Warren); John Doucette (Whitey); Charlita (Mexican Girl in Bar); Ralph Sanford (Politician); Lane Chandler (Sheriff Hardy); Fuzzy Knight (Barber); Fred Graham (Ace Maguire); Dick Wessel (Deputy); Dick Eliott (Storyteller); William Haade (Sheriff Bullock).

The penchant for psychological Westerns in the 1950s resulted

in the teaming of director Fritz Lang and star Marlene Dietrich
(who fought all through production) in an attempt to recreate the
bawdy success of the star's earlier DESTRY RIDES AGAIN (1939)
(see B/V) with a Freudian bent. While Hal Mohr's technicolor is delightful and some parts of the feature are actionful, the film as a
whole is dull and disappointing considering those involved. JOHNNY
GUITAR (see B/V) emerged two years later with Joan Crawford in a
similar older female-with-a-past starring role, and that film took on
a cult status, but RANCHO NOTORIOUS has no such reputation or
following.

When his fiancée Beth (Gloria Henry) is brutally murdered by
an outlaw gang in a small Wyoming Town in the 1870s, cowboy Vern
Haskell (Arthur Kennedy) gets on the gang's trail. He finds one
(John Doucette) of the men, who has been left for dead, but only
gets the words "Chuck-a-Luck" from him before he dies. Finally he
learns that the term is associated with one-time saloon entertainer
Altar Keane (Marlene Dietrich), who now runs a horse ranch which
is really a sanctuary for wanted men. He also learns that Altar's
man, Frenchy Fairmont (Mel Ferrer), is in jail, and Vern gets himself arrested and put on the same cell with Frenchy. Together the
men pull a successful jail break and head for Altar's "Chuck-a-Luck"
ranch, where Vern becomes one of the hands. He then makes a play
for Altar but she rebuffs him. However, when Vern sees her wearing a brooch he gave to Beth before she died, he demands to know
how she got it. Altar tells him that gang member Kinch (Lloyd
Gough) gave it to her as her cut from a robbery. Vern realizes
Kinch is the man he is after, and in town he faces the outlaw in a
showdown. Kinch refuses to fight and is arrested, but the other
gang members help him to escape and they head back to the ranch.
Kinch thinks Altar has betrayed him, and he tries to kill Frenchy.
Altar gets in the way of the bullet and dies as Vern shoots Kinch.
Vern and Frenchy leave the ranch.

In The Films of Marlene Dietrich (1968) Homer Dickens terms
the film "at best a poor man's DESTRY RIDES AGAIN," but added,
"the story, however, did move along at a good pace and there was
plenty of excitement, tension, and bold, bawdy humor, especially in
Dietrich's flashback scenes showing her as various men remembered
in days gone by." Commenting on the production, Dickens observed,
"the limited budget [was] painfully noticeable. There were painted
backdrops, cheap interiors, etc."

Regarding director Fritz Lang's contribution to the feature,
Paul M. Jensen wrote in The Cinema of Fritz Lang (1968), "RANCHO
NOTORIOUS rounds out Lang's experience with Westerns, and it is
probably his best because it emphasises character relationships over
action. The plot contains such solid Lang topics as revenge, justice, a femme fatale, a secret criminal organization and its leader.
These elements are not just added sidelights; they are part and
parcel of the story's development and the characters' motivations.
The picture actually makes a point, instead of referring to the ideas
and assuming that that will cause an immediate response.... Despite
even the presence of Marlene Dietrich, RANCHO NOTORIOUS is

small-scale in its scope and casting, but it is more than usually interesting."

THE RANGE BUSTERS (Monogram, 1940) 54 mins.

Producer, George W. Weekes; director, S. Roy Luby; screenplay, John Rathmell; camera, Edward Linden; editor, Roy Claire.
Ray "Crash" Corrigan (Crash); John King (Dusty); Max Terhune (Alibi); Luana Walters (Carol Thorpe); Earle Hodgins (Uncle Rolf); Frank LaRue (Doc Stegle); Leroy Mason (Torrence); Kermit Maynard (Wyoming); Bruce King (Wall); Elmer (The Dummy); and Duke Mathews, Horace Murphy, Karl Hackett.

Following the success of Republic's "The Three Mesquiteers" series two former members of that group, Ray "Crash" Corrigan and Max Terhune, were teamed with actor-singer John King in a new trio called "The Range Busters." Produced by George Weekes for Monogram, the series lacked the budgets of the Republic series but the three stars worked well together and the resulting films were quite entertaining, although they varied in quality. Corrigan departed the series after sixteen films and was replaced by stunt man David Sharpe for five films; then he left, as did John King, with Corrigan returning and Dennis Moore added to complete the series' two dozen episodes.
THE RANGE BUSTERS, the initial film for the new grouping, was a good one which film historian Dave Rowland, in Wild West Stars magazien (Volume 2, Number 8, no date), judged, "An excellent film on all counts." With its eerie mystery angle and well-staged fight sequences in an abandoned mine tunnel, the movie is very entertaining and a good springboard for the modest, but well-received series.
Crook Torrence (LeRoy Mason) murders Thorpe (Horace Murphy) for his ranch and gold mine. The Range Busters (Ray "Crash" Corrigan, John King, Max Terhune) arrive looking for "The Phantom," whom the locals believe is a ghost. The mystery may hides out on the Thorpe ranch, which is now run by the dead man's daughter, Carol (Luana Walters). The Ranger Busters unmask The Phantom, who turns out to be the local druggist (Frank LaRue).

RANGE RIDERS see THE BOSS COWBOY

RANGER OF CHEROKEE STRIP (Republic, 1949) 60 mins.

Associate producer, Melville Tucker; director, Philip Ford; story, Earl Snell; screenplay, Bob Williams; music, Stanley Wilson; art director, Frank Hotaling; set decorator, James Redd; assistant director, Herb Mendelson; makeup, Howard Smith; sound, Earl

Crian, Sr.; camera, Ellis W. Carter; editor, Irving M. Schoenberg.
    Monte Hale (Steve Howard); Paul Hurst (Jug Mason); Alice
Talton (Mary Bluebird); Roy Barcroft (Mark Sanders); Douglas Ken-
nedy (Joe Bearclaws); George Meeker (Randolph McKinnon); Frank
Fenton (Eric Parsons); Monte Blue (Chief Hunter); Neyle Morrow
(Tokata); and Lane Bradford.

    Joe Bearclaws (Douglas Kennedy) breaks out of prison and
escapes to the independent Cherokee Indian Nation to see his girlfriend Mary (Alice Talton). On the way to see his chief (Monte
Blue) he is captured by Ranger Steve Howard (Monte Hale), who
finds out that Joe wants to stop the chief from leasing Indian lands
to cattlemen led by McKinnon (George Meeker). Meanwhile McKinnon's henchman Mark Sanders (Roy Barcroft) masquerades as Joe
and kills the chief, and Joe is hunted for the crime. Steve and
lawman Jug Mason (Paul Hurst) believe in Joe's innocence and, as
Jug is taking Joe out of the territory, the two are captured by Mark
and the gang, but Steve comes to their rescue. The lawmen then
find out that a salesman (Frank Fenton) is actually a forger and
that he counterfeited the dead chief's signature to the land grant
papers. The two trap McKinnon into confessing his guilt and then
try to stop Mark and the gang from bringing in their cattle herd,
which they turn back. Bark is captured and Joe is proven innocent
and is reunited with Mary.
    Set in the 1890s in the locale of the Cherokee Indian Nation,
and even including a brief cameo of the character of Will Rogers,
this Monte Hale series Western finds hero Hale overshadowed by
Douglas Kennedy's performance as Indian Joe Bearclaws.

THE RANGERS TAKE OVER (Producers Releasing Corp., 1943) 59
    mins.

    Producers, Alfred Stern, Arthur Alexander; director, Al
Herman; screenplay, Elmer Clifton; songs: Robert Hoag, Jack Wil-
liams, Tex Coe; music director, Lee Zahler; camera, Robert Cline;
editor, Charles Henkel, Jr.
    Dave O'Brien (Tex Wyatt); Jim Newill (Jim Steele); Guy Wil-
kerson (Panhandle Perkins); Iris Meredith (Jean Lorin); Forrest
Taylor (Captain Wyatt); I. Stanford Jolley (Rance Blair); Charles
King (Kip Lane); Carl Matthews (Weir Slocum); Harry Harvey (Bill
Summers); Lynton Brent (Block Nelson); Bud Osborne (Pete Daw-
son); Cal Shrum and His Rhythm Rangers (Singers); Slim Whittaker
(Jake).

    Having worked together in the "Renfrew of the Royal Mounted"
series, James Newill and Dave O'Brien were teamed again by producers Alfred Stern and Arthur Alexander for PRC's "Texas
Rangers" series, with Guy Wilkerson providing the comedy relief.
As Les Adams noted in Yesterday's Saturdays (No. 14, May, 1978),
"...most of the genuine laughs in this series are of an unintentional

kind caused by bad dialogue, continuity goofs and sloppy editing."
After fourteen entries Jim Newill left the series in 1944 and was replaced by Tex Ritter for the eight remaining films. THE RANGERS
TAKE OVER was the initial series entry in 1942 and Don Miller
observed of the film in Hollywood Corral (1976), "...from the start
it looked like a long, hard road."

A rustling gang is operating on the Texas border but the
Rangers have trouble locating them. A group of new recruits ar-
rives at the Ranger station and one of them is Tex Wyatt (Dave
O'Brien), the son of the commander, Captain Wyatt (Forrest Taylor).
He is assigned to work with veteran ranger Jim Steele (Jim Newill)
and scout Panhandle Perkins (Guy Wilkerson). The trio trace the
gang to the Oasis Trading Post run by pretty Jean Lorin (Iris
Meredith) and Tex disobeys orders and arrests the gang leader,
Dawson (Bud Osborne). When Dawson escapes, Captain Wyatt dis-
charges his son for disobedience. Embittered, Tex goes to work
for Rance Blair (I. Stanford Jolley), not knowing he is in cahoots
with Dawson. When the rustlers kidnap Captain Wyatt, Tex tells the
Rangers the locale of the outlaws' hideout and fights side by side
with his father until Jean arrives with reinforcements and the outlaws are subdued.

Throughout the Newill-O'Brien-Wilkerson teaming, songs were
used in the "Texas Ranger" series, several of them penned by Tex
Coe, a pseudonym for the song-writing team of Jim Newill and Dave
O'Brien. The songs here included: "Roll Out Cowboys," "The
Rangers Take Over," "High in the Saddle," and "Campfire on the
Prairie."

RAWHIDE (Twentieth Century-Fox, 1938) 60 mins.

Producer, Sol Lesser; director, Ray Taylor; story, Dan Jarrett; adaptors, Jarrett, Jack Natteford; songs: Cecil Mack and
Albert Von Tilzer; Eddie Cherkose and Charles Rosoff; Bob Russell
and Lionel Newman; camera, Allen Q. Thompson; editor, Robert
Crandall.

Smith Ballew (Larry Kimball); Lou Gehrig (Himself); Evelyn
Knapp (Peggy Gehrig); Arthur Loft (Ed Saudners); Carl Stockdale
(Bascomb); Si Jenks (Pop Mason); Cy Kendall (Sheriff Kale); Lafe
McKee (McDonnell); Dick Curtis (Butch); Cecil Kellog (Gillam);
Slim Whittaker (Biff); Tom Foreman (Rudy); Cliff Parkinson (Pete);
Harry Tenbrook (Rusty); Lee Shumway (Johnson); Ed Cassidy
(Fuller); and Al Hill.

Baseball great Lou Gehrig teamed with bandleader Smith Ballew for the fourth and next-to-last film in the latter's starring "B"
Western series for producer Sol Lesser's Principal Pictures; the
series was released by Twentieth Century-Fox. Gehrig is surprisingly effective as the second lead in this actioner and he and Ballew
made a good team, although after one more film, 1983's PANAMINT'S
BAD MAN, the series was dissolved. A good script and strong

Evelyn Knapp and Smith Ballew in Rawhide (1938).

production values, along with the appeal of the two diverse stars, make RAWHIDE good viewing.

Baseball player Lou Gehrig (Himself) retires from the sport and moves with his sister (Evelyn Knapp) to the small Western town of Rawhide, where they have purchased a ranch. Once there they find that Ed Saudners (Arthur Loft), the president of the local ranchers' protective group, is trying to take over the valley by charging high prices for grain from his group's warehouses. Opposing Saunders is local lawyer Larry Kimball (Smith Ballew), and he and Gehrig join forces to stop the injustice. When the ranchers buy several wagonloads of hay for their cattle, Saunders sends his henchman (Dick Curtis) and gang to burn it. Larry and Lou unite the ranchers to bring down Saunders and his minions.

Thanks to its baseball-playing star and major studio release, RAWHIDE was even reviewed by the New York Times, which was usually apathetic about "B" Westerns. The newspaper even liked the film: "Even without the Yankees' cleanup man as its star de resistance, RAWHIDE would be better than average entertainment in its field. Ray Taylor, the director, keeps the story progressing at a lively pace and Smith Ballew fits nicely into the role of a crooning cowboy-lawyer...."

RED FORK RANGE (Big Four, 1931) 59 mins.

Director, Alvin J. Neitz [Alan James]; story, Henry Taylor; adaptor/dialogue, Neitz; camera, William Nobles.

Wally Wales (Wally Hamilton); Ruth Mix (Ruth Farrel); Al Ferguson (Black Bard); Cliff Lyons (Skeeter Beldon); Bud Osborne (Whip Reden); Lafe McKee (Charles Farrell); Will Armstrong (Sergeant O'Flaherty); George Gerwin (Steve Alden); Jim Corey (Apache Joe); Chief Big Tree (Chief Barking Fox).

Promoted as "An All Talking Action Western," this National Players release starred Wally Wales, who had been a popular screen cowboy in the silent days in a series of low-budget actioners for producer Lester F. Scott. Wales continued to star and have supporting roles in low-budget actioners well into the mid-1930s, and then changed his name to Hal Taliaferro (his real name was Floyd Alderson Taliaferro) and became a steady character actor, mostly in bad guy parts. Here, however, he is appearing at the bottom of poverty row in the lowest of low-grade Westerns; a stilted, slow moving and badly recorded feature which did nothing to advance the star or the genre. Films of this type were made for quick playoffs in small towns, and RED FORK RANGE's only notoriety is that it co-starred Tom Mix's daughter Ruth, who billed herself as a "Chip Off the Old Block."

Stagecoach driver Wally Hamilton (Wally Wales) finds out that outlaw Black Bard (Al Ferguson) has enlisted the aid of Indian chief Barking Fox (Chief Big Tree) in attacking an incoming wagon train on which Wally's girl (Ruth Mix) is a passenger. Bard is also in cahoots with express company owner Roden (Bud Osborne) in a scheme to get a government contract by winning a race between the towns of Hangtown and Placerville, in competition with a wagon driven by Wally and owned by his girl's father, the owner of a rival express operation. When the renegades attack the wagon train, a fight ensues. Tom arrives with the cavalry, only to find that the girl has been kidnapped. When the girl's father is blackmailed into leaving the race in order to save his daughter, Tom finds the gang's hideout, rescues her, and then engages in the race. He wins the contract for his future father-in-law.

RED RAIDERS (First National, 1927) 7,050'

Presenter, Charles R. Rogers; supervisor, Harry Joe Brown; director, Albert Rogell; screenplay, Marion Jackson; titles, Don Ryan; camera, Ross Fisher.

Ken Maynard (Lieutenant John Scott); Ann Drew (Jane Logan); Paul Hurst (Sergeant Murphy); J. P. McGowan (Captain Ortwell); Chief Yowlachie (Scar Face Charlie); Harry Shutan (Private Izzy); Tom Day (Earl Logan); Hal Salter (Spike Dargan).

After winning a reputation as a top rodeo cowboy and circus

star, Ken Maynard came to films in 1923, and two years later headlined his first series for independent producer Clifford S. Elfelt.
These actioners proved so popular that Maynard was signed by First
National Pictures; from 1926 to the coming of the sound era, he made
eighteen features for the company with budgets in the $75,000 to
$80,000 range, filmed at such diverse locations as Arizona, California,
Montana, South Dakota, and Wyoming. RED RAIDERS was the
seventh films in the First National series, and "...in many ways remains Ken's best silent picture. Packed with fast and furious action, it contains extreme close-ups of Ken performing almost unbelievable stunts before the relentless eye of the camera" (Jon Tuska,
Views & Reviews, Summer, 1969).

In 1868, young Army Lieutenant John Scott (Ken Maynard) is
assigned to a military post in Sioux Indian territory, where a renegade, Scar Face Charlie (Chief Yowlachie), is trying to stop the
formation of a reservation. John stops the Indians from raiding a
stagecoach and rescues attractive Jane Logan (Anne Drew), the
sister of a local rancher. He also wins the admiration of his men by
riding an outlaw horse. He encounters the ire of his immediate
superior (J. P. McGowan), however, when he objects to the use of
Scar Face Charlie as an army scout, since he feels the Indian is a
spy. Charlie then causes the tribe to go on the warpath and John
takes on the guise of an Indian medicine man in an attempt to scare
them into peace. Charlie, however, sends a message which draws
the troops away from the fort, and then he and his braves attack.
But John returns with the cavalry and defeats the renegades.

RED RAIDERS is a well made action film highlighted by its
riding sequences, excellent battle scenes, and Ross Fisher's topnotch photography; still, the film owes its main success to its star
and his athletic prowess. Raymond E. White wrote in his essay,
"Ken Maynard: Daredevil on Horseback" in Shooting Stars (1987),
"Perhaps his [Maynard's] most spectacular performance occurred in
RED RAIDERS, in which he did hair-raising stunts including retrieving the dragging reins of a runaway stagecoach while galloping
at full speed on Tarzan [his horse]. Not only did he get the
reins, but he also stood up on Tarzan and then jumped to the team
of horses, momentarily being dragged along on the ground by one
of the runaway horses. He quickly flipped himself upon its back
and then dropped down between the team to pick up the remaining
reins before climbing to the driver's box.... These daredevil stunts
became the hallmark of Maynard's First National pictures, and they
immediately established him as one of the top Western stars of the
1920s."

RED SUN (National General, 1971) C 115 mins.

Producer, Robert Dorfmann; director, Terence Young; screen-
play, L. Koenig, D. B. Petitclerc, W. Roberts, L. Roman; music,
Maurice Jarre; camera, Henri Alekan; editor, Johnny Dwyre.
Charles Bronson (Link); Ursula Andress (Christina); Toshiro

Ursula Andress, Charles Bronson, and Toshiro Mifune in RED SUN
(1971).

Mifune (Kuroda); Alain Delon (Gauche); Capucine (Pepita); Satoshi Nakamoura (Japanese Ambassador).

In the early 1870s the Japanese ambassador to the United States (Satoshi Nakamoura) is taking a stagecoach through the West to Washington D.C., where he intends to present a Samurai sword to President Grant. Outlaws led by Link (Charles Bronson) rob the coach but gang member Gauche (Alain Delon) shoots Link, leaves him dead, and steals the sword. Kuroda (Toshiro Mifune), samurai aide to the ambassador, revives the injured Link and forces him to join him in recovering the sword. The two have seven days to accomplish this before Kuroda must commit suicide to maintain his honor. In tracking down Gauche and the sword, the two men develop a mutual respect for each other. Finally they locate buxom Christina (Ursula Andress), a whore in Pepita's (Capucine) brothel, who is Gauche's woman. They take Christina prisoner, forcing Gauche to save her, but as soon as he arrives so does a band of Comanche Indians and the three men unite to defeat the marauders. Gauche then kills Kuroda and, in turn, is dispatched by Link. The conniving Christina tries to convince Link to keep the valuable weapon but he rejects her, hands it over to the authorities, and leaves town.

This international co-production, based on an actual historical event, was filmed in Spain, and the combination of Charles Bronson, Toshiro Mifune and Alain Delon made it dynamite box office everywhere except in the United States, where it was released to tepid returns by the about-to-go-defunct National General Pictures. Naturally American critics were unkind. Judith Crist in New York magazine called it a "mindless movie," while the New York Times judged it "a little above routine." More accurate were Kevin Thomas' words in the Los Angeles Times: "This release is at its best in its humorous, affectionate treatment of the uneasy truce between Bronson and Mifune that develops into friendship when these two proud, strong men realize that they are going to have to depend upon each other. Unfortunately, the various incidents and characters they encounter along the way have not been handled with the same kind of care, and therefore undermine the film's credibility."

RED TOMAHAWK (Paramount, 1967) C 82 mins.

Producer, A. C. Lyles; director, R. G. Springsteen; story, Steve Fisher, Andrew Craddock; screenplay, Fisher; music, Jimmie Haskell; assistant director, James Rosenberger; sound, Harold Lewis, John Wilkinson; camera, W. Wallace Kelly; editor, John F. Schreyer.

Howard Keel (Captain Tom York); Joan Caulfield (Dakota Lil); Broderick Crawford (Columbus Smith); Scott Brady (Ed Wyatt); Wendell Corey (Elkins); Richard Arlen (Telegrapher); Tom Drake (Bill Kane); Tracy Olsen (Sal); Ben Cooper (Lieutenant Drake); Donald Barry (Bly); Reg Parton; Roy Jenson (Prospectors); Gerald Hann (Wu Sing); Dan White (Ned Crane); Henry Wills (Samuels); Saul Gorss (Townsman).

Joan Caulfield, Scott Brady, and Howard Keel in RED TOMAHAWK (1967).

Army Captain Tom York (Howard Keel) arrives in Deadwood to warn the citizens of a pending Sioux Indian attack following the battle at the Little Big Horn River in which Custer and his men have been killed.   York, however, is accused of being a deserter until gunman Ed Wyatt (Scott Brady) tells the locals that Tom is a special Army agent.   Both men know that two Gatling guns are buried in the vicinity but only dance hall hostess Dakota Lil (Joan Caulfield) knows their whereabouts, and she refuses to tell because the guns were responsible for the death of her husband and sons. York tells her the guns are needed to save the town from the Indians.   She leads him to their location but they are stolen by gambler Elkins (Wendell Corey), who plans to sell them to the Indians.   Tom then leads the town's citizens in killing Elkins, taking back the guns and barricading the town.   Word comes that the Sioux have pinned down a cavalry troop.   Tom, Ep, and scout Columbus Smith (Broderick Crawford) take the guns to aid the soldiers, and Smith is killed.   The regiment is saved and the Sioux are scattered.   Tom then returns to Deadwood to Lil.

Another in producer A. C. Lyles' extensive series of low-budget Westerns with veteran casts, RED TOMAHAWK was one of the weakest of the group. Variety reported, "Cast and promises of action strongest selling points but it will all seem familiar." Despite its "name" cast, the movie is all talk and no action. Several battle sequences are promised but nothing spectacular (or costly to the budget) materializes. In terms of performances the movie holds up okay, with Howard Keel doing his best to enliven the proceedings. But Broderick Crawford and many of the other over-the-hill performers seemed bored with their screen assignments. Joan Caulfield was a last-minute replacement for Betty Hutton.

RENFREW OF THE ROYAL MOUNTED (Grand National, 1937) 57 mins.

Producer/director, Al Herman; based on the novel by Laurie York Erskine; screenplay, Charles Logue; music, Arthur Kaye; songs, Betty Laidlow and Robert Lively; camera, Francis Corley; editor, Holbrook N. Todd.

James Newill (Renfrew); Carol Hughes (Virginia Bronson); William Royle (George Hollis); Donald Reed (McDonald); Chief Thundercloud (Pierre); David Barclay (Nolan); William Austin (Constable); Dickie Jones (Tommy); Herbert Corthell (Bronson); Robert Terry (Duke); Kenneth Harlan (Carroll); William Gould (Inspector Newcomb); Lightning (The Dog).

Based on the popular books by Laurie York Erskine, "Renfrew of the Royal Mounted" came to radio in the mid-1930s with House Jameson playing the title role of the Mountie hero. In 1937 the character was translated to the screen by Grand National Pictures, with James Newill, a one-time band and radio singer, in the lead, and the movie proved popular enough to start a series.

In RENFREW OF THE ROYAL MOUNTED, the Royal Canadian Mounted Police are out to stop counterfeiters who have been smuggling currency out of the country. Sergeant Renfrew (James Newill) is assigned to the case and meets a pretty girl (Carol Hughes) who is searching for her lost father. It turns out that the gang is forcing the father to make the bogus money which they are exporting in fish being shipped below the border. Renfrew traps the gang.

The success of the initial entry resulted in more installments being churned out, but in 1938 Grand National went bankrupt. The series was picked up by Monogram and a total of eight "Renfrew" features were produced through 1940. Many of the films co-starred Dave O'Brien, and in 1942 the duo worked for PRC in "The Texas Ranger" series for a baker's dozen entries. Since the "Renfrew" movies proved popular when shown on TV in its early days, the character was revived in 1953 for thirteen half-hour syndicated "Renfrew of the Royal Mounted" TV shows, with James Newill again in the lead and Dave O'Brien co-starring. The feminine lead was done by Louise Stanley, who was the leading lady in two of the earlier theatrical features, YUKON FLIGHT (1939) and SKY BANDITS (1940).

James Newill in RENFREW OF THE ROYAL MOUNTED (1937).

REQUIEM FOR A GUNFIGHTER (Embassy, 1965) C 91 mins.

Executive producer, Pat B. Rooney; producer, Alex Gordon; director, Spencer Gordon Bennet; story, Evan W. Cornell, Guy J. Tedesco; screenplay, R. Alexander; art director, Don Ament; music, Ronald Stein; assistant director, Clark Paylow; sound, Harry Lindgren; camera, Frederick E. West; editor, Charles H. Powell.

Rod Cameron (Dave McCloud); Stephen McNally (Red Zimmer); Chet Douglas (Larry Young); Mike Mazurki (Ivy Bliss); Tim McCoy (Judge Irving Short); Johnny Mack Brown (Enkoff); Chris Hughes (Billy Parker); Olive Sturgess (Bonnie Young); Lane Chandler (Bryan Comer); Bob Steele (Max); Raymond Hatton (Hoops); Dick Jones (Fletcher); Rand Brooks (Gentry); Dale Van Sickel (Kelly); and Doris Spiegel, Zon Murray, Frank Lackteen, Ronn Delanor, Edmund Cobb, Margo Williams, Dick Alexander, Fred Carson, Red Morgan.

Gunmay Dave McCloud (Rod Cameron) is witness to the murder by an outlaw gang of Judge Irving Short (Tim McCoy), who was going to the town of Stopover Flats to investigate a murder. Riding into town, Dave stops a fight between a young rancher (Chet

Douglas) and an outlaw gang member, and the townspeople mistake him for the judge. He finds the area is overrun by Red Zimmer (Stephen McNally) and his outlaws and when one of the gang members, Comer (Lane Chandler), is accused of murder, the rancher and his wife (Olive Sturgess) ask Dave to keep up the masquerade and bring the gang to justice. During the trial, however, gunman Fletcher (Dick Jones) arrives and reveals McCloud's true identity. In a shoot-out between the two, Dave injures the man, but does not kill him. McCloud then throws away his gun and leaves town, but the citizens band together to arrest Zimmer and his men and persuade Dave to return and settle down with them.

Made at the same time as THE BOUNTY KILLER (q.v.), this Alex Gordon production is full of veteran genre players and is a delight for Western film buffs. Rod Cameron, who had only a cameo in THE BOUNTY KILLER, here carries the picture and is quite good as the gunman turned judge. Tim McCoy is also impressive in his brief assignment as the about-to-be-murdered judge; the scene in which he is dragged across the country by the outlaw gang who ambushed him is particularly harrowing.

THE RETURN OF A MAN CALLED HORSE (United Artists, 1976)
     C 125 mins.

     Executive producers, Sandy Howard, Richard Harris; producer, Terry Morse, Jr.; director, Irvin Kershner; based upon a character by Dorothy M. Johnson; second unit director, Michael D. Moore; production designer, Stewart Campbell; set decorator, Ernesto Carrasco; costumes, Dick La Motte; stunt coordinator, Mickey Gilbert; music, Laurence Rosenthal; special effects, Joe Zomar, Federico Farfan; sound, Bill Daniels; camera, Owen Rizman, Jorge Stahl, Ron Taylor.

     Richard Harris (John Morgan); Gale Sondergaard (Elk Woman); Geoffrey Lewis (Zena Morro); Bill Lucking (Tom Gryce); Jorge Luke (Running Bull); Claudio Brook (Chemin D'Fer); Enrique Lucero (Raven); Jorge Russek (Blacksmith); Ana De Sade (Moonstar); Pedro Damien (Standing Bear); Humberto Lopez-Pineda (Thin Dog); Patricia Reyes (Grey Thorn); Regino Herrerra (Lame Wolf); Rigoberto Rico (Owl); Alberto Marsical (Red Cloud).

     See A MAN CALLED HORSE.

THE RETURN OF WILDFIRE (Screen Guild, 1948) 80 mins.

     Producer, Carl K. Hittleman; director, Ray Taylor; screenplay, Betty Burbridge, Hittleman; music, Albert Glasser; camera, Ernie Miller; editor, Paul Landres.

     Richard Arlen (Dobie); Patricia Morison (Pat Marlowe); Mary Beth Hughes (Judy Marlowe); James Millican (Frank Keller); Chris-Pin Martin (Pancho); Stanley Andrews (Pop Marlowe); Holly Bane (Dirk); Highland Dale (Wildfire the Horse); Reed Hadley (Quinn).

Jorge Russek and Richard Harris in THE RETURN OF A MAN
CALLED HORSE (1976).

Drifter Dobie (Richard Arlen) comes to a ranch and is hired
by the owner, Pop Marlowe (Stanley Andrews), to work there and
capture the wild horse Wildfire, which has been ferreting off his
mares. Kelly (James Millican), the ranch foreman, is a gambler who
has been romancing one of Marlowe's daughters, Judy (Mary Beth
Hughes), although both she and her sister Pat (Patricia Morison)
are attracted to Dobie. Having lost much money to crooked gambler
Quinn (Reed Hadley), Kelly shoots Marlowe so that the girls will be
forced to sell their horse herd to Quinn. With Dobie's aid they use
Wildfire to round up the herd but the gambler and his men steal
them and Wildfire kills Kelly. Dobie then defeats Quinn, saves the
ranch for the sisters, and sets Wildfire free. Dobie and Pat fall in
love.

Despite its title, this leisurely drama is not a sequel to WILD-
FIRE (Screen Guild, 1945), starring Bob Steele; the only thing they
have in common is the title horse used in both features. This outing is highlighted by fine acting and camera work; the stock footage
that is used is interpolated well. Although nearing fifty years of
age, Richard Arlen proved to be a stalwart hero contrasting with
Reed Hadley's slimy villain, while Patricia Morison, who sings "Just
an Old Sombrero," and Mary Beth Hughes more than adequately
handle the distaff side of the movie's romantic triangle.

RHYTHM OF THE RANGE see PARDNERS

RIDDLE GAWNE (Ince-Artcraft, 1918) 4,757'

> Producer/director, William S. Hart; based on the short story "The Vengeance of Jefferson Gawne" by Charles Alden Seltzer; screenplay, Seltzer; art director, C. Harold Percival; assistant director, Lambert Hillyer; camera, Joseph August.
> William S. Hart (Jefferson "Riddle" Gawne); Katherine Mac-Donald (Kathleen Harkless); Lon Chaney (Hame Bozzam); Gretchen Lederer (Blanche Dillon); Gertrude Short (Jane Gawne); Leon Kent (Jess Cass); Milton Ross (Reb Butler); E. B. Tilton (Colonel Harkless); George Field (Nigger Paisley).

> William S. Hart's "audience appeal and established box-office drawing power" (Wid's, August 18, 1918) continued with the release of this topnotch melodrama of the Old West, produced and directed by Hart. Here Lambert Hillyer, who had directed the previous year's THE NARROW TRAIL (q.v.), served as assistant director, but after a few more features directed by the star, Hillyer would take over as Hart's helmsman for several additional features. Like moste of Hart's movies, RIDDLE GAWNE is strongest in its stark recreation of the Old West and in the star's handling of the title role. "Hart's interpretation of the character is manly and forceful, and there is a subtle reason for his popularity in fighting roles in this hour of battle. He looks thoroughly representative ... of the American soldier abroad, a determined character of few words and swift deeds," wrote Louis Reeves Harrison in the Moving Picture World trade paper.
> After his brother is killed and the man's faithless wife runs off, Riddle Gawne (William S. Hart) vows to gain revenge for his orphaned niece Jane (Gertrude Short). When two cattle rustlers who work for outlaw Hame Bozzam (Lon Chaney) abduct pretty Kathleen Harkness (Katherine MacDonald), Gawne rescues her and they fall in love. Bozzam, however, wants the woman for himself and has Gawne shot, but the outlaw's mistress, Blanche Dillon (Gretchen Lederer), nurses him back to health. She also attempts to turn Kathleen against Gawne but when the outlaw kidnaps the girl Gawne goes in pursuit, and in a fight his leg is broken. Thinking his adversary is dead, Bozzam brags how he killed Gawne's brother and took his wife, and in a rage Gawne strangles the bad man. Kathleen then admits her love for Gawne and the two adopt Jane.
> William S. Hart had seen Lon Chaney performing villainous roles in Universal films and wanted him for the part of Hame Bozzam despite the fact that others concerned with the production felt Chaney was physically too short to work with Hart. The star persisted and his faith proved correct: Chaney gave a strong performance as the bad man, which helped to launch his screen career as a character star.

Forrest Stanley, Fred Kohler, and Tom Mix in RIDERS OF DEATH VALLEY (1932).

RIDERS OF DEATH VALLEY (Universal, 1932) 76 mins.

Associate producer, Stanley Bergerman; director, Albert Rogell; story, Bergerman, Jack Cunningham; dialogue, Al Martin; camera, Dan Clark.

Tom Mix (Tom Rigby); Lois Wilson (Helen Joyce); Fred Kohler (Lew Grant); Forrest Stanley (Doc Larribe); Willard Robertson (Bill Joyce); Edith Fellows (Betty Joyce); Tony (The Horse); Mae Busch (Dance Hall Girl); Otis Harlan, Max Ascher, Pete Morrison, Edmund Cobb (Citizens); and Iron Eyes Cody.

In the early 1930s Tom Mix returned to the screen to make a series of high-grade, well-budgeted actioners for Universal. RIDERS OF DEATH VALLEY is one of the best of the group and one of the outstanding "B" Westerns of the 1930s. Strong direction by Albert S. Rogell, coupled with a topnotch script, fine acting, and satisfying camera work by Daniel Clark on location in Death Valley, make this film both highly entertaining and picturesque. Although well into his fifties, Tom Mix still rode tall in the saddle, although this outing depends more on histrionics than on strong action.

Prospector Bill Joyce (Willard Robertson) finds gold in Death Valley and gold hunters Lew Grant (Fred Kohle) and Doc Larrabee (Forrest Stanley) find out about it. Grant kills Bill but does not find the secret of the gold's location. Cattleman Tom Rigby (Tom Mix) takes in Bill's orphaned daughter Betty (Edith Fellows) and fears that she too may be killed in an attempt to find the gold, since the girl holds a map of the claim. Believing that the two gold hunters had something to do with her father's murder, Tom divides her map into three parts, with his portion containing the location of the mine. Tom then goes with Betty's aunt Helen (Lois Wilson), Grant and Larrabee into Death Valley to search for the mine, and in a fight Grant causes their buckboard to be lost and all their supplies are destroyed. With only two canteens of water left, the group finds the mine, and to insure their safety Tom gets rid of all their guns. Tom puts a message for help on the mane of his horse Tony and sends the animal home. Lacking water, Grant dies of thirst; meanwhile Larrabee puts sand in Tom's canteen. Trekking across the desert, Tom nearly dies before he is rescued by his ranch hands, who have found Tony's note. The group returns to the site in time to save Helen, and Larrabee, in an attempt to find the mine's source of water, dies in an explosion.

Made the same year as Edward L. Cahn's Universal genre classic LAW AND ORDER (q.v.), this Tom Mix vehicle is just as austere and has a similar penchant for the psychological approach. Here the main plot is the lust for gold, a dramatic device that is well carried out within the conventions of the "B" Western plot-line. The movie is greatly enhanced by Fred Kohler's outstanding performance as the low-life murderous gold hunter, and he is well complemented by Forrest Stanley as his partner.

The locale and a similar plot-line were utilized the next decade in the Cinecolor release, DEATH VALLEY (Screen Guild, 1946), in which a basically decent cowboy (Nat Pendleton) is turned into a madman in his lust for gold while prospecting a Death Valley.

TV title: RIDERS OF THE DESERT.

RIDERS OF DESTINY see WESTWARD HO

RIDERS OF OLD SANTA FE (Universal, 1944) 60 mins.

Producer, Oliver Drake; director, Wallace W. Fox; screenplay, Ande Lame.

Rod Cameron (Matt Conway); Jennifer Holt (Carla [Paula Anderson]); Eddie Dew (Larry Anderson); Fuzzy Knight (Bullseye); Ray Whitley (Hank); Lane Chandler (Sheriff Earl Duncan); Earle Hodgins (Ed Milton); George Douglas (Tom Benner); Dick Alexander (Biff Macauley); Budd Buster (Otis Wade); Ida Moore (Luella Tucker); Al Ferguson (Bartender); Ray Whitley's Bar-6 Cowboys (Entertainers).

Cowboy Matt Conway (Rod Cameron) becomes the new lawman in the town of Red Mountain, throwing out crooked sheriff Earl Duncan (Lane Chandler), who works for saloon owner Tom Benner (George Douglas), the head of the town's council. Armed with a bogus land survey map, Benner hopes to control the area by charging cattlemen a dollar a head to water their stock on the way to market. But he is opposed by local rancher Larry Anderson (Eddie Dew). Realizing the situation, Conway comes to Anderson's aid. Benner cooks up a false murder charge which gets both men put in jail and in danger of being lynched by the local folk. Meanwhile, Matt's pal Bullseye Johnson (Fuzzy Knight) takes on the guise of a woman, breaks into the safe at Benner's saloon and finds the real map, which proves that the water claimed by Benner actually belongs to the town. As a result, the sheriff and Anderson are set free; they stop a raid by Benner and his men on Anderson's ranch and bring in the crooks.

Rod Cameron made six "B" Universal Westerns in 1944 before going on to "A" productions, and RIDERS OF OLD SANTA FE is typical in its actionful script, unobtrusive music by Ray Whitley and his Bar-Six Cowboys, and the comedy antics of perennial sidekick Fuzzy Knight. Comely Jennifer Holt (Jack's daughter and Tim's sister) provided the romantic interest here as Larry Anderson's feisty sister, while Eddie Dew was the second lead as Anderson. Dew also teamed with Rod Cameron for THE OLD TEXAS TRAIL (1944), and earlier had headlined two "John Paul Revere" series films, BEYOND THE LAST FRONTIER and RAIDERS OF SUNSET PASS, at Republic. He proved to be a weak Western star, but later developed into a more than competent director of TV shows and theatrical programmers.

RIDERS OF THE DESERT see RIDERS OF DEATH VALLEY

RIDERS OF THE NORTHWEST MOUNTED see THE VIGILANTES RIDE

RIDIN' THE LONE TRAIL (Republic, 1937) 56 mins.

Producer, A. W. Hackel; director, Sam Newfield; story, E. B. Mann; screenplay, Charles Francis Royal; camera, Robert Cline; editor, S. Roy Luby.

Bob Steele (Bob McArthur); Claire Rochelle (Jean Randall); Charles King (Dusty Williams); Ernie Adams (Peters); Lew Meehan (Sparks); Julian Rivero (Pedro); Steve Clarke (Sheriff); Hal Price (Furman); Frank Ball (Randall); and Jack Kirk.

For two decades Bob Steele reigned as one of the most popular of screen cowboys, coming to films in the silent days at FBO and continuing as a "B" oater hero through 1946. During the interim he starred in more than one hundred feature films for a variety of companies. Many cowboy film fans consider him one of the best genre stars, especially in the areas of acting, riding, and fight sequences. During the mid-1930s Steele made a number of pictures for producer A. W. Hackel, typical of which is RIDIN' THE LONE TRAIL, a very exciting and well executed production with a great performance from Bob Steele, solid fight sequences, and nicely underplayed comedy.

Texan Bob McArthur (Bob Steele) aids a lawman (Steve Clark) in trying to catch a band of road agents who use a ranch owner's daughter's (Claire Rochelle) white horse in their killings and robberies. The gang is led by a masked man, but eventually Bob proves that the culprit is none other than Peters (Ernie Adams), the foreman of the Randall ranch.

RIP ROARIN' BUCKAROO (Victory, 1936) 58 mins.

Producer, Sam Katzman; director, Robert Hill; screenplay, William Buchanan.
Tom Tyler (Scotty McWade); Beth Marion (Miss Hayden); Sammy Cohen (McWade's Sidekick); Forrest Taylor (Luke Slater); John Elliott (Colonel Hayden).

Boxer Scotty McWade (Tom Tyler) gets involved in a prize-fight promoted by dishonest Luke Slater (Forrest Taylor), and during the match is kayoed when his opponent uses illegal brass knuckles. Recovering, Scotty sets out for the ranch of Colonel Hayden (John Elliott), who hires him as a wrangler. The colonel hopes to race his prize bronc in an upcoming race and Scotty is assigned to tame and ride the animal. Meanwhile, Tom is romancing the boss's daughter (Beth Marion). Slater arrives and uses blackmail to force Hayden to wager his ranch on the race and on another prize-fight. Tom realizes the situation and comes to the colonel's rescue, defeating the machinations of the crooked promoter.

Coming at the end of his days as a solo Western star, this Tom Tyler low-achieving effort for producer Sam Katzman's Victory Pictures makes little sense in terms of its plot. Obviously churned out to fill a series quota, the movie has little to recommend it: star Tom Tyler appears confused by the meandering plot, while talented Beth Marion is allowed only to look alluring. Yiddish comedian Sammy Cohen is completely out of place with his wheezy gags. Only Forrest Taylor as the corrupt promoter and John Elliott as the ranch owner manage to make anything of their ill-written roles.

RIVER OF DOLLARS see THE HILLS RUN RED

RIVER OF NO RETURN (Twentieth Century-Fox, 1954) C 91 mins.

Producer, Stanley Rubin; director, Otto Preminger; story,

Marilyn Monroe, Robert Mitchum, and Tommy Rettig in RIVER OF NO
RETURN (1954).

Louis Lantz; screenplay, Frank Fenton; music, Cyril Mockridge;
songs, Ken Darby and Lionel Newman; choreography, Jack Cole;
assistant director, Paul Helmick; art directors, Lyle Wheeler, Ad-
dison Hehr; special effects, Ray Kellogg; camera, Joseph La
Shelle; editor, Louis Loeffler.
    Robert Mitchum (Matt Calder); Marilyn Monroe (Kay); Rory
Calhoun (Harry Weston); Tommy Rettig (Mark Calder); Murvyn Vye
(Dave Colby); Douglas Spencer (Sam Benson); Ed Hinton (Gambler);
Donn Beddoe (Ben); Claire Andre (Surrey Driver); Jack Mather
(Dealer at Crap Table); Edmund Cobb (Barber); Will Wright (Trader);
Jarma Lewis (Dancer); Hal Baylor, Mitchell Lawrence, John Veich,
Larry Chance (Young Punks); Barbara Nichols, Fay Morley (Dan-
cers); Arthur Shields (Priest); Ralph Sanford (Bartender); Harry
Seymour (Man); Jeanne Schaeffer, Anna McCrea, Geneva Gray
(Dance Hall Girls); John Cliff (Leering Man); Mitchell Kowal (Rough-
neck); Paul Newlan (Prospector); John Doucette (Onlooker).

    In the Pacific Northwest in the 1870s, Matt Calder (Robert
Mitchum) is just out of jail and plans to go down a Canadian Rockies
river by barge with his motherless son Mark (Tommy Rettig) to
their new farm home. At a gambling house Matt meets pretty singer
Kay (Marilyn Monroe), who has been fighting off the attentions of

gambler Harry Weston (Rory Calhoun). As a result, Matt agrees to
take the girl on the treacherous river journey. Along the way they
are forced to do battle with the river hazards as well as with local
Indians, and also discover that Weston is on their trail. He is determined to kill Matt and retrieve his woman. In a showdown, it is
Weston who dies, and Matt and Kay realize they are in love. They
journey on to their new home with Mark.

     With CinemaScope and Technicolor, shapely Marilyn Monroe and
the popularity of Robert Mitchum, plus Otto Preminger's direction,
RIVER OF NO RETURN appeared to be a winner. At the box office
it proved to be so, but as a production it is surprisingly weak.
While some of the river sequences are exciting, the movie generally
is mundane, leaving the viewer too much time to guess just when
Mitchum will give into temptation, since the production does everything possible to exploit Monroe's most exploitable body. The New
York Times weighed the feature, "A resoundingly flat showcase for
the physical allure of Marilyn Monroe, playing the guitar in a
spangly costume, shivering in water-soaked, skin-tight dude-
rancher duds or merely wrapped in a blanket." That contemporary
review is substantiated by one in retrospect in Movies on Video
(1983), which noted, "Robert Mitchum has risen above many terrible
scripts in his long career--and this is certainly one of them."

ROAD AGENT (Universal, 1941) 69 mins.

     Producer, Ben Pivar; director, Charles Lamont; story, Sher-
man Low, Arthur St. Claire; screenplay, Morgan Cox, Arthur
Strawn, Maurice Tombragel; song, Jimmy McHugh and Harold Adam-
son; camera, Jerome Ash; editor, Frank Gross.
     Dick Foran (Duke); Leo Carrillo (Pancho); Andy Devine (An-
dy); Anne Gwynne (Patricia); Samuel S. Hinds (Leavitt); Richard
Davies (Martin); Anne Nagel (Lola); Morris Ankrum (Big John);
John Gallaudet (Steve); Reed Hadley (Shayne); Eddy Dams (Lewis);
Ernie Adams, Lew Kelly (Jake and Luke).

ROAD AGENT (RKO, 1952) 60 mins.

     Producer, Herman Schlom; director, Lesley Selander; screen-
play, Norman Houston; camera, J. Roy Hunt; editor, Paul Weather-
wax.
     Tim Holt (Tim); Noreen Nash (Cora Drew); Richard Martin
(Chito Rafferty); Mauritz Hugo (Milo Brand); Dorothy Patrick
(Sally Clayton); Bob Wilke (Slab); Tom Tyler (Larkin); Guy Edward Hearn (Sheriff); William Tannen (Bill Collins); Sam Flint
(George Drew); Forbes Murray (Adams); Stanley Blystone (Barton);
and Tom Kennedy.

     After Richard Arlen left Universal Pictures in 1941 to go to
Paramount, one-time Western star Dick Foran was teamed with Andy
Devine to carry on the popular series of adventure films the studio

had made with Arlen and Devine. After THE KID FROM KANSAS (1941), the duo made a Western called ROAD AGENT, with Leo Carrillo added to the grouping. After ROAD AGENT, however, Foran departed and was replaced by Don Terry. ROAD AGENT looked "like a fugitive from the studio's Johnny Mack Brown hopper, but [was] good enough" (Don Miller, B Movies, 1973). Variety commented, "Despite the familiar situations, director Charles Lamont accentuates the speed of unreeling, with plenty of gun-popping and road-riding."

Cowboys Duke (Dick Foran), Pancho (Leo Carrillo) and Andy (Andy Devine) ride into a small town and are promptly jailed on a murder charge. They have a strong alibi, hwoever, and are released. Duke is made the local lawman and his comrades his deputies. The trio then set out to get the real culprits, who are led by Big John (Morris Ankrum), and they eventually stop him and his gang. It turns out that Duke is a Wells Fargo agent working incognito.

During ROAD AGENT star Dick Foran does a fine job singing "Cielito Lindo" and "Ridin' Home." When the film was reissued by Realart in the early 1950s it was retitled TEXAS ROAD AGENT, perhaps to avoid confusion with Tim Holt's 1952 RKO starrer, ROAD AGENT, the third from the last film in his long studio series. When that film was issued Holt was still among the top five screen cowboys in popularity, but the film is one of his lesser outings.

The 1952 film has cowboys Tim (Tim Holt) and Chito (Richard Martin) at odds over pretty Cora (Noreen Nash), but allied in fighting corrupt Milo Brand (Mauritz Hugo). The two accidentally get the bad man's money after they are overcharged at his toll gate, and they share it with area ranchers who use it to pay off their debts to Brand. The bad man then hires gunman Slab (Bob Wilke) to retrieve the money, but Tim and Chito overcome him in a showdown.

THE ROAMING COWBOY (Spectrum, 1937) 56 mins.

Director, Robert Hill; screenplay, Fred Myton; songs, Stephen Foster and Rudy Sooter; camera, Bill Hyuer.

Fred Scott (Cal Brent); Al "Fuzzy" St. John (Fuzzy); Lois January (Jeanie); Forrest Taylor (Evans); Roger Williams (Walton); Dick Cramer (Morgan); Buddy Cox (Buddy); Oscar Gahan (Tom); Art Miles (Red); and Rudy Sooter, George Chesebro.

Two cowboys, Cal Grant (Fred Scott) and Fuzzy Q. Jones (Al St. John), ride to a ranch where the owner has been murdered, leaving an orphaned son (Buddy Cox). They join the Morgan outfit and get into a range war with crook Evans (Forrest Taylor), who plots to buy up all the area range land and run off the ranchers. It was Evans who killed Morgan, and he convicnes the dead man's niece, Jeanie (Lois January), that Cal committed the homicide. Cal, however, escapes from the law to prove his innocence and win

Jeanie's love.

Despite an obviously small budget and rather stilted dialogue, THE ROAMING COWBOY is a fair entry in Fred Scott's Spectrum series, due mainly to Scott's winning personality and singing. Al St. John's comedy antics and comely heroine Lois January add to the film's pluses. Most of the songs used in the feature are free, public domain tunes by Stephen Foster, and Scott does well by them indeed.

ROCKIN' IN THE ROCKIES see THE OUTLAWS IS COMING

ROCKY MOUNTAIN see SAN ANTONIO

ROCKY RHODES (Universal, 1934) 64 mins.

Producer, Buck Jones; director, Al Raboch; story, W. C. Tuttle; screenplay, Edward Churchill; camera, Ted McCord.

Buck Jones (Rocky Rhodes); Sheila Terry (Nan); Stanley Fields (Harp); Walter Miller (Dan Murtch); Paul Fix (Joe Hilton); Lydia Knott (Mrs. Rhodes); Alf P. James (Street); Silver (The Horse); and Carl Stockdale, Monte Montague, Bud Osborne, Harry Semels.

When Buck Jones (Charles "Buck" Jones) came to Universal in 1934 to take over as the studio's prime Western star after the departure of Ken Maynard, he produced several of his own outings, including this one, which is only fair and certainly not up to the standards of his initial Columbia pictures. The script is more tailored to a Ken Maynard vehicle and the action is slight, although Buck deftly modulates his character to make the film worth viewing.

Rocky Rhodes (Buck Jones), a Chicago stockyard worker, longs to see the Arizona ranch home he left five years before. With pal Harp (Stanley Fields) he heads west to Cactus City, but when he reaches the ranch he finds that his dad has been murdered and that foreman Joe Hilton (Paul Fix) has been arrested for the crime and for the theft of the family savings. In a bogus escape attempt from the local jail, however, Joe is murdered and Rocky realizes that the culprit is businessman Dan Murtch (Walter Miller), who is after all the ranches in the vicinity as well as another rancher's pretty daughter (Sheila Terry).

While Buck Jones shines in his actual stalwart hero's role, the film's best acting comes from former serial star Walter Miller as the villain of the piece.

ROGUES OF THE WEST see RANCHERS AND RASCALS

ROLL ON, TEXAS MOON (Republic, 1946) 67 mins.

Associate producer, Edward J. White; director, William Witney; story, Jean Murray; screenplay, Paul Gangelin, Mauri Grashin; music, Dale Butts; music director, Morton Scott; songs, Jack Elliott, Tim Spencer; art director, Paul Youngblood; set decorator, Earl Wooden; assistant director, Les Lukather; sound, William E. Clark; camera, William Bradford; editor, Lee Orlebeck.

Roy Rogers (Himself); Trigger (The Horse); George "Gabby" Hayes (Gabby Whittaker); Dale Evans (Jill Delaney); Dennis Hoey (Cole Gregory); Elisabeth Risdon (Cactus Kate Taylor); Francis McDonald (Steve Anders); Edward Keane (Frank J. Wilson); Tom London (Bert Morris); Harry Strang (Don Williams); Kenne Duncan (Brannigan); Edward Cassidy (Tom Prescott); Lee Shumway (Ned Burnes); Steve Darrell (Joe Cummings); Pierce Lyden (Stuhler); Bob Nolan and the Sons of the Pioneers (Themselves).

Upon his release from the armed services in 1946, ace serial director William Witney was assigned by Republic to helm its Roy Rogers series, the director having done only one previous "B" Western (HEROES OF THE SADDLE, 1940) for the studio. From 1946 to 1951 Witney directed twenty-seven consecutive Roy Rogers features, and most genre followers insist that they include some of the finest work by the screen star with their combination of hard action and stunts, good plot structure, and well integrated music. When Witney took over the Rogers' pictures, the emphasis on over-staged production numbers and flashy garb was dropped and the entertainment value of the features increased, keeping Roy Rogers the "King of the Cowboys" and the number one box-office draw in the field.

ROLL ON TEXAS MOON, the first of the Witney-directed features, is an interesting example, with a complicated plot, lots of pacing and surprisingly little music. Set in modern-day Texas, the narrative tells of a long-time feud between cattlemen Gabby Whittaker (George "Gabby" Hayes) and sheep rancher Kate Delaney (Elisabeth Risdon). Gabby is falsely accused of murder, but is cleared. However, the trouble remains between the two factions and the cattle syndicate sends agent Roy Rogers (Himself) to investigate. He discovers that Kate's lawyer, Cole Gregory (Dennis Hoey), is responsible for the problems since he wants both spreads for himself. Roy brings peace to the range.

ROLLIN' PLAINS (Grand National, 1938) 61 mins.

Producer, Edward Finney; director, Al Herman; story, Jacques and Clela Jacquard; screenplay, Lindsley Parsons, Edmund Kelso; song, Walt Samuels, Leonard Whitcup, Teddy Powell, Frank Harford; camera, (not credited); editor, Fred Bain.

Tex Ritter (Tex Lawrence); Horace Murphy (Ananias); Snub Pollard (Pee Wee); Harriet Bennet (Ruth Moody); Hobart Bosworth (Gospel Moody); Edward Cassidy (Sheriff Tomlin); Karl Hackett (Dan Barrow); Charles King (Trigger Gargan); Ernest Adams (Cain Moody);

Lynton Brent (Lope); Hank Carpenter (Hank Tomlin); Hank Worden
(Squint); Augie Gomez (Weevil); Oscar Gahan (Telegraph Clerk);
Beverly Hillbillies (Themselves); White Flash (The Horse); and Hank
Worden, Rudy Sooter, Carl Mathews, George Morrell.

Texas Rangers Tex Lawrence (Tex Ritter); Ananias (Horace
Murphy) and Pee Wee (Snub Pollard) investigate trouble between
cattle ranchers and sheep herders. They discover the problem is
over water rights and that rancher Gospel Moody (Hobart Bosworth)
is having his cattle rustled. When a sheepman is murdered, Gospel
is accused, convicted of the crime and sentenced to be hanged. In
the meantime, Tex tries to find the actual murderer. He suspects
that Gospel's half-brother Cain (Ernie Adams) is involved and learns
that he is in cahoots with corrupt sheepman Dan Barrow (Karl
Hackett), who is responsible for the killing. Tex convinces the
governor to pardon Gospel but the crooks steal the pardon and Gospel, forced to make a jail break, is wounded. To force a confession
from Cain, Tex informs him that Gospel is dead and then has him
appear before his half-brother with eerie music playing in the background, scaring a confession from Cain. Tex and the rangers arrest Dan and his henchman, Trigger Gargan (Charles King).
Tex Ritter was to make only one more feature, UTAH TRAIL
(1938), before he and producer Edward Finney left the defunct
Grand National for Monogram. ROLLIN' PLAINS was the star's
eleventh feature for Grand National and is one of his best. In addition to a good, actionful script, the movie is benefitted by veteran
actor Hobart Bosworth as the wronged rancher, and the scene where
he pretends to be a ghost to frighten Ernie Adams is especially effective. The movie also produced one of Tex Ritter's best movie
songs, "Rollin' Plains," although, surprisingly, he never recorded
it commercially. The tune was not put on record until Tex Ritter's
good friend and biographer, Johnny Bond, recorded it on the 1977
album, "The Return of the Singing Cowboy" (CMH 6213), four years
after Ritter's death.

ROUGH RIDERS' ROUND-UP (Republic, 1939) 55 mins.

Director, Joseph Kane; screenplay, Jack Natteford; music, Cy
Feuer; songs: Eddie Cherkose and Cy Feuer; Tim Spencer; camera,
Jack Marta; editor, Lester Orlebeck.
Roy Rogers (Himself); Mary Hart (Dorothy Blair); Raymond
Hatton (Rusty Coburn); Eddie Acuff (Tommy); William Pawley (Ari-
zona Jack); Dorothy Sebastian (Rose); George Meeker (Lanning);
Jack Rockwell (Harrison); Guy Usher (Blair); George Chesebro
(Mosby); Glenn Strange (Boggs); Duncan Renaldo (Alcalde); Trig-
ger (The Horse); Jack Kirk (Jim Horn); Hank Bell (Patrolman Kit
Grant); Dorothy Christy (Blondie); Fred Kelsey (Agitator); John
Merton, Dan White (Patrolmen); George Montgomery (Telegrapher);
Frank McCarroll (Rough Rider); Chris-Pin Martin (Hotel Keeper);
Soledad Jiminez (Old Woman); and Eddy Waller, Al Haskell, Frank
Ellis, Augie Gomez.

Former Rough Riders Roy Rogers (Himself) and Rusty Coburn (Raymond Hatton) work as border patrolmen and are at odds with a gang involved in a gold shipment robbery. The daughter, Dorothy Blair (Mary Hart), of the robbed mine owner comes West not knowing that gang leader Arizona Jack (William Pawley) is working with her fiancé, Lanning (George Meeker), the mine foreman. The crooks capture the girl but she is rescued by Roy and Rusty, and the Rough Riders cross the border to bring the crooks to justice.

With a good story and plenty of action, ROUGH RIDERS' ROUND-UP is a solid entry in the early phase of Roy Rogers' starring career. The movie also has little music, depending on fast direction and a fine supporting cast to keep it moving. The movie co-starred Mary Hart (also known as Lynn/Lynne Roberts) and was one of seven in which she shared billing with Roy Rogers.

ROUGH RIDIN' JUSTICE (Columbia, 1941) 58 mins.

Producer, Jack Fier; director, Derwin Abrahams; screenplay, Elizabeth Beecher; art directors, Lionel Banks, Charles Clague; set director, Fay Babcock; assistant director, Earl Bellamy; sound, Lambert Day; camera, George Meehan; editor, Aaron Stell.

Charles Starrett (Steve Holden); Dub Taylor (Cannonball); Betty Jane Graham (Gail Trent); Wheeler Oakman (Virgil Trent); Jack Ingram (Nick Dunham); Forrest Taylor (Padgett); Jack Rockwell (Sheriff Kramer); Edmund Cobb (Harns); Dan White (Mike); Bob Kortman (Pete); George Chesebro (Lacey); Robert Ross (Bob); Carl Sepulveda, Kermit Maynard, Elmo Lincoln (Guards); Bud Osborne (Driver); Steve Clark (Gray); Butch and Buddy (Themselves); Jimmy Wakely and His Oklahoma Cowboys (Themselves).

Charles Starrett began starring in series Westerns for Columbia in 1935 and continued for that studio through 1952. In 1945 he took on the permanent role of "The Durango Kid," but just prior to that movie he made one of his strongest outings, ROUGH RIDIN' JUSTICE. Variety called the feature "solid Western fare," and added, "Entertainment values are sturdy...."

Charles Starrett is Steve Holden, the head of a gang which harasses the members of a local cattlemen's association. Actually Starrett is an undercover agent out to stop the lawlessness created by crooks Virgil Trent (Wheeler Oakman), Sheriff Kramer (Jack Rockwell) and Harns (Edmund Cobb). The locals decide that the best way to handle the outlaws is to hire Steve Holden to protect their wagon train shipments. He agrees to do so, bringing several gang members with him. It turns out that there is a spy among the gang who aids the crooks. Eventually Steve ferrets out the head of the operation and has his underlings arrested. He rides away to his next assignment.

As with most Westerns of the day, ROUGH RIDIN' JUSTICE had comedy relief, here provided by Dub Taylor, and music by Jimmy Wakely and His Oklahoma Cowboys.

Charles Starret and Wheeler Oakman in ROUGH RIDIN' JUSTICE (1941).

ROVIN' TUMBLEWEEDS (Republic, 1939) 62 mins.

Associate producer, William Berke; director, George Sherman; screenplay, Betty Burbridge, Dorrell McGowan, Stuart McGowan; music supervisor, Raoul Kraushaar; songs: Autry and Fred Rose, Johnny Marvin; camera, William Nobles; editor, Tony Martinelli.

Gene Autry (Himself); Smiley Burnette (Frog Milhouse); Mary Carlisle (Mary); Douglass Dumbrille (Holloway); William Farnum (Nolan); Lee "Lasses" White (Storekeeper); Ralph Peters (Satchel); Gordon Hart (Fuller); Vic Potel (Zeke); Jack Ingram (Blake); Sammy McKim (Eddie); Reginald Barlow (Higgins); Eddie Kane (Congressman); Guy Usher (Craig); Pals of the Golden West (Themselves); Champion (The Horse); Horace Murphy (Sheriff); and David Sharpe, Jack Kirk, Rose Plummer, Robert Burns, Art Mix, Horace B. Carpenter, Fred "Snowflakes" Toones, Frank Ellis, Fred Burns, Edward Cassidy, Forrest Taylor, Tom Chatterton, Crauford Kent, Maurice Costello, Charles K. French, Lee Shumway, Bud Osborne, Harry Semels, Chuck Morrison.

Corrupt politicians fail to pass a flood control bill and a flood causes great damage. Gene Autry (Himself) leads the citizens who fight the raging waters and fail, but Gene's singing proves to be popular and radio announcer Mary (Mary Carlisle) bails him out of jail after he gets into a fight with the sheriff (Horace Murphy) over jobs for the homeless. Gene agrees to sing on the radio to gain money for his friends and he is soon in much demand. Crook Holloway (Douglass Dumbrille) wants all the land before the flood bill is passed and he persuades Gene to run for Congress. Gene does, and wins. Once in office, however, Gene pushes for the passage of the flood bill, but fails. When another flood hits, Gene forces Holloway to give up opposing the bill and it passes. Holloway also consents to assist those affected by the floods. Gene marries his lady love, Mary.

ROVIN' TUMBLEWEEDS is an offbeat (which hurt box-office receipts) yet very good Gene Autry film, especially with its fine photography and special effects, including the well-staged flood sequences. In this film Gene Autry introduces the song which would become his trademark theme, "Back in the Saddle Again," a tune he co-wrote with Ray Whitley. An interesting comedy aspect of the film has two storekeeper characters doing a take-off on the popular radio program, "Lum 'n' Abner." It was no accident that this film appeared in the same year as Frank Capra's MR. SMITH GOES TO WASHINGTON, the latter providing much of the plot structuring for the former.

A.k.a.: WASHINGTON COWBOY

THE ROYAL MOUNTED RIDES AGAIN see COVERED WAGON TRAILS

RUGGLES OF RED GAP (Paramount Pictures, 1923) 7,590'

Presenter, Jesse L. Lasky; director, James Cruze; based on the play by Harry Leon Wilson; screenplay, Walter Woods, Anthony Coldeway; camera, Karl Brown.

Edward Everett Horton (Ruggles); Ernest Torrence (Cousin Egbert Floud); Lois Wilson (Kate Kenner); Fritzi Ridgeway (Emily Judson); Charles Ogle (Jeff Tuttle); Louise Dresser (Mrs. Effie Floud); Anna Lehr (Mrs. Belknap Jackson); William Austin (Mr. Belknap-Jackson); Lillian Leighton (Ma Pettingill); Thomas Holding (Earl of Brinstead); Frank Elliott (Honorable George); Kalla Pasha (Herr Schwitz); Sidney Bracey (Sam Henshaw); Milt Brown (Senator Pettingill); Guy Oliver (Judge Ballard); Mister Barkerrt (The Dog).

RUGGLES OF RED GAP (Paramount, 1935) 90 mins.

Producer, Arthur Hornblow, Jr.; director, Leo McCarey; based on the novel by Harry Leon Wilson; screenplay, Walter DeLeon, Harlan Thompson; adaptor, Humphrey Pearson; songs, Ralph Rainger and Sam Coslow; camera, Alfred Gilks.

Charles Laughton (Ruggles); Mary Boland (Mrs. Effie Floud); Charlie Ruggles (Egbert Floud); ZaSu Pitts (Mrs. Judson); Roland Young (Earl of Burnstead); Leila Hyams (Nell Kenner); Maude Eburne (Ma Pettingill); Lucien Littlefield (Charles Belknap-Jackson); Leota Lorraine (Mrs. Charles Belknap-Jackson); James Burke (Jeff Tuttle); Clarence Wilson (Jake Henshaw); Augusta Anderson (Mrs. Wallaby); Brenda Fowler (Mrs. Judy Ballard); Sarah Edwards (Mrs. Carey).

Harry Leon Wilson's 1915 story, "Ruggles of Red Gap," was adapted to the stage by Harrison Rhodes, with music by Sigmund Romberg, and it opened on Broadway late in 1915 with Ralph Herz in the title role. The play proved enormously popular and, in 1918, Essanay Pictures brought it to the screen with Taylor Holmes as Ruggles. It was remade by Paramount in 1923, starring Edward Everett Horton.

The story for the 1923 film followed the play closely. Newly rich, but crude, Egbert Floud (Ernest Torrance) wins the services of British butler Alfred Ruggles (Edward Everett Horton) in a poker game in Monte Carlo from his employer the Earl of Brinstead (Thomas Holding). Floud and his social-climbing wife (Louise Dresser) bring the butler with them to their home in the rawboned frontier town of Red Gap, where they pass him off as a visiting colonel. The Earl, however, arrives and falls in love with Klondike Kate Kenner (Lois Wilson), whose family background is not acceptable to the snooty Flouds. Ruggles learns that all people are equal in America, proves his true identity, opens a restaurant, and marries young widow Emily Judson (Fritzi Ridgeway). Photoplay magazine termed this version a "...highly amusing comedy ... Ernest Torrance and Edward Horton provide the bulk of the many laughs."

A decade after the 1923 version, Paramount produced the gentle east-versus-west vehicle for a third go-round, this time as a project for Charles Laughton. The British actor provides one of the finest performances of his career, and a highlight of the well-mounted film has him reciting the Gettysburg Address. Like the 1923 edition, this expensive mounting follows the plot-line quite faithfully, and it contains a superb cast: Charles Ruggles and Mary Boland as the Flouds, ZaSu Pitts as the widow, Leila Hyams as Klondike Kate, Roland Young as the Earl of Brinstead, and Maude Eburne as the earthy Ma Pettingill. Variety judged the feature a "...fast and furiously funny film ... it has the unusual elements of combining adults and sophisticated class draw with that of family audiences." With Leo McCarey directing, the feature has a soft edge which does not harm the focus of the social satire.

For his performance in RUGGLES OF RED GAP, coupled with his portrayal of Captain Bligh in M-G-M's MUTINY ON THE BOUNTY the same year, Charles Laughton received the New York Film Critics' first annual Circle Award as best actor of the year.

The old chestnut came to the screen for the fourth time in 1950. Paramount called it FANCY PANTS and it now starred Bob Hope

ZaSu Pitts, Charles Laughton, Charles Ruggles, and Maude Eburne in RUGGLES OF RED GAP (1935).

as the British butler, renamed Humphrey. Lucille Ball co-starred and the locale of the film was switched from Washington to New Mexico. While the new version was fairly amusing, it was not in the same league with the previous Paramount versions. Three songs were written for the updated outing by Ray Evans and Jay Livingston.

Two television versions of "Ruggles of Red Gap" were aired in the 1950s. In 1951 CBS-TV presented the play on "Prudential Family Playhouse," starring Cyril Ritchard as Ruggles and Walter Abel and Glenda Farrell as the Flouds. Six years later NBC-TV presented the play as a video color special, with Michael Redgrave as Ruggles and Imogene Coca and David Wayne as the Flouds. Over the years, there have been assorted stage musical versions of the property.

RUN OF THE ARROW (Universal, 1957) C 86 mins.

Producer/director/screenplay, Samuel Fuller; assistant director, Ben Chapman; music, Victor Young; camera, Joseph Biroc; editor,

Charles Bronson, Rod Steiger, Sarita Montiel, and H. M. Wynant in
RUN OF THE ARROW (1957).

Gene Fowler, Jr.
    Rod Steiger (O'Meara); Sarita Montiel (Yellow Moccasin);
Brian Keith (Captain Clark); Ralph Meeker (Lieutenant Driscoll);
Jay C. Flippen (Walking Cyote); Charles Bronson (Blue Buffalo);
Olive Carey (Mrs. O'Meara); H. M. Wynant (Crazy Wolf); Meyle Mor-
row (Lieutenant Stockwell); Frank de Kova (Red Cloud); Colonel
Tim McCoy (General Allen); Stuart Randall (Colonel Taylor); Frank
Warner (Ballad Singer); Billy Miller (Silent Tongue); Chuck Hay-
ward (Corporal); Chuck Roberson (Sergeant).

    At the end of the Civil War, Confederate soldier O'Meara
(Rod Steiger) fires his last bullet and wounds Union Army Lieutenant
Driscoll (Ralph Meeker). At the war's finale, O'Meara refuses to
accept the defeat of the South and goes West, where he is received
as a member of the Sioux Indian nation after passing an endurance
test. O'Meara becomes the Sioux negotiator with the whites and
signs a peace treaty for them with the government. Chief Blue
Buffalo (Charles Bronson) then marries him to squaw Yellow Moccasin

(Sarita Montiel), but brave Crazy Wolf (H. M. Wynant) stirs up trouble and war breaks out between the tribe and officers led by Driscoll. During the fight Driscoll is captured and tortured by the Sioux. Out of mercy O'Meara kills him and then leaves the tribe to take the wounded soldiers back to Fort Laramie.

Originally titled THE LAST BULLET, this film is a downbeat melodrama pushed out of kilter by Rod Steiger's hammy performance. Variety noted, "...Steiger frequently lapses from Southerner into Irish dialect, difficult to understand, and footage occasionally is impeded by irrelevant sequences." The movie, however was a vanguard for the violent, blood-laced Westerns of Sam Peckinpah during the next decade. Wrote the British Monthly Film Bulletin, "Samuel Fuller's films have now achieved some notoriety for their use of excessive violence; in RUN OF THE ARROW, killings, butcherings, beatings and arrow-pierced flesh are used as deliberate shock tactics, often quite gratuitous to the confused and rambling narrative. The climactic scene of torture, with the Cavalry officer being cut to pieces by vengeful Indians, remains a disturbing experience."

To be noted: the casting of old-time cowboy star Tim McCoy as the dignified General Allen, and the dubbing of Mexican actress Sarita Montiel's voice on the soundtrack by Angie Dickinson.

RUSTLER'S HIDEOUT (Producers Releasing Corp., 1944) 60 mins.

Producer, Sigmund Neufeld; director, Sam Newfield; screenplay, Joe O'Donnell; assistant director, Melville DeLay; sound, Glen Glenn; camera, Jack Greenhalgh; editor, Holbrook N. Todd.

Buster Crabbe (Billy Carson); Al "Fuzzy" St. John (Fuzzy Q. Jones); Patti McCarty (Barbara); Charles King (Buck Shaw); John Merton (Harry Stanton); Terry Frost (Jack Crockett); Hal Price (Dave Crockett); Lane Chandler (Hammond); Al Ferguson (Steve); Frank McCarroll (Squint); Ed Cassidy (Sheriff); and Bud Osborne.

Between 1941 and 1946 Buster Crabbe and Al St. John starred in three-dozen feature Westerns for Producers Releasing Corporation (PRC) and the series has the reputation of being one of the shoddiest cowboy series ever produced. While many of the films in the Crabbe-St. John canon are inferior, though, not all of them are sub-par, as evidenced by RUSTLER'S HIDEOUT.

Billy Carson (Buster Crabbe) and Fuzzy Q. Jones (Al St. John) lead a large Wyoming cattle herd to market and come across an outlaw gang wanting to take the cattle to start their own business. When the outlaws murder a crooked gambler (Lane Chandler), it is Billy who is blamed, but later the real killers tip their hand and Billy brings them to justice.

RUSTLERS OF RED DOG (Universal, 1935) twelve chapters

Director, Louis Friedlander [Lew Landers]; story, Nathaniel

Eddy; screenplay, George Plympton, Basil Dickey, Ella O'Neill, Nate
Gatzert, Vin Moore; art director, Ralph Berger; camera, Richard
Fryer, William Sichner; editors, Alvin Todd, Edward Todd, Saul
Goodkind, Irving Applebaum.

Johnny Mack Brown (Jack Woods); Joyce Compton (Mary Lee);
Walter Miller (Deacon); Raymond Hatton (Laramie); Harry L. Woods
(Rocky); Fredric McKaye (Snakey); Charles K. French (Tom Lee);
Lafe McKee (Bob Lee); William Desmond (Ira Dale); J. P. McGowan
(Captain Trent); Edmond Cobb (Buck); Bud Osborne (Jake);
Monty Montague (Kruger); Artie Ortego (Chief/Scout/Henchman);
Jim Thorpe (Chief Scarface); Chief Thunderbird (Chief); Ann Darcy,
Fritzi Burnette, Grace Cunard, Virginia Ainsworth (Bits); Wally
Wales (Wally); Chief Many Treaties [William Hazlitt] (Chief); Charles
Murphy (Kruger); Art Mix (Waiter/Henchman).

Chapters: 1) Hostile Redskins; 2) Flaming Arrows; 3) Thundering Hoofs; 4) Attack at Dawn; 5) Buried Alive; 6) Flames of
Vengeance; 7) Into the Depths; 8) Paths of Peril; 9) The Snake
Strikes; 10) Riding Wild; 11) The Rustlers Clash; 12) Law and Order.

RUSTLERS OF RED DOG was Johnny Mack Brown's second
serial (the first being Mascot's FIGHTING WITH KIT CARSON in
1933) and his first for Universal, followed by WILD WEST DAYS
(1937), FLAMING FRONTIERS (1938) and THE OREGON TRAIL
(1939). Nicely helmed by Louis Friedlander [Lew Landers], RUST-
LERS OF RED DOG is an actionful cliffhanger with good work by
Raymond Hatton in his usual sidekick role and comely Joyce Compton
as the heroine, and it effectively provided silent serial ace Walter
Miller with the co-starring hero's role. Also fun for Western fans
were the appearance of such genre favorites as Harry Woods,
Charles K. French, Lafe McKee, William Desmond, Bud Osborne, J.
P. McGowan, and Monte Montague in supporting parts.

Three pals, Jack Woods (Johnny Mack Brown), Deacon (Walter
Miller) and Laramie (Raymond Hatton) fight together to protect
settlers moving westward. The trio arrive in Red Dog and agree to
join a wagon train bringing in businessman Tom Lee's (Charles K.
French) daughter Mary (Joyce Compton) and brother Bob (Lafe
McKee0. Rustlers led by Rocky (Harry Woods), however, have also
joined the train and plan to steal the $50,000 in gold being carried
in one of the wagons. Indians attack the train and are fended off
and the Army escorts the wagons to a nearby fort. The Indians
attack the fort and capture its inhabitants, and the outlaws use the
attack to escape with the gold wagon. Jack is spared because he had
once saved the chief's life, but Mary is to become a squaw and
Deacon and Laramie must die. The army arrives with reinforcements
and the four are able to escape from the Indian village. Jack and
his pals retrieve the safe and return it to the wagon train, and
when it reaches town Jack becomes the marshal. Rumors of a gold
strike leave the town empty and Rocky and his gang loot the place,
but Jack and his cohorts return and Jack shoots Rocky when the
latter attempts to escape.

RR-5054-30A

Marilu Henner, Tom Berenger, and Sela Ward in RUSTLERS' RHAP-
SODY (1985).

RUSTLERS' RHAPSODY (Paramount, 1985) C 88 mins.

Executive producer, Jose Vicuna; producer, David Giler; associate producer, Michael Green; director/screenplay, Hugh Wilson; production designer, Gil Parrondo; costumes, Wayne Finkelman; assistant director, Green; music, Steve Dorff; sound, David Lee; camera, Jose Luis Alcaine; supervising editor, John Victor Smith.

Tom Berenger (Rex O'Herlihan); G. W. Bailey (Peter); Marilu Henner (Tracy); Andy Griffith (Colonel Ticonderoga); Fernando Rey (Railroad Colonel); Sela Ward (Colonel's Daughter); Patrick Wayne (Bob Barber); Brant Van Hoffman (Jim); Christopher Malcolm (Jud); Jim Carter (Blackie); Billy J. Mitchell (Doctor).

Following a dormant period, the big-screen Western returned with RUSTLERS' RHAPSODY, quickly followed by PALE RIDER and SILVERADO (qq.v.). The revival was a brief one for the genre, although all three features turned a profit of sorts. Of the trio, only the initial one is a comedy, the other two being straight melodramas. In RUSTLER'S RHAPSODY, director/scripter Hugh Wilson attempts to spoof the musical Westerns of the 1930s and 1940s, and the result is a tame comedy which is only passable entertainment. (It nowhere matches the biting if heavy-handed satire of Mel Brooks' BLAZING SADDLES, 1974--see B/V).

Singing cowboy Rex O'Herlihan (Tom Berenger) travels from town to town with sidekick Peter (G. W. Bailey) and horse Wildlife. The duo right wrongs, sing a few songs, and then drift on to the next locale for more of the same. In Oakwood Estates they discover that corrupt cattle baron Colonel Ticonderoga (Andy Griffith) is riding roughshod over the local citizens with the aid of an equally corrupt railroad tycoon (Fernando Rey) and his gang. In town, the singing cowboy becomes involved with the local prostitute (Marilu Henner), who has a heart of gold, and he also romances the colonel's daughter (Sela Ward). When the colonel discovers that Rex is a formidable opponent, he brings in another good guy cowboy (Patrick Wayne) to oppose him. Eventually the colonel and his minions are defeated by the forces of good and the singing cowboy moves on.

While RUSTLERS' RHAPSODY is a pleasing enough take-off on the "B" genre outings of yore, it is an empty comedy. Its main appeal might have been to "B" Western buffs had not the script gone out of its way to alienate the very audience it most needs.

SAN ANTONIO (Warner Bros., 1945) C 111 mins.

Producer, Robert Buckner; directors, David Butler, (uncredited) Raoul Walsh; screenplay, Alan LeMay, W. R. Burnett; assistant director, William Kissel; dialogue director, Frederick De Cordova; art director, Ted Smith; set decorator, Jack McConaghy; wardrobe, Milo Anderson; makeup, Perc Westmore; music, Max Steiner; orchestrator, Hugo Friedhofer; songs: Ted Koehler,

Alexis Smith and Errol Flynn in SAN ANTONIO (1945).

M. K. Jerome and Ray Heindorf; Jack School and Charles Kisco; Larry Spier; choreography, LeRoy Prinz; color consultant, Leonard Doss; sound, Everett A. Brown; special effects, Willard Van Enger; camera, Bert Glennon; editor, Irene Morra.

Errol Flynn (Clay Hardin); Alexis Smith (Jeanne Starr); S. Z. Sakall (Sacha Bozic); Victor Francen (Legare); Florence Bates (Henrietta); John Litel (Charlie Bell); Paul Kelly (Roy Stuart); John Alvin (Pony Smith); Monte Blue (Cleve Andrews); Robert Shayne (Captain Morgan); Robert Barrat (Colonel Johnson); Pedro de Cordoba (Ricardo Torreon); Tom Tyler (Lafe McWilliams); Chris-Pin Martin (Hymie Rosas); Charles Stevens (Sojar Harris); Poodles Hanneford (San Antonio Stage Driver); Doodles Weaver (Square Dance Caller); Dan White (Joey Sims); Ray Spiker (Rebel White); Al Hill (Hap Winters); Wallis Clark (Tip Brice); Harry Cording (Hawker); Chalky Williams (Poker Player); Bill Steele (Roper); Howard Hill (Clay's Henchman); Arnold Kent (Dancer); Don McGuire, John Compton (Cowboys); Eddie Acuff (Gawking Cowboy); Si Jenks (Station Boss); Denver Dixon (Barfly); Snub Pollard (Dance Extra); Cliff Lyons (Errol Flynn's Double); Harry Semels (Mexican); Francis Ford (Old Cowboy Greeting Coach); William Gould, Jack Mower (Wild Cowmen); Brandon Hurst (Gambler).

Following his successful DODGE CITY (1939), VIRGINIA CITY (1940), SANTA FE TRAIL (1940), and THEY DIED WITH THEIR BOOTS ON (1942) (see B/V for all), Errol Flynn returned to the Western motif for SAN ANTONIO. Hardly a Westerner by birth or inclination, swashbuckling Flynn had great success as a screen cowboy, as Tony Thomas, Rudy Behlmer, and Clifford McCarty discuss in their The Films of Errol Flynn (1969): "By no means a Western type, Flynn was the only non-American actor to become successful in this kind of film in the United States. He confessed to being baffled by this success, and referred to himself as the 'rich man's Roy Rogers.' By the time he made SAN ANTONIO, he had surrendered himself, and obviously decided to enjoy the nonsense along with the customers."

Cattleman Clay Hardin (Errol Flynn) returns home to the Texas city from Mexico with proof that Roy Stuart (Paul Kelly), the owner of a big dance hall, is actually behind a well-trained band of cattle rustlers. When New York actress Jeanne Starr (Alexis Smith) arrives to entertain at Stuart's saloon, Hardin suspects her of being part of his activities. After romancing her, however, he realizes she is innocent. He eventually thwarts Stuarts and his gang.

The New York Times dubbed SAN ANTONIO "A routine beef opera, dressed ostentatiously in Technicolor," and in his book Warner Brothers Presents (1972) Ted Sennett judged it "...a routine but expensively produced Technicolor tale.... It offered lavish sets, including a reproduction of the Alamo, but little else." (Not to be overlooked was Max Steiner's rich score, nor Bert Glennon's eye-catching cinematography. Also, of course, there was the able assist of the Warner Bros.' stock company of flavorful performers.)

Following this actioner, Flynn returned to the Western for three more Warner Bros. productions: SILVER RIVER (1948), MONTANA (1950), and ROCKY MOUNTAIN (1950); none of them matched the standards of SAN ANTONIO.

SANTA FE UPRISING see OREGON TRAIL SCOUTS

DER SCHATZ IM SILBERSEE see THE TREASURE OF SILVER LAKE

SENIOR JIM see TRAIL'S END

SFIDA A RIO BRAVO see GUNMEN OF THE RIO GRANDE

SHEPHERD OF THE HILLS (Wright Pictures, 1919) 5 reels.

George Hackathorne (Old Matt); and Johnny Jones, Lon Poff.

THE SHEPHERD OF THE HILLS (First National, 1928) 8, 188'

Presenter, Richard A. Rowland; producer, Charles R. Rogers; director, Albert Rogell; based on the novel by Harold Bell Wright; screenplay, Marion Jackson; titles, Dwinelle Benthall, Rufus McCosh; camera, Sol Polito; editor, Hugh Bennett

Alec B. Francis (David Howitt, the Shepherd); Molly O'Day (Sammy Lane); John Boles (Young Matt); Matthew Betz (Wash Gibbs); Romaine Fielding (Old Matt); Otis Harlan ("By Thunder"); Joseph Bennett (Ollie); Maurice Murphy (Little Pete); Edythe Chapman (Aunt Mollie); Carl Stockdale (Jim Lane); Marian Douglas (Maggie); John Westwood (The Artist).

THE SHEPHERD OF THE HILLS (Paramount, 1941) C 98 mins.

Producer, Jack Moss; director, Henry Hathaway; based on the novel by Harold Bell Wright; screenplay, Grover Jones, Stuart Anthony; assistant director, Dink Templeton; camera, Charles Lang, Jr., W. Howard Greene; editor, Ellsworth Hoagland.

John Wayne (Young Matt Matthews); Betty Field (Sammy Lane); Harry Carey (Daniel Howitt); Beulah Bondi (Aunt Mollie); James Barton (Old Matt); Samuel S. Hinds (Andy Beeler); Marjorie Main (Granny Becky); Ward Bond (Wash Gibbs); Marc Lawrence (Pete); John Qualen (Coot); Fuzzy Knight (Mr. Palestrom); Tom Fadden (Jim Lane); Olin Howland (Corky); Dorothy Adams (Elvy); Virita Campbell (Baby); Fern Emmett (Mrs. Patterson).

THE SHEPHERD OF THE HILLS (Howco International, 1964) C 110 mins.

Producer, Jim McCullough; director/Ben Parker; based on the novel by Harold Bell Wright; screenplay, Parker; art director, Sterling Merritt; music, Marlin Skiles; songs; Skiles, Skiles and Gregg Hunter; wardrobe, Don Mitchell; sound, LeRoy Robbins; camera, Ted Saizis, Vincent Saizis; second unit camera, Henry Kokojan; editor, Marcell Greco.

Richard Arlen (Old Matt); James W. Middleton (Daniel Howitt); Sherry Lynn (Sammy Lane); James Collie (Wash Gibbs); Lloyd Durre (Doc Coughlan); Hal Meadows (Young Matt); James Bradford (Sheriff); Joy N. Houck, Jr. (Ollie Stewart); Gilbert Elmore (Jess Lane); George Jackson (Jed Holland); Delores James (Aunt Mollie); Danny Spurlock (Pete); Reubin Egan (Howard); Tom Pope, Roy Idom, Jim Teague, Roger Nash, Jim Greene (Baldknobbers).

Harold Bell Wright's classic 1907 novel was first brought to the screen in 1919 by Wright Pictures, with George Hackathorne in the title role. Toward the end of the silent era, First National Pictures mounted a big-budget production of the work, with Alec B. Francis in the lead, John Boles as Young Matt, and Molly O'Day as the feminine lead. Photoplay magazine declared it, "Pure Harold Bell Wright and very sweet and clean," but complained that it was a "bit slow."

The best-known screen version of the work was released by

Paramount in 1941. Like its predecessors it remains close to the Wright novel. Set in the Ozark mountains where the people still led a pioneer existence, the narrative centers around inarticulate young Matt Matthews (John Wayne), who loves pretty Sammy Lane (Betty Field) but is bitter with hatred for the father he has never seen since the man deserted his mother years before, causing her death and making Matt a local outcast. A stranger, Daniel Howitt (Harry Carey), moves into the locality, buys Matt's mother's home, and begins to change the attitude of the people by his good deeds. This upsets charming moonshiner Wash Gibbs (Ward Bond) because his liquor business declines. He threatens Howitt and ends up fighting Matt, who comes to the man's rescue. When old Granny Becky (Marjorie Main) has her sight restored, she recognizes the resemblance between Matt and Howitt, and Matt then realizes that the man is his dad. Matt sets out to kill Howitt but in a shoot-out is himself wounded. Howitt explains that years before, he killed a man under similar circumstances and went to prison, and that is why he never returned home. Matt understands the truth about his father, loses his hatred for him, and plans to marry Sammy.

Filmed in Technicolor, THE SHEPHERD OF THE HILLS is a visually satisfying feature with a good (albeit over-sentimental) story-line and fine characterizations. John Wayne, looking far more like a cowboy than a mountain man, competently underplays the role of Young Matt, while Betty Field is fetching and effective as his love. Harry Carey contributes one of his well-etched performances as the good samaritan Howitt, but the film's acting honors must go to Beulah Bondi and Marjorie Main. The former is exceptional as the hateful and vengeful Aunt Mollie, and usually boisterous Marjorie Main gives one of the most touching performances of his long career as Granny Becky. The famous scene where she has her sight restored, set on a high peak and surrounded by her family and friends whom she has never seen, is highly charged drama.

In 1964 a fourth screen adaptation of the Wright book was made on location in and around Branson, Missouri. This outing was highlighted by a topnotch performance by Richard Arlen as Old Matt, although the supporting cast and the film's production values were mediocre. The plot underwent changes and two songs were added. This time out Daniel Howitt (James W. Middleton), befriended by the Matthews clan, hopes to make amends for his son Howard's (Reubin Egan) desertion, years before, of Old Matt's (Richard Arlen) daughter, who died in childbirth. Young Matt (Hal Meadows) loves local girl Sammy Lane (Sherry Lynn) but she is promised to city slicker Ollie Stewart (John N. Houck, Jr.). Two locals (James Collie, Gilbert Elmore) rob the bank, but Ollie overhears their plans and informs the law. The robbers' hideout is surrounded and one of them is killed and the other wounded. The latter escapes and takes Howitt's runaway grandson (Danny Spurlock) hostage. The boy is saved and the robber killed by Howard, who has been living as a hermit mining gold. Daniel then tells Old Matt the truth and the latter forgives him; they use the gold Howard has mined to aid the drought-stricken area, and Young Matt and Sammy plan to marry.

In the late 1960s, the movie was reissued as THUNDER MOUNTAIN.

EL SHERIFF DEL O.K. CORRAL see GUNMEN OF THE RIO GRANDE

SHERIFF OF CIMARRON (Republic, 1945) 56 mins.

Associate producer, Thomas Carr; director, Yakima Canutt; screenplay, Bennett Cohen; music director, Richard Cherwin; set decorator, Earl Wooden; sound, Ed Borschell; camera, Bud Thackery; editor, Tony Martinelli.

Sunset Carson (Himself); Linda Stirling (Helen Burton); Olin Howlin (Dr. Pinky Snyder); Riley Hill (Ted Cartwright); Jack Kirk (John Burton); Jack Ingram (Brace McCord); Bob Wilke (Shad); Edward Cassidy (Sheriff); George Chesebro (Ed Martin); Dickie Dillon (Boy); Tom London (Frank Holden); Sylvia Aslan (Girl); Henry Wills (Prisoner); Hal Price (Passenger); Carol Henry (Townsman); Jack O'Shea (Brody); Gertrude Short (Portly Woman); George Sowards (Caller).

After taking second billing to sidekick comedian Smiley Burnette in four features, Sunset Carson took on his first solo starring film in SHERIFF OF CIMARRON. Thanks to Yakima Canutt's direction, the film proved to be a fast-moving one from start to finish, although Sunset's thespian abilities showed no improvement over his earlier efforts. The lanky young screen cowboy nevertheless developed quite a following and by the next year was ranked number eight in the Motion Picture Herald's poll of top money-making Western film stars.

After spending three years in prison, framed on a cattle rustling charge, Sunset Carson (Himself) is released and rided into the outlaw-plagued community of Cimarron where he captures three bad men and as a result is appointed sheriff. He meets stage driver Ted Cartwright (Riley Hill), who in reality is Sunset's brother and the leader of the local outlaws together with McCord (Jack Ingram). Ted pretends not to know Sunset so as not to expose his prison record, and Sunset does not know that it was Ted who framed him. Sunset encounters pretty Helen Burton (Linda Stirling), the daughter of the express officer operator (Jack Kirk), through his pal, veterinarian Pinky Snyder (Olin Howlin). Later the gang pulls a stage hold-up but Sunset has substituted horse shoes for money in the strong box, and McCord tells Ted his brother must be stopped. They set up a fake lawman who exposes Sunset's past but Sunset escapes. When gold is shipped out by stage the gang attempts to steal it, and Sunset captures the gang, proving his own innocence.

SHERIFF OF WICHITA (Republic, 1949) 60 mins.

Associate producer, Gordon Kay; director, R. G. Springsteen;

screenplay, Bob Williams; camera, John MacBurnie; editor, Tony Martinelli.

Allan "Rocky" Lane (Himself); Black Jack (The Horse); Eddy Waller (Nugget Clark); Roy Barcroft (Sam Stark); Lyn Wilde (Nancy Bishop); Clayton Moore (Raymond D'Arcy); Trevor Bardette (Ira Flanders); Eugene Roth (Howard Thornton); House Peters, Jr. (Jack Thorne); Earle Hodgins (Jenkins); Edmund Cobb (James); John Hamilton (Warden); Steve Raines (Will); Jack O'Shea (Joe); and Dick Curtis, Lane Bradford.

Raymond D'Arcy (Clayton Moore) escapes from prison and Wichita marshal Allan "Rocky" Lane (Himself) follows and captures him at a desert fort. A number of men, all members of Sam Stark's (Roy Barcroft) outlaw gang, receive letters from a major who, along with D'Arcy, was accused of stealing a gold shipment years before. The lawman encounters Nancy Bishop (Lyn Wilde), the major's daughter, who claims that her father was murdered. She tells Lane she sent the letters to get the gang members to the fort so that she could find the killer, and Lane agrees to help her. Shot by one of the gang, Flanders (Trevor Bardette) confesses that he and Thornton (Gene Roth) were in cahoots with Stark in the robbery and that the major and D'Arcy were innocent. With the assist of pal Nugget Clark (Eddy Waller), Nancy and D'Arcy, Lane captures the gang, but Stark and Flanders escape and return to the scene of the robbery looking for the payroll. When the others follow, the two outlaws capture the girl, but they let her go as they try to escape with the loot. Lane captures them.

Well directed by R. G. Springsteen, this above-average entry in Allan "Rocky" Lane's Republic series is highlighted by a good mystery motif, especially in the movie's early scenes in which the suspects gather at the deserted fort. Although it contains too much sound-stage scenery, the movie stages a well-executed fight sequence between Lane and Gene Roth, plus an exciting climax.

THE SHOOTIST (Paramount, 1976) C 99 mins.

Presenter, Dino Di Laurentiis; producers, Mike Frankovich, William Self; director, Don Siegel; based on the novel by Glendon Swarthout; screenplay, Miles Hood Swarthout, Scott Hale; music, Elmer Bernstein; production designer, Robert Boyle; set decorator, Arthur Parker; assistant director, Joe Cavalier; sound, Arthur Piantadosi, Les Fresholtz, Michael Minkler, Alfred J. Overton; camera, Bruce Surtees; editor, Douglas Stewart.

John Wayne (J. B. Books); Lauren Bacall (Bond Rogers); Ron Howard (Gillom Rogers); Bill McKinney (Cobb); James Stewart (Dr. Hostetler); Richard Boone (Sweeney); Hugh O'Brian (Pulford); Harry Morgan (Marshal); John Carradine (Beckum); Sheree North (Serepta); Richard Lenz (Dobkins); Scatman Crothers (Moses); Gregg Palmer (Ambusher); Alfred Dennis (Barber); Dick Winslow (Streetcar Driver); Melody Thomas (Streetcar Passenger); Kathleen O'Nalley (School Teacher).

John Wayne in THE SHOOTIST (1976).

Without a doubt, THE SHOOTIST is the finest Western of the 1970s and one of the best all-time genre productions. Best known for being John Wayne's final screen appearance, the motion picture is a well-paced, finely performed drama which depicts the last days of the frontier era and the coming of the twentieth century. Although the film grossed an acceptable $6,000,000 at the box office and received substantial critical acclaim, it was entirely bypassed by the Oscars.

Successfully thwarting an attempted hold-up by a would-be road agent (Gregg Palmer), legendary gunfighter John Bernard Books (John Wayne) rides into Carson City in 1901 to consult Dr. Hostetler (James Stewart), who diagnoses him as having incurable cancer. Wanting to die with dignity, Books takes a room at the boarding house home of widow Bond Rogers (Lauren Bacall) and her teenage son Gillom (Ron Howard). Soon Books' identity becomes known and the local sheriff (Harry Morgan) tells him to get out of town; the gunman counters that he cannot leave because he is going to die. When his fate becomes generally known, several people--including a grasping newspaper man (Richard Lenz), the local undertaker (John Carradine) and Books' former girlfriend (Sheree North)--try to take advantage of him. Also two toughs, trying to make a reputation for themselves, attempt to ambush Books while he sleeps, but he kills both of them in a shoot-out. Through Gillom, whom the gunman has befriended, Books learns that the town tough, Cobb (Bill McKinney), old enemy Sweeney (Richard Boone), and flashy gambler Pulford (Hugh O'Brian) want a showdown with him. Putting his affairs in order, and reluctantly halting a romantic relationship he has begun with Bond, Books makes an appointment to meet the three men at the local saloon on his birthday. During the gunplay at the bar, Books dispatches all three gunmen but is injured in the fracas, then fatally shot in the back by the bartender, who in turn is killed by Gillom. The boy then throws away the gun, realizing that he does not want to follow in his dead friend's footsteps.

While excerpts from some of his early movies are used at the beginning of THE SHOOTIST, the John Wayne in this motion picture is drastically different from the Wayne seen in typical actioners. While the film contains well choreographed action sequences, especially the shoot-outs in the boarding house and the saloon, the movie is basically a highly polished melodrama which allows John Wayne full opportunity to really act. Here he reacts with his eyes instead of his fists, with philosophy rather than gunplay, and exemplifies the wisdom of a man who has led a life he is not entirely proud of but for which he offers no apologies. The movie is a strong testament to the vanishing frontier. The legendary gunman (or shootist) arrives in a quickly modernizing western town the day the news arrives of the death of Queen Victoria, thus ending an era. The death of J. B. Books, and his extermination of the town's vermin, also mark the end of an era--the last gasp of the gun as the law of the West.

Packed with superb performances, fine pacing and direction and a most literate script, THE SHOOTIST is nonetheless dominated by John Wayne in his final and most magnificent screen role. Sadly, the part of the dying gunman proved prophetic: the Duke himself succumbed to cancer three years after this feature was released.

SHOWDOWN (Paramount, 1940) 63 mins.

Producer, Harry Sherman; director, Howard Bretherton; based on characters created by Clarence E. Mulford; story, Jack Jungmeyer; screenplay, Harold and Daniel Kusel; music, John Leipold; song, Foster Carling and Phil Ohman; camera, Russell Harlan; editor, Carroll Lewis.

William Boyd (Hopalong Cassidy); Russell Hayden (Lucky Jenkins); Britt Wood (Speedy); Morris Ankrum (Baron Rendor); Jane [Jan] Clayton (Sue Willard); Wright Kramer (Colonel White); Donald Kirk (Harry Cole); Roy Barcroft (Bowman); Kermit Maynard (Johnson); Walter Shumway (Snell); The King's Men (Themselves); Eddie Dean (Sheriff); Topper (The Horse).

A bogus European baron, Rendor (Morris Ankrum), plans to rustle an old colonel's (Wright Kramer) racing horses. Hopalong Cassidy (William Boyd) tries to aid the rancher and expose the crook. The old man, however, dies of a heart attack and his niece Sue (Jane Clayton) inherits the ranch. Lucky Jenkins (Russell

Hayden) falls for the girl, becomes angry with Hoppy over her, and quits his job, but agrees to help in moving the ranch's horses. The baron ties up Hoppy, steals the animals and plans to burn down the barn with Hoppy inside, but Cassidy escapes and, joined by the sheriff (Eddie Dean), rounds up the gang. Hoppy patches up his friendship with Lucky.

Only an average entry in the long-enduring "Hopalong Cassidy" series, this thirteenth outing does not have much action except at the finale. It does contain an amusing gambling sequence, with the hero outwitting the crooks, and also an ingenious use of a covered hay wagon as a getaway vehicle. Future genre singing star Eddie Dean appears briefly as the sheriff. Britt Wood's comedy relief as sidekick Speedy pales very quickly.

SHOWDOWN AT BOOT HILL (Twentieth Century-Fox, 1958) 71 mins.

Producer, Harold E. Knox; director, Gene Fowler, Jr.; screenplay, Louis Vittes; music, Albert Harris; camera, John M. Nickolaus, Jr.; editor, Frank Sullivan.

Charles Bronson (U.S. Marshal Luke Welsh); Robert Hutton (Sloane); John Carradine (Doc Weber); Carol Mathews (Jill); Fintan Meyler (Sally); Paul Maxey (Judge); Thomas B. Henry (Con Maynor); William Stevens, Martin Smith (Cowhands); Joseph McGuinn (Mr. Creavy); George Douglas (Charles Maynor); Michael Mason (Patton); George Pembroke (Sheriff); Argentina Brunetti (Mrs. Bonventura); Ed Wright (Brent).

In the late 1950s Charles Bronson had a brief taste of screen stardom when he headlined a quartet of low-budget programmers, including SHOWDOWN AT BOOT HILL. The others were: MACHINE GUN KELLY (1958); GANG WAR (1958) and WHEN HELL BROKE LOOSE (1958). Thereafter he returned to supporting roles until he emerged as an international (super)star in the late 1960s. SHOWDOWN AT BOOT HILL is an engaging psychological "B" Western in which "Bronson gives a good performance that promises well for his screen future..." (The Hollywood Reporter). Not everyone liked the picture, however, as evidenced by the British Monthly Film Bulletin: "Though it promises to be a study of the psychology of a man who kills for money, the film degenerates into a sentimental and clumsily acted story of a man who decides that not all problems can be solved by violence."

U.S. Marshal Luke Welsh (Charles Bronson) rides into a small town to collect the bounty money for outlaw Con Maynor (Thomas Browne Henry). In a hotel dining room he has a shoot-out with the man and kills him. When he attempts to collect the reward, he finds that the local citizens were fond of Maynor, and a judge (Paul Maxey) refuses to honor the bargain. Staying in town to prove his money claim, Welsh has to fight attempts by some of the people to kill him or run him out of the area. He finds an ally in the local barber/undertaker, Doc Weber (John Carradine), and also meets timid waitress Sally (Fintan Meyler), the daughter of saloon madam Jill (Carole Mathews). Local crook Sloane (Robert Hutton) tries to stir up the people to hang Luke, but eventually the marshal realizes he loves Sally more than the money and the two agree to leave town together.

In addition to Charles Bronson's underplayed performance in the lead assignment, John Carradine is delightfully hammy as his pal and Fintan Meyler is especially good as the repressed young woman who falls in love with the bounty hunter.

THE SIGN OF THE WOLF (Metropolitan, 1931) ten chapters

Producers, Harry S. Webb, Flora E. Douglas; directors, Forrest Sheldon, Webb; story/screenplay, Betty Burbridge, Bennett Cohen; assistant director, Melville DeLay; sound, Ralph Like; camera, William Nobles, Herbert Kilpatrick; editor, Fred Bain.

King the Dog (Muro); Rex Lease (Tom Lanning); Virginia Brown Faire (Ruth Farnum); Joe Bonomo (Bud); Jack Mower (Butch Kohler); Josephine Hill (Pearl); Al Ferguson (Winslow); Robert Walker (Joe); Edmund Cobb (Chief Kuva); Harry Todd (John Farnum); Billy O'Brien (Bud); Jack Perrin (Jack).

Chapters: 1) Drums of Doom; 2) The Dog of Destiny; 3) The Wolf's Fangs; 4) The Fatal Shot; 5) The Well of Terror; 6) The Wolf Dogs; 7) Trapped; 8) The Secret Mark; 9) Tongues of Flame; 10) The Lost Secret.

One of the earliest independent sound serials, THE SIGN OF THE WOLF was promoted as "The Unleashed Fury of Primeval Vengeance!" Given top billing was King, "The Emperor of All Dogs," with hero Rex Lease relegated to supporting billing. In this ten-chapter cliffhanger, King performed in the tradition of Rin-Tin-Tin, but he failed to make much of an impression, perhaps because of the poverty-row surroundings provided him by this picture. The next year Syndicate issued a 55-minute feature version of the serial called THE LONE TRAIL.

Ranger Tom Lanning (Rex Lease) leaves his dog Muro (King) to take care of his sister, but upon his return he finds the girl has been murdered by the mysterious "Tiger" and his gang. The ranger gets on the gang's trail and learns that they have built a wilderness town and that pretty Ruth Farnum (Virginia Browne Faire) and her father (Harry Todd) are being held prisoners. Lanning, with Muro at his side, rescues Ruth and her dad and takes revenge on the cutthroats for his sister's killing.

In 1936 Harry S. Webb, who co-directed THE SIGN OF THE WOLF, remade the script for Bernard B. Ray's Reliable Pictures, as SKULL AND CROWN, this time as a Rin-Tin-Tin, Jr. vehicle. This new version claimed to be based on a James Oliver Curwood work but it was nearly a carbon copy of the 1931 serial created by Betty Burbridge and Bennett Cohen (Carl Krusada is credited with writing the 1932 feature version). In fact, Jack Mower was cast as the arch villain in both Webb productions.

SILENCE OF THE NORTH (Universal, 1981) C 94 mins.

Executive producer, Bob Baylis; producer, Murray Shostak; director, Allan Winston King; based on the book by Olive Fredrickson, Ben East; screenplay, Patricia Louisiana Knop; production designer, Bill Brodie; costumes, Olga Dimitrov; music, Allan Macmillan; music adaptor, Jerrold Immel; camera, Richard Leiterman; editor, Arla Saare.

Ellen Burstyn (Olive Fredrickson); Tom Skerritt (Walter Reamer); Gordon Pinsent (John Fredrickson); Jennifer McKinney (Little Olive); Donna Dobrijevic (Viola); Colin Fox (Arthur Herriott); Chappelle Jaffe (John's Girlfriend); Ken Pogue (Wild Man); Tom Hauff (Billy); Murray Westgate (Doctor); Ken James (Ralph); Booth Savage (Flyer); Louis Banks (Louis); Sean McCann (Man on Soup Line); Frank Adamson (Trapper).

Based on Olive Frederickson's book (1972) about her life as a pioneer woman in Canada's north country in the early part of this century, SILENCE OF THE NORTH studies the pioneer spirit from the woman's viewpoint. "The big-budget female adventure yarn scores its points with breathtaking outdoor footage, but falls down in a corny, melodramatic script," complained Variety, and the trade paper is essentially correct. While the movie is highlighted by Richard Leiterman's stunning cinematography of the north country, the film's plot reads like a daytime soap opera, with the heroine encountering one tragedy after another. Except for Ken Pogue's delightful cameo as a crazed trapper, the picture's performances are mostly uninspired.

In 1919 in a rural but settled part of southern Canada, young Olive (Ellen Burstyn) meets handsome trapper Walter Reamer (Tom Skerritt) at a community outing and the two fall deeply in love. They marry and she goes with him to the north country for the trapping season and has their first child. During the harsh winter they battle wild animals and the elements and are nearly killed by a wild man (Ken Pogue) who takes their provisions. Then, their young baby accidentally causes a fire which burns their cabin. They almost die trying to return to civilization and are finally rescued by adventurer John Frederickson (Gordon Pinsent). The young couple then resettles in a frontier town where Olive has a second daughter. Pregnant with her third child, she learns her husband has been killed while trapping. After the birth of her son, Olive takes her family to Calgary, in the grip of the Depression, and gets a job in a soup kitchen. She again meets Frederickson and they eventually marry, but a sickness takes her son's life.

THE SILVER BULLET (Reliable, 1935) 58 mins.

Producer, Bernard B. Ray; associate producer, Harry S. Webb; director, Ray; story, William L. Nolte; screenplay, Rose Gordon, Carl Krusada; assistant director, Gene George; camera, J. Henry Kruse; editor, Fred Bain.

Tom Tyler (Tom Henderson); Jayne Regan (Nora Kane); Lafe McKee (Dad Kane); Charles King (Luke Hargrave); George Chesebro (Slim Walker); Slim Whitaker (Scurvy); Lew Meehan (Pete); Franklyn Farnum (Marshal Mullane); Walt Williams [Wally Wales/Hal Taliaferrol] (Dick); Blackie Whiteford (Henchman); Nelson McDowell, Robert Brower, Hank Bell, Allen Greer.

Taking the job as sheriff of a small town, Tom Henderson (Tom Tyler) arrests a bandit leader, Slim Walker (George Chesebro), over the protests of banker Luke Hargrave (Charles King), who advises caution. While Tom is dining that evening with pretty Norah Kane (Jayne Regan) and her dad (Lafe McKee), he receives a call telling him that troopers will be in town that night to pick up Slim. The call is a bogus one from Hargrave, who is behind the outlaw gang plaguing the area. At the jail, the fake officers knock out the sheriff, Slim is set free, and the gang robs the bank. When Tom is suspected of being in league with the outlaws he sets out to find them and locates them in a canyon. A shoot-out takes place and a wounded outlaw confesses that Hargrave planned the robbery. Tom arrests the banker and receives a reward.
One of nineteen features Tom Tyler made for Reliable pictures between 1934 and 1936, THE SILVER BULLET is one of the better entries in a generally shoddy run of films. The picture moves well, the story holds up, and Jayne Regan is a most comely heroine. Star Tom Tyler is justly stalwart as the sheriff and in one memorable scene a close-up of his eyes is used very effectively.

SILVER CANYON (Columbia, 1951) 71 mins.

Executive producer, Gene Autry; producer, Armand Schaefer; director, John English; story, Alan James; screenplay, Gerald Geraghty; music director, Mischa Bakaleinikoff; music, Paul Mertz; songs: Autry and Smiley Burnette; Dick Reinhart; art director, Charles Cague; set decorator, Frank Tuttle; assistant director, Paul Donnelly; sound, George Cooper; camera, William Bradford; editor, James Sweeney.
Gene Autry (Himself); Pat Buttram (Cougar Claggett); Gail Davis (Dell Middler); Jim Davis (Wade McQuarrie); Bob Steele (Walt Middler); Edgar Dearing (Colonel Middler); Richard Alexander (Luke Anders); Terry Frost (Irv Wyatt); Peter Mamakos (Laughing Jack); Steve Clark (Dr. Seddon); Stanley Andrews (Major Weatherly); Duke York (Sergeant Laughlin); Eugene Borden (Gus Poppalardo); Champion, Jr. (The Horse); and Bobby Clark, Frankie Marvin, Boyd Stockman, Sandy Sanders, Kenne Duncan, Bill Hale, Jack O'Shea, Frank Matts, Stanley Blystone, John Merton, Jack Pepper, Pat O'Malley, Martin Wilkins, Jim Magill, John R. McKee.

At the start of the Civil War, guerrilla Wade McQuarrie (Jim Davis) leads a band which raids Yankee silver shipments, allegedly with the blessing of the Rebel government. The raids take place near a fort where the commandant's son (Bob Steele) is one of the gang, and his sister (Gail Davis) is loyal to him. The Army hires Gene Autry (Himself) to bring in the guerrilla leader. The latter decides to carry out one last hold-up after the Confederate government denounces his activities.

Made on a $400,000 budget, this Gene Autry production is a handsome one, laced with veteran genre players who greatly enhance the proceedings. The movie, despite its 70-minute running time, moves at a nice clip and is made particularly effective by Jim Davis' work as the hardened thug McQuarrie and Bob Steele's performance as the innocent corraled into illegal activities.

SILVER CITY see ALBUQUERQUE

SILVER ON THE SAGE (Paramount, 1939) 68 mins.

Producer, Harry Sherman; director, Lesley Selander; based on characters created by Clarence E. Mulford; screenplay, Harrison Jacobs; music director, Boris Morros; art director, Lewis J. Rackmil; camera, Russell Harlan; editor, Robert Warwick.

William Boyd (Hopalong Cassidy); George "Gabby" Hayes (Windy Halliday); Russell Hayden (Lucky Jenkins); Stanley Ridges (Brennan/Talbot); Frederick Burton (Hamilton); Ruth Rogers (Ethel); Jack Rockwell (Marshal); Roy Bancroft (Ewing); Ed Cassidy (Pierce); Jim Corey (Martin); Sherry Tanzey (Baker); Bruce Mitchell (Bartender); Topper (The Horse); and Dick Dickson, Buzz Barton, Herman Hack, George Morrell, Frank O'Connor.

Running since 1935, the "Hopalong Cassidy" series celebrated its 25th entry with SILVER ON THE SAGE, an actionful feature with an amusing finale. Stanley Ridges, usually associated with gangster melodramas, is especially strong in this film, in a dual role as a crook and the look-alike he uses for an alibi.

Outlaws are after Bar 20 cattle and Lucky Jenkins (Russell Hayden), accused of killing a man, is put in jail and held for trial. Hopalong Cassidy (William Boyd) and Windy Halliday (George "Gabby" Hayes) help Lucky to escape from the law after he breaks jail. Hoppy then proves that the outlaw rustling gang is controlled by supposedly honest businessman Brennan (Stanley Ridges), who is also guilty of the murder for which Lucky was arrested. Brennan, however, has an alibi, but Hoppy discovers he has a look-alike, Talbot (Stanley Ridges), whom he uses to cover up his crimes. The Bar 20 boys bring in the bad man and his cohorts.

SILVER ON THE SAGE was George Hayes's next-to-last series entry in the role of Windy Halliday. After vacating the series he moved to Republic and became Roy Rogers' sidekick, immortalizing the role of Gabby Whittaker.

SILVER RIVER see SAN ANTONIO

SILVER SPURS (Republic, 1943) 68 mins.

Associate producer, Harry Grey; director, Joseph Kane; screenplay, John K. Butler, J. Benton Cheney; songs, Tim Spencer, Bob Nolan, Smiley Burnette, Hugh Farr; music director, Morton Scott; art director, Russell Kimball; set decorator, Otto Siegel; assistant director, Art Siteman; sound, Thomas Carman; camera, Reggie Lanning; editor, Tony Martinelli.

Roy Rogers (Himself); Trigger (The Horse); Smiley Burnette (Frog Milhouse); John Carradine (Lucky Miller); Phyllis Brooks (Mary Hardigan); Jerome Cowan (Jerry Johnson); Joyce Compton (Millie Love); Dick Wessel (Buck Walters); Hal Taliaferro (Steve Corlan); Forrest Taylor (Judge Pebble); Charles Wilson (Mr. Hawkins); Byron Foulger (Justice of the Peace); Bob Nolan and the Sons of the Pioneers (Themselves); and Charles Wilson, Pat Brady, Jack O'Shea, Slim Whitaker, Arthur Loft, Eddy Waller, Tom London, Bud Osborne, Fred Burns, Henry Wills.

Roy Rogers (Himself) and Frog Milhouse (Smiley Burnette) work for playboy rancher and heel Jerry Johnson (Jerome Cowan), who is being swindled out of his lands by crook Lucky Miller (John Carradine), who wants them for a railroad right-of-way. Mary Hardigan (Phyllis Brooks), a reporter for a large city paper, is after a big story and pretends to be a mail order bride for Jerry. Lucky wants the marriage to take place, as he plans to frame Jerry on a murder charge. Roy has an argument with the arrogant Jerry and quits. Lucky has his henchman Steve Corlan (Hal Taliaferro) murder Jerry, and Roy is blamed for the crime. Roy is also arrested for the killing of another of Miller's henchmen, Buck Walters (Dick Wessel), although the crime was actually perpetrated by Miller when Buck threatened to expose him. Roy escapes from jail and, with the assist of the Sons of the Pioneers (Themselves), has a shoot-out with Lucky and his gang. Roy forces the crook to confess all.

SILVER SPURS is a high-level Roy Rogers vehicle, with a bit more budget than was generally afforded the series, particularly in the use of noted screen villain John Carradine and comely Phyllis Brooks as the leading lady. Along for the ride, as usual, is perennial sidekick, Smiley Burnette, once again doing his Frog Milhouse characterization. With an exciting chase sequence, a nicely arranged climactic shoot-out, excellent stunt work, and a solid script, the movie is consistently entertaining.

SILVER TRAILS see WYOMING ROUNDUP

SILVERADO (Columbia, 1985) C 132 mins.

Executive producers, Charles Okun, Michael Grillo; producer,

Lawrence Kasdan; associate producer, Mark Kasdan; director, Lawrence Kasdan; screenplay, Lawrence Kasdan, Mark Kasdan; production designer, Ida Random; set designers, Charles Butcher, Richard
McKenzie; set decorators, Arthur Parker, Anne D. McCulley; music,
Bruce Broughton; orchestrators, Chris Boardman, Donald Nemitz;
costumes, Kristi Zea; makeup, Daniel C. Striepeke, Gerald O'Dell;
title designer, Wayne Fitzgerald; special effects, William Lee, Robert
W. Ramage, Floyd Van Wey, Richard S. Wood; camera, John Bailey;
editor, Carol Littleton.

Kevin Kline (Paden); Scott Glenn (Emmett); Kevin Costner
(Jake); Danny Glover (Mal); Brian Dennehy (Cobb); Linda Hunt
(Stella); Jeff Goldblum (Slick); Rosanna Arquette (Hannah); John
Cleese (Sheriff Langston); Marvin J. McIntyre (Clerk); Brad Wil-
liams (Trooper); Sheb Wooley (Cavalry Sergeant); John Kasdan (Boy
at Outpost); Todd Allen (Deputy Kern); Kenny Call (Deputy Block);
Bill Thurman (Proprietor); Meg Kasdan (Barmaid); Dick Durock,
Gene Hartline (Bar Fighters); Autry Ward (Hat Thief); Jacob Kas-
dan (Stable Boy); Rusty Meyers (Conrad); Zeke Davidson (Mr.
Parker); Lois Geary (Mrs. Parker); James Gammon (Dawson); Troy
Ward (Baxter); Roy McAdams (Tall Outlaw); Ray Baker (McKendrick);
Joe Seneca (Ezra); Lynn Whitfield (Rae); Jeff Fahey (Tyre); Patricia
Gaul (Kate); Amanda Wyss (Phoebe); Earl Hindman (J.T.); Tom
Brown (Augie); Jim Haynie (Bradley); Richard Jenkins (Kelly);
Jerry Biggs (Bartender); Sam Gauny (Deputy Garth); Ken Farmer
(Deputy Kyle); Bill McIntosh (Deputy Charlie); Charlie Seybert
(Shopkeeper); Jane Beauchamp (Woman Neighbor); Jerry Block, Ben
Zeller (Townsmen); Pepe Serna (Scruffy); Ted White (Hoyt); Ross
Loney (Red); Walter Scott (Swann); Bob Terhune (Guard Cowboy).

Brothers Jake (Kevin Costner) and Emmett (Scott Glenn) are
homeward bound to the small town of Silverado after serving time in
separate jails. Along the way they meet black cowboy Mal (Danny
Glover), who is also heading there to say goodbye to his mother and
sister before heading westward. The trio encounter drifter Paden
(Kevin Kline), who joins up with them. When they reach their destination they discover the vicinity is controlled by the evil McKendrick (Ray Baker) and his hired gun, lawman Cobb (Brian Dennehy),
who also runs the local Midnight Star saloon. Mal finds his sister is
now a prostitute working for Cobb; Paden is strangely attracted to
the saloon's diminutive plain-faced hostess Stells (Linda Hunt); and
the two brothers are at odds with Cobb, who is Paden's ex-partner.
The four men are soon opposed to McKendrick and Cobb, who are
also trying to keep settlers out of the area.

SILVERADO was released the same summer as RUSTLERS'
RHAPSODY and PALE RIDER (qq.v.) in an attempt to revive the
theatrical Western, and of the three films SILVERADO received the
most critical dissecting. In the Los Angeles Times, Sheila Benson
wrote that producer/director/co-scripter Lawrence Kasdan "...sees
the West as a place where each character seeks his or her own kind
of family, and Kasdan lightens the search with deadpan humor."
She added, "For a generation of kids to whom the Western is a new

adventure, there probably will be action and distraction enough to dazzle. Those who need to be deeply stirred by this redoubtable form will still have to wait: SILVERADO is good but not great." Variety labeled it "...an entertaining but not totally satisfying attempt to revive the western genre": while Kirl Ellis in The Hollywood Reporter assessed, "...this Columbia release falls considerably short of the lofty, epic goals it sets for itself. Overlong, overreaching and so top heavy with climaxes that it practically self-destructs in gunfire...."

SILVERADO proved to be for the Western genre what THE COTTON CLUB (1985) was to the gangster film genre: a highly expensive, carefully-mounted exercise that was all show and no substance. Like THE COTTON CLUB, SILVERADO was ballyhooed as the return of a genre form in the grand style. However, an enormously costly soufflé which sinks from lack of body cannot satisfy a filmgoer, nor can it recoup for its backers the tremendous costs from overproduction and a saturation publicity campaign. (SILVERADO was reputed to have a $40,000,000 price tag before all was said and done.).

SING, COWBOY, SING (Grand National, 1937) 60 mins.

Producer, Edward F. Finney; director, Robert North Bradbury; screenplay, Robert Emmett [Tansey]; songs: Ritter, Bradbury, Ted Choate, Frank Sanucci; camera, Gus Peterson; editor, Fred Bain.

Tex Ritter (Tex Archer); Louise Stanley (Madge Summers); Al St. John (Biff); Karl Hackett (Kalmus); Charles King (Red Holman); Robert McKenzie (Judge Dean); Budd Buster (Marshal Pinker); Hank Worden, Chick Hannon (Henchmen); White Flash (The Horse); and Horace Murphy, Snub Pollard, Tex Palmer, Jack C. Smith, Oscar Gahan, Herman Hack.

Crooked shippers Kalmus (Karl Hackett) and Red Holman (Charles King) ambush and kill members of a rival shipping firm to gain the area shipping franchise, and the only survivor is Madge Summers (Louise Stanley). Cowboys Tex Archer (Tex Ritter) and Duke Evans (Al St. John) agree to help the distressed young woman retain her contracts. The duo masquerade as entertainers at the local judge's (Bob McKenzie) saloon and also make the stage runs for Madge. In a fight with Tex, Red is thought to be killed, and Tex is tried and found guilty of the crime. It turns out that Red is only injured, but Kalmus has him shot before he can talk. Tex and Duke are held for questioning but they break jail and with the help of the citizens fight Kalmus. In the big shoot-out the bad man is killed. Tex and Madge go into partnership.

Made as SWING, COWBOY, SWING, this easy-to-take Tex Ritter vehicle was the sixth film in his Grand National series for producer Edward Finney. It boasts good scenic locations and a very actionful climax plus two excellent songs: "Sing, Cowboy, Sing" and the standard "Goodbye, Old Paint." The only drawback to the feature is a couple of other tunes which seem out of place, especially one performed by a group called Tex Ritter's Tornadoes.

It should be noted that veteran silent-film comedy star Snub Pollard has a small role as a prisoner. Since Pollard was Tex Ritter's favorite silent film comedian, the star persuaded producer Finney to put Pollard on contract as a series regular.

SINGING GUNS (Republic, 1950) C 91 mins.

Producer, Abe Lyman; associate producer, Melville Tucker; director, R. G. Springsteen; based on the novel by Max Brand; screenplay, Dorrell and Stuart McGowan; music, Nathan Scott; songs: Johnny Lange, Fred Glickman, Hy Heath, William Moore, Al Vann, Sunny Skylar; camera, Reggie Lanning; editor, Richard L. Van Enger.

Vaughn Monroe (Rhiannon/John Gwenn); Ella Raines (Nan Morgan); Walter Brennan (Dr. Jonathan Marks); Ward Bond (Sheriff Jim Caradak); Jeff Corey (Richards); Harry Shannon (Mike); Barry Kelley (Mike); Tom Fadden (Express Agent); Ralph Dunn (Traveler); Rex Lease (Stage Driver); George Chandler (Smitty); Billy Gray (Albert); Mary Bear (Mother); Jimmie Dodd (Stage Guard).

In 1949 singer/bandlearder Vaughn Monroe had a million-selling record with "Riders in the Sky" for RCA Victor. The same year the ballad was used for the title of a Gene Autry Columbia film. Autry's old studio, Republic, signed Vaughn Monroe to star in SINGING GUNS, an "A" production which furnished the star a straight dramatic role (he sings only "I'm Singin' My Way Back Home" in a saloon sequence). He proved to be a stalwart hero and the feature was an entertaining one. Had Monroe come along at a better time, perhaps he would have developed into a fine screen hero.

Rhiannon (Vaughn Monroe) has his lands stolen by the Great Western Mining Company and he has taken to robbing stages carrying their gold shipments. On one of the stages is Sheriff Jim Caradak (Ward Bond), who is out to capture the highwayman. Rhiannon, however, gets the drop on the lawman and when the gold shipment turns out to be only sand, he humiliates the lawman by forcing him to walk into town wearing a lady's hat and bloomers. Caradak then gives chase to Rhiannon and in a showdown the lawman is shot. The highwayman then takes Caradak to Jonathan Marks (Walter Brennan), the local doctor/preacher. Marks talks the stranger into giving a blood transfusion which saves Caradak. The next day Rhiannon, with new clothes and minus his beard, becomes John Gwenn and the mayor (Harry Shannon) offers him the post of deputy sheriff, since Caradak is out of commission. Taking the job, Rhiannon develops a yen for the local saloon hostess (Ella Raines), tames hard drinking miner Mike Murphy (Barry Kelley), who becomes his pal, and makes an enemy of corrupt mine foreman Richards (Jeff Corey). When a cave-in and explosion occur at the Great Western mine, the sheriff teams with Murphy to save the trapped miners. Having fallen in love with the saloon girl, Rhiannon decides to redeem himself and returns all the stolen mine gold, but he is forced to face Richards and his men in a showdown. Caradak, who now knows the truth about his deputy's identity, joins with him and they defeat the crooks. Now a respectable citizen, Gwenn is free to marry the woman he loves.

Two years after the release of SINGING GUNS, Vaughn Monroe and director R. G. Springsteen reteamed at Republic for TOUGHEST MAN IN ARIZONA. Almost as good as their initial effort, this outing gave Monroe an opportunity to sing a bit more, but he also had a more austere role as a lawman who is on the trail of a gun runner (Victor Jory) whose activities have resulted in the massacre of settlers by rampaging Indians. He falls in love with a pretty widow (Joan Leslie) who takes in his motherless children. Edgar Buchanan, as the local sheriff, and Harry Morgan, as a coward, provide particularly substantial supporting performances.

The inroads of television into movie box-office receipts prevented Vaughan Monroe from making any more theatrical Westerns, but his career continued to flourish via records, television, personal appearances, and as a long-term spokesman for RCA.

SINISTER JOURNEY see HOPPY'S HOLIDAY

SIX BLACK HORSES (Universal, 1962) C 80 mins.

Producer, Gordon Kay; director, Harry Keller; screenplay, Burt Kennedy; music, Joseph Gershenson; assistant director, Ivan Volkman; camera, Maury Gertsman; editor, Aaron Stell.

Audie Murphy (Ben Lane); Dan Duryea (Frank Jesse); Joan O'Brien (Kelly); George Wallace (Boone); Roy Barcroft (Mustanger); Bob Steele (Puncher); Henry Wills (Indian Leader); Phil Chambers (Undertaker); Charlita Regis (Mexican Girl).

Cowboy Ben Lane (Audie Murphy) captures a wild mustang in the desert, but a gang of locals accuse him of being a horse thief. They plan to hang him, but he is rescued by gunfighter Frank Jesse (Dan Duryea). The duo ride into Perdido and pretty Kelly (Joan O'Brien) hires them to escort her to meet her husband in a town on the other side of hostile Indian territory. Along the way the trio take refuge in an old mission and fight attacking Indians. During the skirmish Kelly nearly shoots Frank in the back, but she is stopped by an Indian spear. Only wounded, she tells Ben that her husband is dead and that Frank killed him, and she wants revenge. Frank then refuses to turn back because he wants the money Kelly has in the Santa Rita bank; he knocks out Ben and forces Kelly to go with him. Ben follows and kills him in a showdown, then rides on to Santa Rita with Kelly.

Audie Murphy and Joan O'Brien in SIX BLACK HORSES (1962).

With location filming in south Utah, SIX BLACK HORSES is one of several Western actioners Audie Murphy made in the 1960s, making him a genre staple at the time. The type of picture he starred in, however, would be replaced by the end of the decade with TV movies. SIX BLACK HORSES is one of the better in the Murphy series, with a compact plot, a solid script (full of jokes) by Western aficionado Burt Kennedy, and steady pacing by veteran director Harry Keller. Dan Duryea provides a sterling performance as the likable but murderous Frank Jesse; and there is the presence of Bob Steele and Roy Barcroft for added verisimiltude.

SIX-GUN LAW (Columbia, 1948) 54 mins.

Producer, Colbert Clark, director, Ray Nazaro; screenplay, Barry Shipman; camera, George F. Kelley; editor, Henry Demond.
Charles Starrett (Steve Norris); Smiley Burnette (Himself); Nancy Saunders (June Wallace); Paul Campbell (Jim Wallace); Hugh Prosser (Boss Decker); George Chesebro (Bret Wallace); Billy Dix (Crowl); Bob Wilke (Larson); Bob Cason (Ben); Ethan Laidlaw (Sheriff Brackett); Pierce Lyden (Jack Reed); Bud Osborne (Barton); Budd Buster (Bank Clerk Duffy); Raider (The Horse); Curley Clement and His Rodeo Rangers (Themselves).

   From 1944 to 1952 Charles Starrett played the role of the masked avenger, "The Durango Kid," in scores of features. While many of them appear to be carbon copies of one another, the actioners proved to be profitable and the durable Starrett was still active at the demise of the genre in the early 1950s, long after most of his saddle pals of yore had corraled their horses, holstered their firearms, and hung up their lariats. SIX-GUN LAW is typical of "The Durango Kid" series, although its plot is more complicated than most.

   Rancher Steve Norris (Charles Starrett) is at odds with crooked lawman Brackett (Ethan Laidlaw). When the latter accuses Steve of cattle rustling there is a shoot-out and Brackett pretends to be killed by his own trick pistol. Meanwhile, the real leader of the rustlers, dishonest businessman Decker (Hugh Prosser), has his henchman Larson (Robert Wilke) murder Brackett. He then forces Norris to become his new pawn sheriff. As a result the ranchers come to hate Steve, but he enlists the aid of rancher Bret Wallace (George Chesebro) and donning the disguise of the Durango Kid, robs the local bank so that Decker cannot get its money. He leaves the loot with Wallace, but Decker has the latter killed and tries to frame the man's son Jim (Paul Campbell) on the bank job. Decker learns of Steve's true activities when he finds a letter the lawman has sent to a U.S. marshal (Pierce Lyden) asking for help. Decker schemes to murder Steve with a gun planted in the town photographer's (Smiley Burnette) camera, but this fails. When he attempts to kill the U.S. marshal during a stage hold-up, the Durango Kid saves the day. Later Steve uses the camera weapon to trap a confession from the outlaws.

SKULL AND CROWN see THE SIGN OF THE WOLF

SKY BANDITS see RENFREW OF THE ROYAL MOUNTED

A SON OF THE PLAINS (Syndicate, 1931) 61 mins.

   Producer, Trem Carr; director/screenplay, Robert North Bradbury; assistant director, Paul Malvern; sound, R. L. Hickson; camera, Archie Stout; editor, Robert Johns.
   Bob Custer (Bob Brent); Doris Phillips (Anne Farrell); Edward Hearn (Dan Farrell); Gordon DeMain (Sheriff); J. P. McGowan (Buck Brokoff); Eve Humes (Roxie); Jane Crowell (Saloon Girl); Al St. John (Drunk).

   One-time trick rider Bob Custer starred in Westerns from 1924 to 1936, but after seeing many of his features, one can only wonder how he lasted so long. In silent films, Custer, who also appeared in non-sagebrush pictures under the screen name of Raymond Glenn, was barely passable. In talkies he seemed totally at a loss. He could scarcely read his lines and his stoical expression never seemed to change. In the silent days he worked for poverty-row outfits, but by the time talkies came along he had worked his way up to Films Booking Office (FBO), which also boasted such talents as Tom Mix, Bob Steele, and Fred Thomson. Later he went on to work at Big 4 and in 1936 he turned up briefly for the last time in an anemic series for Reliable.

A SON OF THE PLAINS was one of four starrers Bob Custer did for Syndicate in 1931. He is the sheriff torn between his duty to catch the notorious Polka Dot bandit (J. P. McGowan) and the love of a girl (Doris Phillips) whose father (Edward Hearn) aids the bandit in a hold-up. Silent film comic Al St. John, in his pre-Fuzzy Q. Jones characterization days, has a few good comic moments as a drunk.

Writer/director Robert North Bradbury would use the story-line, including the character of the Polka Dot bandit, to much better advantage three years later in the John Wayne picture, BLUE STEEL, made by producer Paul Malvern for the Monogram-Lone Star series.

SONG OF ARIZONA (Republic, 1946) C 66 mins.

Associate producer, Edward J. White; director, Frank McDonald; story, Bradford Ropes; screenplay, M. Coates Webster; songs: Jack Elliott, Ira Schuster, Larry Stock, J. Cavanaugh, Mary Ann Owens, Bob Nolan, Gordon Forster; camera, Reggie Lanning; editor, Arthur Roberts.

Roy Rogers (Himself); George "Gabby" Hayes (Gabby Whit-taker); Dale Evans (Clare Summers); Lyle Talbot (King Blaine); Tommy Cook (Chip Blaine); Johnny Calkins (Clarence); Sarah Edwards (Dolly Finuccin); Tommy Ivo (Jimmy); Michael Chapin (Cyclops); Edmund Cobb (Sheriff); Tom Quinn (Tom); Kid Chissell (Jim); Robert Mitchell Boy Choir (Themselves); Bob Nolan and the Sons of the Pioneers (Themselves); Trigger (The Horse).

Gangster King Blaine (Lyle Talbot) and his gang pull off a big robbery and King hides the loot. Only his young son Chip (Tommy Cook) knows its location. King is killed by lawmen and Chip is taken in by ranch owner Gabby Whittaker (George "Gabby" Hayes). Meanwhile Chip's half-sister, Claire Summers (Dale Evans), arrives on the scene. Cowboy Roy Rogers (Himself) and pals The Sons of the Pioneers (Themselves) are charged with rounding up the gangsters. The gang members, however, want the loot and they tell Chip that it was Gabby who shot his father. Later they shoot Gabby when he tries to protect the boy from them. Chip uses the money to pay off Gabby's debts so that he will not lose his ranch. At a party, the gang steals the money but Roy and the Pioneers recover it and bring the gang to justice.

This lively motion picture is a refreshing, well-made entry in Roy Rogers' Republic series, coming at a time when most of his films were overloaded with music and production numbers. This film deftly mixes elements of the Western and gangster film genres and its well-conceived script is packed with action. Lyle Talbot is especially impressive in his brief role as the dying gangster, and George "Gabby" Hayes has good dramatic scenes in his relationship with the orphaned lad.

SONG OF OLD WYOMING <u>see</u> LAW OF THE LASH

SONG OF THE GRINGO (Grand National, 1936) 62 mins.

Executive producer, Edward L. Alperson; producer, Edward Finney; director, John P. McCarthy; story, McCarthy, Robert Emmett (Tansey); screenplay, McCarthy, Emmett (Tansey), Al Jennings; camera, Gus Petersen; editor, Fred Bain.

Tex Ritter (Tex); Joan Woodbury (Dolores Del Valle/Lolita); Fuzzy Knight (Tony); Monte Blue (Sheriff); Richard [Ted] Adams (Evans); Warner Richmond (Cherokee); Martin Garralaga (Don Esteban Del Valle); Al Jennings (Judge); William Desmond (Court Clerk); Glenn Strange (Blackie); Jack Kirk (Cowboy); White Flash (The Horse); and Bob Burns, Forrest Taylor, Robert Fiske, Earl Dwire, Slim Whitaker, Budd Buster, Murdock McQuarrie, Ethan Laidlaw, Edward Cassidy.

Tex Ritter was best known as a radio personality when producer Edward F. Finney signed him to star in a series of "B" Westerns for the newly-formed Grand National company. Tex quickly became the studio's most popular Western star and, when that outfit went bust in 1938, Finney transferred the unit to Monogram where the duo made thirty-two features before Tex left to co-star with Bill Elliott at Columbia Pictures. Tex Ritter's solo starring Westerns contained authentic use of true Western songs rather than the Tin Pan Alley or show tunes which often populated series oaters. In addition, the star who originally planned to be an attorney and studied law at Northwestern University, was a rugged Westerner himself and he gave his cowboy roles an authentic feeling which endeared him to genre fans.

Lawman Tex (Tex Ritter) infiltrates an outlaw gang which operates along the Mexican border. He joins the Evans' (Richard "Ted" Adams) gang whose members pose as cowboys as a front for their criminal activities. The outlaws work on a ranch run by Don Esteban (Martin Garralaga). Tex romances the Don's pretty daughter Lolita (Joan Woodbury), but is blamed for Don Esteban's murder after the old man orders him off the ranch for wooing the girl. Tex is arrested for the crime, but in court he proves his innocence and in a shoot-out the real killer, Evans, is shot.

Tex Ritter performs six songs in SONG OF THE GRINGO, including one of his later big record hits for Capitol, "Rye Whiskey." In the cast is old-time outlaw and silent Western star Al Jennings, who taught Tex to shoot a gun properly during the making of this film.

SONG OF THE RANGE (Monogram, 1944) 55 mins.

Producer, Phil N. Krasne; associate producer, Dick L'Estrange; director, Wallace Fox; screenplay, Betty Burbridge; set decorator, Vin Taylor; assistant director, Bobby Ray; music, Frank Sanucci; sound, Glen Glenn; camera, Marcel LePicard; editor, Martin G. Cohen.

Jimmy Wakely (Jimmy); Dennis Moore (Denny); Lee "Lasses" White (Lasses); Kay Forester (Dale Harding); Sam Flint (McDonald); Steve Clark (Sheriff Duncan); Johnny Bond (Johnny); Edmund Cobb (Gang Leader); and Bud Osborne, Ken Terrell, Carl Mathews, Carl Sepulveda, The Sunshine Girls, Johnny Bond's Red River Valley Boys.

Jimmy Wakely came to Hollywood as part of a trio with Johnny Bond and Dick Rinehart and they were soon providing music for a variety of genre stars, plus supporting Gene Autry on his radio show. After successfully recording with Decca Records, Jimmy Wakely went solo and in 1944 landed a starring Western series at Monogram which lasted until 1949. It is hard to comprehend how the series lasted so long, since most of the films are arid affairs and Wakely at best was a mediocre thespian.

Set in the modern-day West, SONG OF THE RANGE tells of cowboy Denny (Dennis Moore) being falsely accused of murdering a man who was a member of an outlaw gang. Cowpokes Jimmy (Jimmy Wakely), Lasses (Lee "Lasses" White) and Johnny (Johnny Bond) help him escape and he finds the real killer, a dying federal agent. Denny then assumes that man's identity and aids agent Dale Harding (Kay Forrester) in trying to bring in an outlaw smuggling operation dealing in stolen gold. Denny joins the gang, pretending to be the dead outlaw, and finds they are using an underground tunnel to carry the ore across the state line. With the help of the local sheriff (Steve Clark), the outlaws are rounded up and Denny is cleared.

SONGS AND SADDLES (Colony, 1938) 65 mins.

Producers, Max Alexander, Arthur Alexander; director, Harry Fraser; screenplay, Wayne Carter; songs, Gene Austin; camera, Robert Cline, Harry Forbes; editor, Charles Henkel.

Gene Austin (Himself); Lynne Barkeley (Carol Turner); Joan Brooks (Lucy); Charles King (Falcon); Walter Wills (Pop Turner); Henry Rocquemore (Jed Hill); Karl Hackett (George Morrow); Ted Claire (Mark Bowers); John Merton (Rocky); Ben Corbett (Sparks); Bob Terry (Klinker); John Elliott (John Lawton); Lloyd Ingraham (Judge); Russell "Candy" Hill (Slim); Otto "Coco" Heimel (Porky).

Gene Austin had sold some 86 million records in the 1920s, with perennial hits like "My Blue Heaven," "Ramona," "The Sweetheart of Sigma Chi," and "I Can't Give You Anything But Love."

In 1938 he made his one solo starring feature film, playing himself as a cowboy hero in the independent production, SONGS AND SADDLES. In <u>Hollywood Corral</u> (1976) Don Miller termed the feature "...a haphazard indie that encouraged no followup, and merited none." Nevertheless, when the film was released, Austin made a personal appearance tour to accompany the film, and the movie did good business, especially in the South.

Austin and his troupe arrive in a small Western town where they try to aid pretty Carol Turner (Lynne Barkeley) and her father, Pop Turner (Walter Wills), whose ranch is coveted by a crook (Charles King). The outlaws kidnap Gene but he escapes and eventually brings them in.

During the film's one-hour running time Gene Austin performs five songs, all of which he wrote for this feature: "Song of the Saddle" (the film's original title), "I'm Comin' Home," "I Fell Down and Broke My Heart," "Why Can't I Be Your Sweetheart Tonight?" and "That Rootin' Tootin' Shootin' Man from Texas." Featured herein were Austin's stage co-stars: Joan Brooks and Candy (Russell "Candy" Hall) and Coco (Otto "Coco" Heimel).

SONG AND SADDLES had a quick playoff by Roadshow Attractions in 1938, but it was not until 1949 that it was released in Great Britain. One of the songs from the film, "That Rootin' Tootin' Shootin' Man from Texas" was refilmed by Austin in 1942 as a three-minute short for the Soundies Corporation of America.

SOUTH OF CALIENTE (Republic, 1951) 67 mins.

Associate producer, Edward J. White; director, William Witney; screenplay, Eric Taylor; music, R. Dale Butts; songs, Jack Elliott, Lee Wainer; camera, Jack Marta; editor, Harold Minter.

Roy Rogers (Himself); Dale Evans (Doris Stewart); Trigger (The Horse); Pinky Lee (Pinky); Douglas Fowley (Dave Norris); Ric Roman (Josef); Leonard Penn (Commandante); Willie Best (Willie); Lillian Molieri (Gypsy Dancer); Charlita (Rosina); Pat Brady (Pat); Frank Richards (Studsy); Roy Rogers Riders (Themselves); and Marguerite McGill, George J. Lewis, Lillian Molieri.

Towards the end of his series film career Roy Rogers returned to the action format, spiced with some music. Directed by William Witney, these productions were typically fast-paced, well-scripted and highly entertaining. SOUTH OF CALIENTE, however, is one of the weaker of the lot, and is hampered by sidekick Pinky Lee's inane comedy antics. Another plot weakness was allowing the brutal murder of the character played by lovable black actor Willie Best.

Outlaws steal ranch owner Doris Stewart's (Dale Evans) prize racing horse, which she must sell to save her ranch. Racing trainer Dave Norris (Douglas Fowley) is behind the gang and he wants both the animal and the spread. Cowboy Roy Rogers (Himself), on the trail of stolen horses, finds the missing racer and also discovers that Norris is the culprit engineering the rustling.

Roy Rogers and Dale Evans in SOUTH OF CALIENTE (1951).

SOUTH OF THE RIO GRANDE <u>see</u> THE GAY AMIGO

SOUTHWARD HO! (Republic, 1939) 58 mins.

Associate producer/director, Joseph Kane; story, John Rath-mell, Jack Natteford; screenplay, Gerald Geraghty; music director, Cy Feuer; songs, Walter G. Samuels; Fred Rose; camera, Jack Marta; editor, Lester Orlebeck.

Roy Rogers (Himself); Mary Hart (Ellen Denbigh); George "Gabby" Hayes (Gabby Whittaker); Trigger (The Horse); Wade Boteler (Colonel Denbigh); Arthur Loft (Jeffries); Lane Chandler (Crawford); Tom London (Hadley); Charles Moore (Skeeter); Edwin Brady (Mears); and Charles Moore, Fred Burns, Frank Ellis, Jack Ingram, Frank McCarroll, Curley Dresden, Jim Corey, Rudy Bowman, George Chesebro.

In Texas after the Civil War, ex-Confederates Roy Rogers (Himself) and Gabby Whittaker (George "Gabby" Hayes) return home to take over Gabby's share of his ranch, the other owner being the new military governor of the territory, Colonel Denbigh (Wade

Boteler). A group of outcast Yankee soldiers working for crook Jeffers (Arthur Loft) pretend to be government soldiers in order to ransack the area. In retaliation, ranchers kidnap Denbigh's daughter Ellen (Mary Hart), but Roy rescues her. Later he tells the colonel his men are robbing the ranches, and Denbigh agrees to investigate. Jeffers plans to murder Denbigh and shoots him, and the blame is put on Gabby. Roy, however, gets the ranchers together and they stop the thieves. Roy and Ellen fall in love.

SPIRIT OF THE WEST (Allied, 1932) 65 mins.

Producer, M. H. Hoffman, Jr.; director, Otto Brower; story, Jack Natteford; screenplay, J. G. White, art director, Jean Hornbustel; sound, Wilbur McGaugh; camera, Harry Newman, Tom Galligan; editor, Mildred Johnson.

Hoot Gibson (Johnny Ringo); Doris Hill (Dorothy); Hooper Atchley (Ryder); Alan Bridge (Tom Fallon); Lafe McKee (Moore); and George Mendoza, Charles Brindley, Walter Perry, Tony Sanford.

When Universal dropped program Westerns at the start of the sound era--in the mistaken notion that they could not fit into the talkie format--studio president Carl Laemmle sadly cancelled the contract of his personal favorite, Hoot Gibson. Gibson then signed with independent producer M. H. Hoffman, Jr. for a series to be released on a states right basis through Allied Pictures. The "B" oater proved to be quite successful in the new sound medium, but Gibson was unable to cancel his contract with Hoffman in order to accept Universal's offer to return there. He was replaced by Ken Maynard, who had been released by Universal at the same time as Hooter. SPIRIT OF THE WEST is one of Hoot's Hoffman features and, like most of this grouping, it emphasizes comedy over violence and contains only one fight sequence and a single shooting. Alan Bridge adds much as villain Tom Fallon.

Rodeo rider Johnny Ringo (Hoot Gibson) returns home to stop bad men who have injured his brother. He masquerades as a vagabond to gain information on the culprits and, one by one, he waylays the gang members and brings in their leader (Alan Bridge). In the course of events, he romances a pretty rancher (Doris Hill).

SPOILERS OF THE FOREST see TIMBERJACK

SPRINGFIELD RIFLE (Warner Bros., 1952) C 93 mins.

Producer, Louis F. Edelman; director, Andre De Toth; story, Sloan Nibley; screenplay, Charles Marquis Warren, Frank Davis; music, Max Steiner; orchestrator, Murray Cutter; assistant director, Frank Mallison; technical adviser, Ben Corbett; art director, John Beckman; set decorator, G. W. Bernsten; makeup, Gordon Bau;

Phyllis Thaxter and Gary Cooper in SPRINGFIELD RIFLE (1952).

sound, Charles Lang; camera, Edwin Du Par; editor, Robert L. Swanson.

Gary Cooper (Major Alex Kearney); Phyllis Thaxter (Erin Kearney); David Brian (Austin McCool); Paul Kelly (Lieutenant Colonel Hudson); Philip Carey (Captain Tennick); Lon Chaney (Elm); James Millican (Matthew Quint); Martin Milner (Olie Larsen); Guinn "Big Boy" Williams (Sergeant Snow); Jerry O'Sullivan (Lieutenant Evans); James Brown (Private Ferguson); Jack Woody (Sims); Alan Hale, Jr. (Mizzell); Vince Barnett (Cook); Fess Parker (Jim Randolph); Richard Lightner (Lieutenant Johnson); Ewing Mitchell (Spencer); Poodles Hanneford (Corporal Hamel); George Ross (Riley); Eric Hoeg (Southerner); Wilton Graff (Colonel Sharpe); Ned Young (Sergeant Poole); William Fawcett (Corporal Ramsey); Richard Hale (General Halleck); Ben Corbett (Sergeant Major); Guy E. Hearn (Calhoun); George Eldredge (Judge Advocate); Rory Mallinson; Ralph Sanford (Barflies); Paula Sowl (Woman); Ric Roman, Jack Mower (Guards); Holly Bane (Red); Ray Bennett (Commissioner); Michael Chapin (Jamie).

During the Civil War the Union cause needs a steady supply of horses from the West for the cavalry, but that influx has diminished

and Major Alex Kearney (Gary Cooper) is sent to find out who is
behind the sabotaging of the horse shipments. He keeps his assignment a secret from his wife (Phyllis Thaxter) and this causes personal friction. Reaching his destination, Kearney masquerades as a
cowboy and puts together a counter-espionage plan to renew the
union's horse shipments. He finds that when a cavalry outpost
plans to move a horse herd, renegades ambush them and corral the
steeds and sell them to the Confederacy. It develops that Elm (Lon
Chaney) is responsible for the rustling.

Released following the major success of Gary Cooper's HIGH
NOON (1952) (see B/V), SPRINGFIELD RIFLE, despite a good script,
fine cast, and plenty of action, was not as successful as it might
have been had it not been so unfavorably compared to the Stanley
Kramer classic. Still, SPRINGFIELD RIFLE received good reviews,
as in the Film Daily trade paper: "This is a well-told tale that was
concocted by Sloan Nibley and it received able direction from the
hand of Andre De Toth. The narrative is projected with imagination
and suspense. Gary Cooper in the saddle, and a good cast of
worthies to back him up, gives SPRINGFIELD RIFLE solid entertainment substance to render satisfaction." The New York Herald-
Tribune commented that the movie is "...tinged with just enough
historical importance to make it worth a hero's grandiose efforts."

SPRINGTIME IN THE ROCKIES (Republic, 1937) 60 mins.

Producer, Sol C. Siegel; director, Joseph Kane; screenplay,
Gibert Wright, Betty Burbridge; songs: Gene Autry, Frank
Harford; Autry, Johnny Marvin; camera, Ernest Miller; editor,
Lester Orlebeck.

Gene Autry (Gene); Smiley Burnette (Frog Milhouse); Polly
Rowles (Sandra); Ula Love (Silly Sylvia); Ruth Bacon (Peggy);
Jane Hunt (Jane); George Chesebro (Morgan); Alan Bridge (Briggs);
Tom London (Tracy); Edward Hearn (Thorpe); Frankie Marvin
(Frankie); William Hole (Bub); Edmund Cobb (Sheriff); Fred Burns
(Harris); Jimmy LeFuer's Saddle Pals (Orchestra); Champion (The
Horse); and Art Davis, Lew Meehan, Jack Kirk, Frank Ellis,
George Montgomery, Robert Dudley, Jack Rockwell, Oscar Gahan,
Victor Cox, Jim Corey.

Singer Gene Autry (Himself) becomes involved in a range feud
between cattle ranchers and sheepherders. When the female owner
(Polly Rowles) of the ranch he manages buys a herd of sheep, Gene
tries to convince her that her ranch is run down so that she will
sell the sheep. A crook (Alan Bridge) who wants to steal the ranch
shoots a cowboy (George Chesebro) and Gene is blamed for the
crime. Gene's pal Frog Milhouse (Smiley Burnette) gets him out of
jail and Gene stops the girl from selling her ranch and brings in the
crook.

Despite the use of the old saw of cattlemen versus sheepherders, SPRINGTIME IN THE ROCKIES is an actionful and entertain-

ing Gene Autry opus which highlights the famous title song as well
as another country/Western perennial: "You're the Only Star in My
Blue Heaven." Alan Bridge does his usual outstanding job as the
villain of the piece.

SQUARE DEAL SANDERSON (Paramount-Artcraft, 1919) 4,800'

Producer, William S. Hart; directors, Hart, Lambert Hillyer;
story, Charles Alden Seltzer; screenplay, Hillyer; art director,
Thomas A. Brierly; art titles, Irwin J. Martin; camera, Joseph
August.
William S. Hart (Square Deal Sanderson); Ann Little (Mary
Bransford); Lloyd Bacon (Will Bransford/Barney Owen); Frank
Whitson (Alva Dale); Andrew Robson (Judge Graney); Edwin Wallace
(Sheriff Maison).

In 1919 William S. Hart again teamed with Lambert Hillyer to
make SQUARE DEAL SANDERSON, with Hart producing and co-
directing with Hillyer from the latter's scenario. The feature is a
sturdy one and includes rather violent sequences, including Hart's
shooting a crooked banker, the attempted rape of the heroine by
the villain, and Hart's killing the villain at the climax by hanging
him from a transom. It is interesting to note that even at this
early stage in film history, so many Westerns had been made that
the genre was old hat to some reviewers, as can be seen in Wid's
trade paper comments on the feature: "Considering the hundreds
of thousand of feet of cowboy melodrama that have been produced
since the days of Broncho Billy Anderson, it is something of an ac-
complishment to find a new stunt for a thrilling climax. Bill Hart
found one for SQUARE DEAL SANDERSON and it goes over big...."
In a ravine, Square Deal Sanderson (William S. Hart) locates
the dead bodies of two men. On one of them he finds a letter a
young woman has written to her long lost brother, begging him to
help her fend off an unwanted suitor. Sanderson decides to help
the woman and goes to her ranch where he finds the man, gang
leader Alva Dale (Frank Whitson), about to hang one of Mary
Bransford's (Ann Little) ranch hands, Barney Owen (Lloyd Bacon).
Sanderson saves the man, who in reality is the girl's brother, but
Mary mistakes Sanderson for her sibling and he is unable to convince her of the truth. Owen tells Sanderson the facts about his
identity but Dale has the local corrupt sheriff (Edwin Wallach) arrest him and then poison all the water holes, thus killing Mary's
cattle. Owen helps Sanderson break out of jail and the latter forces
the local banker--a cohort of Dale's--to pay Mary the cash value for
her cattle herd. At Mary's ranch, Dale traps Sanderson and then
tries to rape the girl, but Sanderson breaks his bonds and throws a
noose around Dale's neck, hanging him. He tells Mary the truth
about his identity and they plan to wed.
The plot of SQUARE DEAL SANDERSON was unofficially reworked three years later for the poverty-row galloper, ANOTHER

MAN'S BOOTS, issued by Anchor. Here a man called The Stranger (Francis Ford) agrees to take on the identity of his pal, Ned Hadley (Harry Smith), who has been shot by outlaws. He is accepted by pretty Nell Hadley (Elvira Weil) and her blind father as their long lost relative, but crooked Sly Stevens (Robert Kortman), who is after the Hadley ranch and Nell, sees through the ruse and has "Ned" charged with a killing he and his henchman (Frank Lanning) have committed. The real Ned arrives, however, and saves his friend from being hanged. The two bad men are arrested, leaving The Stranger free to court Nell.

STAGE TO MESA CITY (Eagle Lion, 1948) 52 mins.

Producer, Jerry Thomas; director, Ray Taylor; screenplay, Joseph F. Poland; music, Walter Greene; music director, Dick Carruth; set decorator, Gene Redd; makeup, Max Asher; sound, Glen Glenn; camera, James Brown, Sr.; editor, Hugh Winn.

Lash LaRue (U.S. Marshal Cheyenne Davis); Al "Fuzzy" St. John (U.S. Marshal Fuzzy Q. Jones); Jennifer Holt (Margie Watson); George Chesebro (Padgett); Brad Slaven (Bob Watson); Marshall Reed (Baxter); Terry Frost (Ed); Carl Mathews (Jim); Bob Woodward (Pete); Steve Clark (Watson); Frank Ellis (Stocker); Lee Morgan (Sheriff); and Dee Cooper, Wally Wet, Russell Arms.

A family-owned stage line is being harassed by bandits as the owner (Steve Clark), his daughter (Jennifer Holt), and son (Brad Slavin) try to get the mail contract for the territory. U.S. marshals Cheyenne Davis (Lash LaRue) and Fuzzy Q. Jones (Al St. John) are sent to Mesa City to investigate. They try to stop the gang and discover that it is being led by the town's postmaster (George Chesebro).

The sixth in Lash LaRue's starring series for PRC, STAGE TO MESA CITY is a fast moving "B" oater with realistic fight sequences and plenty of stirring music. The supporting cast is particularly good, with lovely Jennifer Holt as the heroine, Marshall Reed and Terry Frost as bad guys, and a fine characterization by genre veteran George Chesebro as the big boss villain.

STAGECOACH (CBS-TV, 5/18/86) C 100 mins.

Executive producers, Raymond Katz, Willie Nelson; producers, Hal W. Polaire, Jack Thompson; director, Ted Post; based on the story "Stage to Lordsburg" by Ernest Haycox and the screenplay by Dudley Nichols; teleplay, James Lee Barrett; music, Willie Nelson, David Allan Coe; art director, Bill Conford; camera, Gary Graves; editor, Geoffrey Rowland.

Willie Nelson (Doc Holliday); Kris Kristofferson (Billy "Ringo" Williams); Waylon Jennings (Hatfield); Johnny Cash (Marshal Curley Wilcox); John Schneider (Buck); Elizabeth Ashley (Dallas); Tony

WILLIE NELSON

JOHNNY CASH

KRIS KRISTOFFERSON

WAYLON JENNINGS

A Journey They Had To Take.
An Adventure You'll Never Forget.

STAGECOACH

Also Starring ELIZABETH ASHLEY
JOHN SCHNEIDER · TONY FRANCIOSA
MARY CROSBY · ANTHONY NEWLEY
Written By JAMES LEE BARRETT
Directed By TED POST

WORLD PREMIERE
CBS SUNDAY NIGHT MOVIES

9PM CBS●2

Franciosa (Henry Gatewood); Mary Crosby (Lucy Mallory); Anthony
Newley (Trevor Peacock); Merritt Butrick (Lieutenant Blanchard);
June Carter Cash (Mrs. Pickett); Alex Kubic (Ike Plummer); Lash
LaRue (Lash); Jessi Colter (Martha); David Allan Coe (Luke Plum-
mer); John Carter Cash (Billy Pickett); Michael Hayes (Captain Mal-
lory); Billy Swan (Bartender); Joe Unger (Captain Nikel); Bob
McClean (Chris).

Following the dismal 1966 remake of the 1939 classic John Ford
STAGECOACH (see B/V), it seemed inconceivable that a third version
of Ernest Haycox' story "Stage to Lordsburg" would ever be filmed.
With the signing of country music stars Willie Nelson, Waylon Jennings, Kris Kristofferson and Johnny Cash, however, the project
was made at a cost of slightly over $3,000,000 at Arizona's Old Tuc-
son prefabricated tourist attraction. While TV Guide critic Judith
Crist grumbled, "Skip this one for the sake of both cast and classic," the TV version is a pleasant outing which thankfully lacks the
big-budget pretentions of the limpid 1966 version.

Like the two previous editions, this TV-lensed galloper tells
the tale of a motley group of stagecoach passengers who leave the
town of Tonto for their destination, Lordsburg, under the shadow
of the rampaging Geronimo and his braves. The group is made up
of driver Buck (John Schenider); lawman Curley Wilcox (Johnny
Cash), who rides shotgun to Lordsburg to arrest the murderous
Plummer brothers; pregnant Lucy Mallory (Mary Crosby), who wants
to be with her Army captain husband; hooker Dallas (Elizabeth
Ashley), disappointed by romance; gambler Hatfield (Waylon Jennings), who takes a liking to Lucy because her Army general father
once saved him from a courtmartial; banker Gatewood (Tony Franciosa), who has just robbed his own bank; British whiskey salesman
Trevor Peacock (Anthony Newley); and the consumptive Doc Holliday
(Willie Nelson). En route they pick up wanted outlaw Ringo (Kris
Kristofferson), who is escaping from a posse, and Wilcox puts him
under arrest. At a way station the passengers learn that they will
lose their Army escort. Peacock returns to Tonto with the soldiers
and the others continue on, but they are forced to stop at a burned
out rest stop where Doc Holliday delivers Mrs. Mallory's infant
daughter. The next day they resume their journey with their teams
of weary horses. Geronimo and his braves attack, and Gatewood is
killed and Buck and the lawman injured before they are rescued by
the arrival of the cavalry. In Lordsburg Wilcox deputizes Ringo
and they are aided by Doc Holliday and Hatfield in standing up to
the Plummer brothers. Ringo kills Luke Plummer (Alex Kubic), the
murderer of his brother and the man whose false evidence sent him
to prison. Ringo then returns to his Mexican ranch, accompanied by
Dallas.

The main asset of this version of STAGECOACH is its fine,
moody cinematography by Gary Graver. In addition, the telefilm
has an appealing cast, although Anthony Newley is wasted as the
whiskey salesman and Elizabeth Ashley is too quirky as the good-
hearted whore. Of course, the main interest lies in the casting of

the country music stars in the lead assignments. To placate Willie Nelson, who did not want to play a drunk, the role of the doctor memorably played by Thomas Mitchell in the 1939 edition was changed to the historical character Doc Holliday, shown here as a rather obnoxious proponent of Indian rights. While Kris Kristofferson is acceptable as Ringo, Johnny Cash barely makes it as the lawman. Waylon Jennings steals the films in his underplayed work as gambler Hatfield, who does not die in this version. The movie is a family affair as Cash's wife, June Carter, and son, John Carter Cash, appear briefly as way station operators, while Jennings' lovely wife, Jessi Colter, is none too impressive as banker Gatewood's grasping mistress. For genre buffs, there is the pleasant appearance of old-time star Lash LaRue as the Plummers' ally who deserts them at the showdown.

STAGECOACH EXPRESS (Republic, 1942) 55 mins.

Associate producer/director, George Sherman; story, Doris Schroeder; screenplay, Arthur V. Jones; camera, John MacBurnie; editor, William Thompson.
Don "Red" Barry (Dave Gregory); Lynn Merrick (Ellen Bristol); Al St. John (Dusty Jenkins); Robert Kent (Griff Williams); Emmett Lynn (Charles Haney); Guy Kingsford (Sam Elkins); Ethan Laidlaw (Lou Hawkins); and Eddie Dean.

Three outlaws hold up a stagecoach with the owner, Ellen Bristol (Lynn Merrick); on board, but cowboy Dave Gregory (Don "Red" Barry) scares them away. She asks him to drive the stage for her full-time but he tells her he has come to Pandhandle to locate his pal Dusty Jenkins (Al St. John) who has struck it rich on a gold claim grubstaked by Dave. He finds out, however, that Dusty has lost the mine in a poker game, so the two men agree to work for Ellen. Meanwhile, saloon owner Griff Williams (Robert Kent) and Ellen's partner, Sam Elkins (Guy Kingsford), are secretly working together to cheat miners out of their gold, and they plan to stop Ellen from renewing her stage franchise. When the government sends word that the Panhandle is now part of Texas, Haney gets himself elected commissioner but Dave suspects him of trying to murder Ellen during a stage robbery planned for the next day. Dave abducts Haney and puts him on the stage, and the crook confesses to the planned murder. Dave and a posse stop at a way station where they capture Elkins and the rest of the gang.
By 1942 Don Barry was listed in the Motion Picture Herald's poll of top ten money-making Western stars, a place he would retain through 1945.
After establishing himself as a genre star in THE ADVENTURES OF RED RYDER, a 1940 cliffhanger, Don Barry, who had kicked around Hollywood since 1932, landed his own series at Republic. His fine acting ability and competently made features made him one of the most popular of Western players and STAGECOACH EXPRESS is a

Lois Wilde, Chuck Morrison, and Rex Bell in STORMY TRAILS (1936).

pleasant, if bit slow, diversion. The film contains several well handled riding and chase sequences.

STORMY TRAILS (Colony, 1936) 60 mins.

    Producers, Max Alexander, Arthur Alexander; director, Sam Newfield; based on the story "Stampede" by E. B. Mann; adaptor, Phil Dunham.
    Rex Bell (Tom Storm); Bob Hodges (Billy Storm); Lois Wilde (Connie Curlew); Lane Chandler (Dunn); Earl Dwire (Stephen Varick); Lloyd Ingraham (Curlew); Karl Hacket (Durante); Earl Ross (Thurman); Murdock McQuarrie (Sheriff); Jimmy Aubrey (Shives); Roger Williams (Daniels); and Chuck Morrison, George Morrell.

    Rex Bell is probably best remembered today as the husband of silent screen "IT" Girl, Clara Bow, and later as lieutenant governor of Nevada. He also starred in three "B" Western series in the 1930s; one each for Monogram, Resolute and Grand National. STORMY TRAILS is from the last-named series and although it contained some fine action it was plagued with a complicated, twisty plot, shoddy production values, and the use of poor stock footage of a cattle stampede.

Louis Jean Heydt in STRANGER AT MY DOOR (1956).

Brothers Tom (Rex Bell) and Billy Storm (Bob Hodges) own a heavily mortgaged ranch and crooks are after the land because it contains gold. Tom finds that Billy is mixed up with the outlaws but when he tries to turn in the gang, Billy is chased by them and when they try to rustle the Storm cattle herd, Billy is killed defending it. The gang plans to stampede the cattle so that Tom cannot pay the interest on his mortgage. They capture him but Tom escapes and brings in his brother's killers.

STRANGER AT MY DOOR (Republic, 1956) 85 mins.

Producer, Sidney Picker; director, William Witney; screenplay, Barry Shipman; music, R. Dale Butts; camera, Bud Thackery; editor, Howard Smith.

Macdonald Carey (Hollis Jarret); Patricia Medina (Peg Jarret); Skip Homeier (Clay Anderson); Stephen Wootton (Dodie Jarret); Louis Jean Heydt (John Tatum); Howard Wright (Doc Parks); Slim Pickens (Ben Silas); Malcolm Atterbury (Reverend Hastings).

Outlaw Clay Anderson (Skip Homeier) and his gang pull off a bank robbery and then split up, with Clay taking sanctuary at the farm of minister Hollis Jarret (Macdonald Carey), who has a young second wife. Peg (Patricia Medina), and a hero worshipping young son, Dodie (Stephen Wootton). Clay sees a chance to redeem the outlaw and lets him stay; the restless young wife is attracted to him and the boy is thrilled to have a real life outlaw at his home. Jarrett, however, believes the Lord will convert the outlaw and the miracle does occur, although Clay is eventually killed in a shoot-out near the minister's unfinished church.

STRANGER AT MY DOOR is a fine melodrama which Variety termed "an exceptionally well-done family trade offering...." Macdonald Carey gives one of the best performances of his career as the faithful preacher and is aided by a fine supporting cast, including Louis Jean Heydt as the town lawman and Slim Pickens' as the horse trader. According to Francis M. Nevins, Jr., in his chapter on director William Witney in Close Up: The Contract Director (1976), STRANGER AT MY DOOR is Witney's favorite of his eighty-none features and serials. Nevins noted that the film "...deals with the interactions of an outlaw on the run [and] a preacher of unshakable simple-minded faith ... and Witney elicits such vivid performances from the players that we can see each of the main characters, both as each views himself and as he is perceived by each of the others." Nevins, however, claims the ending is the "ruination of what might have been a magnificent film," but added, "....the three action sequences, especially the eye-popping scene of a killer horse going wild in the middle of the picture, are as filled with maniacal energy as anything Witney did in the serials."

A STRANGER IN TOWN see COMIN' AT YA

THE STRANGER RETURNS see COMIN' AT YA

THE STRAWBERRY ROAN (Universal, 1933) 62 mins.

Producer, Ken Maynard; director, Alan James; story/screenplay, Nate Gatzert; song, Curley Fletcher; camera, Ted McCord, editor, Charles Harris.
Ken Maynard (Ken Mawsters); Ruth Hall (Alice Edwards); Harold Goodwin (Bart Hawkins); Frank Yaconelli (Shanty); Charles King (Curley); William Desmond (Colonel Brownlee); James Marcus (Big Jim Edwards); Jack Rockwell (Beef); Robert Walker (Bat); Ben Corbett (Slim); Tarzan (The Horse); Bill Patton, Roy Bucko, Art Mix, Buck Bucko, Bud McClure (Cowboys).

THE STRAWBERRY ROAN (Columbia, 1948) C 76 mins.

Presenter, Gene Autry; producer, Armand Schaefer; director, John English; story, Julian Zimet; screenplay, Dwight Cummings, Dorothy Yost; music, Paul Mertz; music director, Mischa Bakaleinikoff; songs: Paul Herrick, Allie Wrubel; Fred Holland, Nat Vincent; Autry, Curt Massey, Mary Milland; art director, Harold MacArthur;

set decorator, George Montgomery; assistant director, Earl Bellamy; sound, Lambert Day; camera, Fred H. Jackman; editor, Henry Batista.

Gene Autry (Himself); Champion, Jr. (The Horse); Gloria Henry (Connie Bailey); Jack Holt (Walt Bailey); Dick Jones (Joe Bailey); Pat Buttram (Hank); Rufe Davis (Chuck); John McGuire (Bud Williams); Eddy Waller (Steve); Redd Harper (Andy); Jack Ingram (Pete Lucas); Eddie Parker (Jake); Ted Mapes (Smitty); Sam Flint (Dr. Nelson).

Curley Fletcher's song "The Strawberry Roan" is a classic Western tune which has become a part of western folklore. In 1933 Ken Maynard purchased the rights to the song from Fletcher and used it as the title for his popular Universal series outing. In it Ken Maynard played a devil-may-care bronco-busting cowboy who sets his sights on taming a beautiful strawberry roan and on winning the love of a pretty young woman (Ruth Hall). Two pals (Charles King, Frank Yaconelli) aid him with the horse, which fights a duel to the death with a wild stallion before finally becoming the spirited steed of master Maynard. The film was the second in Maynard's second Universal series, and as in the first entry, THE FIDDLIN' BUCKAROO (1933), the star employed music to good advantage, even accompanying himself on the fiddle. The movie proved to be a box-office winner, both here and abroad, and it was said to be Ken Maynard's favorite of his features. For the action sequences of the two horses doing battle, stock footage from the silent serial THE DEVIL HORSE (Pathé, 1926) was deftly interpolated.

In 1946, Gene Autry, who has always admired Ken Maynard and who made his film debut in Maynard's IN OLD SANTA FE (1934-- q.v.), bought the rights to the song and story from Maynard and used it for his first Cinecolor feature at Columbia. Just as THE STRAWBERRY ROAN was one of Ken Maynard's most popular films, so the title spelled success for Gene Autry. The story has ranch foreman Autry capturing a wild horse which causes injury to the ranch owner's (Jack Holt) young son (Dick Jones). The owner vows to kill the animal but Gene comes to its defense and is fired. To save the animal, he takes it with him, and is charged with theft and becomes a wanted man. Through the aid of the horse, however, the boy walks again and all ends well. Gene Autry's horse, Champion, Jr., enacted the title role, as did Ken Maynard's steed Tarzan in the 1933 version.

There is also a 1944 British film called STRAWBERRY ROAN, but in this feature the title animal is a young heifer calf, not a horse.

SUNRISE TRAIL see NEVADA BUCKAROO

SUNSET RANGE (First Division, 1935) 52 mins.

Director, Ray McCarey; story/screenplay, Paul Schofield;

assistant director, George Sherman; camera, Gilbert Warrenton; editor, Ralph Dietrich.

Hoot Gibson (Reasoning Bates); Mary Doran (Bonnie Shay); James Eagles (Dan); Walter McGrail (Grant); Kitty McHugh (Maid); Lee Fong (Cook); and John Elliott, Eddie Lee, Ralph Lewis, Fred Gilman, Martha Sleeper.

Sandwiched between his Allied series for producer M. H. Hoffman and his First Division oaters for Walter Futter, Hoot Gibson starred in two well-made actioners released by First Division, SUNSET RANGE and RAINBOW'S END (q.v.). SUNSET RANGE has a very exciting climax but despite its rather melodramatic plot, combining the western and gangster genres, the movie has a heavy emphasis on comedy. Well staged is the opening sequence of riders chasing Hoot and roping him, only to extract one of his teeth. Later, the new owner of the ranch, a pretty young woman, wants to dress all the ranch hands like Hollywood cowboys.

Pretty Bonnie Shay (Mary Doran) is given the ownership of the family ranch by her brother, who is actually a gangster. Cowboy Reasoning Bates (Hoot Gibson) wants to buy the spread but stays on because he likes his new boss. The gang to which the former owner belongs has hidden stolen loot in the girl's case, and they try to involve her in their activities. When her brother tries to protect her, he is shot by the other gang members, but he manages to call for help and gets Hoot on the trail of the hoodlums who have kidnapped his sister. Hoot and the ranch hands rescue Bonnie.

To be noted is that George Sherman was the assistant director on this film. He went on to direct many top Westerns.

SUTTER'S GOLD see KAISER VON KALIFORNIEN

SWING, COWBOY, SWING see SING, COWBOY, SING

TAKE ME BACK TO OKLAHOMA (Monogram, 1940) 57 mins.

Producer, Edward F. Finney; director, Al Herman; screenplay, Robert Emmett [Tansey]; music, Frank Sanucci; songs: Slim Andrews, Tex Ritter; Jimmie Davis, Charles Mitchell; Johnny Lange, Lew Porter, Bob Wills, Tommy Duncan; camera, Marcel LePicard; editor, Fred Bain.

Tex Ritter (Tex Lawton); Arkansas Slim Andrews (Slim); Bob Wills (Himself); Johnny Lee Wills, Leon McAuliffe, Sonny Lansford, Wayne Johnson, Eldon Shamblin (Bob Wills' Texas Playboys); Terry Walker (Jane Winters); Bob McKenzie (Ames); Karl Hackett (Storm); Donald Curtis (Snapper); Gene Alsace (Red); Olin Francis (Mule Bates); and Carleton Young, Ruth Rodgers.

Crook Storm (Karl Hackett) and his gang are after the mail franchise and sabotage the operations controlled by pretty Jane Walker (Terry Winters). When the gang attacks the way station and a stagecoach on which Jane is a passenger, cowboy Tex Lawton (Tex Ritter) and his pals Slim (Arkansas Slim Andrews) and Bob (Bob Willis) come to her rescue. Later, during a benefit show, Storm's men steal the profits and place the blame on Tex, but the cowboy is aided by former convict Mule Bates (Olin Francis), a gunman actually on Storm's payroll to kill Lawton. When Storm finds out about Bates' change of heart, he murders him, but in a stagecoach race for the mail contract, Tex drives a stage against Storm and, with the assist of Bob's friends (The Texas Playboys), corrals Storm and his gang.

TAKE ME BACK TO OKLAHOMA was Tex Ritter's 29th series Western and his seventeenth outing since he and producer Edward Finney had joined Monogram two years before. With scenic north country locales, fast action, and a good plot, the movie is considered one of Tex Ritter's better efforts. An asset to the proceedings is the inclusion of Bob Wills and His Texas Playboys in both the musical numbers and the action. In fact, the movie includes nine songs, but they do not get in the way of the story and are well integrated into the plot. Among the tunes are Jimmie Davis's perennial classic, "You Are My Sunshine," a trio of Wills' regulars--"Take Me Back to Oklahoma," "Lone Star Rag" and "Bob Wills Special"--and the novelty tune, "They're Hangin' Pappy in the Morning."

TALES OF THE APPLE DUMPLING GANG see THE APPLE DUMPLING GANG

TEX RIDES WITH THE BOY SCOUTS (Grand National, 1937) 60 mins.

Producer, Edward F. Finney; supervisor, Lindsley Parsons; director, Ray Taylor; story, Parsons, Edmund Kelso; screenplay, Kelso; music director, Frank Sanucci; camera, Gus Peterson; editor, Frederick Baen.

Tex Ritter (Tex); Marjorie Reynolds (Norma); Horace Murphy (Stubby); Karl Hackett (Kemp); Edward Cassidy (Sheriff); Tim Davis (Tommie); Snub Pollard (Pee Wee); Charles King (Stark); Philip Ahn (Sing Fong); Tommy Bupp (Buzzy); Lynton Brent (Pete).

The Boy Scouts of America, to whom this picture is dedicated, figured previously in a "B" Western, in Ken Maynard's DRUM TAPS (1933) for World Wide. Here a Los Angeles scout troup is involved in the plot, but producer Edward Finney later reported that the national organization almost prevented the release of the film after viewing the scouts chasing the bad guys. Finney prevailed by pointing out that the film emphasized the victory of the ideals of the Boy Scouts over the wrongdoings of the film's cattle rustlers.

TEX RIDES WITH THE BOY SCOUTS is one of Tex Ritter's best known films, the ninth release in his Grand National series. It is a decent production with plenty of action and music, and the opening sequences detail the history of the Boy Scouts. The Motion Picture Film Daily trade paper noted the "ready made exploitation angle evident in the title," while Film Curb called it Ritter's "best to date."

Mine ore geologist Tex Collins (Tex Ritter) and his pals Stubby (Horace Murphy) and Pee Wee (Snub Pollard) have trouble with the unfriendly Stark (Charles King), and then camp with a troup of Boy Scouts near the spot where a million-dollar train robbery took place. Gold miner Dorman (Forrest Taylor), Stark and their gang are the robbers hiding behind the facade of gold mine operators. Tex finds out about Dorman's gang but Stark and some of the gang members double-cross Dorman and plan to escape across the border with the gold. When Boy Scout Buzzy (Tommy Bupp) overhears their plans, Dorman shoots him. He then captures Stark and his boys and leaves them to hang for the killing of the boy, but it turns out that Buzzy is only wounded. Tex and his pals round up the Boy Scout troup and they hunt the outlaws, capturing Stark and his men. Tex prevents Dorman from escaping with the gold.

THE TEXAN (Paramount, 1930) 79 mins.

Associate producer, Hector Turnbull; director, John Cromwell; based on the story "The Double-Dyed Deceiver" by O. Henry; screenplay, Daniel Nathan Rubin; adaptor, Oliver H. P. Garrett; songs, L. Wolfe Gilbert, Abel Baer; assistant director, Henry Hathaway; sound, Harry M. Lindgren; camera, Victor Milner; editor, Verna Willis.

Gary Cooper (Enrique [Quico--The Llano Kid]); Fay Wray (Consuelo); Emma Dunn (Senora Ibarra); Oscar Apfel (Thacker); James Marcus (Sheriff John Brown); Donald Reed (Nick Ibarra); Solidad Jiminez (Duenna); Veda Buckland (Mary the Nurse); Cesar Vanoni (Pasquale); Edwin J. Brady (Henry); Enrique Acosta (Sixto); Romualdo Tirado (Cabman); Russ Columbo (Singing Cowboy at Campfire).

The Llano Kid (Gary Cooper), a bandit wanted by the law, stops in a small town run by a Bible-quoting lawman, Sheriff Brown (James Marcus), and gets into a poker game with a young man whom he is forced to shoot after catching him cheating. Escaping, the Kid boards a train where he meets crooked Thatcher (Oscar Apfel), who plans to bilk an old widow (Emma Dunn) by passing the Kid off as her long lost son. The Kid goes along with the ruse but at the woman's hacienda comes to realize that the gambler he killed was actually the woman's offspring. Meantime, he falls in love with her beautiful niece Consuelo (Fay Wray). The Kid refuses to carry out his part of the bargain, and Thacker organizes a gang to steal the old lady's gold. In the meantime, Sheriff Brown tracks the Kid to rancho but holds off arresting him. When the gang attacks, the Kid and the lawman fight together and Thacker is killed.   The sheriff agrees to identify Thacker as the wanted Llano Kid so that the young man can remain with Consuelo.

THE TEXAN, Gary Cooper's third of seven screen appearances in 1930, was sandwiched between his more important genre outings, THE VIRGINIAN (1929) (see B/V) and the first sound version of THE SPOILERS (1930) (see B/V).   While Photoplay magazine termed the feature "picturesque," it was a slow-moving, creaking entry, derived from O. Henry's 1905 story, "The Double-Dyed Deceiver." Cooper was typically laconic in the title assignment, while Fay Wray was a visual delight as Consuelo.   The movie also offers a glimpse of future singing idol Russ Columbo, cast as a campfire cowboy singer.

In 1939 Paramount remade the film as THE LLANO KID, as a vehicle for Mexican singer Tito Guizar who, ironically, did not sing in the feature.   Guizar would be used to much better screen advantage nearly a decade later at Republic Pictures, in the Trucolor Roy Rogers' vehicle, THE GAY RANCHERO (1948).

TEXAS ACROSS THE RIVER (Universal, 1966) C 100 mins.

Producer, Harry Keller; director, Michael Gordon; screenplay, Wells Root, Harold Greene, Ben Starr; music, Frank DeVol; assistant directors, Terry Morse, Jr., John Anderson; camera, Russell Metty; editor, Gene Milford.

Dean Martin (Sam Hollis); Alain Delon (Don Andrea Baldasar); Rosemary Forsyth (Phoebe Ann Naylor); Joey Bishop (Kronk); Tina Marquand (Lonetta); Peter Graves (Captain Stimpson); Michael Ansara (Iron Jacket); Linden Chiles (Yellow Knife); Andrew Prine (Lieutenant Sibley); Stuart Anderson (Yancy); Roy Barcroft (Morton); George Wallace (Willet); Don Beddoe (Mr. Naylor); Kelly Thordsen (Turkey Shoot Boss); Nora Marlowe (Emma); John Harmon (Gabe); Dick Farnsworth (Medicine Man).

Filmed in Julian, California, TEXAS ACROSS THE RIVER is a smartly made Western comedy which never takes itself seriously in its lampooning of the Old West.   Variety termed the film a "boisterous western spoof with belly laughs galore," and the movie did good box-office business thanks to the casting in the lead of Dean Martin, then at the height of his TV popularity.   Having international screen star Alain Delon on hand also helped the film's grosses.   In addition, Western buffs were delighted at the strong supporting cast, which included such favorites as Roy Barcroft, George Wallace, Don Beddoe, Kelly Thorsden, John Harmon, and future star Dick Farnsworth.

Spanish nobleman Don Andrea Baldasar (Alain Delon) is set to marry lovely southern belle Phoebe Ann Naylor (Rosemary Forsyth), but on the eve of the nuptials one of her former boy friends is accidentally killed and Don Andrea is blamed for the death.   To save his hide, he heads to Texas in the company of rowdy gun-running Sam Hollis (Dean Martin) and the latter's Indian comrade Kronk (Joey

Advertisement for TEXAS ACROSS THE RIVER (1966).

Bishop). On the way Don Andrea rescues Indian maiden Lonetta (Tina Marquand) from the Comanches, who plan to kill her. Phoebe catches up with the group, but Sam is drawn to her and Don Andrea challenges him to a duel over his fiancée. The arrival of the cavalry and an Indian attack prevent the shoot-out. When the duel is finally about to take place, the two women get into a fight and oil begins spouting from an open grave. Finally Don Andrea decides he really loves Lonetta, Sam and Phoebe fall in love, and the locals complain about the useless sticky oil. Sam suggests they return the area to the Indians.

TEXAS LEGIONNAIRES see MAN FROM MUSIC MOUNTAIN (1943)

TEXAS MARSHAL see THE GUNMAN

THE TEXAS RANGER (Columbia, 1931) 65 mins.

Producer, Sol Lesser; director, D. Ross Lederman; story/
screenplay, Forrest Sheldon; song, Jack Scholl, Phil Boutelje;
camera, Teddy Tetzlaff; editor, Gene Milford.

Buck Jones (Texas Ranger Jim Logan); Carmelita Geraghty
(Helen Clayton); Harry Woods (Matt Taylor); Silver (The Horse);
and Ed Brady, Nelson McDowell, Billy Bletcher, Harry Todd, Budd
Fine, Bert Woodruff, Edward Piel, Sr., Blackie Whiteford, Lew
Meehan.

Buck Jones' seventh starring talkie, THE TEXAS RANGER is
another outstanding effort in his first season at Columbia, and
typical of the strongly-made features which elevated him to number
one "B" Western star at the box office in the early 1930s. With a
tight script and outstanding photography, the movie is highly entertaining and gives perennial genre bad guy Harry Woods one of
his finest screen roles, that of a murderous, land-grabbing rancher.

In Laredo Valley, a rancher has been murdered and his pretty
daughter, Helen Clayton (Carmelita Geraghty), is out to find the
culprit. She soon realizes that the killer is rival rancher Matt Taylor
(Harry Woods), who owns the Syndicate Ranch, and who employs his
gang to burn out homesteaders so that he can control the entire
valley. The young woman begins a fight with Taylor's men but ends
up being accused of the killing of another rancher. Arriving in
town is Texas Ranger Jim Logan (Buck Jones), who is investigating
the trouble in the valley. He pretends to be a drunk in order to
gain information at the local saloon, and then signs on as a wrangler
on the Clayton ranch. Jim is soon romancing Helen, and also finds
that Taylor is behind all the trouble. When Jim and Helen are
captured by Taylor's men, other Texas Rangers arrive and rescue
them.

TEXAS ROAD AGENT see ROAD AGENT

TEXAS TO BATAAN see OUTLAWS OF THE DESERT

TEXAS TROUBLE SHOOTERS (Monogram, 1942) 55 mins.

Producer, S. Roy Luby; associate producer, Richard Ross;
director, Luby; story, Elizabeth Beecher; screenplay, Arthur Hoerl;
music, Frank Sanucci; camera, Robert Cline; editor, Roy Claire.

Ray "Crash" Corrigan (Crash); John King (Dusty); Max Ter-
hune (Alibi); Julie Duncan (Judy Wilson); Roy Harris (Bret Travis);
Eddie Phillips (Wade); Frank Ellis (Duke); Ted Mapes (Slim); Kermit
Maynard (Pete); Gertrude W. Hoffman (Granny); Steve Clark (Ames);
Jack Holmes (Perry); Glenn Strange (Roger Danby); Richard Cramer
(Bartender); Elmer (The Dummy).

The Range Busters (Ray "Crash" Corrigan, John King, Max
Terhune) set out to aid Bret Travis (Roy Harris), who has been
dry-gulched while claiming a ranch he inherited. Three crooks
(Frank Ellis, Kermit Maynard, Ted Mapes) have another man (Eddie
Phillips) masquerade as the young man, and steal the ranch from
the late owner's pretty daughter Judy (Julie Duncan), who has part
interest in the property with Bret. It turns out there is oil on the
range and the trio of crooks want it, but the Range Busters thwart
them and save the spread for Bret and Judy.

Early in TEXAS TROUBLE SHOOTERS the Range Busters spot
Bret being chased by the three bad men, but only Alibi (Max Terhune) comes to his rescue. It is only after Alibi tells Crash (Ray
Corrigan) and Dusty (John King) that a pretty girl is involved in
the caper that the duo agree to help Brett. Such an uncavalier-like
attitude is hardly in accord with the cowboy code and, even if played
for comedy, hurts the credibility of this series entry. After this,
however, the movie becomes fairly actionful. The film includes the
tunes: "Deep in the Heart of Texas" and "Light of the Western
Skies."

THREE AMIGOS (Orion Pictures, 1986) C 105 mins.

Executive producer, Steve Martin; producers, Lorne Michaels,
George Folsey, Jr.; director, John Landis; screenplay, Martin,
Michaels, Randy Newman; production designer, Richard Sawyer; set
decorator, Richard Goddard; set designers, Mark Faybus, Stan Tropp;
costumes, Deborah Madoolman; music, Elmer Bernstein; songs, Newman; second unit director, Folsey; assistant director, David Sosna;
sound, William Kaplan; camera, Ronald W. Browne; editor, Malcolm
Campbell.

Chevy Chase (Dusty Bottoms); Steve Martin (Lucky Day);
Martin Short (Ned Nederlander); Patrice Martinez (Carmen); Alfonso
Arau (El Guapo); Tony Plana (Jefe); Joe Montegna (Studio Boss).

Three silent-screen singing cowboys, Dusty Bottoms (Chevy
Chase), Lucky Day (Steve Martin), and Ned Nederlander (Martin
Short), are fired by the boss (Joe Montegna) of Goldsmith Studios.
Down on their luck, they get a telegram from Carmen (Patricia
Martinez), who begs them to come to her Mexican town of Santa Poco
to save it from the wicked bandit El Guapo (Alfonso Arau) and his
gang. The young woman has mistaken the screen cowboys' persona
for real. Believing they have been hired for a new movie, the trio
head south of the border where they confront the bandito and his
flier German pals and defeat them. Along the way, the heroes romance and win the local senoritas.

If one can appreciate the special bravura comedy style of Steve
Martin and Chevy Chase, then THREE AMIGOS has its appeal, but
otherwise it has little to offer genre followers. A takeoff of THE
MAGNIFICENT SEVEN (1960) (see B/V), the movie has a "few
choice morsels of brilliant humor ... [but] is a reheated mishmash

of old oaters that teases one's buds with familiarity without enough new flavoring to make it a completely satisfying concoction" (Variety). Duane Byrge leveled a valid complaint against the film in The Hollywood Reporter because of its "heavy-handed character stereotypes among the Mexican villagers," and added, "surely, the Hispanic Academy of Motion Picture Arts and Sciences will not be putting this one up for any commendation awards."

With Western movie releases down to a mere trickle in the mid-1980s, it is a shame that THREE AMIGOS could not have been a better feature. It is a bit hard to take seriously a genre effort which uses a trio of heroes from silent movies, since the concept did not take hold until the 1930s. Even more appalling is the fact the heroes are cowboy crooners of silent movies!

THREE MEN FROM TEXAS (Paramount, 1941) 75 mins.

Producer, Harry Sherman; director, Lesley Selander; based on characters created by Clarence E. Mulford; screenplay, Norton S. Parker; music, Victor Young; camera, Russell Harlan; editor, Carroll Lewis.

William Boyd (Hopalong Cassidy); Russell Hayden (Lucky Jenkins); Andy Clyde (California Carson); Morris Ankrum (Morgan); Morgan Wallace (Andrews); Thornton Edwards (Pico); Esther Estrella (Paquita); Davison Clark (Thompson); Dick Curtis (Gardner); Topper (The Horse); and Glenn Strange, Meyle Marx, Robert Burns, Jim Corey, George Morrell, George Lollier, Frank McCarroll, Lucio Villegas.

It is unusual for a long-running film series to produce its best effort in the middle of its run, but that is what happened with the "Hopalong Cassidy" series, which ran from 1935 to 1948. Probably its best entry is THREE MEN FROM TEXAS, distributed in 1940 and introducing the continuing character of California Carlson, deftly played by veteran screen comic Andy Clyde. Much of the film's success is due to scripter Norton S. Parker, who fashioned a highly entertaining scenario which director Lesley Selander kept moving at a fast clip. With its well-honed plot, exciting climax, and more brutality than normal for the series, THREE MEN FROM TEXAS is a standout "B" Western.

Ranger Hopalong Cassidy (William Boyd) arrests good-natured outlaw California Carlson (Andy Clyde) and the latter's gang tries to kill him to keep him quiet. Hoppy, however, rounds up the outlaws and takes California west with him to reform the varmint. The two join Lucky Jenkins (Russell Hayden) as the law team in the rough town of Santa Carmen, where a criminal, Morgan (Morris Ankrum), is trying to steal land from its owners. Now a federal marshal, Hopalong Cassidy is out to get Morgan and his gang. In the fracas, Lucky's girl friend (Esther Estrella) is killed before the bad men are forced to atone for their crimes.

THE THREE STOOGES MEET THE GUNSLINGERS see THE OUTLAWS IS COMING

THUNDER IN THE DESERT (Republic, 1938) 56 mins.

Producer, A. W. Hackel; director, Sam Newfield; screenplay, George H. Plympton; camera, Robert Cline; editor, S. Roy Luby.

Bob Steele (Radford); Louise Stanley (Betty Andrews); Don Barclay (Rusty); Ed Brady (Reno); Charles King (Harris); Horace Murphy (Sheriff); Steve Clark (Andrews); Lew Meehan (Mike); Ernie Adams, Richard Cramer (Tramps); Budd Buster (Oscar).

Bob Radford (Bob Steele) and Rusty (Don Barclay) are mistaken for outlaws by gang leader Reno (Ed Brady) and they join his outfit as he is trying to take over a ranch. Bob is after the men who killed his uncle Jim and he has Rusty pretend to be the killer. (Actually Rusty is the rightful owner of the ranch Reno and his boss Curt [Charles King] are trying to take.) Bob proves that Curt is behind all the trouble, saves the ranch for pretty Betty Andrews (Louise Stanley) and her father (Steve Clark), and brings about the downfall of the two bad men.

A solid entertainment entry in Bob Steele's lengthy run of pictures for producer A. W. Hackel, the title of this outing refers to dynamite used to blow up waterholes. Although the film lacks proper story development, it moves quickly and has some well-done comedy. Bob Steele is stalwart, as always, as the revenge-seeking hero, and genre fans will be delighted to see Charles King as a romantic interest for the heroine.

THUNDER MOUNTAIN (Fox, 1935) 60 mins.

Producer, Sol Lesser; director, David Howard; based on the novel by Zane Grey; adaptors, Dan Jarrett, Don Swift; camera, Frank B. Good; editor, Robert Crandell.

George O'Brien (Cal Emerson); Barbara Fritchie (Sydney Blair); Frances Grant (Nugget); Morgan Wallace (Rand Leavitt); George "Gabby" Hayes (Foley); Edward LeSaint (Samuel Blair); Dean Benton (Steve Sloan); William Norton Bailey (Cliff Borden).

Prospectors Cal Emerson (George O'Brien) and Steve Sloan (Dean Benton) get financial backing from Sam Blair (Edward LeSaint) to prospect for gold on Thunder Mountain. They make a strike and Steve goes to file a claim. He is dry-gulched by corrupt saloon owner Rand Leavitt (Morgan Wallace). Later Cal is joined by Blair and his daughter Sydney (Barbara Fritchie) in trekking to the gold claim site, which he finds inundated with prospectors who have established a mining camp. Cal finds that Steve is missing and that Leavitt has filed on their claim. He promises Blair he will get to the bottom of the situation. Cal romances the pretty Sydney, but is also

attracted to saloon singer Nugget (Frances Grant), a decent young
woman who works for Leavitt. At the camp of another miner (George
"Gabby" Hayes), Steve turns up and informs Cal that Leavitt had
left him to die in the desret, but that he was rescued by a wagon
train party. When Cal informs Blair of the situation, Sydney overhears and warns Leavitt, since by now she too is greedy for gold.
Just as Steve is about to testify before a miner's court, Leavitt
murders him, and Cal gets on the trail of the killer and his pal
(William Norton Bailey). The latter double-crosses Leavitt and Leavitt
murders him. In a mountain-top fight between Cal and Leavitt, the
wrongdoer falls to his death. Back at the camp Cal rejects the advances of Sydney for the honest love of the saloon girl.

    Based on the Zane Grey novel of the same title, which was pub-
lished the same year as this film was released, THUNDER MOUNTAIN
is an entry in the top-notch George O'Brien oater series for Fox.
Here, however, action is downplayed for dramatics, with good results,
and the movie is highlighted by Frank G. Good's excellent timber
country cinematography. In 1947 RKO used the title again for its
Tim Holt series, but completely revamped the plot. In this version
the star returns home from college and ends up in the midst of a
feud.

THUNDERING HOOFS (Film Booking Offices of America, 1924) 5,033'

    Director, Albert Rogell; screenplay, Marion Jackson; camera,
Ross Fisher.
    Fred Thomson (Dave Marshall); Fred Huntley (John Marshall);
Charles Mailes (Don Juan Estrada); Charles De Revenna (Don Carlos);
Ann May (Carmelita); Carrie Clark Ward (Duenna); William Lowery
(Luke Sever); Silver King (The Horse).

    Fred Thomson was one of the most popular cowboy stars of the
1920s, having given up plans to be a minister after marrying scenar-
ist Frances Marion. During the 1920s he made a successful series of
oaters for Film Bookings Office (FBO), but after making JESSE JAMES
in 1928 he became seriously ill and died on Christmas night of that
year. THUNDERING HOOFS is a fine example of Fred Thomson's
starrers: solid production values, lots of action, and nice comedy
relief. Here, the star's beautiful horse, Silver King, plays a major
role in the action. The film also sports intriguing bull ring sequences.
    Rancher's son Dave Marshall (Fred Thomson) wins prize horse
Silver King (Himself) from Luke Severn (William Lowery), who has
mistreated the animal. Dave later foils an attempt by Severn to rob
rancher Don Estrada (Charles Mailes) of money he plans to use to
buy Dave's father's (Fred Huntley) horses. Dave also rescues Estrada's pretty daughter Carmelita (Ann May) from a runaway stagecoach. Severn, however, tells Estrada that Dave is a desperado
and the girl gets engaged to Severn even though she despises him.
Dave and Carmelita, however, fall in love and intend to marry, but

Estrada takes his daughter to Mexico. Lawmen discover Severn is
the bandit leader and Dave goes to Mexico to save Carmelita form
him and is put in jail there. Silver King comes to his rescue and
Dave and the law catch up with the bandit. Dave and Carmelita
wed.

TIMBERJACK (Republic, 1955) C 94 mins.

Producer, Herbert J. Yates; director, Joseph Kane; based on
the novel by Dan Cushman; screenplay, Allen Rivkin; music, Victor
Young; songs: Paul Francis Webster, Johnny Mercer, Ned Washing-
ton, Hoagy Carmichael; choreography, Jack Baker; assistant direc-
tor, Herbert Mendelson; costumes, Adele Palmer; art director, Frank
Arrigo; set decorators, John McCarthy, Jr., George Milo; sound,
Roy Meadows; camera, Jack Marta; editor, Richard L. Van Enger.
Sterling Hayden (Tim Chapman); Vera Ralston (Lynne Tilton);
David Brian (Croft Brunner); Adolphe Menjou (Swiftwater Tilton);
Hoagy Carmichael (Jingles); Chill Wills (Steve); Howard Petrie (Axe-
Handle Ole); Jim Davis (Poole); Ian MacDonald (Paquette); Wally
Cassell (Veazie); Elisha Cook, Jr. (Punky); Karl Davis (Red Bush);
Tex Terry (Charley); George Marshall (Fireman).

North woods melodramas have always been a strong part of the
Western motif, as evidenced by the many picturizations of the works
of James Oliver Curwood and the popular "Renfrew of the Royal
Mounted" series. Occasionally big-budget features have also tackled
this offshoot of the Western. TIMBERJACK, highlighted by Jack
Marta's gorgeous on-location cinematography in Montana's Glacier
National Park, is a brawling, fast-paced melodrama with lots of action
to compensate for its moderate script. The New York Herald-Tribune
opined, "...the scenery is by far the most intriguing point of the
mvie," while Variety termed it a "lusty actioner."
Tim Chapman (Sterling Hayden) returns to the timber country
to seek his rightful inheritance after Croft Brunner (David Brian),
the owner of the Talka River Logging Company, has murdered his
father and stolen his lands. There Tim encounters and renews his
romance with his childhood sweetheart, Lynne Tilton (Vera Ralston),
the singer/owner of the Vermillion Belle saloon. She is also sought
after by Croft, and she tries to keep peace between the two men.
Her alcoholic lawyer father (Adolphe Menjou) turns on Croft and is
murdered by him. When Lynne finds out, she joins Tim in defeating
Croft in a rifle shoot-out.
In addition to all the action, TIMBERJACK contains several
musical numbers by exotic Vera Ralston and Hoagy Carmichael, the
latter cast as her salty cabaret piano player. Ms. Ralston's singing
was dubbed by Virginia Rees.
Enough footage was left over from TIMBERJACK to be used
for some of the action sequences in another Vera Ralston "opus,"
SPOILERS OF THE FOREST (1957), also directed by Joseph Kane.
Here Vera and her father (Carl Benton Reid) are being swindled out

of their Montana timber lands by crooked Ray Collins, who hires
honest lumberjack Rod Cameron to make love to the heroine.

TO THE LAST MAN (Paramount, 1923) 6,965'

Presenter, Jesse L. Lasky; director, Victor Fleming; based on
the book by Zane Grey; adaptor, Doris Schroeder; camera, James
Wong Howe, Bert Baldridge.
Richard Dix (Jean Isbel); Lois Wilson (Ellen Jorth); Noah
Beery (Colter); Robert Edson (Gaston Isbel); Frank Campeau (Blue);
Fred Huntley (Lee Jorth); Edward Brady (Daggs); Eugene Pallette
(Simm Bruce); Leonard Clapham (Guy); Guy Oliver (Bill); Winifred
Greenwood (Mrs. Guy).

TO THE LAST MAN (Paramount, 1933) 70 mins.

Producer, Harold Hurley; director, Henry Hathaway; based on
the story by Zane Grey; adaptor, Jack Cunningham; camera, Ben
Reynolds.
Randolph Scott (Lynn Hayden); Esther Ralston (Ellen Colby);
Buster Crabbe (Bill Hayden); Jack LaRue (Jim Daggs); Noah Beery
(Jed Colby); Barton MacLane (Neil Standing); Muriel Kirkland (Molly
Hayden); Fuzzy Knight (Jeff Morley); Gail Patrick (Ana Hayden
Standing); Egon Brecher (Mark Hayden) James Eagles (Ely Bruce);
Eugenie Besserer (Granny Spelvin); Harlan Knight (Grandpa Spelvin);
Shirley Temple, John Carradine (Bits).

Two screen adaptations of Zane Grey's 1921 novel have been
made by Paramount, beginning in 1923. A decade later the studio
used stock footage from the first rendition for a talkie remake in a
series it was doing with Randolph Scott. Both movies are solid actioners which retain the full flavor of the Grey book.
In the 1923 version, Richard Dix stars as Jean Isbel, a member
of a cattle ranching family at odds with the sheepherding Jorths.
Jean's father (Robert Edson) accuses his rival, Lee Jorth (Fred
Huntley), of cattle thefts but he says he is innocent. His daughter,
Ellen (Lois Wilson), is being romanced by Jean but when he sees a
horse belonging to him at their farm, he realizes that Jorth is a thief
and a range war breaks out between the two families. Only Jean and
Ellen survive to find happiness together. Photoplay magazine termed
the film "A real, red-blooded Western, filled with fights and other
exciting episodes."
Directed by Henry Hathaway and the sixth of eight topnotch
"B" Westerns he did for Paramount between 1932 and 1934 based on
Zane Grey works (seven of them with Randolph Scott), the remake
sticks to the plot-line of the 1923 movie although it opens with an
interesting prologue of the two families, now called Hayden and Colby, beginning their feud in the hills of Kentucky and then transfer-
ring it to Nevada. Here Randolph Scott stars as Lynn Hayden while
beautiful Esther Ralston is Ellen Colby, the daughter of the rival

Esther Ralston and Randolph Scott in TO THE LAST MAN (1933).

family. The remake has a most austere finale with Billy Hayden
(Buster Crabbe), Lynn's younger brother, being murdered, mounted
on his horse and sent home. The movie greatly benefits from
Esther Ralston's raw sex appeal. If one looks closely, the movie
contains bit performances by Shirley Temple and John Carradine, the
latter being killed in the mountain feud sequence.

TOM HORN (Warner Bros., 1980) C 98 mins.

Executive producer, Steve McQueen; producer, Fred Weintraub;
director, William Wiard; based on the book Life of Tom Horn; Gov-
ernment Scout and Interpreter by Tom Horn; screenplay, Thomas
McGuane, Bud Shrakel; art director, Ron Hobbs; set decorator,
Rick Simpson; music, Ernest Gold; assistant director, Cliff Coleman;
costumes, Luster Bayless; sound, Jerry Jost, Joe Kite; camera, John
Alonzo; editor, George Grenville.
Steve McQueen (Tom Horn); Richard Farnsworth (John Coble);
Linda Evans (Glendolene Kimmel); Billy Bush (Joe Belle); Slim
Pickens (Sam Creedmore).

Steve McQueen's penultimate film, TOM HORN, is considered
one of the worst Westerns ever produced. Made in the late 1970s,
the film did not receive release until the spring of 1980, and then
its distribution was sparse. Variety pinpointed the film's artistic

problems: "Imagine a film that opens up with dialog that can't be heard at all, then proceeds to build up to a fistfight that's never seen, that cuts away to sunsets to fill in other scenes that have no dramatic point, that presents a meal [scene] where the sounds of knives and forks drown out what's being said, and you have just the beginning of what's wrong with TOM HORN." Furthermore, film star Steve McQueen (then suffering from fatal cancer) gives a listless performance, meandering through his scenes in a poorly-directed, written and edited fiasco.

Famous as the man who captured Geronimo, Tom Horn (Steve McQueen) ekes out a living as a bounty hunter, and is hired by a rancher (Richard Farnsworth) to deal with incoming homesteaders and rustlers. Horn, however, proves to be too efficient, and to get him out of the way, the rancher has one of his men (Billy Green Bush) frame Horn on a fake charge. He is convicted, although the local lawman (Slim Pickens) is sympathetic because he knows Horn is innocent. Tom escapes from jail and goes into the desert, but is returned to town for execution.

Linda Evans appears as the distaff love interest, but her carelessly interpolated scenes are accomplished in flashback and confuse the viewer even more than the rest of the dull proceedings.

A much better telling of the Tom Horn saga appeared in 1979 in the two-part CBS-TV movie, MR. HORN, starring David Carradine in the title role. The telefeature told of Horn capturing Geronimo and how he later became a bounty hunter and a Pinkerton agent before ending up as a pawn for both sides in a Wyoming cattle war.

TOUGHEST MAN IN ARIZONA see SINGING GUNS

TOWN TAMER (Paramount, 1965) C 89 mins.

Producer, A. C. Lyles; director, Lesley Selander; based on the novel by Frank Gruber; screenplay, Gruber; music, Jimmie Haskell; song, Haskell and By Dunham; assistant director, Howard Roessel; sound, Hugo Grenzback; camera, W. Wallace Kelley; editor, George Gittens.

Dana Andrews (Tom Rosser); Terry Moore (Susan Tavenner); Pat O'Brien (Judge Murcott); Lon Chaney (Mayor Leach); Bruce Cabot (Riley Candor); Lyle Bettger (Marshall Lee Ring); Coleen Gray (Carol Rosser); Barton MacLane (James Fenimore Fell); Richard Arlen (Dr. Kent); Richard Jaeckel (Honsinger); Philip Carey (Sim Akins); DeForrest Kelley (Guy Tavenner); Sonny Tufts (Carmichael); Roger Torrey (Flon); James Brown (Davis); Richard Webb (Kevin); Jeanne Cagney (Mary); Don Barry, Robert Ivers (Vagrants); Bob Steele (Vigilante).

TOWN TAMER, adapted to the screen by Frank Gruber from his novel, is one of the series of low-budget Westerns producer A. C. Lyles prepared for Paramount Pictures in the 1960s. The series is noted for using veteran stars and this outing boasted more than a dozen such one-time headliners, along with an interesting plot and spirited direction by veteran genre helmsman Lesley Selander.

In a small Kansas town Riley Condor (Bruce Cabot) hires gunslinger Lee Ring (Lyle Bettger) to murder lawman Tom Rosser (Dana Andrews), but the latter's wife (Coleen Gray) is killed. Two years later, Tom comes to White Plains, ostensibly to buy real estate. In actuality he wants to gun down Condor, who has been using his gang to stop engineer Fell (Barton MacLane) from completing a railroad which will bring law and order to the area. Two corrupt lawmen, Ring and Honsinger (Richard Jaeckel), frame Rosser on a fake charge and try to get the drunken local judge (Pat O'Brien) to arrest him. Meanwhile, townsmen led by Mayor Leach (Lon Chaney) and Dr. Kent (Richard Arlen) form a vigilante committee to protect the town, and they come to Rosser's defense. In the meantime, Tom stops drunken Glen Tavenner (DeForest Kelley) from abusing his wife Susan (Terry Moore). When the vigilantes try to kill Condor, the latter's gang repels them and Rosser tells the townspeople to halt their attacks. Law and order is finally restored and Rosser plans to marry the now-widowed Susan.

In its performances, TOWN TAMER is a boon for the fans of the old-timers in the cast. While Pat O'Brien has a disappointingly small assignment as the judge, others, like Lon Chaney, Richard Arlen, Bruce Cabot, Lyle Bettger, and Barton MacLane, have meaty roles, and Dana Andrews is substantial as the revenge-seeking lawman.

THE TRAIL BEYOND (Monogram, 1934) 55 mins.

Producer, Paul Malvern; director, Robert N. Bradbury; based on the novel The Wolf Hunters by James Oliver Curwood; screenplay, Lindsley Parsons; art director, E. R. Hickson; camera, Archie Stout; editor, Charles Hunt.

John Wayne (Rod Drew); Noah Beery (George Newsome); Noah Beery, Jr. (Wabi); Verna Hillie (Felice Newsome); Iris Lancaster (Marie); Robert Frazer (Jules LaRocque); Earl Dwire (Benoit); Eddie Parker, (Mountie Ryan); Reed Howes, James Marcus (Henchmen).

Between 1933 and 1936 John Wayne headlined two dozen "Lone Star" westerns for producer Paul Malvern and the films helped to establish him as one of the most popular American screen cowboys. In the last year of the series, the initial Motion Picture Herald poll of top money-making Western stars placed John Wayne in seventh position. THE TRAIL BEYOND was the first entry for the series' second season (1934-35) and, unlike the others for Malvern, it is based on an original work--James Oliver Curwood's book, The Wolf Hunters, 1908.

Rod Drew (John Wayne) accompanies his half-Indian college pal Wabi (Noah Beery, Jr.) to the north country. Along the way they escape from cardsharks on a train, after Wabi is accused of murdering one of the gamblers. Drew is supposed to locate a missing girl and on the trail he and Wabi find two skeletons in a cabin and a map to a hidden gold mine which belongs to the missing girl, Felice (Verna Hillie). An outlaw gang led by LaRocque (Robert Frazer) wants the map once they learn it has been put in a safe at the general store run by Newsome (Noah Beery). Felice works for Newsome and the gang kidnap her and try to get her to open the safe, but Rod saves her. LaRocque and the gang plan to attack Newsome's store and take the map and Felice, but Rod, who has gone for the Mounties, arrives to stop them. Wabi is cleared of the murder charge and Rod and Felice look forward to a life of happiness.

THE WOLF HUNTERS had first been filmed in 1926 by Rayart Pictures with Ben Wilson producing. That outing had a pretty girl (Virginia Browne Faire) accused of killing a man interested in her, and a Mountie (Robert McKim), who also loves her, being forced to bring in the young woman. She is eventually cleared of the murder charge. In 1949, Kirby Grant starred in the third screen version of the James Oliver Curwood novel, again called THE WOLF HUNTERS. This edition was directed by Oscar (Budd) Boetticher who was to make a name for himself when he helmed Randolph Scott in a topnotch series of "A" Westerns for producer Harry Joe Brown in the mid- and late 1950s. Also of interest is that this Monogram (the studio which also issued THE TRAIL BEYOND) feature was produced by Lindsley Parsons, the screenwriter for the 1934 version. Here a Mountie (Kirby Grant) and his dog Chinook are on the trail of fur thieves and a lost gold mine.

THE TRAIL OF ROBIN HOOD (Republic, 1950) C 67 mins.

Producer, Edward J. White; director, William Witney; screen-play, Gerald Geraghty; music/music director, Nathan Scott; songs, Jack Elliott, Foy Willing; art director, Frank Arrigo; set decorators, John McCarthy, Jr., James Redd; assistant director, Jack Lacey; makeup, Bob Mark; sound, Tom Carman; camera, John MacBurnie; editor, Tony Martinelli.

Roy Rogers (Himself); Trigger (The Horse); Penny Edwards (Toby Aldridge); Gordon Jones (Splinters); Rex Allen, Allan "Rocky" Lane, Monte Hale, William Farnum, Tom Tyler, Ray "Crash" Corrigan, Kermit Maynard, Tom Keene (Guest Stars); Jack Holt (Himself); Emory Parnell (J. Corwin Aldridge); Clifton Young (Mitch); James Magill (Murtagh); Carol Nugent (Sis); George Chesebro (Himself); Edward Cassidy (Sheriff); Foy Willing and the Riders of the Purple Sage (Themselves).

One-time Western movie star Jack Holt (Himself) raises Christ-mas trees and is the rival of a conglomerate run by J. Corwin Al-dridge (Emory Parnell). Roy Rogers (Himself), an agent for the Conservation Service, finds out that evergreens are being cut il-legally and has a confrontation at Aldridge's camp, where he has chased the fir thieves. Holt comes to the camp and refuses an offer

from Aldridge's camp manager McCall (Clifton Young) to form a partnership. Holt also rejects the same offer from Aldridge's pretty daughter Toby (Penny Edwards). Meanwhile, McCall and Henchman Murtagh (James Magill) plan to steal evergreens from Holt and sell them, thus cheating Aldridge by getting their trees to market before his are delivered. Aldridge, however, masquerades as a worker and takes a job at his own camp, but he is found out and held hostage by McCall and Murtagh. The latter then sets fire to the town hall where Holt's trees are stored, and the former movie star suffers badly from smoke inhalation. When it appears that all is lost, the town blacksmith's (Gordon Jones) little sister (Carol Nugent) writes to Western film stars Ray "Crash" Corrigan, William Farnum, Tom Keene, Monte Hale, Allan "Rocky" Lane, Kermit Maynard, and Tom Tyler (Themselves) and asks for help. They arrive, but so does movie villain George Chesebro (Himself). They help Roy in stopping the villains who have set fire to the bridge over which the evergreen shipment must pass. The delivery is finally made. McCall falls from a dam and is killed. Jack Holt and Aldridge form a partnership.

THE TRAIL OF ROBIN HOOD is a topnotch "B" Western, handsomely filmed in Trucolor in California timber country at a budget of nearly $250,000. Besides a strong script and fast action, the movie has great nostalgic appeal in its casting of Jack Holt as the old-time movie star, and there is even a sequence where one of the star's old films is shown, although the footage is obviously new material and not one of Jack Holt's vintage starrers. Also a nice bit of casting is the use of former cowboy stars who come to Holt's aid (a ploy also used in BELLS OF ROSARITA, q.v.), and especially enjoyable is the appearance of veteran Western villain George Chesebro, who asks to join up with the good guys for a change.

TRAIL OF THE MOUNTIES (Screen Guild, 1949) 41 mins.

Producer, Carl K. Hittleman; director, Howard Bretherton; based on the story by James Oliver Curwood; screenplay, Leslie Schwabacher, Elizabeth Burbridge; music, Albert Glasser; camera, Benjamin Kline; editor, Paul Landres.

Russell Hayden (Lucky Sanderson/Johnny); Jennifer Holt (Kathie); Terry Frost (Gumdrop); Harry Cording (Hawkins); Charles Bedell (Maurice).

Russell Hayden, known mainly in Westerns for his Lucky Jenkins role in the "Hopalong Cassidy" series, his co-starring with Charles Starrett at Columbia, and various solo efforts for that studio and others, starred in a quartet of Northwest Mountie featurettes which Screen Guild issued in 1946 and 1947. These streamlined efforts were picturesque in their locales and speedy in plot due to their limited running times, but sometimes the action got in the way of proper plot development.

TRAIL OF THE MOUNTIES is the last of the quartet and it is cheaply made, but still entertaining. Hayden is a Mountie who is sent to a small Canadian village to capture the killer of a fellow officer. He learns that his twin brother (Hayden), the leader of a gang of fur thieves, is the culprit.

This film, like the other three entries--'NEATH CANADIAN SKIES (1946), NORTH OF THE BORDER (1946) and WHERE THE NORTH BEGINS (1947)-- was allegedly based on the works of James Oliver Curwood.

TRAIL OF THE SILVER SPURS (Monogram, 1941) 58 mins.

Producer, George W. Weekes; director, S. Roy Luby; story, Elmer Clifton; screenplay, Earl Snell; music director, Frank Sanucci, song, Lew Porter, Johnny Lange; camera, Robert Cline; editor, Roy Cline.

Ray "Crash" Corrigan (Crash); John King (Dusty); Max

Terhune (Alibi); I. Stanford Jolley (Jingler); Dorothy Short (Nancy Nordick); Milburn Morante (Nordick); George Chesebro (Wilson); Eddie Dean (Stoner); Elmer (The Dummy); and Kermit Maynard, Frank Ellis, Carl Mathews, Steve Clark.

The government puts the Range Busters (Ray "Crash" Corrigan, John King, Max Terhune) on the trail of a gold thief. They wind up in a ghost town called Bottleneck, where a man (Milburn Morante) and his pretty daughter (Dorothy Short) are being harassed by a mysterious figure called "The Jingler," who uses "ghost writing." Alibi (Max Terhune) salts an abandoned mine and brings about a gold rush. When the Jingler uncovers the plot, the Range Busters capture him and find that the gold he has been stealing is from the Denver Mint. A rich vein of gold is found in the mine and Bottleneck becomes a boom town once more.

A good mystery plot element highlights TRAIL OF THE SILVER SPURS, the third entry in Monogram's "The Range Busters" series, which was filmed at star Ray "Crash" Corrigan's ranch. While the film is better than some of the entries in the series, Dave Rowlands wrote in Wild West Stars magazine (Volume 2, Number 8, no date), "The film somewhat lacks appeal, emphasized by the lack of direct action and by the use of patently stock shots (from silent films?) for the gold digging and gold rush scenes." A nice addition to the film was the song, "The Rainbow Is Ridin' the Range," sung by John King.

TRAIL OF VENGEANCE (Republic, 1937) 55 mins.

Producer, A. W. Hackel; director, Sam Newfield; story, E. B. Mann; screenplay, George H. Plympton, Fred Myton; camera, Bert Longenecker; editors, S. Roy Luby, Tom Neff.

Johnny Mack Brown (Duke Ramsey); Iris Meredith (Jean Warner); Warner Richmond (Link Carson); Karl Hackett (Mart Pierson); Earl Hodgins (Buck Andrews); Frank LaRue (Tilden); Frank Ellis (Red Cassidy); Lew Meehan (Bill O'Donnell); Frank Ball (Steve Warner); Dick Curtis (Cartwright); and Jim Corey, Horace Murphy, Dick Cramer, Steve Clark, Budd Buster, Jack C. Smith, Jack Kirk, Francis Walker, Tex Palmer.

Gunman Duke Ramsey (Johnny Mack Brown), searching for the killer of his brother, finds a man dying in the desert and learns that he has a mine. He is ambushed by outlaws but escapes and takes papers regarding the mine to the dead man's daughter Jean (Iris Meredith). He learns that she and her father have been involved in a range war with businessman Link Carson (Warner Richmond) and his gang, and Duke thwarts an attempt by the outlaws to abduct the girl as the gang ambushes the ranchers. Duke learns that the murdered man's partner, who was also killed by Carson, was his brother, and he sets out for revenge, shooting Carson in a showdown as the sheriff captures the outlaws.

A well-made entry in Johnny Mack Brown's Republic series for producer A. W. Hackel, this film had a strong supporting cast and a tight, dramatic script, plus slick direction by Sam Newfield in the days before he turned out films via the PRC assembly-line. Using the old revenge motif, the movie is more austere than the average series oater of the period. It benefits greatly from Warner Richmond's effective performance as the steely-eyed villain, Link Carson.

TRAIL'S END (Beaumont, 1935) 61 mins.

Producer, Mitchell Leichter; director, A. Herman; based on the story "Trail's End" by James Oliver Curwood; screenplay, Jack Jevne; camera, William Tuers; editor, William Austin.
Conway Tearle (Jim "Trigger" Malloy); Claudia Bell (Janet); Baby Charline Barry (Mary Jane); Fred Kohler (Wild Bill Holman); Ernie Adams (Lefty); Pat Harmon (Gimpy); Victor Potel (Red); Gaylord Steve Pendleton (Ed "Kid" Malloy); Stanley Blystone (Randall); Jack Duffy (Deke); Tom London, Hank Bell (Ranch Hands), Black King (The Horse).

During the 1920s, Conway Tearle had been one of the most popular leading men on the screen, usually specializing in sophisticated melodramas, although he did have a few rugged outings such as THE GREAT DIVIDE (1925) and SMOKE BELLEW (1929). He weathered the coming of sound, but his screen career thereafter was mostly confined to poverty row. In the mid-1930s he starred in four very low-grade Westerns for producer Mitchell Leichter, with release on a states rights basis through Beaumont Pictures. Although in his fifties, Tearle was still handsome and made more than an acceptable screen cowboy, even doing some of the rough stunts himself. Nevertheless, THE JUDGEMENT BOOK, SENIOR JIM, DESERT GUNS and TRAIL'S END are bottom-rung productions and it is sas to see an actor of Tearle's stature toiling in them.
TRAIL'S END was prophetic for Conway Tearle, since he died the year after its release. It has the star (Jim "Trigger" Mallooy) coming out of prison and gaining revenge on the man who sent him there. He drifts into a small town where the citizens are being harassed by toughs from a nearby ranch, and when he beats their leader, the townsfolk make him the sheriff. Tearle finds himself attracted to young widow Janet (Claudia Dell) and he is especially liked by her young daughter (Baby Charline Barry). All goes well until Jim's old gang shows up and their new leader (Fred Kohler) tries to force him to steal the local mine payroll which is stored in a safe in Janet's house. The sheriff saves the funds and brings in the outlaw.

THE TRAIN ROBBERS (Warner Bros., 1973) C 92 mins.

Producer, Michael Wayne; director/screenplay, Burt Kennedy;

Ben Johnson, John Wayne, Ann-Margret, and Rod Taylor in THE
TRAIN ROBBERS (1973).

music, Dominic Frontiere; art director, Ray Moyer; set decorator,
Alfred Sweeney; assistant director, Fred Simpson; camera, William
H. Clothier; editor, Frnak Santillo.
    John Wayne (Lane); Ann-Margret (Mrs. Lowe); Rod Taylor
(Grady); Ben Johnson (Jesse); Christopher George (Calhoun);
Bobby Vinton (Ben); Jerry Gatlin (Sam); Ricardo Montalban (Pin-
kerton Man).

    Pretty widow Mrs. Lowe (Ann-Margret) enlists the aid of
aging drifter Lane (John Wayne) in helping her find a half-million
dollars in gold which has been hidden in the desert by her late
husband. She wants the money in order to clear her name, and
the reward to help her raise her small child. Lane agrees to help
and calls on his pals Grady (Rod Taylor) and Jesse (Ben Johnson)
to assist. The former brings along Calhoun (Christopher George),
to whom Lane takes a dislike. The group looks for the gold but
they find themselves being trailed by an outlaw gang as well as by
a mysterious man (Ricardo Montalban). Arriving in a small, deserted town, they discover one old man who has been murdered by

the gang. Eventually they locate the gold, fight off the outlaws, and get away with the money, only to have Mrs. Lowe, who turns out not to have a child, steal it from them. Lane and his buddies trail the female con artist and recover the stolen riches.

While THE TRAIN ROBBERS has memorable moments, it is a disappointing film. John Wayne's role as Lane is not an uninteresting one, especially on his camaraderie with pals Rod Taylor and Ben Johnson and his growing to like and respect hothead Christopher George. Of course, the most intriguing character interaction is between John Wayne and Ann-Margret, with its May-September romance western style, and the Duke telling the young lovestruck woman he owns a saddle older than her. Overall, though, the movie is drab in its plot, except for the twist finale, and lacks the action usually associated with a John Wayne feature. As Allen Eyles assessed in John Wayne and the Movies (1976), "THE TRAIN ROBBERS is most disappointing for just using Wayne for what he stands for and not really making him work at a part."

THE TRAMPLERS (Embassy, 1966) C 105 mins.

Producer/director, Albert Band; based on the novel Guns of North Texas by Will Cook; screenplay, Band, Ugo Libertore; assistant directors, Franco Prosperi, Francois Dupont-Midy; camera, Alvaro Mancori; editor, Maurizio Lucidi.

Joseph Cotten (Temple Cordeen); Gordon Scott (Lon Cordeen); James Mitchum (Hoby Cordeen); Ilaria Occhini (Edith Wickett); Franco Nero (Charley Garvey); Emma Vannoni (Bess Cordeen); Georges Lycan (Longfellow Wiley); Muriel Franklin (Alice Cordeen); Aldo Cecconi (Jim Hennessy); Franco Balducci (Pete Wiley); Claudio Gora (Fred Wickett); Romano Puppo (Paine Cordeen); Dario Michaelis (Bert Cordeen); Ivan Scratuglia (Adrian Cordeen); Carla Calo (Mrs. Temple Cordeen); Dino Desmond (Sheriff); Silla Bettina (Hogan); Edith Peters (Emma).

Filmed in Italy and Spain as GLI UOMINI DAL PASSO PE-SANTE, this European co-production boasts an international cast, good direction, and plenty of action, but it is weighted down by a convoluted plot. Joseph Cotten is especially impressive in the pivotal role and the film proved to be one of the better Spaghetti Westerns of the period.

After the Civil War ends, Texas rancher and Confederate General Temple Cordeen (Joseph Cotten) will not accept the defeat of the South and plans to continue the conflict. The patriarch puts together his own army to keep Northerners out of his cattle lands, but two of his sons, Lon (Gordon Scott) and Hoby (Jim Mitchum), do not agree with their father and aid their sister Bess (Emma Vannoni) in eloping with rival rancher Charley Garvey (Franco Nero). Cordeen's wife (Carla Calo) dies from the stress of her husband's vigilante actions, which include the hanging of a Northerner whose daughter, Edith Wickett (Ilaria Occhini), is loved by Lon. Eventually

With hate blinding their hearts—and guns blazing at their hips—father and son face each other in a bold, bitter battle to the end...!

JOSEPH COTTEN
GORDON SCOTT
JAMES MITCHUM in

THE TRAMPLERS

WITH
Ilaria Occhini · Frank Nero · Emil Jordan · Albert Band · Ugo Liberatore & Albert Band
PRODUCED AND DIRECTED BY   SCREENPLAY BY

Based on the novel "Guns of North Texas" by WILL COOK · Prints by PATHE · An Embassy Pictures Release   IN COLOR

Advertisement for THE TRAMPLERS (1966).

three sons loyal to Temple shoot it out with Hoby and all four are killed. The deed pushes Cordeen to madness and the fighting ends. Lon and Edith return Cordeen to the family ranch and the two lovers plan a life together.

THE TREASURE OF SILVER LAKE (Rialto/Jadran Film, 1963) C 102 mins.

Director, Dr. Harald Reinl; based on the novel Der Schatz im Silbersee by Karl May; screenplay, Harald G. Petersson; music, Martin Boettcher; camera, Ernst Kalinke; editor, Hermann Haller.
Lex Barker (Old Shatterhand); Gotz George (Fred Engel);

Herbert Lom (Cornel Brinkley); Karin Dor (Ellen Patterson); Eddi
Arent (Castlepool); Marianne Hoppe (Mrs. Butler); Pierre Brice
(Winnetou); Jan Sid (Patterson); Ralf Wolter (Sam Hawkins); Mirko
Bauman (Gunstick Uncle).

In 1962 the West German feature DER SCHATZ IM SILBERSEE
was released; it was the first of fourteen films to be based on the
works of popular author Karl May. The movie's success also
launched a whole series of European Westerns, including the
Spaghetti Western craze from Italy. Well-mounted and with an international cast headed by Lex Barker as old Shatterhand, Pierre
Brice as Winnetou, and Britain's Herbert Lom as the chief villain,
the movie is an exciting entry and a fine vanguard for the Conti-
nental oaters that followed.
      When bandits attack a stagecoach and murder a passenger,
scout Old Shatterhand (Lex Barker) and his Indian blood brother
Winnetou (Pierre Brice) investigate and learn that the murdered man
was carrying one-half of a map, the other part belonging to settler
Fred Engel (Gotz George). The map shows the location of long-
hidden Indian gold which is being sought by outlaw gang leader
Cornel Brinkley (Herbert Lom). Obtaining the other half of the map,
Brinkley heads for the secreted gold, but is pursued by Old Shatterhand, Winnetou, Engel, and the latter's girlfriend, Ellen Patterson
(Karin Dor). Brinkley does find the treasure, but is caught in a
secret trap which results in his demise.
      Lex Barker and Pierre Brice played Old Shatterhand and
Winnetou respectively in eight feature films, the last being WINNETOU
UND SHATTERHAND IM TAL DER TOTEN [Winnetou and Shatterhand
in the Valley of Death] in 1968. In addition, Brice played Winnetou
in three films with Stewart Granger (as Old Surehand) and one with
Rod Cameron (as Old Firehand). Lex Barker made two other Karl
May features with Pierre Brice, who has also performed the part of
Winnetou on West German television and stage. Guy Madison starred
in still another Karl May feature, THE LEGACY OF THE INCAS
(1961).

THE TREASURE OF THE SIERRA MADRE see MacKENNA'S GOLD

THE TRIAL OF BILLY JACK see BILLY JACK

TRIBUTE TO A BAD MAN (Metro-Goldwyn-Mayer, 1956) C 95 mins.

      Producer, Sam Zimbalist; director, Robert Wise; based on the
short story by Jack Schaeffer; screenplay, Michael Blankfort; art
directors, Cedric Gibbons, Paul Broesse; set decorators, Edwin B.
Willis, Fred Maclean; music, Miklos Rozsa; costumes, Walter Plunkett;
assistant director, Arvid Griffin; makeup, William Tuttle; color consultant, Charles K. Hagedon; sound, Dr. Wesley G. Miller; camera,

Irene Papas and James Cagney in TRIBUTE TO A BAD MAN (1956).

Robert Surtees; editor, Ralph E. Winters.
    James Cagney (Jeremy Rudock); Don Dubbins (Steve Miller);
Stephen McNally (McNulty); Irene Papas (Jocasta Constantine); Vic
Morrow (Lars Peterson); James Griffith (Barjak); Onslow Stevens
(Hearn); James Bell (L. A. Peterson); Jeanette Nolan (Mrs. L. A.
Peterson); Chubby Johnson (Baldy); Royal Dano (Abe); Lee Van
Cleef (Fat Jones); Peter Chong (Cooky); James McCallion (Shorty);
Clint Sharp (Red); Tony Hughes, Roy Engel (Buyers); Carl Pitti
(Tom); Bud Osborne, John Halloran, Tom London, Dennis Moore,
Buddy Roosevelt, Billy Dix (Cowboys).

    TRIBUTE TO A BAD MAN, filmed on location in Colorado, is
a Western which seems to grow in stature as the years pass, mainly
because of James Cagney's strong performance as a hateful land
baron and for its realistic portrayal of life on the frontier. When
first released, Variety complained it was "somewhat spotty in entertainment impact," while the New York Times wrote that it was "A
Western drama that is all James Cagney," but also noted, "The story
sags now and then...."
    Eastern lad Steve Miller (Don Dubbins) comes West looking for
adventure and happens on the spread owned by Jeremy Rodock
(James Cagney). He aids the land baron in a showdown with rustlers
and the older man befriends him and takes him to his ranch. There
he meets the old man's young Greek mistress, Jocasta (Irene Papas).

Staying on the spread, he learns that Rodock's word is law on his vast range and that the penalty for going against it is the end of a rope. Tired of the older man's overbearing attitude, the young woman initiates a romance with Steve, but eventually Rodock sees the error of his ways. After thwarting a rebellion against him among his own men, he reaffirms his relationship with Jocasta. Steve leaves the ranch.

The film was originally scheduled for M-G-M contract star Spencer Tracy.

TRIGGER TRICKERS see CLEARING THE RANGE

TRIUMPHS OF A MAN CALLED HORSE (Jensen Farley, 1984) C 86 mins.

Executive producer, Sandy Howard; producer, Derek Gibsson; associate producer, Donald R. Borchers; director, John Hough; based on the story by Jack DeWitt and a character created by Dorothy M. Johnson; screenplay, Ken Blackwell, Carlos Aured; music, George Garvarentz; assistant director, Kuki Lopez; production designer, Alan Roderick-Jones; art director, Marilyn Taylor; sound, Manuel Rincon; camera, Joel Alcott, John Cabrera; editor, Roy Watts.

Richard Harris (Man Called Horse); Michael Beck (Koda); Anna DeSade (Redwing); Vaughn Armstrong (Captain Cummings); Anne Seymour (Elk Woman); Buck Taylor (Sergeant Bridges); Simon Andreu (Gance); Lautaro Murua (Perkins); Roger Cudney (Durand); Jerry Gatlin (Winslow); John Davis Chandler (Mason); Miguel Angel Fuentes (Big Bear).

See A MAN CALLED HORSE.

TUCSON RAIDERS (Republic, 1944) 55 mins.

Associate producer, Edward White; director, Spencer G. Bennet; based on the comic strip by Fred Harman; story, Jack O'Donnell; screenplay, Anthony Coldeway; art director, Gano Chittenden; set decorator, Otto Siegel; music, Joseph Dubin; assistant director, Harry Knight; sound, Thomas Carman; camera, Reggie Lanning; editor, Harry Keller.

Wild Bill Elliott (Red Ryder); George "Gabby" Hayes (Gabby); Bobby Blake (Little Beaver); Alice Fleming (Duchess); LeRoy Mason (Banker); Stanley Andrews (Governor); and Ruth Lee, Peggy Stewart, John Whitney, Bud Geary, Karl Hackett, Tom Steele, Tom Chatterton, Edward Cassidy, Edward Howard, Fred Graham, Frank McCarroll, Marshall Reed, Stanley Andrews, Frank Pershing, and the voices of Roy Barcroft, Kenne Duncan, Tom London, Jack Kirk.

Don "Red" Barry had the title role in the popular cliffhanger THE ADVENTURES OF RED RYDER (see B/V) in 1940 and four years

later Republic brought back Fred Harmon's comic strip character in
the guise of Bill Elliott. Elliott played the part for two seasons before branching out into "A" features, and was succeeded by Allan
"Rocky" Lane. TUCSON RAIDERS, Elliott's initial series entry, was
an actionful episode hindered by a mediocre plot-line.

Slickly directed by veteran Spencer Gordon Bennet, Anthony
Coldeway's mundane plot has a crooked banker (LeRoy Mason) in
cahoots with a dishonest governor (Stanley Andrews) to control the
territory, but Red Ryder (Bill Elliott) and his pals Gabby (George
"Gabby" Hayes), Little Beaver (Bobby Blake) and The Duchess
(Alice Fleming) stop them after the duo falsely accuses Red of murder.

Don Miller wrote in Hollywood Corral (1976) that TUCSON
RAIDERS "started the Ryder series in okay fashion," and added,
"Elliott didn't particularly fit one's conception of Ryder, being a mite
too sophisticated and austere in his portrayal, but he made the
character over in his own image and nothing was lost. Young Blake
was a fine Little Beaver, a child actor who wasn't obnoxious and
could lend his talents to the comedy sequences."

TUMBLING TUMBLEWEEDS see GUNS AND GUITARS

TWILIGHT IN THE SIERRAS (Republic, 1950) C 67 mins.

Associate producer, Edward J. White; director, William Witney;
screenplay, Sloan Nibley; songs, Sid Robin, Foy Willing; music/music
director, Stanley Wilson; art director, Frank Redd; assistant director,
Jack Lacey; makeup, Steve Drumm; camera, John MacBurnie; editor,
Tony Martinelli.

Roy Rogers (Himself); Trigger (The Horse); Dale Evans (Pat
Callahan); Estelita Rodriguez (Lola Chavez); Pat Brady (Sparrow
Biffle); Russ Vincent (Ricardo Chavez); George Meeker (Matt Brun-
ner); Fred Kohler, Jr. (Mason); Edward Keane (Judge Wiggins);
House Peters, Jr. (Williams); Pierce Lyden (Blake); Don Frost (Bar-
tender); Joseph A. Garro (Henchman); William Lester (Paul Clifford);
Foy Willing and the Riders of the Purple Sage (Themselves); and
Bob Burns, Bob Wilke.

Toward the end of his feature film series career, Roy Rogers
reverted to the type of action motion pictures which launched him as
a cowboy hero. While his early films contained some music, they
were mostly straight cowboys-versus-bad men affairs, and this plot
format was reinstigated when William Witney took over as Rogers'
series director in 1946. By the time TWILIGHT IN THE SIERRAS
came along in 1950 the series was back to a bit of music, but the
films were mostly still action.

On a sheep ranch which employs parolees, parole officer Roy
Rogers (Himself) gets involved with crooks who are making counterfeit gold certificates. Roy is falsely accused of murdering one of the

gang members and is arrested, but he is placed on parole. He uncovers the gang's crooked scheme and also captures the killer.

TWO-GUN SHERIFF (Republic, 1941) 56 mins.

    Associate producer/director, George Sherman; story, Bennett
Cohen; screenplay, Cohen, Doris Schroeder; music, Cy Feuer;
camera, William Nobles; editor, Tony Martinelli.
    Don "Red" Barry (The Sundown Kid/Bruce McKinnon); Lynn
Merrick (Ruth); Jay Novello (Albo); Lupita Tovar (Nita); Milton
Kibbee (Jones); Fred Kohler, Jr. (Keller); Marin Sais (Mrs. McKin-
non); Fred Toones (Snowflake); Dirk Thane (Duke); Archie Hall
(Dunn); Charles Bob Thomas (Tex); Lee Shunway (Sheriff Blake);
and John Merton, Carleton Young, Curley Dresden, Bud McClure,
Buck Moulton, Tex Parker, Herman Nolan, George Plues.

    Having played the lead in the serial THE ADVENTURES OF RED
RYDER (1940), Donald Barry was billed as Don "Red" Barry and
given the lead in a series of Republic Westerns produced and directed
by George Sherman. With Barry's fine thespian abilities and Sherman's strong production and direction savvy, plus the usual Republic
entertainment gloss, the series proved quite successful and lasted
from 1940 to 1945, when the star graduated to non-Western programmers. In the late 1940s Barry returned to Westerns for a Lippert
series and then developed into a topnotch character player.
    In TWO-GUN SHERIFF, Don Barry is The Sundown Kid, who is
turned over to the law by Spanish dancer Nita (Lupita Tovar). He
is rescued, however, by an outlaw gang who take him to their hideout, and their chief (Jay Novello) convinces him to masquerade as
his look-alike, the local sheriff, whom they kidnap. Now the gang
can get their stolen cattle to market without hindrance from the law.
Unknown to both the sheriff and the Kid, the two men are long lost
brothers. Nita arrives in town and spots the Kid, and the chief
kills her to keep her silent. Upset by Nita's murder, the Kid double-
crosses the gang and rescues his brother, and together they stop
the shipment of stolen cattle. When the chief tries to escape, the
Kid prevents him, but is gunned down by henchman Tex (Fred
Kohler, Jr.), who in turn is killed by the sheriff. At the finale,
the sheriff weds his sweetheart Ruth (Lynn Merrick).
    Offering a complicated plot, plenty of action and a rousing
music score by Cy Feuer, TWO-GUN SHERIFF is a fine example of
the superior series Don Barry turned out for Republic in the early
1940s.

TWO RODE TOGETHER (Columbia, 1961) C 108 mins.

    Producer, Stan Sheptner; director, John Ford; based on the
novel Comanche Captives by Will Cook; screenplay, Frank Nugent;
art director, Robert Peterson; set decorator, James M. Crown; music,

Advertisement for TWO RODE TOGETHER (1961).

George Duning; orchestrator, Arthur Morton; makeup, Ben Lane; assistant director, Wingate Smith; sound, Charles J. Rice, Harry Mills; camera, Charles Lawton, Jr.; editor, Jack Murray.

James Stewart (Guthrie McCabe); Richard Widmark (Lieutenant Jim Gary); Shirley Jones (Marty Purcell); Linda Cristal (Elena); Andy Devine (Sergeant Darius P. Posey); John McIntire (Major Frazer); Paul Birch (Edward Purcell); Willis Bouchey (Mr. Wringle); Henry Brandon (Quanah); Harry Carey, Jr. (Jackson Clay); Olive Carey (Abby Frazer); Ken Curtis (Boone Clay); Chet Douglas (Ward Corbey); Annelle Hayes (Belle Aragon); David Kent (Running Wolf); Anna Lee (Mrs. Malaprop); Jeanette Nolan (Mrs. McCandless); John Qualen (Ole Kundsen); Ford Rainey (Henry Clay); Woody Strode (Stone Calf); O. Z. Whitehead (Officer); Cliff Lyons (William McCandless); Mae Marsh (Hannah Clay); Frank Baker (Captain Malaprop); Ted Knight (Lieutenant Chase); Major Sam Harris (Post Doctor); Jack Pennick (Sergeant); Bill Henry (Gambler); Bob Kenneally, Ed Sweeney (Officers); Big John Hamilton Settler).

Director John Ford said he did not like the story for this film and that he directed it only as a favor to Columbia boss Harry Cohn. The movie is one of the least discussed of Ford's Westerns, even from the 1960s, but it is generally a very satisfying production. The

New York Times judged it "...an unorthodox Western of uncommon
honesty and persuasion. The story is strong and ugly.... Frank
Nugent's scenario spares little anguish, told in direct, uncompromis-
ing terms." Like all John Ford motion pictures, the movie is blessed
with delightful character performances, the best being silent film star
Mae Marsh's as the white woman, long ago captured by the Indians,
who explains why she does not want to return to her people.

In the 1880s, hard-drinking Texas lawman Guthrie McCabe
(James Stewart) agrees to aid cavalry Lieutenant Jim Gary (Richard
Widmark) in rescuing whites takes prisoner by Comanche Indians.
Their first success comes when they get custody of Running Wolf
(David Kent), a young white boy, in return for two rifles. They
also obtain the release of Elena (Linda Cristal), a young Mexican
girl who was forced to be the squaw of warrior Stone Calf (Woody
Strode). The latter tries to recapture her, but is killed by McCabe.
They return to the fort, but no one there claims Running Wolf until
the mad Mrs. McCandlesss (Jeanette Nolan) says he is her son.
When she frees him, the boy murders her. The people in the fort
hang the boy and it is then discovered that he is the brother of
Marty Purcell (Shirley Jones). Gary's girlfriend. Elena, because
she has been an Indian's squaw, is snubbed at the fort, and McCabe
learns that he has lost his job. McCabe and Elena leave the fort,
hoping for a better future together.

UNCONQUERED (Paramount, 1947) C 146 mins.

Producer/director, Cecil B. DeMille; based on the novel by
Neil H. Swanson; screenplay, Charles Bennett, Frederic M. Frank,
Jesse Lasky, Jr.; art directors, Hans Dreier, Walter Tyler; set
decorators, Sam Comer, Stanley Jay Sawley; assistant director,
Edward Salven; second unit director, Arthur Rosson; costumes, Gwen
Wakeling, Mme. Barbara Karinska; makeup, Wally Westmore; technical
supervisors, Captain Fred F. Ellis, Iron Eyes Cody; Technicolor con-
sultants, Natalie Kalmus, Robert Brower; music, Victor Young; song,
Ray Evans and Jay Livingston; choreography, Jack Crosby; sound,
Hugo Grenzbach, John Cope; special camera effects, Gordon Jen-
nings, Farciot Edouart, W. Wallace Kelley, Paul Lerpae, Devereux
Jennings; camera, Ray Rannahan; editor, Anne Bauchens.

Gary Cooper (Captain Christopher Holden); Paulette Goddard
(Abigail Martha Hale); Howard Da Silva (Martin Garth); Boris Karloff
(Guyasuta, the Chief of the Senecas); Cecil Kellaway (Jeremy Love);
Ward Bond (John Fraser); Katherine DeMille (Hannah); Henry Wil-
coxon (Captain Steele); Sir C. Aubrey Smith (Lord Chief Justice);
Victor Varconi (Captain Simeon Ecuyer); Virginia Grey (Diana);
Porter Hall (Leach); Mike Mazurki (Dave Bone); Robert Warwick
(Pontiac, the Chief of the Ottawas); Richard Gaines (Colonel George
Washington); Virginia Campbell (Mrs. Fraser); Gavin Muir (Lieutenant
Fergus McKenzie); Alan Napier (Sir William Johnson); Nan Sutherland
(Mrs. Pruitt); Marc Lawrence (Sioto); Jane Nigh (Evelyn); Griff
Barnett (Brother Andrews); John Mylong (Colonel Henry Bouquet);

Lloyd Bridges (Lieutenant Hutchins); Oliver Thorndike (Lieutenant Baillie); Jack Pennick (Jim Lovat); Paul E. Burns (Dan McCoy); Davison Clark (Mr. Carroll); Dorothy Adams (Mrs. Bront); Clarence Muse (Jason); Raymond Hatton (Venango Scout); Julia Faye (The Widow Swivens); Chief Thundercloud (Chief Killbuck); Charles B. Middleton (Mulligan); Tiny Jones (Bondswoman); Fred Kohler, Jr. (Sergeant); Jeff York (Wide-Shouldered Youth); Dick Alexander (Slave); Syd Saylor (Spieler for Dr. Diablo); Si Jenks (Farmer); Noble Johnson (Big Ottowa Indian); Buddy Roosevelt (Guard); Lex Barker (Royal American Officer); Byron Foulger (Townsman); Jay Silverheels (Indian); John Miljan (Prosecutor); Denver Dixon (Citizen).

In 1763 poor English girl Abby Hale (Paulette Goddard) is sentenced by the courts to serve fourteen years as a bond servant and then is sent to the American colonies. On the ship taking her to her destination she meets Christopher Holden (Gary Cooper), a Virginia militiaman, but she also draws the attention of Martin Garth (Howard Da Silva), a dishonest trader. When Abby refuses Garth's attentions, he orders her sold and Holden buys her and sets the girl free. At Fort Pitt on the frontier, Garth sets up a plan to sell rifles to the Seneca Indians, who want them in order to rid the area of incoming settlers. To become part of the tribe's war council, Garth marries the chief's (Boris Karloff) daughter Hannah (Katherine De Mille), but he still yens for Abby, who has also come to the fort. Arriving there too is Holden's fiancée (Virginia Grey), who tells him she loves another. Meanwhile Garth convinces Abby that Holden's purchase of her was a jest, since Garth has stolen her indenture papers. Holden finds this out and rescues the girl from a tavern run by Bone (Mike Mazurki), Garth's henchman. When Abby attends the King's Ball at Fort Pitt with Holden, Garth holds her up to ridicule by proving she was a bond servant. News arrives that the Senecas have wiped out a small settlement and when the men go to fight the Indians, jealous Hannah has Abby kidnapped and taken to the Indian camp. Holden, however, rescues her and back at the fort, kills Garth as the Indians are defeated. Realizing they are in love, Holden and Abby plan to wed.

Producer/director Cecil B. DeMille again turned to American history for this $5,000,000 tale of love and adventure during the French and Indian War. Reuniting Gary Cooper and Paulette Goddard from NORTH WEST MOUNTED POLICE (1940) (see B/V), this beautifully photographed (by Ray Rennahan) film well conveyed the look and flavor of the 1760s frontier, and this is its chief asset, along with a superb cast and several exciting action sequences. Most memorable is the section where Cooper and Goddard trek through the treacherous wilderness following his rescue of her from the Indian camp. Although running a long 146 minutes, the movie never falters and provides a solid history lesson as well.

THE UNDEFEATED (Twentieth Century-Fox, 1969) C 118 mins.

John Wayne and Rock Hudson in THE UNDEFEATED (1969).

Producer, Robert L. Jacks; director, Andrew V. McLaglen; story, Stanley L. Hough; screenplay, James Lee Barrett; art director, Carl Anderson; set decorators, Walter M. Scott, Chester L. Bayhi; stunt supervisor, Hal Needham; music/music director, Hugo Montenegro; costumes, Bill Thomas; assistant director, Jack Cunningham; sound, Richard Overton, David Dockendorf; camera, William Clothier; editor, Robert Simpson.

John Wayne (Colonel John Henry Thomas); Rock Hudson (Colonel James Langdon); Tony Aguilar (General Rojas); Roman Gabriel (Blue Boy); Marian McCargo (Ann Langdon); Lee Meriwether (Margaret Langdon); Merlin Olsen (Big George); Melissa Newman (Charlotte Langdon); Bruce Cabot (Jeff Newby); Michael Vincent (Bubba Wilkes); Ben Johnson (Short Grub); Edward Faulkner (Anderson); Harry Carey, Jr. (Webster); Paul Fix (General Joe Masters); Royal Dano (Major Sanders); Richard Mulligan (Dan Norse); Carlos Rivas (Diaz); John Agar (Christian); Guy Raymond (Giles); Don Collier (Goodyear); Big John Hamilton (Mudlow); Dub Taylor (McCartney); Henry Beckman (Thad Benedict); Victor Junco (Major Tapia); Robert Donner (Judd Mailer); Rudy Diaz (Sanchez); Pedro Armendariz, Jr. (Escalante); Gregg Palmer (Parker); Kiel Martin (Union Runner); Bob Gravage (Joe Hicks).

At the end of the Civil War, Yankee Colonel John Henry
Thomas (John Wayne) leads his men in an attack on a Southern position, but just as victory is apparent, word arrives that the War is
over. Thomas resigns from the service and with his adopted Indian
son, bugler Blue Boy (Roman Gabriel) and ten of his loyal followers,
heads West to secure wild horses for the army. At the same time,
in Louisiana, Confederate Colonel James Langdon (Rock Hudson) takes
a wife (Lee Meriwether), daughter (Melissa Newman), and widowed
sister-in-law (Marian McCargo), along with about one hundred other
men, women, and children, and heads for Mexico rather than live in
a defeated land. The group evades federal troops and gets into
Mexico. There they encounter Thomas and his men, who have
rounded up a horse herd, only to find that the buyers were crooks
and have now agreed to take the herd to Durango to sell to Emperor
Maximillian's forces. When a Mexican bandit (Pedro Armendariz, Jr.)
and his gang threaten the Southern settlers, Thomas and his men
come to their rescue; the result is in an uneasy alliance between the
two one-time enemies. Langdon and his party go to Durango and
are made prisoners of General Rojas (Antonio Aguilar), an ally of
Juarez, and he threatens to kill the Confederates unless Thomas
turns the herd over to him. Thomas's men agree to this, but the
French arrive with an army to stop them and the Yankees use the
herd as a battering ram, break through the government lines, and
get the herd to Durango. The Southerners are set free and join
Thomas's contingent in a search for new homes.

Coming right after John Wayne's Academy Award performance
in TRUE GRIT (1968) (see B/V), THE UNDEFEATED benefitted at
the box-office (it grossed $4,000,000 in domestic rentals) as a result.
Otherwise the movie is not one of Wayne's best, although it does
have exciting sequences and an excellent supporting cast, topped by
one-time "B" Western comedy sidekick Dub Taylor as Thomas's can-
tankerous cook. At nearly two hours, the film is just too long and
rambling. It is certainly one of John Wayne's lesser cinematic efforts.

UNDER WESTERN STARS (Republic, 1938) 65 mins.

Producer, Sol C. Siegel; director, Joseph Kane; story, Dorrell
and Stuart McGowan; screenplay, the McGowans, Betty Burbridge;
songs: Jack Lawrence, Peter Tinturin; Charles Rosoff; Johnny
Marvin, Eddie Cherkose; camera, Jack Marta.

Roy Rogers (Himself); Trigger (The Horse); Smiley Burnette
(Frog Milhouse); Carol Hughes (Eleanor); The Maple City Four (Them-
selves); Guy Usher (Fairbanks); Tom Chatterton (Marlowe); Kenneth
Harlan (Richards); Alden Chase (Andrews); Brandon Beach (Senator
Wilson); Earle Dwire (Mayor Biggs); Jean Fowler (Mrs. Wislon);
Dora Clemant (Mrs. Marlowe); Dick Elliott (Scully); Burr Caruth
(Larkin); Charles "Slim" Whittaker (Tremaine); Jack Rockwell
(Sheriff); Frankie Marvin (Deputy Pete); and Tex Cooper, Bill
Wolfe.

Leonard Slye had attained some measure of success as a member of the singing group The Sons of the Pioneers, who had become popular on radio and recordings and had appeared in several movies, including "B" Westerns. With his name changed to Dick Weston he appeared in a few features at Republic. In 1938 that studio's biggest box-office draw, Gene Autry, departed over a contract dispute, and Leonard Slye was redubbed Roy Rogers and assigned to star in a production intended for Autry, UNDER WESTERN STARS. The movie successfully launched Roy Rogers' film career and later, dubbed "The King of the Cowboys," he became the genre's top star after Autry entered World War II service.

When released, UNDER WESTERN STARS was a topical film, dealing with farm lands plagued by dust storms resulting from drought and poor cultivation methods. Roy Rogers (Himself) is drafted into running for Congress in opposition to the incumbent (John Elliott), who is the pawn of a large water company which overcharges ranchers for the water they must purchase in their drought-stricken locale. Rogers is elected and gains the support of fellow congressmen to pass a water bill. Prosperity returns to the farm area.

Handsomely mounted and well-written, UNDER WESTERN STARS has Smiley Burnette as Roy Rogers' sidekick (as he had been to Gene Autry), but he has little to do herein. Besides singing "That Pioneer Mother of Mine," Roy Rogers also performs the Academy Award-nominated ballad "Dust," which was written by one-time singing idol Johnny Marvin. This song is particularly effective as Roy sings it while films are shown of the drought-engulfed areas he is seeking to help.

UNEXPECTED GUEST see HOPPY'S HOLIDAY

UNKNOWN VALLEY (Columbia, 1934) 64 mins.

Director; Lambert Hillyer; story, Donald Lee; /screenplay, Hillyer; camera, Al Sielger; editor, Clarence Kolster.
Buck Jones (Joe Gordon); Cecilia Parker (Sheila); Carlotta Warrick (Mary James); Arthur Wanzer (Tim); Wade Boteler (Elder Crossett); Frank McGlynn (Debbs); Charles Thurston (Younger); Ward Bond (Snead); Steve Gaylord Pendleton (Bennson); Silver (The Horse); and Alf James.

One-time Army scout Joe Gordon (Buck Jones) discovers that his father is missing in the desert and sets out to find him. Eventually he runs out of water and begins seeing mirages of water holes. He finally collapses but is found by attractive Sheila (Cecilia Parker), a member of a religious sect which has come to the wasteland to get away from society. She nurses Joe back to health and the two fall in love. Then he learns the girl is supposed to marry an older man in the congregation. The elders suspect Joe of trying to aid the

girl and her brother in their desire to leave the group. Joe finds
that his father is a prisoner of the sect and is being forced to mine
gold for them. Joe helps his father, along with Sheila and her
brother, to escape from their captors.

In some respects, UNKNOWN VALLEY is reminiscent of the type
of austere Westerns William S. Hart made in the silent years, yet this
is a topical film, since it deals with a secretive religious sect. Well
directed by Lambert Hillyer, with a low-key performance from Buck
Jones and pleasant support from comely Cecilia Parker, the movie is
much more of a melodrama in a Western setting than a "B" actioner.

UTAH (Republic, 1945) 78 mins.

Producer, Donald H. Brown; director, John English; story,
Gilbert Wright, Betty Burbridge; screenplay, Jack Townley, John K.
Butler; music, Morton Scott; choreography, Larry Ceballos; songs:
Ken Carson; Dave Franklin; Bob Nolan; Bob Palmer; Tim Spencer;
Glenn Spencer; Charles Henderson; art director, Gano Chittenden;
set decorator, Otto Siegel; assistant director, George Webster; sound,
Thomas A. Carman; camera, William Bradford; editor, Harry Keller.

Roy Rogers (Himself); Trigger (The Horse); George "Gabby"
Hayes (Gabby Whittaker); Dale Evans (Dorothy Bryant); Peggy
Stewart (Jackie); Beverly Lloyd (Wanda); Grant Withers (Ben Bow-
man); Jill Browning (Babe); Vivien Oakland (Stella Mason); Hal
Taliaferro (Steve Lacey); Jack Rutherford (Sheriff MacBride); Em-
mett Vogan (District Attorney); Bob Nolan and the Sons of the
Pioneers (Themselves); and Edward Cassidy, Ralph Colby.

Out of work, Dorothy Bryant (Dale Evans) and her show girl
pals (Peggy Stewart, Beverly Lloyd, Jill Browning) come to her Utah
ranch, which she plans to sell to raise funds to produce a musical
show. Cowboy Roy Rogers (Himself) and foreman Gabby Whittaker
(George "Gabby" Hayes) try to dissuade her from selling the spread,
because they do not want sheepmen controlling the range. Crook
Ben Bowman (Grant Withers), however, buys the ranch and Roy and
Gabby go to jail for trying to impede the sale. They escape and go
to Chicago to regain control of Dorothy's cattle by capturing Bowman
and his henchman (Hal Taliaferro). Dorothy, thanks to the sale of
the cattle, now has sufficient funds to save her ranch and, to celebrate, she puts on a musical show.

Another of the Roy Rogers' films which is more of a musical
than a Western, UTAH does sport a gripping plot and is actionful
due to serial ace John English's speedy direction. The dull production number finale is a detriment to the film's overall effect.

UTAH TRAIL see ROLLIN' PLAINS'

VALDEZ IS COMING (United Artists, 1971) C 90 mins.

Burt Lancaster in VALDEZ IS COMING (1971).

Executive producer, Roland Kibbee; producer, Ira Steiner; associate producer, Sam Manners; director, Edwin Sherin; based on the novel by Elmore Leonard; screenplay, Kibbee, David Rayfiel; music, Charles Gross; art director, Jose Maria Tapiador; set decorator, Rafael Salazar; costumes, Louis Brown; makeup, Mariano Garcia Rey, Alberto Comenar; assistant director, Tony Ray; sound, Bud Alper; special effects, Chuck Gaspar, Linc Kibbee; camera, Gabor Pogany; editor, James T. Heckart.

Burt Lancaster (Bob Valdez); Susan Clark (Gay Erin); Jon Cypher (Frank Tanner); Barton Jeyman (El Segundo); Richard Jordan (R. L. Davis); Frank Silvera (Diego); Hector Elizondo (Mexican Rider); Phil Brown (Malson); Lex Monson (Rincon the Fugitive); Juanita Penaloza (Apache Woman); Roberta Haynes (Polly); Maria Montez (Anita); Marta Tuck (Rosa); Jose Garcia (Carlos); James Lemp (Bony Man); Werner Hasselman (Sheriff); Concha Hombria (Inez); Per Barclay (Bartender); Vic Albert, Allan Russell (Ranchers); Michael Hinn (Merchant); Rudy Ugland, Joaquin Parra (Trackers); Santiago Santos, Losardo Iglesias (Riders); Joan Fernandez (Mexican Buyer); Tony Eppers (Bodyguard); Mario Barros,

Raul Castro, Nick Cravat, Santiago Garcia, Jeff Kibbee, Linc Kibbee, Ian MacLean, Tom McFadden, Jose Morales, Mario Sanz, Lee Thaxton, Robin Thaxton, Julian Vidrie, Manolin Vidrie (Gang Members); Sylvia Poggioli (Segundo's Girl).

The sad state of the Western film in the early 1970s is exemplified by this Hollywood-produced Spanish-filmed concoction which was heavy on murder and bad language but light on overall violence and likable characters. While the revenge motive dominates the plotline, the title character is not much more desirable than the villain he is after, and leading lady Susan Clark appears to have been thrown into the proceedings for feminine interest and little else. Variety correctly dubbed the feature "a sluggish meller" and opined, "Story collapses from premise of a man attempting to right a wrong, to reels of boring mayhem."

Southwest lawman Bob Valdez (Burt Lancaster) is on the trail of a fugitive (Lex Morson) accused of murdering a man. Valdez accidentally kills his quarry. Local rancher Tanner (Jon Cypher) has stolen Gay (Susan Clark), the wife of the man the fugitive was accused of murdering. When Valdez refuses to give $100 to the fugitive's pregnant widow (Juanita Penaloza), Tanner has him brutally beaten, and Valdez vows revenge. With the aid of pal Diego (Frank Silvera), Valdez gets on Tanner's trail and has to fight off his hired killers before finally getting even with the man and liberating the woman.

Surprisingly, VALDEZ IS COMING was quite popular in Great Britain, where audiences took to star Burt Lancaster's character donning his old army uniform and going on his revenge mission.

THE VALIANT HOMBRE see THE GAY AMIGO

THE VANISHING LEGION (Mascot, 1931) twelve chapters

Producer, Nat Levine; directors, B. Reeves Eason, Ford Beebe; screenplay, Wyndham Gittens, Ford Beebe, Helmer Bergman; camera, Benjamin Cline, Ernest Miller, Jo. J. Novak; editor, Ray Snyder.

Harry Carey (Cardigan); Edwina Booth (Caroline Hall); Rex (The Horse); Frankie Darro (Jimmie Williams); Philo McCullough (Stevens); William Desmond (Sheriff of Milesburg); Joe Bonomo (Stuffy); Edward Hearn (Jed Williams); Al Taylor (Sheriff of Slocum); Lafe McKee (Hornback); Dick Hatton (Dodger); Peter Morrison (Dopey); Dick Dickinson (Rawlins); Bob Kortman (Larno); Paul Weigel (Laribee); Frank Brownlee (Bishop); Yakima Canutt (Cowboy); Tom Dugan (Warren); Bob Walker (Allen); and Olive Fuller Golden.

Chapters: 1) The Voice from the Void; 2) The Queen of the Night Riders; 3) The Invisible Enemy; 4) The Fatal Message; 5) The Trackless Trail; 6) The Radio Riddle; 7) The Crimson Clue;

8) The Doorway of Disaster; 9) When Time Stood Still; 10) Riding the Whirlwind; 11) The Capsule of Oblivion; 12) The Hoofs of Horror.

As the silent era came to a close, Mascot Pictures began to compete with Universal and Pathé in the production of serials. With the coming of sound, Mascot continued to improve its product and market, and the studio's initial 1931 cliffhanger, THE VANISHING LEGION, proved to be popular and important. It introduced primitive science fiction plot ploys involving a mysterious masked figure called "The Voice." In addition, the film featured a triad hero combination--here a man, boy, and a horse--and for box-office bait there was the re-teaming of Harry Carey and Edwina Booth, the co-stars of the previous year's box-office blockbuster from M-G-M TRADER HORN. Shot in eighteen days with stock footage from films like THE DEVIL HORSE (1926) and THE GREAT K & A TRAIN ROBBERY (1927), this twelve-chapter production paved the way for the use of multi-heroes and master villains, and settings in the modern-day West. This cel-luloid format would continue in future Mascot cliffhangers and there-after when that studio joined others to become Republic Pictures, which produced some of the finest chapterplays of the sound era.

Chapter One of THE VANISHING LEGION was entitled "The Voice from the Void" and it begins the story of how a mysterious madman called "The Voice," who is never seen but who is heard giving orders by shortwave radio, tries to take over and destroy the Milesburg Oil Company. He has the head of the company, Jed Williams (Edward Hearn), framed on a murder charge. The accused man's son, Jimmie (Frankie Dorro), enlists the help of Cardigan (Harry Carey) as well as the horse Rex (Himself) in proving his father's innocence. Meanwhile, a group of mystery riders called The Vanishing Legion come to the aid of beautiful Caroline Hall (Edwina Booth), Williams' secretary and the rightful heir to the oil company. In a showdown with the Voice's gang, The Vanishing Legion defeats the villain's minions, saves its own leader (Philo McCul-lough), who has been captured by the Voice, and unmasks the bad man. The charges against Williams are proved false and Caroline takes her rightful property.

THE VIGILANTES ARE COMING (Republic, 1936) twelve chapters

Producer, Nat Levine; supervisor, J. Laurence Wickland; directors, Mack V. Wright, Ray Taylor; story, Maurice Geraghty, Winston Miller; screenplay, John Rathmell, Geraghty, Leslie Swa-backer; music, Harry Grey; camera, William Nobles, Edgar Lyons.

Bob Livingston (Don Loring); Kay Hughes (Doris); Guinn "Big Boy" Williams (Salvation); Raymond Hatton (Whipsaw); Fred Kohler (Jason Burr); Robert Warwick (Count Raspinoff); William Farnum (Father Jose); Bob Kortman (Petroff); John Merton (Talbot); Ray Corrigan (Captain John Fremont); Lloyd Ingraham (Colton); William Desmond (Anderson); Yakima Canutt (Barsoum); Tracy Layne Peters); Bud Pope (Ivan); Steve Clemente (Pedro); Bud Osborne

(Harris); John O'Brien (Robert Loring); Henry Hall (Señor Loring); Phillip Armenta (Dark Feather); Stanley Blystone (Kramer); Vinegar Roan (The Horse); and Jerome Ward, Al Taylor, Sam Garrett, Herman Jack, Jack Ingram, Jack Kirk, Jack Inney, Pascale Perry, Len Ward, Lloyd Saudners, Wally West, Frankie Marvin, Fred Burns, Joe De La Cruz.

Chapters: 1) The Eagle Strikes; 2) Birth of the Vigilantes; 3) Condemned by Cossacks; 4) Unholy Gold; 5) Treachery Unmasked; 6) A Tyrant's Trickery; 7) Wings of Doom; 8) A Treaty with Treason; 9) Arrow's Flight; 10) Prison of Flame; 11) A Race with Death; 12) Fremont Takes Command.

THE VIGILANTES ARE COMING was Republic's third serial and the first of all eighteen Western cliffhangers. Basically a remake of the 1925 Rudolph Valentino feature, THE EAGLE (which had its setting in Russia), this twelve-episode chapterplay proved to be popular, mainly due to its swift pace and fine casting. Robert Livingston, at the beginning of his Republic tenure, was the likable hero and Kay Hughes the pretty heroine, with sidekick comedy support from Guinn "Big Boy" Williams and Raymond Hatton. Fred Kohler and Robert Warwick were outstanding villains, silent star William Farnum was delightfully hammy as a Franciscan friar who aids the hero, and Ray Corrigan (soon to co-star with Livingston in "The Three Mesquiteers" series) was a stalwart Captain John Fremont. Still, the serial had a few deficits, as Edward Connor noted in his article "The First Eight Serials of Republics" in Screen Facts magazine (Number 7, 1964). Connor termed the film "somewhat slower than its two predecessors" (DARKEST AFRICA, 1935, and THE UNDERSEA KINGDOM, 1936) and added, "It also cheats mercilessly in getting hero Livingston out of his predicaments at the end of the chapter, and Harry Grey's musical score made frequent use of Beethoven's 'Egmont Overture' which is just not serial music."

Set in Old California in 1840, the cliffhanger has ruthless General Jason Burr (Fred Kohler) planning to take over the territory and make himself dictator. To do so, he needs the mines and lands of Loring (Henry Hall), and he enlists the aid of Cossack soldiers and Russian emissary Count Raspinoff (Robert Warwick). Burr has Loring and his son Robert (John O'Brien) murdered and confiscates their holdings. The murdered man's other son, Don Loring (Robert Livingston), who has been in the Northwest Territory fighting with Captain John Fremont (Ray Corrigan), returns home to find his family dead and his property gone. To fight Burr and his gang, Don wears a mask and a black robe and calls himself "The Eagle." He organizes the locals, along with pals Salvation (Guinn "Big Boy" Williams) and Whipsaw (Raymond Hatton), in opposing Burr's scheme. Fremont and his men join Loring in overcoming Burr.

VIGILANTES OF BOOMTOWN (Republic, 1947) 56 mins.

Producer, Sidney Picker; director, R. G. Springsteen; based

394 / THE VIGILANTES RIDE

on the comic strip "Red Ryder" by Fred Harman; screenplay, Earle
Snell; art director, Fred A. Ritter; set decorators, John McCarthy,
Jr., Bob Mark; music director, Mort Glickman; assistant director,
Eddie Stein; sound, Fred Stahl; camera, Alfred Keller; editor, Wil-
liam P. Thompson.

Allan "Rocky" Lane (Red Ryder); Bobby Blake (Little Beaver);
Martha Wentworth (The Duchess); Roscoe Karns (Delaney); Roy
Barcroft (McKean); Peggy Stewart (Molly McVey); George Turner
(Corbett); Eddie Lou Simms, Bobby Barber (Sparring Partners);
George Chesebro (Dink); George Lloyd (Thug); Ted Adams (Sheriff);
John Dehner (Bob Fitzsimmons); Earle Hodgins (Governor); Harlan
Briggs (Judge); Budd Buster (Goff); Jack O'Shea (Referee); Black
Jack (The Horse); and Tom Steele.

In Carson City, Nevada in 1897, factions oppose the sanction-
ing of the James J. Corbett-Bob Fitzsimmons heavyweight boxing
title fight. Red Ryder (Allan "Rocky" Lane) get into the fracas to
keep the peace, and outlaws decide to come to town to rob the
banks of the receipts. At the same time the fight opponents plan
to kidnap Corbett (George Turner); instead they get Red. Pretty
Molly James (Peggy Stewart) helps him to escape and he stops the
outlaws. The fight takes place, with Bob Fitzsimmons (John Dehner)
winning the bout.

This "Red Ryder" series entry is a bit different in that it
pivots around a famous boxing match, although the fight itself is
not actually presented; viewers only see the knockout of Corbett
by Fitzsimmons. In addition, the film presents Red Ryder as none
too level-headed at times, although he does acquire boxing skills
which he employs to defeat bad guy McKean (Roy Barcroft) at the
finale.

THE VIGILANTES RIDE (Columbia, 1944) 56 mins.

Producer, Leon Barsha; director, William Berke; story/screen-
play, Ed Earl Repp; assistant director, William O'Connor; art director, Lionel Banks; set decorator, Frank Tuttle; sound, Edward
Bernds; camera, Benjamin Kline; editor, Jerome Thomas.

Russell Hayden (Lucky Saunders); Dub Taylor (Cannonball);
Shirley Patterson (Jane Andrews); Jack Rockwell (Captain Randall);
Tristram Coffin (Anse Rankin); Bob Kortman (Drag); Dick Botiller
(Rogan); Jack Kirk (Lafe Andrews); Stanley Brown (Rod Saunders);
Blackie Whiteford (Hench); Bob (John) Cason (Henchman); Bob
Wills (Bob Allen); The Texas Playboys (Musicians).

Much to the puzzlement of his pals Bob Allen (Bob Wills),
Cannonball (Dub Taylor), and the Texas Playboys (Themselves),
Texas Ranger Lucky Saunders (Russell Hayden) leaves the service
when his younger brother Rod (Stanley Brown) is murdered. Lucky
goes to the wrong side of the law and robs a bank, but also romances
a rancher's daughter (Shirley Patterson). Eventually he joins with
the gang which killed his brother. The outfit is led by supposedly

Olin Howland in WAGON WHEELS (1934).

respectable citizen Anse Rankin (Tristram Coffin) and his henchman Drag (Bob Kortman). It turns out that Lucky's activities have been a ruse to bring the murderer to justice, and with the assist of his pals, he accomplished his mission.

Having come to genre stardom as Lucky Jenkins in the "Hopalong Cassidy" series, Russell Hayden headlined in a group of pictures for Columbia, with musical interludes by Bob Wills and His Texas Playboys and comedy relief by Dub Taylor as Cannonball. Variety said, "The formula plot has been well put together in the story and screenplay by Ed Earl Hepp to furnish plenty of action and a number of suspenseful moments as directed by (William) Berke."

The film's plot-line, however, is somewhat similar to the previous year's entry, RIDERS OF THE NORTHWEST MOUNTED, except that that film had a Canadian setting and Hayden was a Mountie who leaves the force to gain needed evidence against a fur theft gang led by trading post operator Dick Curtis.

WAGON WHEELS (Paramount, 1934) 56 mins.

Director, George Barton; based on the novel Fighting Caravans by Zane Grey; screenplay, Jack Cunningham, Charles Logue, Carl A. Buss; camera, William Mellor.

Randolph Scott (Clint Belmet); Gail Patrick (Nancy Wellington);
Billy Lee (Sonny Wellington); Leila Bennett (Hetty Masters); Jan
Duggan (Abby Masters); Monte Blue (Murdock); Raymond Hatton
(Jim Burch); and Olin Howland, J. P. McGowan, James Marcus,
Helen Hunt, James Kenton, Alfred Delcambre, John Marston, Sam
McDaniels, Howard Wilson, Michael Visaroff, Eldred Tidbury, Julian
Madison, E. Alyn Warren, Pauline Moore.
See FIGHTING CARAVANS.

WAGONS WESTWARD (Republic, 1940) 70 mins.

Producer, Armand Schaefer; director, Lew Landers; screenplay,
Joseph Moncure March, Harrison Jacobs; music director, Cy Feuer;
camera, Ernest Miller; editor, Ernest Nims.
Chester Morris (David Cook/Tom Cook); Anita Louise (Phyllis);
Buck Jones (Sheriff McDaniels); Ona Munson (Julie); George "Gabby"
Hayes (Hardtack); Guinn "Big Boy" Williams (Hardman); Douglas
Fowley (Marsden); John Galludet (Blackie); Virginia Brissac (Angela
Cook); Trevor Bardette (Alan Cook); Selmer Jackson (Major Marlowe);
Charles Stevens (Elma); Wayne Hull (David as a Boy); Warren Hull
(Tom as a Boy); and Tex Cooper.

Twins Dave and Tommy grow up on opposite sides of the law,
with outlaw Tom (Chester Morris) protected by crooked Sheriff
McDaniels (Buck Jones). Lawman Dave (Chester Morris) has his
brother arrested and then assumes his identity in order to round up
the rest of his gang. He becomes romantically involved with two
women, falling in love with Julie (Ona Munson) but marrying Phyllis
(Anita Louise). Tom escapes from jail and when he finds his brother,
Dave's ruse is uncovered. Indian Pima (Charles Stevens) helps Dave
escape from the outlaws. Tom kills Phyllis for marrying Dave but
the gang is routed by Dave and the crooked McDaniels is shot. In
the showdown, Dave kills Tom, and now Dave and Julie can wed.
WAGONS WESTWARD is an engaging adult Western produced by
Republic, obviously one of its big-budget pictures for the year. The
movie is well done and Chester Morris is especially effective in his
dual assignment as the twin brothers, while George "Gabby" Hayes
provides his customary effective comedy relief as the contrary Hardtack. The least satisfying element of the film is the casting of cowboy hero Buck Jones in the villainous role of the crooked lawman.
Seeing him riding his beautiful horse Silver, it must have been difficult for Buck's legions of loyal film fans to accept him on the wrong
side of the law, a fate which often met Western film heroes at low
points in their careers. For Buck Jones, however, it was only a
brief departure from the screen's cowboy code, for he was soon back
starring in the "Rough Riders" series for Monogram with Tim McCoy
and Raymond Hatton.

WANTED WOMEN see JESSI'S GIRLS

Ona Munson and Buck Jones in WAGONS WESTWARD (1940).

WAR OF THE WILDCATS see IN OLD OKLAHOMA

WASHINGTON COWBOY see ROVIN' TUMBLEWEEDS

THE WAY OF THE WEST see BREED OF THE WEST

WELCOME TO HARD TIMES (Metro-Goldwyn-Mayer, 1967) C 103 mins.

Producers, Max E. Youngstein; David Karr; associate producer, Hank Moonjean; director, Burt Kennedy; based on the novel by E. L. Doctorow; screenplay, Kennedy; art directors, George W. Davis, Carl Anderson; set decorators, Henry Grace, Joseph J. Stone; music, Harry Sukman; makeup, William Tuttle; assistant director, Al Jennings; sound, Franklin Milton; camera, Harry Stradling, Jr.; editor, Aaron Stell.

Henry Fonda (Will Blue); Janice Rule (Molly Riordan); Aldo Ray (Man from Bodie); Keenan Wynn (Zar); Janis Paige (Adah); John Anderson (Ezra/Isaac Maple); Warren Oates (Jenks); Fay Spain (Jessie); Edgar Buchanan (Brown); Denver Pyle (Alfie); Michael Shea (Jimmy Fee); Arlene Golonka (Mae); Lon Chaney (Avery); Royal Dano (John Bear); Alan Baxter (Jack Millay); Paul

Lon Chaney and Aldo Ray in WELCOME TO HARD TIMES (1967).

Birch (Mr. Fee); Dan Ferrone (Bert Albany); Paul Fix (Major Munn); Elisha Cook (Hanson); Kalini Liu (China); Ann McCrea (Flo); Bob Terhune (Drinker); Ron Burke (Young Miner).

Hard Times is a small frontier settlement inhabited by some fifty citizens. One day a mysterious stranger (Aldo Ray) rides into town. He rapes a saloon girl (Fay Spain), murders her husband (Paul Birch), and threatens everyone in the community. Local lawyer Will Blue (Henry Fonda) runs rather than face the bad man. Meanwhile, the stranger kills the saloon owner (Lon Chaney), sets fire to the town, and rides away. Most of the inhabitants leave, but a few remain, and urged on by his girl friend Molly (Janice Rule), who was also raped by the stranger, Will takes over the rebuilding of the town. The settlement's success is cemented by the arrival of madam Adah (Janis Paige) and her girls. The town begins to prosper again, but the stranger returns and terrorizes the inhabitants. Again Will turns coward in a showdown with him, and it is Molly who finally brings about the demise of the bad man.

Originally made for television but issued theatrically because it was initially deemed too violent for the small screen, WELCOME TO HARD TIMES is not an unlikable Western, although much of its interest revolves around its sterling cast and its borrowing from other genre films (e.g., the bad man's murder of Elisha Cook is straight out of SHANE, 1953--see B/V). Aldo Ray is especially impressive in the nonspeaking role of the Big Bad Man from Bodie. It was Time magazine which pinpointed the film's basic appeal: "Fortunately for the film, even the small roles are in the hands of some of the oldest pros in the business--among them Edgar Buchanan as a government man and Lon Chaney as a bartender. Handling the cliches with the care of a cowpoke tending a tired palomino, they make HARD TIMES seem better than it is because they have been there before--many times. So has the audience."

The movie proved to be a box-office dud and was soon issued to TV. In Great Britain it was retitled KILLER ON A HORSE.

WELLS FARGO (Paramount, 1937) 115 mins.

Producer, Frank Lloyd; associate producer, Howard Estabrook; director, Lloyd; story, Stuart M. Lake; screenplay, Paul Schofield, Gerald Geraghty; Frederick Jackson; song, Ralph Freed, Burton Lane; camera, Theodor Sparkuhl; editor, Hugh Bennett.

Joel McCrea (Ramsay McKay); Bob Burns (Hank York); Frances Dee (Justine); Lloyd Nolan (Dal Slade); Porter Hall (James Oliver); Ralph Morgan (Mr. Pryor); Mary Nash (Mrs. Pryor); Robert Cummings (Trimball); Henry O'Neill (Henry Wells); Johnny Mack Brown (Talbot Carter); Jane Dewey (Lucy Dorsett Trimball); and Peggy Stewart, Bernard Siegel, Stanley Fields, Frank McGlynn, Barlowe Bourland.

The formation and history of the Wells Fargo Express Company was the basis for this big-budget feature, but these historical events were relegated to the second shelf and the film focused mainly on a love affair torn apart by the Civil War. While the movie is well produced, its main drawback is its running time, as noted by Variety: "...115 minutes is a bit overlong, and some of the midway footage, explaining the development of the coast-to-coast delivery service, might be expunged as obvious or repetitious." In fact, the film was cut to 94 minutes when issued to television.

Beginning in the mid-1840s, the film relates how Henry Wells (Henry O'Neill) began running a mail and passenger service across the United States. Blazing the trail for the company is Ramsay MacKay (Joel McCrea), who meets and falls in love with pretty Justine Pryor (Frances Dee). After setting up a West Coast office in San Francisco following the 1949 California gold strike, Ramsey marries Justine. The company continues to prosper but when the Civil War breaks out, President Lincoln orders it to carry gold shipments for the Union cause. This angers Justine, who is loyal to the South, and her mother (Mary Nash), who has always disliked Ramsey, finds her daughter has written in anger and gives it to her daughter's former suitor, Confederate officer Talbot Carter (Johnny Mack Brown). He attacks the gold train with his troops and is killed. Ramsey finds the letter and believes Justine has betrayed him. After the war, however, he learns the truth and is reunited with Justine through the efforts of their now grown daughter.

George N. Fenin and William K. Everson essayed in The Western: From Silents to Cinerama (1962): "Frank Lloyd's WELLS FARGO was a grandiose production, but the epic theme of national progress was too often lost sight of by excessive attention to historical details and the business aspects of the Wells Fargo organization. An artificial love triangle further slowed the proceedings, which came to life only twice: in a brief attack by Indians on a stagecoach, and, more notably, in a spectacular action sequence showing a troop of Confederate rebels attacking a wagon convoy."

WEST TO GLORY (Producers Releasing Corp., 1947) 60 mins.

Producer, Jerry Thomas; director, Ray Taylor; screenplay, Elmer Clifton, Robert B. Churchill songs, Eddie Dean, Hal Blair, Pete Gates; assistant director, F. O. Collings; set decorator, Louis Diage; sound, Glen Glenn; camera, Milford Anderson; editor, Hugh Winn.

Eddie Dean (Himself); Roscoe Ates (Soapy Jones); Dolores Castle (Maria); Gregg Barton (Barrett); Jimmy Martin (Cory); Zon Murray (Avery); Alex Montoya (Juan); Harry Vejar (Don Lopez); Carl Mathews (Vincente); The Sunshine Boys (Themselves).

Two crooks steal the gold of Don Lopez (Alex Montoya), which represents his life's savings, but they overlook a necklace containing a valuable diamond and try to go back for it. Cowboys Eddie (Eddie Dean) and Soapy Jones (Roscoe Ates) come to the aid of the man and his pretty daughter Maria (Dolores Castle) and bring the bad men to justice.

WEST TO GLORY is a poorly conceived, dull Western in Eddie
Dean's PRC series. Cinecolor, which had highlighted early entries
in the program, had been abandoned in a cost cut and this black
and white oater is a mundane entry livened only by a few songs
written by the star and Hal Blair: the title tune and "Cry, Cry,
Cry," a song closely associated with Eddie Dean's career. A
further detriment to the film is an unfunny dream sequence in which
sidekick Soapy thinks he is Eddie Dean while the cowboy star becomes his yokel pal.

WESTERN RACKETEERS see BORDER MENACE

WESTERN RACKETEERS see GHOST CITY

WESTWARD BOUND (Monogram, 1944) 54 mins.

Producer/director, Robert Tansey; screenplay, Frances Kava-
naugh; assistant director, Arthur Hammond; music director, Frank
Sanucci; songs, Mack David, David Mendoza; sound, Roy Zoray;
camera, Marcel LePicard; editor, John C. Fuller.
Ken Maynard (Himself); Hoot Gibson (Himself); Bob Steele
(Himself); Betty Miles (Enid Barrett); John Bridges (Ira Phillips);
Harry Woods (Roger Caldwell); Karl Hackett (Henry Wagner);
Weldon Heyburn (Albert Lane); Hal Price (Jasper Tuttle); Roy Brent
(Will); Frank Ellis (Judd); Curly Dresden (Monte); Al Ferguson
(Henchman).

Made on a budget of about $15,000, WESTWARD BOUND was
the fifth entry in producer Robert Tansey's "The Trail Blazers"
series for Monogram Pictures, the penultimate entry with Ken Maynard, and the second to include Bob Steele among its trio of heroes.
The picture is a fast-paced composition which nicely showcases the
individual screen personas of its three stars: Ken and Bob handling
the action with fists and guns while Hooter relies more on comedy
antics to subdue the villains. The film's only flaw is at the finale,
in which Hoot Hurls dynamite at the bad guys and the camera picks
up the unexploded props as they lay untouched on the ground.
United States marshals Ken Maynard, Hoot Gibson, and Bob
Steele (Themselves) arrive in the Montana territory and find a pretty
rancher Enid Barrett (Betty Miles) being harassed by thugs (Al
Ferguson, Frank Ellis, Curley Dresden) who are actually in the pay
of townsman Henry Wagner (Karl Hackett). The latter, in turn, is
the local agent for territorial official Albert Lane (Weldon Heyburn).
Lane is behind a scheme in which ranchers are heavily taxed and
their cattle rustled so that he can obtain their lands, which will have
a big resale price when Montana becomes a state. The three lawmen
stop the outlaws from bothering the girl and after seeing Ken defeat
one of his men in a fight, Wagner, believing that Ken can be bought

off, makes him the local sheriff. Ken, however, establishes Hoot and Bob as his deputies and sets out to stop the outlaws from bothering the ranchers. The lawmen build the needed evidence to bring Lane and Wagner to justice.

WESTWARD HO (Republic, 1935) 60 mins.

Producer, Paul Malvern; director, Robert N. Bradbury; story, Lindsley Parsons; screenplay, Parsons, Robert Emmett (Tansey), Harry Friedman; sound, Dave Stonert; camera, Archie Stout; editor, Carl L. Pierson.

John Wayne (John Wyatt); Sheila Mannors (Mary Gordon); Frank McGlynn, Jr. (Jim Wyatt); Jack Curtis (Ballard); Yakima Canutt (Red); Bradley Metcalfe (Young John Wyatt); Hank Bell (Mark Wyatt); Mary MacLaren (Hannah Wyatt); James Farley (Lafe Gordon); Dickie Jones (Young Jim Wyatt); Glenn Strange (Cowboy); The Singing Riders (Singing Cowboys); and Lloyd Ingraham, Frank Ellis, Earl Dwire, Fred Burns, Jack Kirk, Tex Palmer.

This was John Wayne's first "Lone Star" production for Paul Malvern to be issued by the newly formed Republic Pictures. WEST-WARD HO is a topnotch "B" actioner which cost $15,000 to make and grossed some $500,000 (or ten times the usual gross for a series oater) at the box office. In addition to a solid plot and steady direction by Robert North Bradbury, the movie benefits from unobtrusive music, including star John Wayne (dubbed) singing "The Girl I Loved Long Ago" and campfire numbers by a group labeled "The Singing Riders," which included Glenn Strange.

Outlaws attack a family traveling Westward, the parents are killed and the older brother left for dead. The younger one is taken by the gang. Fifteen years later John Wyatt (John Wayne) still searches for his little brother and for the outlaws who murdered his parents. Actually the younger sibling is Jim (Frank McGlynn, Jr.), a member of Ballard's (Jack Curtis) outlaw band. John joins a wagon train going West, and so does Jim, who has infiltrated the train to aid his gang's plans to attack the settlers. Both men fall in love with pretty Mary Gordon (Sheila Mannors) and when the gang attacks the group, Jim sacrifices his life to save Mary. John realizes the truth and sets out to get Ballard and his henchman Red (Yakima Canutt). When this is accomplished, he returns to Mary.

John Wayne occasionally sang in his films for producer Paul Malvern, commencing with RIDERS OF DESTINY (1933) (see B/V), in which he played a lawman named Singin' Sandy. He was dubbed throughout the series, although it has never been clarified who did the singing for Wayne. Some sources claim that Wayne actually did the vocalizing; other researchers insist that Glenn Strange or Smith Ballew did the dubbing. Ballew, however, denied this and in a 1983 interview with historian Ray White, Paul Malvern said the singing was accomplished by director Robert North Bradbury's son Bill (twin brother of Bob Steele), then a Los Angeles physician.

Richard Widmark and Frederic Forrest in WHEN THE LEGENDS DIE (1972).

WHEN THE LEGENDS DIE (Twentieth Century-Fox, 1972) C 105 mins.

Producer/director, Stuart Millar; based on the novel by Hal Borland; screenplay, Robert Dozier; music, Glenn Paxton; songs, Paxton and Bo Goldman; art director, Angelo Graham; set decorator, Jerry Wunderlich; assistant director, Pepi Lenzi; sound, Richard Overton, Theodore Soderberg; camera, Richard H. Cline; editor, Louis San Andres.

Richard Widmark (Red Dillon); Frederic Forrest (Tom Black Bull); Luana Anders (Mary); Vito Scotti (Meo); Herbert Nelson (Dr. Wilson); John War Eagle (Blue Elk); Tillman Box (Tom as a Boy); John Gruber (Tex).

"Tom Black Bull came out of the wilderness at the end of a rope ... a wild Indian boy. He hasn't been tamed yet." Thus ran the ads for Stuart Millar's initial directorial feature (he was the producer of LITTLE BIG MAN, 1970--see B/V), and it appears that the distributor intended to rely on the action motif to bring in customers to a basically cerebral movie. Newsweek noted, "Deftly, Millar makes his points about exploitation and racism, subtly sketching the love-hate relationship of the two men, while his camera probes the dusty emptiness of those tacky, small rodeo towns."

Based on the 1963 novel, the film relates how, following the deaths of his parents, fourteen-year-old Ute Indian boy Tom Black Bull is taken forcefully from his Colorado Mountains home and sent to a reservation school. He is promised that he can teach others the old ways, but instead is taught the ways of the white man. Growing up and showing a proclivity as a bronc rider, Tom (Frederic Forrest) comes under the tutelage of one-time rodeo star Red Dillon (Richard Widmark), now a heavy drinker and womanizer. Red takes Tom on the tank town circuit, showing him how to win and how to throw events, and making money for himself to spend on booze and whores. Finally Tom is satiated with Red and this kind of life; he leaves and becomes a big attraction on the main rodeo circuit. There he earns the nickname "Killer" because he rides the horses until they drop. With all the hatred in him eventually evaporated, Tom returns to the reservation to tend its horse herd.

Writing in the New York Times, Vincent Canby said, WHEN THE LEGENDS DIE "...may be too intelligent, too gentle and too reticent for its own good.... It deals in small betrayals, hurt feelings and interim relationships, the sort of things more likely to send you out of the theater talking about good taste than feeling any particular elation." Time magazine commented that director Millar "...has a good eye for the landscape of the Southwest and a talent for conveying a sense of rootlessness and change.... Widmark is in top form and Forrest is a real find...."

WHERE THE NORTH BEGINS see TRAIL OF THE MOUNTIES

THE WHITE BUFFALO (United Artists, 1977) C 97 mins.

Presenter, Dino De Laurentiis; producer, Pancho Kohner; director, J. Lee Thompson; based on the novel by Richard Sale; screenplay, Sale; music, John Barry; production designer, Tambi Larsen; set decorator, James Berkey; wardrobe/costumes, Eric Seelig, Dennis Fill; assistant director, Jack Aldworth; stunt coordinator, Ben Dobbins; sound, William McCaughey, Lyle J. Burbridge, Michael J. Kohut, Harlan Riggs; camera, Paul Lohmann; editor, Michael F. Anderson.

Charles Bronson (Wild Bill Hickok [James Otis]); Jack Warden (Charlie Zane); Will Sampson (Crazy Horse); Kim Novak (Poker Jenny); Clint Walker (Whistling Jack Kileen); Stuart Whitman (Coxy); Slim Pickens (Pinkney); John Carradine; (Briggs); Cara Williams (Cassie); Shay Duffin (Brady); Douglas V. Fowley (Bixby); Cliff Pellow (Holt); Ed Lauter (Captain Tom Custer).

Haunted by dreams of a monstrous white buffalo, Wild Bill Hickok (Charles Bronson) returns to the West under the alias of James Otis. At the same time, the buffalo invades an Indian camp and murders the wife and the infant daughter of Crazy Horse (Will Sampson), who vows revenge. Hickok meets old friend Charlie Zane

(Jack Warden) and in a saloon fight with wicked Whistling Jack Kileen (Clint Walker), saves the frontiersman. In the same town, Hickock finds his former mistress, Poker Jenny (Kim Novak), and they resume their affair, but Bill wants to find the white buffalo and he and Charlie set out to locate and kill it. On the trail they encounter Crazy Horse and form an uneasy truce with him to destroy the beast. In the final showdown with the animal, Hickock's gun jams and the Indian finally kills the white buffalo with his knife, destroying the spectre which haunts both men. Now friends, the two part to meet their individual destinies.

THE WHITE BUFFALO--which owes a lot to the MOBY DICK revenge theme--has a mystical look which makes it appear more like a horror film than a true Western. The proceedings seem like a dream and this is abetted by the film's murky photography (some sources claim the final prints were accidentally made too dark) and the archaic dialogue. Still, the film is wonderfully cast, from the stars through the brief supporting parts, and it has several exciting sequences, including the saloon shoot-out and the final confrontation with the beast, although the buffalo itself is more tacky than frightening. Upon its release, the movie was lambasted by the critics: the "white elephant of the year. It is a film that defies description" (San Francisco Chronicle); "a turkey" (Variety); a "fiasco" (The Washington Post). Only Roger Osbourne, in The Hollywood Reporter, was on the mark when he wrote, "...THE WHITE BUFFALO deserves better than a quick, inconspicuous burial." Sadly, this is what the film got, since the distributor sent it out mostly to drive-in theatres where its dim photography and muffled soundtrack made it practically incomprehensible.

When the film was telecast on NBC-TV in the summer of 1983 it was retitled HUNT TO KILL.

THE WHITE OUTLAW (Exhibitors Film Corp., 1929) 4,478'

Director, Robert J. Horner; screenplay, Bob McKenzie; camera, Ernest Laszlo; editor, William Austin.

Art Acord (Johnny Douglas, the White Outlaw); Lee Meehan (Jed Izbell); Walter Maly (Bud Mason, the Deputy); Howard Davies (Colonel Holbrook); Vivian May (Janice Holbrook); Bill Patton (Ted Williams); Art Hoxie (Sheriff Ralston of Grant Pass); Slim Mathews (Joe Walton); Dick Nores (Chet Wagner); Betty Carter (Mary Wagner).

During the 1920s, Art Acord was one of the screen's most popular Western players, on an equal footing with Harry Carey and Hoot Gibson at Universal, where he starred in a long series of "Blue Streak" Westerns. With the coming of the sound film, he was dropped by Universal and ended his screen career in a series of cheap silents for J. Charles Davis Productions before his mysterious death in 1931. Sadly, these Davis films are the only Acord starrers available today, and they must certainly be a pale example of the work that made him so popular in his cinematic heydey.

Johnny Douglas (Art Acord) is a good guy outlaw who wears a white bandana. Wrongdier Jud Izbell (Lew Meehan) pulls a robbery and The White Outlaw (Acord) is blamed. Under an assumed name, Johnny Douglas, he goes to work for the Holbrooks. Their ranch mortgage is held by Chet Wagner (Dick Nores), who also wants Colonel Holbrook's (Howard Davies) daughter Janie (Vivian May), who is loved by foreman Ted Williams (Bill Patton). Janice agrees to wed Chet to cancel her father's debts and the foreman then pretends to be The White Outlaw and holds up the stage, but he is recognized and arrested. Johnny comes to the rescue by staging a hold-up and Ted is released from jail. A posse follows Johnny and he gets into a fight with an old enemy Jed. When the latter is killed in a fall, Johnny exchanges identities with him and gets the reward for The White Outlaw, which he uses to save the Holbrook ranch. At the finale, Johnny hits the trail.

WIDE OPEN TOWN (Paramount, 1941) 76 mins.

Producer, Harry Sherman; associate producer, Lewis J. Rachmil; director, Lesley Selander; based on characters created by Clarence E. Mulford; screenplay, Harrison Jacobs, J. Benton Cheney; assistant director, Frederick Spencer; camera, Russell Harlan; supervising editor, Sherman A. Rose; editor, Carroll Lewis.

William Boyd (Hopalong Cassidy); Russell Hayden (Lucky Jenkins); Andy Clyde (California Jack Carlson); Evelyn Brent (Belle Langtry); Victor Jory (Steve Fraser); Morris Ankrum (Jim Stuart); Kenneth Harlan (Tom Wilson); Bernice Kay (Joan Stuart); Roy Barcroft (Red); Glenn Strange (Ed Stark); Ed Cassidy (Brad Jackson); Jack Rockwell (Rancher); Topper (The Horse); and Bob Kortman, George Cleveland.

Hopalong Cassidy (William Boyd), Lucky Jenkins (Russell Hayden), and California Carlson (Andy Clyde) ride into a town looking for their stolen Bar 20 cattle herd. They find that saloon owner Belle Langtry (Evelyn Brent) and crook Steve Fraser (Victor Jory) are out to get rid of the town's newspaperman/mayor Jim Stuart (Morris Ankrum), a rival for control of the area. This pair tries to wreck Stuart's office but the Bar 20 boys stop them. Hoppy agrees to become the town's sheriff and clean up the community. He thwarts Stuart's gang in their attempt to rob gold from a train and captures most of them. The remaining members are then captured in a trap by Hoppy and his pals and the Bar 20 cattle are recovered. The outlaws hold up at the saloon and the law raids the place. Seeing that he will lose, Steve tries to use Joan as a pawn to escape. Belle stops him but he shoots her; she and Joan, however, escape and Hoppy captures Steve. Belle agrees to leave town.

Silent screen star Evelyn Brent played a role here very similar to the one she performed in HOPALONG CASSIDY RETURNS (see B/V) six years earlier. It should be noted that young actress Bernice Kay later changed her name to Cara Williams.

As Phil Hardy assessed in The Film Encyclopedia: The Western (1983), "...[this is] one of the best of [the] Hopalong Cassidy's outings.... Boyd, Brent, and, in particular, Jory bring real conviction to their parts and, with Selander's snappy direction, the result is a superior series entry."

WILD HORSES (CBS-TV, 11/12/85) C 100 mins.

Executive producers, Ken Kragen, Dick Lowry; supervising producers, Frank Konigsberg, Larry Sanitsky; producer, Hunt Lowry; director, Dick Lowry; teleplay, Roderick Taylor, Danile Vining; production designer, Linda Pearl; art director, Dena Roth; costume designer, Jack Buehler; music, Stanley Myers, Hans Zimmer; stunt coordinator, Dave Cass; sound, Ron Judkins; camera, Keith Wagstaff; editor, Byron (Buzz) Brandt.

Kenny Rogers (Matt Cooper); Pam Dawber (Daryl Reese); Ben Johnson (Bill Ward); David Andrews (Dean Ellis); Richard Masur (Bob Browne); Karen Carlson (Ann Cooper); Richard Farnsworth (Chuck Reese); Richard Hamilton (Blue Houston); Jack Radar (Dick Post); Ritch Brinkley (Wedge Smithfield); Buck Taylor (Cowboy); Kelly Yunkerman (Ted Holmes); Cathy Worthington (Lynda); R. W. Hampton (Himself); Brian Rogers (Matt Cooper, Jr.); Jamie Fleenor (Debbie); Dawn Holder (Katie Cooper); Roddy Salazar (Carlos); Beckie Hinton (Girl); Charles H. Hunt (Auctioneer); Dave Lowry (Wrangler); Jay H. Zirbel (Leon); Riders in the Sky (Themselves).

Following the rating successes of KENNY ROGERS AS THE GAMBLER (1980) and KENNY ROGERS AS THE GAMBLER--THE ADVENTURE CONTINUES (1983) (qq.v.), country music star Kenny Rogers returned to the Western with still a third TV movie, WILD HORSES, set in the modern-day West. In TV Guide, Judith Crist noted, "It's a very pleasing and predictable entertainment, with beautiful horses and unwild women."

With the advertising catchlines "Today there's a place a man can be free. And he'd risk everything for the life he loves," this telefilm tells of former rodeo champion Matt Cooper (Kenny Rogers) who grows tired of his factory job in Texas and leaves his wife (Karen Carlson) and family and heads to Wyoming with his pal (David Andrews) to work a mustang herd belonging to old-time cowboy (Ben Johnson). He meets a rancher (Richard Farnsworth) and has an affair with the rancher's pretty daughter (Pam Dawber). He also uncovers a plot by a crooked bureaucrat (Richard Masur) to sell wild horses for a huge profit and tries to thwart the official's scheme.

Filmed on location in Sheridan, Wyoming, this telefeature was a satisfying outing, although its acting honors go to veterans Ben Johnson and Richard Farnsworth rather than to star Kenny Rogers. The film is light on music other than its title theme, "Wild Horses," and Rogers performing his self-penned "Eight-Second Hero."

WILD WEST see LAW OF THE LASH

WILD WEST (Producers Releasing Corp., 1946) C 78 mins.

 Producer/director, Robert Emmett Tansey; screenplay, Frances
Kavanaugh; songs, Dorcas Cochran, Charles Rosoff; Eddie Dean;
Ruth and Louis Herscher; music director, Karl Hajos; art director,
Edward C. Jewell; assistant director, Louis Germonprez; sound, Ben
Winkler; camera, Fred Jackson, Jr.; editor, Hugh Winn.
 Eddie Dean (Himself); Roscoe Ates (Soapy Jones); Al "Lash"
LaRue (Stormy Day); Robert "Buzz" Henry (Skinny Bannister);
Sarah Padden (Carrie Bannister); Louise Currie (Florabelle); Jean
Carlin (Mollie); Les Bennett (Butler); Terry Frost (Drake Dawson);
Warner Richmond (Judge Templeton); Lee Roberts (Captain Rogers);
Chief Yowlachie (Chief Black Fox); Bob Duncan (Rockey); Frank
Pharr (Doctor); Matty Roubert (Halfbreed Charlie); John Bridges
(Constable); Al Ferguson (Kansas); Bud Osborne (Cactus); Flash
(The Horse).

 Eddie Dean's finest series Western, and his fifth and final
Cinecolor starrer, WILD WEST is one of the best oaters made by
PRC. The film was also the third and final teaming of Eddie Dean
and Al "Lash" LaRue before the latter began his own starring series
for the studio. Topnotch in all departments, from script to action
to music (including Eddie Dean's self-penned parody, "Elmer, the
Knock-Kneed Cowboy"), WILD WEST was so good that in 1948 it was
reissued, minus fifteen minutes and with an added framing scene,
in black and white as PRAIRIE OUTLAWS. Critics, not alerted that
it was a re-release, praised it as a new feature.
 In the territory around the small town of Preston, a telegraph
company is stringing wire but is plagued by outlaws who are inciting
the Indians. The engineer (Les Bennett) heading the project asks
for help, and three agents--Eddie Dean (Himself), Soapy Jones
(Roscoe Ates) and Stormy Day (Al "Lash" LaRue)--are sent to investigate. They ask the aid of rancher Carrie Bannister (Sarah
Padden), whose late husband started the territorial rangers before
his murder. She sends her son Skinny (Robert "Buzz" Henry) to
bring the Indian chief (Chief Yowlachie) to her ranch and they convince him that the telegraph will help the territory. Meanwhile, the
leader of the outlaws, Drake Dawson (Terry Frost), who is behind
the Indian attacks (his gang has been killing buffalo and then
blaming the settlers), sends his men to destroy telegraph equipment
at the Bannister ranch. Dawson also pays crooked Judge Templeton
(Warner Richmond) to help his cause and the judge causes Soapy
and Skinny to be ambushed by the gang. Soapy, however, connects
Dawson to the elder Bannister's killing and the lawmen, helped at
the last minute by the arrival of the Captain (Lee Roberts) of the
territorial rangers and his men, confront the gang in town.

Duane Eddy, Bob Steele, Harry Lauter, James Philbrook, and Nancy
Kovack in THE WILD WESTERNERS (1962).

THE WILD WESTERNERS (Columbia, 1962) C 70 mins.

Producer, Sam Katzman; director, Oscar Rudolph; screenplay,
Gerald Drayson Adams; music, Duane Eddy; assistant director, Sam
Nelson; camera, Gordon Avil; editor, Jerome Thoms.
James Philbrook (U.S. Marshal Jim McDowell); Nancy Kovack
(Rose Sharon); Duane Eddy (Deputy Marshal Clint Fallon); Guy
Mitchell (Deputy Johnny Silver); Hugh Sanders (Chief U.S. Marshal
Reuben Bernard); Elizabeth MacRae (Crystal Blummer); Marshall
Reed (Sheriff Henry Plummer); Nestor Paiva (Governor John Bullard);
Harry Lauter (Judas); Bob Steele (Deputy Marshal Casey Banner);
Ilse Burkert (Yellow Moon); Terry Frost (Ashley Cartwright); Hans
Wedemeyer (Wasna); Don Harvey (Hanna); Elizabeth Harrower
(Martha Bernard); Frances Osborne (Lulu); Tim Sullivan (Reverend
Thomas); Pierce Lyden (Jake); Joe McGuinn (Sam Clay); Charles
Horvath (Moose); Marjorie Stapp (Lily).

In Montana Territory in 1864, show girl Rose Sharon (Nancy
Kovack) tricks U.S. Marshal Jim McDowell (James Philbrook) into
marrying her and accompanies him on his mission to take gold out of
the area for the Union cause. Along the way they are attacked first
by marauding Indians and then by a gang of gold-hungry cutthroats

led by another lawman, Deputy Johnny Silver (Guy Mitchell). With the aid of his deputy (Duane Eddy), McDowell brings down Silver and his minions and saves the gold. He also discovers that his bride, who fights at his side, is worth having.

A minor Western from economy producer Sam Katzman, THE WILD WESTERNERS is a well-written "B" picture which moves quickly and is bolstered by a fine cast, including then popular recording artists Guy Mitchell and Duane Eddy. James Philbrook, who had headlined many minor Westerns both in the U.S. and Europe, nicely handles the title role and attractive Nancy Kovack complements him as the new bride. Another virtue of the film is its topnotch supporting cast, including such genre old-timers as Marshall Reed, Hugh Sanders, Nestor Paiva, Harry Lauter, Bob Steele, Terry Frost, Don C. Harvey, Pierce Lyden, Joe McGuinn, and Charles Horvath.

Dubbed a "Lively if minor Western" by F. Maurice Speed in Film Review 1963-64 (1963), the film's main drawback is the interpolation of stock footage of Indian raids, which does not match Gordon Avil's otherwise attractive cinematography.

WILDFIRE see DRIFTIN' RIVER

WINNERS OF THE WEST (Universal, 1940) thirteen chapters

Producer, Henry MacRae; directors, Ford Beebe, Ray Taylor; screenplay, George Plympton, Basil Dickey, Charles R. Condon; dialogue director, Jacques Jaccard; art director, Harold MacArthur; song, Everett Carter, Milton Rosen; camera, Jerome Ash, William Sickner, John Hickson; supervising editor, Saul A. Goodkind; editors, Alvin Todd, Louis Sackin, Joseph Glick.
Dick Foran (Jeff Ramsay); Anne Nagel (Claire Hartford); James Craig (Jim Jackson); Tom Fadden (Tex Houston); Charles Stevens (Snakeye); Trevor Bardette (Raven); Harry Woods (King Carter); Chief Yowlachie (Chief War Eagle); Edward Keane (John Hartford); William Desmond (Brine); Edmund Cobb (Maddox); and Chuck Morrison, Edgar Edwards, Jack Voglin, Roy Barcroft, Edward Cassidy.
Chapters: 1) Redskins Ride Again; 2) The Wreck at Red River Gorge; 3) The Bridge of Disaster; 4) Trapped by Redskins; 5) Death Stalks the Trail; 6) A Leap for Life; 7) Thundering Terror; 8) The Flaming Arsenal; 9) Sacrificed by Savages; 10) Under Crashing Timbers; 11) Bullets in the Dark; 12) The Battle of Blackhawk; 13) Barricades Blasted.

The construction of the first transcontinental railroad was screen fodder for many years, appearing in such classics as THE IRON HORSE (1925--see B/V) and UNION PACIFIC (1939--see B/V). WINNERS OF THE WEST, a 1940 Universal serial in thirteen installments, also examines the cross-country railroad construction, but unlike the previously mentioned features, does so in a totally fictional context. In fact, the cliffhanger is a remake of the studio's earlier chapterplay, HEROES OF THE WEST (q.v.), made eight years earlier, and this new effort rather unconvincingly interpolates stock footage from that production. The two serials share the same director, Ray Taylor having helmed the 1932 version and co-directed the remake with Ford Beebe.

John Hartford (Edward Keane) and his foreman, Jeff Ramsay (Dick Foran), are working to get the Hartford Transcontinental Railroad through Hellgate Pass, but their efforts are opposed by self-appointed local dictator King Carter (Harry Woods), who is allied with half-breed Snakeye (Charles Stevens) in stirring up the local Indians to oppose the incoming railroad. Carter is afraid the railroad will cause him to lose control of the area and he does everything possible to see it thwarted, including having the Indians raid the railroad construction camps, robbing stagecoaches, stealing wagon train supplies, and destroying the telegraph and railroad lines. Ramsay is aided in opposing Carter by frontiersman Tex Houston (Tom Fadden) and scout Jim Jackson (James Craig), but their efforts are often unintentionally hurt by Hartford's snooty daughter Claire (Anne Nagel), who ends up being captured by Snakeye and his braves since the lecherous Carter desires her. Ramsay and his pals rescue Claire and in a shoot-out in Carter's town of Blackhawk, the bad man and his henchmen are defeated and Carter is turned over to federal authorities. A peace treaty is signed with Chief War Eagle (Chief Yowlachie) and the railroad is completed.

WINNERS OF THE WEST was re-edited into eight chapters and telecast as part of the fourth season of the PBS-TV series, "Matinee at the Bijou," in 1983.

WINNETOU AND SHATTERHAND IN THE VALLEY OF DEATH see THE TREASURE OF SILVER LAKE

WINNETOU UND SHATTERHAND IM TAL DER TOTEN see THE TREASURE OF SILVER LAKE

WITH GENERAL CUSTER AT LITTLE BIG HORN (Sunset, 1926) 5,094'

Producer, Anthony J. Xydias; director, Harry L. Fraser; story, Carrie E. Rawles; camera, L. William O'Connell.

Roy Stewart (Lem Hawks); Helen Lynch (Betty Rossman); John Beck (General George A. Custer); Edmund Cobb (Captain Page).

In the mid-1920s independent producer Anthony J. Xydias made a series of romantic historical dramas for his Sunset Productions. Among them were WITH KIT CARSON OVER THE GREAT DIVIDE (1925), DANIEL BOONE--THRU THE WILDERNESS (1926),

DAVY CROCKETT AT THE FALL OF THE ALAMO (1926) and SITTING
BULL AT THE SPIRIT LAKE MASSACRE (1927).

WITH CUSTER AT THE LITTLE BIG HORN is typical of the
series--a low-budget but adequately made melodrama which is well
acted by its cast. The movie takes great pains to show the
gathering of the Indians before the big battle, and the staging of
the Little Big Horn massacre is surprisingly well done for an
economy independent feature.

In 1976, frontier scout Lem Hawks (Roy Stewart) and Army
Captain Page (Edmund Cobb) are at odds over the affections of
pretty pioneer girl Betty Rossman (Helen Lynch). Page causes the
Indians led by Chief Sitting Bull (Running Dear) to unite in op-
posing General Custer (John Beck) and, despite Hawks' efforts,
Custer and his men are led into a fatal trap and massacred by the
Indians.

For the record, actor John Beck, who made a good, if rather
harried Custer, was made up to resemble Henry B. Walthall in THE
BIRTH OF A NATION (1914).

A.k.a.: GENERAL CUSTER AT LITTLE BIG HORN

THE WOLF HUNTERS (Rayart Pictures, 1926) 5,976'

Producer, Ben Wilson; director, Stuart Paton; based on the
novel by James Oliver Curwood.
With: Robert McKim, Virginia Browne Faire, Alan Roscoe,
Mildred Harris, David Torrence, Al Ferguson.

THE WOLF HUNTERS (Monogram, 1949) 70 mins.

Producer, Lindsley Parsons; director, Oscar (Budd) Boet-
ticher; based on the novel by James Oliver Curwood; screenplay,
W. Scott Darling; music, Edward J. Kay; camera, William Sickner;
editor, Ace Herman.
Kirby Grant (Rod); Jan Clayton (Greta); Chinook (The Dog);
Edward Norris (Henri); Helen Parrish (Marcia); Charles Lang
(McTavish); Ted Hecht (Muskoka); Luther Crockett (Cameron);
Elizabeth Root (Minnetaki).
See THE TRAIL BEYOND.

WOLF TRACKS (Sunset, 1923) 4,818'

Producer, Anthony J. Xydias; director, Robert North Brad-
bury; screenplay, William Lester; assistant director, Jack Pierce;
camera, Bert Longenecker.
Jack Hoxie (John Hastings); Andree Tourneur (Jean Meredith);
Jim Welch (Bob Meredith); Albert J. Smith (Steve "Wolf" Santell);
Tom Lingham (Lemuel Blatherwick); William Lester (Laroque); Marin
Sais (Rose Blatherwick); Kate Price (Kitty Blatherwick).

Cowboy John Hastings (Jack Hoxie) is mistaken for an outlaw called The Wolf (Albert J. Smith) who is after a mine an old man has left to his daughter (Andree Tourneur). Escaping from the law, Hastings finds the old man before he dies, hears his story and sets out to save the girl's mine and capture the elusive Wolf.

Jack Hoxie was one of the more popular Western stars of the 1920s, although he reached his apex in the middle of the decade in his Universal series. He earned that series, however, based on the success of his features for producer Anthony Xydias' Sunset Pictures, and WOLF TRACKS is a solid programmer in that group. Not only is the plot of the movie interesting, but director Robert North Bradbury keeps it moving at a steady pace and Jack Hoxie is quite good in the role of the likable cowboy hero. In later years, especially in his brief talkie career in Majestic features like GOLD (q.v.), Hoxie was deprecated as being oafish and a poor actor. He is anything but those things here, coming across quite well in the silent film medium and proving why he attracted such a following in the years before the movies learned to talk.

WYOMING ROUNDUP (Monogram, 1952) 53 mins.

Producer, Vincent M. Fennelly; director, Thomas Carr; screenplay, Dal Ullman; assistant director, Melville Shyer; dialogue director, Stanley Price; sound, John Kean; camera, Ernest Miller; editor, Sam Fields.

Whip Wilson (Himself); Tommy Farrell (Bob Burke); Phyllis Coates (Terry); Henry Rowland (Howard); House Peters, Jr. (Randolph); I. Stanford Jolley (Earl Craven); Dick Emory (Jack Craven); Bob Wilke (Wyatt); Stanley Price (Clark).

WYOMING ROUNDUP (made as HIRED GUNS) was the last of the 22 features Whip Wilson starred in for Monogram between 1949 and 1952. First introduced in the Jimmy Wakely vehicle, SILVER TRAILS (1948), the singing, whip-wielding cowpoke was given his own series beginning with CRASHING THRU (1949). Most of his films were only average, although Wilson, while a bit stilted on camera, was an acceptable horse opera star. He failed to make the needed impression with filmgoers and the series was dropped after WYOMING ROUNDUP, which ironically is one of his best starrers. The movie has a tight, fast-moving plot and plenty of enjoyable action.

Seeking work, cowpoke Whip Wilson (Himself) and Bob Burke (Tommy Farrell) drift into the small town of Willows in Wyoming and stop a fight between Jack Craven (Dick Emory) and Wyatt (Robert Wilke), a gunman who has just murdered the town's sheriff. Impressed with the duo, the town's leading citizens ask them to become deputy marshals, and the two quickly accept. Jack's father, Earl Craven (I. Stanford Jolley), and businessman Randolph (House Peters, Jr.) tell the new lawmen that the area's trouble is being caused by rancher Bill Howard (Henry Rowland), who has hired

Whip Wilson in WYOMING ROUNDUP (1952).

gunmen to rid the range of ranchers. Whip and Bob find out that Howard is innocent of the charges and that he believes the elder Craven is after his ranch. The two lawmen get Howard and Craven together and resolve their differences. Whip proves that it is Randolph who wants the local range land and is behind the trouble. The two factions meet in a shoot-out. Randolph is arrested after most of his gang is wiped out.

YODELIN' KID FROM PINE RIDGE (Republic, 1937) 62 mins.

Producer, Armand Schaefer; director, Joseph Kane; story, Jack Natteford; screenplay, Natteford; Stuart McGowan, Dorrell McGowan; songs, Gene Autry, Smiley Burnette, Frank Harford, Jack Stanley, William Lava; camera, William Nobles; editor, Lester Orlebeck.

Gene Autry (Himself); Champion (The Horse); Smiley Burnette (Colonel Milhouse); Betty Bronson (Milly Baynum); LeRoy Mason (Len Parker); Charles Middleton (Autry, Sr.); Russell Simpson (Bayliss Baynum); Tennessee Ramblers (Themselves); Jack Dougherty (Jeff Galloway); Guy Wilkerson (Clem); Frankie Marvin (Luke); Henry Hall

(Sheriff); Fred "Snowflake" Toones (Sam); Jack Kirk, Bob Burns (Ranchers); Al Taylor (Hank the Turpentiner); George Morrell (Towsman); Lee Meehan, Jack Ingram (Henchmen); Art Dillard (Rodeo Spectator); Art Mix (The Fake Autry); Bud Osborne (Deputy Carter); Tom Smith (Rodeo Performer); Jack Montgomery (Joe, the Rodeo Performer); Herman Hack, Oscar Gahan (Turpentiners).

Released in Great Britain as THE HERO OF PINE RIDGE, this Gene Autry opus is novel: it takes place in modern-day Florida, not in the West. Containing captivating musical interludes, good cinematography and location shooting, and lots of action in a gripping story, the movie is very entertaining. Fans of silent cinema will enjoy Betty Bronson in one of her final heroine roles. Also, in this feature, Smiley Burnette does not play his usual role of Frog Milhouse but the part of Colonel Milhouse, the leader of a traveling carnival show.

In the Turpentine Pine Forests of Florida and Georgia, where many large cattle ranches are located, trouble brews between ranchers who want to burn off trees for more grazing land and the turpentiners who need the trees to make their living. Gene Autry (Himself), the son of a rancher (Charles Middleton), tries to stop the trouble. He is called a traitor and his father disowns him. He joins a traveling wild west show led by Colonel Milhouse (Smiley Burnette) and later returns home with the show. He is abducted by cattlemen but escapes; meanwhile a double for him at the show is shot and his father is murdered. Gene is arrested for the killing of the leader (Russell Simpson) of the turpentiners, whose daughter Milly (Betty Bronson) he has been romancing. Gene Learns that cattleman Parker (LeRoy Mason) and his rustlers are behind all the trouble. After a gun battle, Gene captures Parker and proves him guilty of both murders.

YOUNG BILL HICKOK (Republic, 1940) 59 mins.

Associate producer/director, Joseph Kane; screenplay, Norton S. Parker, Olive Cooper; music director, Cy Feuer; songs: Roy Rogers; Peter Tinturin; Eddie Cherkose, Raoul Kraushaar; Mola Sweet, Nat Vincent; camera, William Nobles; editor, Lester Orlerlebeck.

Roy Rogers (Bill Hickok); George "Gabby" Hayes (Gabby); Trigger (The Horse); Jacqueline Wells [Julie Bishop] (Louise Mason); John Miljan (Nicholas Tower); Sally Payne (Calamity Jane); Archie Twitchell (Phillip); Monte Blue (Marshal Evans); Hal Taliaferro (Morrell); Ethel Wales (Mrs. Stout); Jack Ingram (Red); Monte Montague (Major); and Iron Eyes Cody, Fred Burns, Frank Ellis, Slim Whitaker, Jack Kirk, Hank Bell, Henry Wills, Dick Elliott, William Desmond, John Elliott, Jack Rockwell, Bill Wolfe, Tom Smith.

In the early days of his film career, Roy Rogers often appeared in films of a historical nature, even playing well known characters in

pseudo-historical dramas. He played a look-alike for the title character in BILLY THE KID RETURNS in 1939 and followed this with DAYS
OF JESSE JAMES (1939) (q.v.), with Don Barry in the title role;
YOUNG BUFFALO BILL (1940), this outing, and JESSE JAMES AT
BAY (1941), with Roy as the famous bandit. All of these films were
solidly produced and directed by Joseph Kane and, while they may
have been short on historical fact, were entertaining little efforts
with plenty of solid action. YOUNG BILL HICKOK is no exception.
    Set in California at the time of the Civil War, YOUNG BILL
HICKOK tells of a foreign agent, Nicholas Tower (John Miljan),
getting the aid of a gang called the Overland Raiders, led by ma-
rauder Morrell (Hal Taliaferro), in taking part of California for his
country. His actions are opposed by Pony Express rider Bill Hickok
(Roy Rogers), but Bill is suspected of being a member of the gang
after his fiancée, Louise Mason (Jacqueline Wells), accidentally gives
information to the agent which causes a gold shipment to be robbed.
Bill, however, is able to convince the law of his innocence and he
assists in rounding up the Overland Raiders and putting a stop to
their nefarious plot.

YUKON FLIGHT see RENFREW OF THE ROYAL MOUNTED

ZANDY'S BRIDE (Warner Bros., 1974) C 116 mins.

    Producer, Harvey Matofsky; director, Jan Troell; based on the
novel The Stranger by Lillian Bos Ross; screenplay, Marc Norman;
music, Michael Franks; production designer, Al Brenner; set
decorator, George Gaines; assistant director, Miles Middough; sound,
Charles Knight; camera, Jordan Croneweth; editor, Gordon Scott.
    Gene Hackman (Zandy Allan); Liv Ullmann (Hannah Lund);
Eileen Heckart (Ma Allan); Susan Tyrrell (Maria Cordova); Sam
Bottoms (Mal Allan); Joe Santos (Frank Gallo); Frank Cady (Pa
Allan).

    Director Jan Troell and star Liv Ullmann teamed for this Holly-
wood-produced frontier saga after making the critically acclaimed
THE EMIGRANTS (1971) and THE NEW LAND (1972) (see B/V) in
their homeland of Sweden. While ZANDY'S BRIDE did a fine job of
recapturing the raw frontier, it lagged as a melodrama despite the
inclusion of a bear fight and a showdown with cattle thieves. Gene
Hackman is appropriately stoical as the emotionless Zandy, while
Liv Ullmann is rightly emotional as his imported, confused bride.
It is Frank Cady (best known as the easy-going store proprietor
Sam Drucker in the "Petticoat Junction" and "Green Acres" teleseries) who gives the film's best characterization, as Zandy's stern
father, while Eileen Heckart has a few moments as his downtrodden
mother.
    In the Big Sur area of California in the 1870s, Zandy (Gene
Hackman) makes a living farming and trapping. He has never

Liv Ullmann and Gene Hackman in ZANDY'S BRIDE (1974).

married and feels the time has come to raise a family. He buys a
bride, Swedigh immigrant Hannah (Liv Ullmann), who in her thirties
has a need for romance. When she arrives, Zandy marries her but
is unhappy because he feels she is too old to bear him children,
and on their wedding night he ends up raping her. Their married
life is not a congenial one; Zandy finds his new wife has a quick
tongue and a will of her own, and Hannah realizes that her husband
is an uncouth frontiersman. Eventually Zandy deserts Hannah for
a tart (Susan Tyrrell), but after being away for a time, realizes he
loves his wife. Returning home, Zandy finds Hannah has given
birth to healthy twins, and he and his wife are reconciled.

Michael Buckley wrote over-enthusiastically in Films in Review
magazine (June-July, 1974), "The characters are realistic and most
interesting in their relations to the background of American pioneer
life; and though the action moves slowly at times, the film is never
dull.... This is a fine film which almost everyone should enjoy."

ZORRO, THE GAY BLADE (Twentieth Century-Fox, 1981) C 93 mins.

Executive producer, Melvin Simons; producers, George
Hamilton, C. O. Erickson; director, Peter Medak; story, Hal Dresner, Greg Alt, Don Moriarty, Bob Randall; screenplay, Dresner;
production designer, Herman A. Blumenthal; art director, Adrian
Gorton; costumes, Gloria Gresham; assistant director, Daniel J.
McCauley; music, Ian Fraser; sound, Bob Henderson, Alan Murray;
camera, John A. Alonzo; editor, Hillary Jane Kranze.

George Hamilton (Don Diego Vega/Bunny Wigglesworth);
Lauren Hutton (Charlotte Taylor Wilson); Brenda Vaccaro (Florin-
da); Ron Leibman (Esteban); Donovan Scott (Paco); James Booth
(Velasquez); Helen Burns (Consuelo); Clive Revill (Garcia);
Eduardo Noriega (Dolores).

In 1979 George Hamilton produced and starred in the box-
office success, LOVE AT FIRST BITE, which spoofed horror films.
He attempted to recreate his success by kidding Westerns with
ZORRO, THE GAY BLADE, but the result was a dull film which
"climaxes at a snail's pace to the proverbial happy ending"
(Variety). While Hamilton is adequate both as stalwart Don Diego
and as his limp-wristed brother Bunny (and even as their sister in
a far-out sequence), the rest of the cast appears to be doing a
road show version of "Ten Nights in a Bar Room" with their un-
subtle acting techniques--especially Ron Leibman, overblown as the
villain.

The narrative follows the accepted Zorro film story-line, with
the locals in Spanish California being harassed by a tyrant,
Esteban (Ron Leibman). When his father is killed by the villain's
gang, Don Diego Vega (George Hamilton) takes on the guise of the
masked avenger Zorro to bring the bad man to justice, but while
righting wrong he injures his foot and is put out of action. He
then sends for his effete brother Bunny (George Hamilton), who has

George Hamilton and Lauren Hutton in ZORRO, THE GAY BLADE (1981).

been residing in England. Bunny's light-handed methods prove to be the opposite of his brother's, but eventually the mincing hero does bring the villain to justice. Don Diego wins the love of pretty Charlotte (Lauren Hutton), who is also opposed to the local tyranny.

RADIO WESTERN PROGRAMS
(ADDITIONS TO BASE VOLUME)

BLAIR OF THE MOUNTIES (Syndicated, 1930)

CALL OF THE RANGE (Syndicated, 1946)

THE CARSON ROBISON SHOW (Syndicated, 1949)
    w. Carson Robison and His Buckaroos

THE CHALLENGE OF THE YUKON (ABC, 1947)
    w. Paul Sutton, Jay Michael, Bruce Beemer
    (a.k.a. SERGEANT PRESTON OF THE YUKON)

CHUCKWAGON JAMBOREE (Syndicated, 1950)
    w. Ken Curtis, The Novelty Aces

THE DEERSLAYER (1930s--serial)

THE DUDE RANCH PARTY (Syndicated, 1940s)
    w. Harry V. "Pappy" Cheshire

FOY WILLING AND THE RIDERS OF THE PURPLE SAGE (Teleways--
    Syndicated, 1947)
    w. Foy Willing and the Riders of the Purple Sage

THE LAST OF THE MOHICANS (1930s--serial)

THE LUCKY RANCH (Syndicated, 1953)
    w. Ken Curtis, Shug Fisher

LUKE SLAUGHTER OF TOMBSTONE (1958)
    w. Sam Buffington

MACK McGUIRE AND HIS HARMONY RANGERS (Syndicated, 1951)
    w. Mack McGuire and His Harmony Rangers

THE NIGHT HAWK RIDE (1930s--serial)

THE OLD CORRAL (ZIV Syndicated, 1940s)
    w. Harry V. "Pappy" Cheshire

THE OPEN SPACES (Syndicated, 1935)
    w. The Sons and Daughters of the Pioneers

PATSY MONTANA & SLIM (ABC, 1940s)
    w. Patsy Montana and Slim

PINTO PETE AND HIS RANCH HANDS (1940s)
    w. Pinto Pete and His Ranch Hands

RED RIVER DAVE (Mutual, 1944)
    w. Red River Dave [McEnery]

RENFREW OF THE ROYAL MOUNTED (CBS, 1936)
    w. House Jameson

RIDERS OF THE PURPLE SAGE (1937) (delete entry from base volume)

ROMANCE OF THE RANCHO (1941--serial)

SADDLE ROCKIN' RHYTHM (1940s)

SANDERS OF THE CIRCLE X (NBC, 1941)

SONGS OF THE B-BAR-B (1930s--1940s)
    w. Tex Ritter, Tex Fletcher, Al Hodge, Herb Ride, Ivan Curry,
    Don Knotts

SONGS OF THE WEST (Syndicated, 1938)
    w. Cactus Mack and His Saddle Tramps

TALES FROM THE DIAMOND K (Syndicated, 1955)
    w. Ken Maynard

TOWN HALL PARTY (NBC, 1950s)
    w. Tex Ritter, Johnny Bond

THE ZANE GREY SHOW (1947)

TELEVISION WESTERN PROGRAMS:
(ADDITIONS TO BASE VOLUME)

THE AMERICANS (NBC-TV, 1961)
    w. Darryl Hickman, Dick Davalos.

BRET MAVERICK (NBC-TV, 1982-83)
    w. James Garner, Darleen Carr, Stuart Margolin, Ramon Bieri.

THE CHISHOLMS (CBS-TV, 1980)
    w. Robert Preston, Rosemary Harris, Ben Murphy, James Van
    Patten, Delta Burke, Mitchell Ryan, Susan Swift.

COWBOY THEATRE (NBC-TV, 1957)
    w. Monty Hall (host).

COWBOYS AND INJINS (ABC-TV, 1950)
    w. Rex Bell (host).

CRASH CORRIGAN'S RANCH (ABC-TV, 1950)
    w. Ray "Crash" Corrigan.

THE DRIFTER (Syndicated, 1967)
    w. Marty Robbins.

FIVE-STAR JUBILEE (NBC-TV, 1961)
    w. Tex Ritter, Jimmy Wakely, Rex Allen, Carl Smith, Snooky
    Lanson.

GUESTWARD HO (ABC-TV, 1963-64)
    w. Joanne Dru, Mark Miller, J. Carrol Naish, Flip Mark,
    Earle Hodgins, Jolene Brand.

GUN SHY (CBS-TV, 1983)
    w. Barry Van Dyke, Bridgette Anderson, Keith Mitchell, Tim
    Thomerson, Henry Jones, Geoffrey Lewis.

HAPPY TRAILS THEATRE (Nashville Network, 1986-88)
    w. Roy Rogers, Dale Evans (hosts).

HOW THE WEST WAS WON (ABC-TV, 1978)
    w. James Arness, Fionnula Flanagan, Bruce Boxleitner,
    Kathryn Holcomb.

KLONDIKE (NBC-TV, 1960-61)
    w. Ralph Taeger, James Coburn, Mari Blanchard, Joi Lansing.

KUNG FU (ABC-TV, 1972-75)
    w. David Carradine, Keye Luke, Philip Ahn, Radames Pera.

THE LIFE AND TIMES OF GRIZZLY ADAMS (NBC-TV, 1977-78)
    w. Dan Haggerty, Denver Pyle, Don Shanks, John Bishop.

THE MARSHAL OF GUNSIGHT PASS (ABC-TV, 1950)
    w. Russell Hayden, Roscoe Ates.

MELODY RANCH THEATRE (Nashville Network, 1987)
    w. Gene Autry, Pat Buttram (hosts).

THE MONROES (ABC-TV, 1966-67)
    w. Michael Anderson, Jr., Barbara Hershey, Keith Schultz,
    Kevin Schultz, Tammy Locke.

NAKIA (ABC-TV, 1974)
    w. Robert Forster, Arthur Kennedy, Gloria De Haven, Taylor
    Lacher.

THE NEW LAND (ABC-TV, 1974)
    w. Todd Lookinland, Debbie Lytton, Kurt Russell, Lou Frizzell.

NORTHWEST PASSAGE (NBC-TV, 1958-59)
    w. Keith Larsen, Buddy Ebsen, Don Burnett, Philip Tonge.

THE OREGON TRAIL (NBC-TV, 1977)
    w. Rod Taylor, Darleen Carr, Charles Napier, Andrew Stevens.

OUTLAWS (CBC-TV, 1987)
    w. Rod Taylor, Richard Roundtree, Charles Napier.

THE QUEST (NBC-TV, 1976)
    w. Kurt Russell, Tim Matheson.

RANCH PARTY (Syndicated, 1957)
    w. Tex Ritter (host).

RHYTHM RODEO (Dumont Network, 1950-51)
    w. Art Jarrett (host).

RIVERBOAT (NBC-TV, 1960-61)
    w. Darren McGavin, Burt Reynolds, Jack Lambert, Noah
    Beery, Jr.

RORY CALHOUN WESTERN THEATRE (Syndicated, 1985)
    w. Rory Calhoun (host).

THE ROUGH RIDERS (ABC-TV, 1958-59)
w. Kent Taylor, Jan Merlin, Peter Whitney.

THE ROUNDERS (ABC-TV, 1966-67)
w. Ron Hayes, Patrick Wayne, Chill Wills.

ROY ROGERS THEATRE (Syndicated, 1977)
w. Roy Rogers (host).

SERGEANT PRESTON OF THE YUKON (CBS-TV, 1955-58)
w. Richard Simmons.

SIX-GUN HEROES (PBS-TV, 1984-87).
w. Sunset Carson (host).

TOWN HALL PARTY (KTTV-TV-Los Angeles, 1952-61)
w. Tex Ritter, Johnny Bond, Merle Travis, Tex Carmen.

TUMBLEWEED THEATRE (Nashville Network, 1984-87)
w. Riders in the Sky (hosts)

WILDSIDE (ABC-TV, 1985)
w. William Smith, Howard E. Rollins, Jr., John Di Aguino,
Terry Funk, Meg Ryan, Jason Hervey.

YOUNG DAN'L BOONE (CBS-TV, 1977)
w. Rick Moses, Devon Ericson.

THE YOUNG REBELS (ABC-TV, 1970-71)
w. Rick Ely, Lou Gossett, Alex Henteloff, Hilarie Thompson.

ZORRO (ABC-TV, 1957-59)
w. Guy Williams, George J. Lewis, Henry Calvin.

ABOUT THE AUTHORS

JAMES ROBERT PARISH, Los Angeles-based direct marketing consultant was born in Cambridge, MA. He attended the University of Pennsylvania and graduated Phi Beta Kappa with a degree in English. A
graduate of the University of Pennsylvania Law School, he is a member
of the New York Bar. As president of Entertainment Copyright Research Co., Inc. he headed a major research facility for the film and
television industries. Later he was a film reviewer/interviewer for
Motion Picture Daily and Variety. He is the author of over 70
volumes, including: THE FOX GIRLS, GOOD DAMES, THE SLAP-
STICK QUEENS, THE RKO GALS, THE TOUGH GUYS, THE
JEANETTE MACDONALD STORY, THE ELVIS PRESLEY SCRAPBOOK,
and THE HOLLYWOOD BEAUTIES. Among those he has co-written
are THE M-G-M STOCK COMPANY, THE DEBONAIRS, LIZA!, HOLLY-
WOOD CHARACTER ACTORS, THE HOLLYWOOD RELIABLES, THE
FUNSTERS, THE BEST OF M-G-M, and his ongoing series, ACTORS'
TELEVISION CREDITS. With Mr. Pitts, he has co-written such
tomes as THE GREAT WESTERN PICTURES, THE GREAT SCIENCE
FICTION PICTURES, HOLLYWOOD ON HOLLYWOOD, FILM DIRECTORS
GUIDE: THE U.S., THE GREAT SPY PICTURES (I & II) and THE
GREAT GANGSTER PICTURES (I & II).

MICHAEL R. PITTS is a freelance writer who has written or co-
authored fifteen books, including WESTERN MOVIES, HOLLYWOOD
AND AMERICAN HISTORY, HORROR FILM STARS, FAMOUS MOVIE
DETECTIVES, HOLLYWOOD ON RECORD, THE BIBLE ON FILM and
two editions of RADIO SOUNDTRACKS. With Mr. Parish he co-
authored THE GREAT ... PICTURE SERIES and its second volumes.
In addition he has contributed to several other published books and
his magazine articles have been published both here and abroad.
A graduate of Ball State University, Muncie, IN, with degrees in
history and journalism, Mr. Pitts writes columns on record collecting
for The Big Reel and Classic Images magazines. He has written
record album liner notes and lectures on film history and entertainment. Mr. Pitts resides in Chesterfield, IN with his wife Carolyn
and daughter Angela.